Space Between Words

The Origins of Silent Reading

Figurae

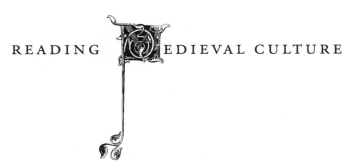

READING MEDIEVAL CULTURE

Space Between Words

The Origins
of Silent Reading

Paul Saenger

Stanford University Press, Stanford, California

Published with the assistance of Roger S. Baskes;
The Holzheimer Fund; The Otto L. and Hazel T. Rhoades Fund.

Stanford University Press
Stanford, California
© 1997 by the Board of Trustees of the
Leland Stanford Junior University
Printed in the United States of America

CIP data appear at the end of the book

For Nadine

Preface

In October 1978 in Saint Louis, Missouri, I presented a paper at the Fifth Saint Louis Conference on Manuscript Studies at Saint Louis University. In that paper, I outlined the thesis that the separation of words, which began in the early Middle Ages, altered the physiological process of reading and by the fourteenth century enabled the common practice of silent reading as we know it today. My research on the history of reading was motivated by my dissatisfaction with the explanation given by H. J. Chaytor in *From Script to Print: An Introduction to Medieval Literature* (Cambridge, 1945) and by others that the transition from oral to silent reading was the consequence of the introduction of printing in the late fifteenth century. As a teacher of paleography, I had found that my students quite properly had difficulty distinguishing an illuminated incunable page of Colard Mansion from a fifteenth-century manuscript leaf. I therefore wondered whether the average medieval reader would have changed his or her mode of reading because of a change in book production that on casual observation was scarcely discernable.

An abstract of my 1978 paper was published in *Manuscripta* 23 (1979): 20–21. The reaction of the audience at the conference and a letter from the late Professor Lynn White in response to the abstract encouraged me to revise my essay into an article, published as "Silent Reading: Its Impact on Late Medieval Script and Society," *Viator* 13 (1982): 366–414. In the summer of 1981, while the article was still in manuscript, I had the opportunity to meet and discuss my ideas on the origins of silent reading with Professor Henri-Jean Martin while he was on a brief visit to Chicago. Following our encounter, I sent him a copy of the future *Viator* article, which he read and circulated to colleagues in Paris, including Roger Chartier. Some weeks later, I received a letter from Professor Jean

Vezin inviting me to prepare a résumé of my findings for publication in the *Histoire de l'Edition française*, vol. 1, *Le livre conquerant du moyen âge au milieu du XVIIe siècle* (Paris, 1982), 130–41.

The apparent interest in my research on silent reading led me to write a number of additional articles on the history of reading and finally this book, which, I would stress, is not a general history of literacy. Instead, I have attempted to explain the physiological and psychological influence of word separation on the reading process and to trace, in far greater detail than my knowledge in 1980 would have permitted, the path of the adoption of word separation — the crucial element in the change to silent reading — in medieval Latin script. Numerous readers have been kind enough to suggest that interest in the particular developments covered here extends beyond the world of paleography, and even beyond that of medieval studies, to a broader range of readers concerned with later developments in the history of reading and the history of the book. Because such readers may be unfamiliar with the technical language of paleography, the textual genres and practices of medieval writing, or both, I have included both brief, in-text glosses and a glossary explaining the terminology employed throughout, including the terminological innovations this study proposes. I trust that those for whom such aids are superfluous will not mind these efforts to open the study of paleography to those who have not experienced the exciting results it can produce.

In order to document the history of word separation, I set for myself the challenge of examining medieval manuscripts according to new criteria of description that I deemed essential for the discipline of the history of reading. Primarily in 1984–85, under the auspices of an American Council of Learned Societies fellowship, I was able to examine the necessary manuscripts in the libraries of France, England, and the Netherlands. This book is largely the result of that year's research on original sources in their original state.

A volume so closely tied to primary sources as is this study could not have been written without the help and support of many institutions and individuals. I am particularly indebted to the American Council of Learned Societies, Northwestern University, the Newberry Library, and the Herzog August Bibliothek in Wolfenbüttel for fellowship aid and grants for travel. Numerous scholars made invaluable suggestions in regard to methodology and guided me to potentially interesting manuscripts. In Paris, a generous invitation from Jean-Claude Schmitt and Roger Chartier permitted me to present my preliminary findings in a series of lectures at the Ecole des Hautes Etudes en Sciences Sociales. Jean Vezin, François Dolbeau, and Patricia Stirnemann brought a host of specific codices at the Bibliothèque Nationale to my attention. The erudite staff of the Latin and Codicological Sections of the Institut de Recherche et d'Histoire des Textes constituted an indispensable resource. Bernard Barbiche provided invaluable assistance for the Archives Nationales. In Rome, Armando Petrucci encouraged my efforts and offered invaluable guidance in regard to research methodology and the bibliography of Italian codices. David Olson and Insup Taylor provided crucial counsel on recent studies in cognitive psychology. I am particularly indebted to David Ganz, who read much of the entire manuscript and made numerous corrections and helpful suggestions. I am indebted, too, to Roger S. Baskes, the Holzheimer Fund, and the Otto L. and Hazel T. Rhoades Funds for their support in providing the illustrations for this volume. Finally, Brian Stock kindly encouraged me and generously assisted me through the final revision and publication of my manuscript; and Ellen Smith, with skill and tact, guided the manuscript through the press. All translations in the text are my own.

P.S.

Contents

Chapter 1   Introduction   1
        The Physiology of Reading 1; Ancient Readers and
        Unseparated Texts 6; Ancient *Scriptura Continua* 9;
        Word Separation and Word Order 14

Chapter 2   The Nomenclature of Word Separation   18
        Word Separation and Paleographic Studies 18;
        Separated Script: An Overview 26; Linguistic
        Implications of Separation 30; Aerated Script 32;
        Canonical Separation 44

Chapter 3   Complements to Word Separation by Space   52
        Medieval Signs for Word Separation 53; Medieval
        Signs for Word Unity 65; Construction Notes 70;
        Punctuation 71; Musical Notation 74; *Nota* Signs and
        Tie Notes 75; Indications of Page Locus 77; Résumé
        Notes and Schematic Diagrams 79; Post-Factum
        Emendation 79

Chapter 4   Insular Culture and Word Separation in the
        Seventh and Eighth Centuries   83
        The Grammarians of Separation 83; New Genres of
        Books 90; New Modes of Reading 98

Chapter 5   Exceptions to Continental Aerated Text Formats in
        the Ninth and Tenth Centuries   100
        Regional Differences 101; Insular Intellectuals on the
        Continent 106; Tironian Notes 115

xiv   Contents

Chapter 6   The Origins of Continental Word Separation,
950–1300   120
    Protoscholasticism 120; Arabic Influence on
    Continental Word Separation 123

Chapter 7   Word Separation and the Transcription of Numbers
and Music   131
    Numbers as Language 131; The Reformatting of
    Roman Numerals 135; Fractions 137; New Modes of
    Graphic Display 138; Musical Notation 139

Chapter 8   The Early Protoscholastics   143
    Gerbert of Aurillac 143; Abbo of Fleury 152; Heriger
    of Lobbes 162

Chapter 9   The Proliferation of Word Separation in the
Eleventh Century   165
    Fulbert of Chartres 165; Fulbert's Students 168;
    Gerbert's Students in the Eleventh Century 170;
    Heriger's Students 171; Authors of Unseparated
    Texts 177; Robert the Pious and French Royal
    Charters 178; Otto III and German Imperial
    Documents 182

Chapter 10   The Spread of Word Separation from England to
the Low Countries and Lorraine   183
    English Benedictine Reform and Caroline Script 183;
    The Reformed Abbeys 185

Chapter 11   The Spread of Word Separation from England to
Northern France   202
    Norman Benedictine Piety and Silent Reading 202;
    Fécamp 204; Mont Saint-Michel 208; Jumièges 209;
    Bec 212

Chapter 12   Cluniac Monasticism: Eastern and Southern France   215
    Cluny 215; Saint-Bénigne of Dijon 221; Saint-Martial
    of Limoges 223; Saint-Pierre of Moissac 227; The *Ars
    lectoria* in Aquitaine 231; Aurillac and Saint-Sever 233;
    The Reform of Saint-Victor of Marseille 233; La
    Grasse 234

Contents   xv

Chapter 13   Italy   235

Chapter 14   Reading and Writing in Northern Europe in the
               Twelfth and Thirteenth Centuries   243
               The Spread of Canonical Separation 244; The Author
               and the Book 249; Book Production 252; Changes in
               Scholastic Grammatical Theory 253; Changes in the
               Language of Mathematics 255

Chapter 15   Written Culture at the End of the Middle Ages   256
               Gothic Cursive Script and the Manuscript Book 257;
               The Classroom 258; Libraries 261; Private Study and
               Heresy 264; Lay Society and Vernacular Texts 265;
               Italy 271; Private, Silent Reading and Personal
               Expression 273

               Appendix: Characteristics Relating to Word
               Separation in Manuscripts Surveyed   279

               Notes   293

               Glossary   433

               References   437

               Index of Manuscripts Cited   449

               General and Topical Index   469

Figures

1. Livy's *History of Rome* written in *scriptura continua*.   5
2. The book of Haggai written in *cola et commata*.   16
3. Separated script in Pseudo Jerome, *Epistola degradus Romanorum*, copied by an Anglo-Saxon scribe ca. 900.   31
4. Letter blocks in the *Cathach Psalter*.   34
5. Syllable blocks in the *Antiphonary of Bangor*.   35
6. Hierarchical letter blocks in a patristic miscellany.   36
7. Hierarchical word blocks in the *Regiensis Livy*.   37
8. The psalms written in hierarchical word blocks with syllables pedagogically marked by interpuncts.   38
9. Morphemic hierarchical word blocks in the English translation of Orosius's *Seven Books Against the Pagans*, the Tollemache manuscript.   42
10. Summary of nomenclature for space in script.   45
11. Canonical separation in the writing of the scribe Goderan in Josephus, *De bello iudaico*.   46
12. The successor note to the *diastole, trait d'union,* and accenting of double *ii* used by an emendator to remove ambiguity from unseparated script in Boethius's *De consolatione philosophiae*.   56
13. The successor note to the *diastole* used to separate words in Philippus's *In Job*.   58
14. The terminal capital *S* in Beranger of Tours' *Rescripta contra Lanfrancum*.   60
15. A ligature breaching intersyllabic space in the Old Testament.   67
16. Alphabetical construction notes in Aldhelm's *De virginitate*.   71

17. Table with references to folios in Gregorio di Cantino's
    Liber largitorius.   78
18. A schematic tree diagram accompanying Boethius's
    De topicis differentiis.   80
19. The text format of Bede's description of the *diastole* in the
    De orthographia.   86
20. Word separation in the earliest treatise on word order, the
    *Quomodo septem circumstantiae rerum in legendo orchinande
    sint*.   104
21. The Psalms in word-separated Greek, Latin Greek, and
    Latin in the *Psalter of Sedulius*.   112
22. Word images in a tironian psalter and glossary.   116
23. Word separation in the earliest Latin treatise on the
    astrolabe.   128
24. Signs for fractions in Victorius's *Calculus*.   138
25. Word separation and related characteristics in Gerbert's
    Scholium ad Boethii Arithmeticam institutionem.   145
26. The authorial manuscript of Richer's *Historia francorum*.   148
27. Abbo's possible autograph script in Boethius's translation
    of Aristotle's *Categoriae*.   156
28. The word separation in syllogisms transcribed at Fleury in
    Abbo's *De propositionibus et syllogismis categoricis et
    hypotheticis*.   157
29. The authorial copy of Gérard I of Florennes's *Gesta
    episcoporum Cameracensium*.   172
30. Script attributed to the scribe Wichard, in Terence's
    Comoediae, ca. 1030.   199
31. Word separation in a contemporary copy of John of
    Fécamp's *Epistula ad monachos dyscolos*.   206
32. A pen sketch of a motionless reader in a manuscript from
    Fécamp containing Gerbert's *Regulae de numerorum abaci
    rationibus*.   207
33. The authorial manuscript of Anselm's *Epistola de sacrificio
    azimi et fermentati*, written in canonically separated script.   213
34. Pedagogical word separation by points and space in the
    Dicta Leonis.   229
35. Word separation in Pope Gregory VII's *Dictatus Papae*.   240
36. Silent reading in the mid-fifteenth century, an illumination
    from Jacque Le Grand's *Livre des bonnes moeurs*.   262

Tables

A.1 Early Manuscripts of Works by Gerbert   281
A.2 Early Manuscripts of Works by Adson   282
A.3 Early Manuscripts of Works by Abbo of Fleury   283
A.4 Early Manuscripts of Works by Fulbert   284
A.5 Early Manuscripts Originating from the Abbey of Mont
     Saint-Michel   285
A.6 Early Manuscripts Originating from Cluny   287
A.7 Early Manuscripts Originating from Saint-Martial of
     Limoges   288
A.8 Manuscripts Originating from Saint-Pierre of Moissac   290

Space Between Words

The Origins of Silent Reading

Chapter I

Introduction

~~~~~

The Physiology of Reading

Modern reading is a silent, solitary, and rapid activity. Ancient reading was usually oral, either aloud, in groups, or individually, in a muffled voice. Reading, like any human activity, has a history. It cannot be assumed that the cognitive processes that enable today's reader to decipher the written page have been the same throughout the recorded past.[1] Contemporary evidence for this assertion can be drawn from diverse cultures throughout the world where literate men and women use different cognitive processes to read different forms of handwritten and printed text. The text format in which thought has been presented to the reader has undergone many changes in order to reach the form that the modern Western reader now views as immutable and nearly universal. As the format of text has varied historically from culture to culture, so, too, have the cognitive skills necessary for its deciphering.[2]

The cognitive skills required for the decoding of text depend on a variety of neurophysiological processes that historically readers in different civilizations have employed in different ways to extract meaning from the page. Two factors intrinsic to all written documents determine the nature of these physiological processes. The first is the structure of the language itself.[3] The frequency of polysyllabic words, the absence or presence of inflection, and the different conventions for word order all determine which mental capacities are required for the decoding of written as well as oral language.[4] The second factor is the way the language is transcribed, that is, the full range of graphic conventions used for its representation. It is the second factor that is central to this book on the history of reading.

The conventions for the transcription of language are quasi-independent of the structure of language. Languages that are linguistically closely related have been transcribed by radically disparate forms of notation. Examples of this phenomenon are numerous among today's languages. Chinese, the Tibeto-Burman languages, and Vietnamese, all closely related structurally, have been transcribed by radically different writing systems.[5] Within the Chinese language group, the dialects of Chinese have since earliest times been transcribed by graphs that in most cases are nearly identical to modern Chinese characters, the Tibeto-Burman languages have employed the Devanagari alphabet of Sanskrit, and Vietnamese, since the seventeenth century, has been transcribed phonetically by a version of the Roman alphabet based on conventions first introduced by Italian and Portuguese Jesuit missionaries.[6] Korean, a non-Chinese language, can be transcribed either in Chinese characters or in *hangul*, an indigenous alphabet invented in the fifteenth century.[7]

It is a premise of this book that given such differences in transcription, there is a correlation between a propensity to read orally in both past and contemporary cultures and the threshold in the duration of cognitive activity needed to achieve lexical access in that culture's script. The differing ways in which oral or silent reading depends on the duration of cognitive activity required by differing transcription systems in different cultures appear most clearly in modern languages as differences in language pedagogy.[8] In general, graphic systems that eliminate or reduce the need for a cognitive process prior to lexical access facilitate the early adaptation of young readers to silent reading, while written languages that are more ambiguous necessitate the oral manipulation of phonetic components to construct words. These latter writing systems require a longer training period, one that features oral reading and rote memorization and that continues, in some instances, even into adulthood. Examples from several modern languages, as well as from ancient Greek and Latin, help illustrate these differences.

Parallel research in the disciplines of cognitive and educational psychology indicates that the Chinese graphic tradition provides optimal conditions for rapid lexical access and allows Chinese children to develop silent reading at an earlier age than in Burma or in the West.[9] As an apparent consequence, many skilled adult Chinese readers are able to achieve a proficiency in rapid, silent reading perhaps unequaled in modern occidental languages.[10]

The relationship between the cognitive skills characterizing reading in a given national or ethnic tradition and the conventions of graphic representation has been further elucidated by experiments and clinical observations conducted in Japan. In contrast to Chinese, Japanese has a dual structure of transcription, one character-based (*kanji*) and one phonetic (*kana*).[11] A Japanese text may be transcribed graphically, using Chinese logograms, or phonetically, using either of two varieties of *kana*, or syllabary characters. Clinical studies of Japanese patients with cerebral lesions have identified individuals apparently unable to read one system of transcription or the other, depending on which areas of the brain have been affected.[12] This correlation suggests that the cerebral processes necessary for recognizing characters have loci in the brain that are distinct from those used to decode phonetic transcriptions. Recent experiments in Hong Kong suggest a right-hemisphere advantage for the recognition of Chinese one-character and two-character words.[13] It would appear that the right hemisphere plays a more active role in reading scripts in which words have discrete images. Research indicates that English-speaking subjects also have discrete systems within the brain for the aural understanding and the silent visual understanding of language.[14] The introduction of proton-emission tomography scanners allowing technicians to observe the inner workings of the brain during cognitive activities may one day soon permit more precise study of the differences in hemispheric functions necessitated by the different conventions of graphic transcription.[15]

In the dual system of transcription used for Japanese, syllabic characters, limited in number, are used to instruct young children.[16] The exclusive use of a syllabary method of presenting text to novice readers, necessitating the oral reconstruction of units of meaning from phonetic components by means of a limited set of cues corresponding to sounds, makes this mode of transcription preferable, in the initial phase of elementary education, to a system consisting of a much larger number of complex Chinese word-characters. Japanese syllabary transcription, however, contains no regular word separation, and it imposes on the young reader the formidable burden of recognizing units of meaning through the synthetic reconstruction of words from initially ambiguous phonetic signs offering no distinction between word and syllabic boundaries. To aid the young Japanese reader, group oral recitation is essential.[17]

The young reader who progresses soon begins to read more difficult texts, which are transcribed increasingly in Chinese characters, and the syllabary characters are relegated to a secondary role of representing function, that is, to short or linking words. A similar progression occurs among young readers of Korean.[18] In both Japanese and Korean, the prevalence of Chinese characters in more difficult texts is predicated on the greater mnemonic capacity of the physically mature reader to retain lexical images.[19] The infusion of characters also in effect divides many, if not all Japanese words for the reader and largely eliminates the task of word reconstruction based on a synthetic combination of phonetic elements.[20] The increased presence of Chinese characters accompanies the transition to rapid, silent reading and is particularly efficacious for the intrusive and rapid, silent perusal of text in the quest for specific information that is known as "reference reading."[21]

The skills associated with reference reading are characteristic of both advanced occidental and oriental civilizations. In the West, as this book will narrate, these skills emerged first in the British Isles in the early Middle Ages and on the Continent beginning in the late tenth century. In Japan, a blend of syllabary and ideographic transcriptions of Japanese allows pedagogues to lead pupils in a smooth transition from an oral mode of reading suitable to young readers but irksome to adults to one that, while still making use of the initially learned syllabary-decoding skills, is better suited to the rapid, silent reading required of experienced readers in a modern industrial society. However, Japanese pedagogy has judged this more efficient mode of reading to be too difficult for young readers to master in the initial phase of instruction.

In Liberia, the Vai ethnic and linguistic group uses a form of phonetic syllabary transcription that originated as an attempt to emulate the written documents of Portuguese explorers of the sixteenth century but that subsequently developed as an autonomous written language in isolation from European or Arabic influence.[22] It also strikingly resembles the opening of an ancient Greek or Roman manuscript written in *scriptura continua* (Figure 1).[23] In Vai, we find the rare instance of a modern language form of polysyllabic words that is transcribed syllabically without word separation, diacriticals, punctuation, or the presence of initial capital forms. In both Vai and the ancient Greek and Roman books, the reader encounters at first glance rows of discreet phonetic symbols that have to be manipulated within the mind to form properly articulated and accented entities equivalent to words. In all three languages, the phonetic components of words have at best only limited consistent meanings. In a written language such as Vai that requires extensive phonetic activity prior to the reader's understanding of a word's meaning, it

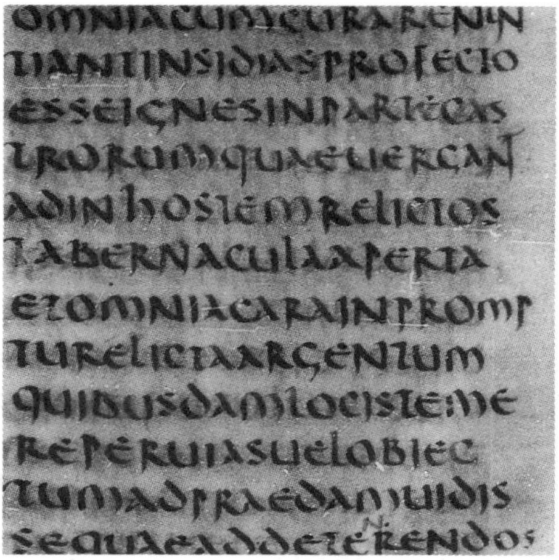
OMNIACUMSECURARENIN
TIANTINSIDIASPROFECTO
ESSEIGNESINPARTECAS
TRORUMQUAEUERGAN
ADINHOSTEMRELICTOS
TABERNACULAAPERTA
ETOMNIACARAINPROMP
TURELICTAARGENTUM
QUIBUSDAMLOCISTEMNE
REPERUIASUELOBIEC
TUMADPRAEDAMUIDIS
SEQUAEADDETERENDOS

Figure 1. Livy's *History of Rome* written in *scriptura continua*. Paris, Bibliothèque Nationale lat. 5730, f. 59 recto, col. 2; reproduced by permission.

is not surprising to find that oral recitation forms an important part of elementary reading instruction. Moreover, in the form of mumbling to sound out a text, it is a normal part of the habits of experienced adult readers when reading privately. The reading habits of the Vai people, like those of the ancient Greeks and Romans, are phonosynthetic, and all three written languages employ similar modes of decoding polysyllabic words written in unseparated script. Thus, in historically unrelated circumstances, similar reading processes make use of the same human cerebral structures and mental capacities (which have remained biologically unchanged during the brief period of recorded civilization) to resolve analogous forms of graphic ambiguity.[24]

As should be clear from the last example, in Western scripts, spatial organization is a determinative element in the effect of different transcription systems on the cognitive processes required for lexical access and hence on the propensity to read orally or silently. Experiments performed on adult, English-speaking readers confirm that the total suppression or partial obfuscation of spatial boundaries between words increases the duration of the cognitive activity necessary for reading, which in turn produces physiological reactions associated with vocal and subvocal activity.[25] Conversely, although young readers who are obliged to read silently may encounter difficulties in comprehension, deletion of interword space does not affect them, for the pattern of their ocular movements remains unchanged by the absence of cues the use of which they have not yet mastered.[26] If one gives a text typed in uppercase letters without word separation or punctuation to a class of fifth graders, they automatically read it aloud. This phenomenon is a continuation of a habit that originates when the child initially pronounces words syllable by syllable in order to gain access to meaning. When visual access to meaning is blocked, the brain's redundant aural system for word recognition predominates. Young children also tend initially to write in *scriptura continua* because they see its continuity as a faithful representation of uninterrupted oral speech.[27] However, the ever-present space between words allows young occidental readers, in a manner analogous to young Japanese readers progressing from syllabary characters to logograms, to develop easily from reading skills based on synthetic recognition of a word by means of its syllabic component to the global recognition of the word as an entire unit with a single meaning and pronunciation.[28]

In beginning readers, measurements of the eye-voice span, the variable quantity of text that a reader has decoded but not yet pronounced at any given moment during oral reading, indicate that the number of characters perceived during each of more numerous ocular fixations often falls within the limits of longer words.[29] The suppression of space between words causes a similarly reduced visual field, or tunnel vision, in adults.[30] Under these conditions, adult readers experience radically reduced parafoveal vision, the span of fifteen to twenty letters in separated printed English text adjacent on either side of what is clearly perceived by the reader's fovea, the area of acute vision. In other words, they experience a reduction of the span within which preliminary details of words or letters can be recognized. They also experience reduced peripheral vision, the broader field within which only the grossest characteristics of signs, words, and spatial arrangement can be perceived. Only scripts that provide a consistently broad eye-voice span to oral readers can sustain rapid, silent reading as we know it.

Ancient Readers and Unseparated Texts

In the West, the ability to read silently and rapidly is a result of the historical evolution of word separation that, beginning in the seventh century, changed the format of the written page, which had to be read orally and slowly in order to be comprehended.[31] The onerous task of keeping the eyes ahead of the voice while accurately reading unseparated script, so familiar to the ancient Greeks and Romans, can be described as a kind of elaborate search pattern.[32] The eye moves across the page, not at an even rate, but in series of fixations and jumps called "sac-cades." Without spaces to use for guideposts, the ancient reader needed more than twice the normal quantity of fixations and saccades per line of printed text. The reader of unseparated text also required a quantity of ocular regressions for which there is no parallel under modern reading conditions in order to verify that the words have been correctly sepa-rated.[33] The ancient reader's success in finding a reasonably appropriate meaning in the text acted as the final control that the task of separation has been accurately performed.

A useful analogy is to a computer program written to verify correct spelling. The use of a typed space to signify word termination vastly sim-plifies this process. A program written for texts without word separation would be infinitely more complex, for it would have to incorporate a thesaurus of licit syllables, syllable divisions, and syllable combinations, as well as syntactical, morphological, and contextual constraints for con-trolling all the phonetically plausible but inappropriate points for divid-ing a stream of continuous letters. The brain of the ancient reader had to perform this difficult task constantly. Such readers were better at this process than a computer program could be because they didn't simply proceed mechanically. Psychologists concede that readers who habitu-ally read unseparated writing would adapt and improve their reading rates over time. However, they maintain that these readers' brains would always compensate for the extra cognitive burden by more numerous ocular fixations and regressions.[34]

A radically reduced field of vision and an increased number of fixa-tions reduced the quantity of written text that could be perceived at each of the reader's fixations. This reduction in the length of each unit of tex-tual intake meant that at the end of each fixation, the reader's memory, unaided by contextual cues and parafoveal vision, instead of retaining the coded images of the contours of one, two, or three words, as is cus-tomary when reading modern separated English text, could retain only the phonic trace of a series of syllables, the boundaries of which were in need of identification and verification.[35]

These syllables sometimes helpfully might correspond to monosyl-labic or bisyllabic words or morphemes, that is, to sense-conveying syl-labic prefixes or suffixes. In the many intellectually difficult *scriptura con-tinua* texts that have survived from ancient Greece and Rome, however, they corresponded to syllabic fragments of words of which both the ter-mination and the sense were apt to remain uncertain during the moment

between ocular saccades. This ambiguity was increased by ancient grammatical structures relying on parataxis and inflection that lacked and even
purposely avoided conventional word order and failed to group grammatically related words consistently. In these circumstances, the ancient
reader in his initial preparation or *praelectio* of a text normally had to read
orally, aloud or in a muffled voice, because overt physical pronunciation
aided the reader to retain phonemes of ambiguous meaning.[36] Oral activity helped the reader to hold in short-term memory the fraction of a
word or phrase that already had been decoded phonetically while the cognitive task of morpheme and word recognition, necessary for understanding the sense of the initial fragment, proceeded through the decoding of
a subsequent section of text.[37] The aural retention of inherently ambiguous fragments often was essential until a full sentence was decoded.

In this manner, ancient readers of unseparated writing were able to
retain and understand written text in a fashion somewhat comparable to
the series of signs that modern readers of separated text can decode visually, either when reading silently or when rapidly "sight reading" a text
in oral performance. The only way in which ancient scribes aided the
reader in the task of grasping letters for syllable recognition was, especially in formal book scripts, by regularly placing relatively more space
between letters than is customary for medieval or modern handwritten
and printed text.[38] It was the very absence of word boundaries that made
the technique of the identification and memorization of those sequences
of letters representing licit syllables a fundamental aspect of ancient and
early medieval pedagogy.[39]

The fragmentation of text into the minute sections characteristic
of ancient textual commentaries was a profound aspect of the ancient
mentality of *belles lettres*,[40] and given the physiological constraints of
the medium, there was little incentive for an ancient reader to suppress
the exterior voice in reading, for such a conscious effort could not increase the speed of the reading process. Ambrose's peculiar habit of reading silently with only the eyes and mind amazed Augustine, but when
Ambrose read silently, given the constraints of ancient writing, he could
not have read rapidly in the manner of the modern silent reader, even if
he had wanted to do so.[41] Indeed, Augustine suggests that Ambrose read
silently either to seek privacy by concealing the content of his book or to
rest his voice.[42] Other ancient authors occasionally described the reading
of letters and documents, whether silently in the strict sense, or more
probably, quietly with suppressed voice, in order to retain privacy or to

concentrate on understanding the text, but no classical author described rapid, silent reference consultation as it exists in the modern world.[43] For the ancients, *lectio*, the synthetic combination of letters to form syllables and syllables to form words, of necessity preceded *narratio*, that is, the comprehension of a text.[44]

Ancient *Scriptura Continua*

The uninterrupted writing of ancient *scriptura continua* was possible only in the context of a writing system that had a complete set of signs for the unambiguous transcription of pronounced speech. This occurred for the first time in Indo-European languages when the Greeks adapted the Phoenician alphabet by adding symbols for vowels. The Greco-Latin alphabetical scripts, which employed vowels with varying degrees of modification, were used for the transcription of the old forms of the Romance, Germanic, Slavic, and Hindu tongues, all members of the Indo-European language group, in which words were polysyllabic and inflected. For an oral reading of these Indo-European languages, the reader's immediate identification of words was not essential, but a reasonably swift identification and parsing of syllables was fundamental.[45] Vowels as necessary and sufficient codes for sounds permitted the reader to identify syllables swiftly within rows of uninterrupted letters. Before the introduction of vowels to the Phoenician alphabet, all the ancient languages of the Mediterranean world—syllabic or alphabetical, Semitic or Indo-European—were written with word separation by either space, points, or both in conjunction.[46] After the introduction of vowels, word separation was no longer necessary to eliminate an unacceptable level of ambiguity.

Throughout the antique Mediterranean world, the adoption of vowels and of *scriptura continua* went hand in hand. The ancient writings of Mesopotamia, Phoenicia, and Israel did not employ vowels, so separation between words was retained. Had the space between words been deleted and the signs been written in *scriptura continua*, the resulting visual presentation of the text would have been analogous to a modern lexogrammatic puzzle.[47] Such written languages might have been decipherable, given their clearly defined conventions for word order and contextual clues, but only after protracted cognitive activity that would have made fluent reading as we know it impractical. While the very earliest Greek inscriptions were written with separation by interpuncts, points placed at midlevel between words, Greece soon thereafter became the first ancient civilization to employ *scriptura continua*.[48] The Romans, who borrowed their letter forms and vowels from the Greeks, maintained the earlier Mediterranean tradition of separating words by points far longer than the Greeks, but they, too, after a scantily documented period of six centuries, discarded word separation as superfluous and substituted *scriptura continua* for interpunct-separated script in the second century A.D. In Hebrew, the introduction of vowels in the manuscripts of the high Middle Ages resulted in the evolution of not fully separated Masoretic script that was probably modeled, directly or indirectly, on what I will be calling the "aerated" writing of the contemporary Carolingian Latin West.[49] In India, the Brahmi syllabary alphabet, whose ultimate relationship to ancient Greek is uncertain but whose Middle Eastern origin appears likely, incorporated vowels that permitted Sanskrit to be transcribed in its own form of *scriptura continua*.[50] The various vernacular dialects transcribed in writing derived from the Greek, including Coptic, Glagolitic, Cyrillic, and Gothic, also have medieval traditions of transcription originating in antiquity that employed neither points nor intratextual space. In contrast, the Semitic languages (Hebrew, Aramaic, Arabic, and Syriac), when written without vowels, were virtually always written with word separation in antiquity and continued to be so transcribed into modern times, with the quantity and even the mode of separation, however, varying according to the epoch.

The parallel development of vocalic writing without separation and consonantal transcription with separation seems at first glance to be paradoxical, and this dual phenomenon long has puzzled students of the history of writing, who have condemned the dominance of *scriptura continua* in late antiquity as a retrograde development in human history. From the modern point of view, it seems inexplicable that two modes for facilitating lexical access, the use of vowels and word separation, were not combined at an early date to form a hybrid transcription that would have greatly facilitated reading by incorporating redundant cues for word recognition similar to those of the modern separated printed page. The mnemonic advantage of permitting the association of specific information with spatially defined loci on the page would have been created.[51] However, in contradiction to our expectation, the Roman Empire, which for a time enjoyed the widespread use of interpunct-separated Latin script with vowels, chose to discard that form of writing for *scriptura continua*.[52]

This failure to achieve a lasting hybridization of separated consonantal script with unseparated vocalic script in any of the Indo-European languages of antiquity cannot be explained away by the ignorance of the scribes in one language of the conventions of the other, for the survival of numerous bilingual fragments written on papyrus suggests that the Romans, Greeks, and Jews in late antiquity were aware of each other's differing graphic traditions regarding word separation.[53] The answer to our query lies rather in an analysis of the unique features of ancient reading habits, as well as in the social context in which ancient reading and writing took place.

Stated summarily, the ancient world did not possess the desire, characteristic of the modern age, to make reading easier and swifter because the advantages that modern readers perceive as accruing from ease of reading were seldom viewed as advantages by the ancients. These include the effective retrieval of information in reference consultation, the ability to read with minimum difficulty a great many technical, logical, and scientific texts, and the greater diffusion of literacy throughout all social strata of the population.[54] We know that the reading habits of the ancient world, which were profoundly oral and rhetorical by physiological necessity as well as by taste, were focused on a limited and intensely scrutinized canon of literature. Because those who read relished the mellifluous metrical and accentual patterns of pronounced text and were not interested in the swift intrusive consultation of books, the absence of interword space in Greek and Latin was not perceived to be an impediment to effective reading, as it would be to the modern reader, who strives to read swiftly.[55] Moreover, oralization, which the ancients savored aesthetically, provided mnemonic compensation (through enhanced short-term aural recall) for the difficulty in gaining access to the meaning of unseparated text. Long-term memory of texts frequently read aloud also compensated for the inherent graphic and grammatical ambiguities of the languages of late antiquity.

Finally, the notion that the greater portion of the population should be autonomous and self-motivated readers was entirely foreign to the elitist literate mentality of the ancient world. For the literate, the reaction to the difficulties of lexical access arising from *scriptura continua* did not spark the desire to make script easier to decipher, but resulted instead in the delegation of much of the labor of reading and writing to skilled slaves, who acted as professional readers and scribes.[56] It is in the context of a society with an abundant supply of cheap, intellectually skilled labor that ancient attitudes toward reading must be comprehended and the ready and pervasive acceptance of the suppression of word separation throughout the Roman Empire understood. Even during the early empire, when the Romans separated words by interpuncts that were only sometimes accompanied by limited additional space, a period when the Greeks did not, the philosopher Seneca viewed this difference in graphic presentation as an indication of two divergent styles of oratorical delivery. He identified the Roman use of the interpunct as an indication of the Latin emphasis on measured and expressive oral delivery, in contrast to what he deemed the gushing quality of Greek orations. His remarks suggest that he thought interpuncts were a sign of the Latin reader's slower cadence, rather than an aid to augment the speed of decoding.[57]

A century after Seneca's death in A.D. 65, the Roman page had become increasingly similar to that of Greek, as the Romans gave up separation by interpuncts and adopted the Greek convention of *scriptura continua*. In Rome after the Golden Age, interword space, except as an occasional sign of punctuation, was virtually unknown.[58] The similarity of Roman *scriptura continua* text format to that of the Greek was further enhanced by the adoption of Latin uncial script. This script was an emulation, if not of the specific *ductus* or strokes that formed Greek letters, at least of the general visual impression of the unseparated Greek script that paleographers since the eighteenth century have termed uncial.[59] The Romans, however, were reluctant to emulate other Greek practices that may have helped Greek scribes and readers to control unseparated text. Foliation, pagination, and catchwords, all present in Greek papyri codices, were never employed by the Romans, and paragraphing was received into Latin only with hesitancy and often confined to certain genres of texts.[60] At the end of antiquity, in both Greek and Latin texts, intratextual space had ceased entirely to serve as a code to separate words and had become instead an occasionally used code for the punctuation of texts. Most late Roman and many Greek texts were copied totally without intratextual space or other signs of intratextual punctuation.[61]

The absence of interword space and interpunctuation at the end of antiquity was a reflection of the particular relationship of the antique reader to the book. The reintroduction of word separation by Irish and Anglo-Saxon scribes marks a dramatic change in that relationship and constitutes the great divide in the history of reading between antique cultures and those of the modern Occident. It is clear from the evidence of any page chosen at random from any northern European university text written in the thirteenth century that for Latin, the practice of placing an easily perceptible unit of space between every word, including monosyllabic prepositions, pronouns, conjunctions, interjections, articles (borrowed from the vernacular), and certain freestanding particles, all of which had not been regularly pronounced as separate words in antiquity, was the norm of scholastic culture.[62] An examination of Greek texts copied in the British Isles, Italy, and Greece reveals how the separation of words in Greek originated in manuscripts copied by Irish scribes in the early Middle Ages and became a frequent practice in Renaissance Italy and France well before it became normal in Byzantium in the second half of the sixteenth century.[63] In the Slavic languages, written in the Cyrillic alphabet, word separation became standard by the beginning of the seventeenth century.[64] For Indian languages devolving from Sanskrit, word separation seems to have become standard only in the modern period.[65]

However, it has yet to be determined by what date and geographic route word separation, rejected by the literate culture of late antiquity, came to be the unfailing hallmark of the written Latin of the central Middle Ages, where it provided the model for the ultimate reintroduction of separation into Greek, as well as for the modern quantity of space in Hebrew and Arabic. Clearly, during the course of the nine centuries following Rome's fall, the task of separating written text, which had been for half a millennium a cognitive function of the reader, became instead the task of the scribe. But by what historical process did this remarkable change, fundamental to the history of reading, transpire? The response to this question is the subject of this book.

The importance of word separation by space is unquestionable, for it freed the intellectual faculties of the reader, permitting all texts to be read silently, that is, with eyes alone. As a consequence, even readers of modest intellectual capacity could read more swiftly, and they could understand an increasing number of inherently more difficult texts. Word separation also allowed for an immediate oral reading of texts, which eliminated the need for the arduous process of the ancient *praelectio*. Word separation, by altering the neurophysiological process of reading, simplified the act of reading, enabling both the medieval and modern reader to receive silently and simultaneously the text and encoded information that facilitates both comprehension and oral performance.[66]

Word Separation and Word Order

Ancient Latin was also profoundly modified in the postclassical period by the emergence of word order as an adjunct to the ancient principle of inflection.[67] Word order in medieval Latin affected the neurophysiology of reading in a way that was complementary to word separation, and together they laid the foundation for rapid, silent reading. Although word separation will be the central concern here and throughout this volume, the importance of word order to the genesis of silent reading must be recognized.

It is generally acknowledged that conventions of word order were a significant new dimension of medieval Latin and its vernacular derivatives.[68] Indeed, the philosophes of the eighteenth century regarded the constraints of French word order as a sign of the superiority of French in comparison with both classical Greek and Latin.[69] However, the imposition of conventions of word order on medieval Latin prose has often been regarded as a symptom of the degeneration of classical norms of style due to the influence of vernacular models, rather than as a positive achievement of medieval culture.[70] The modern mode of word separation by clearly perceptible unities of space, also a product of the medieval experience, was in its early manifestations similarly viewed as a degeneration of ancient cultural norms. Within the larger context of the history of Latin, word separation and word order represented linguistic simplifications that distinguished the written language of scholasticism from that of Tacitus and Augustine. In conjunction, they were already present in early Insular codices, where they made Latin a more analytic vehicle for the expression of thought.

Whereas word order in the written form of modern western European languages is syntactically essential, its absence in written ancient Greek and Latin was syntactically indifferent.[71] In the latter languages, as in Sanskrit and other ancient Indo-European languages, the relationship between words was conveyed by inflection, and not by permutations of sequence.[72] In ancient Latin, permutations of sequence only very rarely had an impact on sense, but they were fundamental elements of mellifluous style.[73] We have already noted that in the periodic sentences of antiquity, which were often logically imperfect in their syntax, long portions of text had to be read and retained in memory without being fully understood before ambiguity in construction could be resolved and meaning rendered apparent,[74] and that the grammatical ambiguity of classical Latin, compounded by the graphic ambiguity of *scriptura continua*, encouraged the practice of oral reading as a short-term mnemonic tool for extracting meaning from texts. By contrast, this compounded ambiguity was reduced in the Latin of the central Middle Ages and in the emerging written Romance vernacular languages written with interword space when conventions of word groupings and word order became an important adjunct to inflection, and, for the vernacular, an alternative to it.[75] However, this new, rigorous word order was inherently antithetical to the ancient quest for metrical and rhythmical eloquence.

The medieval sensitivity to word order formed part of a broader tendency to group syntactically related words into linear arrangements that medieval grammarians referred to as "contiguous continuations of letters."[76] To grammarians of the twelfth century, the *continuatio* of an ancient Latin text implied its construing or rephrasing into unambiguous and "correctly" ordered medieval Latin prose. In the thirteenth century, Roger Bacon and Johannes de Balbis explicitly recognized proximity as a determinant of meaning.[77] This development reflected the medieval propensity to structure Latin syntax according to the principles of logic.[78] Grammarians of the thirteenth and fourteenth centuries, particularly the modists, regularly referred to this analytical order imposed on prior classical norms as Latin's "natural order."[79] *Hyperbaton*, or departure from ordinary word order, defined only vaguely by the ancients, was linked by Insular grammarians to a violation of this "natural" order and of the boundaries of word grouping or *sectiones* within sentences.[80] The restructuring of written language that originated in the British Isles and began to spread on the Continent in the word-separated manuscripts of the tenth and eleventh centuries was a necessary prerequisite for the introduction of consistent signs of syntactic punctuation, which guided the reader through complex and compound sentences that departed from simple subject-verb-object order.[81] The sentence as "a total statement . . . conveyed by a series of propositions that follow rapidly one after another and each of which has a conclusion apparently complete" was fundamental for the genesis of modern notes of punctuation, the minimal use of short-term memory to achieve comprehension, and rapid, silent reading as we now know it.[82]

A notion of word order, and more generally of word groupings within sentences, had been foreshadowed in the vulgar Latin of the very end of the Imperial period.[83] The tendency not to pronounce word endings distinctly tended to make sequence more significant. The influence of

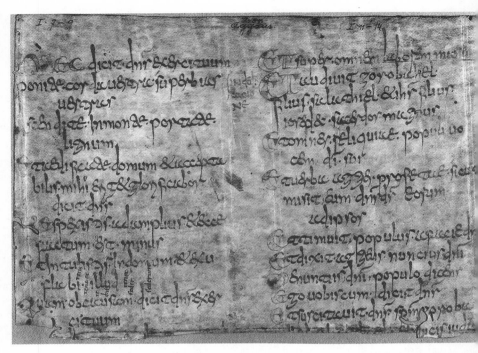

Figure 2. The book of Haggai written in *cola et commata*. Chicago, Newberry Library fragment 1; reproduced by permission.

this simpler and more direct language may be detected in Augustine's sermons and in Jerome's Vulgate, which reproduced to a degree greater than is usually appreciated the fixed sequence of words that was an attribute of ancient Hebrew and New Testament Greek.[84] The Latin of the Vulgate, with its simpler and shorter sentences and limited tendency toward subject-verb-object word order, made far fewer demands on the reader's ability to maintain ambiguous text in memory than the Latin of Cicero's orations or of Jerome's own epistles. The *per cola et commata* text format, which Jerome introduced as an essential element of the manuscript text of the Vulgate, complemented this effect by creating contextual space in which each line represented either a phrase, a clause, or a sentence (Figure 2).[85] The Vulgate became a primary model for medieval Latin. Conventional word groupings and shorter grammatical constructions eventually became normal in written Old French and Provençal.[86] Another, entirely independent precursor of medieval word order occurs in Boethius's Latin translations and commentaries on Aristotle's *Logica vetus*, where the need to express syllogisms without ambiguity also encouraged the use of conventional word groupings.

In medieval Latin prose, the enhanced observance of conventions of word order and word grouping reduced the time lag between the phonetic conversion of signs into words (whether internal or external) and the reader's full comprehension of the word based on its syntactical context.[87] Indeed, laboratory experiments on eye movements confirm that English texts in subject-verb-object order are more easily and efficiently read than those in a convoluted order, much as word-separated text is more easily read than unseparated text.[88] It has also been shown that the observance of fixed conventions of word sequence facilitates the reader's identification of word boundaries in unseparated text, and in separated text, word order extends the reader's field of vision as measured by the eye-voice span.[89] Finally, experiments have shown that word-separated writing enhances the reader's short-term memory of word order, and it is surely no coincidence that in modern European languages, word order is also far more rigorous in printed and written text intended to be read visually than in informal speech.[90] The evolution of rigorous conventions, both of word order and of word separation, had the similar and complementary physiological effect of enhancing the medieval reader's ability to comprehend written text rapidly and silently by facilitating lexical access. Although word order and word separation are thus intimately linked in the linguistic history of medieval Latin, for our story of the history of reading, we will continue to concentrate principally on the methodological problems posed by the evolution of word separation.[91]

Chapter 2

The Nomenclature of Word Separation

Word Separation and Paleographic Studies

In recent years, the thrust of manuscript studies has been to isolate the paleographic and codicological features linking a specific manuscript codex to the time, place, and mode of its manufacture. The insights gleaned from this approach have relevance for this study only insofar as the accurate dating and localization of codices establishes the matrix of artifacts necessary for the narration of the introduction of space into text and the related changes in text format that gave rise to modern reading habits. Thus, certain standard aspects of the descriptions of early medieval books, such as the arrangement of hair and flesh sides within the quire, each potentially useful for establishing date and place of origin, have no direct relevance for the history of reading. Other elements of the manuscript that on occasion have been consistently recorded, such as abbreviation, punctuation, and ruling, are of direct importance to this study.

In the existing tradition of manuscript scholarship, classical paleography, as defined by Ludwig Traube, E. A. Lowe, and Wallace M. Lindsay, is more pertinent to the history of reading than the more modern science of codicology. However, several defining characteristics of paleography have conspired to divert paleographers' attention from the development of word spacing in medieval texts.

While the paleographer's principal focus has been on the classification of individual letter forms, the student of the history of reading in the medieval West is primarily concerned with the evolution of word shape, and letter forms are important only to the degree that they play a role in determining that shape.[1] Thus, the adoption of minuscule, that is, lowercase letters, as a book script is significant for the historian of reading insofar as it contributed, in conjunction with word separation, to giving each word a distinct image. Modern psychologists call this image the "Bouma shape."[2] It is peculiarly characteristic of Western writing, in contrast to Chinese, whose characters each have a similar-sized square outline.[3] Since changes in letter forms after the evolution of minuscule in the early Middle Ages had in most instances only an indirect impact on Bouma shape, the medieval alterations that distinguished pre-Caroline and Caroline minuscule are of marginal significance for the history of reading. The individual letters within specific western European medieval minuscule scripts, unlike those of the Hebrew and Hindu tradition, have only occasionally been so similar as to be ambiguous and require contextual cues for the recognition of words.[4] Colette Sirat has stated that the working tool of the paleographer, the magnifying glass, is indicative of an orientation toward graphic traits that are obscure to the naked eye.[5] In contrast, the historian of reading focuses on the word, the graphic image that is most readily detectable and exploitable through normal vision.

In addition to the study of letter forms, a second major concern of paleographers has been instruction in the skills of transcribing difficult hands. Like the paleographer's focus on small graphic traits, this preoccupation, too, has inadvertently obscured the impact on normal reading of the insertion of space, a phenomenon that more than any other set the medieval book apart from its ancient antecedents. While it is true that transcribing letter by letter a fifth-century codex of Virgil or Livy written in rustic capitals is initially an easier task for the untrained modern student than transcribing some fourteenth-century scholastic texts, it would be wrong to conclude that the fourteenth-century texts were harder to read. To the contrary, scholastic Latin, when written by a professional scribe with complete word separation, allowed the medieval scholar familiar with its conventional abbreviations, preferred modes of construction, and vocabulary to read swiftly and skim easily in a fashion not readily distinguishable from the perusal of a modern printed book.[6] The difficulty encountered by the modern manuscript cataloguer or editor of a diplomatic edition (which attempts an exact reproduction of the original) in determining and noting in transcription within brackets the absence in scholastic writing of a given letter or minim stroke—the short, vertical lines forming the minuscule letters *i*, *u*, *n*, and *m*—was of no concern to a medieval reader, who easily grasped the correct meaning of the whole word as a unit, even when a single minim stroke or even an entire letter was wanting. In contrast, the relatively easy task of artificially deciphering, one by one, the individual letter forms of *scriptura continua* masks the profound difficulties of reading with understanding in an ambiguous medium where almost all grammatical units were obscured.

Reading scholastic Latin, with its grouping of syntactically related words, ample punctuation, and clear identification of word boundaries, was a relatively easy task for one who possessed the requisite specialized intellectual training. The modern student, once he or she has learned the apposite signs, can skim and take notes directly from late medieval codices. This contrasts with the modern reader of ancient texts, who finds it useful to read ancient script orally, using a tape recorder, and invariably even the most thoroughly initiated of modern classicists will begin work on an edition of a manuscript in *scriptura continua* by preparing a word-separated transcription.[7] Empirical evidence has corroborated the importance of separation by demonstrating that the suppression of the boundaries between words interferes with reading far more profoundly than changes in type font or even the omission of letters within words.[8] The impact on reading of even the most dramatic changes in Latin letter forms within the minuscule tradition is difficult to document.[9] Thus, the most crucial change in the relationship of the reader to the book from antiquity to modern times was the consequence of the medieval evolutionary process through which space was introduced into text. This change, complemented in certain instances by modest changes in letter shapes (for example, the distinction between *c* and *t* introduced in eleventh-century Caroline script by making the *t*'s vertical stroke protrude above the horizontal one), produced word shape, the prerequisite for the modern reading process.

This study of word shape in no way disparages the paleographer's concern with the accurate identification and description of letter forms as an essential tool for accurate dating. Indeed, such dating is essential for the narrative of this volume. Nevertheless, focusing uniquely on letter forms has helped to create a schema of historical periodization poorly suited to narrating the historical evolution of reading habits. In the now traditional paleographic time frame, the ninth-century Carolingian graphic reform marked the crucial point of transition between the book and documentary scripts of the late Roman Empire and those of the medieval and modern periods.[10] In the nearly four centuries during which Caroline minuscule gradually spread from its initial cradle in Corbie in eastern France to the rest of France, Lorraine, Germany, Spain, much of Italy, and the British Isles, according to conventional descriptions, the script remained substantially unchanged until resurgent chancelleries and burgeoning cathedral schools generated the Gothic "distortions" of Caroline letter forms that dominated the handwriting of the late Middle Ages.[11] Overall, if judged only by the form of individual letters, the script of books and documents of the ninth century through the early twelfth seems strikingly similar, for Caroline letter forms, considered in isolation from other aspects of the page, changed only slightly during these four centuries. Nevertheless, certain minor changes in letter shape, such as the protruding vertical stroke of the *t*, the accenting of the double *ii*, the descending *r* and *s*, the *ct*, *st*, and *et* intraword ligatures, and the use of the capital *S* at word extremities, coincide historically with the dramatic emergence of word separation in Caroline script. Each of these innovations enhanced the perception of the word as a graphic sign.

The general continuity in letter forms in the centuries after Charlemagne has generated the view of a static society that venerated ancient models. When using only changes in letter forms as a criterion, even expert paleographers have sometimes disagreed by over two centuries on the dating of books written in Caroline script.[12] However, when attention is focused on details of central importance to the study of the history of reading, such as space, abbreviation, *prosodiae* (signs that aided recognition and pronunciation of syllables and words), punctuation, terminal forms, and other related graphic innovations that enhanced word image, the period from the ninth century to the eleventh on the Continent emerges as an epoch of revolutionary changes. During this period, when the shape of individual letters changed but slightly, the Bouma shape first emerged on the written page, and as a consequence, Continental reading habits began to undergo a fundamental restructuring. So dramatic was this change that it is unsurpassed by any other alteration in the act of reading between the patristic age and the sixteenth century.

Existing paleographic and codicological literature, precisely because it has been based on an incomplete topology for manuscript description in regard to reading, also offers only very limited guidance as to the time and place of origin of aerated and separated script. Paleographers specializing in Irish and Anglo-Saxon books, citing the oldest monuments of Insular paleography, chiefly Bibles and Gospel books, have tended, correctly, to place the beginnings of word separation in the seventh and eighth centuries.[13] In contrast, a generation of German and American paleographers, either trained by Ludwig Traube or directly influenced by his school, have tended to look to the Carolingian reform as the period when word separation became if not normal, at least a predominant scribal practice. Traube's student, E. A. Lowe, avoided commenting on word separation in the *Codices latini antiquiores* except to note its absence in manuscripts of late antiquity.[14] In his various studies, Lowe rarely commented directly on word separation, but in his *Scriptura Beneventana*, he remarked on the absence or presence of the pattern he termed word separation only for manuscripts written during the ninth century, implicitly accepting separation as standard at Monte Cassino after the Carolingian era.[15] C. W. Barlow, whose work exemplifies the philological preoccupations of early-twentieth-century manuscript scholarship in Germany, saw no anachronism in ascribing to the ninth-century emendations intended to correct an aerated codex the standards of what I will define below as canonical separation, historically the most advanced and complete form of separation.[16] The late Bernhard Bischoff, in keeping with prewar German scholarship, stated that word separation began in the ninth century, and he modified the older view only in noting that separation did not include monosyllabic prepositions until the tenth century.[17]

French scholars have placed word separation in a somewhat different chronological framework. The seventeenth-century founder of diplomatics and paleography, Jean Mabillon, thought word distinctions to be anachronistic in all charters and books before Charlemagne, and indeed, spurious canonical separation of words is found in many eleventh-century attempts to replicate Merovingian acts.[18] The Maurist monks Charles François Toustain and René Prosper Tassin, in their *Nouveau traité de diplomatique*, an eighteenth-century vernacular expansion of Mabillon's work, engaged in a far more extensive discussion of word separation, which, despite some obscure references to codices and charters in eighteenth-century depositories, remains among the most useful general inquiries into the matter. Toustain and Tassin recognized the occasional connection between space and punctuation in antique and early medieval manuscripts, particularly those copied from examplars written *per cola et commata*, and accurately noted that in the mid-seventh century, erratic interword space supplanted space signifying or complementing punctuation.[19] They also realized that readers of Mabillon erred if they thought imperfect separation of words ceased with the ninth century, and using charters, Toustain and Tassin accurately traced the absence of separation through the reign of Hugh Capet. They correctly observed the relation between the *trait d'union* (the modern hyphen) and the separation of words, describing the post-factum addition of *traits d'union* to a ninth-century unseparated royal charter.[20] Natalis de Wailly, whose nineteenth-century compendium of Maurist scholarship was prepared as a manual for early students of the École des Chartes, reiterated Toustain's chronology for word separation by noting its absence in tenth-century French codices, but he prudently refrained from stating precisely when word separation became a conventional element in medieval writing.[21] In the twentieth century, Jean Vezin has accurately stated that word separation became normal in French manuscripts in the course of the eleventh century.[22]

Scholars from other national traditions have varied greatly in estimating the date of the advent of word separation. Etienne Sabbe, the only Belgian paleographer to address the problem directly, correctly placed the beginning of separation in Ghent after the mid-tenth century.[23] Until very recently, no Italian paleographer has attempted to date the appearance of word separation in Italian scripts. This hesitancy has perhaps been a result of the diverse nature of Italy's written tradition, ranging from the precocious practices of Irish scribes of seventh-century and eighth-century Bobbio to the pervasive reluctance to separate words characteristic of late-twelfth-century and thirteenth-century centers in central and southern Italy. Nevertheless, in 1984, Armando Petrucci, in part responding to a previous publication by this author, identified the eleventh century as the period in which word separation became normative in Italian codices.[24] Spanish paleographers have entirely eschewed discussion of the question, and not without cause, for enclaves of Mozarabic influence in the Iberian peninsula and the ensuant influence of the spacial patterns of Arabic on Visigothic script make generalizations particularly difficult.

The contradictory statements and general uncertainty concerning the dating and the nature of word separation in Latin medieval manuscripts have led to the generalization that word separation evolved between the sixth and the eleventh century in a desultory manner at the whim of individual scribes. This was an early view held by Robert Marichal, and as an explanation, it has a certain seductive charm.[25] If the history of word separation from the seventh to the twelfth century reflected the random habits of diverse scribes, a general chronology for its development would not be possible, and the careful analysis of the use of space in surviving dated and datable manuscripts would be neither necessary nor useful. However, a lengthy and detailed examination of hundreds of pre-twelfth-century manuscripts has convinced me that a geographical chronology for the development of word separation exists.[26]

Experts have often disagreed as to the origin of word separation because they have described different manuscripts with diverse vocabularies. This has been true in part because of the physical and technical constraints limiting scholarly investigations in the late nineteenth and early twentieth centuries, a period otherwise correctly recognized as the golden age of paleographic research. Scholars before World War I, due to the national orientation of paleographic training, the cost and difficulty of travel, and the great expense and limited availability of photographic reproductions, tended to base their general observations and conclusions implicitly on manuscript materials that were immediately accessible. In this light, their diverse chronologies for word separation, while parochial, are far less contradictory than they might at first appear, for they were often based on an extensive examination of manuscript *fonds* having historically homogeneous origins. Although a hasty attempt to synthesize their judgments in order to offer a chronological overview for all western Europe can easily create confusion, their apparently contradictory statements offer important insights for tracing the generally southward spread of word separation from Ireland and England to France and Germany, and onward to the shores of the Mediterranean.

Scholars have lacked a standard nomenclature for describing intratextual space, in particular. This lack has contributed to the failure to define with precision the role of space in Latin medieval manuscripts. Paleographers from the eighteenth century to the twentieth have not communicated effectively with each other, and in some cases, they have disagreed about the date at which separation commenced solely because of the lack of a consistent terminology for describing the variety of ways in which, from the seventh century onward, scribes intermingled space and text on the written page. Whereas all paleographers would agree that the term *scriptura continua* describes the rustic capitals of the oldest Virgil codices and that the term "separated" describes thirteenth-century Parisian manuscripts of Bonaventure and Albertus Magnus, few since the Maurists have ventured to categorize those manuscripts originating in the gray period of transition between the fall of Rome and 1200, when space appeared, often erratically, between groups of letters, syllables, or words, creating configurations of letters neither wholly contiguous nor fully separated. The lack of an appropriate vocabulary has resulted in codices being labeled by some as separated when in fact space irregularly separates letter, syllabic, or word blocks.[27] Also, some authorities, in describing word separation, have employed the phrase "word division," which properly connotes the division of words at line endings. This has caused confusion between two discrete phenomena that, although they are in certain instances closely related, remain fundamentally distinct. For example, the ninth-century scribe Lupus of Ferrières observed the Greco-Latin syllabic rules of correct word division at line endings while not regularly separating words within the line by space or other marks.[28]

New resources for research exist today, making possible a rigorous study of the history of reading based on a consistent nomenclature for the introduction of space into medieval manuscripts. First among these is the published corpus of photographic reproductions of pre-twelfth-century Latin manuscripts, which has grown comulatively since the end of the nineteenth century.[29] These reproductions, taken together, are a formidable instrument of research for formulating and resolving questions regarding word separation that the original compilers of these works never could have envisioned.[30] Of special value are the ongoing collections of *manuscrits datés*.[31]

A second resource not available in the last century is the corpus of unpublished photographic reproductions available in great repositories such as the Porcher Collection at the Bibliothèque Nationale in Paris and especially the collective holdings of the Institut de Recherche et d'Histoire des Textes, the IRHT. The IRHT collection of microfilms for textual study and photographs for paleographic study provide systematic access to hundreds of unpublished facsimiles from manuscripts of common origin that are today dispersed in depositories throughout Europe. As an aid to researchers, reference is regularly provided to these reproductions, as well as to those in the Porcher Collection, in the notes of this study.[32] The IRHT has also greatly advanced the reconstruction of the holdings of medieval libraries. It is now possible to establish origins and provenances for far more pre-thirteenth-century books than would have been imaginable a century ago, when Léopold Delisle published his monumental *Cabinet des manuscrits de la Bibliothèque Nationale*.[33]

A third boon to the systematic study of word separation has been the establishment of art history as an academic discipline. Art historians have been responsible for publishing thousands of examples of script incidentally accompanying illuminated miniatures and minor decorations.[34] The discipline of art history has also introduced its own criteria for establishing the date and origin of important groups of manuscripts, thus significantly augmenting the number of eleventh-century and twelfth-century codices of known origin.

Separated Script: An Overview

Although in the classical age, and very occasionally until the end of antiquity, Roman books and inscriptions were written with separation by medial points or interpuncts placed at midlevel in the line, these points were not usually accompanied by quantities of space any greater than that ordinarily placed between adjacent letters within a word, and never of the dimensions customary in medieval manuscripts.[35] In the second century A.D., words in inscriptions were frequently separated by an ivy-leaf-like decorative design, forming a special, space-filling intraword character known as a *hedera*, which more closely resembled a letter of the alphabet than a point.[36] While from a grammatical point of view texts separated by either space, interpuncts, or *hederae* may all be separated, neurophysiologically, the effect of these three modes of separation on the reading process is very different.[37] Points, and especially *hederae*, are not susceptible to rapid visual detection, while space of sufficient quantity is readily perceived. Experiments demonstrate that the placing of symbols within the spaces between words, while preserving separation in a strictly grammatical sense, greatly reduces the neurophysiological advantages of word separation and produces ocular behavior resembling that associated with unseparated text.[38]

In the early medieval period, the *scriptura continua* format of ancient manuscripts changed as space began to be introduced between words. In order to record the steps of this historical process, a terminology for the accurate description of interword space must be established. Paleographical and epigraphical literature offers little guidance, and the measurement of intratextual space in millimeters or points (as is customary among printers) is of only limited usefulness because absolute measurements of the quantity of space do not indicate how easily that space can be perceived in the context of a given script or type font.[39] Because individual letters of disparate origins vary greatly in proportion and density, simple linear measurements fail to reveal the relative perceptibility of space as a visual code, especially when comparing manuscripts written in different scripts and in different epochs.

Recently, students of Roman antiquity have suggested that space may be measured in relation to the equivalence with the space occupied by the width of a letter. This approach is helpful in that it makes measurement of space relative to a given hand.[40] For Hebrew, Maimonides in the twelfth century declared correct interword space to be the breadth of a small letter.[41] However, for Latin, the breadth of a letter as a unit of measure is too vague for both the antique and medieval periods. From the reader's vantage point, the salient quality of intratextual space is not its relative width in comparison with a letter, but the rapidity with which the eye can distinguish it from the spaces otherwise contained within a text, that is, the space between letters and within letters.[42] Therefore, the space used for the separation of words in manuscripts should be measured relative to whichever of these is greater in a given script. In the formal book scripts of antiquity, the maximum unit of space found within letters was customarily, but not always, greater than that existing between them, and this was always the case for medieval scripts. For ancient Latin manuscripts written in majuscule characters, the unit of comparison can usually be established from the internal space of the letters *D*, *O*, or *U*. In ancient cursive and minuscule scripts of the Middle Ages, the unit of space can usually be determined from the distance between the minum stroke of the "lowercase" letters *u*, *m*, or *n*, or more rarely the internal breadth of the letter *o*.[43] During the medieval period, the unit or, as I term it, unity of space was usually the same in the various letters, but the broadest of these measurements should be selected if a distinction exists among them. For consistency, the measurement between words is made between two words beginning and ending with a vertical stroke, measuring from one stroke to the other.

The norms established by the separated manuscript books and documents surveyed in this study suggest that for rapid perception in reading, a space of 1.5 unities of interletter space is minimal and 2 unities sufficient for the identification of word boundaries by the parafovea, the portion of the eye that perceives images at the margin of the eye's point of principal focus.[44] Parafoveal vision extends for six degrees, or about fifteen characters in modern printed text. Space of fewer than 1.5 unities of interletter space appears to help the reader to define word boundaries only within foveal vision, the portion of the visual field, about two degrees, where images of letters are perceived in full detail. Such spacing acts much like interpuncts or *hederae* between words in classical papyri. These symbols required purposeful scrutiny on the part of the reader, eliminating the creation of Bouma shape and the ensuant involvement of the right hemisphere in reading. The interpuncts and *hederae* of ancient separated script thus could help the reader by facilitating the phono-synthetic combination of phonemic signs in *praelectio*, but they did not enable the ancients to encode information on word boundaries prior to the ocular fixation, in the manner of modern separated writing. In this sense, interpuncts and *hederae* were ineffective aids to the physiological process of reading when compared with the interword spaces familiar in late medieval manuscripts and modern printed books. Space, in contrast with other antique forms of word separation, offers a principal advantage in that it gives a central role to parafoveal and (at greater distance from the eye's central focus) peripheral vision for the perception of words, as well as of *prosodiae* and signs of punctuation.

In modern printed text separated by 2 times the unity of space, the eye can identify letters at a range of seven to ten characters to the right of the point of fixation, and it can detect the presence of unities of space in parafoveal vision at a range of up to fifteen characters to the right of the reader's point of ocular fixation.[45] The eye uses this information to orient and organize saccadic movements in a regular and efficient manner. When reading printed texts in English, the eyes avoid fixations focused on a space and instead systematically group short words. Largely avoiding fixations on monosyllabic articles and prepositions, the brain centers fixations on long words, avoiding intraword saccadic movement.[46] When a fixation occurs on a long word, the center of the fixation is consistently on the anterior portion of the word. The eye movements of the modern reader are thus determined by graphic units delineated by space, and there can be little doubt that the later medieval reader reacted similarly to these spatial patterns.

The extra unities of space regularly allocated to signs of punctuation also affect eye movement. Information about space and punctuation is garnered by the reader of modern separated text through parafoveal and peripheral vision at least one line in advance of the portion of text being decoded.[47] All these complex neurophysiological processes for the decoding of visible language in the West, that is, the efficient organization of saccades, the prerecognition of capitalization and punctuation, and the recognition of Bouma shape, especially of short words, are dependent on the eye's use of intratextual space greater than 1.5 unities of space.

In the relatively small corpus of extant interpunct-separated Latin papyri, ancient scribes never accompanied interpuncts with 1.5 unities of space.[48] The maximum space I have recorded is 0.67 unities of space, and even this advantage was greatly lessened due to the absence of a distinction between uppercase and lowercase letters, which eliminated much of the potential difference in the Bouma shape or silhouette of each word.[49] Separation by interpuncts alone was primarily a phenomenon of Latin antiquity prior to the end of the second century A.D. When interpuncts were used by the original scribes in medieval manuscripts in the British Isles and on the Continent from the eighth century through the eleventh and revived again in the Renaissance for display scripts, the interpuncts were almost always accompanied by 1.5 or more unities of space.

An unambiguous distinction between interword and interletter space is fundamental to the modern reading of separated writing and to the economy of mental effort that today's reading habits represent. For this reason, fusions and intraword ligatures that enhanced word shape were common in the fully separated Gothic script of the late Middle Ages. Studies conducted in the first half of this century on the Fraktur type font, a direct descendent of medieval Gothic script, have suggested that fusion is advantageous for the mature reader.[50] In scripts where words are distinguished by the scribe and where perception of the Bouma shape is regularly exploited for word recognition, too easy a perception of interletter space can be detrimental to the rapid perception of the word as a whole. A compact representation of the word also modestly enhances the average number of words visible in parafoveal vision.[51]

In contrast, unseparated script is easier to read where interletter space is roughly comparable to the maximum quantity of space contained within letters. The phonosynthetic process of reading *scriptura continua* by mentally grouping letters within uninterrupted rows to form syllables, and then of grouping syllables to form words, is physiologically easier when individual letters are framed by space so as to be distinct one from another. The presence of interpuncts in Roman manuscripts of the Golden Age facilitated this grouping process. Even in Roman cursive script, which emphasized speed of transcription rather than legibility, ligatures between letters were avoided and space between letters generally remained.[52]

The tendency toward compaction characteristic of scripts separated by readily perceptible unities of space complemented the compaction already achieved by signs at word endings, such as the *e* cedilla and the ampersand or *et* ligature, which used a symbol to replace two or more letters. Generally, script compaction is measurable by variations in the ratio of letter width to height. In separated script, the ratio of width to height tends to be consistently less than in unseparated script, which is another way of saying that letters in unseparated writing tend generally to be broader. For the sake of comparison between scripts of widely disparate epochs, the letter *o* can be conveniently used as a benchmark. In the *scriptura continua* of Roman antiquity, the letter *o* was often entirely circular or broader than its height; in medieval script separated by space, the letter *o* was normally higher than its breadth.[53]

Linguistic Implications of Separation

In addition to a graphic definition of what constitutes a unit of intratextual space, consistent grammatical criteria for what constitutes word separation are also needed. Modern linguists have tended to begin their study of language by accepting as an element in their initial definition of the word the units delineated by space in printed books.[54] This is an understandable premise because in books and documents of the modern period, the principal function of space within sentences has been word separation, even if the conventions for inserting space, and thereby distinguishing words from bound morphemes, on close analysis often seem arbitrary.[55] However, it has often erroneously been assumed that in ancient and medieval books, all spaces falling within lines of text, in the absence of notes of punctuation, were intended to serve as signs of word separation. Certain ancient fragments, written on papyrus and wood, in which space was used as a form of punctuation, and numerous medieval manuscripts dating from the seventh century to the twelfth have been described by one observer or another as separated, when in fact properly speaking they are not, because space did not fall predictably between each word.[56] In manuscripts or inscriptions in *scriptura continua*, where space was used as a mode of punctuation, such occasional spacing naturally fell between words, but did not systematically mark individual word boundaries. In many other early medieval manuscripts that will be described in this book, space unrelated to any function of punctuation fell between words, but not between every word. In this study, for writing to be described as separated, spaces, interpuncts, or other signs of separation must fall regularly between every word, with the exception only of monosyllabic prepositions and certain other short and generally monosyllabic function words (Figure 3).

The failure to separate words from monosyllabic prepositions that proceed them has a long tradition, beginning in antiquity and continuing, especially for vernacular manuscripts, to the end of the Middle Ages.

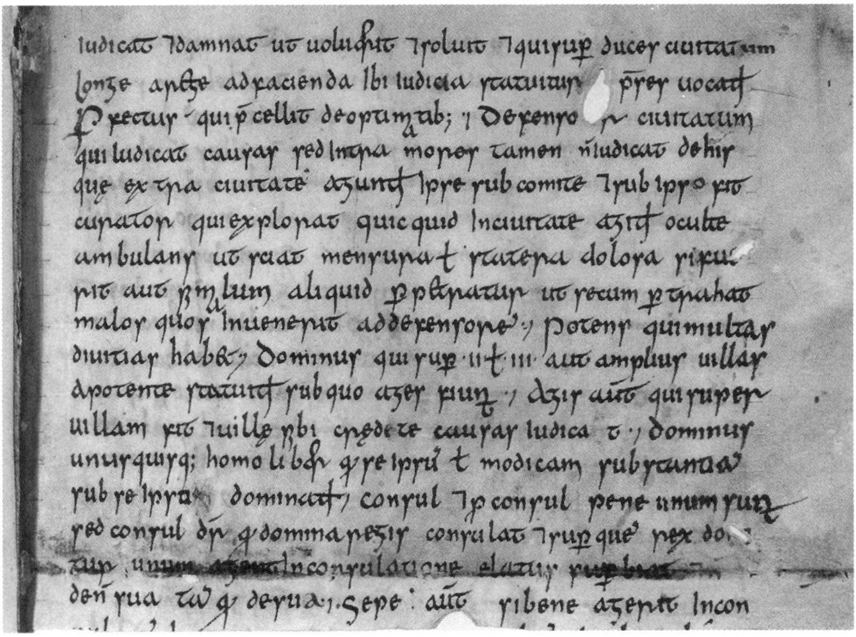

Figure 3. Separated script in Pseudo Jerome, *Epistola degradus Romanorum*, copied by an Anglo-Saxon scribe ca. 900. Chicago, Newberry Library 1.5, no. 9 recto; reproduced by permission.

In many ancient Latin manuscripts, the interpunct was frequently omitted between a monosyllabic preposition and its subsequent object.[57] In medieval manuscripts, space after prepositions and other monosyllables, sometimes including conjunctions, particles, and forms of the verb *esse*, were often either omitted or of reduced quantity. This form of separation was particularly prevalent in Latin manuscripts of northern Europe dating from before the mid-eleventh century, and in Italy until the end of the Middle Ages. Its origin lies in the ancient rules of pronunciation, where proclitic and enclitic words received neither tonic nor rhythmic accentuation.[58] Ancient grammarians, whose notion of the graphic word was amorphous, failed to distinguish between prepositions and homographs that were bound morphemic syllables.[59] For example, Priscian, in defining the *dictio* as a minimal part of speech, did not clearly distinguish between *in* as a freestanding preposition, *in-* as a bound preposition, and *in-* as a bound negative particle.[60] The cognitive demands made on the reader who must only separate prepositions from their objects are far less onerous than those imposed on a reader who is obliged to separate all words in a text written in *scriptura continua* or most words in a text written in word blocks composed of two or more polysyllabic words, for in script in which spaces are omitted only after prepositions, potential points of ambiguity necessitating the intervention of memory and intellectual judgment based on context are relatively few.

Aerated Script

Unlike late ancient manuscripts that were unseparated or separated only by interpuncts accompanied by minimal space, manuscripts written in the British Isles in the late seventh century, and in other regions far later, were regularly separated by space complemented by incipient and terminal signs and by monolexic abbreviations (clearly delimited signs that stood for words) or by suspension abbreviations (sequences of initial letters), all of which were susceptible to ready exploitation by parafoveal vision.[61] Thus, in some medieval handwritings at an early date, there was a clear shift toward signs that, in addition to performing a grammatical function, aided the reader to organize efficient saccadic movements and to recognize certain preliminary attributes of a word before the word as a whole was fixed in foveal vision. In many other early medieval manuscripts, space was present, but not consistently between every word. I identify this large and important group of manuscripts as "aerated."

The common characteristic of all aerated Latin manuscripts is that inserted space delimits units that do not necessarily correspond to either units of meaning or rhetorical pauses. In general, modern students of paleography have either insisted upon a grammatical basis for such spacing (without offering satisfactory documentary proof of its consistent presence) or, accepting the aeration as eclectic, have regarded it as a sign of the general cultural decline of the early Middle Ages.[62] When comparing aerated scripts with fifth-century and sixth-century Roman manuscripts in which space was used as an adjunct to or in lieu of punctuation, some have judged them to constitute no more than a degeneration of scribal understanding of the ancient units of the *cola et commata*. These paleographers interpret the emergence of aeration as an indication that scribes no longer fully understood ancient grammar—and by implication, the texts they copied.[63] Other scholars, viewing these manuscripts from the vantage point of the truly separated manuscripts of the later Middle Ages, have judged early medieval aerated manuscripts to be the work of scribes too ignorant of basic Latin vocabulary to be able to recognize the boundaries that ought to separate words.[64] Aerated manuscripts have rarely been appreciated in their own right as a valid and important innovation in textual display, an intermediate stage between *scriptura continua* and separation, that facilitated reading.

The ancient manuscripts that did use space as punctuation to set off a paragraph as an aid to oral recitation were a precedent for the aerated texts copied on the Continent during the seventh and eighth centuries. In numerous instances, the evolution from spatial punctuation to aeration may be traced in the textual tradition of specific patristic works, such as the *Regula magistri* and Hilary of Poitier's *De Trinitate*.[65] Many of the earliest aerated manuscripts preserved the distinction of the *cola et commata* by the periodic insertions of major spaces to form distinctions of about twenty characters in length, divided by erratically inserted minor space. In effect, this devolutionary process altered the composition of the written page from long word blocks roughly corresponding to grammatical units of meaning to shorter sub-blocks devoid of any but coincidental correspondence to syntactical units. While this process did not enhance the role of space as a cue to meaning, the greater frequency of space within texts must have had direct and salutary implications for saccadic ocular movement.

Text regularly permeated by space, even when that space is capriciously inserted so as to correspond regularly neither to words nor to larger grammatical units, is still physiologically easier to read than *scriptura continua*. While the reader of aerated script cannot identify a word by its Bouma shape or regularly rely on parafoveal vision to glean preliminary information about word meaning, aeration helped the reader to reduce ocular regressions by providing points of reference for orientation of the eye movements within a line of text as the reader grouped letters to form syllables and words. The insertion of intratextual space at irregular intervals implied the possibility of fixations and fewer regressions, with greater quantities of text decoded at each fixation, potentially measurable by an enhanced eye-voice span. Thus, aeration made it possible for the reader to begin the cultivation of cognitive skills that had not been exploited by either the ancient Greeks or Romans. Far from being a symptom of grammatical incompetence or faulty scribal orthography, the aeration of script was a sign of an unconscious quest for a mode of textual display that enhanced the reader's exploitation of his hitherto untapped neurophysiological faculties.

The temporal span of the production of aerated manuscripts varied

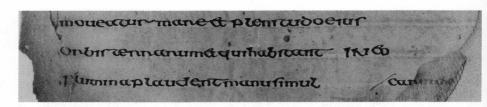

Figure 4. Letter blocks in the *Cathach Psalter*. Dublin, Royal Irish Academy, f. 52 recto; reproduced by permission.

greatly in different geographic regions of Europe. In Ireland, aerated manuscripts were uniquely a transient phenomenon of the seventh century, after which all Latin writing was separated, although vernacular manuscripts continued to be aerated according to special rules into at least the twelfth century.[66] In England, Wales, and Brittany, the earliest extant Latin manuscript books and documents were separated, but vernacular texts were usually aerated, at least through the eleventh century. In France, the Low Countries, Germany, and the Iberian peninsula, aerated Latin manuscripts were common from the seventh century through the eleventh, and they prevailed in central and southern Italy even into the thirteenth century. Formal texts of Roman law were still produced in aerated script in central Italy in the fourteenth century. In Byzantium, aerated Greek manuscripts were normal from the ninth century to the sixteenth.[67] Not only did the chronological limits of aerated manuscripts differ dramatically from northern to southern Europe, but the configuration of the intrusion of space also varied greatly between regions.[68]

Of all the aerated manuscripts, those in which intratextual space was inserted without or with minimal respect for either words or syllabic boundaries represent only a minuscule subset. These may be identified as being written in "letter blocks" (Figure 4). In general, this group is restricted to the oldest aerated manuscripts, which were produced only in Ireland or in Irish colonies on the Continent.[69] Space aids reading most efficaciously when it corresponds to units of sound or meaning.[70] Medieval Irish scribes, within three-quarters of a century of their initial experimentation with intratextual space, developed varieties of aerated writing in which space served as a cue to the recognition of syllables and words, establishing a correlation between space and phonemic or morphemic units. In this group of manuscripts, scribes placed space, usually of inconsistent quantity, only between words or between syllables within words. The boundaries for syllables were set by the conventions of spo-

ken Latin, and not by the arbitrary rules stated by the ancient grammarians, which the Romans themselves did not observe when dividing
words at line endings.[71] Space did not identify every syllable or word,
but nevertheless it aided the reader by highlighting a certain number
of syllabic or word boundaries, without distinguishing the former from
the latter. Such manuscripts are properly denoted as being written in
"syllable blocks" (Figure 5).[72] This use of space simplified the cognitive
process of word identification, extended the eye-voice span of the reader
with greater total efficiency, and contributed to the reduction of ocular
regressions. In the British Isles, space was from a very early date more
frequently used to denote words and morphemic syllables, and this morphemic configuration of space soon evolved into both true word separation in Latin and the morphemic blocks characteristic of aerated Celtic
and Anglo-Saxon vernacular codices. Other Irish manuscripts had a variant format in which major spaces set off word blocks that were parsed by
erratically inserted spaces. This format can be termed "hierarchical letter
blocks" (Figure 6).[73]

A still more sophisticated form of aerated manuscripts became the
prevalent textual format on the Continent in both pre-Carolingian and
post-Carolingian times. In it, the scribe made a hierarchical distinction
between a larger quantity of space placed exclusively between words
and a smaller quantity of space placed indiscriminately between either
syllables or words, creating word blocks with subdistinctions denoting
either words or syllables that made no distinction between morphemic
syllables and other syllables. This most important group of manuscripts

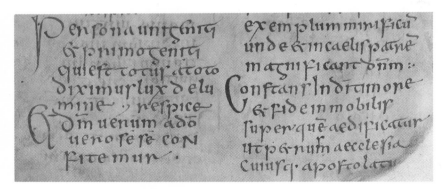

Figure 5. Syllable blocks in the *Antiphonary of Bangor*. Milan, Biblioteca Ambrosiana C. 5 inf., f. 13 verso; reproduced by permission.

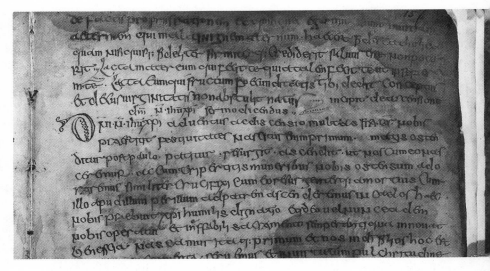

Figure 6. Hierarchical letter blocks in a patristic miscellany. Milan, Biblioteca Ambrosiana O. 212 sup., f. 15 recto; reproduced by permission.

may be described as having been written in "hierarchical word blocks" (Figures 7 and 8). The coded intratextual space of manuscripts written in hierarchical word blocks facilitated recognition of words and improved the reader's ability to recognize simultaneously words, punctuation, and other paratextual signs.

Alcuin's injunction to denote units of sense by signs of punctuation was addressed to the scribes of the Caroline scriptoria of Tours, who produced aerated codices in hierarchical word blocks replete with marks of punctuation.[74] Emblematic forms of punctuation imported from the British Isles permeated this variety of aerated script, and new forms of punctuation evolved on the Continent. The most innovative of these was a sign of interrogation, unknown in antiquity and first enumerated among *positurae* (the ancient term for signs of punctuation) by Isidore of Seville. Similarly, the earliest forms of musical notation by neumes, nonexistent in the Latin manuscripts of antiquity, also spread in ninth-century and tenth-century aerated texts written in hierarchical word blocks.[75] The compatibility of punctuation and musical signs is evidence of the advantages for ocular movement and text perception that intra-textual space afforded the oral reader who in the new medium could more readily decode not only the text's meaning but also indications for pitch, intonation, and tempo. Intratextual space was a prerequisite for maintaining an eye-voice span sufficiently broad to enable the fluent matching of syllable to pitch necessary for the performance of medieval chant.[76] In general, in texts written for musical notation, the musical portion is more intensely aerated and consequently contains more free-standing syllables and words than the normal prose sections written by the same scribe in the same codex.[77]

Most manuscripts in hierarchical word blocks were written in minus-cule scripts, and this significantly aided the recognition of syllables as units, as well, thereby creating the potential for more rapid word recog-nition. The relative prevalence of intratextual space in hierarchical word blocks compared with *scriptura continua* determined the degree to which the reading of these scripts may have approached that of separated writ-ing. Manuscripts in which a hierarchical word block was more than twenty-five characters in length (exceeding the outer limits of parafoveal vision) must have been read much like *scriptura continua* itself. Where word blocks were fifteen to twenty-five characters in length, the reader's use of parafoveal and peripheral vision must regularly have exceeded that

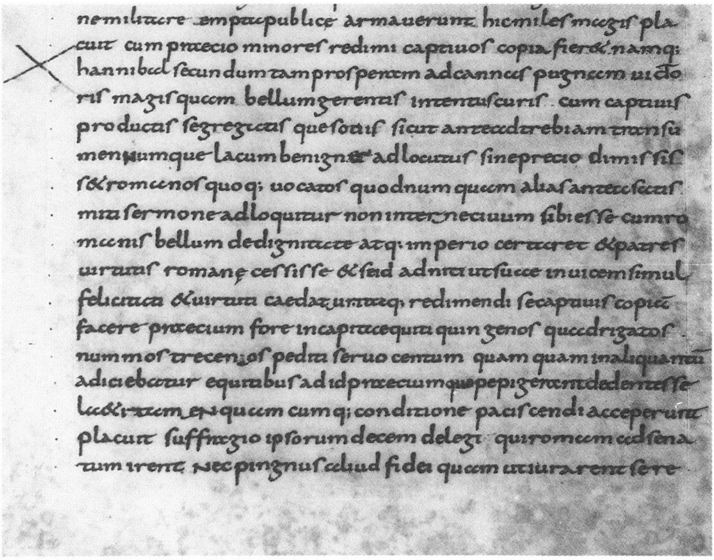

Figure 7. Hierarchical word blocks in the *Regiensis Livy*. Vatican Library Reg. lat. 762, f. 28 verso; reproduced by permission.

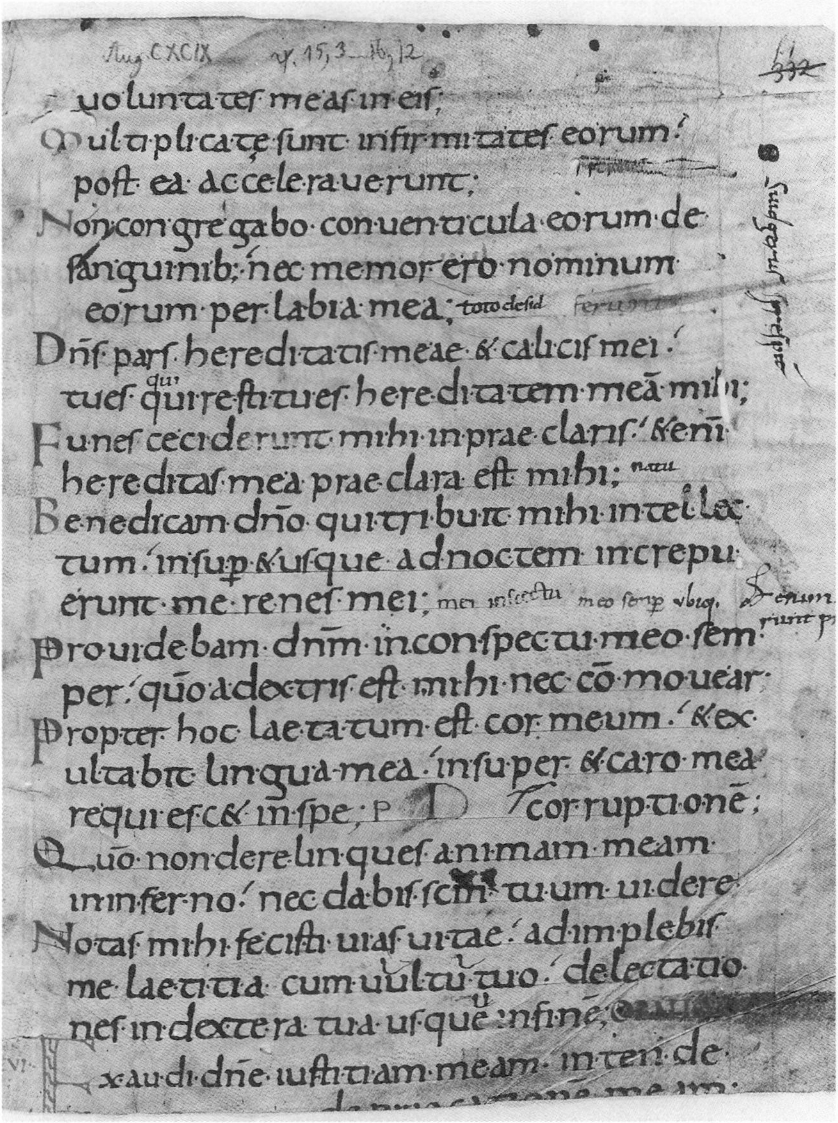

Figure 8. The psalms written in hierarchical word blocks with syllables pedagogically marked by interpuncts. Karlsruhe, Badische Landesbibliothek Aug. Fragment 8; reproduced by permission.

of *scriptura continua* manuscripts punctuated by space. Space in these hierarchical word blocks was sometimes supplemented by capitals and monolexic or terminal abbreviations that effectively subdivided the word blocks. Even in highly aerated scripts, the frequent presence of inter-word ligatures and intersyllabic space often obstructed the perception of words as images. It is possible that some very highly aerated text formats similar to those that facilitated reading musical notation may also have facilitated the silent, devotional reading of familiar private prayer books. The nomenclature for devotional reading in early medieval Continental monastic rules and customaries is too ambiguous for us to be certain that silent reading was in fact practiced by Continental monks of the Carolingian age. However, many literary sources suggest that reading was oral.[78] Unlike Insular monks, Continental monks did not use the verb *videre* to mean "to read." Certainly, rapid, silent reference reading was not possible even within highly aerated early medieval Continental minuscule scripts.

The limit of fifteen characters has not been arbitrarily established. Although we cannot place Carolingian readers in a laboratory, experiments with modern separated script demonstrate that this length represents the approximate limit of the quantity of text visible in parafoveal vision to the right of the reader's point of ocular fixation. Fifteen characters is also roughly equivalent to the eye-voice span in normal reading of separated print.[79] The absence of separation in medieval aerated script undoubtedly reduced the quantity of text visible in parafoveal vision, implying more frequent intrablock saccadic movements. In long word blocks, the reader confronted at first glance many false syllables and phonetically plausible pseudosyllables that inevitably slowed the decoding process.[80] In contrast, many of the saccades that the reader of intensely aerated script performed must have been aided by the presence of the occasional interword space perceived in parafoveal vision. The graphic isolation of word beginnings or endings facilitated lexical access, reinforced contextual cues, and generally reduced reliance on aural recall in the reading process.

In Latin, fifteen letters roughly conform to the maximum length of two common words. Therefore, in codices written in hierarchical word blocks of fewer than fifteen characters, the word blocks were typically composed of either two polysyllabic words or a monosyllabic and polysyllabic word. The shorter the word blocks, the easier they were for the reader to parse. Also, the reader encountered more freestanding graphic words, each with its own Bouma shape. Consequently, in these manuscripts, ocular movements more closely resembled those of a modern reader of separated print. A consistent absence of interword ligatures in highly aerated manuscripts in the ninth and tenth centuries would have further abetted word recognition, especially when ligatures were present within words, but such was rarely the case.

In addition to the relative prevalence of intertextual space, a second variable pertinent to texts written in hierarchical word blocks was the quantity of space employed relative to a text's basic unity of space. For ease in reading, it was crucial that the distinction between larger quantities of space inserted only between words and lesser quantities used to denote both the boundaries of words and syllables be readily perceptible. The model developed for measuring separated script is applicable to measuring the interword spaces in aerated script, that is, the interior unit of space between minim strokes of the letters *m*, *n*, and *u* relative to the amount of interword space falling between the boundaries of two hierarchical word blocks, with measurement made between words ending and beginning with vertical strokes. The same unity of space also provides the reference point for the smaller quantities of space used to distinguish words or syllables within these word blocks. The interword spaces at word-block boundaries in pre-Carolingian and Carolingian scripts were almost uniformly equal to or greater than 1.5 times the unity of space, while spaces within the hierarchical word blocks were generally shorter than 1.5 unities of space or less. Such minor spaces were therefore not readily identifiable in parafoveal vision. The tendency toward the convention of a larger unit for interword space equal to 2 times the unity of space, already evident in many eighth-century northern European aerated manuscripts, was the precursor of the normal quantity of space placed between all words in the separated manuscripts of the central Middle Ages. The minor space of generally less than 1.5 unities was the precursor of intersyllabic space that was still regularly present in many Continental separated scripts through the mid-eleventh century, but that tended to disappear in northern Europe at the end of the century. It was also often the precursor for the quantity of space placed after monosyllabic prepositions in many early separated scripts.

Geographical patterns exist for the various classes of hierarchical word blocks. Short word blocks of fewer than fifteen characters in length were particularly common in southern Germany in the late ninth and tenth centuries.[81] In contrast, the relatively long word blocks of greater than fifteen characters in length and not infrequently of greater than twenty characters were characteristic of scripts in southern France and Italy. In northern France, the Low Countries, and northern Germany, hierarchical word blocks varied greatly, some being fewer than and some more than fifteen characters in length. It is noteworthy that in general, script contained more intratextual space in those regions where the vernacular was Celtic or Teutonic than in France and Spain, where the vernacular, a derivative of Latin, was not consciously recognized to be a distinct language.[82] Within Romance-speaking Europe, where consciousness of the vernacular as a language developed later, word blocks were generally longer because the need for the artificial graphic aid of interword space was less pronounced.

In England, Ireland, Wales, and Brittany, where separation as opposed to aeration prevailed by the eighth century in Latin manuscripts, a special form of hierarchical word block evolved for the vernacular. In these "morphemic hierarchical word blocks," major spaces were inserted exclusively between words, and minor spaces were inserted either between words or between morphemic syllables (Figure 9).[83] In a few instances, this format also reoccurred in Insular Latin manuscripts. In eleventh-century and twelfth-century Italy, as part of that region's prolonged evolution toward regular word separation, we frequently encounter word blocks unparsed by minor spaces. I will term this configuration "solid word blocks."

In describing aerated manuscripts copied in hierarchical word blocks, it can also be important to enumerate the terminal signs and abbreviations used in addition to space to separate either syllables or words within the blocks. These scribal practices, along with the use of monolexic abbreviations and the rejection of interword ligature, were on occasion signs of evolving word consciousness. Virtually the only terminal sign in ancient Latin was the capital *NT* ligature. It was present in ancient inscriptions and manuscripts where it signified the end of a physical line of undivided writing without necessarily corresponding to the termination of a word. Its chief function was to save space, rather than to guide the eye movements of the reader.[84] In manuscripts of the ninth, tenth, and eleventh centuries written in hierarchical word blocks, the capital *NT* ligature reentered the graphic *langue* as a sign of syllabic termination that could be placed within a line of text, either at the end of a syllable or at the end of a word. However, some ninth-century scribes, notably Lupus of Ferrières, reserved the capital *NT* ligature exclusively for word endings.[85] The *NT* ligature in the context of minuscule script became much

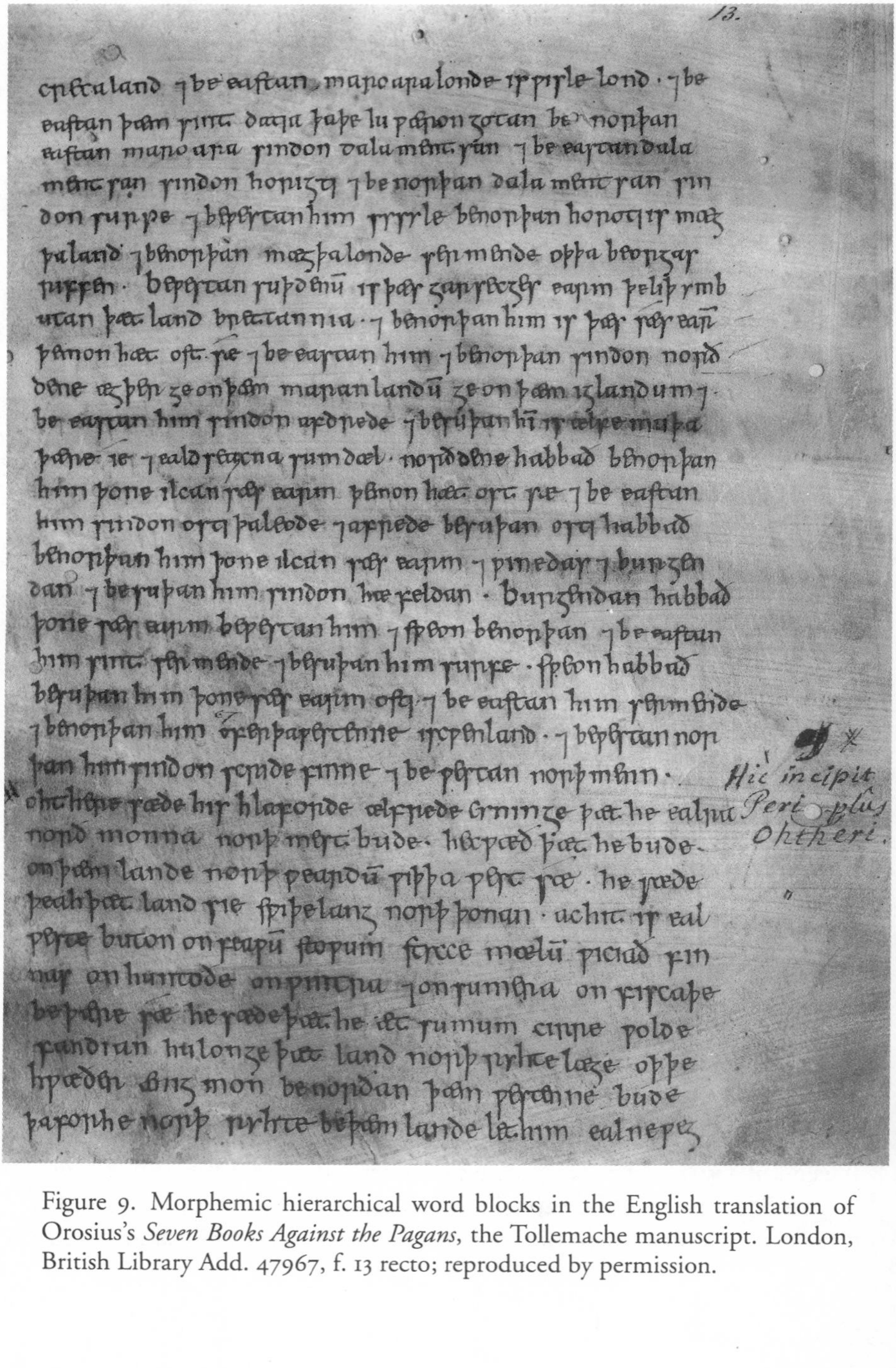

Figure 9. Morphemic hierarchical word blocks in the English translation of Orosius's *Seven Books Against the Pagans*, the Tollemache manuscript. London, British Library Add. 47967, f. 13 recto; reproduced by permission.

more conspicuous in peripheral vision than it had been in the uppercase writing of antiquity. Capital forms of the letters *N*, *S*, and *Z* were similarly used in aerated manuscripts as signs of syllabic boundary. Other signs of intraword syllabic boundary present in Caroline script were the *ct* and *et* ligatures, often breaching intersyllabic space. They were a sign of word unity that did not, however, create word shape.[86] In addition, the suprascript stroke, or *virga*, and the apostrophe were used to denote omitted letters at the end of either a syllable or word.

In the period directly preceding the proliferation of separated script, scribes in northern France reserved certain signs with increasing frequency for syllables at the ends of words, particularly those falling at the end of a hierarchical word block. These included, in addition to the *NT* ligature, the suprascript stroke for *m*, the Insular symbol for *-tur*, the apostrophe for *-us*, the symbol for *-bus*, and the *et* ligature.[87] With the advent of word separation at the end of the tenth century, these same signs came to be restricted to word endings.

Abbreviations were absent or extremely rare in *scriptura continua*. They were abundant in Irish and Anglo-Saxon separated manuscripts, as well as in the separated Continental manuscripts. In Continental aerated manuscripts written in hierarchical word blocks, abbreviations were composed of a mixture of syllable and word signs, rather than of signs for words or morphemes alone, and the same sign was often used to connote more than one syllable. Abbreviations in aerated writing thus typically lacked the regular correspondence to units of meaning characteristic of the monolexic abbreviations of Insular and subsequent Continental separated writing. The broader span of vision for the reader that resulted from aerated text provided an advantage for the resolution of the inherent ambiguity of many abbreviations. Space in scripts written in hierarchical word blocks thus compensated the reader for the more difficult lexical access that the use of ambiguous abbreviations imposed, thereby having a role analogous to that of space in Semitic scripts. Indeed, an important form of abbreviation originating and spreading exclusively in the medium of aerated script was vowel suppression, a normal occurrence in ancient Phoenician, Hebrew, and very early Arabic, where the absence of vowels had been tolerable only because of the compensatory presence of intratextual space. Thus, in contrast to Insular separated writing, where monolexic abbreviations complemented and enhanced the image of words, the abbreviations characteristic of aerated script, while they expedited writing, were often fraught with ambiguities that only the presence of space alleviated. They frequently did not expedite word recognition.

Canonical Separation

A final category, "canonical separation," is needed to bring this nomenclature for the evolution of intratextual space to its conclusion. (A summary of this nomenclature is given in Figure 10.) Canonical separation describes the configuration of space that has since the twelfth century become characteristic of almost all written or printed Latin texts. In canonically separated manuscripts, all words, including conjunctions (except, as in modern printed Latin, the postpositional -*cum*, the enclitics -*que* and -*ve*), monosyllables, and particles (except the interrogative -*ne* and the inseparable *in*- and *ve*-), were separated solely by space with interword space equivalent to an average minimum of twice the unity of space.[88] Canonical separation was usually accompanied by the suppression of intrasyllabic space (except in the presence of conventional ligatures), reinforcing the reader's ability to identify a word as a single unit. Syllabic space, which had played an important role in the aerated Continental manuscripts of the high Middle Ages and continued to be present in early-eleventh-century separated manuscripts, was absent or only minimally present in canonically separated manuscripts of the late eleventh and twelfth centuries. Monosyllabic prepositions were separated by space comparable to that accorded to other words. Canonically separated manuscripts were the dominant text format for both the late Middle Ages and the Renaissance (Figure 11). Later, I will employ the term "*fere* canonical script" to describe manuscripts that occasionally lapse into separated script, often by sometimes omitting space after one or more monosyllabic prepositions.

The aspect of canonically separated script that fundamentally distinguishes it from separated script was the presence of spaces after every word, including all short function words. In the classical period, these short words had not received tonic accentuation when pronounced, and subsequently, at the end of antiquity, these same words did not receive rhythmic stress.[89] Thus, in oral discourse, they were not separated.[90] Canonical separation was therefore a graphic form that implied a far more rigorous definition of the word than that provided by ancient grammarians. The regular separation of function words that became common in the twelfth century in northern Continental books was accompanied by

Scriptura continua (see Figure 1)
Cola et commata (see Figure 2)
Punctuation by space
Aeration by: letter block (see Figure 4)
              syllable blocks (see Figure 5)
              hierarchical letter blocks (see Figure 6)
              hierarchical word blocks (see Figures 7 and 8)
              morphemic hierarchical word blocks (see Figure 9)
              solid word blocks
Separation (see Figure 3)
Canonical separation (see Figure 11)

Figure 10. Summary of nomenclature for space in script.

a new grammar permeated by Aristotelian logic, which, in the thirteenth century, culminated in the grammatical school of the Modists, for whom word distinction and word order were key tools of analysis.[91] Instead of mirroring oral accentuation, grammarians and scribes isolated the maximum number of words playing a syntactical role within the sentence consistent with minimizing graphic ambiguity. Canonical separation as a text format not only ceased to reflect speech, but may have on occasion generated departures from ancient pronunciation. Modern scholars have noted in the accentual patterns of the *cursus*, the set rhythms observed by some authors of medieval prose, a presumption of the oral accentuation of monosyllables, and a spoken accentuation of monosyllabic prepositions is assumed in certain thirteenth-century scholastic discussions of accenting.[92]

As has been noted, psychologists have observed that the presence of graphically distinct short function words, including articles (not present in classical Latin) and prepositions, is very important for organizing eye movement because such short words are particularly easy to decode in parafoveal vision.[93] The new text format of canonical separation made the use of parafoveal vision optimal in two ways. First, for saccadic co-ordination, by isolating the maximum number of short words, it permitted ocular fixations to be centered on long words; and second, short words could be grouped with the maximum efficiency characteristic of modern printed text.[94] The increasing tendency of scribes from the mid-eleventh century onward to set monosyllabic prepositions off by space was strengthened by the increasingly analytical nature of medieval Latin, as evidenced by the adoption of patterns of word order employing the prepositions where ancient authors had relied on inflection.[95] Physiologically, the combined use of short words and the separation of short words

Figure 11. Canonical separation in the writing of the scribe Goderan in Josephus, *De bello iudaico*. Brussels, Bibliothèque Royale Albert Ier, II, 1179, f. 3 verso, col. 1; reproduced by permission.

enhanced fluid reading. Since the meaning of short words was easier to extract through parafoveal vision, speed of comprehension was increased. Canonical separation thus capitalized on a shift away from parataxis to expedite the reading process. Because in canonically separated script every block of letters invariably represented a word, intrablock saccadic movement was largely eliminated, producing the eye movements of modern rapid reading, that is, saccades of maximum mean length with minimal deviations from the mean. In canonically separated script, each word could be recognized by a Bouma shape, and therefore word recognition was minimally subject to the fallible intervention of the reader's contextual or grammatical judgment. Canonical separation also eliminated reader reliance on contextual and grammatical constraints to distinguish syllabic prepositions and bound morphemes from freestanding words.

However, the process of separating morphemes playing a syntactical role by the insertion of space was suspended in cases of the conjunctions *-que* and *-ve*, the interrogative particle *-ne*, the negative particle *-ve*, and the postpositioned *-cum* in expressions like *vobiscum* and *tecum*. In these instances, introducing space would have increased ambiguity.[96] Written separately, the conjunction *-que* would have been confused, in the context of the evolving orthography of the central Middle Ages, with the pronoun *quae*, written either as *que* (*e* cedilla) or *que*. Similarly, the graphic binding of *-ve* eliminated confusion between the conjunction and the proclitic negative particle *ve-*. The graphic binding of the interrogative particle *-ne* eliminated homography with the adverb and interjection *ne*. The graphic form *vobis cum* could easily have led to confusion with the use of *cum* as a conjunction. Thus, at the inception of canonical separation, the dominant criterion of eleventh-century scribes was the minimization or elimination of ambiguity, rather than the separability invoked by modern linguists.[97]

In the late eleventh and twelfth centuries, when conventions governing the new format of canonical separation were still uncertain, the interword space of canonically separated script varied from between 1.5 to over 3 times the unity of space. As the new medium took hold, books intended for normal reading usually contained script separated with a standard interword space equivalent to twice the unity of space. This pattern of spacing, standard in today's printed books, dominated in codices copied in northern Europe, and it prevailed with somewhat less frequency in southern Europe. In certain ordinary northern European books written in the fourteenth and fifteenth centuries in canonically separated Gothic *textualis* and *hybrida*, scribes sometimes added vertical terminal strokes to enhance word separation, usually where the threshold of interword space fell below 1.5 unities of space.[98] This practice was even continued into incunables by monastic correctors and emendators.[99]

The effect of canonical word separation on manuscript production was profound. It brought about a revolution in the practices of the scriptorium. The preponderance of textual evidence suggests that the ancients copied manuscripts by dictation.[100] Each copy of an ancient Latin book was before all else a record of a public or private oral performance of a written text. In his *Letter to Atticus*, for example, Cicero spoke of dictating a text syllable by syllable to his secretary.[101] Nevertheless, some students have proposed that *scriptura continua* was highly suitable for visual copying because its widely spaced letters could easily have been transcribed, sign by sign, by scribes unable to understand the meaning of the text. If ancient scribes had copied visually, rather than by transcribing texts read orally, one would anticipate encountering errors of transposition such as those that occur in the copying of large, unpunctuated numbers digit by digit. Such purely graphic errors are not found in *scriptura continua* codices, which instead are marked by divergences explicable only by errors caused by copying from texts read aloud — errors of pronunciation, decoding, and memory due to either a lector dictating to a scribe or to a scribe pronouncing to himself.[102] It is indeed possible that the scribe, and even the dictator reading to the scribe, might not have understood the sense of the copy being produced, but this is because *scriptura continua* is a particularly ambiguous medium for the transcription of oral speech, a problem augmented by the ambiguous script and syntax of a given exemplar. Several factors probably contributed to the preference for oral rather than visual transcription of texts, including the lack of specialized furniture in antiquity, which rendered the ocular gestures necessary for visual contact between exemplar and copy awkward and clumsy.[103] The ancient posture of writing on one's knee, which left little room for manipulating an exemplar, certainly would not have been conducive to such visual copying. It is worthy of note that the first manuscript miniature depicting a writing table was painted by an eighth-century Anglo-Saxon artist.[104]

The absence of visual copying in antiquity for all languages other than Hebrew and Syriac is also dramatically documentable in the period of medieval aerated writing. Scribes copying aerated texts written in letter blocks, syllable word blocks, or hierarchical word blocks never reproduced exactly the same pattern of spatial distinctions, even in codices that textual critics and codicologists have determined with a high degree of probability to have been copied one from another. Rather, each scribe aerated his copy according to individual conceptions of what constituted a physiologically satisfying pattern. Writing a copy correctly in hierarchical word blocks required reading the text with a modicum of comprehension not necessary for *scriptura continua*, for the scribe had to distinguish the greater quantities of space used only between words from the lesser quantity used between either words or syllables, and to punctuate while writing. A subtle indication of the level of scribal comprehension in aerated scripts was the habit of some scribes to alter word order and substitute synonyms as they wrote.[105] Aural memory is not as conducive to the precise replication of word order as the reliance on visual copying characteristic of late medieval scriptoria,[106] and studies suggest that such rearrangements and substitutions occurred when scribes found it easier to retain the meaning of short sections of text rather than to recall a fixed series of words from memory.[107] The oral nature of early medieval copying is confirmed by the colophon of Vat. Pal. lat. 46 (s. ix), copied in aerated script, in which the scribe wrote: "Three fingers write, two eyes see, one tongue speaks, the whole body works."[108] This awkward oral process of reading, remembering, and replicating nevertheless had certain benefits for the reader. The synonyms that the scribe substituted often represented the Latinized form of the vernacular, and these, like the infusion of space, eventually effected a simplification for the reader. Scribal word rearrangements that grouped together grammatically related words also frequently simplified the task of the reader.

Once texts were definitively reformatted, as a result of canonical separation, they could be copied visually as a series of images, enabling scribes to copy accurately writing which they could not and did not have to understand.[109] Evidence of the change to visual copying on the part of scribes can be detected at an early date. In his colophon, the seventh-century scribe Mulling boasted of having copied the entire text of the Gospels in twelve days. Speedy copying had not been a preoccupation of the ancients, but references to rapid transcriptions were frequent for the small Irish books written in separated script. The *Vita* of Saint Lasrianus related that the monks of Delcan copied from the exemplar with great speed a Gospel book for their abbot.[110] The *Vita* of Finnian Clonard attributed to his monastic school the production of large numbers of Gospel books.[111] The *Book of Dimma*, according to the *Vita* of Saint Cronan, was reputed to have been written in a single day.[112] Physiologically and historically, there is no doubt that visual copying, swift copying, and word separation were closely related.

Further evidence of visual copying can be gleaned from the new graphic similarity that might exist between the exemplar and the copy. London, BL Cotton Tiberius A xiv was one of the first identifiable surviving manuscripts to be copied visually from a separated exemplar, the Leningrad Bede. There can be little doubt that the scribe worked visually, since certain passages are an exact line-by-line replication of his exemplar, a process for which no precedent exists, even in codices written *per cola et commata*.[113] The errors that the scribe of Tiberius A xiv made suggest the problems posed for visual replication by certain aspects of his exemplar. The scribe of the Leningrad Bede, like those of earlier Irish codices, evinced respect for the word as a unit of meaning not only by separating words by space, but by avoiding the division of words at line endings. However, when forced to divide a word, he followed the Irish practice of writing the remainder of the word, and frequently one or two following words, in space left blank above the end of the line. These continuations were often overlooked by the scribe of the Cotton manuscript. Cognizant of possible error, the scribe of Tiberius A xiv abandoned Irish practice and placed word continuations on the following line signaling the divided word with either the *trait d'union* or a suspended ligature. Cotton Tiberius A xiv is one of the earliest books to employ the *trait d'union*.[114]

In contrast to aerated manuscripts, not only was the distinction of words usually identical in both the exemplar and the copy of Insular separated manuscripts, but the pattern of abbreviations, terminal forms, and punctuation was often highly similar.[115] The similitude of punctuation and *prosodiae* was related to the new capacity of the scribe to reproduce visually a properly punctuated text as a series of discrete images and emblematic signs without necessarily comprehending them. The scribe also was able to recognize words, terminal abbreviations, tie notes, and musical notation as distinct images, and for this the regular presence of interword space was a necessity.[116] The scribe Mac Regol, abbot of Birr (d. 822) in Ireland, referred to himself ambiguously as both the painter and writer of his *Book*.[117] Giraldus Cambrensis recorded an Irish legend that surrounded an ancient Gospel book he saw in 1185–88. According to Giraldus, an angel had held an open Gospel book as an exemplar before the scribe so that he could replicate its illustrations and page format, in addition to its text.[118] The cognitive skills of the medieval copyist of canonically separated script in fact resembled those of a modern typist, and studies indicate that the reading process of the typist who copies mechanically is different from that of the normal reader.[119] Insular scribes, like typists, read with an invariable eye-hand span while replicating the black-on-white images of their exemplar.

Chapter 3

Complements to Word Separation by Space

⁓

As we have seen, other forms of separation existed in both antique and medieval Latin manuscripts as either supplements or alternatives to the use of space for separating words. These principally consisted of encoded graphic marks or signs. In the British Isles and subsequently on the Continent, Europe witnessed an evolution from "a system that separates words by signs and units of sense by spaces" to one "that separates words by spaces and units of sense by signs."[1] The rapid perception of these various encoded signs was physiologically predicated upon the enhanced eye-voice span created by word-separated text. Such signs could be exploited by oral readers, especially during liturgical performance, but they could also be used by silent readers for rapid visual comprehension. Studies confirm that the skilled reader, whose decoding is more visual than aural, is best able to extract meaning from punctuation.[2] This use of visual signs for meaning further suggests a reallocation of hemispheric faculties.

During the evolution of Western writing from *scriptura continua* to canonically separated script, medieval scribes both employed ancient signs of separation and developed other techniques of separation as aids to reading and copying. These included various ancient *prosodiae*, newly invented signs for word separation, special letter forms, including the capitalization of proper nouns, and monolexic and suspension abbreviations. Conversely, they employed or developed signs designating the unity of words, including *traits d'union*, suspended ligatures, accent marks, and Greek hyphens. They also developed encoded graphic marks or "construction notes" that were used to identify the grammatical function of particular words, and they employed a variety of marks of punctuation, including the question mark and a predecessor of the quotation mark. In addition to these, they devised other signs to aid in decoding and comprehending a text, including musical notation, marginal conventional *nota* signs, encoded tie notes (the progenitor of modern footnotes), foliation, *résumé* notes, and schematic diagrams. Beginning with the resources originally provided by ancient textual practices, they gradually developed many of the textual foundations of the modern scholarly book, including this one.

Medieval Signs for Word Separation

Medieval Uses of Ancient Prosodiae

Prosodiae was a term employed by ancient grammarians to signify a group of signs added in the classroom to guide the inexperienced reader in the correct pronunciation of text.[3] One type of *prosodia* was points, usually referred to as "interpuncts" for the texts of antiquity, as we have seen, and their use without space as a means of separation had a long history in prevocalic languages. Their use in Latin is particularly well documented in the inscriptions of the first and second century A.D.[4] Points were used only on rare occasions to separate words in the manuscripts of late antiquity.

In medieval codices, primarily from the eighth century to the tenth, points were occasionally used to alleviate the ambiguity of unseparated script.[5] However, they were also placed between syllables within words in ancient inscriptions and in early medieval texts intended to instruct beginning readers.[6] In certain manuscripts and inscriptions of Irish and Anglo-Saxon origin, points were used often, but not always in conjunction with space, to separate words. The seventh-century lapidary inscriptions of the Abbey of Jouarre, founded by Irish monks, contained words separated by interpuncts without the insertion of additional space, in apparent emulation of Roman lapidary inscriptions dating from before the end of the second century A.D.[7] Eleventh-century France witnessed a resurgence of this practice, notably in monastic lapidary inscriptions.[8] Points as signs of separation also formed integral parts of certain conventional abbreviations, and they were often used to designate the transcriptions of numerical expressions. The point as a sign of separation was still reflected in certain grammatical definitions of the thirteenth century.[9]

While interpunctuation for word separation is consistently recorded in the major catalogues of papyrus fragments, for example Grenfell and Hunt's *Oxyrhynchus papyri*,[10] other works on both ancient and medieval

lapidary inscriptions have systematically suppressed points in their transcriptions by silently substituting either points and space or space alone.[11]
The presence of points to separate words has never been recorded in catalogues of medievalia, and only one short (but valuable) contribution on
this phenomenon, by Wallace M. Lindsay, exists in the extensive corpus
of medieval paleographical literature.[12]

The *diastole*, a second *prosodia* used for word separation, is a sign resembling an enlarged comma. It was originally employed in Greek texts
written in the second century B.C. in *scriptura continua* as an occasional
aid to correct pronunciation, separating for the reader words or syllables
with ambiguous boundaries.[13] Among the Romans, it came to replace
the point as the grammar teacher's usual means of separating words at
points of ambiguity in the second century A.D., when points took on
the value of punctuation, rather than serving as signals for distinguishing
words.[14] The *diastole* was never used by ancient Latin scribes in copying
text. However, medieval scribes as early as the seventh century used it
to separate words or to insert an omitted word, and they subsequently
developed for it a number of variant shapes. In catalogues of medieval
manuscripts, the use of the *diastole* either by scribes, correctors, or readers
has scarcely been noted.

A third *prosodia* used to separate words that was occasionally noted in
descriptions of ancient epigraphs and papyri is the sign that the Romans
termed the *apex* but that I shall refer to by its modern name, the acute
accent mark. The acute accent mark was used in antiquity as a sign of
vowel length.[15] According to Quintilian (ca. 40–ca. 118 A.D.), this practice avoided the ambiguity of homographs in certain contexts.[16] After
Rome's general acceptance of *scriptura continua*, the acute accent mark
was also used, usually in school texts, to indicate the doubling of vowels and occasionally to designate the final syllable of each word or each
syllable within a word, or to identify the syllable receiving the tonic accent.[17] Since, according to the ancient Roman rules of accentuation,
only one syllable in each word could receive the tonic accent, the presence of the acute accent performing the last function aided the reader,
at least indirectly, to determine word boundaries and thus reduced the
ambiguity of text written either in *scriptura continua* or in aerated script.
Thirteenth-century scholastics made this point explicitly, although by
this date, word separation, rather than the presence of *prosodiae*, was the
usual cue for correct accentuation.[18] In certain ancient Latin books from
Egypt and in lapidary inscriptions throughout the Roman Empire, acute

accents were used to designate monosyllabic words, usually containing long vowels, and in a few instances a reverse *apex*, the modern grave accent, was reserved exclusively for identifying monosyllabic words, while the acute accent was reserved to denote the syllable receiving the tonic accent in polysyllabic words.[19]

In general, in antiquity acute accent marks, diastoles, and other *prosodiae* were used chiefly on wax tablets or the papyri used by beginning readers engaged in the difficult process of the oral *praelectio*. Because of the difficulty of *scriptura continua*, training in reading persisted into adolescence.[20] In London, BL Add. 33293, a third-century school tablet, occasional interword space and accents were used to denote words in the difficult-to-understand dialect of the *Iliad*.[21] The presence of acute accents in lapidary inscriptions may be interpreted as aids for the semilettered. Accent marks and other *prosodiae* were never used by scribes in the confection of formal Latin books in either the eastern or western empires. When present, they were added by readers. In the early seventh century, Isidore of Seville commended the traditional uses of accent marks as aids to young readers seeking to reduce the ambiguity of problematic texts by distinguishing words and averting homographs.[22] In Continental manuscripts of the sixth and seventh centuries, as in antiquity, *prosodiae* in manuscripts were almost invariably added by readers, and they were never used with frequency by scribes.[23]

In the late seventh century, first in Ireland, then in England and Wales, and subsequently in zones of profound Celtic and Anglo-Saxon influence on the Continent, scribes began to employ the acute accent with great regularity in conjunction with word separation. Acute accents as a regular accoutrement to text emerged more or less contemporaneously on the Latin and Greek page, but subsequent to the diacritical points prevalant on the Syriac written page. This is significant because considerable evidence indicates that the Irish were exposed to Syriac influence at an early date.[24] On the Continent, the practice of inserting accents in confected books won general acceptance only in the tenth and eleventh centuries, at the time of the adoption of word separation. Pseudo-Priscian's *Liber de accentibus*, dating from about the year 1000 and titled in one of the earliest manuscripts *Liber prosodiae*, was the first Continental manual to explain their use as an aid in text presentation.[25]

One of the purposes for which Irish scribes used the acute accent was to denote monosyllables, especially monosyllabic prepositions. Initially, scribes seem to have designated only those prepositions containing

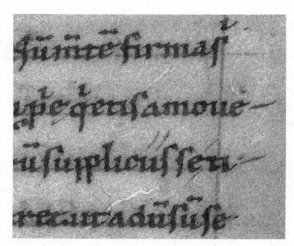

Figure 12. The successor note to the *diastole*, *trait d'union*, and accenting of double *ii* used by an emendator to remove ambiguity from unseparated script in Boethius's *De consolatione philosophiae*. Chicago, Newberry Library 10, f. 38 recto; reproduced by permission.

long vowels, but later, they marked monosyllables regardless of vowel length. Irish scribes also employed the acute accent to mark long vowels in tonic syllables and the first and second declension dative and ablative *-is* terminations. The latter practice spread in the eighth and ninth centuries throughout England, Wales, Brittany, and to Irish and Anglo-Saxon centers elsewhere on the Continent, almost always in the context of Insular script.[26] Later, Insular scribes extended the use of the acute accent to other terminal syllables. The use of the terminal acute accent with Caroline letter forms was almost unknown in England and rare on the Continent, where through the mid-tenth century it remained as a sign of direct or indirect Anglo-Saxon or Irish influence.[27] The use of the accented *-is* as a terminal form turned it into a quasi-construction note, aiding the reader at once both to group nouns with their modifying adjectives and to identify their syntactical function. The accenting of the terminal double *ii* achieved a similar effect.

A third Insular function of the acute accent that emerged in the late tenth century was to place it over long vowels in the tonic syllable containing ambiguities resulting from the use of minim strokes in minuscule script to form the consonant letters *m* and *n* and the vowels *u* and *i*.[28] A fourth and closely related function of the acute accent was to define word unity by identifying the tonic syllable in compound words, particularly those formed by the addition of bound syllabic prepositions or of enclitic conjunctions such as -ve and -que. Here, the acute accent prevented the reader from separating into two words what was meant to represent a single unit of pronunciation and, excluding enclitic conjunctions, of meaning. Soon after this use had become current in England and on the Continent, it was described in Pseudo-Priscian's *Liber de accentibus*.[29] The acute accent was also used on the final syllable to identify adverbs and on the penultimate syllable to distinguish the infinitives of the second conjugation from those of the third conjugation. Finally, the acute accent was used to denote the double *ii*, averting confusion between it and the letters *u*, *n*, and *m*, thereby distinguishing the Bouma shapes of many words (Figure 12).

New Medieval Signs for Separation

Medieval scribes not only evolved new uses for ancient *prosodiae*, they also invented new signs, both as occasional reader aids and as systematically exploited alternatives to interword space.[30] The new medieval signs for word separation were essentially variant forms of the ancient *diastole*. The variant forms, for the most part, consisted of three basic types. The most common form employed in the central Middle Ages was the oblique double slash ⁄, a sign of Insular origin that in some manuscripts dating from as late as the eleventh century was composed of a *diastole* below and an acute accent mark above (Figure 13; and see Figure 12). Its form suggests that this notation for separation originated, or was at the very least occasionally conceived of, as a synthesis of two discrete signs that ancient Roman schoolboys had sometimes employed to denote separation. I will refer to this sign as "the successor note to the *diastole*." The successor note to the diastole disappeared after the early thirteenth century, and I have found only rare examples of its revival by humanists in manuscripts of the fifteenth century.[31]

A second and rarer sign was a *J*-shaped vertical stroke. Certain unseparated central medieval manuscripts of works by Donatus present this sign as the normal form of the *diastole*, but it is unknown in ancient codices and fragments.[32] This mark, like the *diastole*, was from the ninth century onward employed for correcting omitted interword space, as well as for inserting corrections, the latter especially in Anglo-Saxon manuscripts.[33] Also, in English manuscripts, a descender from a word or fragment of a word to be inserted as an interlinear correction was frequently written so as to resemble this mark.

A third form of the *diastole* was the vertical stroke, sometimes placed

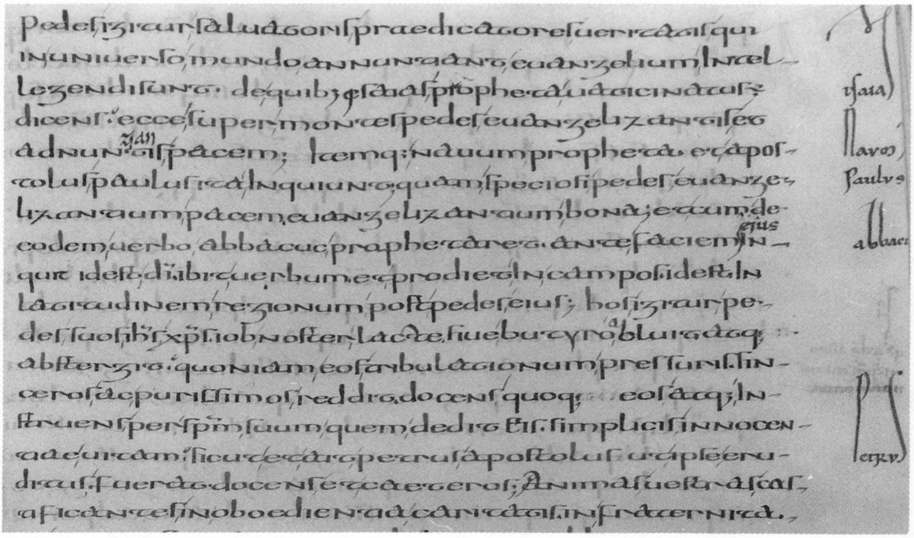

Figure 13. The successor note to the *diastole* used to separate words in Philippus's *In Job*. Cambrai, Bibliothèque Municipale 470, f. 129 recto; reproduced by permission.

at a slightly oblique angle. It seems to have originated on the Continent and was current in certain French monasteries in the eleventh century, notably the Abbey of Saint-Bénigne of Dijon and at Fécamp at the time of Abbot John. This sign became by far the most prevalent mark of post-factum separation at the end of the Middle Ages, and it is present as a handwritten mark of emendation in some incunables.[34] The story of the historical evolution and dissemination of these medieval forms of the *diastole* remains, to date, untold. Their narrative is crucially linked to the history of word separation by space, for which these signs ultimately served as substitutes, and therefore to the history of the use of word images in reading. Various ersatz marks, the interlinear *dasia*, ˥ and ˦, the Greek characters for aspiration, the *dasia*'s Latin equivalent, the letter *h*, and in certain instances, what are now called "construction notes," which will be discussed below, also sometimes served as signs of separation.[35]

Letter Forms and Abbreviations as Signs of Separation

In addition to space and *prosodiae*, special letter forms to delineate words have also been used, either for the initial or for the terminal letter. These included initial and terminal capitals, related alternative letter forms, and conventional abbreviations at the end of words. The use of special initial and terminal forms has a rich history, beginning in antiquity in languages transcribed in the Semitic alphabets, where it has consistently been a principal mode of separation in Hebrew, Arabic, and Syriac.[36] Syriac codices in particular may have provided the model of page format for the first separated Latin manuscripts produced in Ireland. In contrast to the Semitic languages, initial and terminal forms never consistently separated words in medieval Latin. However, Latin scribes did occasionally use terminal forms, much as they did *prosodiae*, to supplement space and aid the reader in resolving ambiguities created by an infelicitous sequence of words within aerated writing. They also used them widely as a redundant sign of separation in early separated script.

The use of capital forms and special symbols at word endings in the tenth and eleventh centuries has been noted by a few paleographers.[37] However, the evolution of these marks from the occasional, haphazardly selected large letters placed at the end of the line in ancient lapidary inscriptions and manuscripts into an integral part of the graphic *langue* of the Middle Ages has been overlooked.[38] From the ninth century to the twelfth, in some regions of Europe where word separation had not yet become prevalent, the use of distinctive forms for the initial letter of a word, for the final letter, or for both, was an important aid to the reader in separating words. Modern studies demonstrate word extremities to be crucial for word recognition, helping parafoveal vision to pre-identify the significant features of words and thereby increasing reading speed.[39] In conjunction with the judicious use of space, these other aids to separation — capitals, special terminal forms, and abbreviations — created a subclass of protoscholastic manuscripts, notably at Fleury, in which all words were immediately perceptible to the reader, although not consistently separated by space.[40]

The use of capital forms at the beginning of proper nouns, a practice unknown in antiquity, became an important aid in establishing boundaries for those words, which, when they appeared in aerated script, were often particularly difficult for medieval readers to parse.[41] Initial capitals combined with writing containing the ascending and descending strokes characteristic of minuscule script gave proper nouns a readily identifiable image. The practice of selective capitalization also provided a code for the visual recognition and swift retrieval of specific kinds of information relating to individual persons and places, as well as to corporate

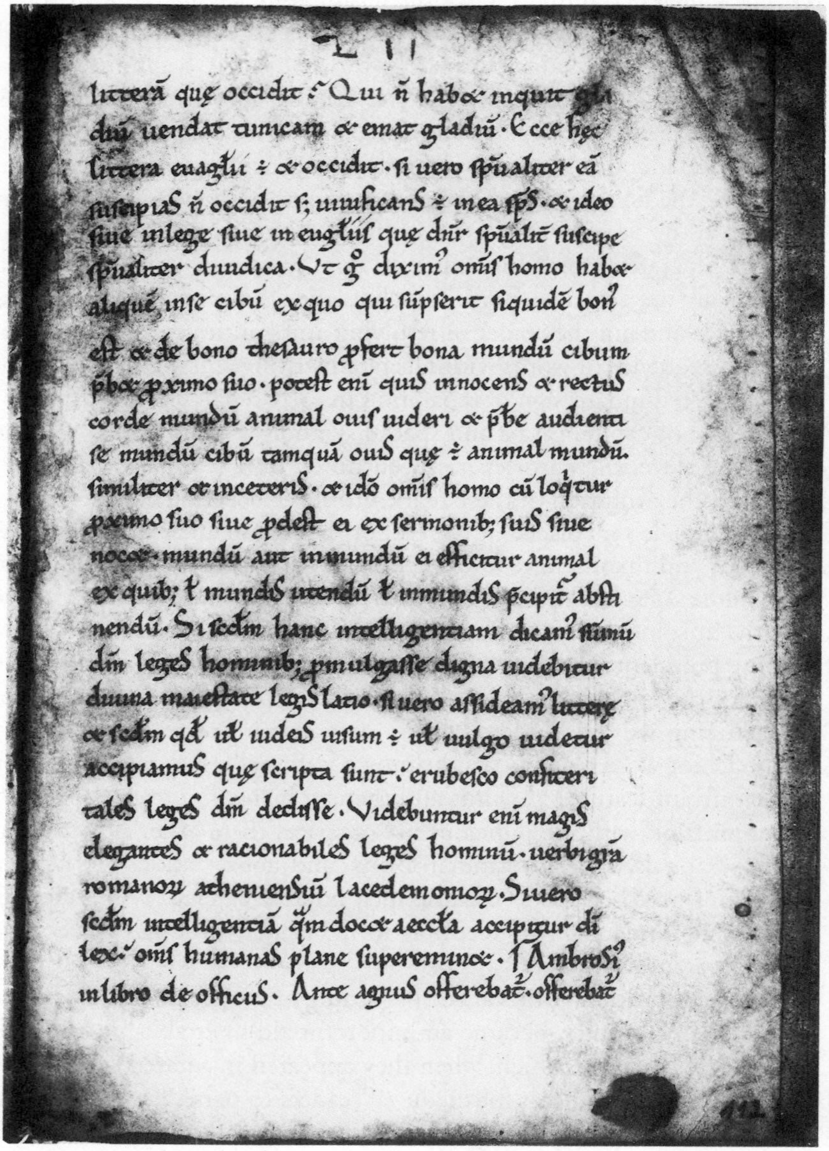

211

littera que occidit. Qui n̄ habet inquit d̄m
d̄n uendat tunicam & emat gladiū. Ecce hec
littera euagl̄ii ÷ & occidit. si uero sp̄ualiter eā
suscipias n̄ occidit s; uiuificans ÷ in ea ips̄. & ideo
siue inlege siue in euḡliis que d̄r sp̄ualit suscipe
sp̄ualiter diuidica. Vt q̄ diximꝰ om̄is homo habet
aliquē inse cibū ex quo qui sūpserit siquidē bon̄

est & de bono thesauro pfert bona mundū cibum
pbet p̄ximo suo. potest enī quis innocens & rectus
corde mundū animal ouis uideri & pbe audienti
se mundū cibū tamquā ouis que ÷ animal mundū.
similiter & inceteris. & ideo om̄is homo cū loq̄tur
p̄ximo suo siue pdest ei ex sermonib; suis siue
nocet mundū aut inmundū ei efficitur animal
ex quib; t mundis utendū t inmundis p̄cipit absti
nendū. Si sec̄m hanc intelligentiam dicam stimū
d̄m leges hominib; pmulgasse digna uidebitur
diuina maiestate leḡslatio. si uero assideam littere
& sec̄m q̄d ut uides usum ÷ ut uulgo uidetur
accipiamus que scripta sunt. erubesco confiteri
tales leges d̄m dedisse. Videbuntur enī magis
elegantes & racionabiles leges hominū. uerbigra
romano⁊ atheniensiū lacedemonio⁊ Si uero
sec̄m intelligentiā q̄m docet aeccl̄a accipitur d̄i
lex. om̄s humanas plane supereminet. ¶ Ambrosiꝰ
inlibro de officiis. Ante agnus offerebat. offerebat

Figure 14. The terminal capital *S* in Berangar of Tours' *Rescripta contra Lanfrancum*. Wolfenbüttel, Herzog August Bibliothek Weissenburg 101, p. 211; reproduced by permission.

entities. The adoption of this convention in separated script was an indication that a new form of reading, rapid, silent reference consultation, had begun to flourish in the central Middle Ages. The capitalization of proper nouns was often neglected by late medieval scribes, but the practice was revived by humanist scribes and has since been systematically regularized and rendered canonical by modern typographical usage in English, the Romance languages, and, with different encoded significance, in German.[42]

From the seventh century to the twelfth, the use of all capitals and the use of accents, particularly in transliterations of Hebrew, Greek, and Arabic names, existed as an alternative to initial capitalization as graphic cues for denoting proper nouns for reference consultation.[43] The same or related graphic conventions were also on occasion used to set off words and phrases written in languages other than Latin or the vernacular, like Greek, Arabic, and Hebrew.[44] Traces of this practice remain detectable in certain humanistic type fonts. In addition to marking sentence beginnings and proper nouns, the long *j* was used in the Middle Ages simply to denote word beginnings.[45] The capital *A* (in England) and the capital *N* (in Spain) were sometimes used toward the end of the tenth century at word beginnings. In Insular script, the acute accent was employed on occasion to signal the initial vowel in certain words.[46]

Terminal capitals (or occasionally the capitalization of the end of the morpheme stem) were used by scribes even more often than initial capitals, first in Irish centers on the Continent and eventually more generally on the Continent in the tenth and eleventh centuries, as a common adjunct to word separation.[47] Such practices, like the use of initial capitals, had no antecedent in antiquity.

Among terminal forms, the capital *S*, which in the final analysis was a sign of Insular origin, was the most common (Figure 14).[48] Its use, as opposed to the long *s* at word endings, generated a more readily identifiable word image. The terminal capital form of *R*, *S*, and *A* was normal in the Insular majuscule scripts, which unlike the continental pre-Caroline scripts, were derived exclusively from uncial forms. In Insular books written in the script that Julian Brown brilliantly characterized as hybrid, these letters were often retained at word endings, where they ambiguously served to enhance separation by space.[49] When Continental scribes in the eighth, ninth, and tenth centuries wrote under Insular influence in Caroline minuscule script, they sometimes retained the capital form of *R*, *S*, or *A* solely at word beginnings and endings, thereby preserving the

Bouma shape of the word in peripheral vision when written in Insular script.[50] Ultimately, the terminal capital *S* form evolved into two new forms, the superscript round *S* and the small round *s*; the latter becoming the normal terminal *s* of Gothic script. In the fourteenth century, it was the presence of the Gothic round *s* that preserved a modicum of word separation in Italian juridical manuscripts, particularly the *Decretals* of Gratian, when Bolognese university scribes launched a short-lived experiment of reducing and even occasionally eliminating interword space in their codices in order to produce a text format of genuine imperial allure.[51] However, special initial and terminal forms, despite their great importance for the separation of words and the expanded role of parafoveal vision, have never been systematically recorded in manuscript catalogue descriptions of Western books and documents, to the great detriment of the history of reading.

Other signs that designated word endings were symbols used as abbreviations for the terminations *-tur*, *-us*, *-bus*, *-orum*, *-ra*, and the superscript *o*. All save the usual *4* sign for *-orum*, the rare ' sign for *s*, and the long *j* were of Insular origin.[52] In the late Middle Ages, a few of the special forms, such as the small capital form or round *s*, and abbreviations, such as that for *-tur*, became standard in Gothic script, and later some entered the Fraktur type fonts. Others, such as the ' sign for *s*, the crossed capital *S* for *-orum*, and the terminal capitals *S, R, M, X, A*, and *T* (the last particularly popular in Italy in the eleventh and twelfth centuries), passed entirely into oblivion, only to be selectively readopted by fifteenth-century humanist scribes as part of their conscious emulation of eleventh-century and twelfth-century exemplars.[53]

The *e* cedilla as an abbreviation for the diphthong *ae* is a special case. Most scribes used it anywhere within the word, but in word-separated text it acted as a terminal form by enhancing the visibility of the *-ae* ending. The tendency toward compaction characteristic of scripts separated by readily perceptible units of space was complemented by the compaction of signs such as the *e* cedilla and the ampersand, which used a symbol to replace two letters. The *e* cedilla originated in Insular separated script in the seventh century and certain eleventh-century scribes used it only in the terminal position.[54]

Directly following the definitive adoption of separation by space, terminal letter forms became even more common. In the age of transition, when the general acceptance of the meaning of intratextual space as a cue to word separation was not yet secure, scribes made copious use of terminal forms to make word separation emphatically clear. In separated manuscripts, one cannot be entirely sure whether the use of terminal forms was simply a holdover from aerated texts of a needless linguistic redundancy or an additional enhancement of word image that could be exploited because of the extended parafoveal and peripheral vision that separation created.

  While signs of word termination might occur anywhere within a written line, during the period of transition from aerated to separated script, they, like signs of word continuation, were most often placed at line endings. This was particularly true of the *NT* ligature and the capital *S* and *R*. The occurrence of a large letter at a line ending in classical Latin had been without encoded meaning. To the medieval reader, terminal signs at line endings eliminated the burden of unnecessarily retaining in mind an unresolved phonetic element of uncertain meaning while the reader's eyes were displaced to the beginning of the next written line to verify whether elements of a word remained to be decoded. Neurophysiologically, these signs played a role analogous to interpuncts at line endings in the interpunct-separated script of the classical period. However, interpuncts at line endings were rare in antiquity, while terminal forms at line endings were abundant in early separated Continental manuscripts. Terminal abbreviations had the added advantage of contributing to a linear compression of text that helped to maximize the efficiency of ocular saccades and increased the eye-voice span in a manner analogous to Japanese written in *kanji* as opposed to *kana*.[55]

Monolexic Abbreviations and Suspension Abbreviations

  Another mode of word separation that was especially prevalent in the medieval period of transition to word separation by space was the use of monolexic abbreviations, which were conventional symbols or fixed, stylized combinations of letters that invariably corresponded to a specific uninflected short word or to a specific case of an inflected short word. Examples include various symbols used for *et* and *est*. Because of the minimal length of monolexic abbreviations, their Bouma shape was especially easy for readers to recognize in parafoveal vision, much as the shape of the article "the" is recognizable for the modern reader of English.[56] Monolexic abbreviations included not only monograms, but other invariable alphabetic ligatures and abbreviations, as well as conventional signs, a few of logographic origin, representing words. The critical feature of monolexic abbreviations distinguishing them from other abbreviations was that they were immediately recognizable as specific words, often regardless of the presence or absence of space.

In informal Greek documentary papyri, symbolic characters had sometimes been used as abbreviations. Of these abbreviations, the only one that had been used in formal Greek books was the *coronis*, an ideograph meaning "the end." [57] In ancient Rome, monolexisms, except for certain numerical symbols, were absent in documents as well as books. However, a variety of monolexic abbreviations were employed in the ancient shorthand used by secretaries for rapidly transcribing oral statements.[58] The earliest surviving examples of these notes date from late Imperial papyri and lapidary inscriptions.

Monolexic abbreviations of very marginal significance in the normal writing of Greco-Roman antiquity assumed central importance in the Insular Latin manuscripts of the early Middle Ages. As early as the late seventh century, they were prominent in Irish manuscripts as a redundant expression of word separation in scripts that also separated by space.[59] The Insular and probably Irish grammarian Virgilius Maro describes the use of a monolexic abbreviation for the conjunction *et*.[60] Some of the Irish and Anglo-Saxon monolexisms were drawn from the shorthand notes of antiquity; others were indigenous inventions (see Figure 3).[61] On the Continent, excluding the Insular colonies, from the end of the tenth century to the twelfth, monolexic abbreviations constituted an important complement to word separation by space and by codes denoting word beginnings and endings. They also contributed to the linear compression that maximized the efficiency of ocular saccades. After the twelfth century, many of them became an essential element of the scripts used for scholastic discourse.[62] Although paleographic literature is rich in studies on particular monolexic abbreviations, their presence as a class has never been specifically enumerated in the descriptions of medieval manuscripts.

Closely related to monolexic abbreviations were suspension abbreviations, or sequences of initial letters, which had their origin in the interpunct-separated Roman writing of the republican period. In these abbreviations, of which perhaps the most famous is S.P.Q.R., the point after the initial letter indicated the conclusion of a syllable or word and the omission of letters. In interpunct-separated script, suspension abbreviations were used exclusively for words or morphemes. In the context of *scriptura continua*, they evolved into *notae iuris*, the abbreviations used by lawyers, in which individual letters could represent either suspended words or syllables.[63] The *notae iuris* were inherently ambiguous, and Imperial law eventually forbade their use. In medieval manuscripts, suspension abbreviations were extremely rare until the tenth century, when they emerged again frequently in the context of aerated and separated Continental script. They were then used exclusively for words, and separated by space as well as by points.[64]

Suspension abbreviations became increasingly prevalent in the eleventh and twelfth centuries as a compact device for citing verses from the Psalms and Gospels and for liturgical formulae, texts that many monks retained by heart and for which the initial letters served as convenient mnemonic cues. Unlike monolexic abbreviations, which were inherently unambiguous, sequences of initial letters were heavily dependent for their comprehension on contextual cues. However, in using a sign for each word, suspension abbreviations reflected a new general orientation of the reader toward a page where words were separated by space. Late-tenth-century authors and scribes began to use capital suspension abbreviations for proper nouns. Gerbert, Richer, Fulbert, and Abbo commonly employed them for this purpose. Used exclusively for words, suspension abbreviations remained a standard feature of script until the end of the age of the incunable.

Medieval Signs for Word Unity

Traits d'Union

Closely related to the signs indicating word separation were other symbols connoting word unity. A sign shaped like a half circle, indicating that an incomplete word at the end of a line would be continued on the next line, was present in at least one fragment of unseparated Latin script written before the end of the third century A.D.[65] In earlier interpunct-separated script, a more common but still relatively rare sign of word continuation had been a negative one: the absence of an interpunct at the line ending when a word was left incomplete in writing where points were regularly placed at lines ending in a complete word.[66] This sign disappeared of necessity with the prevalence of *scriptura continua* in late antiquity.

Signs of word continuation first reappeared in the separated script of the early and central Middle Ages in the British Isles.[67] This reappearance in conjunction with word-separated script after an interval of more than half a millennium and in a region where there was not the remotest possibility of the emulation of ancient Roman models is suggestive of a psychological link to changed reading habits. Word separation meant a greater awareness of the graphic unity of the word, which signs of continuation were intended to preserve. The concern with graphic signs for denoting the unity of the word suggests a decoding process oriented toward morphemes rather than toward the phonemes that had been fundamental to the synthetic reading techniques of antiquity. At the same time, the broader field of vision afforded by separated script enabled readers to perceive readily in parafoveal vision the new cues pertaining to word continuation.

Seventh-century Irish scribes began the practice of inserting an unfinished portion of a word in the interlinear space above the line.[68] Bede, in his *De orthographia*, showed concern for the correct division of written words, a subject not directly addressed by ancient grammarians.[69] Medieval signs signifying the continuation of words seem first to have reappeared in English manuscripts of the late eighth century. However, signs for word continuation did not become popular in England until the late tenth century.[70] A few ersatz signs with related functions are to be found in ninth-century aerated Continental codices.[71] *Traits d'union* first became common on the Continent in the late tenth and eleventh centuries. In modern English, the Insular sign of word continuation is customarily termed a "hyphen," but in this study I will identify it as a *trait d'union* to avoid confusion with the true hyphen, a sign of ancient Greek origin regularly enumerated by Roman and medieval grammarians and used by medieval scribes for a related but, as will be seen, distinctly different function. It is this sign that I will call simply the "hyphen." Only in a very few instances—three, to my knowledge—did tenth-century and eleventh-century scribes use the true hyphen to indicate interline word continuation, and medieval grammatical treatises never applied the term "hyphen" to the *trait d'union*. The sign for the *trait d'union* remained without a proper grammatical name until the fifteenth century, when grammarians titled it a *semipunctus* or *virgula* and listed it among either *prosodiae* or signs of punctuation.[72]

Traits d'union vary in shape, position, and ink, and these variants offer important clues to their dating. Horizontal *traits d'union* at midletter or at the base of the letter were characteristic early forms. The presence of *traits d'union* at both line endings and beginnings or even at line beginnings only is also an indication of an early date. Oblique *traits d'union* and the double stroke or = form were late, the former being unknown

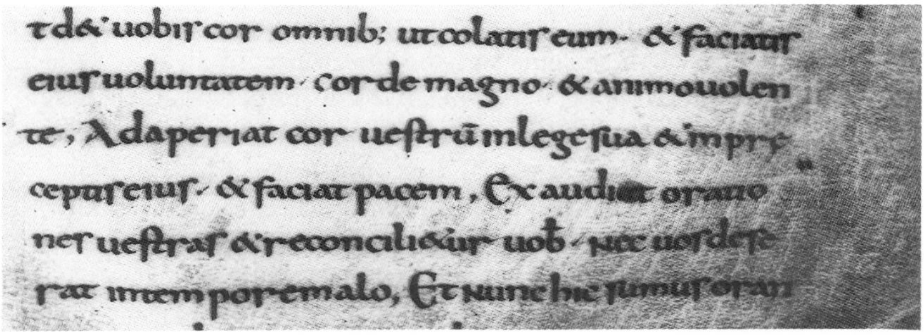

Figure 15. A ligature breaching intersyllabic space in the Old Testament. Amiens, Bibliothèque Municipale 11, f. 58 recto; reproduced by permission.

before the late twelfth century and the latter dating only from after 1300. Where the ink of the *trait d'union* differs from that of the adjacent text, it can often be compared with the ink of other portions of the text, with other added reading aids, or with marginalia as clues for accurate dating.

Variations in the grammatical function of the *trait d'union* are equally worthy of attention. Their presence after monosyllabic prepositions or other monosyllables was often evidence not of error but of ambiguity in the scribe's conception of what constituted a word, and therefore this occurrence is an indication of an early date. Although geographically and chronologically closely tied to word separation, *traits d'union* were occasionally adopted by scribes writing in aerated script. Instances of this practice continued in Italian manuscripts into the early thirteenth century.[73]

The Suspended Ligature

Another early sign of interline word continuation found occasionally in some late aerated manuscripts and with far greater frequency in separated script was the suspended ligature. In some aerated scripts, ligatures extending across syllabic space indicated in some instances that an ambiguous syllable, *cor*, for example, which might be either a freestanding word or a bound syllable, formed part of a word, as in *cor-de* (Figure 15). By a suspended ligature, I mean an extended stroke attached to the last letter at the end of a line, suggesting the presence of a disrupted continuation to the next letter and forming an incipient bridge to the end of the word on the following line. Sometimes the scribe also added a continuation stroke at the beginning of the next line. A suspended ligature thus served as a sign that a line ended with an incomplete word. The most unequivocal of these signs was the interrupted *ct* ligature, which was sometimes added along with *prosodiae* and punctuation by emendators reworking unseparated script. Of a more ambiguous nature were the *e* with prolonged cross stroke and the prolonged forms of *r* and *g*, and *n* and *m* with extended feet.[74] These signs, in conjunction with word termination signs, provided guidance to the reader in recognizing word boundaries and controlling eye movements. However, the value of suspended ligatures was mitigated by the fact that in other codices, similar strokes might occur without any encoded meaning.

The Acute Accent

A third medieval sign of the continuation of a word from one line to the next was the acute accent, used to designate the last syllable on a line ending with an incomplete word. This practice had its origin in the more general use of acute accent marks to denote the tonic syllable discussed above. According to the ancient rules of Latin accentuation, the accented syllable in polysyllabic words could not fall on the last syllable.[75] Therefore, placing an accent on the last syllable of the written line signaled the reader that additional syllables of the same word remained. Initially, acute accents were placed only on the tonic syllable, but by the late tenth century they seem to have been placed on the last syllable of incomplete words, regardless of that syllable's tonic value.[76] This use of the acute accent was identical to that of a *trait d'union*, and the acute accent's earliest appearance in this role was approximately contemporary with the earliest general use of the *trait d'union*. It is therefore plausible that the *trait d'union* developed from this specialized use of the acute accent, rather than from the suspended ligature. This uniquely medieval use of the acute accent mark was never included by medieval grammarians in their discussions of *prosodiae*, although the acute accent was used for precisely this purpose by the scribe of one of the earliest copies of Pseudo-Priscian's *Liber de accentibus*.[77] In this instance, as with the *trait d'union* and suspended ligature, grammarians of the early and central Middle Ages preferred to repeat the commonplaces of late antiquity (with rare concessions to changes in pronunciation), rather than to take stock of the graphic inventions that scribes in their own time had perfected to facilitate reading.

The use of the tonic accent to denote the division of a word at a line ending, a device intended to reduce ambiguity, created possible confusion with the accented *-is* termination, the accenting of monosyllables, the accenting of the final syllables of adverbs, and other uses of the acute accent in manuscripts in the period of transition from unseparated to separated writing. The eventual disappearance of accentuation as a sign of interline continuation (in the eleventh century in England and France, in the twelfth century in Italy) and the ensuant exclusive reliance on the *trait d'union* were symptomatic of an evolving scribal quest for the elimination of graphic ambiguity.

The Hyphen

This mark, the "true hyphen" of Greek origin, was shaped like a semicircle and was written below the line. It had its origin in ancient Greek *scriptura continua* and was introduced into written Latin along with other Greek diacritical signs, critical signs, and marks of punctuation in the late second or third century A.D. when the Romans adopted *scriptura continua* in emulation of the Greeks.[78] Both Greek and Roman grammarians described the hyphen as an artificial aid to the reader, and Roman schoolmasters employed it when teaching pupils to read from wax tablets.[79] Both the hyphen and the *diastole* helped to overcome the difficulty of the correct pronunciation and comprehension of oral verse when the juxtaposition of certain words and syllables rendered word boundaries, and therefore correct accentuation, ambiguous in unseparated script. Occasional examples of the hyphen survive in the extensive corpus of Greek papyri, but none occur in the far smaller corpus of classical Latin papyri and patristic parchment codices.[80]

In contrast, medieval scribes regularly used the hyphen to correct errors in spacing in aerated manuscripts of the early Middle Ages, when space as a cue for both words and syllables began to intrude into text. The hyphen continued to be used in the central Middle Ages with separated script. It thus evolved in medieval Europe from a pedagogical mark intended to facilitate the private pronunciation by the schoolboy preparing for the *praelectio* of a text written in *scriptura continua* to a consistently used sign, placed in books either by the scribe or a professional emendator and intended to facilitate both oral and silent reading. In its new role, the hyphen's chief function was to correct an inappropriately placed space in separated writing or a space of inappropriate quantity in aerated writing. The use of the hyphen by scribes from the eighth century onward reflected a change in mentality, for it indicated the acceptance of an encoded significance for space as an interword boundary rather than as an occasional sign of punctuation.[81] Recording the presence of hyphens is therefore of considerable significance for the history of reading, but like the *trait d'union* and so many other pertinent details indicating the changing nature of the Latin page, it has seldom been regularly recorded in descriptions of medieval manuscripts.

Construction Notes

Among the new marks that complemented word separation by space were those identifying the grammatical function of particular words known to modern scholars as "construction notes." These marks, of which equivalents were almost entirely unknown in antiquity except in Syriac, emerged for the first time in separated Insular writing of the eighth century.[82] As early as the second half of the sixth century, when standards of education were in decline, Gregory of Tours linked the reader's task of separating words and reordering them as impediments to the understanding of elegant Latin.[83] In seventh-century Ireland and England, the accented *-is* termination and the terminal *e* cedilla acted as primitive construction notes when they denoted both a noun and the adjective modifying it. In the eighth century, interlinear emblematic syntactic notes, perhaps inspired by Syriac models, denoted words with common grammatical functions and in some instances identified, in encoded form, specific grammatical functions, such as those of the adjective, adverb, subject, verb, and object.[84] In the light of recent neurophysiological studies indicating that nouns and verbs are processed by different regions of the brain, the utility of such signs is evident.[85] In the ninth century, sequential construction notes using letters of the alphabet provided this information by directing the reader to reorganize a sentence in what thirteenth-century authors termed its "natural order" so that its sense could be more easily understood (Figure 16).[86] It is likely that the principle of using letters of the alphabet sequentially was inspired by Greek numerical notation.[87]

The expanded vision of text physiologically created by word separation and quantifiable in terms of an enhanced eye-voice span enabled the reader to use these signs effectively. The presence of sequential construction notes, in particular, implied a shift on the part of the reader from the aural retention in memory of words with their terminal inflections to visual memory and a direct visual access to meaning derived by mentally arranging encoded images on the page. In the context of classical

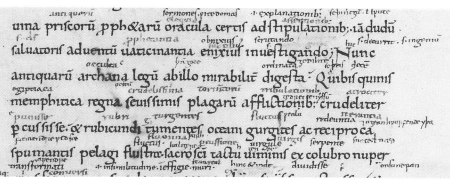

Figure 16. Alphabetical construction notes in Aldhelm's *De virginitate*. Brussels, Bibliothèque Royale Albert Ier 1650, f. 3 recto; reproduced by permission.

and patristic texts transcribed in the British Isles, sequential construction notes constituted the rudiments of syntactical punctuation, which employed new emblematic *notae* that also originated in the British Isles.[88] In modern times, syntactical gestures, analogous to written syntactical signs, have been integrated into the standard American Sign Language for the deaf to accelerate access to meaning and thereby to avoid excessively burdening visual memory with the retention of ambiguous strings of words in series, a task for which the brain's redundant system of aural memory plays such a significant role among the hearing.[89]

Punctuation

Other early sense-conveying signs, juxtaposed with text, emerged on the medieval page to provide supplementary information to guide the reader to the meaning of text. Although these "silent" paratextual signs did not form part of the text itself, the reader was expected to perceive them simultaneously with the text. They included encoded notes for the punctuation of sense, notes for the identification of citations, tie notes, and musical notation. Of these, the signs for the punctuation of sense were of particular importance. They had a precedent in the word-separated Syriac biblical codices of late antiquity, known in Ireland at an early date.

The same lack of conventions of word order in ancient Latin and the ensuant avoidance of syntactical word groupings that stimulated the invention of construction notes made the rigorous syntactical punctuation of the sort used in modern European languages awkward and sometimes impossible. Indeed, twentieth-century editors who have attempted to use modern signs of punctuation to parse classical Latin sentences into logical units and contiguous blocks of meaning are often frustrated by the problem of the displacement of words in rhetorical devices and the ambiguities stemming from using the same word or words to perform discrete functions within two or more discrete constructions.[90] The primary punctuation of ancient Latin was the metrical and rhythmical *clausulae*, which ambiguously signaled to the aural reader the end of either a clause or sentence.[91] The interrogative was frequently conveyed by enclitic particles and more ambiguously by interrogative adverbs and pronouns, and to some degree both subordinate clauses and sentences were defined by terminal verb position.[92] Identification of direct quotation remained uncertain. As an aid to the reader confronting these oratorical complexities, ancient readers of the classical period, when written Latin was separated by interpuncts, used occasional visual signs to denote amorphous units of sense and their related rhetorical pauses.[93]

With the shift from interpunct separation to *scriptura continua*, the old signs for punctuation of sense disappeared, and new Greek marks of punctuation based on a system of elevated points and linked closely to rhetorical phrasing were introduced, almost exclusively for pedagogical purposes. In manuscript books, these new signs of punctuation were rare, and when present, they, like *prosodiae*, were added by the reader rather than the scribe. In the late Imperial period, punctuation notes (which grammarians termed *positurae*) were tools intended primarily for the inexperienced reader, who employed them when mastering a text by copying it onto wax tablets, and they were not generally considered appropriate for a formal book.[94] For Augustine, the responsibility of parsing an ambiguous text into orthodox and meaningful distinctions lay explicitly with the reader.[95] At the end of antiquity, the only "punctuation" sometimes present in formal Roman books was spaces setting off paragraphs. Only after Rome's fall did Christian writers like Cassiodorus seem to envison the scribe making use of *positurae* in confected books to aid the reader (particularly the liturgical reader) with difficult passages.[96] Cassiodorus believed that they aided the reader to recognize words.[97] However, the actual evidence of the scribal insertion of such marks, always in the presence of additional space and capital letters, prior to the insertion of intratextual space under Insular influence, is generally limited.

The reintroduction of space within texts in the early Middle Ages corresponded to a precipitous expansion of scribal punctuation and the birth of a more rigorous effort to relate punctuation to units of sense. The use of capital letters and a hierarchy in the quantity of interword space played an important role in the development of this encoded punctuation. Similar values were communicated by patterns of points, comma-like marks, the sign of interrogation, and a predecessor of intratextual quotation marks, all of which I term "emblematic punctuation."

Most of the earliest emblematic marks emerged in the British Isles in manuscripts written with word separation.[98] This Insular emblematic punctuation was formed by patterns of points and commas that were recognized by the eye of the reader as a unity. Scribal use of these graphic signs was an indication of the heightened importance of parafoveal vision in aerated and separated script. The most enduring of Insular emblematic punctuation was the three-point cluster, resembling the musical symbol, or neume, known as the *trigon*, and the point over the comma identified by later medieval writers as the *punctus versus*. The three-point cluster was usually used as a terminal mark for a sentence or larger textual unit, for which function it is still used by modern printers. It is reasonable to suppose that this sign was inspired by an analogous mark employed in the same Syriac codices that also provided Insular culture with models of word separation, terminal forms, and ornamental decoration.

An encoded system of elevated points at two levels, probably inspired by Isidore's instructions for pedagogical punctuation, was employed in ninth-century separated Breton manuscripts.[99] The same system was employed by scribes in aerated and separated codices written at Tours in about 820, and it was used increasingly in Germany, Lorraine, and northern France in the late tenth and early eleventh centuries. In other manuscripts, simple points, when placed in conjunction with letters of different size, also had different syntactical values. The *metron*, a bow-shaped mark beneath a point that was used to delimit sentences, originated on the Continent in ninth-century aerated script. Two other marks, the *punctus flexus* to indicate clauses and the *punctus elevatus* to indicate phrases evolved three and one-half centuries later, when word separation spread from England to Normandy.

Other forms of emblematic punctuation evolved on the Continent. One of the most innovative was the sign of interrogation, a mark unknown in antiquity and first enumerated among *positurae* by Isidore of Seville. In ancient Latin, interrogation was either left to the reader to determine or conveyed solely by particles and interrogative pronouns and adverbs, easily confused with the same words employed for other functions.[100] Isidore's early-seventh-century enumeration of the question mark was as a pedagogical sign to be used by schoolmasters. Its subsequent use by scribes was an important stride toward a form of graphic Latin that transcended the mere phonetic transcription of speech. However, centuries before Western scribes used the new interrogation mark, Syriac scribes had employed interlinear points, called accents by modern scholars, as a preferred alternative to the interrogative particle.[101] Intratextual space, which had the effect of broadening the field of vision of both the reader and the scribe, was a prerequisite for the perception and interpretation during normal reading of the signs of interrogation of both Syriac and medieval Latin. Subsequently, in the Vulgar Latin and the Romance vernacular, inverted word order emerged as a complementary mode of signaling the interrogative.[102]

In the same Insular word-separated manuscripts that contained syntactic signs and signs of punctuation, the diple, or ancient wedge-shaped marginal note for identifying quotations, rare in Greek codices and unknown in Latin, came to be used with great frequency. These signs, which aided the comprehension of a text without affecting its pronunciation, were subsequently replaced by intratextual citation notes, which, like the new mode of punctuation of sense, had no antecedent in antiquity.[103]

Musical Notation

The earliest Latin musical notation, which first developed in the ninth century, in either Germany or northern France, was another group of intratextual signs linked to the emergence of the new text format.[104] The first neumes occurred in the presence of aerated and separated script and closely resembled marks of punctuation and *prosodiae* in their form.[105] Early musical notation also consisted of interlinear letters and tironian word notes to indicate both pitch and tempo.[106] As signs, they were at times identical to the letters used for the notation of syntax, and experienced scholars have more than once mistaken the one for the other. The same neurophysiological processes that necessitated space for the effective reception of signs for word sequence were required for the perception of these *notae*, which provided encoded information for the oral performance of liturgical texts. Intratextual space was essential for sufficient clarity in the primary text to allow the reader to achieve a broader eye-voice span and thereby to turn his faculties to the perception of supplementary material necessary for the coordination of musical pitch with the syllables of the text.[107] Such reading drew upon the same neuro-physiological capacities used to decode construction notes or the signs of punctuation that guided pronunciation of a liturgical text.

Nota Signs and Tie Notes

A type of encoded marginalia denoting place in the text and closely linked to the presence of intratextual space was the conventional *nota* sign, in its earliest form a monogram formed from the letter *N*. The *nota* sign was used to draw the reader's attention to significant passages in the text. Its use suggests a degree of interaction between the scribe or reader and the texts of which we find only limited traces in ancient codices written on papyri or parchment and occasional mention in patristic texts.[108] Readers of separated script, who relied increasingly upon the left visual field for recognition of words as images, showed greater receptivity to reading these emblematic signs, which came into prominence for the first time in the ninth century.[109]

Another reader sign (closely related physiologically to *nota* signs, *prosodiae*, punctuation, construction notes, and musical *notae*) are the tie notes that attached interlinear and marginal *scholia*—commentaries and annotations—to their referents in the text. Tie notes, too, had only rudimentary antecedents, in the form of the critical signs and notes indicating and sometimes attaching omitted passages occasionally present in books written in Greek and Latin in *scriptura continua*.[110] These notes mushroomed in conjunction with the aeration and separation of text in the early Middle Ages. In the British Isles in the eighth century and on the Continent in the eighth, ninth, and tenth centuries, tie notes became a frequent feature of school texts, especially the Psalms, the classical poets, and from the eleventh century onward, juristic texts. The dramatic effusion of tie notes occurred more or less simultaneously in northern Europe, most notably in Lorraine and northeastern France, and in Byzantium. The fact that many of the early Latin tie notes were Greek letters of the alphabet or signs inspired by them might suggest that tie notes originated in the Eastern Empire. However, the earliest Insular symbolic tie notes antedate Byzantine examples, and the use of Greek more probably represents Insular interest in the Greek language than an emulation of Greek models. Elsewhere in the East, models may have existed for Insular tie notes. Syrian manuscripts with tie notes, such as Paris, BN Syr. 27, a copy of the Pentateuch in Syriac dating from the end of the seventh century or from early in the eighth, contain signs very similar to those of subsequent Insular codices.[111]

A second type of medieval tie note, the tie note of explication, coded each symbol to help the reader distinguish the subjects of different notes by the form of the note serving as a referent.[112] These were related to the critical notes or marginal signs intended to communicate supplementary information about content that schoolboys of ancient Greece employed to annotate philosophical texts.[113] Marginal critical signs, originally artificial aids of the schoolroom, entered fully confected Latin codices for the first time at Vivarium, where Cassiodorus formally introduced them into his commentaries on the Psalms. Sophisticated marginal notes were widely used in Continental manuscripts written by Irish scribes in the early ninth century. These critical notes also served as tie notes when additional information was appended to them and a referent note was placed within the text.[114] Hincmar, archbishop of Reims from 845 to 882, described his own use of such symbols in his correspondance with Odon of Beauvais.[115] In the twelfth century, Hugh of Saint-Victor enumerated in a list of *prosodiae* the tie notes and critical notes that could convey meaning directly to the reader, without need of the phonetic transcription of oral discourse.[116]

A third type of tie note that increased dramatically in quantity and complexity as an accompaniment to the regular use of intratextual space was the tie note of correction, by means of which scribes could include omitted lines and phrases. These tie notes, which antedate tie notes of explication, appeared in late classical Latin codices as the marginal suspension abbreviations *hd* and *hs*.[117] In Insular separated codices, they became complex emblems, with forms similar to neumes and marks of punctuation.

Tie notes were also used to establish fixed and readily identifiable loci on the page. In the period immediately preceding the separation of words by space, an innovative form of tie note proliferated on the Continent. It used Latin letters of the alphabet in sequence to establish a series of fixed loci within the text on the leaf. These, and marginal alphabets designating place, are found in word-separated books of the eleventh century. Alphabetical sequential tie notes appear in numerous late medieval manuscripts and incunabula, or books printed before 1501, where they are the direct ancestors of the modern numbered footnote.

Indications of Page Locus

The evidence of surviving fragments does not permit us to determine if page numbering began first in tablets, codices, or scrolls. The codex as a format for a published confected book originated in the first century A.D. in Rome, when it enjoyed popularity, at least in a restricted circle, because it was smaller than the roll, and hence more portable.[118] The script of these early codices was separated by points. No evidence of foliation exists on any surviving Latin codex.[119] In Greek codices, written in *scriptura continua*, pagination or foliation can be documented as early as the third century A.D., and in some rare instances, the vertical columns of Greek papyri scrolls of approximately the same date were also numbered, as were the leaves used in Greek writing tablets.[120] It is also uncertain whether Greek foliation, or in some instances pagination, was intended as an aid in assembling books, as seems probable, or as an aid to the reader. However, it is clear that the Greeks produced no tables referring to specific folios similar to those found in any medieval Latin reference work. Greek and Coptic scribes continued the practice of foliation and pagination into medieval times, and Byzantium may have provided a model for the development of foliation in the medieval West.[121]

Although leaf signatures appear in certain eighth-century Insular separated codices, the first indications of foliation of Latin manuscripts occur in aerated codices dating from the tenth century, when space had already assumed a prominent role.[122] The first evidence of its repeated use in centers in France and Italy followed within a century of the adoption of word separation by space.[123] The practice, however, did not become in any sense current until after 1200. By facilitating the retrieval of specific information within the codex, foliation served the reader in a manner analogous to that of word separation. Both innovations artificially divided the book into a series of physically defined loci, independent of literary structures inherent in the text, that were generated simply and automatically by the process of transcription. As early as the first years of the twelfth century, scribes produced for Latin manuscripts sophisticated tables with references to folio number (Figure 17).[124] The ultimate popularity of both word separation and foliation was consonant with the ocular gestures that became essential features of the new reading habits in the late Middle Ages.

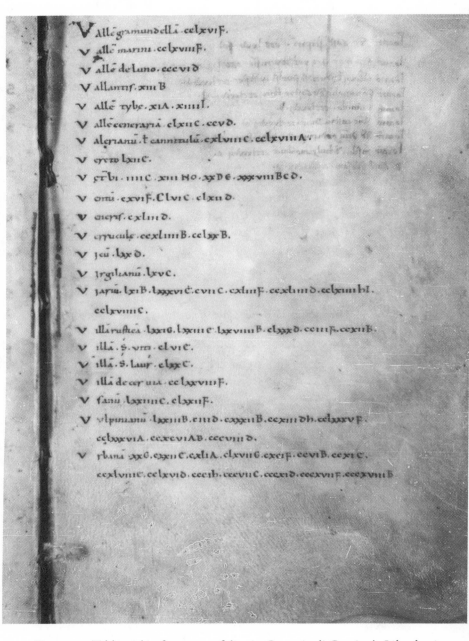

Figure 17. Table with references to folios in Gregorio di Cantino's *Liber largitorius*. Rome, Biblioteca Nazionale Centrale, Vittorio Emanuele II, Farfa 2, f. 19 recto; reproduced by permission.

Résumé Notes and Schematic Diagrams

Marginalia of another type provided brief graphic *résumés* of portions of text to aid the reader in finding information on a particular subject and in retaining that information in memory. *Résumé* notes were an important artificial device for abetting the mastery of written text.[125] *Résumé* notes, often framed in irregular boxes, designated multiple points of entry into texts, thereby providing an alternative to reading texts from beginning to end, the traditional mode of the ancient reader. These notes were often added after the confection of the book, and in some instances they were added by the same hand that separated words and modified punctuation.[126] Another related practice was the writing in the margin of a book the proper names of the principal authorities referred to in the text.

In the late tenth and early eleventh centuries at Reims, Fleury, and Chartres, *résumé* notes evolved into marginal treelike schematic diagrams (Figure 18). Totally unknown to both ancient *scriptura continua* and early medieval aerated writing, schematic diagrams by their inherent format were intended for silent, visual inspection, and not for oral recitation.[127] They became characteristic of central and late medieval school texts, achieving their zenith in the circle of Raymond Lull at the University of Paris in the early fourteenth century.[128] They were present as well in the margins of fifteenth-century humanist manuscripts of Aristotle and Plato. Schematic diagrams gave a symbolic and pictorial *résumé* of relationships or logical statements contained within the body of the text, and as such, represented a pedagogical innovation demonstrably useful for the learning process.[129] The presence of schematic diagrams in difficult texts implied a new use by the reader of the right hemisphere. The use of schematic diagrams is so fundamental to modern students that it is easily forgotten that no equivalent visual notation existed in antiquity.[130] The reading of such tabular presentations of information, in which imagery was critical for the organization of concepts and logical relationships, neurophysiologically resembled the reading by word-image of separated text.

Post-Factum Emendation

The post-factum emendation of unseparated early medieval pre-Caroline and Caroline manuscripts provides historical documentation of the linkage in the mind of medieval readers between word separation

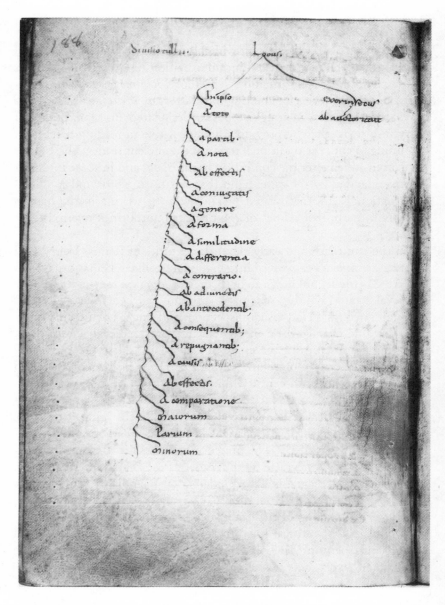

Figure 18. A schematic tree diagram accompanying Boethius's *De topicis differentiis*. Vatican Library, Vat. lat. 8591, f. 94 verso; reproduced by permission.

and the perceived need for signs to clarify higher levels of textual division: the clause, the sentence, the paragraph, and the chapter. Reworked manuscripts also provide invaluable sources for tracing the comparative chronology of word separation in various regions of Europe. Indeed, for the historical narration of word separation, the subsequent reworkings of manuscripts, particularly by the use of the successor note to the *diastole*, are of an importance equal to the separation exhibited in new codices.

The emendation of earlier manuscripts was a common phenomenon of the central and late Middle Ages. It was discussed in tracts on the art of reading, beginning with Pseudo-Priscian's *Liber de accentibus*, and in monastic customaries.[131] The practice of separating unseparated writing demonstrates the perceived advantages of word separation for reading. It also documents the frustrations of readers who had evolved new reading habits when they confronted old books. The reworkings, unfortunately, often go unreported in paleographic literature, except in the prefatory material to certain volumes of *Early English Manuscripts in Facsimile* and isolated instances commented upon by E. A. Lowe in his *Codices latini antiquiores*.

Scribal reworking to create separation is first evident in Continental aerated manuscripts that were emended in England in the late tenth century.[132] Such emendation continued through the sixteenth century, when old books, even if unseparated or imperfectly separated, were still consulted, read, and copied. Monastic customaries, the books that recorded the rules governing an abbey, and the remarks of scholastic authors confirm that the emendation of these books was an official task of the scriptorium.[133] A dramatic example of subsequent emendation is an eleventh-century reader's revision of a seventh-century biblical commentary, *Philippus in Job*, Cambrai, BM 470, written in half uncial *scriptura continua* (see Figure 13).[134] Here, the reader marked the separation of every word, including monosyllabic prepositions, by adding successor notes to the *diastole* and by denoting the division of words at line ending with the *trait d'union* and suspended ligature. The *trait d'union* was used only after prepositions that were not used as freestanding words. It was more common, however, for books to be emended with varying degrees of separation and punctuation at a time closer to their transcription. An example of a narrower chronological gap is Charleville, BM 196c, copied at the Cistercian Abbey of Notre-Dame de Signy near Reims in the twelfth century, in which emendators working within a century of the initial confection of the codex added *prosodiae*, sequential construction notes, and altered punctuation.[135]

An occasional aspect of reworked manuscripts was the altering of terminal letters into forms reserved for this position. Such reworking facilitated the recognition of words by contributing to giving each word its own shape. Examples of post-factum terminal letters are present in Cambrai, BM 470, Charleille 196c, Venice, Marcianus Z.L. 497, and Vat. lat. 4929, a ninth-century codex from Fleury or its region that included Pomponius Mela's *De chorographia libri III*.[136] In Cambrai, BM 470, other reworkings included the addition of the suspended *ct* ligature to enhance word shape. The same emendator also placed acute accents on the double *ii* and adapted the punctuation to give clarity to the meaning of the text.[137]

The corpus of manuscripts in which separation and punctuation were added by a single emendator documents the emergence of a new reader expectation: finding books with both words and larger distinctions of sense clearly demarcated.[138] This historical evidence is consistent with the results of laboratory experiments suggesting that in the absence of word separation, punctuation cannot be readily decoded by the reader.[139] The presence of word separation was thus inextricably linked to the evolution of a system of unambiguous signs for denoting larger units of meaning.

Chapter 4

Insular Culture and Word Separation in the Seventh and Eighth Centuries

The Grammarians of Separation

The origins of rapid, silent reading lie in the scribal techniques and grammatical teachings that developed in Ireland and England in the seventh and eighth centuries. The first separated Latin manuscript books in western Europe were Irish, and their text format was probably inspired by Syriac Gospel books. The first datable word-separated manuscripts are Dublin, Trinity College 60 (A.I.15), the *Book of Mulling* (before 692),[1] and Schaffhausen, Stadtsbibliothek Generalia I, Adomnan's *Vita Columbae* (before 713).[2] The first seventh-century Irish grammarian who has left even indirect indication of the appeal of separated script was Virgilius Maro. His graphic distinctions between the conjunction *et* (written with the ligature) and the word termination *-et* (written without the ligature), the conjunction *ac* and the demonstrative *hac*, and the demonstrative *hic* and the adverb written *hiic* are indicative of the desire of Irish scribes to avoid ambiguity.[3] The Irish grammatical text *Anonymous ad Cuimnanum* from the seventh or eighth century emphasized that readers of liturgical texts needed to recognize *dictiones*, or words, and *distinctiones sententiarum*, that is, the distinction into sentences.[4] The author's description of the *figura*, or shape, of prepositions suggested a graphic image for the morphological distinction between prepositions acting as syllabic prefixes and those acting as separate words.[5] *Anonymous ad Cuimnanum* also emphasized the importance of terminal letters. In the eighth century, the anonymous Irish author of the *Ars anonyma Bernensis* defined *figura* as the shape of an object or of the noun denoting it, a formulation that clearly implied the graphic representations created when words were set off by space.[6]

In eighth-century England, we find grammatical treatises composed in separated script by Anglo-Saxon authors trained by Irish masters that begin to offer direct insight into the pedagogical implications of word separation. Two Anglo-Saxon authors who commented on the classical texts took note of word separation. The earliest was Aldhelm (ca. 640–709), bishop of Sherborne, the first Anglo-Saxon to leave a substantial corpus of Latin prose.[7] Aldhelm, whose writings remained popular until the eleventh century, as a youth had studied under Irish masters in the second half of the seventh century, when separation and certain important adjuncts to script, including accentuation, had become normal in Irish codices. Unfortunately, no authorial and only one eighth-century word-separated fragment of an Insular copy of Aldhelm's works survives.[8] However, the text of his *Epistola ad Acircium sive liber de septenario et de metris et enigmatibus ac pedum regulis* reveals a new relationship between the reader and the book. Aldhelm redefined ancient *prosodiae*, which had been the interpretive marks added by the reader, as signs regularly provided by the scribe for the reader's correct distinction of words.[9] He associated the *apex*, or acute accent, not only with tone, but with vowel length, in keeping with the actual practice of Insular scribes, who used the apex to denote vowel length in monosyllables and for the dative termination *-is*.[10] Aldhelm enumerated the *dasia* as a mark of aspiration found almost always at word beginnings, suggesting that it was to be used as a 'sign of word boundaries, which in fact the early Irish scribes did. Virgilius Maro also was likely alluding to word boundaries in his distinction of *ac* from *hac*, for both the *h* and the *dasia* in medieval Latin were silent characters.[11] Their development as marks for word boundaries was probably influenced by Greek and the Germanic languages, where the *h* (both the sound and subsequently the graphic symbol) served to demarcate word beginnings. The graphic role for the *dasia* and the *h* as scribal marks of word boundaries continued until the eleventh century.[12]

Aldhelm's most original comments concern the explicit signs for word demarcation that he termed *passiones*, notably the hyphen and *diastole*. The term *passiones*, meaning "feelings," was unknown to the technical vocabulary of ancient grammarians. Aldhelm apparently preferred it to *prosodiae* because in confected books these signs removed ambiguity and enabled the reader to lend suitable expression to his voice by not mistaking two words for one or one word for two.[13] Using vocabulary borrowed from the abstract ancient discussion of each word's *figura*, Aldhelm defined the hyphen—the hyphen of Greco-Roman heritage—as a sign uniting two graphic parts into one compound word.[14] In antiquity, the primary referent of *figura* had been the letter. According to both Donatus and the Anglo-Saxon grammarians of the eighth century, six of the eight parts of speech had the quality of *figura*.[15] However, to the ancients who wrote in unseparated script, *figura* in this context constituted a vague metaphorical abstraction used to teach students writing on wax tablets to distinguish between simple and compound words. For the Continental grammarian Julian, bishop of Toledo from 667 to 690, who knew only *scriptura continua*, groups of letters having *figura* were distinguishable from other groupings of letters only in that the former represented units of meaning. When viewed on the page, the two types of letter groupings were identical.[16] However, for Anglo-Saxon grammarians, beginning with Aldhelm, *figura* literally implied the outline of the block of letters on the page, where space separated one *pars*, or part, from another, and in England, *figura* came to serve as a regular visual confirmation of the *pars* or *dictio*, that is, the word. Aldhelm defined the *diastole* as a sign that removed ambiguity by indicating the division of two words written as a single unit of grouped letters (*compositae litterae*). Thus, Aldhelm's new terminology could distinguish between two words written as a single composite of letters, or in our nomenclature, as a word block, and two words written separately. These definitions confirm the normal use of space as a cue for word separation.

Aldhelm's description of the *diastole* and the hyphen as *passiones* indicates that these Insular graphic innovations were not meant merely to avert misplaced stress, but also to speed the comprehension necessary for reading with expression. Well-separated Insular text, replete with *prosodiae* and *positurae*, permitted the distinct antique activities of *lectio*, that is, pronunciation, and *enarratio*, that is, comprehension, to merge into a single physiological process.[17] Word separation, the *diastole*, the hyphen, and eventually the *trait d'union* in Insular books provided shortcuts for achieving the reading skills that an elite among the ancients had mastered only through a prolonged and arduous grammatical apprenticeship.

A second Anglo-Saxon grammarian of preeminent authority, the Venerable Bede (d. 735), a monk from the twin Abbeys of Wearmouth-Jarrow and author of the *Liber de orthographia*, datable to ca. 700, also was among the early proponents of innovations that promoted rapid, visual reading. Bede was more explicit in his discussion of the *diastole*. At one point in his brief treatise (Figure 19), Bede defined the *diastole* as follows: "*Diastole*, Greek for the Latin term *interdictum*, or interword, is moreover a mark placed at the foot of a letter that separates incorrectly joined let-

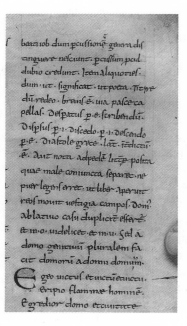

Figure 19. The text format of Bede's description of the *diastole* in the *De orthographia*. Cambridge, Corpus Christi College 221, f. 14 recto, col. 2; reproduced by permission of the Master and Fellows of Corpus Christi College, Cambridge.

ters so that a youth will not make the error of reading: '*Liber apervit reos movit vestigia campos*' " (a sentence of licit Latin words of which the syntax and meaning are obscure).[18] In the version reproduced here, a tenth-century copy of Bede's text that was almost certainly written in England or on the Continent by an Insular scribe, the erroneous word separation that the *diastole* and the hyphen could have corrected was unambiguously communicated to the reader by the same purposefully erroneous pattern of interword space reproduced above in italics.[19] The correct reading of the verse from Sedulius should have been "Libera per vitreos movit vestigia campos."[20] It is likely that the Corpus Christi 221 transcription accurately represented authorial intent, for Bede's statement makes sense only in a manuscript written with interword space. Indeed, all of Bede's works were disseminated in the British Isles only in separated script.[21]

Bede's definition of the *diastole* contrasts sharply with Isidore's, written in *scriptura continua* in Spain a century earlier. Isidore (d. 636) had distinguished the *diastole* from the hyphen in a manner that in no way presupposed the presence of interword space.[22] His definition, like those of the Silver Age Latin grammarians Donatus, Victorinus, and Diomedes, assumed the *diastole* to be a classroom mark added to a text written in *scriptura continua* to clarify pronunciation where the boundary between two words might easily be misconstrued.[23] While Bede, too, saw the *diastole* as performing this function, his phrase "incorrectly linked" (male coniuncta), where the ancients had stated "incorrectly discerning what went together (male cohaerentia discernens)," suggests in the context of a treatise that repeatedly emphasized correct writing that the *diastole* was a mark in a confected book intended to correct a scribe's omission of the interword space that ordinarily guided the inexperienced reader. Bede's discussion of word division at line endings similarly assumed the written word to be a unit of linked letters.[24] Indeed, space for word separation was regularly inserted in the earliest surviving English books, and the first English documents, which date from the end of the seventh century, were all separated.[25] On folio 4 of the seventh-century *Book of Durrow*, the original scribe appears to have used the *diastole* in precisely the function that Bede envisioned.[26]

Another indication that Bede's view of the writing process embodied the notion of separated script can be found in the first paragraph of his *Liber de orthographia*, in which he explained the significance of suspension abbreviations for proper names. The use of initial letters as abbreviations originated in the period when Roman script was separated by interpuncts. Bede, following late Roman practice in *scriptura continua*, retained the *virga* (the superscript bar) for certain multiletter abbreviations for set phrases that were not suspension abbreviations and in which each letter did not represent a word. Here, the *virga* signaled the reader that the letters were not to be read phonetically, for example, "VV" for *verbi gratia*, "VV.CC" for *viri clarissimi*.[27] For single-letter abbreviations, including proper names, and for some multiletter abbreviations, letters alone sufficed, without the *virga*, reflecting a presumption that interword space and interpuncts could isolate each letter and render it a symbol for a freestanding word.[28] This notion of a suspension abbreviation presupposed a one-to-one graphic correspondence between symbol and word that had been totally absent in early medieval Continental glossaries of ancient abbreviations that had been transcribed in aerated writing.[29] However, in one respect, Bede continued antique tradition, for like Priscian and other ancient grammarians, he did not have a clear conception of the distinction between the preposition as a freestanding word and as a bound syllabic prefix in composite words.[30] This lack was consistent with the practice of eighth-century Wearmouth-Jarrow scribes, who, like many of their Irish counterparts, failed to insert space consistently after monosyllabic prepositions.[31]

The transformation of *figura* from an abstraction to a concrete graphic reality gave a new dimension to Anglo-Saxon grammatical instruction. Tatwine, bishop of Canterbury from 731 to 734, in a grammatical treatise probably written before 731, gave great importance to *figura*. No authorial or contemporary manuscripts of Tatwine's works survive.[32] However, Tatwine's discussion of suspension abbreviations confirms that he, like Aldhelm and Bede, wrote in separated script.[33] His idea of the word was more advanced than the ancients' or Bede's, for in his consideration of prepositions, he distinguished between prepositions as bound morphemic prefixes forming one *pars* with the syllables that followed them and prepositions functioning as separate words requiring interword space.[34] For Tatwine, all parts of speech had *figurae*, including by implication not only prepositions, but conjunctions and interjections, words not separated in ancient pronunciation.[35] In his *Aenigma*, he spoke of the reader going directly from the letters to the recognition of the word, without reference to the syllable, the crucial unit in ancient phonosynthetic reading.[36] From the visually perceived form of the termination, the student could rapidly and artificially determine a word's grammatical function.[37]

Boniface (ca. 675–754), the celebrated Anglo-Saxon missionary to the Germans and Frisians and commentator on Donatus, prepared a handbook of grammar in which he carefully enumerated the *figurae* of nouns, verbs, adverbs, and conjunctions as graphically visual forms immediately perceptible to the reader.[38] The word separation of an Insular transcription of Boniface's text made terminations readily visible, thus giving them a redundant physiological function.[39] The characteristically Insular paradigms that constituted the major portion of his text provided readers with the opportunity of visually familiarizing themselves with all the variant silhouettes of inflected nouns and verbs.[40] Profiting from the physiological accessibility of word beginnings and endings that separation afforded, Boniface proceeded to enumerate the cues to grammatical function that readers could deduce from word terminations, particularly when distinguishing adverbs from related nouns, verbs, and adjectives.[41]

The promotion of rapid visual reading with understanding evident in Aldhelm's *Epistola ad Acircium*, Bede's *De arte metrica*, and Boniface's grammar also appears subsequently, in the writings of the Irish schoolman Dicuil, who flourished in the first half of the ninth century and expounded on a short text, the *De finalibus*, generally attributed to the

fourth-century grammarian Servius. Capitalizing on the fact that reading in separated script extended the scope and enhanced the accuracy of
parafoveal vision, all these Insular authors stressed how the initial and terminal portion of words provided cues to understanding, as well as to pronunciation.[42] The scribal conventions for the use of distinctive terminal
forms, in effect, encoded identification of case and facilitated comprehension.[43] In this way, the reader could often visually recognize syntactically linked parts of speech and using the visible signs understand swiftly
the grammatical relationship necessary for comprehension of the text,
relying on short-term visual memory. The use of acute accents on the -is
termination and the terminal e cedilla complemented this phenomenon.

The *Corpus Glossary*, the earliest Anglo-Saxon Latin glossary, dating
from the second half of the eighth century, and the *Leiden Glossary* that
was derived from it, provide additional textual evidence of word separation's penetration into the consciousness of Insular grammarians.[44] In
the latter, we find a definition of *figura* as an image corresponding to the
separated *dictio*.[45]

The same eighth-century Anglo-Saxons who explicated grammar
graphically also began to examine the question of word order. Ancient
grammarians had enumerated eight parts of speech, roughly corresponding, save for the adjective, to the entities we recognize today as the names
for parts of a sentence, but they gave few rules for the way in which these
parts of speech were to be ordered within the sentence. The scant dicta
on word order that the ancient grammarians provided were often taken
much more literally in the Middle Ages than they had been by classical
authors, who generally exhibited a very free order.[46] For example, Quintilian's expressed preference for placing the verb in the final position was
more scrupulously honored by certain early medieval authors than any
Roman author would have deemed reasonable. Similarly, in the thirteenth century, Priscian's casual statement that adverbs should proceed
the verbs they modified was lifted from its context and made an artificial
rule for eliminating ambiguity in logical texts.[47]

Beginning in the sixth century, Celtic and Anglo-Saxon authors of
Latin began to make word order conventions a regular feature of their
prose. The resulting rigid artificial word orders were evident in the *Hisperica famina*, Gildas's *De excidio Britanniae*, and in the works of Columbanus, the first great Irish missionary to the Continent and founder of
the monastery of Bobbio.[48] Early Anglo-Saxon authors, notably Ald-

helm, adopted them and employed other conventional word orders, including that of subject-verb-object, which had come to characterize vulgar Latin.[49]

Tatwine was the first Insular grammarian to make Donatus's ordering
of the parts of speech the one that words should follow within a sentence
so as to avoid ambiguity.[50] He thus began the imposition onto classical rhetoric of conventions of word order based on the logical relation
between grammatical elements. If an author observed his rule that the
subject should precede the verb, a reader was more apt to comprehend
the sense of a phrase. Tatwine's emphasis on grammatical order must
also be viewed in the context of the modification of word order made by
Irish and Anglo-Saxon scribes when transcribing biblical texts and the
introduction of sequential construction notes by Insular scribes of the
following century.[51] Unlike classical grammarians, Irish and Anglo-Saxon
monks came to view sentences as a series of dedicated grammatical loci
existing in the mind of the reader that, once filled with the appropriate sequence of words, convey meaning. Bede, in his *De schematibus et
tropis*, offered guidance to Anglo-Saxons who had to search for meaning
in the complex word order of late Latin poetry.[52] These new aspects of the
written Latin *langue* of the British Isles supplemented the ancient intricate codes of inflected terminations. Among the Irish and Anglo-Saxon
authors, the sequencing of graphic images was valued for the readily
perceived clarification it gave to the relationship between words, and to
achieve this effect sonority was sacrificed.

New Genres of Books

Alphabetical Glossaries

Five new genres of books originated in England and Ireland from the
seventh to the ninth centuries, after separated script had already become
habitual. The first and perhaps the most important was the alphabetical
glossary. It is difficult to imagine an alphabetical dictionary functioning as a reference tool when written in *scriptura continua*, even after the
codex had supplanted the scroll. For the Greeks and Romans, alphabetical order was chiefly an aid to grammarians in assembling collections of
grammatical definitions, such as that of Pompeius Festus, and as a mnemonic tool for relatively short lists of names. The alphabetical principle
was never used to facilitate rapid consultation, as in modern indexes.[53]
Even for Pliny the Elder (A.D. ca. 23–79), who knew interpunct-separated

script, the principle of alphabetization in long sequences functioned as an aid to the compiler, rather than as an avenue for the silent and swift retrieval of information from an ancient scroll.

Extensive alphabetical glossaries and dictionaries were a uniquely medieval innovation, diffused only in aerated or separated script and originating in the zone of Europe where the vernacular was not a derivative of Latin. They were an aid to those readers of Latin for whom the vernacular offered no phonic clues for comprehension. The earliest substantial alphabetical glossaries were bilingual documents, an indication that the impetus to establish alphabetical reference tools arose from the peculiar tension generated by the early Middle Ages' consciously bilingual cultures.

In ancient Rome, the only foreign language had been Greek, which Roman children learned naturally as a spoken tongue. Since the educated Roman elite culture was essentially bilingual, there had been little need for special reference works to give word-by-word equivalents.[54] However, in what Peter Brown has termed "middlebrow" Christian circles, where bilingualism was less prevalent, certain manuscripts, such as Oxford, BL Laud. Gr. 35, containing the biblical book of Acts, both in the original Greek and in Latin translation, were written in a special text format, a modification of *per cola et commata*, in which often only one word was written per line. This format allowed an inexperienced reader instantly to perceive word-by-word equivalents.[55]

In contrast to the way in which young Romans learned Greek, Irishmen and Englishmen learned Latin not as a spoken language, but artificially, in the schoolroom, from word-separated grammars and glossaries. As a result, Insular pedagogy emphasized word-to-word correspondence. Perhaps inspired by the bilingual biblical format of antiquity, which had reached the British Isles before the time of Bede in manuscripts like Oxford, BL Laud. Gr. 35, Insular monks created Latin and bilingual glossaries written in separated script. These glossaries included Bede's *Liber de orthographia*, the *Epinal Glossary*,[56] and the *Corpus Glossary*, this last consisting of sixty-two folios, lengthy enough to warrant justly the title of being the first European dictionary.[57] The development of the alphabetical glossary as a pedagogical tool was part of the process of linguistic simplification that facilitated the learning of a foreign tongue.

In Bede's *De orthographia*, the principle of alphabetical arrangement can be traced to the very end of the seventh century. Although the earliest surviving manuscripts date from the eighth and ninth centuries, there is no doubt that this was a genuine work by Bede.[58] In essence, the *De orthographia* was an incipient dictionary, primitive in comparison to the much larger *Corpus Glossary*, but highly significant as an example of the pedagogical impulses leading to the latter's compilation. The *De orthographia* was composed by Bede either when he was a student or as a pedagogical aid for his own students. In either event, as an ephemeral effort, it might not have survived had it not been the work of a saint who in his own time was revered as an exceptional scholar. Bede's short book provided an alphabetically arranged compilation of words deemed difficult to spell, conjugate, understand, or divide at line endings. The inconsistent form of the entries and the eclectic selection of the words confirm that the work was not meant to be a formal grammatical opus. However, as an example of early Insular pedagogy, the *De orthographia* shows that the study of Latin was already tied to the memorization of words by their written images for eventual use as building stones for sentences.

All early medieval alphabetical glossaries, whether copied in England, Ireland, or on the Continent, evince directly or indirectly the influence of glossaries compiled in separated script in the British Isles or in Insular colonies on the Continent.[59] The earliest Continental manuscripts of alphabetical glossaries dating from the ninth century contain glosses of Insular composition, and the entries in Latin/German alphabetical glossaries were modeled on Latin/Anglo-Saxon ones.[60] When written in aerated script, Continental alphabetical glossaries employed either space, interpunctuation in the presence of space, or capitalization to set off the *figura* of the entry word from an explication written in word blocks.[61]

Like word separation, alphabetical glossaries spread in a generally southward direction, first to Germany and France, and only finally to Italy. Alcuin's *Orthographia* was in essence an Insular alphabetical glossary.[62] Papias's *Dictionarium*, composed in northern Italy in the mid-eleventh century and often arbitrarily referred to as the first Latin dictionary, was created from a synthesis of older glossaries, including alphabetical texts of Insular origin, just at the time when word separation was first penetrating this region. While alphabetical glossaries were copied on the Continent from the ninth century onward, many other glossaries originating on the Continent as early as the sixth century were not alphabetically arranged.[63] Glossaries of tironian notes, the uniquely Continental form of separated writing, totally lacked the convenience of alphabetical access to their *figurae*.[64]

Interlinear Translations

A second type of book born in the British Isles was the interlinear translation. For this genre of text, too, there was no classical antecedent. The juxtaposition of a bilingual translation on a single opening had been known in the ancient world. The most famous example of this format is the Rosetta Stone.[65] Bede had access to a biblical manuscript in a variety of this format, Oxford, BL Laud. Gr. 35, which he consulted for his *Expositio actuum apostolorum* and *Retractio*.[66] However, no classical precedent existed for the eighth-century Irish and English bilingual books in which each line of Latin was interpolated with a word-for-word vernacular translation. Irish interlinear translations of Latin were followed by Anglo-Saxon, Welsh, and Breton ones. The same format was also used for Insular bilingual Greco-Latin books. The ninth-century Irish interlinear translations of Greek are among the earliest examples of word-separated Greek texts. From the vantage point of the reader, bilingual glossaries and interlinear texts had much in common, for both assumed the practice of frequent and facile ocular gestures to retrieve verbal images to explicate in a familiar tongue what had been written in an esoteric one.

Pocket Gospel Books

Ancient paintings depicting reading suggest that to resist the tunnel vision imposed by *scriptura continua*, the reader tended to distance himself physically from the page.[67] The medieval shift of attention from the *figura* of the letter to the *figura* of the word produced a compacted and smaller script that brought the reader closer to the page, creating a greater intimacy between the writer, the reader, and the book. Among the earliest signs of this intimacy was the new Irish miniature pocket Gospel book.

Although miniature Latin books separated by interpuncts and space had existed in the first century A.D., they do not seem to have enjoyed wide popularity and apparently vanished after the general Roman acceptance of *scriptura continua*.[68] The Irish pocket Bibles of the seventh, eighth, and ninth centuries measure from 125 mm to 175 mm in height and from 112 mm to 142 mm in width.[69] In them, the use of separated or canonically separated script was standard, as was the presence of monolexic abbreviations. Irish artists employed one of these, the *nomen sacrum*, "XPI," as a prominent decorative image in illuminating both large and small manuscripts.

Eight Irish pocket Gospels and a number of similar Anglo-Saxon codices survive, and literary sources suggest that such books were copied in far larger numbers. As a sign of the new intimacy, their colophons included for the first time in the West the name of the scribe and other personal details, as well as short pious private messages intended for the reader.[70] It is probable that these personal colophons were patterned on those used by Syriac monks as early as the beginning of the fifth century.[71] The earliest datable separated pocket Gospel book, the Gospel of Saint John, Dublin, Trinity College 60, (A.N. 23) was written by the scribe Tech Mulling, who died in 696. Mulling asked for the prayers of future readers who would copy, scrutinize, or scan his book.[72] Mulling's use of the verb *videre,* "to see," as a synonym for reading came to be a commonplace of the late Middle Ages. In the seventh century, it was a new and peculiarly Insular word for reading. Private written dialogues between scribe and reader, of which Mulling's colophon is an example, became so much a part of the book culture of the Middle Ages that it is easily forgotten that in Roman antiquity, similar inscriptions did not exist, and that their equivalent did not fully emerge on the Continent until the eighth century, after the influence of the Irish missionaries and aerated writing had become pervasive.

Pocket Gospel books were an integral part of Irish monastic life. Each was very much a monk's private book and was carried among his personal possessions. The close relationship between the reader and his books continued even after death. A pocket Gospel, purportedly interred with Martin of Tours, was later removed and transported to Derry as a relic.[73] Private religious devotion tied to the portable Gospel book was unique to the culture of the West, and it had no equivalent in Byzantium. This early, devout attachment to the book among the Irish was a precursor of the acknowledged intimacy between Anglo-Saxon Gospel books and their tenth-century owners. According to tradition, the Gospel of Chad was buried with its owner. Other small Anglo-Saxon books include Priscian's Latin translation of Pseudo-Denis's *Periegesis,* which was illustrated by one of the early surviving medieval maps in London, BL Cotton Tiberius B V.[74]

Irish pocket Gospels and other biblical manuscripts, discussed above for their script and format, display a peculiar textual pattern of considerable interest for the history of reading. The oldest biblical codices written on the Continent in script closest to *scriptura continua* tended to preserve either a pure Old Latin or pure Vulgate version of Scripture. In contrast, Irish pocket Gospels and other Irish biblical codices were very frequently conflated texts, drawn both from the Old Latin translation, which was the earliest version of Scripture known in Ireland, and the Vulgate of Jerome. Although in some instances a scribe copied entire sections from one version or the other, Irish, and more broadly, Anglo-Celtic scribes typically produced an eclectic mixture of variant Vulgate, Old Latin, and on occasion, Syriac readings, greatly accelerating a process that had already begun in Roman codices.[75] Inadvertently, Irish scribes sometimes copied the same passage twice from variant translations, creating the phenomenon that modern textual scholars have termed "doublet readings." Doublet readings, absent from classical texts written in *scriptura continua*, abound in Insular codices and fragments written in separated script.[76]

The emergence of biblical transcriptions that were compilations of two variant versions of the same text within the new medium of separated script was not purely coincidental. The task of manipulating more than one text at a time was simplified by the use of a separated exemplar.[77] Irish hybrid biblical texts were precursors of the books that became prevalent in Insular circles at the end of the eighth century, in which variant readings were transcribed interlinearly, usually by the monolexic abbreviation for *vel*, itself a note of Insular origin.[78] The precocious interest of Irish scribes in textual variants between manuscripts had existed only in rudimentary form in Greco-Latin antiquity, an absence that scholars have correctly associated with *scriptura continua*.[79] From a neurophysiological viewpoint, the Irish innovation of separation contained the seeds that would generate the medieval tradition of textual conflation exemplified by scholars such as Roger Bacon, Nicolaus de Lyra, and Raoul de Presles and that would subsequently bear fruit in the quest for textual purity characteristic of the fifteenth-century humanists, several of whom insisted on the advantages of word-separated codices. It must, however, be understood that Irish scribes were not seeking to establish a text free of barbarisms, but rather that they sought one that was unambiguous and easy to read. They frequently inserted short function words to facilitate rapid decoding.[80] Perhaps most significantly, Irish scribes altered word order in a manner generally consistent with the patterns of the sequential construction notes that had begun to appear in Irish manuscripts at the end of the eighth century. These editorial practices, like the introduction of word separation, reflected a mentality in which reading was primarily a visual process for which the stylistic virtue of mellifluous sound was subordinate to rapid access to meaning.

Personal Prayer Books

The private prayer book, probably intended for silent scanning, emerged in England in the medium of separated script. *The Harleian Prayer Book*, London, BL Harley 7653, *The Royal Library Prayer Book*, BL, Royal 2.A XX, and *The Book of Nunnaminster*, Harley 2965, all dating from the early ninth century and written in separated script, included prayers in the first-person singular intended for intense private devotion; no equivalent can be found in unseparated manuscripts.[81] The legibility of these books no doubt encouraged the development of private religious devotion, which was transported to the Continent from the eleventh century onward, when separated writing became normative on the other side of the Channel.

Cartularies

Insular separated script, and to a lesser extent, Continental aerated script, can be identified with the birth of the cartulary, a book containing copies of the charters that served as title deeds for the property of a monastery or similar ecclesiastical institution. The cartulary was among the two or three oldest medieval reference tools after the glossary.[82] Cartularies, unknown in classical antiquity, were a new and unique medieval genre of reference book, emerging for the first time principally in Germany in the ninth century. They had their origin in the English custom of copying charters in separated script into Gospel books, a practice engaged in as early as the seventh century.[83] One of the oldest of all cartularies, that of the monastery of Fulda, was begun in separated script by an Anglo-Saxon scribe between 828 and 842.[84] Its text format was far clearer than the aerated leaves of the Parisian monastic record book *Liber de domibus et redditibus monasterii Sancti Germani a Pratis*, Paris, BN lat. 12832.[85] A few surviving cartularies of German and Belgian origin, including the cartulary of the Abbey of Werden and the first cartulary of Saint Peter's of Ghent, were written in the ninth and tenth centuries in aerated script.[86] However, the overwhelming majority of medieval cartularies were composed and disseminated in separated script, beginning in the mid-eleventh century.

Vernacular Texts

The last new genre of text was the non-Latin vernacular book written in Latin characters. It is unequivocal evidence that the medieval spoken tongue was different from Latin. Writing in the vernacular, like word separation, was a way of accommodating reading. The first transcriptions of a European vernacular other than Latin using the Latin alphabet occurred in the same geographical regions and at approximately the same time as the acceptance of the separation of words by space,[87] first in Ireland and England, then on the Continent, first in Germany in the eighth and ninth centuries, and last in Italy in the twelfth and thirteenth centuries.

In Ireland and England, the earliest inscriptions in the Irish ogam and Germanic runic alphabets, whatever the relation of these characters to Greek script, were written in *scriptura continua*.[88] In bilingual Irish inscriptions, the ogam was in *continua*, the Latin aerated. The earliest vernacular Celtic and Anglo-Saxon texts written in Latin characters were aerated and showed profound graphic affinities to separated Latin. They were generally written in morphemic hierarchical word blocks, with major spaces between words and minor spaces denoting either words or morphemic syllables. The earliest Irish-language grammatical treatise, probably composed between the seventh century and the tenth in Latin and Celtic, exemplified a consciousness of word boundaries and word length in Latin and Celtic that had been entirely absent among ancient Greek and Latin grammarians.[89] In Old Anglo-Saxon, for which a far more copious documentation exists than for Old Irish, scribes tended, at least until the mid-eleventh century, to write in morphemic hierarchical word blocks.[90] In both Irish and English vernacular texts, canonical word separation had not yet been achieved, even by the end of the Middle Ages.[91]

Like word separation and alphabetical sequencing, vernacular transcriptions spread in a generally southward path within a chronological framework paralleling that of the other graphic innovations. The relatively less rigorous separation of Celtic and Anglo-Saxon vernacular texts as compared with contemporary Latin texts was subsequently replicated in more phonemic form in German, French, Provençal, and finally, Italian texts.[92] The recurring phenomenon of less rigorous word separation for the vernacular can be explained both by the oral character of vernacular literature, which had a broader, semiliterate audience, and by the fact that reading one's native tongue required fewer graphic aids.[93] In Irish and Anglo-Saxon vernacular texts antedating the year 1200, major interword space fell far more frequently below the threshold of 1.5 unities of space than in Latin texts written in separated script.

The restrained use of *prosodiae* in vernacular texts, in which the *diastole* and the hyphen occurred rarely, is yet another sign of the greater ease of reading one's own language.[94] The *trait d'union*, which first appeared in Latin manuscripts of English origin, was used freely in vernacular Anglo-Saxon texts, where it was employed as a sign not only of word continuation but also of phrase continuation within morphemic word blocks, notably after monosyllabic prepositions falling at line endings.[95] Runic characters were used in Anglo-Saxon and acute accents were employed in both Irish and Anglo-Saxon, and later in Welsh, Old German, Slavic, French, and Provençal, to supplement the deficiencies of the Roman alphabet and to avoid homographs for words distinguished by vowel length. The use of accent marks to denote monosyllables, particularly prepositions, which began in Insular Latin books, was rare in Insular vernacular books.[96] Capitalization of names and punctuation were less lavishly used in vernacular manuscripts, and construction notes were unknown.[97]

New Modes of Reading

The notion of word shape permeated the English and Celtic perception of reading. The ninth-century Breton life of Saint Samson, for example, narrates how the saint, as a precocious child, learned to read by recognizing distinctions of letters as words, and makes no mention of the syllable.[98] Compilations of *Aenigmata*, or Latin riddles written in verse, a favorite Irish and Anglo-Saxon genre of text, reflected the conception of the written page as a field for the artificial mental manipulation of word images, rather than for the transcription of oral speech. Aldhelm, in his *Aenigmatum 30* on the alphabet, in a manner reminiscent of Tatwine, described reading as a silent and rapid extraction of meaning from text.[99] This conception is also expressed by an anonymous early-ninth-century Irish monk at the Abbey of Reichenau, who in a vernacular poem compared the activity of reading to a cat silently stalking a mouse, a metaphor without parallel in classical literature.[100] The manuscript recording the poem was transcribed in Saint Paul in Carinthia, Stiftsbibliothek sec. xxv.d.86, written in morphemic hierarchical word blocks.[101]

The Insular cryptographic system of patterned points, invented by Boniface, presupposed word separation, for without it, the encoded text would have slipped into hopeless ambiguity.[102] Word separation facilitated the decoding of the abstruse constructions of the ancients, as well as the intricate artificial word order that Aldhelm and earlier Celtic writers employed in their verse. It also facilitated the general use of disjunction in the highly artificial word-order pattern that typified much of early Celtic and Anglo-Saxon Latin prose. The Insular scholar was at home in a page bearing a new text format that he emended with emblematic *notae*, expanded upon a base borrowed from ancient Greek and Syriac.[103]

Chapter 5

Exceptions to Continental Aerated Text Formats in the Ninth and Tenth Centuries

The Insular graphic innovation of word separation was not adopted by Continental scribes until the mid-tenth century.[1] Instead, they evolved the entirely new configuration of textual space that I have called aerated script written in hierarchical word blocks, which was the result of a hybridization of the ancient Roman tradition of *scriptura continua* and the tradition that produced Insular word separation. Emblematic forms of punctuation imported from the British Isles permeated this variety of aerated script. As we have seen, Alcuin decreed to the scribes of the Carolingian scriptoria of Tours that units of sense should be denoted by signs of punctuation. New forms of punctuation evolved on the Continent, as well, among which were (as we likewise have seen) the sign of interrogation. Insular intellectuals like Alcuin who were employed on the Continent during this period brought with them true word separation. Its general acceptance there, however, had to await a range of further developments that subsequent chapters will delineate. Properly, the story of the development of word separation on the Continent therefore begins with the few deviations from the general practice of writing aerated script in hierarchical word blocks that predominated from the ninth century until the middle of the tenth.

It is worth recalling here the differences between Continental aerated and Insular separated writing systems at this time. Text separated into hierarchical word blocks depended on a fundamental distinction between intersyllabic space and interword space. This distinction was accompanied by emblematic signs of punctuation in the presence of quantities of space larger than those regularly placed between words, by the coordination of this punctuation with initial capitals, and by the use of ligatures both within and between words. It also employed points as redundant signs of word separation, especially with numbers and abbreviations, and occasionally, especially in glossaries, used the signs for *et* and *est* that Irish and Anglo-Saxon scribes had adapted from the ancient system of shorthand abbreviation. The Insular system, by contrast, used accents to clarify interword boundaries, to denote monosyllables, and to indicate the dative and ablative plural termination *-is*.[2] Script aerated by hierarchical word blocks used the hyphen and the *diastole* as corrections for inappropriate spacing, whereas the Insular separated script used the *trait d'union*. Rare Continental experiments with marks analogous to the *trait d'union* in aerated script did not take hold.[3] The system that was predominant on the Continent was distinguished by the use of the capital *R* and *S* at word endings falling at the end of word blocks or at line endings, while the Insular system was distinguished by its syntactical or sequential construction notes,[4] and by its use of the interlinear page format for translations.

In Ireland and England, Latin always had been consciously viewed as a language distinct from the vernacular, and as we have seen, the origins of separated writing owed much to the existence of a vernacular recognized as differing from Latin. Throughout much of Continental Europe, however, there was no such recognition. In northern France, for example, there is no evidence before about 950 of a conscious awareness that the spoken Romance dialects were languages different from Latin. Consequently, the graphic tradition that had evolved from *scriptura continua* prevailed, so strongly, in fact, that it substantially resisted the innovations brought to the Continent from Insular abbeys. Writing aerated script in hierarchical word blocks was the standard scribal practice. There were, however, exceptions. These included regional differences, the extremely limited appearance of scriptural practices imported by Insular scholars, and a use of tironian notes that was wholly independent of Insular influence.

Regional Differences

Brittany

One region on the Continent that was an exception to the general rule of aeration was Brittany, settled in about A.D. 600 by Celtic immigrants from Cornwall. Here, as in Ireland, England, Scotland, and Wales, the Insular practice of word separation predominated. Early manuscripts of Breton origin, like Orléans, BM 221 (193) and 302 (255), dating from the eighth and ninth centuries, were written in separated Insular script.[5]

They were replete with many of the traits common to Insular manuscripts, including accents, emblematic punctuation, and construction notes.[6] The Latinity of Breton authors was marked by the artificial patterns of word order present in Irish and Anglo-Saxon Latin authors, and Breton Gospel books manifested the same textual variants arising from collation and compilation common to Insular codices. The *Gospels of Marmoutier*, London, BL Egerton 609, containing a mixed Vulgate/Old Latin text, was copied on the Continent from an Insular exemplar in pre-Caroline script, separated with interpuncts and space.[7] The separation of words and the presence of Insular *prosodiae* and punctuation continued in Brittany even after Bretons assimilated Caroline letter forms. The earliest word-separated Caroline manuscripts of Breton origin include the *Harkness Gospels*, copied at Landévennec in the second half of the ninth century,[8] and Cambridge, Corpus Christi College 192, containing Amalarius Metensis's *Liber de officiis*, copied at Landévennec in 952.[9] Oxford, BL Hatton 42,[10] and Paris, BN lat. 3182[11] (containing the same collection of canons as Orléans BM 221), are examples of late-tenth-century manuscripts written in separated Caroline script. The similarity of Breton manuscripts to those of the British Isles was indicative of a common Celtic language and ethnicity, as well as geographic proximity.[12] The Bretons, like the Irish, Welsh, and Anglo-Saxons, had greater difficulty reading Latin than did native speakers of a Romance tongue.

Central and Southern Germany

The manuscript tradition in Germany (which includes today's Switzerland and Austria) also was an exception to the rule of aerated script in hierarchical word blocks. Before the eighth century, Germany shared with Ireland, England, Scotland, Wales, and Brittany the total dissimilitude between its vernacular and Latin, the language of ecclesiastical liturgy and administration.[13] In northern Germany, where the French and Imperial influence on textual format was stronger, the general Continental pattern of aeration prevailed. However, in central and southern Germany, scribes were selectively more receptive to emulating Insular innovations for simplifying written language than their counterparts elsewhere on the Continent. These scribes, after the mid-ninth century, began to write Latin in intensely aerated script, sometimes approaching separation, and began to develop modes for writing the vernacular that were clearly stimulated by Anglo-Saxon models. Centers of Insular activity like Freising, Fulda, and Saint Gall were among the earliest centers to produce German vernacular books and Latin vernacular glossaries.[14] Some of the oldest manuscripts containing German texts have Anglo-Saxon letter forms, and all were written in aerated script.[15]

While Insular influence was notably more intense in southern Germany, only at the Abbey of Saint Gall, one of the larger Continental colonies of Irish and Anglo-Saxon monks, did the evolution of text format go so far as to constitute consistent emulation of Insular word separation. Saint Gall, Stiftsbibliothek 913, the *Vocabularius Sancti Galli*, the personal study book of an Anglo-Saxon monk, is an example of a separated manuscript written in Insular script in about 780–90.[16] The ninth-century catalogue prepared under Grimald, abbot from 841 to 872, recorded fifty manuscript books as "scottice scripte," and most of the surviving Saint Gall codices in Insular script, copied either in Ireland or at the abbey, were word-separated.[17] The catalogue itself, written in Saint Gall, Stiftsbibliothek 728, was written in separated Caroline script.[18] Books written in Continental pre-Caroline and Caroline minuscule at Saint Gall were not generally separated until the Irish scribe Moengal (d. 869) took charge of the abbey's scriptorium.[19] From his administration onward, Saint Gall's charters and books were invariably written in separated Caroline script, a text format that set them apart from those produced at other southern German monasteries.[20] Some ninth-century codices, like Saint Gall, Stiftsbibliothek 869, show distinct Insular influences in their letter forms.[21] Very early examples of the distinct Saint Gall variety of interlinear musical neumes occur in a manuscript written in word blocks from the Abbey of Saint Emmeram in Regensburg.[22] These neumes were disseminated in the medium of separated tenth-century codices like Saint Gall, Stiftsbibliothek 339,[23] 390–91,[24] and 359,[25] and Einsiedeln, Stiftsbibliothek 121.[26] Before his death in 912, Notker Balbulus, who was educated in the abbey school under Grimald, and whose own writing was separated, wrote a treatise on the use of minuscule letters of the alphabet (the same signs employed in the British Isles for the notation of syntax and word order) for giving interlinear instructions on musical tempos. Signs guiding performance complemented the information on pitch provided by the neumes.[27] An anonymous monk of Saint Gall of this period was the author of the *Quomodo septem circumstantiae rerum in legendo orchinande sint*, which is perhaps the earliest grammatical treatise setting forth subject-verb-object as the natural word order.[28] The author was also among the earliest to introduce vocabulary drawn from the corpus of Aristotelian logic to grammatical analysis. The

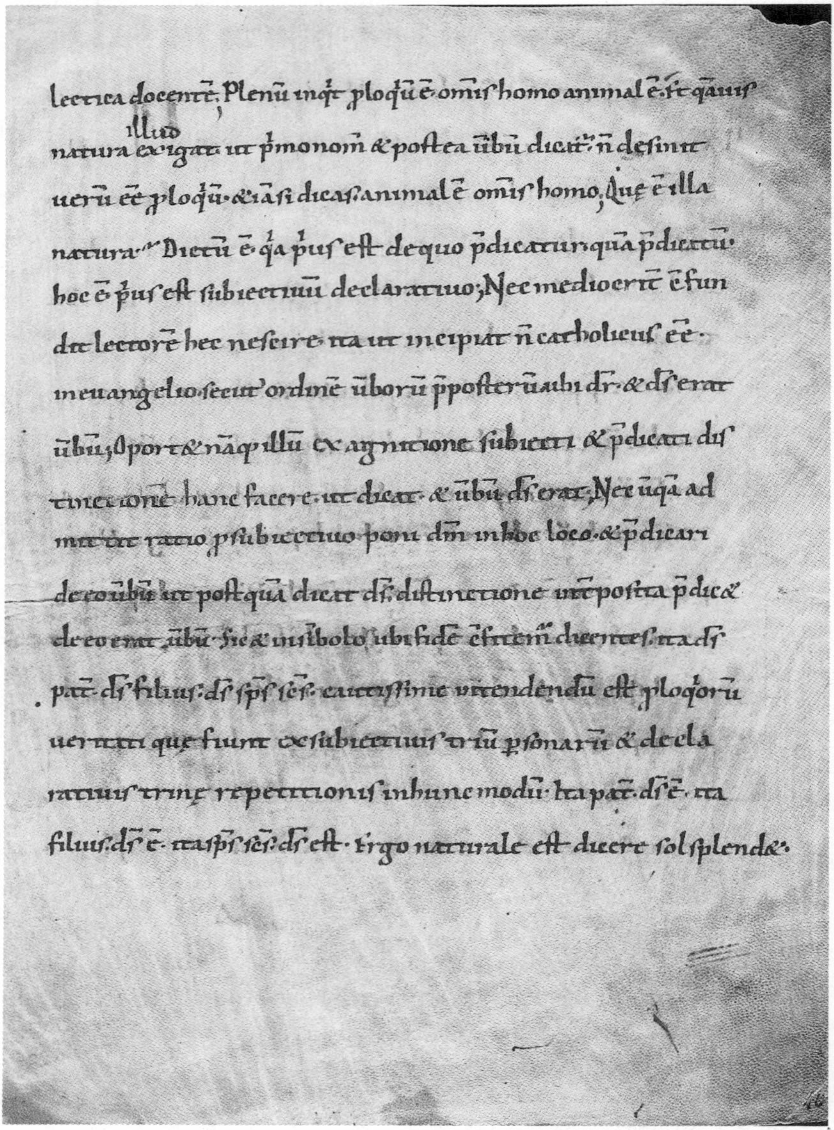

Figure 20. Word separation in the earliest treatise on word order, the *Quomodo septem circumstantiae rerum in legendo orchinande sint*. Zurich, Zentralbibliothek C 98, f. 40 recto; reproduced by permission.

earliest manuscript containing this text was written in Saint Gall in separated script in the tenth century (Figure 20).[29] The scribe restricted the ampersand to word endings and beginnings, and he employed Insular monolexic abbreviations and signs of punctuation.

Although tenth-century Saint Gall manuscripts were separated, many were written with interword space less than 1.5 times the unity of space, so that their separation was not optimal for parafoveal vision and right-hemisphere involvement in reading.[30] Consistent word separation of 2 times the unity of space accompanied by *traits d'union* and successor notes to the *diastole* did not become the norm at Saint Gall until the middle to late eleventh century, when, in emulation of the radical graphic changes that had occurred in northern France, all of southern Germany accepted canonical word separation.

Another, but significantly later isolated instance of the implantation in southern Germany of Insular patterns of spacing in the context of Caroline minuscule transpired at Einsiedeln, where word separation was adopted when the abbey was governed by its third abbot, the Anglo-Saxon Gregory, from 964 to 996.[31] Apart from Saint Gall and the less important center at Einsiedeln, writing in word blocks continued throughout southern Germany into the eleventh century. However, in the mid-ninth century, short word blocks, generally restricted to under fifteen characters and therefore approaching separation, became notably more common than in either France or Italy.[32] In the ninth and tenth centuries, the Abbey of Lorsch produced highly aerated manuscripts with many freestanding words.[33] At Freising, similar patterns of intense aeration prevailed for the first two-thirds of the tenth century.[34] The cartulary of the cathedral chapter prepared by the monk Cozroh for Hitto, bishop from 811 to 835, was written in short hierarchical word blocks.[35] The manuscripts in Munich, Staatsbibliothek Clm. 6430, two distinct mid-ninth-century benedictionals bound together in the late Middle Ages, were written for the cathedral of Freising in separated script, with interword space varying from equivalence to 2 times the unity of space.[36] Both benedictionals are rare examples of frequent use by German scribes of the acute accent to denote monosyllables. The scribes employed Insular emblematic signs for punctuation. However, regular word separation did not arrive at Freising until the period from 992 to 1005, when protoscholasticism permeated the cathedral school.[37]

At Regensburg, the earliest cartulary of the Abbey of Saint Emmeram was written in the ninth century in word blocks shorter than fifteen characters in length,[38] as were the abbey's *Annales*, written before 848.[39] Numerous Regensburg books of the eighth and ninth centuries were written in highly aerated script, with a few appearing to be actually separated.[40] The sacramentarium made at Regensburg for Emperor Henry II documents the continuation of hierarchical word blocks as a normal text format in Bavaria until the early eleventh century.[41] At Tegernsee, manuscripts of the ninth and tenth centuries were transcribed in word blocks of fewer than fifteen characters,[42] and aerated writing continued until the eleventh century.[43] The sacramentarium made for Arno bishop of Salzburg from 785 to 821, Munich, Staatsbibliothek Clm. 29164, was written in hierarchical word blocks.[44] This format seems to have prevailed at Salzburg throughout the ninth century.[45] Dated tenth-century Salzburg codices were aerated.[46] The episcopal cartulary of Salzburg, which probably dates from the eleventh century, was separated.[47] In northern Germany, the pattern of aeration was similar to that of northern France. In Luxembourg, at Echternach, near Trier, word separation had been practiced by the Irish-trained Anglo-Saxon founder of the abbey, Willibrord, but it did not appear again until the eleventh century.[48]

Insular Intellectuals on the Continent

Alcuin

From Bede onward, and during the ninth and tenth centuries, from Alcuin to Johannes Scottus and the circle around Sedulius Scottus, the most original thinkers in the realm of grammar and logic on the Continent were either of Insular or Celtic origin, but their graphic models found infrequent Continental acceptance at best. They employed word separation in their own authorial manuscripts, but it was then suppressed by the Continental scribes who copied their works. Alcuin (ca. 735–804) emigrated from York to help organize Charlemagne's palace library, as well as the scriptorium of Tours. Alcuin's poem *De scriptoribus* confirms that this English master possessed an interest in the punctuation of texts typical of intellectuals of Insular origin.[49] However, early manuscript copies of his own works, apart from those of English origin, were all copied in Caroline script and hierarchical word blocks.[50] Just as word separation had been obliterated from the Continental transcriptions of the works of Bede and Boniface, it was deleted from the Continental branch of Alcuin's manuscript tradition.

Although Alcuin supervised the Imperial scriptorium at Tours, only very minor Insular paleographic influence relating to letter forms, and perhaps to punctuation, can be found among the books copied for Charlemagne's court.[51] The Bible of Maudramnus, abbot of Corbie from 772 to 780, Amiens BM 6, 7, 9, 11, 12, commonly regarded as the earliest example of Caroline minuscule, was written in hierarchical word blocks,[52] as were virtually all the books written at Tours and elsewhere for the Imperial court.[53] The books in Charlemagne's court library were written in hierarchical word blocks that ranged from fewer than fifteen to greater than twenty-five characters in length, with major space reserved for insertion between words equivalent to 2 times the unity of space (see Figure 7). Ligatures occurred both within and between words. However, the *Lorch Gospels*, Vatican Library, Pal. lat. 50, were written in half uncial letter forms arranged in short *scriptura continua* lines of about fifteen characters in length, interrupted only occasionally by insertions of undifferentiated intersyllabic or interword space.[54]

The manuscripts that are generally believed to have been written for the Imperial court under Alcuin's personal direction do not exhibit any special signs of Insular graphic influence. Vatican Library, Reg. lat. 762, the *Regiensis Livy*,[55] written in hierarchical word blocks generally fewer than twenty characters in length, has been identified by classicists as a direct copy of Paris, BN lat. 5730, a sixth-century Italian manuscript written in *scriptura continua*.[56] Continental scribes, like their Insular counterparts, had the task of inserting at the appropriate junctures either minor spaces equivalent to the unity of space or major interword spaces equivalent to 2 times the unity of space. Facilitated by the presence of vowels, the insertion of minor space between syllables was performed with great accuracy, suggesting that the recognition of syllabic boundaries did not pose a problem for ninth-century readers and copyists of *scriptura continua*.[57] However, the recognition of words necessary for the correct insertion of the major spaces was a more onerous task. In Reg. lat. 762, the determination of word boundaries was performed with less success than it had been by the scribes of Irish Gospel books, no doubt because the periodic sentences of Livy's text were far more difficult than the simpler phrases of the Vulgate.[58]

The errors in word separation made by the scribes of Reg. lat. 762 provide insight into the useful function that correctly inserted word blocks could perform for the early medieval reader of a difficult text. In certain instances, the scribe, failing to understand the text, inserted major space, creating a phonetically plausible reading, which, however, formed entities that still did not constitute Latin words.[59] Another error occurred when a scribe created meaningful words by the insertion of major spaces that in turn created sentences either lacking grammatical sense or with inappropriate meaning.[60] Frequently, this type of error stemmed from misattaching the letter *s* or *e* (in an *ae* diphthong) to the end of one word or to the beginning of the next word.[61] Scribal errors in the recognition of word boundaries, which Abbo of Fleury at the end of the tenth century would call *colissio*, offer insight into the emergence from the late ninth century onward of the *NT* ligature, the capitals *R* and *S*, and the *e* cedilla as occasional signs of word separation redundant to major spaces in manuscripts written in word blocks.[62] Other errors of word separation in the *Regiensis Livy* followed from the misconstruction of proper names, suggesting one reason why the conventions of accenting and capitalizing of proper names came to be accepted on the Continent in the course of the tenth century.

The scribes of the *Regiensis Livy* sometimes corrected initial mistakes in the insertion of major spaces by adding hyphens. In other instances, the scribes attempted to correct their own error of spacing by adding letters to give meaning to what would otherwise have been a block of meaningless letters. Here, misconstruction of word boundaries seriously corrupted the text.[63] The scribes had special difficulty in reading the ancient suspension abbreviations and the numerical expressions, for which conventions of ninth-century aerated script differed radically from those of *scriptura continua*.

In the century after Charlemagne, the Imperial court under Louis the Pious (778–840) continued the patronage of Insular scholars. Louis the Pious protected Dicuil, the noted Irish grammarian and mathematician, whose works survive neither in authorial nor other contemporary manuscripts. His grammatical works, when copied in the ninth and tenth centuries, were generally written in hierarchical word blocks similar to the text format used at Tours at the time of Alcuin.[64] However, Valenciennes, BM 386, a copy of his *Liber de astronomia*, was written in separated Caroline script, at the Abbey of Saint-Amand, probably from an exemplar in Insular script in the mid-tenth century, at least two generations before the Abbey of Saint-Amand accepted word separation as its usual text format.[65]

Johannes Scottus

In the early tenth century, the Continental members of the circle of the Irish dialectician Johannes Scottus (ca. 810–877), who seems to have resided for a time at the cathedral school of Laon, also rejected Insular separation. The authorial additions of Johannes Scottus in Bamberg, Staatsbibliothek Philos. 2 (HJ. N. 5–6), and Reims, BM 875, were written in Insular minuscule, with word separation equivalent to 2 times the unity of space.[66] However, the Continental students surrounding this renowned Irish teacher did not in general accept the graphic conventions of their master. Rather, the authorial manuscripts that scribes copied for Scottus and that he himself corrected in separated script were copied in Caroline script in hierarchical word blocks, a format that the Irish master accepted without emendation. In Scottus's circle, word separation was retained by Irish scribes writing in Insular minuscule, but Caroline script never appears to have been written in any text format other than hierarchical word blocks.[67] Johannes Scottus's works, like those of Sedulius Scottus, were disseminated on the Continent exclusively in aerated script.[68]

The Circle of Sedulius Scottus

During the reign of Louis the Pious's successor Charles the Bald (822–77), a group of word-separated manuscripts was written by Irish scribes that the great German scholar and founder of modern paleography, Ludwig Traube, identified with the grammatical scholar Sedulius Scottus or Sedulius Scottigena, active between 848 and 874, whose name is frequently cited in their glosses.[69] These manuscripts (which do not include copies of his own works, which survive only in aerated Continental form) are associated by their Insular script, general provenance, and textual content.[70] It has been suggested that the Irishman Sedulius, who had also resided at the court of King Ruadri of Wales, came to the Continent as part of an embassy sent by the Irish king, Máel-Sechlainn.[71] Thus Sedulius, like Alcuin and Dicuil before him, hailed from a region in which word separation had been standard long before the mid-ninth century. In 845, Sedulius was at Liège as a guest of Bishop Hartgar. He and his circle were also active at Cologne, Metz, Münster, Milan, and Saint Gall.

The scholarship of the circle of Sedulius was distinguished principally by its grammatical expertise and mastery of Greek. Unlike the indigenous Continental manuscripts of his period, all of the Sedulius manuscripts were word-separated and included both interlinear translations, sequential construction notes, and other syntactical marks as an integral part of their confection. Irish vernacular glosses played an important role in these manuscripts,[72] and in the first half of the ninth century, equivalent vernacular glosses existed on the Continent only in Anglo-Saxon and

Teutonic dialects.[73] Leiden BR Voss lat. F.67, from the Abbey of Egmont, containing Priscian's *Periegesis* and *Institutiones grammaticae* and dated April 11, 838, was written in separated script, with interword space varying from equivalence to 1.5 times the unity of space.[74] The manuscript, the product of numerous hands, was signed by the scribe Dubthach, who in the Irish fashion added a colophon with a personal plea for forgiveness from the reader who would scan (*vides*) his book.[75] The codex contained Insular monolexic abbreviations for *et, est, vel, eius,* and *enim,* the acute accent as a redundant sign for the separation of monosyllables, and medial points as redundant signs to separate numerical expressions from the text. The *dasia* was also used as a redundant sign of separation. Emblematic punctuation and additional space marked sentences. Greek citations in the text were separated. Emblematic syntax notes and interlinear Irish translations were added by the scribe to aid the reader's comprehension.

Another codex linked to Sedulius, Bern, Burgerbibliothek 363, a collection of classical and patristic texts, including the writings of Dioscorides, Priscian, Ovid, and Horace, Servius's *Commentary on Virgil,* a *Dialectica* and *Rhetorica* attributed to Augustine, as well as fragments of an eccentric recension of Bede's *Historia ecclesiastica,* different from the standard "M" recension descending from the *Moore Bede,* was also written in separated form.[76] The codex contains numerous emblematic critical notes. The reformatting of classical texts, particularly those of poets such as Horace, whose syntax was complex and difficult to parse, documents the triumph of the application by Irish scholars of their artificial reformatting. The quality of the texts they produced, even when executed in inexpert script, reveals that these Irish scribal editors performed their task with great skill, perhaps owing to the fact that word separation helped them to better their comprehension of inherently difficult grammatical constructions.[77]

It is crucial to note that the manuscripts of the circle of Sedulius exemplify the transfer of the graphic techniques perfected for the comprehension of Latin to the writing of Greek. New graphic conventions for Greek, like those for Latin, originated in Ireland. The scribe of the *Vita Columbae,* in Schaffhausen, Stiftsbibliothek Generalia 1, written before 713, already wrote the Lord's Prayer at the end of his codex in separated Greek script.[78] However, the codices of the circle of Sedulius also document the earliest surviving extended corpus of the Irish application of word separation to Greek. Paris, Arsenal 8407, known as *Sedulius's*

Greek Psalter because its colophon identifies the scribe as Sedulius himself, typified the new Irish format of Greek texts.[79] Sedulius separated Greek words by medial interpuncts, usually in conjunction with space, but he separated the interlinear Latin translation of the Greek titles of each Psalm with space alone, which varies from equivalence to 2 times the unity of space, even inserting space after monosyllabic prepositions. He used emblematic signs similar to those found in earlier Irish transcriptions of the Latin Psalms to punctuate the Greek, and he employed critical signs whose meaning has not yet been elucidated. The *Basle Psalter*, Basel, Universitätsbibliothek A.VII.3, copied by two principal scribes and several supplementary hands, including one Marcellus (probably the same as the Saint Gall monk Moengal, under whom word separation was introduced at that abbey), contained a Greek recension of the Psalms in a text closely related to the *Psalter of Sedulius* in script separated by interpuncts and space of generous proportions, accompanied by an even more generously spaced, canonically separated, word-by-word Latin interlinear translation (Figure 21).[80] The Latin text included monolexic abbreviations; the Greek text included sophisticated forms of emblematic punctuation. In a marginal note, the scribe Marcellus used the acute accent for Latin monosyllables. He also made use of the capital *S* as a terminal form.

Saint Gall, Stiftsbibliothek 48, a copy of the Greek Gospels, displays a similar combination of Greek text, separated by medial interpuncts, accompanied by space and a canonically separated Latin interlinear translation.[81] Confirming the close relationship between form and content, the recension of the Latin translation of Saint Gall 48 is an example of a typical Irish hybrid version of Old Latin and Vulgate texts. Here, however, it also incorporated revisions based on the Greek.[82] As in others of Sedulius's codices, the page was embellished by a variety of Irish critical signs. A final Sedulius codex, the *Codex Boernerianus*, today Dresden, Staatsbibliothek A.145 b, contains the Epistles of Paul in Greek, copied in a Greek minuscule separated by space, with a canonically separated Latin interlinear translation elucidated by encoded Irish critical marks.[83] The Latin text was based on the Old Latin version, revised from the Greek original, reflecting again the nexus between word separation and the techniques of editing perfected by Irish scribes.

Sedulius Scottus, who himself wrote in separated script, like Bede, Alcuin, and Johannes Scottus, was a disciple of visual language, and not surprisingly, he wrote prose that ignored the rhythmical rules of the *cursus*.[84] Building on the precedents of earlier Insular grammarians and

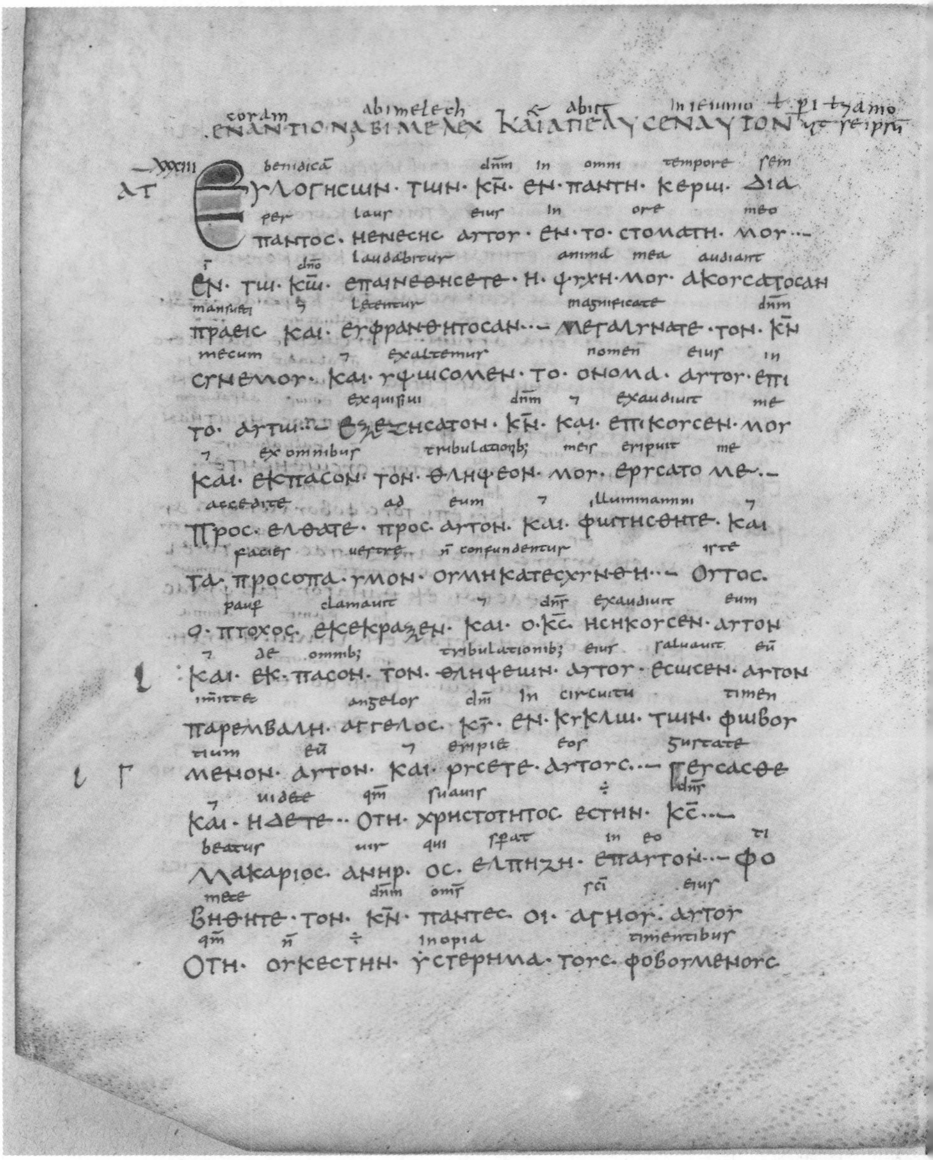

Figure 21. The Psalms in word-separated Greek, Latin Greek, and Latin in the *Psalter of Sedulius*. Basel, Universitätsbibliothek A.VII3, f. 26 verso; reproduced by permission.

incorporating certain principles of Aristotelian logic, Sedulius Scottus advanced ideas that presupposed the separation of words as a normal attribute of the page.[85] He related *figura* to the configuration of the written page. Taking cognizance of the firmly established Irish tradition of setting off grammatical units of sense and words with varying quantities of space, he declared: "*Figura* comes from the verb *fingo* (to mold). Therefore *figura* properly means the contours of a certain phrase, either in respect to its entirety or in regard to length or height, so said from *fingo*, a synonym for compono (to construct)."[86] In his *In Priscianum*, Sedulius went on to explain how written text ought to reflect grammatical structure through its *figurae*, which we would term blocks of letters, and which Sedulius referred to as *partes*. His explanation posited the Insular text format. According to Sedulius, starting with *cola* and *commata*, all text is reducible into the *partes* that constitute minimal units of meaning. These minimal *partes*, each with its *figura* and definable as *dictiones*, were taken to be equivalent to prime numbers in mathematics, the minimum units into which any expression could be reduced.[87]

The proper distinction of words was a prerequisite for correctly analyzing a sentence. In defining *dictio* as the indivisible unit of meaning out of which text is constructed, Sedulius modified the imprecise classical notions of *dictio* as *minima pars orationis*, the minimal part of a text, which failed to distinguish adjectives from nouns, ignored particles, and had only a vague appreciation of prepositions, into one that was consonant with Insular scribal practice. Sedulius's definition made *dictio* virtually equivalent to our notion of "word," as reflected in modern printed editions of Latin texts. Thus, when Sedulius discussed the incorrect division of *vires* into *vi* and *res* in the Virgilian verse "validas vires habet," he meant the kind of error that was common to the reading of *scriptura continua* and that, as we have seen, can be documented by the scribal errors in transcribing the *Regiensis Livy*. For while *vi* and *res* might be valid words in themselves, divided in this context, they could not be construed in a manner leading to the correct understanding of the sentence.

Sedulius's views contrast with those of Julian of Toledo, who read and wrote *scriptura continua*. Julian considered the verb *doleo* to be a compound word containing *figurae* of the verb *do* and the noun *leo*, despite the fact that the meaning of *doleo* was related to neither, and that separately, neither played a role in the construction of the sentence.[88] For Julian, *do* and *leo* were simply useful aids for the mental grouping of letters into words before oralization; for Sedulius, *vires* was an indivisible element that, if divided by space, formed two parts "male intercisae" that obstructed lexical access. Sedulius's presumption that words ought to be correctly spaced is reiterated in his discussion of *prosodiae*. He specifically defined *diastole* as a substitute for space, hence a sign of separation, or an "interword."[89]

A similar acceptance of word separation was evinced by the anonymous author of *Ars Laureshamensis*, a ninth-century commentary on Donatus written by an Irish monk living on the Continent who was a contemporary of Sedulius.[90] The author proposed an ingenious syllogism to reconcile Donatus's failure to enumerate *figura* as an attribute of prepositions with the Irish practice of frequently writing prepositions as a *simplex pars*, or freestanding word. According to his logic, a preposition could not have a *figura* because *figura* distinguished words as either simple or compound, and therefore did not pertain to prepositions, which were never compounded.[91] In discussing separable prepositions, the anonymous author revealed that for him, *separata*, that is, separated, did not simply connote a licit permutation of word order and distinction in pronunciation, as it had for Donatus, but also the insertion of interword space.[92] Thus, a graphic distinction was made between the syllabic prepositions *di-*, *dis-*, *re-*, *se-*, and *am-*, which were always written joined, as one compound word, and did not take objects, and *apud* and *penes*, which, since they were never elements in a compound word, always required an object and always had to be placed on the page as separate words, or in ninth-century Irish grammatical terms, as *duo partes*. Other prepositions (the monosyllables *ab*, *de*, *ex*, *in*, etc.) were either separated or conjoined according to the intention of the author (*voluntas loquentis*), and inconsistent scribal practice in the separation of these words reflected this ambiguity.[93] The *Ars Laureshamensis* also defined the hyphen as a note signaling the reader that a group of letters written by the scribe as two *partes* were to be read as one.[94]

The Irish acceptance of word separation at least partially penetrated the writings of the Continental grammarian Remi of Auxerre (841–918), schoolmaster of the Abbey of Saint-Germain of Auxerre, a center where aerated writing was normal until the eleventh century. He equated *figura* and *pars* as elements of grammatical analysis.[95] Remi, in his *Commentum Einsidlense in Donati Artem maiorem*, surviving only in Einsiedeln, Stiftsbibliothek 172, written in hierarchical word blocks, followed Sedulius and defined the *diastole* not as a simple mark of disjunction, but as an "intercolumnium vel spatium," that is, a unit of space separating words that had been inappropriately conjoined.[96] Indeed, aerated writing incorporated the use of *prosodiae* as signs to correct inappropriately placed space. Thus, Remi took cognizance of the principle that word separation was at least an occasional responsibility of the writer, who in aerated script shared the task of parsing words with the reader.

Tironian Notes

During the Carolingian age, one type of word-separated writing for which there was no Insular and only a limited ancient equivalent was practiced in French monastic and cathedral schools. This alternative system is commonly known as tironian notes.[97] In tironian notes, uninflected words and a small group of common inflected words were represented by a single sign. Other inflected words were represented by two morphemic signs; a large sign or radical represented the stem, and a small sign represented the termination.[98] In this system, words were separated both by space and by the intrinsic character of the signs (Figure 22).[99] In its formal and calligraphic manifestations, it made use of word images. The distinction in size between radicals and adjacent terminations and the redundant interword space inserted between words left little room for ambiguity as to word boundaries. Each word usually constituted a unique image, only with distinctions between preposition and object sometimes obscured. In these manuscripts, an unskilled reader could immediately perceive and count the series of discrete word images on the page.[100]

Although at first glance tironian notes seem very different from Insular separated writing, they had certain common traits. Some of the monolexic abbreviations used in Insular script were modeled on the same scantily documented ancient stenographic systems that were the principal source for the medieval tironian script,[101] and Continental scribes writing tironian script sometimes substituted the Insular sign for a related tironian abbreviation.[102] Although scribes in the British Isles undoubtedly had contact with tironian notes in books imported into Britain, they never employed tironian abbreviations in books or documents before the eleventh century.[103] This lack of interest in tironian signs by Insular scribes suggests that one of their advantages, easy lexical access, was already well provided for in the word-separated Insular system. Tironian notes were also totally absent from the separated codices of the Abbey of Saint Gall. Apart from Cologne and Corvey, few manuscripts containing tironian notes were of German origin, and none came from southern Germany.

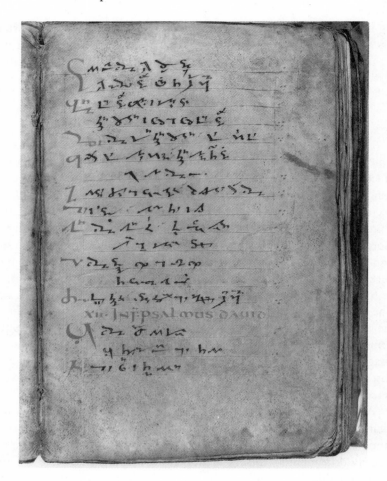

Figure 22 (here and facing page). Word images in a tironian psalter and glossary. Bern, Burgerbibliothek 668, f. 5 recto and f. 128 verso; reproduced by permission.

Tironian glossaries were not arranged alphabetically, as were Insular Latin and bilingual glossaries, but instead, word symbols for related ideas and concepts were grouped together. The manuals explaining the etymologies of the word symbols broke them down into their visual components as a pedagogical aid for memorizing.[104] Visual recall of a word's silhouette, of no importance to the reader of *scriptura continua* and of only limited value for deciphering aerated writing, was thus central to the pedagogy of the fluent reader of calligraphic tironian writing. The neuro-

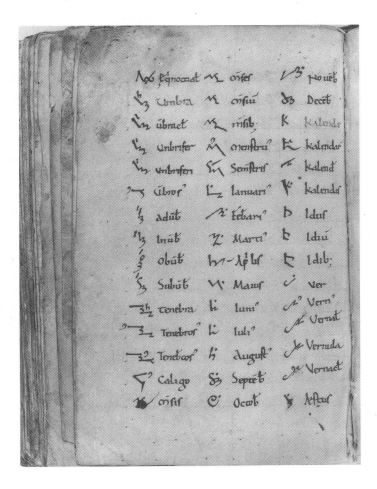

physiological processes for deciphering clearly written tironian notes as images were consequently more like those used in today's reading of separated script than those employed in the syllabic decoding in antiquity.

The enlarged field of vision, similar to that created by Irish and Anglo-Saxon separated script, allowed the reader to profit from signs of punctuation, and tironian transcriptions were frequently punctuated by the same emblematic signs used in Insular separated texts, an indication of the physiological link between the effect of these notes and the effect of separation by space on the ease of reading.[105] The reader of properly written tironian notes thus was freer than the reader of aerated script to receive emblematic encoded instructions concerning larger grammatical units of meaning and intonations, especially for texts intended for chanting and oral recitation, such as hymns and Psalters. In several tironian Psalters, punctuation was written in a special column defined by rulings well to the right of the text. The position of this punctuation suggests a medieval reader with a broad and easily maintained eye-voice span, and therefore with the potential for silent reading.[106]

Tironian notes were most frequently used for marginal and interlinear glosses and as marginal finding aids in school texts written in aerated script.[107] Here the script at times degenerated into a syllabic script that was not easy to read. Hincmar of Reims used tironian characters to write his marginal notes.[108] Tironian notes were highly compact, and at least for certain words, offered superior legibility to readers in search of points of entry to a text written in aerated script.

In most manuscripts, tironian notes were mixed with Caroline *textualis*, the reformed minuscule script favored by the court of Charlemagne. This form of writing I will term tironian *hybrida*.[109] It was not uncommon in manuscripts dating from the ninth and tenth centuries, but precisely when it originated is difficult to determine because of the total lack of firm dates for codices containing tironian *hybrida*.[110] In such codices, scribes often transferred the separation of words, inherent in the tironian text, to adjacent segments written only in Caroline script, just as in several of the tironian Psalters the rubrics giving the titles of the Psalms were written in separated Caroline script, as were the alphabetically transcribed definitions of tironian symbols in certain tironian glossaries.[111] The logographic rather than syllabographic quality of tironian *hybrida* is confirmed by the fact that word boundaries were respected. A single word was never transcribed by mixing both types of characters. In some codices, the separation in the portion written *en clair*, that is, in alphabetical characters, approached canonical separation, as in the homilies in Bern, Burgerbibliothek 611, ff. 87–92, in which space was regularly inserted after monosyllabic prepositions in the portion transcribed alphabetically.[112] In Paris, BN NAL 1595, copied in Tours and containing the works of Augustine, one of the principal scribes wrote alternatively in tironian *hybrida* and canonically separated Caroline script.[113] The same phenomenon occurred in Paris, BN lat. 9603, a lectionary, or book of biblical readings, from Saint-Martin of Tours containing canonically separated tironian *hybrida*.[114] The marginal notes in two codices originating from the Abbey of Saint-Martin of Tours, Paris, BN NAL 1612, a copy of Bede's *De natura rerum*,[115] and Paris, BN NAL 2322, a lectionary,[116] were also written in separated tironian *hybrida*. Other examples in which contiguous portions of Caroline script were written with word separation include Leiden, BR Voss. lat. Q. 98, a fragment of a letter of Pliny the Younger. Chartres, BM 13, a tenth-century codex from the library of the Abbey of Saint-Père near Chartres, contained an extensive commentary on Virgil's seventh *Eclogue*. The commentary was written in tironian *hybrida*, of which the Caroline portion was, although not separated, far more intensely aerated than most manuscripts at Chartres before the general advent of word separation at the time of Fulbert.[117] In a few tenth-century charters written in tironian *hybrida*, words written *en clair* were also separated.[118]

A much larger group of manuscripts related to those exhibiting tironian *hybrida* made use only of the tironian or the standard Insular monolexic abbreviation for *est* and the tironian sign for *et*, and rarely a few other tironian logograms.[119] The hybridization of tironian and Caroline *textualis* played an important role in the evolution of a marginal glossular script found in Continental manuscripts from France and Lorraine that was regularly more intensely aerated than the script used for the principal text of the codex. The selective use of tironian symbols enhanced the legibility of these glosses. Sometimes this type of glossular script was virtually separated by means of a combination of space, terminal forms, and conventional abbreviations. It is especially difficult to date the development of this type of writing because glosses may postdate the text to which they are appended by a considerable period of time. This being said, it nevertheless appears likely that this form of gloss script evolved during the mid-tenth century and became increasingly popular at the end of the tenth century. Geographically, it developed at centers like Reims, Tours, and Fleury, where the first seeds of protoscholasticism were to germinate in the course of the late tenth and early eleventh centuries, when separated Continental writing first appeared.

Chapter 6

The Origins of Continental Word Separation, 950–1300

Protoscholasticism

In addition to the fact that on the Continent there was almost no recognition, outside of Germany, that the vernacular languages differed from Latin, which was written in the aerated script that had evolved from *scriptura continua*, there was another reason why the Insular practice of word separation by space, which seems to the modern mind to have such obvious advantages for reading, was not adopted earlier there. This concerns the nature of the reading material itself.

In the seventh, eighth, ninth, and early tenth centuries, when the primary function of reading was the memorization and oral performance of prayer in a familiar and intensively read corpus inherited from antiquity, libraries were composed predominantly of liturgical, patristic, and grammatical texts.[1] Continental monks perceived no need to make the reading of this corpus easier. Indeed, an ambiguous text format enhanced the mystery and power of clerics, who were the sole dispensers of the Divine Word to a laity almost entirely illiterate. After 950, a profound change occurred in the nature of what monks and other clerics chose to read. From the second half of the tenth century to the twelfth, schools produced a new corpus of protoscholastic texts. They differed from the earlier liturgical, patristic, and grammatical texts in that they obliged the reader to grapple with highly technical concepts expressed in grammatical structures based upon principles of Aristotelian dialectic.[2] The number of dialectical texts in libraries grew steadily in the eleventh and twelfth centuries, and they became the hallmark of new library catalogues. The new and difficult works had to be decoded swiftly and, above all, read with comprehension. The desirability of making reading easier became apparent to Continental scholars, and to this end the word separation by space of Insular manuscripts became an essential linguistic tool. By the thirteenth and fourteenth centuries, when the disciplines of grammar, theology, and law were thoroughly permeated with the principles of Aristotelian logic and systematic word order, scholastic treatises were disseminated only in word-separated text format.[3]

Two protoscholastic authors, Garland, the eleventh-century Lotharingian logician and computist, and the early nominalist Peter Abelard (1079–1142), provided an intellectual framework for the profound grammatical changes that occurred in the reading process. Their fusion of the principles of Aristotelian logic with the study of grammar is evidence that scholars were indeed looking at the written page in a new light. These protoscholastic authors gave the word a precise syntactic definition without precedent among ancient grammarians, for whom the terms *dictio*, *vox*, and *pars* had not fully corresponded to our concept of the word "word."[4] The only limited antecedent for their new concept of the word can be found in the writings of the Insular grammarian Sedulius Scottus. But Garland departed from the early medieval Insular tradition, grounded in the grammatical theories of Donatus, and instead based his conception of the word on grammatical principles grounded in the dialectical theories of Aristotle. He postulated, in his *Dialectica*, the existence of two parts of speech, nouns and verbs.[5] He also distinguished between syllables as units of sound without meaning and *voces significantes*, or sense-conveying utterances, the basic verbal expressions for which the graphic signs corresponded to units of meaning.[6] A noun or verb was a signifying *pars*, which if subdivided yielded *partes* that had no meaning. Here, separability became the explicit criterion for the definition not just of prepositions, but of all words. The separable *pars* constituted the building block for all logical propositions. An evolution driven by logical rigor led Garland in the more "transparent" medium of separated script to posit a grammatical definition of the word consistent both with Irish and Anglo-Saxon graphic practice and with the notion of *pars* that had been expressed by Sedulius Scottus. Garland thus imposed upon written language what students of semeiotics would term an iconic representation of reality, that is, one in which a direct correspondence was supposed to exist between objects or acts and their written symbols.[7] Garland's rigorous identification of meaning with graphic expression went beyond any explicit statements made by Insular grammarians.

For dialecticians, the separation of words, combined with syntactical word grouping, made the transcription of logical statements, particularly syllogisms, a graphic verisimilitude of relations of physical and metaphysical reality.[8] As treatises incorporating rigorous principles of logic became more complex, authors relied on the separation of words, combined with conventions for word order, to formulate increasingly subtle and complex thoughts, which without these tools would not have been possible. Protoscholastic Latin prose written in the new space-separated script relied on extended parafoveal vision for placing the individual word rapidly in context. The reader could now use memory chiefly for the retention of meaning, rather than for stocking ambiguous strings of syllables and words. Separated script was an indispensable medium for this new learning, and intrinsic to it.

Like Garland, Peter Abelard distinguished between words and sounds, and his definition of the word was similar to Garland's. Words were defined as the separable units of meaning within phrases.[9] In a manner that would be perfectly acceptable to modern cognitive psychology, Abelard noted that the understanding of complex ideas rests not on words taken individually, but on the retention of groups of syntactically related words in short-term memory, in which manner general meanings are first extracted and then cumulatively remembered.[10] Thus, both Garland and Abelard presupposed forms of written language that facilitated the cognitive functions necessary for rapidly extracting meaning from texts. Only in this way could the reader assess with sufficient ease the validity of propositions.

Separation by space created as a neurophysiological reality the broader span of text that Abelard held to be necessary for the reader's comprehension of language. Rules of word order were equally necessary for the writing of unambiguous syllogisms. Abelard focused particularly on the importance of the position of adverbs and negative particles for determining the meaning of a sentence.[11] In this, he foreshadowed the concerns of Roger Bacon, Johannes de Balbis, and the modists. Abelard's approach to language, emphasizing graphic clarity and word order rather than sonority, ran counter to the orality and tunnel vision that ancient *scriptura continua* had imposed upon the reader. For while *scriptura continua*, in conjunction with sonorous periodic sentence structure, did not inhibit the reader from decoding the individual word, its limited field of vision obstructed the rapid appreciation of the word within its syntactical context, making the comprehension of propositions neurophysiologically more difficult. Unseparated writing's tunnel vision inhibited precisely those distinctions of meaning that had become fundamental to the new scientific culture of the eleventh and twelfth centuries.

The impediment that unseparated writing imposed on northern European readers had been tolerable in a milieu in which the effective literary corpus was small and where a shared understanding of the general meaning of familiar texts rendered reading errors a problem of largely secondary significance. However, in a world in which complex logical and scientific texts were continually being taught to students whose vernacular language was either a Romance dialect clearly recognized as such or a Germanic tongue, errors in reading could have potentially grave consequences by breaching the subtle distinctions separating orthodoxy from heterodoxy. The men who wrote in separated script were preoccupied with language as a precise instrument for the accurate communication of complex and rigorously defined theological distinctions. In the protoscholastic period, as the message became increasingly complex, scholars came to adopt a less ambiguous graphic medium for Latin expression, and one of their models was Insular. As we shall see, their other model was Arabic.

Arabic Influence on Continental Word Separation

Word separation can be regarded as a product of the frontier civilizations that had developed at the periphery of what had been the Roman Empire. Throughout history, intellectual, technical, and social innovations have often first appeared on the margins of well-established cultures. America and Japan can properly be regarded as frontier civilizations, the former of Europe, the latter of China. Although in the early Middle Ages the impetus for the restructuring of the page had come primarily from the literary achievements at the empire's northern frontier, by the early tenth century, the prominence of the Insular authors identified with word separation such as Bede, Alcuin, Sedulius Scottus, Johannes Scottus, and the anonymous compilers of glossaries had waned. A new corpus of scientific knowledge, and with it a new impetus for the adoption of word separation, sprang forth in another linguistic frontier zone, that of Mozarabic Spain.

In the Arabic world, Aristotelian logic and mathematical computation had been nurtured and augmented in the medium of separated script while these sciences lay quiescent in the West. For the history of reading and the book, Arabic culture was to the medieval Latin West what Greek culture had been to the Roman Empire in late antiquity. In both instances, the prestige of a dominant culture was such that when its superior learning was transmitted by translation into Latin, its text format was emulated as well.[12]

Tenth-century Arabic was separated by both space and special letter forms.[13] Far more consistently than Insular script, it reserved certain letters for word beginnings and endings. Word separation in Arabic was not an optional characteristic to be added in some epochs and omitted in others. It was an intrinsic feature, and as such, a continuation of an ancient Semitic practice clearly evident in the earliest examples of Hebrew writing.[14] Ancient Arabic had been written without vowels, and if it had not been separated by space, identifying word boundaries would have been impracticable. The wide field of vision in medieval Arabic that resulted from word separation, vocalic pointing, and conventions of word order was essential for comprehending and pronouncing Arabic texts.[15] Thus, the separated Arabic translations of *scriptura continua* Greek texts became models for the Latin West, which is indebted to the Arab world for the transmission of the text format as well as for the content of Aristotelian and other scientific works.

The translation of Arabic scientific writings from the tenth century through the thirteenth constituted the most significant corpus of prose translation from a separated Semitic language to Latin since Jerome had translated the Vulgate. Jerome's Vulgate, however, had completely suppressed the word separation of the Hebraic and Aramaic original. While one might speculate that his extensive contact with the separated writing of Hebrew and Aramaic may account for his introduction of *cola et commata* to achieve a level of legibility in Latin appropriate to the middlebrow Christian audience of the late Roman world, there is no literary or textual evidence to confirm this theory.[16] It seems, therefore, that Semitic word separation had its first direct impact on the Latin page when seventh-century Irish scribes were exposed to Syriac models. Documentation of Syriac influence on Ireland, however, is scanty, compared with that of Arabic on tenth-century Continental writing.

On the Continent, the Arabic scientific writings, when translated into Latin, brought word separation with them and formed the earliest body of writings to circulate invariably in word-separated text format. In these writings, untranslated Arabic phrases, written in Latin transliteration, were always separated, unlike analogous Greek passages in Latin texts, which had been written in unseparated script, except when copied by Irish scribes.[17] In some Mozarabic codices, Arabic glosses to aerated Latin codices provided entry points similar to those provided by tironian notes.[18] The separation of words was so essential to the comprehension of Arabic science that tenth-century scholars in Germany, France, and Spain tended to retain word separation not only in transliteration, but in translation as well. This influence of the Arabic text format is clearly evident in Latin glosses to Arabic texts written in Spain by bilingual scribes.

The specific modes of separation in the Mozarabic Latin manuscript corpus were the result of two factors. First, because human visual and cerebral powers had remained unchanged, the same quantity of space, minimally equivalent to 1.5 unities of space, was necessary for word separation to be apparent in the parafoveal vision of Mozarabic readers, as it was for Insular readers. The same quantity of interword space present in the Latin-Arabic corpus and in earlier Irish and Anglo-Saxon manuscripts reflected universal physiological constraints. Second, under the impetus of the Arabic example, the separation of Latin was made more emphatic by the use of initial and terminal strokes inspired by the terminal forms employed in Arabic.[19] To this end, Spanish scribes made great use of the terminal forms that had emerged in Continental manuscripts written under Insular influence during the ninth and tenth centuries. At the Abbey of Santa Maria of Ripoll, for example, scribes made frequent use of the terminal capital *S*. It is significant that the monks of Ripoll, who produced some of the earliest Latin translations from the Arabic, also displayed a renewed interest in transcribing the scientific texts of Bede in separated script. In copying Barcelona, ACA Ripoll 106, Hispanic scribes, consciously or unconsciously, restored Insular signs, notably the monolexic abbreviation for *est*, to their original role as adjuncts to consistent word separation.[20] While no enduring terminal forms in Latin were directly modeled on Arabic letters, certain ones present in Visigothic script, notably the small elevated capital *s* initially used solely for the ablative and dative termination *-bus* and later simply for the terminal *s* and the terminal long *j*, were Mozarabic innovations.[21]

The relatively sparse number of photographed Latin manuscripts of Mozarabic provenance impedes research on the presence of word separation in the Hispanic peninsula, but two abbeys, Santa Maria of Ripoll in Catalonia and Saint Martin of Albelda, located on the frontier of the kingdom of Leon, were clearly important centers for this innovation. At Ripoll, manuscripts written in Caroline script and datable to the time of Arnolf, abbot from 948 to 970, reveal the process by which changes leading toward separation were adopted at a surprisingly early date. Barcelona, ACA Ripoll 106, a collection of treatises on computation and measurement known as the *Geometria Gisemundi* that was drawn from Bede, Pseudo-Boethius's *De geometria* in five books, and a variety of classical authors, was confected in two stages.[22] Folios 27 through 120 were written in aerated Caroline script in hierarchical word blocks of fewer than fifteen characters in maximum length.[23] This codex was annotated by a nearly contemporary hand in separated script, and soon after its initial confection, the book was augmented by the addition of the first twenty-five folios written in separated script, with interword space varying from equivalence to 2 times the unity of space. The scribe of the separated portion made use of Insular monolexisms and punctuation marks and persistently employed the capital *NT* ligature at word endings. On folio 23v, an acute tonic accent mark was used to resolve an ambiguity in separation.

Barcelona, ACA Ripoll 74, a collection of alphabetical glossaries and other texts dating from the second half of the tenth century, was also highly aerated.[24] In headings written in capitals, the penultimate letter preceding a terminal *S* was reduced in size, creating a Bouma shape similar to that occurring in the text when the capital *S* was used at word endings. Folios 1 through 16, containing liturgical texts with neumes, were written in separated script, making prominent use of the terminal long *j*. Barcelona, ACA Ripoll 168, containing extracts of Boethius's *De arithmetica*, was copied at approximately the same date in highly aerated script, with terminal forms that included the elevated round *s*.[25]

In the eleventh century, word separation, accompanied by the frequent presence of terminal forms, notably the elevated round *s* and long *j*, was standard at Santa Maria of Ripoll. At the time of Oliva, abbot from 1008 to 1046, the abbey had close connections with Fleury and other northern French abbeys, where word separation, as we shall see, was practiced at an early date.[26] Word-separated codices included Barcelona, ACA Ripoll 42, a collection of musical texts containing Abbot Oliva's own writings and Boethius's *De musica*, and Ripoll 40 and 59. These manuscripts exhibit the elevated round *s* and long *j* in words and Roman numerals. The capital *N* was used at word beginnings. In Ripoll 59, f. 6v, sequential construction notes were present.

The Albelda scribe Gomesanus, in 951, copied Paris, BN lat. 2855, containing Ildephonsus of Toledo's *De virginitate Mariae*, in separated Visigothic script for a distinguished French pilgrim, Gottescalcus, bishop of Puy, who brought the codex book to France.[27] Upon the bishop's return to Puy, a prologue was added in aerated Caroline script. Also at Albelda, in 976, the scribe Vigila copied Escorial d. I. 2, which included an anonymous *De arithmetica*, as well as a number of patristic and juridical texts, in separated Visigothic script.[28]

In Spain, the use of word separation in the late tenth and early eleventh centuries was reserved to those abbeys that were centers of intense Latin-Arabic interchange, although they did not form a distinct geographic zone. At Saint Pelayo of Cerrato, for example, Paris, BN NAL 2180, copied in 992, was written in hierarchical word blocks,[29] and at the Abbey of Silos, despite the reform of Dominic, abbot from 1041 to 1073, who was influenced by Cluny,[30] charters in 1067 were still being prepared in Visigothic script, in syllabic blocks greater than fifteen characters in length.[31] In contrast, other Spanish charters in Visigothic script dating from 1062 and 1082 were written with both word separation and *traits d'union*.[32] In eleventh-century Silos, the long *j* was frequently used as a terminal form in both aerated and separated script. Only in the twelfth century did emendators at Silos begin to use the successor note to the *diastole* to distinguish words in unseparated texts.[33]

The Cistercian Order was an important nexus for the diffusion of canonically separated script in Spain, as it was in Italy. At the end of the twelfth century at the Cistercian Abbey of Santa Maria of Huerta,[34] an emendator employed the successor note to the *diastole*, *traits d'union*, and acute accents denoting the tonic syllable to facilitate the reading of Soria, Biblioteca publica 31-H, a collection of *Vitae sanctorum*, in which the body of the text was canonically separated.[35] In an unusual act, he added a colophon in the Irish manner, requesting the prayers of the subsequent monks who would read (*legerit*) or scan (*viderit*) the codex that he had clarified.[36]

A corpus of Latin translations of Arabic scientific works brought word separation from Mozarabic Spain to France, Lorraine, and Germany. These works contained some of the most technical and difficult Latin prose to emerge during the Middle Ages. It was the first genre of Latin text to circulate in northern Europe invariably in word-separated form.[37] The word separation that reduced lexical ambiguity made these texts easier to comprehend.

The early Latin translations of Arabic science consisted of two principal groups: treatises on the astrolabe, astronomy, and astrology, and treatises on arithmetical computation. Two separate studies undertaken independently in Spain and Belgium in the 1930's have removed all doubt

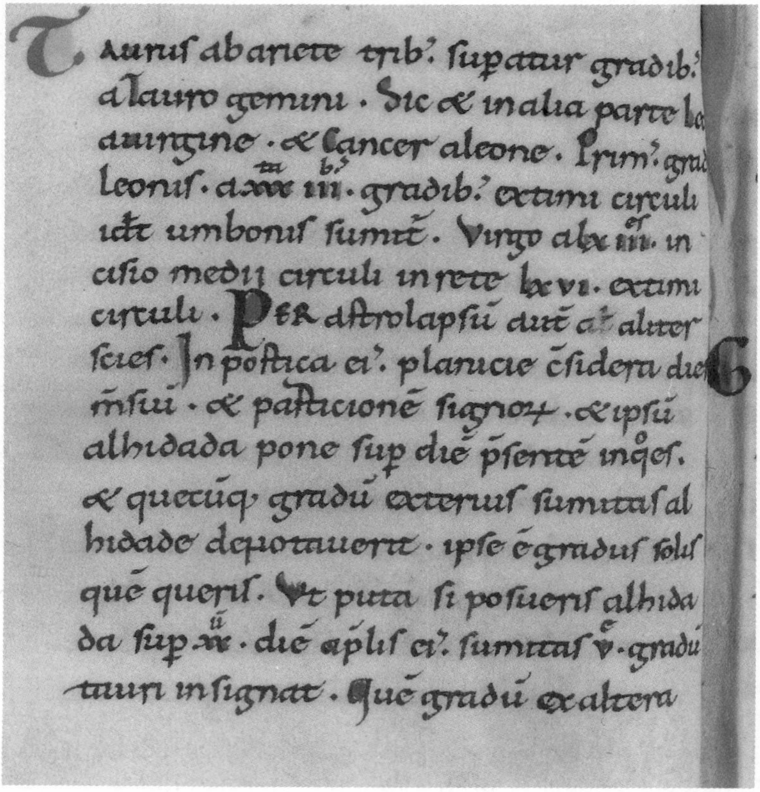

Figure 23. Word separation in the earliest Latin treatise on the astrolabe. Barcelona, Archivo de la Corona de Aragon Ripoll 225, f. 10 verso; reproduced by permission.

that the astrolabe was introduced into western Europe from Mozarabic Spain and that the earliest extant writings explaining its use were translated into Latin in Catalonia, probably by Lobet of Barcelona.[38] These treatises form the single largest subgroup of Arabic scientific writings. All of the extant exemplars were written in separated script. The earliest one, probably written in Catalonia as early as the second half of the tenth century, is Barcelona, ACA Ripoll 225 (Figure 23).[39] In this codex, words were separated by between 2 and 2.5 unities of space, with space often present after monosyllabic prepositions. Terminal forms included the elevated round *s* for -*bus*, the capital *S*, the *4* sign for -*orum*, the apostrophe for -*tur*, the ampersand, and the *e* cedilla. The long *j* and the *NS* and *NT* ligatures were present as terminal forms at line endings. Capital letters set off by interpuncts were used for unknown quantities in mathematical expressions; Roman numerals were punctuated into decimal distinctions and inflected with superscripts. Monolexic abbreviations included sparse superscript forms, the tironian sign for the conjunction *et* (without space), the ampersand (with space), and the Insular sign for *enim*. Arabic words were written all in capitals and separated by space and interpuncts, much as Greek had been in Insular manuscripts. *Prosodiae* were limited to two instances of the acute accent used to denote monosyllables.

The first Latin treatises on the astrolabe with related texts were also contained in a number of French eleventh-century manuscripts, all of which were separated by generous quantities of space. To cite just one example, in Vat. reg. lat. 598, a composite codex formed by Pierre Daniel from material originating in the Loire Valley, possibly at Fleury, on folios 115 through 122, the corpus on the astrolabe was written with interword space equal to 2 times the unity of space.[40] The text was accompanied by diagrams of the astrolabe clearly based on Arabic models. In the text and diagrams, Arabic words were separated and transliterated in capital letters and separated by space. The text contained neither *traits d'union* nor acute accent marks.[41]

The pattern of word separation found in the earliest translations and compendiums of Arabic treatises pertaining to the astrolabe was also present in the manuscripts of the Latin translations of the Syriac version of the astronomical treatises of Alchandreus.[42] The three earliest manuscripts of the Syriac corpus, Paris, BN lat. 17868 (northern France, after 978),[43] London, BL Add. 17808 (northern France ca. 1040),[44] and Munich, Staatsbibliothek Clm. 560 (Germany, eleventh century),[45] were all either separated or canonically separated. The appearance of this corpus marked the first significant Western contact with Syriac writing, either directly, or indirectly, via Hebrew or Arabic translation, since the seventh-century and eighth-century Insular transcriptions of the Gospels.

A comparable pattern of word separation is also found in the earliest Latin manuscripts containing Arabic numerals.[46] The introduction in the eleventh century in the Latin West of Arabic numerals was thus clearly linked to the adoption of word separation. As noted above, in 976, at the Abbey of Saint Martin of Albelda, the monk Vigila copied an anonymous *De arithmetica* in Escorial d. I. 2, f. 12. This text, composed from extracts of Isidore's *Etymologiarum libri* and containing the earliest known Western example of Arabic numerals, was in word-separated script, with space sometimes omitted after monosyllabic prepositions and with occasional monosyllabic run-ons.[47] Escorial d. I. 1, a visually copied, line-by-line twin of d. I. 2 containing the same texts in the same order, was copied in 992 at the Abbey of San Millan of Cogolla.[48] Here, the Arabic numbers were surrounded by words canonically separated by interword space 3 times the unity of space. Another early transcription of Arabic numbers occurs in a tenth-century Saint Gall codex, now Zurich, Zentralbibliothek C 78.[49] As was normal in the tenth-century Saint Gall codices, the surrounding text was written in separated script, but here, interword space was equivalent to 3 times the unity of space.

In 984, Gerbert, the future Pope Sylvester II, wrote to Gerald, abbot of Aurillac, and to Bonifilius, bishop of Girone in the Spanish March, demanding a manuscript of a work of Josephus Hispanus entitled *De multiplicatione et divisione numerorum*, a work that is now believed to have been the same *De arithmetica* contained in the Escorial codices I.d.2. and I.d.1.[50] The earliest extant copy of the Pseudo-Boethius *De geometria (in two books)* (a text containing Arabic numbers closely associated with Gerbert's circle and apparently based on the *De arithmetica*) preserved in Erlangen (ex Alfdorf) Universitätsbibliothek 288 (s. xi), was transcribed in script separated by from 1.66 to 2 unities of space.[51] Among his other contributions, Gerbert introduced the use of Arabic numbers for the abacus. It was Gerbert's goal in employing Arabic numbers to provide a distinct image for each number, just as it was the goal of a scribe of separated script to provide a distinct image for each word. Gerbert's student Richer said of the new Arabic numerals that their direct access to value made calculation more rapid than verbal formulations.[52]

Geographically, the corpus of early Latin manuscripts through which Arabic learning was diffused to the West came from Spain, northern France, Lorraine, and southern Germany. None originated in Italy (except for the very recently discovered Laurenziana codex) or southern France, where protoscholasticism and word separation were late to develop.[53] In addition, this corpus was intermingled with the writings of authors such as Abbo and Heriger of Lobbes, who, as we shall see in the next chapter, were closely identified with word separation and the new and intellectually more rigorous disciplines of science and logic that burgeoned at the end of the tenth century.

Chapter 7

Word Separation and the Transcription
of Numbers and Music

Numbers as Language

Thus far, our discussion of the separation of text by space and other cues complementary and redundant to spaces in the British Isles and on the Continent in the early Middle Ages has been largely confined to the reading of verbal texts. Arabic numbers have been considered only in regard to their historical link to word separation. The moment has now arrived to examine the reading of numbers and statements of mathematical relationships in greater depth. We also need to examine the related matter of musical notation.

Mathematics is a language, and like other languages, its notation has varied over time. The history of the reading of numbers, like that of the reading of words, was profoundly marked by the introduction of separation by space and the related innovations designed to reduce the ambiguity of the page. The understanding of complex mathematical statements, like the comprehension of complex Latin prose, was greatly facilitated by a text format that minimized ambiguity and the ensuant reliance on aural short-term memory and gestures.

Historians of mathematics, far more than students of intellectual and literary history, have been sensitive to the impact of changes in conventions of notation on the progress of mathematical thought.[1] They have determined that in the Western tradition, critical breakthroughs in scientific knowledge have been achieved when easily decoded symbols were employed, either for numbers or as indications for arithmetical operations. The ancient Greek creation of an effective system of geometry was dependent on the existence of an efficient system of notation. In algebra, the Greek contribution was less felicitous because the Greeks progressed only from a rhetorical algebra, that is, an algebra expressed by the use of ordinary language, to a syncopated algebra, an algebra using letter abbreviations to represent unknown quantities. The Greeks' failure to develop a notation based on symbols stunted their subsequent algebraic development. Historians of science have recognized that the fidelity of English physicists to Isaac Newton's system of notation similarly retarded the development of physics in England, while on the Continent, Leibniz (who was also a paleographer) perfected a system of notation that facilitated the advancement of both physics and mathematics. Psychological studies confirm that the mode of notation directly affects the speed with which a mathematical formula can be read and a problem solved.[2] Effective mathematical notation allows a maximum amount of information to be unambiguously displayed in foveal and parafoveal vision.

In mathematical statements, the symbols representing numbers may be regarded as analogous to nouns and the symbols for operations as analogous to verbs. The conventional form of graphic mathematical notation that evolved in the Middle Ages encoded the mathematical equivalence of grammatical distinctions with an efficiency equal to that of the new conventions of written Latin. In mathematics, as in medieval Latin and its derivative Romance vernacular languages, conventions of sequence complemented new modes of transcription in eliminating ambiguity and reducing reliance on memory for decoding components of mathematical computations. In logic, the clearly separated and syntactically sequenced syllogisms of the late-tenth-century and eleventh-century Aristotelian texts were a nascent form of symbolic logic linking the otherwise discrete realms of verbal and mathematical expression.[3] The use of space in protoscholastic syllogisms and schematic "tree" diagrams made them an important transitional stage between the purely rhetorical logic of antiquity and the symbolic logic used by modern mathematicians and philosophers.[4]

The symbols, distinctions, and syntactical conventions present in medieval arithmetical expressions at the end of the Middle Ages had not been present in the mathematical language of antiquity. In ancient Latin literature, numerical expressions, especially in literary texts, were regularly written out as words, and when symbols were used for numbers, they were usually letters of the alphabet, requiring discretionary sequencing as well as addition and subtraction by the reader for their decoding. Greek, and Hebrew in imitation of Greek, employed all the letters of their respective alphabets as numbers. In ancient Latin, however, only

seven letters were used.[5] Some modern scholars of mathematical notation have suggested that the reliance of Latin on seven of twenty-three
characters of the ancient Roman alphabet for numerical expression had
the pedagogical advantage of making it initially easy for children to write
simple numerical statements, much as modern binary notation requires
an initial mastery of a smaller set of symbols than conventional Arabic
decimal notation.[6] However, from a reader's point of view, the Roman
system, at least as it survived in books in the early Middle Ages, was
far more ambiguous than either Greek or Hebrew numbers, for Roman
numerals necessitated prior extensive neurophysiological activity to determine how to combine the values of its discrete symbols in order to
achieve an accurate comprehension of each element in a mathematical
statement.[7] In contrast, Greek notation had clear sequencing and discrete decimal elements that were easy to comprehend. In ancient Egypt
and China, where script was logographic, extremely clear notations for
numbers were employed at an early date.[8]

The process of reading ancient Roman numbers was particularly
complex because the principles governing the relations of the symbols
were both cumbersome and ambiguous. The prior cognitive activity required for adding and subtracting in Roman numerals was analogous to
that required for combining phonemes to achieve lexical access in the
reading of unseparated Greek and Latin text in that both activities relied
on oralization. Although individual Roman numerals are not phonemes,
psychological studies indicate that readers confronting ambiguously written mathematical expressions react with increased oralization in the same
way as readers of phonetically transcribed verbal text. Oralization aided
the ancient reader to retain ambiguous mathematical elements in memory during the process required for manipulating them.[9] As with written
verse and prose, context served as an important cue in resolving the inherent graphic ambiguity in ancient Latin numerical statements.[10]

The relative lack of ambiguity in Greek and Hebrew letter-based
numbers accounts for their popularity in the early Middle Ages, especially in the British Isles, in circles that otherwise were generally ignorant
of these languages. Greek and Hebrew letter-based numbers were used
for ecclesiastical computations, particularly for determining the date of
Easter. Even the ancient Romans may have possessed a rarely used system of integral notation that employed all twenty-three letters of the
alphabet.[11] Bede's *De temporum ratione* and Pseudo-Bede's *De loquela
per gestum digitorum libellus*, a text of eighth-century Insular origin, in-

cluded concordances of minuscule Latin letters and their equivalents in Roman numerals, just as thirteenth-century manuscripts provided concordances of Roman and Arabic numbers.[12] Insular scribes used minuscule letters of the alphabet in lieu of numbers in lunar calendars in the eighth century and used sequential construction notes for the same purpose in the ninth century. Another Insular alternative to cumbersome Roman numerals was to use a structured system of decimal gestures or finger manipulations for calculation.[13]

It is clear that in general, the early medieval chronology for the emergence of new symbols for numbers, mathematical operations, and conventions of order for mathematical statements, as well as their clarification through punctuation, paralleled the emergence of intratextual space and conventions for syntactical sequence in textual manuscripts. Greek numerical characters were recommended in the computational treatises of Bede and Pseudo-Bede, which were first transcribed in England in separated script, then circulated in separated and aerated text on the Continent as part of the general diffusion of Insular culture.[14] Bede expressed approbation for the Greek system because he found it easier to read and to operate.[15] A table of Greek number equivalents is preserved in Oxford, BL Bodley 309, copied in separated script at Vendôme in the eleventh century. This codex is believed to be a Continental copy of the Irish computational material that Bede relied upon when composing his *De temporum ratione*.[16] Concordances of Greek, Hebrew, and Roman numerals were a common feature of early medieval Latin codices written in both aerated and separated script.[17] The same isolation of the British Isles that contributed to the ignorance of much of antique culture created a milieu in which scribes were more open to deviation from the written modes of computation inherited from the Roman Empire. The religious disputations between the English and Irish monks over the correct date for celebrating Easter and related calendrical matters gave a special importance to advances in numerical notation.

Trade with Mediterranean merchants provided the most likely avenue for the introduction of Greek and Hebrew numbers into Insular culture, much as it had for the introduction of Syriac and Greek *prosodiae*, punctuation, and tie notes.[18] It is also possible that Theodore of Tarsus, archbishop of Canterbury from 669 to 690, a native of Greece, and founder of the cathedral school of Canterbury, may have provided the nexus for the dissemination of certain aspects of Greek numerical science to England, and thence to Ireland.

The Reformatting of Roman Numerals

It would be wrong to suppose that the emergence of Arabic numbers in the West in the late tenth and eleventh centuries resulted in the immediate supplanting of Roman numerals in written text by their Arabic equivalents. Excluding the *apices*, or tokens bearing Arabic characters, intended for use with the abacus, the numerical expressions used in the codices containing the first Arabic numbers were always Roman rather than Arabic. For the first two and one-half centuries after their initial appearance on the page, Arabic numbers continued to be employed almost solely in the limited context of treatises explaining the use of the abacus, and in all other contexts, Roman numerals continued to proliferate in separated text. However, scribes often modified them as part of a new emphasis on images directly convertible to meaning. These Roman numerals were clearly differentiated from words by points and space.

One modification to Roman numerals was the adoption on the Continent of the Insular division by points and/or space of Roman numerals into decimals or decimal distinctions. The use of punctuation of large numbers by decimal distinctions, as in m.cc.l.vi for 1,256, had an Insular origin, and it paralleled the Insular use of punctuation employed to reduce the ambiguity of Latin prose. Interpuncts to set off decimal distinctions first appeared in English charters of the eighth century.[19] This practice migrated to the Continent in the late tenth century, just when Gerbert was introducing Arabic numbers for the abacus. Another modification that spread on the Continent in the late tenth and eleventh centuries was the use of the terminal long *j* for the final *i* in composite expressions of integers. The use of the long *j* in numerical notation had no precedent in antiquity, but was adopted for numbers by analogy with the long *j* placed at word endings in Spanish manuscripts. It was used first in Spain as a redundant sign to clarify the boundary between numbers and adjacent verbal text.[20] A third change already present in the eleventh century was the use of a small form of the Roman capital *V* for numbers in place of the minuscule *u*. This distinction greatly reduced the new ambiguity created by the frequently juxtaposed minim strokes in Roman numerals when written with minuscule script instead of with capital or uncial letters.

A fourth graphic convention associated with word separation and useful for representing large numbers was the superscript stroke, or *virga*, employed as a conventional notation for representing multiples of thousands, as in the expression M with a *virga*, which converted 1,000 to 10,000. Historically, this use of the *virga* had its origin in interpunct-separated inscriptions of antiquity.[21] In *scriptura continua*, the Romans borrowed the Greek usage of the *virga*, making it an ambiguous sign for distinguishing numerical expressions and abbreviations from surrounding text. Roman cursive letter forms were also used to distinguish letters representing numbers from those representing syllables in both formal book scripts and lapidary inscriptions. Certain of these Roman cursive numerals, like those for 6, 40, 60, and 550, in effect formed discrete logograms, written and read as single symbols.[22] These emblematic notations for numbers disappeared entirely in the early Middle Ages. In medieval aerated and separated scripts, where space and points identified numbers, scribes returned to using the *virga* exclusively to signal multiples of one thousand, for example, x (with line over it) was equivalent to M, or 1,000. Such encoded information simplified the neurophysiological processes involved in reading large numbers. The *virga* representing multiples of 1,000 was used for expressing large sums until the thirteenth century, when exponential forms and Arabic numerals replaced it.

The Insular principle of decimal punctuation was fundamental to the decoding of both the Roman and the new Arabic numerical symbols of the Middle Ages. It reflected fixed conventions of order based on a sequence of values, whereas in ancient Rome, conventions of order had been obscured by the mixture of addition and subtraction in numerical reading. Thus, in the mid-eleventh century, both in northern Europe and in England, the antique expression MCCLXVII was likely to be transcribed x̄.cc.l.xvij, suggesting a direct visual awareness of decimal units that facilitated the swift conversion of the symbols to verbal expression.[23] Ocreatus combined this form of notation with the Arabic zero in the early twelfth century.[24] Conventions of punctuation were fully transferred to Arabic numbers when, in the early thirteenth century, Leonardo of Pisa commended the use of the inverted hyphen to divide Arabic numerals into decimal groupings of three digits. In the mid-thirteenth century, John of Sacrobosco used medial points for the same purpose.[25]

Another medieval innovation in numerical legibility was the exponential form for inflected cardinal and ordinal numbers, such as $\overset{o}{v}$ and $\overset{m}{v}$, which became current in the eleventh century. Their construction was modeled on Irish and Anglo-Saxon monolexic abbreviations, like ṁ for *modo*, that could be rapidly converted to a verbal expression.[26] It has been suggested that a superscript monolexic abbreviation for eight (*octo*) may have been the origin of the modern "Arabic" sign for that number.[27] Superscript forms of cardinal and ordinal numbers were not recorded before the late tenth or eleventh century, the period of transition from aerated to separated script on the Continent.

Fractions

Like integers, fractions evolved symbolic forms concomitantly with the introduction of space into script. The ancient Roman mode of expressing fractions involving mental combinations of letters and points was as cumbersome as Roman notation for integers. Ancient fractional notations are preserved in lapidary inscriptions, papyri, and certain ninth-century and tenth-century manuscripts of classical texts with Continental textual traditions, such as Volusius Maecianus's *De distributione* and Priscian's *Liber de figuris numerorum*.[28] They were supplanted by emblematic symbols that first emerged in the British Isles. The obligation of establishing the correct date for the celebration of Easter gave duodecimal fractional notation a special and more prominent role in Insular Christian culture than it had had in classical belles lettres. In the earliest Insular Christian calendrical treatises written in *scriptura continua*, the clumsy ancient Roman forms must have been used. However, in Irish and Anglo-Saxon separated codices, the new emblematic forms for fractions derived from them replaced the Roman ones in the complex arithmetic needed to resolve calendrical disputes. Bede employed them in his *De temporum ratione*.[29] They were present in the earliest extant copy of Victorius's *Calculus*, Vat. lat. 5755, ff. 5–6, which preserves an Insular transcription of the late eighth century or early ninth (Figure 24).[30] It was in the context of Continental aerated codices that the same fractional notation emerged in copies of classical texts such as Vitruvius's *De architectura*.[31] The ninth-century Irish monk Dicuil employed them in his *Epistula censuum*.[32]

In the ninth and tenth centuries, these Insular symbols were often either misconstrued or erroneously reproduced by Continental scribes.[33] However, in the late tenth century, one of the first Continental authors to use word-separated script, Abbo of Fleury, enhanced the Insular corpus with additional symbols. By the end of the eleventh century, emblematic representations and *notae* were used in both England and on the Continent as the regular equivalent to duodecimal fractions.[34] Garland's eleventh-century treatise on the abacus treated these signs for fractions

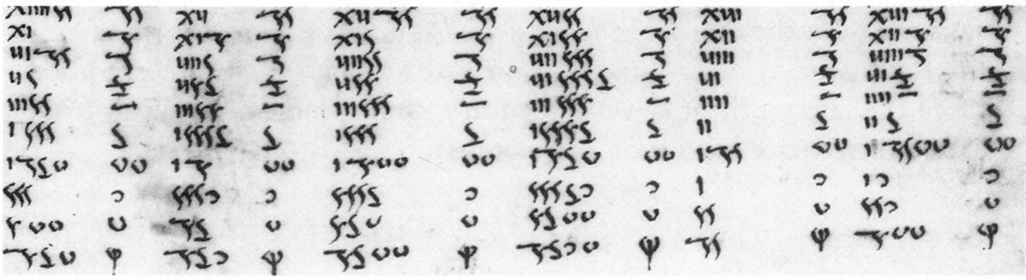

Figure 24. Signs for fractions in Victorius's *Calculus*. Vatican Library, Vat. lat. 5755, f. 5 recto; reproduced by permission.

as *notae* analogous to Arabic numbers. Both sets of characters were to be etched in memory to facilitate mental computation.[35] In fact, the Insular medieval fractional symbols simplified neurophysiologically the task of decoding in precisely the same manner as Arabic integers. The eleventh-century appetite for Insular fractional *notae* was a sign of the new mentality toward reading that made Continental Europe equally receptive both to Arabic numbers and to Insular word separation, punctuation, and *prosodiae*.

New Modes of Graphic Display

Altered manners of reading numbers and text also stimulated the proliferation of new kinds of decoration in mathematical and scientific texts. One of these was the encasement of the written page within graphic designs modeled on architectural motifs of arches and columns. In the papyri of antiquity, this type of presentation of text had been extremely rare, and its use for the tabular representation of mathematical data was unknown.[36] It figured prominently in certain early Christian texts written in *scriptura continua*, where it seems to have been employed first in conjunction with numbers in the canon tables of Jerome's Latin Vulgate translation of the Gospels.[37] In his general preface, *Novum opus*, Jerome described the canons as a form of concordance that would permit the reader to use easily the marginal numbers of the *capitula*, or chapters, to consult rapidly disparate but parallel passages of the Gospel.[38]

Apart from the Vulgate, architectural encasement of words and numbers was not characteristic of manuscripts written in *scriptura continua*, although they may have been present in the earliest eighth-century and ninth-century manuscripts of Isidore of Seville's *Etymologiarum libri*.[39] It was not until after the emergence of aerated and separated writing that architectural motifs gained popularity as a reader's aid. Textual manuscripts incorporated architectural motifs into grammatical, mnemonic, and chronological tables; liturgical manuscripts used them to construct tables for the litany. In mathematical texts, tables set in architectural motifs containing the products of complex multiplications accompanied the explicatory treatises on the use of the abacus, employing Arabic numerals and the Insular signs for fractions.[40] In computative treatises, like Garland's *Tractatus*, these tables were intended to be memorized as visual images. Another graphic complement to scientific texts were the tables showing astrological movement that were present from the tenth century onward in manuscripts written in aerated and separated text.[41]

Musical Notation

A second special variety of reading and writing relates to musical notation. Before the end of the tenth century, most Continental antiphonaries, evangelistaries, Psalters, and benedictionals were written in aerated script, undifferentiated from those of textual manuscripts. Aside from Psalters written in tironian notes that may have been used only for pedagogical purposes, there are examples of codices like the *Benedictionals of Freising*, written in Caroline script with fully developed word separation and with the acute accent used to denote monosyllables and the *-is* termination. These benedictionals also contained emblematic Insular punctuation, and it is reasonable to suppose that the hybridization of Insular textual format and Caroline letter forms was intended to create a book optimally suited for the decorous recitation of public prayer. However, books such as the *Benedictionals of Freising* were extremely rare, even in southern Germany. The presence of intense aeration and frequent separated words and syllables when musical notation was present became consistently more prominent in liturgical books from the ninth century onward. For the ancient reader of Latin *scriptura continua*, the task of chanting a musical text with appropriate pitch and tempo was the responsibility of the reader, much as were the tasks of word separation and punctuation. The modern mode of providing musical instructions to the reader by means of interlinear encoded glosses suitable for the "sight reading" of a melodic line was poorly suited to the cognitive demands of identifying word boundaries in continuous script.

In ancient Greece, alphabetical musical notation, judging from sur-

viving papyri, was relatively rare and was sometimes associated with aeration, and in ancient Latin books no musical notation existed.[42] Augustine
identified music with memory, and Isidore of Seville stated that there
was no notation for church music.[43] Early Christian singers of chants relied exclusively on memory to reproduce melodies accompanying written
sacred texts. The introduction of aerated and separated scripts, first in the
British Isles in the seventh century and later on the Continent, created an
unprecedented potential for the reader to make much wider use of interlinear musical notation than would have been physiologically possible in
the *scriptura continua* of antiquity. It has been suggested that the earliest Latin texts with musical notation may have been copied in Rome,
based on Byzantine models. However, the earliest surviving examples of
Western notation radiated from northern Europe, in particular from two
ninth-century centers of aerated writing, Saint Gall and Laon.[44]

From the ninth century onward, many manuscripts written for musical notation had a text format distinct from that of other books produced
in the same scriptorium. These manuscripts were marked by an increased
aeration, and consequently by a higher number of freestanding words
and syllables.[45] Intense textual aeration can be seen in the section of text
containing early examples of musical notation in the *Musica Enchiriadis*
in Valenciennes, BM 337.[46] The coordination of syllable and pitch, fundamental to the Western chant, was reflected in an altered text format for
portions intended for musical notation within books otherwise written
in hierarchical word blocks, such as Paris, BN lat. 2291, f. lv; Chartres,
BM 47;[47] Montpellier, L'École de Médecine, H. 159;[48] Vat. Reg. lat. 577,
f 77v.[49] The need to coordinate intratextual space and musical notation was equally evident in the earliest musical *probationes pennae*, or pen
trials.[50] In this light, it seems unlikely that neumatic notation (for which
all documentation has been lost) appeared first at the papal court of Pope
Stephen in the mid-eighth century, when Roman scribes were still writing *scriptura continua*.[51]

Early musical manuscripts for which the intratextual space was clearly
influenced by Insular precedents also exhibited other forms of Insular
influence. The shapes of the early neumes at Saint Gall and the abbeys
of Brittany, Normandy, Aquitaine, Chartres, and Catalonia are reminiscent of the forms of *prosodiae* and *positurae*, especially the acute accent
and emblematic punctuation of Insular writing.[52] Tenth-century authors
compared the function of neumes to grammatical notes.[53] Inspired by
Boethius, an interlinear alphabetical mode of pitch notation was per-

fected in eleventh-century Normandy and diffused in northern France, northern Italy, and England, except for a single instance exclusively in separated writing.[54] The careful use of emblematic punctuation and special adaptations of the *trait d'union* also contributed to reducing the ambiguity of pages written with interlinear musical notation.[55]

In the eleventh and twelfth centuries, neumatic musical notation evolved toward a graphic representation of pitch, capitalizing on the enhanced eye-voice span that word separation created.[56] Neumes indicating direction for pitch change were placed diastematically (i.e., between parallel lines) on the page.[57] Toward 1026, Guido of Arezzo (ca. 990–ca. 1050) greatly advanced this process by introducing a staff with fixed, graduated pitch values that made an alphabetical pitch notation sufficiently unambiguous so that a singer might perform an unfamiliar chant exclusively from the written text.[58] This reduction in ambiguity was not unrelated to the emergence on the Continent of word separation. Guido, in his *Micrologus*, underscored the significance of the graphic word when he wrote of the necessary coordination of musical notation with grammatical distinctions,[59] and for an eleventh-century commentator of the *Micrologus*, "the word" meant the *pars*, fundamental to both grammar and music.[60]

This logocentric approach to musical notation meshed well with the text format of the early manuscripts in which the *Micrologus* and Guido's other writings survive. These codices, of which the earliest were copied fifty years after his death, were written with the word separation and schematic diagrams as well as other features that typified protoscholastic books.[61] The textual tradition of Guido's corpus and the implications of his writings for text format lend credence to the assertion by some scholars that Guido had visited abbeys in northern France.

Guido's use of the staff to achieve a diastematic notation of pitch was analogous to the perfection of separated script with full punctuation for prose. Neurophysiologically, both the new musical and the new textual formats presupposed a broad eye-voice span and the extensive use of parafoveal vision in the left visual field to perceive the forms of melody, words, and word groupings.[62] When musical notation accompanied separated text, the use of parafoveal vision could simultaneously anticipate the movement of the melodic line and the grouping of grammatical units. In some books, the matching of syllable to pitch was expedited by the frequent presence of hierarchical distinctions of space, in which major space marked the separation of words and minor space marked the distinction of syllables within words. In other books, extended red *traits d'union* preserved the visual unity of words, aiding the performer to chant a text while comprehending its meaning. In the graphic representation of both music and prose, the scribe assumed burdens that had previously been those of the reader, thereby substituting a rapid and unambiguous comprehension of written text for the ancient dependency on *praelectio* and rote memorization.

The eventual triumph of separated text format for the musical page had clear implications for book production. The reproduction of a chant with its musical notation required a coordination of sign and space and a much greater degree of visual similitude between the exemplar and the copy than had been requisite for the copying of a simple literary text written in *scriptura continua* or aerated script. The use of visual memory in copying, not essential for the scribe who wrote to dictation or who dictated to himself, was intrinsically attractive to the scribe copying musical books in separated script, just as it was for the scribe charged with the added complication of the tie marks, construction notes, and emblematic punctuation characteristic of glossed books. The textual traditions of word-separated eleventh-century chant manuscripts from Aquitaine began to display errors that confirm the emergence of a visual dimension in the transmission of musical texts.[63] In the mid-twelfth century, the visual copying of music was firmly established in the Cistercian Order, and in the thirteenth century, visual replication of standard exemplars was adopted by the Dominicans, Franciscans, and Carthusians.[64]

Chapter 8

The Early Protoscholastics

Three figures dominated the period of protoscholasticism at the end of the tenth century: Gerbert of Aurillac (d. 1003), Abbo of Fleury (d. 1004), and Heriger of Lobbes (d. 1007). In their treatises, they revived the study of Aristotelian logic and diffused the new Arabic scientific learning. All three employed word separation by space and other visual cues to facilitate the comprehension of new and difficult concepts. Their students and anonymous scribes in their circle also wrote in separated script and employed the auxiliary graphic aids inspired by Insular and Arabic models.

Gerbert of Aurillac

Gerbert of Aurillac has long been recognized as the principal intellectual figure of the tenth century. His original mind shaped the curriculum of early protoscholasticism. In mathematics, as we have seen, Gerbert introduced a new form of the abacus that employed tokens or *apices* bearing Arabic characters, an innovation in graphic forms that transcended words by providing symbols for numerical values.[1] In his *Historia francorum*, Gerbert's student Richer related that his master used spheres and planetaria to elucidate his lectures, innovations reflecting a new emphasis on the visual conceptualization of complex astronomical relationships.[2] According to Richer, Gerbert also restructured the basic school texts used at Reims, making dialectic the principal academic discipline.[3] At the heart of his course of study Gerbert placed a series of translations, commentaries, and treatises that formed the foundation of future medieval education. These texts, which came to be known collectively as the *Logica vetus*, included Boethius's translations of the *Isagoge* of Porphyry and of Aristotle's *Categories* and *De interpretatione*, Boethius's monographs on logic, Cicero's *Topica* (a Latin summary of Aristotle's *Topica*), and Pseudo-Apuleius's *De interpretatione*.[4]

Latin translations of Greek logical texts had not made easy reading in Roman antiquity. They were even more difficult to comprehend when read in a foreign tongue, Latin, in late-tenth-century France. To aid the reader to comprehend the difficult concepts of logic, Gerbert introduced special visual aids in the form of tables that mixed words and images.[5] These special tables required the use of the left visual field and para-foveal and peripheral vision.[6] From Gerbert's correspondence, we know that in his continuous quest for manuscripts, he paid keen attention to those containing explicative illustrations.[7] For his lecture before his pupil Emperor Otto III, Gerbert prepared a special table demonstrating the divisions of philosophy, and for private study, he compiled a table of twenty-six leaves, now lost, to help students comprehend the logical distinctions of rhetoric.[8] It is likely that the format of these tables was similar to the schematic tree diagrams that accompanied many of the earliest codices of Gerbert's and Abbo's works. They would become hallmarks of the new schoolbooks of eleventh-century France. Gerbert's enthusiasm for figures and tables as aids in the study of logic was a sign of his keen interest in the simplification of cognitive processes by the use of graphic representations. This same simplification was achieved within the text by word separation, which is clearly evident in the codices of Gerbert's *Regulae de numerorum abaci rationibus*, both those containing and those not containing the table of Arabic numbers.[9]

Milan, Biblioteca Ambrosiana C. 128 inf., from the library of Bobbio, contains the oldest copy of the *Saltus Gerberti*, otherwise known as Gerbert's *Scholium ad Boethii Arithmeticam institutionem* II, i (Figure 25).[10] Because of its provenance, it is reasonable to conclude that it was copied in close physical proximity to the author, for Gerbert was resident abbot at Bobbio from 980 to 983, after he left Reims. In it, words were generously separated by 3 times the unity of space, with space omitted after monosyllables. Terminal forms included the ampersand and the long *j* in numbers. The *ct* and *st* ligatures cloaked intersyllabic space within words. Emblematic punctuation was employed, in conjunction with capitals and increased space. This manuscript, by virtue of its word separation, stands out from other Bobbio codices of the second half of the tenth century.

The early manuscripts containing Gerbert's other writings were also separated. After 1011, the monk Stabilis at the Abbey of Saint-Mesmin

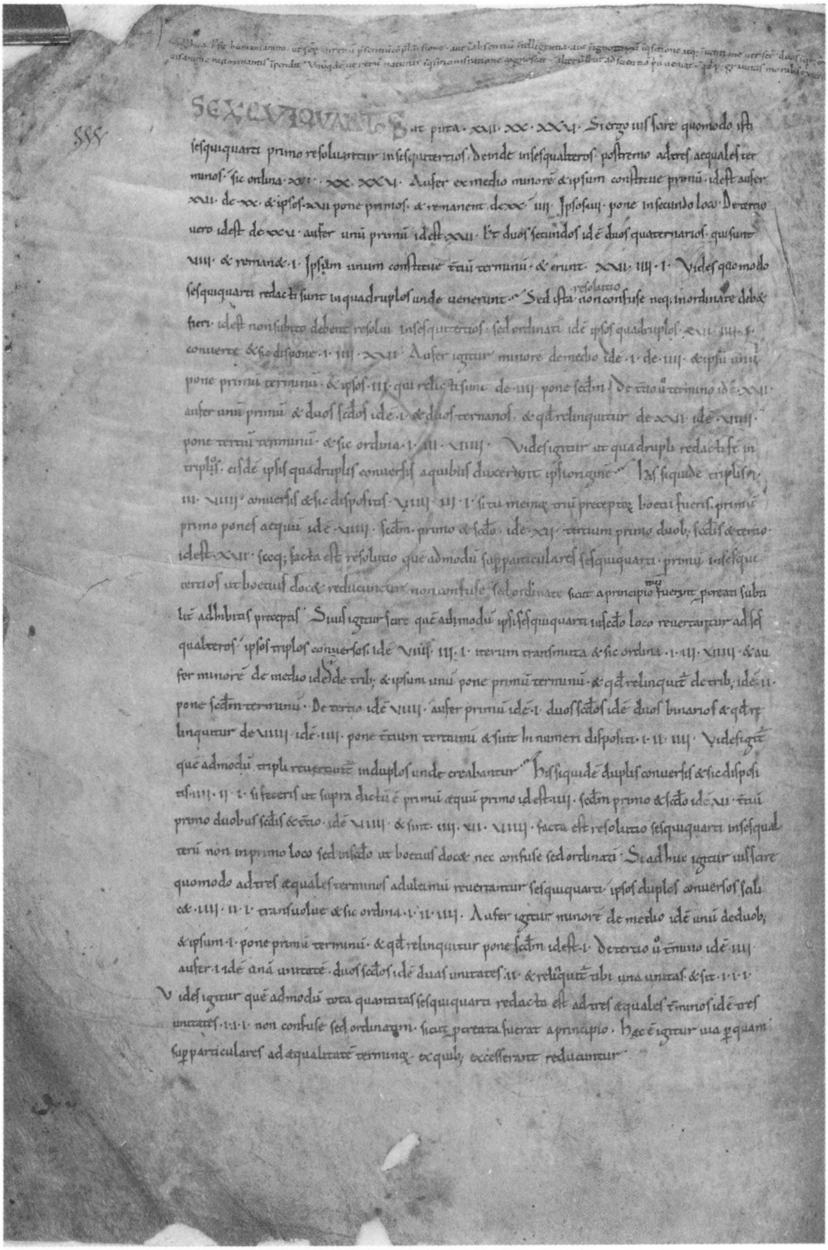

Figure 25. Word separation and related characteristics in Gerbert's *Scholium ad Boethii Arithmeticam institutionem*. Milan, Biblioteca Ambrosiana C. 128, inf., f. 1 verso; reproduced by permission.

of Micy, near Orléans, copied Leiden, BR Voss. lat. Q. 54, the earliest collection of Gerbert's *Epistulae*, in separated script with space often omitted after monosyllabic prepositions and other monosyllables.[11] Interword space varied from 1 to 3 multiples of the unity of space.[12] Terminal forms, including the elevated *o* and monolexic abbreviations, enhanced the separation achieved by space. Initial capitals or all capitals without signs of punctuation were frequently used to signal proper names, and were usually preceded by points. Capital suspension abbreviations were used for proper names. In his *Epitoma vitae regis Roberti Pii*, composed in about 1031–41, Helgaud of Fleury lauded Gerbert and recounted a joke made by Gerbert referring to the use of the suspension abbreviation *R.* for a proper name, a joke that presupposed this word-separated graphic convention that Gerbert shared with both Abbo and Fulbert.[13] Stabilis also added various *nota* signs and capital letters, probably encoded critical notes, in the margins. Suspended ligatures were occasionally present. The other copies of Gerbert's letters were all word-separated, including an even earlier transcription of his *Epistula ad Wilderodum*, a text that circulated separately from the corpus, in Leiden, BR Voss. lat. Q. 17, written at Saint-Mesmin of Micy at the end of the tenth century.[14]

The oldest manuscript of Gerbert's *Geometria*,[15] Munich, Staatsbibliothek Clm. 14836, ff. 24v–41v, from the library of the Abbey of Saint Emmeram in Regensburg, was transcribed in separated script. In Munich, Staatsbibliothek Clm. 14735, from the Abbey of Saint Emmeram, Hartwic transcribed the earliest extant copy of Gerbert's *De rationali et ratione uti* in a rapidly written script separated by approximately 2 times the unity of space. Terminal forms included the capital *US* ligature, as well as the usual signs for *-us* and *-tur*. Monolexic abbreviations consisted of the Insular sign for *est*.[16] In Paris, BN lat. 10444, f. 61–61v, an extract from the *De rationali et ratione uti* was transcribed in script separated by 2 times the unity of space.[17] Monolexic abbreviations included *l* for *vel*. Terminal forms were the usual signs for *-tur*, *-orum*, *-m*, the ampersand, and the elevated *o*. Punctuation included paragraph signs, medial points, and the sign of interrogation. For an overview of separation in the Gerbert manuscripts, see the Appendix, Table A1.

Apart from Monte Cassino, Archivio della Badia 189, containing the *Regulae de numerorum abaci rationibus*, copied at Monte Cassino before the consistent use of word separation at that abbey, only two manuscripts containing texts attributed to Gerbert are in unseparated script. The *Elogium Boethii*, of which the textual tradition was linked to the *Consolatio philosophiae*,[18] was transcribed in Basel, Universitätsbibliothek An. IV. 2 (F.III–VII), f. 7 (s. x ex.), in script with word blocks of fewer than fifteen characters in maximum length and with many freestanding words.[19] Gerbert's authorship of this work is suspect, however, and the lack of word separation tends to justify the doubt that the *Elogium Boethii* was genuinely his.[20] Another text, the *Sermo de informatione episcoporum*, was copied as a text of Gerbert's in Paris, BN lat. 2400, ff. 136–37, an aerated codex prepared under the direction of Adémar de Chabannes at Saint-Martial of Limoges, a scribe who wrote only in aerated script.[21] The *Sermo* belongs to the corpus of Pseudo-Ambrose and is not a genuine work of Gerbert's.[22]

In general, in the textual tradition of Gerbert's students, the earliest surviving manuscripts often greatly postdate the death of the author, and therefore the time of Gerbert's active teaching at Reims (972–80). Such, however, is not the case for Richer, whose authorial manuscript of the *Historia francorum* containing autograph corrections is a unique source for the history of word separation (Figure 26).[23] Because of the numerous details it gives on Gerbert's life, the *Historia* has great historical value, and as a result, Richer has become the best known of Gerbert's students. However, celebrated as he is today, in his own time, Richer and the *Historia* were totally unknown. The three great letter writers of the age, Gerbert, Abbo, and Fulbert, never mention him, and his chronicle seems to have been neither recopied nor read.[24] Indeed, it was from Richer's own copy (Bamberg, Staatsbibliothek Hist. 5, E.5.3), which Gerbert gave to Otto III, that the *Historia francorum* was rescued from oblivion in the mid-nineteenth century.[25]

As an artifact, Gerbert's copy of Richer's *Historia francorum*, which contains the author's rapidly written autograph emendations, is incontrovertible evidence that in Gerbert's circle, separated script was not only the medium of textual dissemination but also the medium of textual composition. Richer's script contained many of the graphic elements found in the early codices of Gerbert. The writing of the *Historia francorum* was separated by space, complemented by the use of terminal forms and monolexic abbreviations, with interword space varying from 1.5 to 3 times the unity of space.[26] Richer and the scribe who worked for him used terminal forms that included the usual signs for *-us*, *-tur*, *-m*, and *-orum*, as well as the ampersand and the capital *NT* ligature. Monolexic abbreviations included superscript forms and the tironian sign for the conjunction *et*. Proper names were denoted by capitals in marginal finding notes,

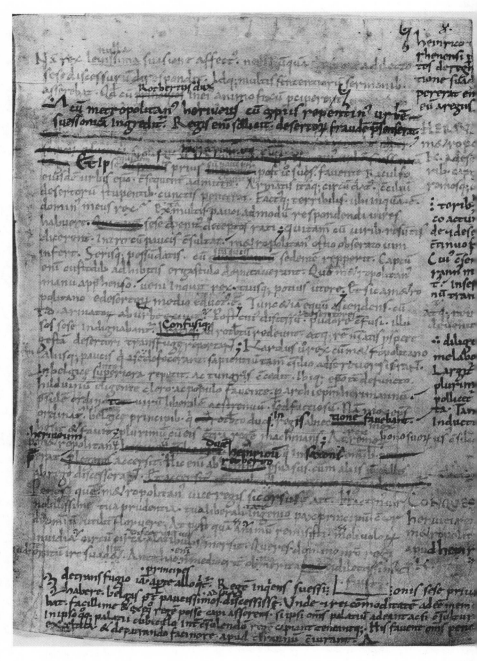

Figure 26. The authorial manuscript of Richer's *Historia francorum*. Bamberg, Staatsbibliothek Hist. 5 E.5.3, f. 8 recto; reproduced by permission.

and many were abbreviated within the text by an initial capital, preceded and followed by a point.[27] Richer's autograph revisions were joined to the text by patterned tie notes, and from the content of these corrections, the Bamburg codex can be dated to between 995 and 997. The terminal capital *S* and *R*, the use of accents, the successor note to the *diastole*, and the *trait d'union*, all tied to Insular tradition, were wanting in Richer's codex, just as they were also largely absent in the early manuscripts of the Arabic scientific corpus and in Gerbert's writings not copied at Fleury.

The regular observance of word separation characteristic of Gerbert's students was evinced by other members of Gerbert's circle who, while not his students, shared his intellectual vision and emphasis on the study of Aristotelian logic. Adson, monk of Luxeuil, taught at the Abbey of Saint-Evre of Toul in Lorraine, where he was in contact with a major infusion of Irish scholars under Gerard, abbot from 963 to 994.[28] In 967, he became abbot of the Abbey of Saint Peter and Paul of Montier-en-Der, two hundred kilometers to the north. Adson corresponded with Gerbert, and Gerbert wrote to him in quest of manuscripts. In a letter that Gerbert addressed to Adalbero of Reims in 983, he mentioned borrowing a manuscript of Caesar from Adson's library to be copied at Reims,[29] and in a letter to Adson in 986, Gerbert clearly implied that Adson was an important source of books.[30] Adson was also a friend of Abbo's, for whom he prepared a now lost versification of Gregory the Great's *Dialogus II*.[31] Adson wrote the *De ortu et tempore Antichristi* for Gerberge, sister of Otto I, and according to Richer's *Historia francorum*, Adson was present at the famous disputation before Otto III in which Gerbert employed his table graphically illustrating the tripartite division of philosophy.[32] Thus, Adson had to be aware of the changes in text format that Gerbert had introduced.

In 992, Adson left Montier-en-Der on a pilgrimage to Jerusalem, during which he perished. At the time of his departure, he left a list of his personal library, copied on a blank leaf of a Montier-en-Der volume, now Paris, BN lat. 5547.[33] Its twenty-two titles included the Latin poets commended by Gerbert, Boethius's translation of Porphyry's *Isagoge*, and Aristotle's *Categories* in the paraphrase of Pseudo-Augustine.[34] The catalogue that records these books was transcribed in separated script, and it is the earliest of a series of library inventories written in separated script that mention logical texts disseminated in separated writing.[35] Proper names were denoted by initial capitals. *Prosodiae* consisted of a *trait d'union* and the *ct* and *st* intraword ligatures.

The manuscript evidence for Adson's literary works confirms the pervasive presence of word separation in their textual tradition. Adson was the author of four saint's lives, of which the early manuscripts are also separated.[36] In Paris, BN lat. 13764, probably from Saint-Remi in Reims, Adson's *Vita Basilii* falls on folios 1 through 48, and its script dates from about 1000. The scribe wrote in separated script, with interword space equivalent to from 2 to 3 times the unity of space. Terminal forms included the ampersand and at least one instance of the terminal capital *S* at a line ending. *Prosodiae* by the scribe and early emendators facilitated the recognition of words. Acute accents denoted certain monosyllables, and, when placed on the tonic syllable, aided the reader in resolving ambiguous word boundaries that resulted either from irregular spacing of compound words formed from prepositions or from an infelicitous conjunction of minim strokes. The acute accent was also used at line endings in conjunction with the *trait d'union* as a redundant sign of interline word continuation. The *diastole* was used by the scribe to correct omitted interword space. Proper names were written both all in capitals and with initial capitals.

The earliest copy of Adson's *Vita Waldebeti* is preserved in The Hague, Koninklijke Bibliotheek 70.H.50, ff. 1–12v. It dates from the late tenth or early eleventh century and was transcribed in separated script, with interword space equivalent to from 3 to 4 times the unity of space. The single scribe used a wide variety of terminal forms, including the elevated round *s*, the capitals *S* and *M*, and the capital *US* and *NT* ligatures. The ampersand, however, was used indiscriminately within and at the end of words. Another codex, containing Adson's *Vitae sanctae*, London, BL Add. 21917, copied at the Abbey of Luxeuil, where he also served as abbot, was written in separated script in the late tenth or early eleventh century.[37] Terminal forms included the usual forms for -*m*, -*tur*, -*orum*, the ampersand, and the capital *US*, *NT*, and variant *NTur* ligatures at line endings. The terminal capital *S*, in some portions restricted to line endings, was present elsewhere in the manuscript.

In the second half of the century, the *De ortu et tempore Antichristi* was transcribed at Saint-Martial of Limoges in Paris, BN lat. 3454 in canonically separated script with *traits d'union*. Adson's *De ortu* was part of the first wave of the textual diffusion that brought northern word separation and *prosodiae* southward. By the end of the century, Adson's text had reached the Abbey of San Sevrino in Naples, where it was copied in Naples, BN, VII, C. 43, ff. 81v–86v, in canonically separated script, with suspension abbreviations for biblical citations.[38] For a survey of word separation in Adson's pre-1000 manuscript corpus, see the Appendix, Table A2.

Ayrard was another of Gerbert's students whose familiarity with word separation can be documented in codices contemporary to Gerbert. A monk from Aurillac, he followed Gerbert to Reims, where he transcribed classical texts for him after becoming abbot of Saint-Thierry in 972. Gerbert corresponded with Ayrard concerning the correction and copying of manuscripts of ancient texts.[39] One of the copies that Ayrard made for Gerbert survives in Erlangen, Universitätsbibliothek 380, containing Cicero's *De oratore*, Priscian's *De figuris numerorum*, and other ancient texts.[40] Apart from occasional run-ons, words were separated by space varying from equivalence to 2 times the unity of space. Terminal forms included the usual signs for *-us*, *-tur*, *-bus*, the *e* cedilla, the ampersand, the capital *NT* ligature, and the capital *S*. Suspension abbreviations were present, as well as the monolexic symbol for *vel* to denote interlinear additions. However, in the text of Priscian, the Insular emblematic forms for fractions were not present, and the Greek citations within Priscian's text were aerated, rather than separated. Reims, BM 250, a lectionary for Saint-Thierry copied under Ayrard's direction, was separated by interword space that varied from equivalence to 2 times the unity of space.[41] Terminal forms included the capital *NT* ligature. Monolexic abbreviations included the ampersand for the conjunction *et*.

A manuscript apparently prepared for Gerbert at Bobbio during Gerbert's residence there as abbot from 980 to 983 is another example of word separation closely associated with Gerbert. In Wolfenbüttel, Herzog August Bibliothek, Gud. lat. 335, containing a collection of classical texts by Cicero, Sallust, and Seneca, Cicero's *Pro rege Dejotaro* corresponds to the copy described by Gerbert in a letter of July 983.[42] The principal texts of this codex, which was apparently copied at Gerbert's request, were separated by interword space varying from 2 to 3 times the unity of space. Monolexic abbreviations included the ampersand, set off by space, and the tironian sign for the conjunction *et*. Capital suspension abbreviations, set off by space and interpuncts, were used for proper names. Terminal forms consisted of the usual signs for *-tur*, the ampersand, the capital *NT* ligature, the capital *S*, and the capital *US* ligature at the end of lines. The scribe used the long or Insular form of the minuscule letter *r*. A second hand added three draft letters on the margins of folios 43, 44v, and 45. These too are likely to have been copied in the milieu of Gerbert. They were written in script separated from 1.5 to 2 times the unity of space. Terminal forms included the *m*, the capital *US* ligature, and the *e* cedilla. *Prosodiae* were limited to the acute accent on the monosyllable *ré*. As in Gerbert's letters and Richer's *Historia*, capital suspension abbreviations were used for proper names. Superscript monolexic abbreviations were also present.[43]

Abbo of Fleury

Abbo of Fleury is the second preeminent tenth-century intellectual whose textual tradition was closely related to the emergence of word separation in late-tenth-century Continental manuscripts. Abbo was introduced to the study of logic, arithmetical computation, and astronomy as a student at Reims, and although his modern biographers assume on the basis of very sketchy documentation that his sojourn there preceded that of Gerbert, the possibility exists that Abbo may have learned word separation from members of Gerbert's circle.[44] However this may be, the similarity of their interests suggests the probability of at least indirect intellectual contact between the two. While it is true that Abbo never mentions Gerbert, and Gerbert mentions Abbo only once, this silence may very well attest to a personal rivalry that may very well have existed between two notable teachers who were on opposing sides in a series of complex conflicts between royal, episcopal, monastic, and papal authority.[45] In a letter written to Constantine in early 980 accompanying a copy of the *Regulae*, Gerbert seems to suggest that Abbo had clumsily plagiarized his writings on the abacus.[46] Indeed, it would be difficult to accept Abbo's ignorance of Gerbert's teachings, for Gerbert addressed complicated mathematical epistles to Constantine of Fleury between 978 and 986, when Abbo was master of Fleury's school, a post he held from 965 to 985. Gerbert also requested manuscripts from Constantine,[47] and Gerbert's works, including the *Regulae de numerorum abaci rationibus*, were copied at Fleury at an early date.[48]

Even if we assume that Abbo never met Gerbert or read his works, Abbo's emphasis on the *Logica vetus* as central to the curriculum paralleled Gerbert's. In addition, Abbo's writings are of interest for the history of word separation because he spent two years in England (from ca. 985 to the end of 987) as schoolmaster at the Benedictine Abbey of Ramsey.[49] In this capacity, he was a principal figure in the revival of intellectual contact between northern France and southern England that played a central role in reforming English and Continental monasticism. Since word separation had been standard in England from the late seventh century onward, we may reasonably infer that Abbo personally acted as a conduit enabling Insular scribal practices to migrate to the Continent.

Abbo was the first indigenous Continental author using Caroline letter forms to broach the problem of regular word separation in a grammatical treatise. In his *Quaestiones grammaticales*, a text written either at Ramsey or directly after returning to Fleury, Abbo underscored the importance of the correct separation of words in both speech and writing when he stated: "Finally, it is to be said to take care to avoid collision, which is commonly committed between two parts, whether in pronunciation or in writing, as *veni trex* where the correct form is *venit rex*, and *par sest* where the correct form is *pars est*, and *feli xes* where the correct form is *felix es*." [50]

Like ninth-century Insular grammarians, Abbo equated *pars* with words. Abbo applied *collisio* to the violation of interword boundaries, rather than to the violation in pronunciation of syllabic boundaries, as had ancient grammarians. [51] For Abbo, correct word separation was a responsibility of the scribe, and the very notion of averting collision between written words presupposed word separation. In the absence of conventions for interword space, the examples that Abbo enumerated would have been nonsensical homographs, just as *scriptura continua* would have vitiated Bede's description of the use of the *diastole* in the *De orthographia*. Another textual indication of Abbo's use of word separation is that in his correspondence, he, like Gerbert, used suspension abbreviations for proper names. [52]

The conclusion that the message of word separation in Abbo's *Quaestiones grammaticales* was inextricably linked to the medium in which the text was diffused is confirmed by the two surviving codices containing the text, both contemporary to Abbo. Although the *Quaestiones* may have been composed in England, these codices were written at Fleury at the time of Abbo. [53] In London, BL Add. 10972, the text of the *Quaestiones* on folios 38 through 48 was written in separated script in a codex containing almost exclusively works of Abbo's composition, all written by scribes writing separated script. [54] The portion containing the *Quaestiones* was written by at least two hands. One of the two principal scribes, responsible for folios 1 through 23v, wrote in canonically separated script. Terminal forms included the usual symbols for *-us* and *m* and the capital *NS* and *NT* ligatures reserved for line endings. At line endings, these were complemented by the presence of suspended ligatures, including the *ct* ligature. This sensitivity to the word as a graphic unit was strikingly reinforced by the scribe's use of the split-line *trait d'union*, a *prosodia* developed by scribes in southern England at the end of the tenth century. Its presence in Add. 10972 was a clear sign of Anglo-Saxon influence in the adoption of word separation at Fleury after Abbo's return from Ramsey. The scribes of Add. 10972 also employed capitals and augmented space in conjunction with punctuation to denote sentences. In addition, proper names were written all in capitals. In some instances, particularly after folio 23v, syllabic space and interword space were not clearly distinguished, a vestigial sign of the tradition of the aerated script characteristic of Fleury.

Vat. Reg. lat. 596, ff. 20–23, the second copy of Abbo's *Quaestiones*, formed one element of a composite codex also containing Abbo's *Libellus de propositionibus hypotheticis*.[55] Here, the copy of the *Quaestiones* was written with word separation by space and terminal forms similar to Add. 10972, but with space omitted after monosyllabic prepositions. On some folios, the scribe's grasp of separation degenerated into the use of short hierarchical word blocks of fewer than fifteen characters in length. The scribe, in keeping with Continental practice, occasionally used medial interpuncts as a supplement to a minor space to clarify the separation of words. The scribe's monolexic abbreviations included Insular superscript forms and the tironian symbol for *est*. The use of the tironian symbol for *est*, rather than the more usual Insular form, was peculiar to the separated manuscripts written at Fleury at the time of Abbo.

In both codices of the *Quaestiones*, the scribes who transcribed the particular passage that explained the necessity of correct word separation ironically made differing errors in spacing that obscured its meaning. The failure of scribes close to Abbo to reproduce accurately intended examples of erroneous written separation was indicative of how fragile the new notion of word separation was in a milieu where, aside from codices brought to Fleury in the tenth century by Breton monks fleeing the Normans, word separation was an innovation in the face of an uninterrupted tradition of aerated writing. Nevertheless, it was in monastic schools like Fleury, where the word separation in new scientific texts was reinforced by the emulation of Anglo-Saxon models, that the new text format was launched on a course of rapidly increasing popularity.

The nexus between form and content was equally present in Abbo's logical writings, which were based upon the same authors of the *Logica vetus* who formed the core of Gerbert's curriculum at Reims. In Paris, BN NAL 1611, formerly one codex with Orléans, BM 267 (223), copied at Fleury, the text of Abbo's *De propositionibus et syllogismis categoricis et hypotheticis* was written in script separated by space, with the redundant presence of numerous terminal forms and monolexic abbreviations and with monosyllabic prepositions usually separated from their objects.[56] Terminal forms included the usual symbols for -*us* and *m*, the capitals *S* and *R*, and the ampersand. While the use of the terminal *S* and *R* was initially an innovation of Insular scribes, the restriction of the ampersand to the terminal position and its use in the presence of readily perceptible space on either side as a monolexic abbreviation for the conjunction *et* were French inventions.[57] Interword space was equivalent to 2 times the unity of space and therefore readily perceptible to parafoveal and peripheral vision. The scribe regularly made a hierarchical distinction between intersyllabic and interword space. An additional sign of Insular influence closely related to separation was the redundant accenting of monosyllables also separated by space.[58] Monolexic abbreviations were the tironian sign for *est*, *e* for *est*, *n* for *non*, and numerous superscript forms. Proper names were written with an initial capital.

In a second copy of the *De propositionibus*, Orléans, BM 277 (233), pp. 74–77, also from Fleury, the text was transcribed in script separated by space equivalent to 2 times the unity of space.[59] The presence of Abbo's face and name in a historiated initial *O* on page 62 establishes this manuscript as having been copied in close proximity to the author (Figure 27).[60] The other copies of this text are also word-separated.

In Leiden, BR BPL 139B, ff. 1–31,[61] a Fleury codex, Abbo's revised second recension of *De propositionibus* was copied with words separated. In this recension, Abbo introduced interlinear capital letters to clarify the syllogisms, thus enhancing their iconic quality. The writing of capitals, as well as the special spacing to represent complex statements of syllogisms, were characteristic of Abbo's new use of format as an adjunct to the comprehension of difficult text (Figure 28). The result was a brilliant example of a graphic innovation for the transcription of logic, analogous to late-tenth-century reforms in transcriptions of numbers.[62] Schematic tree diagrams of logical relationships accompanied the text of Porphyry's *Isagoge* contained in the same codex (compare Figure 24).[63]

Manuscripts of other Abbo texts confirm that word separation was diffused as an integral part of the master's works at Fleury, elsewhere in northern France, and in southern England, where they were copied soon

Figure 27. Abbo's possible autograph script in Boethius's translation of Aristotle's *Categoriae*. Orléans, Bibliothèque Municipale 277 (233), p. 62; reproduced by permission.

after his death. Bamberg, Staatsbibliothek Class 53 (H.J.IV.24), contains an early (ca. 1000) Fleury transcription of the *Commentum super Calculo Victorii* that entered the Imperial library in the eleventh century.[64] The texts of Victorius and Abbo were written by several scribes in script separated by 2 times the unity of space, with space occasionally present after monosyllabic prepositions. One of the scribes (folios 1 through 4v) used a distinctly Insular form of the minuscule *r* descending below the line. The scribe's monolexic abbreviations included the Insular sign for *enim* and *est* and the tironian sign for *et*. Emblematic construction notes were present. *Prosodiae* included suspended ligatures, the acute accent to denote monosyllabic prepositions, and the tonic syllable, suspended ligatures, and *diastole* to insert both omitted space and letters. The *ct* ligature was prominent as a symbol of word unity. In numbers, the superscript stroke or *virga* was used as a sign of thousands. Interlinear Roman numerals were used to explicate Abbo's new signs for fractions, and the text was accompanied by schematic diagrams. The *Commentum super Calculo Victorii* in Bern, Burgerbibliothek 250, also from Fleury, was

separated by 2 times the unity of space.[65] On folio 25, it contains what
has been identified to be the authorial copy of the *Computus vulgaris*,
written in separated script.[66] The same text in Berlin, Staatsbibliothek
138 (Phillipps 1833) was likewise separated.[67]

Separation was an integral part of the textual tradition of Abbo's treatises on calculation when these texts spread in northern France. When
a monk from Ferrières transcribed the *Computus vulgaris* in Vat. Reg.
lat. 1573 in the early eleventh century, he separated words.[68] The monk
Ingelard copied and decorated Paris, BN lat. 12117 at the Abbey of Saint-
Germain-des-Prés under Abbot Adélard between 1030 and 1060, when
word separation was accepted at the abbey.[69] He copied the *Computus
vulgaris* on folios 148 through 167 in script separated by space, using terminal forms and monolexic abbreviations, suggesting the visual influence

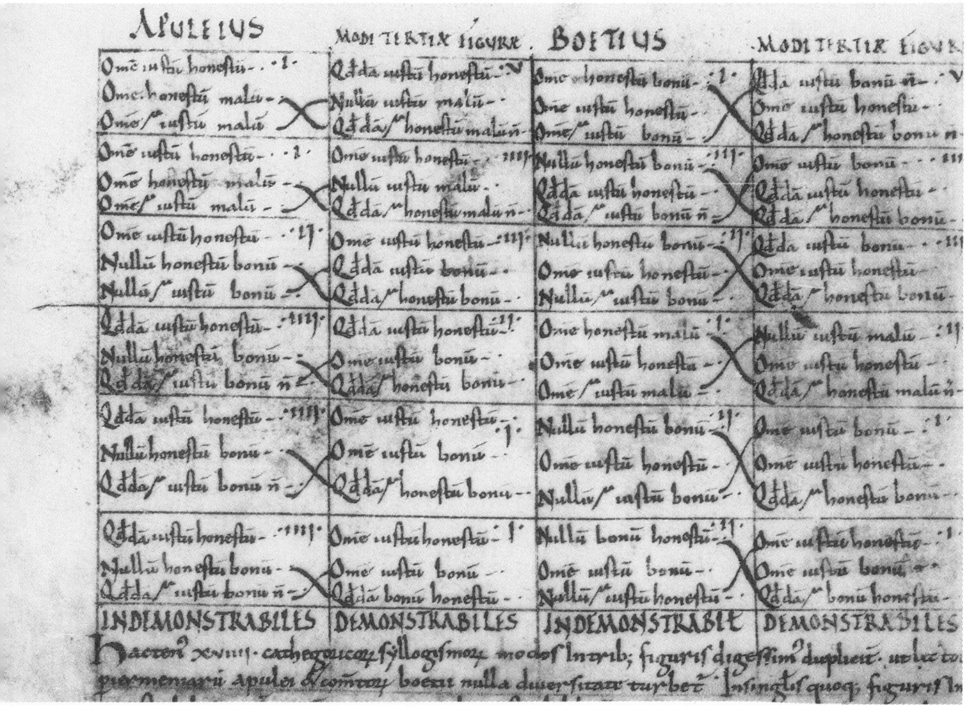

Figure 28. The word separation in syllogisms transcribed at Fleury in Abbo's *De
propositionibus et syllogismis categoricis et hypotheticis*. Paris, Bibliothèque Nationale NAL 1611, f. 10 verso; reproduced by permission.

of an exemplar similar to that of Berlin, Staatsbibliothek 138 (Phillipps 1833). See the Appendix, Table A3, for additional examples of the progress of word separation in the pre-1100 manuscripts of Abbo's works.

The unique copy of Abbo's *Collectio canonum* is the only work of Abbo's to survive in a copy written entirely in hierarchical word blocks. The Fleury copy of Abbo's *Collectio canonum* was already lost by the mid-eleventh century.[70] The sole surviving copy, Paris, BN lat. 2400, ff. 154–162v and 183, was written under the direction of Adémar de Chabannes at Saint-Martial of Limoges, well to the south of Fleury, within the Occitan linguistic zone. It forms part of the same codex that contains Pseudo-Ambrose's *Sermo de informatione episcoporum*, erroneously attributed to Gerbert. The Abbey of Saint-Martial was remote from both England and the intellectual centers associated with the new study of logic, and it was not until the second half of the eleventh century that the first separated manuscripts were transcribed there.

While the *Collectio canonum* is the sole work of Abbo's not to be preserved in word-separated format, it is the one about which we have the most knowledge concerning its composition. Abbo produced the *Collectio* by compiling and rearranging extracts from the Church Fathers and other esteemed sources. The intensive use of this mode of composition was characteristic of protoscholastic authors, for whom the use of word separation surely facilitated their task. To expedite the forming of such compilations, old codices written in aerated script were emended, and according to Fleury's *Customary*, this task would have fallen to Abbo as master of the abbey's school.[71]

Two ninth-century codices, Paris, BN lat. 2278 and lat. 11674, contain respectively parts 1 and 2 of the Fleury copy of Gregory the Great's *Registrum epistolae* that Abbo used to prepare the *Collectio canonum*.[72] Either Abbo or monks working under his direction added marginal summaries to provide points of entry into this aerated codex.[73] These marginalia were written in separated script, with terminal forms that included the capital *NT* ligature. In the marginalia, initial capitals denoted proper names, and acute accents were placed on some monosyllables. Of the two codices, the emendations of lat. 11764 seem textually closer to Abbo's *Collectio canonum* and paleographically closer to the script found in the oldest examples of Abbo's works.[74] Some of the annotations are quite possibly Abbo's autographs. Before Abbo, tenth-century emendators had added marginal summaries and headings in a manner similar to the tenth-century Fleury copy of Quintus Curtius, Bern, Burgerbibliothek

451.[75] However, the tenth-century annotators, who wrote in a highly aerated tironian *hybrida*, had not attempted to reformat the text itself. In
contrast, the emendators working for Abbo entered into the texts to clarify word distinctions, as well as distinctions of higher levels of meaning.
To establish word boundaries in this codex, they used the successor note
to the *diastole* and two other variant signs of word separation. The first
of these was formed from an interpunct and the acute accent, the second from an inverted *J* stroke and an acute accent.[76] The presence of the
successor note to the *diastole* is perhaps its earliest datable appearance in
a Continental manuscript, and it is significant that the scribe-annotator
hesitated between using this mark of Insular origin and the two otherwise unknown signs intended to convey the same meaning. The acute
accent by itself was used to denote monosyllables and the tonic accent in
compound words formed with prepositions. The interpunct was also employed for word separation. The emendators also added split-line *traits
d'union*. In one instance, a *trait d'union* in the form of a hyphen was inserted over an erasure occurring at a line ending.[77] The same emendators
altered medial points into at least two forms of emblematic punctuation,
the *punctus versus* of eighth-century Insular origin and the Continental
metron. The Insular marginal critical note *r* was present.[78] Paris, BN lat.
2278 was less intensely annotated than lat. 11674.[79] Nevertheless, Abbo's
emendators here added *prosodiae* that included *traits d'union* and acute
accents, modified punctuation, and added critical signs in the margins.

If we exclude Paris, BN lat. 2400, copied at a center where the Carolingian practice of hierarchical word blocks flourished three-quarters of
a century longer than at Fleury, an interesting dichotomy remains in the
early Abbo codices copied on the Continent. The literary, historical, and
grammatical texts were separated by space, with only the occasional redundant presence of terminal forms and monolexic abbreviations; the
logical, astronomical, and arithmetical texts were more frequently separated by a combination of space, terminal forms, and monolexic abbreviations, either in lieu of space or as a redundant sign of space. At least
one of the latter manuscripts, Paris, BN lat. 17868, also contains one of
the earliest copies of the first Latin translations of the Syriac astronomical
writings. The mode of separation in Abbo's early scientific manuscripts
strongly resembles that encountered in the early Gerbert corpus. It is
reasonable to suggest the greater reliance of scribes on terminations as
a sign of word boundary when copying Abbo's scientific works was at
least in part an indirect result of Arabic influence introduced into French

monastic circles by Gerbert, and especially by the corpus of Latin translations of Arabic texts. In sifting the evidence of the Abbo manuscripts copied at Fleury during his lifetime, we can conclude that at Fleury there existed, in addition to the initial impetus provided by the new text format developed at Reims, a pronounced Anglo-Saxon influence, notably documented by the presence in Fleury codices of the *trait d'union*, the capitals *R*, *S*, *M*, *X*, and *A* at word endings, the successor note to the *diastole*, and certain Insular monolexic abbreviations that were absent or rarely present in the early manuscripts of Gerbert. Other than Abbo's own works, virtually all manuscripts written at Fleury at the time of Abbo were separated. These include the earliest surviving manuscripts of Boethius's logical monographs and other diverse elements of the *Logica vetus*, in Orléans, BM 277 and Paris, BN NAL 1630. Orléans, BM 267 and Paris, BN NAL 1611, both copied under Abbo, contain important examples of schematic tree diagrams.[80]

There also can be no doubt of Abbo's personal knowledge of Anglo-Saxon vernacular writing, for in his *Quaestiones grammaticales*, he specifically mentioned the *thorn* as a special character used in England for transcribing Old English.[81] Abbo's interest in vernacular writing likely related to the important experiments in writing the Romance vernacular in aerated script that transpired at Fleury.[82] A group of Fleury manuscripts reflect Insular influence in the special sense that they contain vernacular texts. These contain three of the earliest known transcriptions of Occitan. Why monks at Fleury should have preserved and in all probability written texts in Occitan, rather than in Old French, which according to modern philologists should have been their dialect, is not clear. Perhaps monks from southern France came to Fleury, or linguistic lines of demarcation in the eleventh century were other than the evidence of later centuries suggests.[83] Whatever may be the case, English expertise in using Latin letters to transcribe Anglo-Saxon constituted an important example for emulation by the monks at Fleury.

The *Phebi Claro*, a poem of eight lines added in the margin of folio 50v of Vat. Reg. lat. 1462, was set down during Abbo's years at Fleury.[84] It was written in aerated script and was accompanied by a melange of acute accents and accentlike neumes. These Occitan word blocks, however, lacked the morphemic blocks evident in Insular vernacular writing. Approximately one-third of a century later, a verse translation of the Latin *Vita Boethii* was added on pages 269 through 275 of Orléans, BM 444 (649), leaves originally left blank in a tenth-century Latin codex containing extracts of the Bible and sermons in hierarchical word blocks.[85] The vernacular text was written in word blocks, with many freestanding words, and contrasts with a word-separated Latin text also added to the original codex and directly preceding it. As in written Anglo-Saxon and German, acute accents were abundantly present to avert homographs. They were used on the -*is* termination, monosyllables, and within words, apparently as signs of vowel length.

At the same time as scribes at Fleury under Abbo adopted word separation for the transcription of both the ancient and new treatises on logic and science, a linguistic change of great importance for the simplification of reading was also occurring at Fleury. This was the growing adoption of word grouping and patterns of word order. In ancient Latin, the use of word order was essential to avoid ambiguity, most especially in statements of logic, where implicit conventions of sequence, or at least clear groupings of syntactically related words analogous to those that emerge in vulgar Latin, were essential for the unambiguous communication of subtle distinctions. This specialized and peripheral aspect of ancient Latin, which came to be central in scholastic medieval written discourse, was transmitted to the Middle Ages by Boethius in translations and commentaries of the *Logica vetus* that were fundamental to the new education fostered by Abbo and Gerbert in the late tenth century. Because of the inherent difficulty of the subject matter and the need to make precise and subtle distinctions in meaning, the authors of new treatises on logic, like Abbo, observed the same syntactical conventions as Boethian prose, to which they added the additional graphic aid of word separation. Thus, it was not fortuitous that at Fleury, word separation, the new learning, and a concern for conventions of word sequence simultaneously emerged.

The oldest known copy of one of the earliest Latin treatises on word order, the *De ordinatione constructionis*, Orléans, BM 303 (256), ff. 145–48, of which the author is unknown, was copied at Fleury at the time of Abbo in separated script as an addition to a tenth-century aerated codex.[86] The text referred to words as *distinctiones*, here, clearly meaning visible graphic distinctions.[87] In the only other recorded copy of this treatise, Paris, BN lat. 7505, dating from the mid-eleventh century, the text is associated with sequential construction notes. The canons of word order set down were those normally used in Insular construction notes. Briefly and in terse prose, the *De ordinatione constructionis* recommended the sequence subject-verb-object, with adjectives preceding the nouns modified.[88] The anonymous author made use of the Insular grammatical term *adjectiva* not used in antiquity. *Adjectiva* here had a quasi-logical significance, and the treatise as a whole was permeated by the vocabulary of Aristotelian dialectic.[89] The author's use of *adjectiva* implicitly recognized adjectives as a part of speech quasi-distinct from nouns. The treatise went on to define clauses and phrases as word groups within the sentence and gave rules for their correct sequencing. The articulation at Fleury of the notion that a sentence ought to consist of ordered subgroups of correctly ordered words would not only make Latin a far more precise instrument of communication, but it would also have profound implications for the Continental development of syntactical punctuation, in which distinct, encoded emblematic signs, complemented by capitalization, distinguished the boundaries of clauses from those of sentences.

It is possible that the Fleury transcription of the *De ordinatione constructionis* was a copy made of an earlier Insular text. Whether composed in France or not, it was surely inspired by the Anglo-Saxon intellectual models so greatly emulated by the monks of Fleury, for in the British Isles, separation and conventions for word order, as reflected in sequential construction notes, had evolved simultaneously to facilitate the comprehension of written Latin. With the emergence of word separation in Caroline script in northern France under Abbo's influence, sequential construction notes were used for the first time in manuscripts written with purely Continental letter forms. At Fleury, they were present in the copy of Fimicus Maternus's *Mathesis*.[90] In the *Quaestiones grammaticales*, Abbo explicitly used word order as a tool of textual criticism. Postulating a grammatically correct word order, he judged between disparate manuscript readings of Virgil's *Aeneid* 10, 644 in order to restore a "correct" text.[91] Abbo himself also tended to observe certain patterns of word order and word groupings.[92]

Heriger of Lobbes

Heriger shared Gerbert's interest in dialectic and mathematics.[93] The chronicler Sigebert of Gembloux (ca. 1030–1112) compared Heriger to Abbo, Gerbert, and Fulbert.[94] Gerbert corresponded regularly with Notker, who was an intimate of Heriger, and Heriger cited Gerbert in his *Epistola ad Hugonem*. Although the surviving manuscript evidence is not as complete as it is for Gerbert and Abbo, it suggests that Heriger, too, was an early practitioner of word separation. Heriger, with his protector Notker, bishop of Liège from 972 to 1008, was an intimate of the emperors Otto II, Otto III, and Henry II. He is thought to be the author of a work on the use of the abacus, the *Regulae numerorum abaci rationibus*, which did not contain the new Arabic symbols, but which suggests at least indirect contact with Arabic learning.[95] It was frequently copied in the same eleventh-century codices that contained the mathematical writings of Gerbert, to whom it has sometimes been attributed. Like Gerbert's *Regulae*, it was copied only in separated and canonically separated script. As was the case for Gerbert's and Abbo's writings, the scribes who transcribed Heriger's were careful to facilitate the reading of numbers through the use of space, the *virga*, the terminal long *j*, and punctuation.

Heriger wrote a treatise on the Eucharist of which the earliest example dates from the middle to late eleventh century. This text, which in one late-eleventh-century or early-twelfth-century codex was also attributed to Gerbert, made important use of dialectic to reconcile divergent views on transubstantiation.[96] This treatise, like the one on the abacus, circulated exclusively in separated manuscripts.[97] Heriger's *Vita Usmari metrica* survives in an eleventh-century codex from the reformed Abbey of Saint-Vannes in Verdun, where it was copied in separated script.[98]

Heriger was also the author of a *Vita sancti Remacli*, a life of the patron saint of the Abbey of Stavelot. This text was intended to supercede a Merovingian *Vita*, of which the oldest surviving copy was transcribed at the Abbey of Stavelot in the tenth century in hierarchical word blocks.[99] Heriger's *Vita* was far more literate, being constructed out of citations lifted from classical texts that notably included two elements of the *Logica vetus*, Boethius's *In Topica Ciceronis* and Pseudo-Apuleius's *De interpretatione*.[100] Robert Babcock has suggested that Heriger chose these citations by flipping back and forth in a now lost Lobbes codex that contained both these works, a task that would have been facilitated by the word separation regularly present in the *Logica vetus* when it was disseminated in Germany, Lorraine, and France in the late tenth and eleventh centuries.[101] The oldest copy of Heriger's *Vita*, Vat. Reg. lat. 615, dating from the late tenth century, has been judged by Babcock to have been copied under Heriger's direction.[102] It was written in separated script marred only by inconsistent interword space and rare interword ligatures.[103] However, no terminal forms or monolexic abbreviations were employed, and an interpunct in lieu of space, possibly by the original hand, was the only *prosodia*. Punctuation was by the Carolingian system of elevated points. Proper names were not distinguished from common nouns. Slightly later, the hagiographical fragment *Tres furunt sorores . . .*

was added on a blank leaf, with separation exceeding 4 times the unity of space, and with terminal forms that included the *-m*, *-us*, and the elevated round *s*. Monolexic abbreviations consisted of superscripts, and proper names were denoted by initial capitals and by all capitals. The other surviving eleventh-century codices of this text were all separated.[104] A *florilegium*, a collection of extracts drawn from classical authors, contained in Munich, Staatsbibliothek Clm. 6292 appears to be the source of Heriger's classical citations in his *Vita sancti Remacli*, except those drawn from the *Logica vetus*. This work, now judged to be a composition of Heriger's, was copied in separated script between 1006 and 1039 for Egbert, bishop of Freising.[105]

Some scholars have attributed another *florilegium* on the Holy Eucharist to Heriger. The oldest copy survives in a tenth-century manuscript, Ghent, Univ. Lib. 909, transcribed in hierarchical word blocks exceeding fifteen characters in maximum length.[106] However, Bernhard Bischoff has assigned the script of this codex to the early tenth century, making an attribution to Heriger untenable, and the evidence of the unseparated writing tends to confirm that Heriger could not have been its author. In contrast, two marginal annotations on folios 36v and 42v that are currently accepted as Heriger's autograph additions were indeed written in separated script.[107]

Chapter 9

The Proliferation of Word Separation in the Eleventh Century

~~~~~

Fulbert of Chartres

In the generation after Gerbert, Abbo, and Heriger, it was Fulbert of Chartres (d. 1028) who played the most prominent role in continuing the dissemination of separated handwriting in France. According to two eleventh-century chronicles, Fulbert had studied under Gerbert's direction at Reims, and although the earliest of these sources was composed over twenty years after Fulbert's death, there is no reason to dispute an assertion that concords well with Fulbert's intellectual interests.[1] Chartres, BM 100, a codex destroyed under the German occupation during World War II of which no photographs survive, was copied during Fulbert's lifetime and contained extracts drawn from the *Logica vetus*, as well as what was probably the oldest known transcription of Gerbert's *De rationale et ratione uti*.[2] Fulbert's *Tractatus contra Iudeos* indicates an interest in Aristotelian logic, which both Gerbert and Abbo had rekindled.[3] Fulbert's familiarity with the corpus of translated Arabic writings known to Gerbert's circle and his interest in Arabic science are revealed in his poems and *opuscula*, or minor works, which list the Arabic names of the stars and use the terminology of the astrolabe.[4] Fulbert's students, Hartwic, who also studied at Reims, and Ragimbold of Cologne, were familiar with Arabic science. Fulbert, like Gerbert, won respect for his geometrical calculations, and he wrote mnemonic verses for learning the Insular signs of the duodecimal fractions perfected earlier by Abbo.[5] This poem was transcribed in Paris, BN lat. 13955, where it is associated with Gerbert's writings.[6]

Fulbert's poems, letters, and the *Tractatus contra Iudeos* were disseminated in the eleventh and twelfth centuries in a group of codices that, in effect, constituted a manuscript edition of his *opera omnia* (excluding the sermons on the Virgin) prepared by his two secretaries, Hildegar and Sigo.[7] The earliest of these manuscripts, Paris, BN lat. 14167, was copied at the Benedictine Abbey of Saint-Père of Chartres in close proximity to Fulbert's cathedral school, reasonably within a generation of Fulbert's death in 1028 and probably soon after 1030.[8] The manuscript, written by several hands, was entirely in separated script, with some portions approaching canonical separation.[9] The names Fulbertus and especially Robertus were often abbreviated by a capital initial set off by points, a practice current in the epistolary manuscripts of Gerbert and Abbo.[10] Fulbert's mnemonic poem on fractions, *De libra et partibus eius*, was transcribed twice within the codex. In each transcription, the fractions were written out with the verse, but on folio 38v, some of their emblematic signs were written in the margin, and on folio 63, the same signs were written interlinearly. Another of Fulbert's mnemonic poems, *De signis et mensibus et diebus et horis compendium computi*, was accompanied by a marginal tabular recapitulation of the verbal text.[11] Both poems reflect an interest in alternate modes of graphic representation as aids to comprehension and memory reminiscent of Abbo of Fleury's interlinear mode of representing syllogisms in the revised recension of his *De propositionibus*.

Paris, BN lat. 14167 is also significant for its use of Anglo-Saxon *prosodiae*. At least one of the scribes used the split-line form of the *trait d'union* that had also been present in the corpus of Abbo. On folio 26, the scribe used the successor note to the *diastole* to correct an erroneous transcription *docitsuo* to *docit suo*. This use of the successor note to the *diastole* marks its second earliest datable appearance in a Continental manuscript. Traces of Arabic influence on the evolution of word separation are also present in this codex, notably in the list of Arabic names for the stars (folio 65) and in the fragment of the last quire containing various minor works and the third chapter of the *Tractatus contra Iudeos*. Having been separated from the remainder of the original codex at an unknown date, this fragment was bound by Nicolas le Fèvre into a late-sixteenth-century composite book of fragments and transcriptions, now Paris, BN lat. 2872, ff. 25–28v. In this section, entirely written in separated script, the scribe included an Arabic-Latin glossary of terms for the astrolabe in which the Arabic terms were transliterated in Latin letters with full word separation. The scribe used the acute accent mark as an aid in transcribing the Arabic, following Insular precedent for the transcription of

Hebrew and Greek. When the language transcribed was more obscure, graphic aids to render the text less ambiguous were more in evidence.

Paris, BN lat. 2872, ff. 1–24v, a substantial fragment of a second copy of Fulbert's collected *opera*, was written in a script similar to but slightly more consistent in its separation than lat. 14167.[12] It was written entirely by one scribe, who made interword space equivalent to 2 times the unity of space. The scribe placed space after many monosyllabic prepositions and on some leaves came close to achieving canonical separation. In addition to all the terminal forms present in lat. 14167, the scribe used the long form of *j*, the capital *N*, and especially the capital form *S*.[13] He also used the capital *S* at sentence and chapter endings as a terminal sign equivalent in value to a sign of punctuation. Initial capital forms and suspension abbreviations were used to denote proper names. *Prosodiae* included the acute accenting of the double *ii* to aid in word discrimination and of the monosyllabic interjection *O* as a redundant sign of word separation.[14] The scribe used the *trait d'union* placed at the foot of letters, suggesting a suspended ligature, and he also occasionally employed the suspended *ct* and *e* ligatures as alternate indications of interline word continuation.[15]

Vat. lat. 1783, ff. 97–128v, 137r–37v, and 153–62, a composite book, constitutes a fourth mid-eleventh-century French manuscript of the collected *opera* of Fulbert.[16] In the margins of Fulbert's sermons, the scribe placed schematic tree diagrams of the virtues and the vices. Fulbert's *Sermons on the Virgin* was disseminated in a separate corpus of manuscripts, also copied exclusively in separated writing.[17] For additional examples of word separation in the manuscripts of Fulbert's works copied before 1100, see the Appendix, Table A4.

A manuscript copied at about the time of Fulbert's death gives additional insight into the graphic patterns employed at the school of Chartres in this period. Fulbert's *tumulus*, or funeral leaflet, was prepared by the same secretary Sigo who coprepared the manuscript edition of the *opera*. One of the original copies of the *tumulus*, consisting of verses and images, survives in two leaves bound as folios 33 and 34 of Chartres, BM nouv. acq. 4 (formerly Saint-Etienne, BM 104).[18] The *tumulus* text, written immediately after Fulbert's death, was copied in separated script. The *tumulus* was bound into a martyrologium copied for the cathedral chapter of Notre-Dame of Chartres between 1026 and 1028 and written by a single scribe in separated script.[19] The manuscript's *prosodiae* appear to be by an early and perhaps contemporary emendator. They consisted of split-line *traits d'union*, sometimes displaced well into the right margin, in a manner indicating a broad span of parafoveal vision.[20] Acute accents denoted the vowels in tonic syllables, including letters formed from minim strokes, thus aiding the reader to distinguish words with similar global shapes. The double *ii* was accented.

Fulbert's Students

Hartwic

The manuscripts of Fulbert's students confirm word separation as an aspect of Fulbert's pedagogy. Munich, Staatsbibliothek Clm. 14272, containing works on music, arithmetic, and logic from the library of Saint Emmeram's of Regensburg, was copied in separated script under the direction of the monk Hartwic, Fulbert's student, either at Chartres or at Saint Emmeram's, following Hartwic's return from Chartres.[21] This was the same Hartwic who copied works by Gerbert in Clm. 14735. On folio 6v, the manuscript was decorated with a miniature, labeled "Dominus Fulbertus episcopus," depicting two angels conferring a nimbus on Fulbert.[22] Another codex copied under Hartwic, Munich, Staatsbibliothek Clm. 14436, a collection of texts including Boethius's *In Isagogen Porphyrii*, was written in similarly separated script, replete with schematic tree diagrams.[23]

Prosodiae, especially *traits d'union*, so important in the manuscripts of Fulbert's *opera*, are conspicuously absent in Hartwic's manuscripts, suggesting that he may have left Chartres before their use had become normative in Chartres's word-separated script, an interpretation that is plausible because the presence of added *traits d'union* and accents in the martyrologium of Chartres cathedral suggests that *traits d'union* became current only at the end of Fulbert's lifetime, or after his death. Indeed, the surviving manuscripts suggest that *traits d'union* became standard at Chartres in the middle third of the eleventh century, just when the Fulbert corpus was being disseminated. In the mid-eleventh century, *traits d'union* were common not only in the collected Fulbert manuscripts, but in codices containing isolated works of Fulbert's. For example, in Paris, BN lat. 7202, f. 19, an added marginal gloss on Boethius's *De musica* is attributed to Fulbert and written with a *trait d'union*. *Prosodiae* such as the *trait d'union* were common in the diverse corpus of Fulbert's *Sermons on the Virgin* in early-eleventh-century transcriptions made at Fleury, Fécamp, Jumièges, and Cluny.

Bernard of Angers

A similar progression from script separated by space to script separated by space and *prosodiae* can be seen in the writings of Bernard of Angers. Like Hartwic, Bernard studied at Chartres under Fulbert. After 1010, he composed his *Vita sanctae Fidis*, which he dedicated to Fulbert. The authorial manuscript of this work, today located at the Abbey of Conques, was written in script separated by 2 times the unity of space.[24] Terminal forms included the usual signs for *-orum* and *-tur*. *Prosodiae* included the acute accent to denote the tonic syllable in compound words and in the infinitives of verbs of the second conjugation.[25] The acute accent was also used as a redundant sign of word continuation and to denote monosyllables, notably *re* and the interjection *O*. Other *prosodiae* were *traits d'union* of both the split-line and normal variety, and suspended *e*, *r*, and *g* ligatures. The *ct* ligature was used to enhance word shape.[26]

Berengar of Tours

The change after 1030 in separated script at Chartres toward a more regular use of *prosodiae*, notably the *trait d'union*, is also confirmed by the manuscripts of Berengar of Tours (ca. 1000–1088). The supposed authorial codex of his *Rescriptum contra Lanfrancum*, or *De sacra coena*, dating from the early 1060's, was written in script separated by 2 times the unity of space, with *traits d'union* among its *prosodiae*.[27] The *diastole*, used as an insertion mark under the descending stroke of *q*, resembled the successor to the *diastole*. In the Anglo-Saxon manner, elongated descenders were used for insertions in lieu of the *diastole*.[28] In the mid-eleventh century, the use of the terminal capital *S* within the line as a redundant sign of separation became extremely popular, and it was conspicuously present in this codex, as well as in eleventh-century manuscripts of Berengar's correspondence.[29] The scribe used the terminal long *j* and the *v* form to clarify numbers. Berengar's *Confession of 1078* was added in the eleventh century on originally blank leaves in Paris, BN lat. 2076, at Montier-en-Der, and in lat. 8922 at Echternach, in canonically separated script. Berengar's prose was permeated with phrases drawn from the *Logica vetus*.

Other Students

Adelman of Liège (d. 1061), bishop of Brecia, also composed texts that circulated exclusively in separated script containing *traits d'union*.[30] The drawings and script of the principal text in the correspondence of Ragimbold of Cologne with Ralph of Liège, preserved in folios 1 through 14v of a Fleury codex, Paris, BN lat. 6401, are also celebrated for their Anglo-Saxon affinities.[31] The text was transcribed in script separated by from 2 to 2.67 unities of space. Terminal forms included the capital *S* at line endings and at the end of proper names. Capitals were used to denote proper names, and capital initials preceded and followed by a point were used as suspension abbreviations for proper names. Insular emblematic signs denoted fractions (folio 2) and *virgae* were used to indicate thousands in numerals. Schematic tree diagrams accompanied the text. *Prosodiae* included *traits d'union*. A mixture of green, blue, and red initials enhanced the mnemonic quality of each page. Also, before 1063, Arnoul of Chartres composed an office of Saint Evraul transcribed in Rouen, BM 1386 (U.158) with word separation that was accompanied by alphabetical pitch notation.[32] The autograph writing of Olbert (d. 1048), a student of both Heriger's and Fulbert's who will receive further attention later, also was separated with *traits d'union*. In addition, Franco of Liège, who studied with Wazo of Liège, another of Fulbert's students, composed the *De quadratura circuli* that circulated in separated script.[33]

Gerbert's Students in the Eleventh Century

Gerbert's students also extended the developing tradition of word-separated writing on the Continent in the eleventh century. The writings of Bishop Adalbero of Laon were copied exclusively in separated script.[34] His *Dialogus*, or *Epistula ad Fulconem*, a veritable exposition of the new discipline of dialectic, reveals his contact with Boethius's monographs *De syllogismo hypothetico* and *De syllogismo categorico*, as well as with Aristotle's *De interpretatione*, all components of the *Logica vetus* fundamental to the new educational program molded by Gerbert and Abbo. In Paris, BN NAL 1630, f. 19, column a, a fragment of the *Dialogus* was written in the late tenth or early eleventh century in separated script. The scribe who copied the *Dialogus* in Valenciennes, BM 298, ff. 132–35, in canonical or *fere* canonical script in the early eleventh century used terminal endings, such as the capital *S*, and *prosodiae* that included the *trait d'union* and the suspended *ct* ligature.[35] The acute accent was used in conjunction with a suspended ligature as a sign of interline word continuation.

Gérard I of Florennes, canon of Reims and later bishop of Cambrai (d. 1051), authored the *Gesta episcoporum Cameracensium*, of which the authorial manuscript is preserved in The Hague, Koninklijke Bibliotheek 75F12 (Figure 29).[36] The text from Gerard's own hand was separated by 3 times the unity of space; he made frequent use of the Insular monolexic abbreviation for *vel*. His principal scribe also separated words by about 3 times the unity of space, inserting space after many monosyllabic prepositions. The scribe used the ampersand for the conjunction *et* and as a terminal form. Other terminal forms included the capital *NS* ligature and round *s* occasionally at line endings. Punctuation was by the Carolingian system of elevated points. The hyphen was used to correct erroneous separation; the *trait d'union* was not present. Frequently, the vertical stroke of the *t* protruded above its horizontal cap, distinguishing *t* from *c* and enhancing Bouma shape. This manuscript of the *Gesta episcoporum Camaracensium* is the earliest datable example of this important development, which ultimately served to distinguish the silhouettes of many words.

The *Libellus de vita et miraculis sancti patris nostri Vitoni* of another student of Gerbert's, Richard of Saint-Vannes, the great Benedictine reformer and canon of the Cathedral of Reims, was copied at his reformed abbey in word-separated script. Richard will be discussed at length in the next chapter. The only Gerbert student who appears to be closely linked to aerated rather than separated writing was Ingon (d. 1025), successively abbot of Saint-Martin of Massay (1002), Saint-Germain-des-Prés (1004), and Saint-Pierre-le-Vif of Sens. The three abbeys under Ingon's direction did not accept word separation until after his tenure.[37] Ingon left no corpus of writings, and his only surviving brief text was set down by Odoranus of Sens in ca. 1045, in aerated script.

Heriger's Students

Adalbold of Utrecht

Adalbold, cleric at Liège and later archbishop of Utrecht (d. 1026), studied under Heriger at Lobbes, which, like Fleury and Chartres in northern France, had become in the early decades of the eleventh century

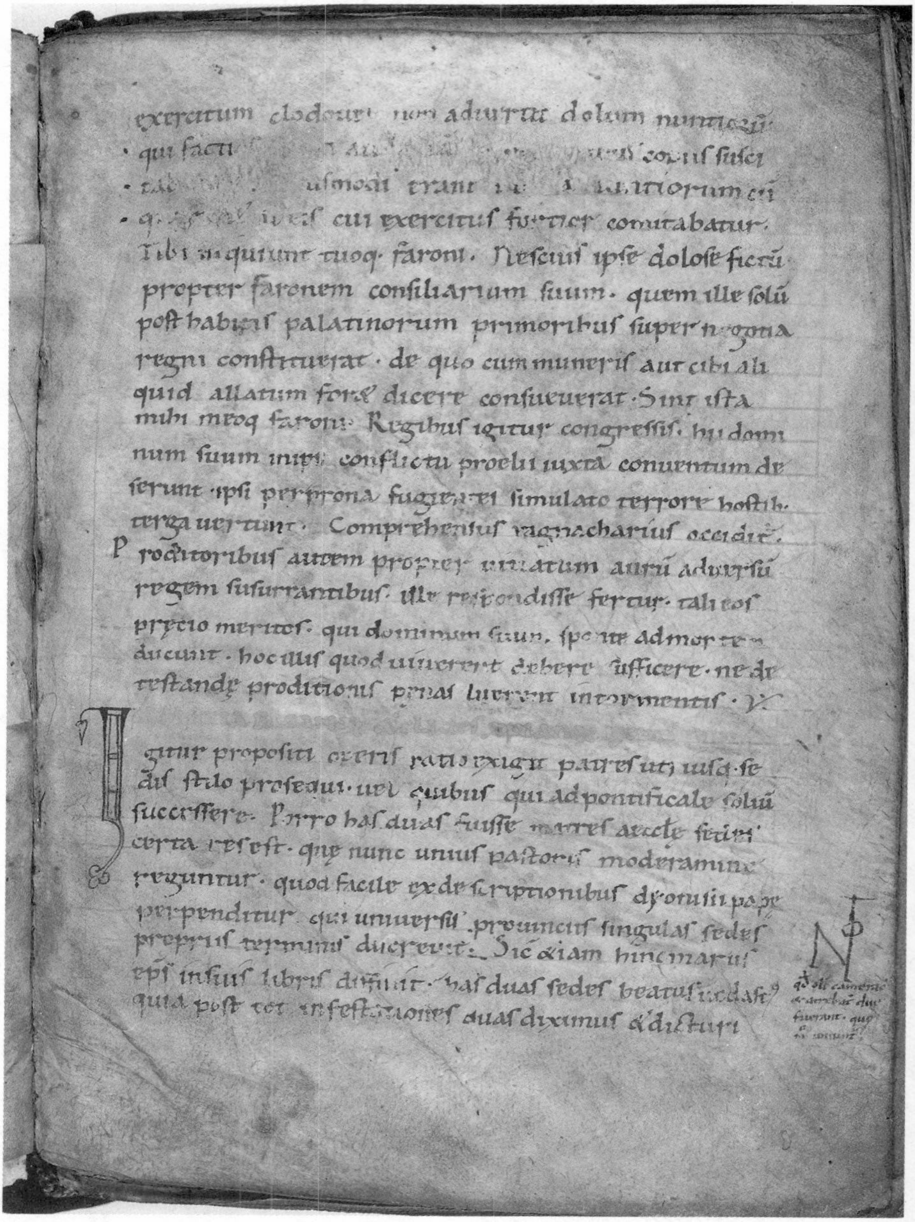

Figure 29. The authorial copy of Gérard I of Florennes's *Gesta episcoporum Cameracensium*. The Hague, Koninklijke Bibliotheek 75F12, f. 4 recto; reproduced by permission.

a center where scholars were taught to employ separated script. Adalbold was associated with Berno of Reichenau, a Benedictine monk who began his career at Fleury at the time of Abbo and corresponded with Gerbert.[38] The earliest copy of Adalbold's commentary on Boethius's *De consolatione philosophiae*, Munich, Staatsbibliothek Clm. 14836, ff. 10–16, written at Saint Emmeram's of Regensburg in the mid-eleventh century, was transcribed in separated script with interword space equivalent to from 1.67 to 3 times the unity of space and with space inserted after monosyllabic prepositions.[39] The scribe's terminal forms included the elevated round *s* and the capital *US* ligature. *Prosodiae* included the successor mark note to the *diastole*, used by the scribe to correct the erroneous omission of space after a monosyllabic preposition. Also present were suspended ligatures attached to the letters *e* and *r*, closely resembling *traits d'union* and indicating word continuation. The same codex contained two transcriptions of Adalbold's letter to Gerbert as Pope Sylvester II, in which he explained how to calculate the volume of a sphere. Both were written in separated script. An even earlier copy of this text on folio 182 of Munich, Staatsbibliothek Clm. 14272 was copied by Hartwic before Fulbert's death, also in separated script. The long *j* was used as a terminal form in both numbers and words. The *v* form was used for numbers and emblematic symbols for fractions. In addition, this important mathematical text was transcribed in separated codices in conjunction with other works by Gerbert.[40] Adalbold, who wrote a *Vita Henrici II*, served in the Imperial chancellery when it was using the new separated text format in its diplomas.[41]

Burchard of Worms

A pattern of word separation is also found in the manuscript corpus of a second of Heriger's pupils, Burchard of Worms (d. 1025), a favorite of Otto III and Henry II, who ranks among the premier intellectual figures of the first half of the eleventh century. Between 1008 and 1012, Burchard, as bishop of Worms, assembled the *Libri viginti decretorum*, a compilation of canon law, arranged by subject, of a size, scope, and thoroughgoing intellectual rigor that had only limited precedent in prior centuries.[42] For all Christendom, it represented the equivalent of his *Lex familiae ecclesiae Wormatiensis* of 1023–25, an episcopal decree in which he set forth in a rigorously logical manner the secular prerogatives of the bishop of Worms.[43] Burchard generally favored the prerogatives of the emperor vis-à-vis the Pope, and his work provided a foundation upon which bishops could expand their episcopal authority in the service of imperial dignity.

Prior to Burchard's *Libri viginti decretorum*, the conception of what constituted church law was extremely fragmented, with each abbey or cathedral school tending to view its own cumbersome collection of canons as authoritative. Collation between codices was scarcely feasible, and the possibility of imaginative fabrication was exploited, as the success of Pseudo-Isidore's *Decretals* bears witness.[44] Burchard's *Libri viginti decretorum* was the first standard compilation of canons to achieve wide dissemination and to establish itself as a standard reference work for church law. Before the end of the twelfth century, when the Gregorian reform was at its apogee and its proponents viewed the *Libri viginti decretorum* with some disfavor, every important abbey from England to Naples and from Germany to Spain seems to have had a copy of Burchard's compilation. Of the more than seventy-four codices of the *Libri viginti decretorum* that are known to be extant and the twenty-four recorded in library catalogues that are now lost, only four date from as late as the thirteenth century.

One reason for the work's popularity was that it was far easier for the average reader to consult than the earlier collections of canon law. Its table of principal sources and its breadth, combined with a rational organization of subject matter, made it ideal for the reader unable or unwilling to rely on the extensive use of memory. A general summary outlined the logical division into twenty books, and each book was prefaced with a detailed table of contents. These features, combined with marginal finding notes and word separation, made the *Libri viginti decretorum* an ideal book for reference consultation. It formed the first in a chain of increasingly more comprehensive collections of papal decrees consciously intended to serve as standard reference works, culminating in the first half of the twelfth century in Gratian's *Concordia discordantium canonum*.

Word separation was prevalent in the early codices of the *Libri viginti decretorum*.[45] Freiburg im Breisgau, Universitätsbibliothek 7, written before 1034 for Eberhard, later bishop of Constance from 1034 to 1046, was transcribed by several scribes in separated and canonically separated script.[46] Suspended ligatures and *traits d'union*, placed in the margin, confirm Anglo-Saxon influence in the transcription of this codex. The *diastole* was used to correct errors of spacing. All but one of the northern European copies of Burchard were in separated script. Only at Echternach, a center that accepted the new modes of writing with peculiar inconsistency, was the *Libri viginti decretorum* copied partially in aerated script. Paris, BN lat. 8922, was copied between 1051 and 1081 for Abbot Regimbert in handwriting that curiously varied between hierarchical word blocks exceeding twenty characters in length (folio 2) and canonical separation.[47]

Word separation played a direct role in the unprecedented, rapid, and wide dissemination of Burchard's *Libri viginti decretorum*. The older compilations of canon law germane to a specific diocese or abbey, like all works disseminated in the medium of hierarchical word blocks, before being copied had first to be read with at least a minimal amount of understanding to ensure a correct distinction between the use of major and minor spaces. In contrast, Burchard's word-separated text could be copied visually and rapidly by scribes unburdened by the task of inserting space, since the separation of words created an invariable pattern of intratextual space. Each freestanding word gave the scribe a target whose shape could be produced semi-automatically, without the burdensome task of word verification. The textual tradition of the *Libri viginti decretorum* suggests a systematic organization of copying, with scribes working from sections resembling the *peciae* of the later Middle Ages, model books that were rented in parts by the university scribes.[48] Direct visual contact between the scribe and the exemplar is reflected in the oblong, two-column page format in which the work invariably circulated. The characteristic *B* initial of the first leaf of most copies of the *Libri viginti decretorum* gave the book a standardized appearance not evident in manuscripts of earlier texts disseminated in aerated script.[49] The scribes of Burchard's manuscripts also tended to use terminal forms in the same positions in the text and to employ the *trait d'union*. This new similitude in the page and text format of Burchard's widely disseminated work can most readily be explained by the enhanced role of word images in the neurophysiological task of copying separated script, for which the apposite cognitive skills came increasingly to resemble those of a modern typist, rather than those of an ordinary reader.

Olbert of Gembloux

For Burchard, we can penetrate beyond the evidence of early manuscript copies of his work. Although we do not have Burchard's authorial manuscript, we know from the *Vita* composed directly after his death that a number of collaborators aided him in compiling the *Libri*. One

was Olbert, the future abbot of Gembloux, whom Burchard brought
from Lobbes to assist in the redaction of the *Libri viginti decretorum*.[50] In
addition to having studied and taught at Lobbes under the direction of
Heriger, he, like Adalbold and Wazo, had also studied under Fulbert. As
abbot at Gembloux between 1025 and 1040, Olbert copied Brussels, BR
5500–03, a large manuscript containing Martin of Braga's *Liber de quattuor virtutibus* in addition to Jerome's *Commentarii in Esaiam*.[51] Olbert's
script, while marred by occasional run-ons, was in general separated
with interword space equivalent to 2 times the unity of space.[52] Terminal forms included the ampersand, the capital *S*, and the capital *NT*
ligature, usually reserved for line endings. *Prosodiae*, either by Olbert or
by an early emendator of the abbey, included suspended ligatures, *traits
d'union*, usually of the split-line form, the successor note to the *diastole*,
and the acute accent to denote monosyllables, especially at line endings.
Olbert used the tripoint Insular emblematic terminal sign of punctuation
in the rubrics only, but he employed the Carolingian system of elevated
points in conjunction with augmented space and capitalization to set off
sentences within the text.

Sigebert of Gembloux

By the mid-eleventh century, word separation was standard and ubiquitous. Sigebert of Gembloux (ca. 1030–1112), whose historical writings
form an important source for reconstructing Burchard's career, was a
student of Olbert's. His autograph working notes for the *Gesta abbatum Gemblacensium*, datable to before 1076, were written in separated
script.[53] These notes and his other drafts are particularly instructive in
that they confirm that the separation of words and the related graphic
practices that accompanied the spread of the new learning in Europe
north of the Alps in the eleventh century were not simply an artificial aid
to the reader, added as a refinement to a text at the final stage of its confection for publication, but rather an integral part of writing, employed
even in drafts prepared in the process of composition. Sigebert's notes
for the *Gesta*, although hastily written and totally devoid of calligraphic
pretension, were separated with interword space regularly varying from
1.5 to 2 times the unity of space. Where interword space was reduced,
terminal forms usually compensated for the lack and maintained interword boundaries. Syllabic space was usually suppressed or breached by
a ligature, except in the instance of prepositional prefixes to compound
words. Terminal forms included the ampersand, which was also used, set

off by space, as a monolexic abbreviation for the conjunction *et*.[54] Proper names were denoted with initial capitals and abbreviated in suspension by a capital and a point. Sigebert punctuated his Roman numerals into decimal distinctions by space and points.

Sigebert's working notes survived because they were written in blank leaves of books in the Gembloux library, most of them copied at the time of Abbot Olbert. They appear to be the vestiges of a larger corpus of documentation from which Sigebert fabricated the *Gesta* by a process of note taking and compilation. Sigebert's mode of autograph composition resembled the techniques employed a generation later by Bernard Itier, in the Abbey of Saint-Martial. Sigebert's method, clearly similar to that used to compose Burchard's *Libri viginti decretorum*, was clearly facilitated by the separation of words. This technique of processing written information was to become the hallmark of scholastic didactic literature.[55]

Authors of Unseparated Texts

While most of the leading intellectuals of the late tenth and eleventh centuries wrote in separated script, it is important to remember that word separation prior to the middle decades of the eleventh century was still not a ubiquitous practice in western Europe. It was totally missing in the works of a small group of authors in the late tenth century and first half of the eleventh who were interested in neither the renewed Aristotelian logic nor the Arabic sciences. The works of these authors continued the Carolingian culture of the previous three centuries, both in form and in substance. Belying the thesis that absence of word separation was a sign of problematic illiteracy, these authors of unseparated texts in the late tenth and eleventh centuries employed a Latinity that by classical standards was in no way inferior to that of the authors who observed word separation. The Italian Gunzo of Novare in the late tenth century wrote Latin prose of high quality and apologized profusely for one instance when he erred in using the ablative instead of the accusative case.[56] Gunzo's *Epistula ad Augienses*, composed in 965, survived in three manuscripts[57] only one of which, Bodmer 80, was copied prior to the end of the tenth century.[58] The text in this codex was written in hierarchical word blocks of a maximum length of fewer than fifteen characters, without trace of the use of capitals for proper names and with only the rudimentary presence of terminal forms.[59]

The poet and grammarian Ratherius, bishop of Verona (d. 974), always wrote in hierarchical word blocks of more than fifteen characters in length, and the earliest scribal copies of his works were also written in aerated script.[60] Only in manuscripts copied at Lobbes after Ratherius's death was word separation introduced into his compositions.[61] The works of the early Cluny abbots, including Odon, abbot from 927 to 942, were initially written and diffused in manuscripts aerated by hierarchical word blocks.[62] Bamberg, Staatsbibliothek Bibl. 126 (B.I.8), the copy of Sucherius's *In Epistulas S. Pauli commentarius ex libris S. Augustini collectus* that Abbot Odilon prepared for the imperial library of Emperor Henry II (1002–24), was written in hierarchical word blocks.[63] Adémar of Chabannes (d. 1034), of the Abbey of Saint-Martial, set down his *Chronicon*, of which the autograph codex is Paris, BN lat. 5943A, in hierarchical word blocks of more than fifteen characters in length, and his consistent use of this format is confirmed by a large corpus of autograph manuscripts.[64] Adémar was most likely cognizant of the new text format, for he and his assistants copied a text by Abbo of Fleury of which the exemplar was probably separated.[65] Odorannus of Sens's *Opera omnia*, Vat. Reg. lat. 577, also was compiled in 1045 in hierarchical word blocks.[66]

Robert the Pious and French Royal Charters

All the authors whose writings have thus far been examined for evidence of word separation were clerics. However, a tradition dating back to Robert the Pious's first biographer and chaplain, Helgaud of Fleury, asserts that the king studied under Gerbert before ascending to the throne.[67] Such an education for Robert is plausible, for before the death of his elder brother, Robert was destined for an ecclesiastical career. Throughout his reign, from 996 to 1031, Robert was close to Gerbert's circle. With his father, he staunchly defended Gerbert's election as archbishop of Reims, and Gerbert numbered the king among his correspondents.[68] Abbo dedicated his *Apologia* to Robert, and he, too, corresponded with the king.[69] Fulbert also exchanged correspondence with Robert.[70] Adalbero of Laon dedicated his celebrated poem to his royal master. Thus, by education, political contacts, and intellectual patronage, Robert was an intimate of the leading thinkers of his age whose writings were circulating in word-separated script.

We might speculate, then, whether word separation entered French royal documents at the time of King Robert. To this question, no simple response is possible, for two salient reasons. First, medieval charters cannot be dated with the same measure of certainty as manuscript books. In the early and central Middle Ages, manuscript books can be dated by liturgical revisions, dedications, and textual content, all of which are very unlikely to have been falsified. In contrast, charters, although very often containing precisely dated documents, were frequently tainted by either forgery or replacement by copies of genuine documents worn out by use, destroyed by fire, or otherwise innocently lost. Production of replacements was facilitated by the fact that people in the Middle Ages did not share the modern idea of a single original. Since there was no Xerox machine, it was normal practice to produce several originals, often varying slightly, to aid the record keeping of the parties to whom the documents pertained. In instances where the span of time between the date of an original and a replacement copy is relatively great, an array of paleographic and diplomatic techniques afford ample possibility for detection of the substitution. But when the substituted copy was prepared within a quarter century of an original act, it is often difficult to detect. Because of the extensive number of such copies among the frequently consulted royal charters, the dating of the beginning of word separation in this genre is a most difficult task, for it must by necessity be based on documents that have been judged original without regard to the presence or absence of word separation.

A second major difficulty in determining the advent of word separation in royal documents is that it is by no means clear that a single staff of royal scribes accompanied the sovereign on his peregrinations. On the contrary, it is probable that the king made use of the monastic or other ecclesiastical scribes who were conveniently available, so that the work of the chancellery was divided between the king's own men and local clerics. The question of who wrote eleventh-century French royal charters has yet to be addressed by modern scholars.[71] However, Françoise Gasparri's important paleographic studies of twelfth-century French royal documents indicate that in the reign of Louis VII (1137–80), the royal chancellery was still making heavy use of monastic scribes, and it seems likely that the first Capetians delegated the writing of charters in a similar manner.[72]

Before the Capetians, aeration in hierarchical word blocks was the normal mode of transcribing French royal documents of the Carolingian dynasty, and many diplomas written in separated script have been recognized as copies or rejected as fraudulent for other reasons.[73] However, because charters were supposed to be legible even to semiliterate laymen, and perhaps because they were by their nature documents of reference, word blocks in Carolingian charters tend to be shorter than those in contemporary books and to have a high percentage of freestanding words.[74] The intensity of the aeration in royal charters appears relatively enhanced after the succession of Hugh Capet as de facto ruler of France, but despite the influence of both Gerbert and presumably Adalbero of Laon, who served as King Lothaire's chancellor, none of Hugh's original charters, either as master of the palace or as king, survive in separated script.

Whenever the transition from aerated to separated script occurred in these documents, we can say with some certainty that a few early Capetian charters display interesting elements of the new patterns of clarity in writing. A charter from Hugh on behalf of the monks of Jumièges dating from 984, before his usurpation of the crown, was written in hierarchical word blocks of more than fifteen characters in length, but with the terminal capital *S* used to denote word endings falling at line endings, sentence endings, and elsewhere within the text.[75] A charter of a royal act of 993 in which Hugh at Paris confirmed the customs of Fleury at the request of Abbo (Archives du Loiret, fonds de Saint-Benoît) was written in hierarchical word blocks generally fewer than fifteen characters in length.[76] In it, the name of Robertus was denoted by an initial capital, and *Sanctae Martae* was set off by space and a terminal *e* cedilla. However, a charter dated June 4, 988, in which Hugh confirmed the privileges of immunity of Sainte-Colombe of Sens was written in long word blocks, without any trace of the influence of new format.[77]

For the reign of Robert the Pious (996–1031), the evidence becomes equivocal. Robert's diploma confirming the privileges of the canons of Sainte-Geneviève in about 1010 was written in hierarchical word blocks with a maximum length of fewer than fifteen characters.[78] The body of the text incorporated many terminal signs (restricted to the end of words) including those for -*m*, -*tur*, -*orum*, and the capital *NT* ligature.[79] The copy of Robert's confirmation of the privileges of the Abbey of Saint-Bénigne of Dijon, dated January 25, 1015, but copied in 1031, was written in word blocks shorter than twenty characters in length.[80] The use of the terminal capital *S* and terminal ampersand was the only sign of contact with the new patterns of writing.

In contrast, the copy of King Robert's act confirming the properties of Saint-Bénigne, dated August 25, 1005, was written in script separated by 2 times the unity of space, with terminal forms that included the long *j* in numerals; proper names were denoted by capitals.[81] The king's diploma confirming an act of September 23, 1030, on behalf of Saint-

Hippolyte of Combertault in Argilly (Burgundy) was written in separated script, with the *diastole* used to insert an omitted word.[82] A royal charter of 1006 or 1014, made at the Abbey of Chelles, in a faubourg of Orléans, was written in generally separated script,[83] and another, datable to 1006–16, was again written in separated script.[84] In 1027, King Robert, at the request of Guillaume, abbot of Jumièges, obliged Albert, seigneur de Creil, to return to the monks a *terre* near Montataire.[85] This document was written in canonically separated script, with interword space equivalent to from 2 to 3 times the unity of space.[86] Some proper names were capitalized. *Prosodiae* included *traits d'union*, the acute accent as a redundant sign for the recognition of the monosyllable *re*, and the use of accents to denote the double *ii*. Other royal charters dating from between 1025 and 1030 were written in separated script.[87] However, two charters of 1028 (Chelles) and 1030 were still written in word blocks.[88]

This problematic array of spacing patterns is somewhat less surprising when account is taken of the total lack of paleographic homogeneity within the received corpus of the original charters of Robert's reign. Substitution of replacement copies may explain some of the variety in spacing, letter forms, and parchment. If the early Capetians used conveniently located monastic scribes, as is likely, the fact that important Benedictine houses near Orléans and in Normandy accepted word separation earlier in Robert's reign than did the Cluniac houses of Burgundy may partially account for the inconsistent pattern of word separation in Robert's charters. Thus, it is not clear that Gerbert had any direct influence through the king's person on the preparation of word-separated French royal acts.

With the earliest surviving original charter of King Henry I (1031–60), the separation of words was definitively established. Henry's original charter confirming the privileges of the canons of Sainte-Geneviève, which may date from as early as 1031, was written in separated script and contained *traits d'union*.[89] His act of May 23, 1048, made at Senlis, was written in separated script, with space often occurring after monosyllabic prepositions and with interword space equivalent to 4.67 times the unity of space.[90] The scribe's terminal forms included the capital *S*, and the *st* and *ct* ligatures as signs of verbal unity were present. He denoted proper names with capitals. Henry's confirmation of the privileges of the monks of Saint-Germain-des-Fossés, given between 1054 and 1058, was written with interword space 3 times the unity of space; *prosodiae* included three *traits d'union*.[91]

Otto III and German Imperial Documents

Gerbert's closest ties were with the kings of Germany. He was first protected by Otto I, and he tutored his sons, Otto II (973–83) and Otto III (983–1002). We have already noted the table of philosophy that Gerbert used to instruct Otto III. Imperial charters, unlike contemporary French royal documents, form a homogeneous paleographic corpus produced by an organized chancellery and scriptorium. Otto I's confirmation of the privileges of the churches of Rome, dated 961, was written in hierarchical word blocks.[92] However, Otto II's illuminated marriage charter, dated 972, was written in script that was separated by 2 times the unity of space.[93] The scribe used the acute accent to denote the adverb *eo*. After 972, Imperial charters were regularly written in word-separated format, but the use of terminal forms and *prosodiae*, particularly the *trait d'union*, trailed well behind their use in documents produced in France.[94]

The advancement of word separation can also be traced in the books of the Imperial library. Otto III had inherited from his father a Psalter, Bamberg, Staatsbibliothek Bibl. 44 (A.I.14), copied at Saint Gall in separated script,[95] and he himself commissioned the monks of Reichenau to copy a word-separated Gospel book that is now part of the treasures of the cathedral of Aachen. Reichenau manuscripts from this period onward were all written in separated script.[96] A collection of canons, Bamberg, Staatsbibliothek Can. 1 (P.III.20), was inscribed with verses by Otto's chancellor, Leo of Vercelli, in about 998–99, in separated script.[97] Richer's *Historia francorum*, a gift of Gerbert to the emperor, was separated (see Figure 26, p. 148), as were the autograph annotations by Johannes Scottus in a volume that also came from Gerbert.[98] Word separation may also have come to the Imperial court via the now lost presentation copy of Abbo of Fleury's poem dedicated to Otto III. Additional books copied for Otto III's successor, Henry II, were written at Seon and Reichenau in separated script.[99] However, the codices produced for Henry II at Echternach were aerated, and not separated.

Chapter 10

The Spread of Word Separation from England to the Low Countries and Lorraine

English Benedictine Reform and Caroline Script

In ninth-century England, monasticism was in decline, and even in the great abbeys the rule of Saint Benedict was not observed. The movement of Benedictine reform that germinated at the end of the tenth century in southern England, with its new emphasis on both *lectio divina*, that is, the oral reading of holy texts, and private study, provided a ready channel for the spread of the newly separated Caroline writing of Latin, both in England and on the Continent. Abbo of Fleury personified the renewed contact between reformed French and English abbeys. During his stay at the Abbey of Ramsey, he encountered the great English Benedictine reformer Dunstan. The books produced for Dunstan and his reformed Benedictine disciples were all written in script separated by space, and all, save one, were written in Caroline letter forms.[1] Dunstan, Abbo, and Oswald, archbishop of York (d. 992), who was trained at Fleury and had invited Abbo to Ramsey, played a major role in the popularization in the British Isles of what I will term the new Caroline *separata*. This was a hybridization of Insular text format and Continental letter forms. In an important eddy within the currents through which the spread of word separation flowed, Caroline *separata* was adopted in England at approximately the same time as English codices were providing the model for the introduction of word separation on the Continent, at Fleury and elsewhere in northern France. This important process produced a new and largely uniform international medium of separated Caroline writing for Benedictine written communication. When Abbo set down Dunstan's narration of the martyrdom of Saint Edmond in the polished prose of the *Passio sancti Edmundi*, he dedicated it to Dunstan.

It was then promptly disseminated in Caroline *separata* to other Benedictine abbeys in the British Isles.[2] Separated Caroline minuscule was also
the medium for the diffusion of Abbo's other works in Britain.[3] However, English scribes copying Abbo's works used the ampersand for the
conjunction *et*, a sign of an emerging Anglo-Saxon tendency to restrict
the tironian symbol to vernacular texts (written in Insular script), where
the sign as an ideograph stood for "and."

The history of the early-eleventh-century additions made at an unknown center, probably in northern or eastern France, to Paris, BN lat.
943, the *Sherborne Pontifical*, offers one of the most dramatic examples
of both the genesis and migration to the Continent of English Caroline
separata.[4] The original liturgical codex, written in separated Anglo-Saxon
hybrida, including a copy of a letter from Pope John XIV (983–84) to
Dunstan (d. 988), was transcribed for Wulfsin or Wulfsige, bishop of
Sherborne from 993 to 1002, a disciple of Dunstan's, who introduced
Dunstan's monastic reforms to Sherborne, where he transformed the
cathedral chapter into a Benedictine monastery.[5] Latin and Anglo-Saxon
texts were added to the codex in the early eleventh century while the Pontifical was still at Sherborne, where the codex remained until ca. 1012.[6]

The original codex exemplified the highest standard of late-tenth-
century Anglo-Saxon techniques for enhancing legibility, including separation by space, the acute accent, and terminal forms. Its Anglo-Saxon
script was separated by space equivalent to 2 times the unity of space,
with intersyllabic space largely suppressed and with space after monosyllabic prepositions frequently present. The monosyllables *si*, *te*, *hic*, *de*, *sic*,
re, *ne*, and *ac* were often marked with the acute accent, either in lieu of
space or as a redundant sign of it. In addition, the acute accent was used
as an alternative to the *trait d'union* as a sign of word continuation at line
endings and to denote the tonic syllable in long words, most often in the
presence of letters formed from minim strokes. Other uses of the acute
accent included the designation of Hebrew names and the terminal *i*,
double *ii*, and dative and ablative plural *-is*. The scribe used both the
usual and split-line form of *trait d'union*, and he employed suspended
ligatures to signal interline word continuation. The interlinear *dasia* also
signaled word boundaries. Monolexic abbreviations included the Insular
symbol for *autem*. Proper names were written with initial capitals.

The process of hybridization of Insular spacing and Continental letter forms began while the codex was still at Sherborne. On folios 2 and
3, the letter of Aelfric, the eminent Benedictine grammarian, to Wolf-

sin, like the other surviving copies of Aelfric's Latin compositions, was transcribed in the Caroline *separata* favored by Dunstan's Benedictine disciples.[7] Aelfric's text was copied with interword space equivalent to the unity of space and with *prosodiae* that included both the split-line *trait d'union* and the acute accent, used in lieu of the *trait d'union*. Terminal forms included the capital *S* and the capital *NT* ligature.

A purely Continental portion, a library catalogue once thought to be that of Notre Dame of Paris, was added to the manuscript when the book was brought across the Channel after ca. 1012.[8] The catalogue itself was written in separated Caroline script with interword space equivalent to 2 times the unity of space. *Prosodiae* included split-line *traits d'union* and acute accents to denote the double *ii*. Initial letters of proper names and titles were capitalized. The contents of this catalogue are of special interest, for they reflect an emphasis on logic and science. The first section, enumerating 106 volumes of *divinorum librum*, included as item 60 (in the edition of De Bruyne), a work possibly by Abbo of Fleury.[9] The second section consisted of elements of the *Logica vetus* (item nos. 125, 127–29, 135, 136–38, and 147) including Boethius's *De topicis differentiis*, one of the monographs rediscovered by Gerbert and Abbo. The library contained as well books by the classical authors taught by Gerbert and various books on mathematics, such as Boethius's *De arithmetica* and Bernelinus's *Liber abaci*. Another title was the *Liber Helperici artis calculatoriae*, a text that Abbo reedited at Fleury and that was fundamental for the revision of the Christian calendar undertaken by Abbo, Heriger, and Garland. As an artifact, the *Sherborne Pontifical* epitomized the three driving forces that spread word separation in northern France. The first two we already have examined: Anglo-Saxon scribal influence and the new learning based on Arabic texts. It is now time to examine the third, Benedictine reform, via a survey of the reformed abbeys.

The Reformed Abbeys

Saint-Vannes of Verdun

On the Continent, word separation was rapidly accepted by reformed Benedictine monasteries, beginning with Saint-Vannes of Verdun. Throughout the tenth century, texts had been written at Verdun in hierarchical word blocks similar to those encountered at Reims before Gerbert and at Fleury before Abbo.[10] In these books, terminal forms and monolexic abbreviations were rare. However, by the end of the tenth century, there was renewed Insular influence at Saint-Vannes with the election as abbot of the Irish monastic reformer Firgen (d. 1005), active at Metz, who installed seven Irish monks.[11] The first example of a separated text at Verdun dates from 1004, when the monk Rudolph prepared for Bishop Haymon, who had studied with Notker of Liège, a word-separated copy of the *Collectio Anselmo dedicata*, Paris, BN lat. 15393.[12]

The leading figure of Benedictine reform on the Continent was Richard of Saint-Vannes (d. 1046), who, as we have seen, was a student of Gerbert's. As abbot of Saint-Vannes from 1004 until his death, Richard gave shelter to Simeon of Syracuse, a Byzantine monk learned in two languages with word-separated graphic traditions, Arabic and Syriac.[13] Richard's own literary output was modest and, in contrast to that of his master, entirely hagiographic. He authored a life of Rouin,[14] an early Irish saint, of which no early manuscript survives, and a *Libellus de vita et miraculis sancti patris nostri Vitoni*,[15] of which Verdun, BM 2, ff. 1–42 is a copy executed in separated script at the Abbey of Saint-Vannes while Richard was abbot.[16] On folio 15v, the scribe used a split-line *trait d'union*. Richard of Saint-Vannes owed his promotion as abbot of Saint-Vannes to Haymon, bishop of Verdun, who himself may have been exposed to Gerbert's new learning at Liège.[17] In contrast to his contemporary Odilon, abbot of Cluny, Richard endorsed the new learning of Gerbert and the reading of classical authors.[18]

All the manuscripts datable to Richard's abbacy at Saint-Vannes were written in separated script, with many incorporating Anglo-Saxon *prosodiae*. Richard's own *Life of Saint Vannes* employed the *trait d'union*. Gregory the Great's *Expositio in Canticum canticorum* and Isidore's *Commentum in Canticum canticorum*, respectively contained on folios 103 through 118 and 148 through 149 of Verdun, BM 2, were written in separated script for Richard early in his abbacy.[19] However, the scribe's colophon in verse on the final leaf was written in word blocks. Here, the distinction between prose and verse text format suggests that the scribe may have judged that where the constraints of rhythmic patterns aided the reader to enhance his comprehension (or as we would say, his eye-voice span), the addition of interword space was not necessary.[20] The scribe Rothardus wrote three manuscripts now preserved in the Bibliothèque Municipale of Verdun, two for the Abbey of Saint-Vannes and one for the Abbey of Saint-Pierre of Lobbes, which had close ties to Saint-Vannes after 1020, when the reformer Wolbodon, bishop of Liège, chose Richard of Saint-Vannes to serve as its abbot.[21] Rothardus copied

Verdun, BM 50 [22] and 75 [23] for the library of Saint-Vannes in canonically separated script. At the end of the century, Verdun, BM 7, containing the *Regula sancti Benedicti* and a *martyrologium*, adjusted for the abbey's use, was copied in canonically separated script. Intersyllabic space, still present in books copied by Rothardus, was suppressed.[24]

On folio 52 of BM 50, a miniature containing a banderole, an unfurled banner that bears text, exemplifies an important new development brought about by the spread of word separation. This is the mixture of script and image. In ancient Greece and Rome, the intermixture of art and written text was limited. Titles identifying the people depicted were sometimes present in mosaics, paintings, and book illustrations, but they played a role distinct from the visual statement made by the work of art itself. This separation of script from art reflected the differences between the visual processes required for the perception of art and the aural skills necessary for decoding text written in *scriptura continua*.[25] Each mode of perception required its own discrete act of concentration, obliging the individual viewing an art object to alternate between the role of perceptor of an image and listener to a text.

The spread of separated writing broke down the perceptual barriers that had isolated these two activities. The first banderoles appeared in the ninth and tenth centuries, in the illuminations for codices, and beginning in northern France during the early eleventh century, banderoles bearing text narrating the scenes depicted in miniature manuscript illustrations, mural paintings, stained glass windows, sculpture, and tapestry became the hallmark of medieval art.[26] Although Gregory the Great's reference to paintings as books for the simple and illiterate was often cited throughout the Middle Ages, and although familiarity with iconographic conventions was widespread, artists frequently deemed the message of the image alone to be unintelligible without lines of text written on banderoles and attached to each protagonist in a narrative picture.[27]

Banderoles first appeared in codices because in the context of the book, an artist could use script with a high degree of confidence that the text and the images would be readily and correctly interpreted. In addition to banderoles, medieval aerated and especially word-separated manuscript illuminations regularly depicted codices and rolls bearing readily legible script.[28] And manuscript miniatures now began to depict readers reading with lips closed, motionless, silently, to themselves.

Saint-Vaast in Arras

From Saint-Vannes, Richard's Benedictine reform, and with it word separation, spread throughout Flanders, northeast France, and Lorraine. In 1009, Baudoin IV, count of Flanders, with the consent of Gerbert's student, Gérard I de Florennes, who had become bishop of Cambrai (and whose own handwriting was separated), forced the Abbey of Saint-Vaast in Arras to accept Richard's reform.[29] In the tenth century, manuscripts copied at Saint-Vaast had been written in aerated script similar to that encountered elsewhere. Typical of these manuscripts was Paris, BN lat. 12052, a sacramentarium, apparently prepared for Ratoldus, abbot of Corbie from 972 to 986, a codex celebrated today for its Franco-Insular decoration.[30] This volume exemplifies the general tenth-century trend of emulating Insular book decoration while rejecting Insular patterns of spacing.

The process of introducing the new mode of separated writing evident in the early-eleventh-century additions to BN lat. 12052 can be observed in Arras, BM 559 (435), the great Bible of Arras, consisting of three volumes copied by a number of scribes from the early to middle eleventh century.[31] In the older portions, the text was in word blocks, with words subsequently separated by *prosodiae*, including vertical strokes, the acute accent on the letter *i* falling in the tonic syllable, and *traits d'union*. The greater portion of the manuscript was separated or canonically separated.

The reforms of the abbey coincided with a greatly augmented quantity of manuscripts, all of which were word-separated. These books include Arras, BM 903 (589),[32] Arras, BM 860 (530),[33] and Cologne, Domsbibliothek 141.[34] In the third quarter of the eleventh century, the scribe Albertus led a team of monks in copying the *Liber miraculorum et officii sancti Vedasti*, Arras, BM 734 (686), in separated script.[35] In Arras, BM 732 (684), containing the works of Pseudo-Jerome and Cassiodorus, separation was accompanied by Insular *prosodiae*, including the acute accent on the interjection *O*.[36] Boulogne-sur-Mer, BM 9, a word-separated Gospel book, shows the influences of the Winchester school of illumination.[37] In the eleventh century, an otherwise unidentified abbot, Siewoldus, made a gift of thirty-three manuscripts, mostly Insular, to the Saint-Vaast library, and the frequency of *prosodiae* in Saint-Vaast manuscripts may also be due to this donation, as well as to the abbey's proximity to the Channel.[38]

Gembloux

We have already seen that Olbert's own writing in Brussels, BR 5500–03 was separated, and from the time of his succession as abbot of Gembloux in 1012, where he introduced the reform of Saint-Vaast, separation was normal in the abbey's scriptorium.[39] The working notes of Sigebert, dating from before 1076, were written here in separated script. The abbey's *Annales*, written before 1079, were in separated script before they were sent to Liège.[40] In the years around 1100, Brussels, BR 5576–604, a collection that included the writings of Sigebert, Lanfranc, Berengar, and Adelman, was transcribed at Gembloux by various hands in separated and canonically separated script.[41]

Saint-Amand

In 1013, Count Boudouin IV of Flanders placed the Abbey of Saint-Amand under Richard's tutelage. Richard remained abbot until 1018, when he named Malbod as his successor.[42] A rich *fond* of tenth- and eleventh-century manuscripts reveals that here, too, the adoption of word separation coincided with the introduction of monastic reform. Valenciennes, BM 510, a mid-tenth-century collection of saints' lives, was copied in hierarchical word blocks exceeding fifteen characters in length.[43] By the end of the tenth century, Saint-Amand's scribes were increasingly reducing the length of word blocks by the use of terminal forms and monolexic abbreviations. Valenciennes, BM 390, a composite book formed in the late tenth and early eleventh centuries, containing Donatus's *De barbarismo*, Arator's *De actibus apostolorum*, Pseudo-Augustine's paraphrase of Aristotle's *Categoriae*, Remi of Auxerre's *Commentum in Bedae De metrica arte et De schismatibus et tropis*, and a leaf of classical epitaphs, bridges the gap from aerated to separated script.[44] The separated portions were written with terminal forms that included the capital *S*. *Prosodiae* included the acute accent for the interjection *O*, and proper names were denoted by initial capitals.[45]

The emergence of word separation at Saint-Amand coincided with the transcription of texts of the new curriculum that Gerbert established at Reims. The twelfth-century catalogue of the abbey's library, Paris, BN lat. 1850, included various elements of the *Logica vetus* and Garland's *Regulae in abacum*.[46] Valenciennes, BM 406, containing a copy of Cicero's *Topica*, Pseudo-Apuleius's *De interpretatione*, and the Boethian monographs on logic, exemplified the influence of proto-

190   Word Separation in the Low Countries and Lorraine

scholasticism at Saint-Amand. In its word separation, this manuscript was similar to the early copies of Boethius's logical works transcribed at Fleury under Abbo.[47] As at Fleury, the separated text format of the *Logica vetus* enhanced a clarifying word order with an iconic dimension totally absent in the works of Aristotle and Boethius as they were copied in late antiquity and the Carolingian period. In the transcriptions of syllogisms, words were separated by even more ample space. *Prosodiae* in this portion of the book included suspended ligatures.[48]

The introduction of word separation was also apparent in the new Saint-Amand copies of classical texts. These included the same titles that Richer enumerated in his description of Gerbert's curriculum. The first ninety-nine leaves of the *Comoediae* of Terence, in Valenciennes, BM 448, were written in canonically separated script, with interword space equivalent to 2 times the unity of space.[49] On folio 2, a contemporary hand added a schematic tree diagram similar to those encountered at Reims, Fleury, and Chartres, a sign of the new visual mode of analysis dependent on parafoveal vision accompanying the new teaching of protoscholasticism. Another codex, Juvenal's *Saturae*, in Valenciennes, BM 410, was written in canonically separated script with generous interword space varying from 2.5 to 4 times the unity of space.[50] The *Odae* of Horace, Valenciennes, BM 408, is a third eleventh-century codex of a classical text transcribed in separated script.[51] The pages of this book were replete with a marginal apparatus of capital and minuscule letters in alphabetical sequence that served as a finding device by designating fixed loci within each leaf.[52] Similar marginalia also occurred in Valenciennes, BM 169, a canonically separated codex containing Johannes Cassianus's *Collationes* and Johannes Chrysostom's *De reparatione lapsi*.[53] Here the letters *b*, *n*, *r*, and *F*, as well as alphanumerical combinations, appear to be encoded either for correction or for the retrieval of information.[54] Greek within the text was separated, with interlinear Latin translations.

By the second half of the eleventh century, the presence of canonical separation was definitely established at Saint-Amand. An art-historical monument, Valenciennes, BM 41, containing exegetical writings of Augustine and datable to after 1087, was canonically separated.[55] Valenciennes, BM 502, the *Vita sancti Amandi*, was copied in separated script with interword space exceeding 3.5 times the unity of space.[56] Intersyllabic space was suppressed, even at the *ct* ligature. Errors of separation were corrected by the *J* form of the *diastole* and by vertical strokes.

The Abbeys of Metz and Toul

Adalberon II, bishop from 984 to 1005, established at Saint-Symphorien, then in ruins, a colony of Irish monks under the Irish abbot Fingen, creating an Insular milieu that may well have fostered the subsequent acceptance of word separation and ancillary practices.[57] Bishop Thierry and Richard of Saint-Vannes introduced reform to the abbeys of the diocese, of which the most prominent was Saint-Symphorien, directed by Constantinus, abbot from 1005 to 1048.[58] The scriptorium of Saint-Symphorien at the time of Abbot Constantinus produced only separated and canonically separated manuscripts, including Paris, BN lat. 5294, a collection of *Vitae sanctae*,[59] and Paris, BN lat. 9394.[60] The scribe Rainier copied Reims, BM 1429, containing the Continental "M" recension of Bede's *Historia ecclesiastica* in separated script, with the terminal long *j* form used at word endings.[61]

Nearby, at the Abbey of Saint-Vincent, which also came under the reforming influence of Bishop Thierry, Oxford, BL Auct. T. 1. 23, was copied during the abbacy of Folcuin, from 1048 to 1072, in separated script.[62] At the Abbey of Saint-Arnoul of Metz, an original charter from Abbot Johannes, dated August 16, 967, had been written in hierarchical word blocks.[63] In contrast, a charter from William, abbot of Saint-Arnoul, dating from 1010–31, was written in separated script of 4 to 5 times the unity of space.[64] Metz, BM 245, also from Saint-Arnoul, containing among other things a letter of the Norman Benedictine reformer John of Fécamp dated in 1064, was copied not long thereafter by several scribes in script separated by 3 times the unity of space, with terminal forms including the capital *US*, *NS* and *NT* ligatures.[65]

In the diocese of Toul, the Abbey of Saint-Pierre of Senones was reformed for Saint-Vannes by Bruno, bishop from 1026 to 1048 and later Pope Leo IX. At Senones, Paris, BN lat. 9392, a Gospel book, was copied under Abbot Suthard before 1023 in script separated by from 2 to 3 times the unity of space, with space irregularly present after monosyllabic prepositions.[66]

Stavelot-Malmédy

Richard of Saint-Vannes's principal assistant, Poppon (ca. 978–1048), a former monk of Saint-Thierry of Reims, reformed the twin Abbeys of Stavelot-Malmédy, where once again the adoption of word separation accompanied an abbey's religious reformation.[67] Remaclus was the patron saint of Stavelot-Malmédy. Bamberg, Staatsbibliothek Hist. 161 (E.III.1), the Stavelot copy of the first *Vita Remacli*, composed in the ninth century, was written in the first part of the tenth century in hierarchical word blocks.[68] Heriger's new version of the *Vita* in Vat. Reg. lat. 615 was sent to Stavelot from Lobbes in separated script at the end of the tenth century, and a copy made at Stavelot, former Chester Beatty 17 (olim Phillipps 12348), was written in about 1000 in similarly separated script.[69] Another manuscript of the new *Vita Remacli*, Brussels, BR II, 1180, was written at Stavelot under Thierry, abbot from 1048 to 1080, in separated script.[70] The adoption of word separation and its ancillaries is further documented by the *fonds* of Malmédy books donated to the Vatican by Pius VII in 1816.[71]

At the end of the eleventh century, the scribe Goderan, the most celebrated European scribe of his age, emigrated from Lobbes to Stavelot, where he transcribed two of the most celebrated paleographic monuments of the period, London, BL Add. 28106 and 28107, a Bible,[72] and Brussels, BR II, 1179, Josephus's *De bello iudaico*,[73] in canonically separated script. The illuminated initals of the former codex, attributed to Goderan himself, contained banderoles replete with separated text.

Waulsort, Saint-Hubert, and Florennes

Poppon also reformed the Abbey of Waulsort, established in 944. The *Waulsort Psalter*, Munich, Clm. 13067, reflecting Insular liturgical models of the mid-eleventh century, was written in canonically separated script.[74] Another disciple of Richard of Saint-Vannes's, Abbot Thierry I (1046–1080), reformed the Abbey of Saint-Hubert.[75] Brussels, BR II 1639, the first volume of the abbey's Bible, dating from about 1082, was written in separated script, with initials decorated with banderoles containing separated script.[76] The abbey's chronicle, composed in the eleventh century, exemplified the new mode of composition through textual manipulation of phrases borrowed from ancient authorities.[77]

The Abbey of Saint-Jean at Florennes, founded by Gerbert's student Gérard I when he was canon of Reims, was populated from its foundation by a colony of monks from Verdun.[78] Namur, Grand Séminaire 37, containing works of Rufinus and Bede, was copied at the abbey in the mid-eleventh century in separated script.[79]

Liège, Trier, and Spire

In the tenth century, hierarchical word blocks had been the standard medium for manuscripts copied in Liège.[80] Wolbodon, bishop of Liège (d. 1021), was a major figure of monastic reform and a patron of both Richard of Saint-Vannes and Poppon.[81] Wolbodon's glossed Psalter, Brussels, BR 9188–89, was long a venerated treasure at the cathedral of Liège.[82] It was certainly written under his supervision, and he has been thought to have been one of its principal scribes. The text of the Psalms was written in narrowly separated script, with interword space varying from 1 to 1.5 unities of space. The glosses, linked to the text by a wide array of emblematic tie notes, of which some resembled neumes and other tironian notes, were more generously separated, with interword space equivalent to 2 times the unity of space. In 1021, he entrusted the newly founded Abbey of Saint-Jacques in Liège to the reformer Olbert of Gembloux, who established a new reformed abbey, Saint-Laurent of Liège. At the Abbey of Saint-Laurent, all manuscripts were written with word separation, including Paris, BN lat. 819, a sacramentarium thought by some scholars to have been written in about 1025, which was copied in canonically separated script.[83]

Wolbodon then reformed the Abbey of Saint-Jacques of Liège, founded in 1015, and Olbert of Gembloux served as abbot from 1021 to 1048. Darmstadt, Hessische Landes- und Hochschulbibliothek 523, a homiliarium from this period, was copied in separated script.[84] Liège, Universiteitsbibliotheek 162, the authorial manuscript of the *Vita Baldrici episcopi Leodiensis*, dating from about 1053, was written in script separated by 2 times the unity of space, with terminal forms that included the elevated round *s*. *Prosodiae* included the *trait d'union* and the acute accent to denote monosyllables.[85] The *Annales Sancti Iacobi Leodiensis minores*, in Darmstadt Hessische Landes- und Hochschulbibliothek 314, begun at Gembloux, was continued at Saint-Jacques in Liège in separated script, as were all other manuscripts from this scriptorium.[86] The earliest charters of the Abbey of Saint-Jacques, modeled on those of the emperor Henry III, were similarly word-separated. Throughout the city of Liège, the support of religious reform by Wolbodon, his successor Réginard, abbot from 1025 to 1037, and the Imperial court was responsible for the rapid adoption of word separation in the first third of the eleventh century.[87] Bamberg, Staatsbibliothek Litt. 3 (Ed.V.4), a sacramentarium from the cathedral of Saint-Lambert dating from about

1015, was written in separated script, with interword space equivalent to 2 times the unity of space.[88] The capital S was notably present as a terminal form. Other terminal forms were the usual signs for -m, -tur, -us, and -orum. In the diocese of Trier, the Abbey of Saint Maximin, reformed by Poppon in 1022, produced separated manuscripts like Paris, BN lat. 1541, a lectionary,[89] and Trier, Stadtbibliothek 171/1626, the *Registrum Gregorii Magni*.[90] The Abbey of Weissenburg in the diocese of Spire, also reformed by Poppon, was already producing separated script under Gerrichus III, abbot from 989 to 1001, during the reign of Otto III.[91]

Saint Peter's of Lobbes

The practice of word separation at some abbeys in Flanders and Artois antedated the acceptance of the reform of Richard of Saint-Vannes because of prior contact with English Benedictine reform and protoscholastism. When in 1020, Wolbodon, bishop of Liège, and Gérard I of Florennes, bishop of Cambrai, removed the incumbent abbot of Saint Peter's of Lobbes and placed the abbey under the administration of Richard, word separation had already been established there, probably as a consequence of the abbacy of Heriger and the proximity of Anglo-Saxon influence.[92] The crucial change to separated writing at Lobbes occurred in the late tenth century, sometime after the deposition in 956 of Abbot Ratherius of Verona (d. 974), who wrote in hierarchical word blocks. Under Ratherius's successor, Folcuin (d. 990), it is probable that word separation had not yet been introduced to the abbey.[93] Folcuin's brief *Vita sancti Folcuini*, a life of his ninth-century namesake, survives in a fragment contained in Saint-Omer, BM 342 bis, f. 104, originating from the Abbey of Saint-Bertin and dating from the end of the tenth century.[94] Reasonably contemporary with the author, it was written in hierarchical word blocks, with neither *prosodiae* nor any other evident sign of graphic innovation.[95] At Folcuin's death in 990, Heriger, whose own works were disseminated only in separated script, as we have seen, was selected abbot, and the Abbey of Lobbes remained under his direction until his death in 1007. The earliest datable manuscript written in separated script at Lobbes was Valenciennes, BM 843, containing the works of Ratherius and the epitaph of Abbot Folcuin, added by the original hand in all probability soon after Folcuin's death in 990.[96] The manuscript was subsequently enumerated in the Lobbes library catalogue of 1049.[97] Taken as a whole, its text format exemplifies the evolution from hierarchical word blocks to canonically separated script. The original flyleaves contain fragments of Ratherius's autograph, written in hierarchical word blocks that on one leaf exceed and on another remain under fifteen characters in length. These remnants of the scribe's exemplar seem to have been discarded and used for binding once the new and more legible copies contained in the codex had been completed. The first folios of the primary texts of Valenciennes, BM 843 were written in hierarchical word blocks shorter than fifteen characters in length, containing conspicuous interword ligatures. Suspended ligatures, but not *traits d'union*, were present at line endings. However, beginning on folio 50, *traits d'union* appear, and from folio 63 onward, word separation was regular and canonical, with interword space equivalent to 2.25 times the unity of space. Terminal forms increased as the book was confected, and came to include the capital *NT* ligature and, uniquely for the epitaph of Folcuin on folio 137, the capital *S* and capital *NS* ligature. In the canonically separated portion, monolexic abbreviations included superscript forms and the tironian sign for the conjunction *et*. The scribe used the acute accent as a redundant sign of word separation for monosyllables. In addition to normal *traits d'union*, the split-line *trait d'union* and *trait d'union* used only at line beginnings were occasionally present. Proper names were denoted by initial capitals in both the unseparated and separated portions of the codex. The elongated Insular form of *r* was present throughout.

Copenhagen, Kongelige Bibliotek, G1. kgl. S. 20,[98] a collection of patristic texts also recorded in the Lobbes catalogue of 1049, was copied at approximately the same date as Valenciennes, BM 843 in narrowly separated script (interword space is equivalent to the unity of space) and with space present after monosyllabic prepositions. Separation was occasionally marred by interword ligatures and run-ons. Verdun, BM 24, copied by Rothardus of Saint-Vannes between 1020 and 1046 for the Abbey of Lobbes, provides a model of word separation as practiced in Verdun. The codex contains Boethius's *De arithmetica*, written in canonically separated script, with interword space equivalent to 2 times the unity of space.[99] The Lobbes catalogue of 1049, preserved in London, BL Royal 6 A V, f. 76, was written in canonically separated script, with interword space equivalent to 3 times the unity of space and with the acute accent regularly used on the double *ii*.[100] The catalogue reveals that in 1049, Lobbes possessed a copy of Abbo of Fleury's *Commentum super Calculo Victorii*.[101] In the second half of the eleventh century, Goderan of Lobbes wrote in the abbey's lectionary and Bible in a canonically separated hand rich in *prosodiae* and terminal forms.[102]

Saint-Bertin

In 1021, Baudouin IV of Flanders, who had reformed Saint-Vaast and Saint-Amand, entrusted the Abbey of Saint-Pierre in Saint-Bertin to Rodriquez of Saint-Vannes, a disciple of Richard's.[103] Here, as at Lobbes, separation preceded the Saint-Vannes reform. A generation earlier, Abbot Odbert, elected ca. 989, had already introduced both Anglo-Saxon Benedictine reform and word separation to Saint-Bertin. Manuscripts written before the election of Odbert, including the fragment of Folcuin's *Vita Folcuini* contained in Saint-Omer, BM 342 bis, were transcribed in hierarchical word blocks.

In 989 and 990, Folcuin's successor, Odbert, addressed two letters to Aethelgar, archbishop of Canterbury from 988 to 990,[104] and Sigeric, his successor, archbishop from 990 to 994.[105] In these epistles, Odbert invoked his friendship with Dunstan and credited Aethelgar with reforming Saint-Bertin. Odbert's close ties to Canterbury were reflected in the decoration and word-separated script of the relatively large number of manuscripts copied during his abbacy. The Anglo-Saxon-style illuminations present on two leaves of the *Boulogne Gospels*, Boulogne-sur-Mer, BM 11, are apparently by Odbert's own hand.[106] The inscriptions contained within its miniatures were canonically separated, and the text of the Gospels was written in separated script. Odbert also wrote the colophon of the collection of texts pertaining to Saint Martin that now forms Saint-Omer, BM 765.[107] The colophon was written in separated script, with interword space exceeding 2 times the unity of space; the text to which the colophon was appended was similarly separated. Paleographic signs of English influence in this book include the descending forms of the minuscule *r* and *s*, which enhanced the Bouma shape.

The colophon of Saint-Omer, BM 168, Saint Gregory's *Dialogi*, indicates that the monk-priests Riculfe and Baudouin of Saint-Bertin copied this book, written in canonically separated script, at the request of Odbert.[108] Dodolin, another priest-monk, copied Saint-Omer, BM 342 bis, containing an evangelistary and the *Passion of Saint Denis*, in separated script.[109] In a transliterated Greek word, the acute accent signaled interline continuation. Dodolin, Hérivé, and Odbert himself collaborated in 999 in the confection of Boulogne-sur-Mer, BM 20, a glossed Psalter written in script separated by 2.66 unities of space.[110] The use of an acrostic colophon to identify the scribes and illuminator was typical of what originally had been an Insular scribal practice. The gloss was attached to the text by emblematic tie notes resembling Greek letters or tironian notes. During Odbert's tenure at Saint-Bertin, at least twenty other codices were written in similarly separated script, many replete with acute accents. These included BM 350, where on folio 2 a scribe or early emendator corrected an error with a variant form of the successor note to the *diastole*, an initially Insular *prosodia*.[111] The so-called *Codex Vossianus Quadratus*, Leiden, BR Voss. lat. Q. 94, a ninth-century codex of Lucretius, was probably at Saint-Bertin in the early eleventh century, when it was copiously emended with the successor note to the *diastole*.[112] Boulogne-sur-Mer, BM 189, containing Prudentius's *Carmina*, either brought to Saint-Bertin from Canterbury or written on the Continent under Odbert's direction, was soon after its confection glossed by an emendator, identifiable as Anglo-Saxon by his scribe, who inserted sequential construction notes.[113] The emendator wrote a marginal note, for the benefit of contemporary readers, identifying the letters as signs of construction.[114] This reworking of the text indicates that at Saint-Bertin, as at Fleury, the reception of word order and word separation was complementary.

Saint-Bertin's simultaneous reception of Anglo-Saxon artistic styles and scribal habits was dramatically exemplified by Boulogne-sur-Mer, BM 188,[115] a *fere* canonically separated copy of Aratus of Soli's *Phaenomena* that is believed to have been transcribed from Leiden, Voss. lat. F. 79, a ninth-century codex written in hierarchical word blocks. Like most of the manuscripts prepared for Odbert, Boulogne-sur-Mer, BM 188 was illuminated by artists who had been trained in the schools of Winchester and Canterbury.[116] Of all the separated manuscripts produced for Odbert, Boulogne-sur-Mer, BM 188 was unique in its scientific content.

Saint Peter's of Ghent

In 1029, Richard of Saint-Vannes personally took charge of the direction of Saint Peter's of Ghent.[117] However, Saint Peter's, like Saint-Bertin, had had prior contact with English Benedictine reform, for in 955–57, Dunstan himself had taken refuge in the abbey for two years, and in 970, monks of Saint Peter's were invited by Dunstan to participate in the compilation of the *Regularis concordia*, the systematic collection of Continental and English monastic customaries.[118] Like reform, word separation in Saint Peter's scriptorium preceded Richard's administration of the abbey. The exceptionally large collection of late-tenth-century charters from Saint Peter's, comparable only to those of Cluny, allows us to place the date of the advent of word separation at about 981–83.[119] Before Wido, abbot from 981 to 985, the original charters from Saint Peter's that date from the ninth and tenth centuries were written in aerated script.[120] In contrast, two charters from Saint Peter's, numbers 69 and 70, copied in 981 and 982–83, were canonically separated, with terminal forms that included the long *j*, the capital *NS* and *NT* ligatures, and capitals *S*, *R*, and *M*.[121] Specific signs of contact with Anglo-Saxon scribal practice included the use of the acute accent as a redundant sign of separation for the monosyllabic preposition *a*.[122] Charters dating from 983 onward were invariably written in word-separated script.

Wido was close to Gerbert, who was a member of the Saint Peter's confraternity. On October 15, 986, Gerbert wrote to his Benedictine confreres at Ghent to demand the return of certain books that Wido had borrowed to be copied.[123] In another letter from Gerbert's epistulary corpus, Archbishop Adalbero of Reims, writing on August 15, 987, demanded the return of the same volumes.[124] Surviving manuscripts attributed to the scriptorium of Saint Peter's under Wido and copied in separated script include Paris, BN lat. 12285, ff. 1–101 (omitting folio 17), Saint Augustine's sermons on the Proverbs of Solomon, and Bede's *Super epistulas catholicas expositio*.[125]

The adoption of word separation after 981 is further confirmed by writing identified with the scribe Wichard, who is known to have been active as a scribe at Saint Peter's first in 986, and who served as Richard of Saint-Vannes's provost, beginning in 1029. Wichard eventually succeeded Richard as abbot in 1034. During his abbacy, the charters written at Saint Peter's were separated or canonically separated by from 2 to 4 times the unity of space, with the capital *NS* and *NT* ligatures, the capital forms of *S* and *X*, and an enlarged *-orum* sign used at word endings. Proper names were capitalized; *prosodiae* included the *trait d'union*.[126] In Paris, BN NAL 2320, f. 1, a charter signed by Wichard and canonically separated, the acute accent was used as a redundant sign of separation.[127] In his subscription to this document, Wichard himself capitalized the initial letters of proper names. Leiden, BR Lipsianus 26 (Geel 341), a codex of Terence's *Comoediae* believed to be copied in Wichard's own hand, was written in canonically separated script (Figure 30). Wichard used the hyphen and the *diastole* to correct errors in spacing and the acute and circumflex accents to denote monosyllables.[128] Another separated manuscript book dating from the time of Wichard, Oxford, BL Rawlinson G, 44, the

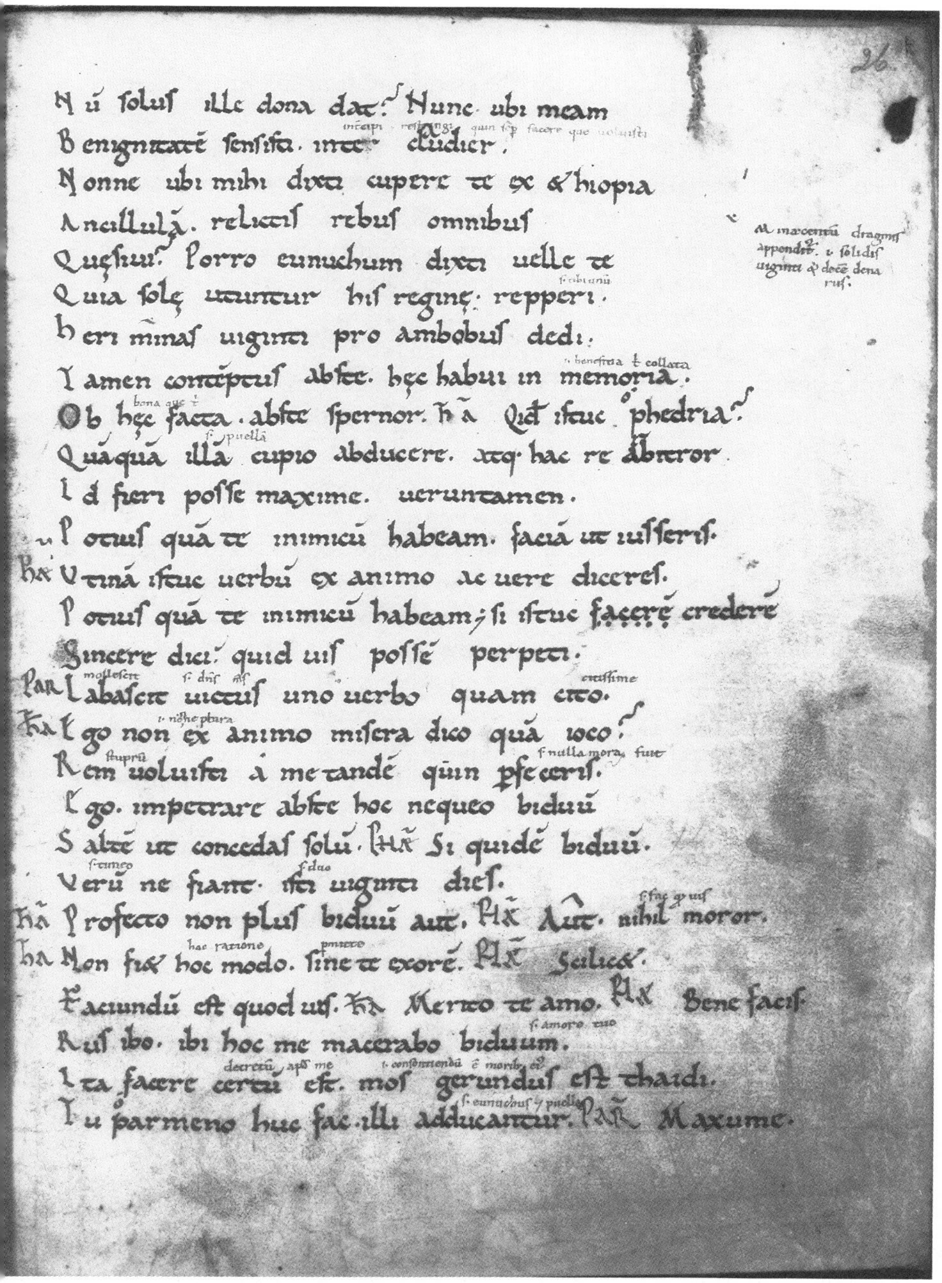

Figure 30. Script attributed to the scribe Wichard, in Terence's *Comoediae*, ca. 1030. Leiden, Bibliotheek der Rijksuniversiteit Lipsianus 26 (Geel 341), f. 26 recto; reproduced by permission.

abbey's copy of Sallust, reveals the transition from unseparated to separated script. The unidentified text of the flyleaves, dating from the tenth century, was written in hierarchical word blocks of fewer than fifteen characters in length. In contrast, the text of Sallust was copied in separated script and included an early use of the *trait d'union* at Saint Peter's.

The new form of the written page at Saint Peter's coincided with the appearance in the subscriptions of the abbey's charters of Insular terminology to describe the activity of reading. In the eleventh century, Saint Peter's verified the accuracy of its charters' contents by having them read and signed by the abbot or by another monk acting as supervisor of the scriptorium. The earliest recorded subscription dates from 1031–34, and a number of them are in Wichard's own hand. In these subscriptions, the Insular term *videre*, to see or to scan, was used in the phrase "vidi et notavi" (seen and signed) as a synonym of *legere*.[129] Its use, implying the scanning of text, would not have been possible in aerated script. The *Liber traditionum*, Ghent, Archives Suppl. 2 bis, an extensive cartulary-chronicle for Saint Peter's compiled under Wichard's direction between 1034 and 1058, was transcribed in canonically separated script.[130]

Under Wichard, changes in the mode of text composition occurred that may be linked to changes in text format. The abbey's copy of Wichard's own *Visio Aldegundis*, Ghent BR 224, was transcribed in canonically separated script and was contemporary with the author.[131] Terminal forms included an enlarged form of the *et* ligature. The *Visio Aldegundis* was in fact a composite work formed from fragments borrowed from earlier hagiographic material. Word separation facilitated the compilation of the *Visio Aldegundis*, just as it had facilitated Burchard of Worms's compilation of the *Libri viginti decretorum*, Dunstan's composition of the *Regularis concordia*, and Sigebert's drafting of his *Chronicle*.

Saint Willibrord of Echternach—An Exception

The only abbey that had not definitively accepted word separation after receiving Richard of Saint-Vannes's reform was the Abbey of Saint Willibrord of Echternach, in the diocese of Trier. An early Insular center for word-separated books, Saint Willibrord's produced books in aerated script in the ninth and tenth centuries. In the early eleventh century, under Humbert, abbot from 1028 to 1051, certain codices linked to the new learning were copied in separated script.[132] These included Paris, BN lat. 11127, containing Boethius's commentary on and translation of Aristotle's *De interpretatione*, Pseudo-Apuleius's *De interpretatione*, and a letter of Gerbert's,[133] as well as lat. 11128, Boethius's commentary on Aristotle's *De interpretatione*,[134] lat. 11129, Boethius's translation of Porphyry's *Isagoge*,[135] and lat. 18195, a collection of classical texts, including writings by Macrobius and Sallust.[136] However, under Humbert's successor, Abbot Regimbert, a series of dated and datable manuscripts were once again produced partly in aerated script.[137]

Chapter II

The Spread of Word Separation from England to Northern France

Norman Benedictine Piety and Silent Reading

The Benedictine reform created particularly strong ties between Insular abbeys and those in Normandy. In Norman reformed Benedictine abbeys such as Mont Saint-Michel and Jumièges, and through the efforts of individuals such as John of Fécamp and, at Bec, Lanfranc and Anselm, writing practices shifted toward word separation and enhancing the clarity of the written page, as the present chapter will document. Devotional practices, and with them, reading practices, changed as well. By spreading word-separated English books among Norman abbeys, the Benedictine reform also encouraged the diffusion of Insular texts of private prayers, exemplified by the *Adoro te*, that during the next four centuries would become some of the most popular texts of silent devotion.[1] More generally, the shift to word-separated text coincided with a greater emphasis on silent, individual reading as a component of Anglo-Norman monasticism.

The provisions for individual monastic reading in Dunstan's *Regularis concordia* had surpassed those of the *Rule of Saint Benedict*, the *Rule of Saint Augustine*, and ninth-century and tenth-century Continental customaries.[2] John of Fécamp (990–1078), abbot of the abbey there, whose own writing was separated, now equated reading with prayer and meditation and assumed that monks would follow a written text for their private devotions.[3] In his treatise *De vita ordine et morum institutione*, of which the only surviving eleventh-century copy comes from the library of Mont Saint-Michel, John set forth an ideal of mental prayer closely tied to reading.[4] For him, reading and private prayer were inextricably linked in a manner that was unprecedented, either in the injunctions of the Latin Fathers of late antiquity or in the customaries of the Carolingian church. He was the first medieval author to employ the term *meditatio* for a written text intended for private spiritual use.[5] The writings of John of Fécamp were an important step toward the late medieval spirituality that was to become centered on individual, silent reading.

At Bec, Lanfranc (ca. 1010–89), in his *Decreta*, reworked the early *consuetudines* or rules of the abbey and Bernard's *Consuetudines* for Cluny to emphasize private reading as an integral part of public liturgy.[6] He commended the practice, unprecedented in early medieval liturgical instructions, of asking monks to read prayers *in silentio* at specific moments during the Mass and the canonical offices.[7] Given the ambiguity of medieval nomenclature, his injunction to read such prayers *in silentio* did not necessarily imply silent, visual reading, but at a minimum, it did require that the voice of the reader not be so loud as to be generally audible and comprehensible.[8] This caveat notwithstanding, word separation in Bec's books must have greatly facilitated individual, truly silent reading within the group. Indeed, Lanfranc used the verb *inspicere*, to gaze, when he enjoined the monks of Bec to refrain from reading books during the most solemn moments of common worship.[9] He was the earliest recorded author to employ this term that, like *videre*, "to see," clearly implied silent reading. As already noted, the use of the banderole in book illustration reflects this shift from the aural to the visual. Banderoles were present, for example, in the illustrations of the *Regularis concordia* contained in London, BL Cotton Tiberius A III, ff. 3–27, one of two surviving copies of the text copied at Christ Church, Canterbury, in about 1040–70.[10] They became prominent in the miniatures decorating the separated manuscripts produced during the twelfth century at Mont Saint-Michel, Jumièges, and other reformed Norman Benedictine abbeys.[11]

Lanfranc's successor, Anselm, who lived from 1033 to 1089, perfected the new Anglo-Norman literary genre of *meditationes*. He composed a book, to which he himself gave the title *Orationes sive meditationes*, with the explicit intent that it be perused and read in private, where it might serve as a spiritual conduit from the author to the reader.[12] Anselm's initial title for the *Monologicon* was *Exemplum meditandi de ratione fidei*, and its first chapter was "Excitatio mentis ad contemplandum Deum." [13] In it, he carefully distinguished between images and logographs, internal mental speech and external oral speech.[14] For Anselm, like John of Fécamp, meditation was the free, speculative thought stimulated by private reading. Anselm became one of the first medieval authors to refer to the punctuation of his own text when he pointed out that his division of the text into paragraphs freed the reader from obligatorily reading from beginning to end by permitting easy entry wherever one wanted.[15] This liberty empowered devout readers to control the process of their own spiritual stimulation.

Anselm also expressed the concern, unprecedented in the writings of the early Middle Ages, that monks should avoid a too rapid reading of devotional texts.[16] In a world in which *scriptura continua* and hierarchical word blocks had been normal, reading had been a slow and laborious task, and reading too rapidly could not have been a vice worthy of condemnation. The endemic fault of early medieval oral readers, denounced by the ninth-century monk Hildemar in his *Commentum in Regulam sancti Benedicti*, was an inaudible mumbling of syllables, reflecting lack of comprehension.[17] In effect, the new word separation that facilitated the reading of difficult texts and enhanced individual spirituality in the eyes of the reformed Benedictines created a new vice. Anselm insisted that spiritual works be read decorously, with the requisite emotion. As reading became a silent and solitary activity, constraints imposed by the group were no longer efficacious, and explicit injunctions against private abuse were required.

Fécamp

In 1028, John of Fécamp (ca. 990–1078) succeeded his aging uncle, the Cluniac William of Volpiano, as abbot of Fécamp, an office he exercised until his death. Although born in northern Italy, John, unlike his uncle, was nurtured in France, and he was the earliest of a series of Norman Benedictine reformers to place special emphasis on private devotional reading and prayer. Before John's election, manuscripts copied at Fécamp had been aerated. A few years after he became abbot, BN lat. 989, containing the *Vita sancti et miracula Taurini*, accompanied by related liturgical and patristic texts prepared in conjunction with the transfer of the relics of Saint Taurin from Evreux to Fécamp in 1035, was written partly in aerated but mostly in separated script, with interword space equivalent to 2 times the unity of space and with terminal forms.[18] As at other Norman abbeys, all heavily subject to Anglo-Saxon influence, the separation of writing was accompanied at Fécamp by a conspicuous increase in the use of *prosodiae*, notably the acute accent. Other *prosodiae* included the medial point used as a *diastole* to correct errors in word separation. However, in midfolio on folio 79v, the hand and script changed, and the next seventeen leaves, as well as folios 118 through 124, were transcribed by a single scribe in hierarchical word blocks regularly exceeding twenty characters in length, but effectively reduced to fewer than fifteen characters by word boundaries denoted by terminal forms and monolexic abbreviations without space. This scribe was probably a senior member of the scriptorium, for on folio 2, acting as a corrector, he substituted unseparated writing over a line of text that had originally been separated. The separated portion of this book contains one of the earliest examples of the encoded alphabetic musical notation characteristic of eleventh-century and twelfth-century Normandy.[19]

The word separation in lat. 989 likely reflected Fécamp's new abbot, for John of Fécamp's own autograph writing was separated. It exists in at least four Fécamp codices containing copies of his devotional prayers.[20] In Paris, BN lat. 1872, John wrote his rhymed prayer "Pater mi," in which he separated words with space equivalent to 3 times the unity of space, inserting space after some monosyllabic prepositions.[21] Paris, BN lat. 1928, ff. 171v–73, contains a contemporary copy of the "Pater mi" in script separated by from 2 to 3 times the unity of space, with the terminal capital S at line endings.[22] The manuscript elsewhere contains the Norman form of encoded alphabetic musical notation (Figure 31).[23] Another contemporary hand added John's *Epistula ad monachos dyscolos* in separated script, with suspension abbreviations used for proper names.[24] In Paris, BN lat. 3088 (a sixteenth-century composite codex), John added on leaves now forming folios 7 through 8 his epistle beginning "Tuae quidem" and his *Deploratio quietatis et solitudinis derelectae*, in which he separated his writing by 3 times the unity of space and employed terminal forms including the usual signs for *m*, *-tur*, and *-bus*, the ampersand, and the capital S at line endings.[25] In Paris, BN lat. 2401, ff. 135–36v, John added a paraphrase of the litany of the saints to a separated copy of Amalarius's *Liber officialis*.[26] Here, John's hand separated the text by 2 times the unity of space, using terminal forms including the crossed capital S for *-orum*. John placed the acute accent on the letter *i* in the tonic syllable of the compound word *ubique* and on the *-es* termination. In all the examples of John's script, the *ct* and *st* intraword ligatures were regularly employed, and in lat. 2461, the suspended *ct* ligature was used to denote a word divided at a line ending. In other codices, ranging from Normandy to Metz to Saint-Martial, the works that John of Fécamp had composed at Fécamp in a separated hand were rapidly diffused in word-

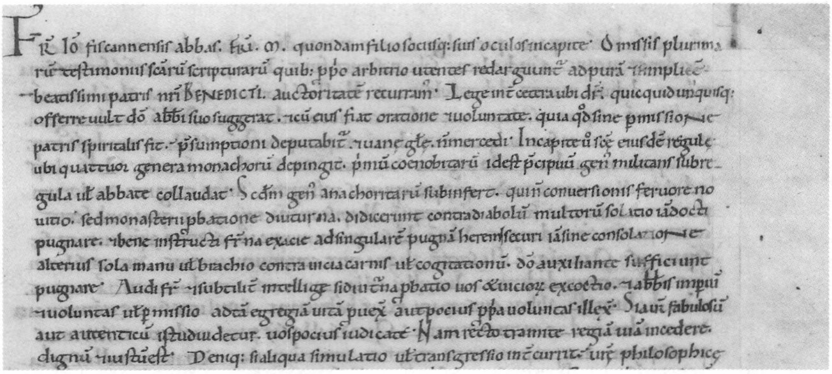

Figure 31. Word separation in a contemporary copy of John of Fécamp's *Epistula ad monachos dyscolos*. Paris, Bibliothèque Nationale lat. 1928, f. 173 recto; reproduced by permission.

separated copies.[27] In Paris, BN lat. 1939, a contemporary note regarding John was written in canonically separated script on folio 171v.[28] Capitals were used to denote proper names.

The religious reform with which John of Fécamp was associated linked Norman abbeys with their counterparts in southern England. Contact with English Benedictines was reflected in the characteristically Insular *prosodiae* and punctuation that appeared at Fécamp after ca. 1030. Further confirmation of English influence at Fécamp comes from art-historical evidence. Paris, BN lat. 2079, containing Augustine's *Contra Faustum*, written in canonically separated script, was decorated by an artist inspired by the school of Winchester.[29] Its *prosodiae* included *traits d'union* and acute accents to denote Hebrew names. Rouen, BM 478 (A. 7), a word-separated volume containing diverse minor works by Augustine, was decorated by an artist of exceptional talent who drew inspiration from English models.[30]

As at Fleury, experiments in writing the vernacular were also a sign of Anglo-Saxon influence. In the early years of the twelfth century, a scribe at Fécamp copied a French and Latin ceremonial for trial by ordeal, Paris, BN lat. 2403, f. 163.[31] In the Latin text, the words were separated, and *prosodiae* included the acute accent on monosyllables, as well as *traits d'union*. The French text was written in aerated script, but unlike Anglo-Saxon vernacular scribes, the French scribe did not attempt to use minor spaces to highlight morphemic units within word blocks.[32]

In one of the Fécamp codices containing Insular artistic motifs, the transcription of texts relating to the new learning converged with Anglo-Saxon scribal practices, giving additional impetus to the adoption of separated script. In Rouen, BM 489 (A.254), dating from the second half of the eleventh century, Gerbert's *Regulae de numerorum abaci rationibus*, accompanied by the anonymous commentary and a table of Arabic numbers with their names (including the symbol and name for zero), was written in separated script, with interword space equivalent to 2 times the unity of space and terminal forms that included the capital *S*, the crossed capital *S* for *-orum*, and the capital *NT* ligature.[33] Alphabetical tie notes connected marginal glosses to the text, and marginal schematic diagrams typical of the protoscholastic tradition emanating from Reims and Fleury were also present elsewhere in the codex. In the table of Arabic numbers (as in the table of contents of another Fécamp codex, Paris, BN lat. 1684), architectural motifs were used as visual mnemonic aids for presenting information. On folio 65, the scribe added a pen sketch of a reader, arms folded, staring at a book (Figure 32). This scene is reminiscent of the posture depicted in Paris, NAL 2196 from Luxeuil.[34] Both are precious iconographic evidence of the anticipated absence of gestures in the silent reader of a word-separated codex.[35]

A second codex linked to the new learning was Rouen, BM 471 (A.291), a collection of Fulbert's *Sermones*.[36] This book, possibly predating Rouen, BM 489 (A.254), was written in narrowly separated script, complemented by the lavish use of Insular and Continental *prosodiae*. The twelfth-century Fécamp catalogue recorded that copies of Bur-

Figure 32. A pen sketch of a motionless reader in a manuscript from Fécamp containing Gerbert's *Regulae de numerorum abaci rationibus*. Rouen, Bibliothèque Municipale 489, f. 65 recto; reproduced by permission.

chard's *Collectio canonum*, Helpericus's *De computo*, and Virgil's *Aeneid*, all associated with the new learning, once formed part of the monastery's library.[37]

Mont Saint-Michel

The Abbey of Mont Saint-Michel was reformed by Abbot Mainhard I, who in 961 virtually reconstituted a Benedictine foundation that had fallen into ruin during the tumult of the Norman invasions. Mainhard I, who was patronized by Richard I, duke of Normandy (933–96), had been trained at the Abbey of Saint Peter's at Ghent, and the earliest Saint-Michel codices written in hierarchical word blocks closely resemble the pre-981 aerated books produced at Saint Peter's scriptorium.

The transition to word separation at Mont Saint-Michel occurred under Mainhard's successor, Mainhard II, abbot from 991 to 1009. During these years, a sacramentarium, Orléans, BM 127 (105), written in separated Caroline script at the reformed Benedictine Abbey of Winchcombe for exportation to Fleury, passed through Mont Saint-Michel before making its way to Fleury, where the book was located at the time of the death of Abbot Gauzelin in 1029.[38] At Mont Saint-Michel, a list of the abbey's monks, living and dead, was added on page 362. It was written in separated script attributed to the same scribe, Hervardus, who signed his name to a word-separated book containing Gregory of Tours's *De gestis francorum* and Ado of Vienne's *Chronicon*, now divided between Leiden, BR Voss. lat. F. 39 and Paris, BN lat. 5920.[39]

Four manuscripts apparently dating from either the period of abbot Mainhard II or his successor, Hildebertus II, abbot from 1009 to 1027, further document the transition to separated writing. Avranches, BM 229, containing Boethius's commentaries on three elements of the *Logica vetus* is one example.[40] Boethius's *Commentarii in Porphyrii Isagogen* was written in hierarchical word blocks greater than twenty characters in length, with terminal forms denoting some word endings in a manner similar to that found in Avranches, BM 50. The commentaries on Aristotle's *Categoriae* and *De interpretatione* were written in separated script, with interword space equivalent to 2 times the unity of space. The initial, unseparated folios of the manuscript containing the *Isagoge* commentary were subsequently separated by an early-eleventh-century emendator who used the successor note to the *diastole* to enhance word boundaries where neither space nor terminal forms were present. The emendator also added acute accents to mark the double *ii* and marginal diples to separate commentary from text and to denote the beginning of a new sentence. In a contemporary marginal note (written in separated script), the scribe marked with an acute accent the penultimate syllable of the compound word *itáque*.[41]

Two of the texts of Gerbert's new curriculum were written and glossed at Mont Saint-Michel in fully perfected separated script.[42] In Persius's *Saturae*, the text was accompanied by separated glosses in which the acute accent denoted the tonic syllable in proximity to letters formed from minim strokes. At the end of the codex, the response to the proto-scholastic question "Utrum corpus a domino sit?" was written in separated handwriting strikingly similar to that used at Fleury for the transcription of Abbo's syllogisms. For an overview of the progress of word separation at Mont Saint-Michel, see the Appendix, Table A5.

The transition to word separation under Mainhard II, abbot from 991 to 1009, is confirmed by the few charters from Mont Saint-Michel that survived long enough to be photographed before the abbey's archives were destroyed during World War I. A charter of a certain Ives on behalf of the abbey, datable to 997, was written in separated script, with widely variable quantities of interword space.[43] Its scribe used initial capitals to denote proper names, as did the scribe of the apparently contemporary charter of a certain Guy, which was written in imperfect hierarchical word blocks.[44] Three charters of Hugh I, count of Maine (d. 1015), recording donations to the abbey and dating from 1014–15, were written in separated script.[45] The other surviving eleventh-century charters of the abbey were all word-separated, including one of Robert II Courte-Heuse, duke of Normandy from 1087 to 1134,[46] which had as terminal forms the round and capital *S* and the crossed capital *S* for *-orum*. Suspension abbreviations were used for proper names, which were either denoted by initial and terminal capitals or written all in capitals. *Prosodiae* consisted of *traits d'union*, and punctuation included the tripoint English emblematic terminal mark. Anglo-Saxon influence was detectable, too, in the descending form of minuscule *r* used by the scribe. Significantly, the minim stroke of the *t* projected above the cross stroke, distinguishing the *c* from the *t* and enhancing word image.

Jumièges

At the Abbey of Saint-Pierre of Jumièges, near Rouen, which was closely linked to Fécamp, Mont Saint-Michel, and the reform movement, the acceptance of word separation developed at a pace similar to that of Fécamp.[47] The few surviving ninth-century and tenth-century codices of Jumièges were written in aerated script. For example, Rouen, BM 26 (A.292), an Old Testament with texts on ecclesiastical computation and astronomy, was written in 852–67 in hierarchical word blocks.[48] The first three leaves of Rouen, BM 1378 (V.40), a collection of *Vitae sanctae* dating from the time of Annon, abbot from 942 to 973,[49] were written in hierarchical word blocks fewer than fifteen characters in length. In the course of the eleventh century, the entire codex was refurbished after serious damage. Occasional accents and *traits d'union* were added to the original leaves to facilitate word recognition, and new quires were added. The purely eleventh-century portion, comprising most of the codex, included Fulbert's sermon on the Virgin Mary, *Approbate consuetudinis*. The script of these leaves was separated. Rouen, BM 395 (Y.127), a *rituale* written for use at Jumièges at the time of Abbot Thierry of Montgommeri (1014–28), who concurrently in 1023–27 was abbot of Mont Saint-Michel, was written in separated script.[50] Rouen, BM 310 (A.293), an evangelistary, was also probably written for Thierry. It was copied in script separated by variable quantities of space, with separation marred by occasional run-ons.[51] Thierry, it may be noted, was subsequently remembered as an abbot who had been preoccupied with the accuracy of the books transcribed for him.[52]

The Abbey of Jumièges was particularly rich in books imported from England. Robert Champart, abbot of Jumièges from 1037 to 1044, sent to the abbey a sacramentarium copied at Winchester, Rouen, BM 274 (Y.6), after he had left Jumièges to become bishop of London (1044–51).[53] The text of the sacramentarium, written between 1006 and 1023,[54] was transcribed in separated script, as was then normal in the British Isles. The acute accent was used to denote the double *ii*, and vernacular Anglo-Saxon rubrics facilitated the use of the book.[55] The note of presentation to Jumièges, written on folio 227v, apparently in Robert's own hand, was written in less consistently separated script (varying from equivalence to 2 times the unity of space), with capital letters used to denote proper names. A separated late-tenth-century volume of Anglo-Saxon origin, a Psalter-hymnal, Rouen, BM 231 (A.44), also may have entered the library of Jumièges as a gift of Abbot Robert.[56] A third English separated manuscript at Jumièges, the *Pontifical of Saint Germans in Cornwall*, Rouen, BM 368 (A.27), copied in southern England in about 1009 and containing Insular neumes, also apparently crossed the Channel at an early date and was yet another potential model for Jumièges scribes.[57]

The presence of so many English volumes on the French side of the Channel is indicative of the interchange between Jumièges and England and helps to explain the frequent presence of Anglo-Saxon terminal forms, *prosodiae*, and punctuation in Jumièges manuscripts of the middle and late eleventh century. The Jumièges scribe who, in the middle third of the century, wrote Rouen, BM 536 (A.389), Smaragdus's *Diadema monachorum*, made abundant use of *prosodiae* to facilitate word recognition in a script written with word separation varying from equivalence to 2 times the unity of space.[58] Oxford, BL Bodley 852, ff. 1–31, Fulbert's *Vita sancti Achardi abbatis Gemeticensis*,[59] datable to 1049–72, was copied in canonically separated script with *prosodiae*, including *traits d'union*.[60] Terminal forms included the capital *R*. The ampersand set off by space was used as a monolexic abbreviation for the conjunction *et*. The table of abbots on folio 31 was framed in an architectural motif; miniatures contained banderoles. The decoration of London, BL Add. 17739, an evangelistary copied at Jumièges ca. 1100, shows profound signs of Anglo-Saxon influence.[61] After the Norman conquest in 1066, the administrative bonds linking Jumièges and England exceeded those of any other Norman abbey.[62]

No early cartulary survives from Jumièges, but of all Norman abbeys, Jumièges possessed the most extensive number of original charters dating from before the year 1060. These documents, preserved in the Rouen Archives Départmentales de Seine-Maritime, confirm the chronology, suggested above, for the adoption of word separation in manuscript books. A charter from Eudes, bishop of Chartres, apparently signed on April 5, 984, by Hugh Capet, giving a rent to the Abbey of Jumièges, was written in hierarchical word blocks of twenty-five characters in maximum length, without capitalization of proper names.[63] Rouen, AD 9H106 (Vernier, no. vii), a convention of 1012–13 between the abbots of Jumièges and Bourgueil, was written in hierarchical word blocks.[64] Rouen, AD 9H27 (Vernier, no. viii), a concession by Hugh, bishop of Bayeux, to the abbey in 1020–30, was still written in hierarchical word blocks, although in two instances it was clarified by the scribe or an emendator with an acute accent and vertical strokes.[65] The use of the terminal capital *S* within the line, emblematic punctuation, including the tripoint terminal sign, and the coordinated use of initial capitalization and interpuncts for proper names are also signs of the influence of new writing habits.

In 1023–27, a charter from Albert, abbot of Saint-Mesmin, Rouen, AD 9H1433 (Vernier, no. ix), was written in script separated by 3 times

the unity of space.[66] Other word-separated charters rich in Insular terminal forms, *prosodiae*, and emblematic punctuation include Rouen, AD
9H30 (Vernier, no. xiii)[67] and Rouen, AD 9H29 (Vernier, no. xvi), written before 1031.[68] After the frontier of word separation had been breached
during the period from 1027 to 1035, there was no relapse to word
blocks, and word separation in Jumièges charters was consistently replete
with the same indicators of English graphic influence as the codices of
Jumièges.

Bec

Aerated script cannot be documented at the celebrated Abbey of Bec,
founded in 1035 and home to both Lanfranc and Anselm, two monks of
northern Italian birth who preeminently came to embody Norman spiritual and graphic reform.[69] The devastation of the French Revolution has
left less than a dozen eleventh-century Bec codices, and if any aerated
manuscripts had ever been written at Bec, they have been destroyed.[70] It
is indeed probable that the new abbey's first scribes viewed word blocks
as *démodé*. In 1041–42, Lanfranc came to Bec from Mont Saint-Michel,
where, as we have seen, Anglo-Saxon Benedictine reform had already
occurred and separated script had been established. In 1070, Lanfranc
brought from Bec to Canterbury a compilation of decretals, the *Collectio
Lanfranci*, Cambridge, Trinity College B.16.44 (405).[71] The principal portion of this codex was written after 1059, the date of the condemnation
of Berengar, which is mentioned in the text; English monks added more
texts in Canterbury. The text copied at Bec and its English additions were
equally well separated. The two Continental scribes wrote separated and
canonically separated script, with interword space equivalent to 2 times
the unity of space and with terminal forms such as the capital *S. Prosodiae* included *traits d'union*. Another Bec book, Augustine's *De pastoribus*, Paris, BN lat. 12211, copied not much later, was written in separated
script replete with *traits d'union*.[72] Rouen, BM 511 (A.361), a copy of
Gregory's *Homilarium in Ezechielem*, dating from the second half of the
eleventh century and originating from Bonne Nouvelle, a Bec priory, displays separated handwriting replete with many signs of Anglo-Saxon influence.[73] The twelfth-century catalogue of Bec, preserved in Avranches,
BM 159, records a number of elements of the *Logica vetus*, the *Epistolae* of
Fulbert, Helperic's *De computo*, and Burchard of Worms's "Collectiones
libri," all among the texts disseminated in separated text format.[74]

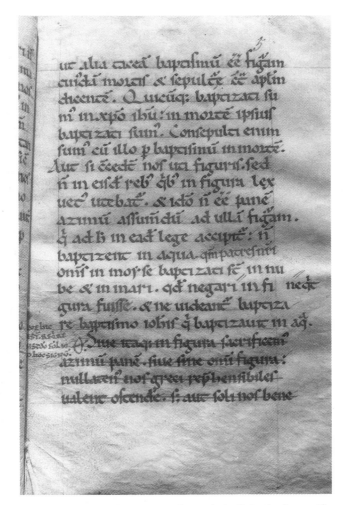

Figure 33. The authorial manuscript of Anselm's *Epistola de sacrificio azimi et fermentati*, written in canonically separated script. Arras, Bibliothèque Municipale 484 (805), f. 5 recto; reproduced by permission.

The textual traditions of the writings of Lanfranc and Anselm, both of whom employed logic in their defense of orthodoxy, document a continuous presence of word separation.[75] The corpus of these Benedictine reformers circulated in England and on the Continent exclusively in separated writing. The earliest manuscript of Lanfranc's *Epistolae*, London, BL Cotton Nero A VII, ff. 1–39v, was separated. *Prosodiae* included *traits d'union*, the acute accent on the double *ii*, and the *-is* termination.[76] Lanfranc was abbot of Saint-Etienne of Caen from 1063 to 1070, during which time he wrote his treatise *De corpore et sanguine Domini* against Berengar of Tours. Clarity in philosophical expression, now made possible by the new medium of separated writing, was exemplified by both parties to the controversy over the nature of the Sacrament.[77] Each author's manipulation of the other's text was undoubtedly facilitated by word separation, as was the manipulation of glosses that led to the *Glossa ordinaria*.[78] A charter from Saint-Etienne datable to 1067–75 was written in script separated by 2 times the unity of space,[79] and Cambridge, Emmanuel College I. 1. 8., from Saint-Etienne, was written in a script similar to that of the *Collectio Lanfranci*.[80] Also word-separated were the early English copies of Lanfranc's *Constitutiones* and *Decreta pontificum*.[81] The charter founding the Abbey of Lessay that Lanfranc, as archbishop of Canterbury, witnessed in 1080, was written in separated script, with terminal forms including the capital *S* and crossed *S* for *-orum*.[82] *Prosodiae* included *traits d'union*.

Anselm's Latinity, which was profoundly influenced by Boethius's Latin translations of Aristotle, provided him with an unambiguous medium for formulating subtle distinctions in logic.[83] He evinced the characteristically medieval propensity to form syntactically related word groupings that was a prerequisite for a more rigorous application of syntactic punctuation.[84] An early collection of most of Anselm's other writings, Rouen, BM 539 (A.366), including the *Monologion*, in which he used logic to prove the existence of God, was written at Jumièges, possibly under the author's supervision, in canonically separated script, with interword space equivalent to 2 times the unity of space, but with reduced space after monosyllables, and with *prosodiae* including the *trait d'union*.[85] Arras, BM 484 (805), the authorial manuscript of Anselm's *Epistola de sacrificio azimi et fermentati*, for example, was written in canonically separated script, with interword space equivalent to 2 times the unity of space and with *prosodiae* that included *traits d'union* (see Figure 33, preceding page).[86]

Chapter **12**

Cluniac Monasticism: Eastern and Southern France

~~~~~~~

Cluny

A discussion of the role of French monasticism in the spread of word separation would not be complete without consideration of Cluny, the largest and most important monastery in western Europe. In the tenth century, the monastic customs of Cluny were adopted by other Benedictine abbeys in France, the Low Countries, and Italy. Although many of these abbeys were subsequently reformed in the eleventh century by Richard of Saint-Vannes and others, the Abbey of Cluny itself did not participate in this reform movement and did not adopt word separation at an early date. However, once it did adopt separation, in approximately 1035, the Order of Cluny, established in the second half of the eleventh century, became the major force for the imposition of word separation in numerous abbeys in southern France and Spain.

Under Maïeul, abbot from 954 to 994, Cluny's manuscript books and documents were invariably written in unseparated script, usually in hierarchical word blocks exceeding fifteen characters in length. London, BL Add. 22820, Rabanus Maurus's *Expositio in Hieremiam*, according to its colophon, was copied for Abbot Maïeul.[1] Its single scribe wrote in hierarchical word blocks exceeding twenty characters in maximum length, with capitalization of proper names limited to the colophon. He tended to reserve terminal forms for the end of word blocks. Another scribe wrote Paris, BN NAL 1442,[2] in the mid-tenth century in hierarchical word blocks greater than twenty characters in length and used the medial point as an occasional aid to separation. Prior to the death of Abbot Maïeul, separated writing was unknown in any book produced in the scriptorium of Cluny, and the corpus of new scientific texts and classical authors fundamental to the curriculum of Gerbert and Abbo went uncopied.[3]

A group of manuscripts written during the half-century-long abbacy of Odilon (994–1049) documents the period of transition at Cluny to separated script. They confirm that Cluny's transition transpired later than at northern monastic centers closely linked to the teachings of Gerbert and to the reformed religious observance of Dunstan and Richard of Saint-Vannes. Paris, BN NAL 2253, was written in hierarchical word blocks exceeding thirty characters in length between 998 and 1008, when word separation had already become normal at monasteries in Reims, Fleury, Ghent, Saint-Bertin, and Verdun.[4] Odilon's presentation copy of Sucherius's *In epistolas S. Pauli Commentarius ex libris S. Augustini Collectus*, Bamberg, Staatsbibliothek Bibl. 126 (B.I.8), prepared for Emperor Henry II (1002–24), was transcribed in hierarchical word blocks at a time when the Imperial circle had already accepted word separation.[5] However, Paris, BN NAL 1447, Augustine's *Contra Faustum*, written at Cluny during the abbacy of Odilon, probably in the first two decades of the eleventh century, shows signs of evolution toward the new format of the written page.[6] The two scribes wrote in hierarchical word blocks exceeding twenty-five characters in length, but the principal scribe made use of the successor note to the *diastole* to mark word boundaries at points susceptible to misconstruction, and he also employed the split-line *trait d'union*.

Several Cluny manuscripts exemplify the evolution from aerated to separated script. London, BL Add. 11873, a collection of the works of Augustine, was begun in hierarchical word blocks but was completed under Odilon in separated script (folios 59 through 136) and in canonically separated script (folio 137 to the end).[7] Paris, BN NAL 1478, included Boethius's *De consolatione philosophiae*, copied at the end of the tenth century, and the *De topicis differentiis*, copied in the eleventh century, with a list of the other logical monographs so important to Gerbert and Abbo.[8] The *De consolatione philosophiae* (folios 1 through 55v) was written in hierarchical word blocks of fewer than fifteen characters. The *De topicis differentiis* (folios 56 through 90) and the list of logical treatises were written in separated script, with interword space equivalent to 2 times the unity of space, but the new Anglo-Saxon *prosodiae* were not yet present.

Paris, BN lat. 15176, called Odilon's Bible because his name is contained in its dedicatory verses, confirms the practice of word separation at Cluny before 1049, the time of Odilon's death.[9] This Bible, including both New and Old Testaments, was an extensive enterprise of over

four hundred folios directed by the scribe Franco. Franco likely under-
took the project to make the word of God available in the new medium,
for Cluny must have already had Bibles of similar dimensions written in
word blocks.[10] Franco's text was entirely separated. Contemporary emendators added *prosodiae* to clarify the text. The successor note to the *diastole* was used to distinguish monosyllabic prepositions from their objects
in instances where misconstruction was easy. The acute accent was added
by the scribe, or possibly by an early emendator, to denote Hebrew names
and as an alternate to the suspended ligature to indicate word continuation.[11] Rare *traits d'union* were also added by an early emendator.

Although word separation was widely practiced at Cluny during Odilon's final years, its dominance was not complete at his death. A compilation of patristic texts and contemporary sermons, today divided between
Paris, BN NAL 1455,[12] containing the greater part of the original codex,
and Paris, BN lat. 17275,[13] an isolated fragment, now separately bound,
were copied at various moments during Odilon's abbacy, with the final
texts added after 1049. The oldest portions were written at the turn of the
eleventh century in hierarchical word blocks regularly exceeding twenty
characters in length.[14] The text of John Chrysostom's *Homilies* was separated by space frequently less than 2 times the unity of space.[15] However,
Remi of Auxerre's *Commentum in Canticum canticorum* was consistently
separated by 2 times the unity of space, which was clearly distinguishable from intersyllabic space.[16] The scribe also used the successor to the
diastole and both *traits d'union* and acute accents to indicate word continuation at line endings. A group of sermons on folios 87 through 90,
134 through 136, and 153 through 166 of Paris, BN NAL 1455 were the
final element of this book to be written, and they were surely added
after Odilon's death, for the scribes in attributing them designated the
abbot as "sanctus" and "beatus."[17] Most of the sermons were written in
separated script, including one that an eleventh-century corrector rightly
attributed to Fulbert.[18] However, on folios 160 through 161v, two leaves
containing the conclusion of a posthumously transcribed sermon of Odilon's were written in word blocks. Thus, even under Abbot Hugh in the
second half of the eleventh century, Cluny scribes were not universally
practicing word separation. However, the lapse into word blocks in NAL
1455 was exceptional, and all other codices datable to the abbacy of Hugh
(1049–1109) were separated and contained abundant *prosodiae*, terminal
forms including the capital *S*, the elevated round *s*, the long *j* in numbers,
and intraword ligatures that enhanced Bouma shape.[19] For an overview

of the progress of word separation at Cluny, see the Appendix, Table A6.

When we turn to Cluny's large corpus of charters, it would also seem that the transition to word separation transpired under Odilon's abbacy as well. However, the considerable number of post-factum copies, many skillfully executed in the eleventh century as facsimiles of lost originals, are problematical. This practice seems to have been as prevalent at Cluny as at Saint Peter's of Ghent, but at Cluny, the originals are particularly difficult to distinguish.

Adding to the problem is the fact that eleventh-century Cluny scribes viewed writing in hierarchical word blocks as a sign of antiquity (and word separation as a sign of modernity), and therefore, in the desire to imitate an earlier practice, they consciously reproduced the unseparated text format of the past. Proof of this can be found in Paris, BN NAL 1497 and NAL 1498, the oldest cartularies of the abbey.[20] Respectively known as "Cartulary A" and "Cartulary B," they reproduce documents beginning with the foundation of the abbey. The two volumes were initially copied at the end of Odilon's abbacy and the beginning of Hugh's administration, and they were subsequently expanded. The writing varies considerably in the original portion, which fills over six hundred leaves. Thus, the *Annales of Cluny* (a historical preface found in "Cartulary A," folios 1 through 4) and the analytical tables were written in canonically separated book script, replete with monolexic abbreviations, the terminal elevated round *s*, the terminal capital *S*, *traits d'union*, and the denoting of monosyllables and the double *ii* by acute accents. Many of the documents were also copied in this canonically separated and extremely legible book script, with proper names regularly denoted by an initial capital to facilitate reference consultation.

However, some documents were copied in a script characteristic of the original charters, and certain sections were written as veritable historical facsimiles of them. Four of these sections, Cartulary "A," folios 7 through 10, 82v through 95 and 168 through 172v, and Cartulary "B," folios 4 through 13v, exemplify this attempt at historicity, for they were transcribed in hierarchical word blocks in an attempt to recreate the unseparated writing deemed by the compilers of the cartularies to be appropriate for the date of the original. Not only were the words on these leaves unseparated, but the terminal forms, accenting, and *traits d'union* were omitted, with the only concession to mid-eleventh-century writing habits being the consistent use of initial capitals to denote proper names. The unseparated sections contained documents whose originals had been written under the tenures of abbots Bernon (910–27), Aimard (942–54), Maïeul (954–94), and Odilon (994–1049). Among the charters of Odilon written in word blocks, the most recent is dated in 1038. Later documents from Odilon's abbacy and the charters of the abbacy of Hugh, even when written in script intended to suggest a facsimile of a documentary hand, were transcribed in separated script. It is therefore reasonable to infer that the monk-compilers under abbots Odilon and Hugh deemed 1038 as an approximate chronological limit after which the use of word blocks in the cartularies would have been inappropriate.

The tenth-century and eleventh-century Cluny charters (some of which are certainly word-separated copies made after the fact) help to confirm the dating of the cartularies. These were collected and bound in the nineteenth century in composite volumes. Those bridging the gap between word blocks and separated script are Paris, BN Collection Bourgogne, volumes 76, 77, 78, lat. 17715, and NAL 2154.[21] These documents permit the determination of the latest date for charters in which word separation was not observed, for even if some are not actually original, they at least reflect the date at which the scribes of the abbey thought that separation would not have been appropriate. NAL 2154, an undated charter of the time of Abbot Odilon, was written in hierarchical word blocks shorter than twenty-five characters in maximum length.[22] In Collection Bourgogne, volume 77, the most recent document in aerated script is charter number 94, dated in 1031, with word blocks greater than twenty characters in maximum length. In Collection Bourgogne, volume 78, the last aerated document was dated in 1040 and written in word blocks greater than twenty characters in maximum length.[23] Thus, the evidence of these documents is consistent with that of the cartularies and books. All three sources indicate an acceptance of the new mode of writing at Cluny early in the fourth decade of the eleventh century, distinctly later than at Reims, Chartres, Fleury, and the reformed abbeys of Flanders and Normandy. The basilica begun by Abbot Hugh in 1088 reflects the change in writing that had occurred just prior to his election. The capitals of the choir were embellished with explicatory legends written in separated script analogous to the banderoles present in the illuminations of separated manuscripts and similarly exemplify the infusion of writing into art.[24]

When word separation did emerge at Cluny, it did so contemporaneously with the appearance of the monastic cartulary, a genre of monastic book already discussed above in the context of Saint Peter's of Ghent.

The two-volume cartulary of Cluny, containing the texts of over two thousand documents, was a medieval reference tool of unprecedented amplitude. Whereas most early cartularies were organized strictly chronologically and were unaccompanied by tables of *capitula*, the Cluny cartularies were arranged geographically for the reign of each abbot according to the lands referred to in the donation. Each abbacy had its own discrete table giving a summary of the content of each document, including a geographic referent, the incipit of the text, and a red reference number also placed in the outer margin of the apposite folio. These reference numbers allowed the reader to identify swiftly a given document in the body of the text. In the Cluny cartularies, canonical word separation, the capitalization of proper names, acute accents, *traits d'union*, and colored ink in most of the text facilitated the rapid reading needed for the retrieval of specific data. Eleventh-century Cluny was an enormous agrarian enterprise, and it may well be that the needs of its archival administration provided part of the impetus for the acceptance of separated writing at the abbey.

The size and complexity of Cluny and the concomitant effort to facilitate the retrieval of information can also be seen in the codices recording the names of deceased monks.[25] The new cult of prayer for the dead in purgatory that was peculiarly characteristic of Cluniac piety made easy access to this particular information especially important.[26] Cluny's obituary codices have been lost, but Paris, BN NAL 348, prepared ca. 1093–94 by the scribe and nun Elsendis from Cluny's priory of Marcigny-sur-Loire (est. 1055), contains about ten thousand names. It made abundant use of the capitalization of proper names and employed a sophisticated two-column page format in which one column was reserved for the monks of Cluny and the nuns of Marcigny and the other column reserved for monks and nuns of other Cluniac houses.[27]

The relatively late date at which word separation was accepted at Cluny was due to the abbey's attachment to its own strong liturgical and scribal traditions. Cluny took little interest in the new Benedictine reform movement emanating from England, Normandy, Lorraine, and the Low Countries, or in the protoscholastic thought of Gerbert, Abbo, and their disciples. With the exception of the aforementioned single copy of Boethius's *De topicis differentiis* and the sermon of Fulbert copied after 1049, none of the authors and texts associated with the new learning were copied in the eleventh century at Cluny, and they were largely absent from the catalogues of the abbey's library.[28] Classical authors such as Virgil, Statius, Terence, Juvenal, Persius, and Horace, deemed by Gerbert to be essential to the study of rhetoric, were also for the most part absent from Cluny, where pagan authors continued to be viewed with suspicion.[29] This may explain why Adalbero of Laon, a student of Gerbert's and writer of word-separated texts, sarcastically referred to the ignorance of the monks of Cluny.[30] A mid-eleventh-century Lenten reading list confirms that the reading tastes of Cluny centered on the Church Fathers, with minimal interest in pagan authors, and none in logical and scientific texts.[31] The influence of scribes from Italy and Spain may also have contributed to making the transition to word separation more gradual at Cluny than at Saint Peter's of Ghent or Saint-Bertin.[32] When word separation did come to Cluny, it likely came from Fécamp, which had been associated with Cluny since 1001 and which practiced word separation after 1028. As we shall see in the next section, Fécamp monks were probably responsible for the introduction of word separation to Saint-Bénigne in Dijon.

Saint-Bénigne of Dijon

The earliest Saint-Bénigne manuscripts were aerated, but certain of these codices, dating from late in the abbacy of William of Volpiano, when his nephew John had already succeeded him at Fécamp, began to incorporate specific features regularly associated with word separation, including *traits d'union*, suspended ligatures, use of the *J* form of the *diastole* to separate words at points of ambiguity, and the accented double *ii*.[33] A part of Dijon, BM 51, was actually written in separated script. The *Tonaire de Saint-Bénigne*, Montpellier, Bibliothèque de l'Ecole de Médecine H 159, was written under William in highly aerated syllabic script.[34] A copy of the charter from Robert the Pious, dated January 25, 1015, confirming the privileges of the abbey and its abbot, but actually copied at Saint-Bénigne in January 1031, was in hierarchical word blocks shorter than twenty characters in length. However, the monk Aldebaldus added a word-separated inscription to Berlin, Staatsbibliothek Stiftung Preussischer Kulturbesitz Hamilton 82, a ninth-century Bible, in which he stated that he was recopying the book for Abbot William.[35] The copy he made is unfortunately lost.

After the election of William's successor Halinard, abbot from 1031 to 1052, who was associated with the reform of Richard of Saint-Vannes, Saint-Bénigne's manuscripts display consistent word separation. Halinard presented to the abbey a copy of the *Pseudo-Clementine Recognitiones*, Paris, BN lat. 9518.[36] The manuscript was the work of several scribes. Words were separated by unstable quantities of space varying from equivalence to 2 times the unity of space. *Prosodiae* included split-line *traits d'union*, in some instances clearly by the scribe, and suspended *ct* ligatures. Acute accents were used in lieu of *traits d'union* as signs of word continuation and for the redundant denotation of monosyllables. In 1036, Halinard received a sacramentarium, Dijon, BM 122, copied at Saint-Germain-des-Prés, where word separation emerged in the middle third of the century under Adélard, abbot from 1030 to 1060.[37] On folio 108v, three texts were added at the Abbey of Saint-Bénigne, two brief liturgical texts and an oath of fidelity to Halinard as abbot of Saint-Martin of Autun and archbishop of Lyon, a see that he occupied from 1041 until his death in 1051. The oath and the liturgical additions were all written in separated script. By the second half of the eleventh century, codices such as Dijon, BM 107, were being routinely written in canonically or *fere* canonically separated script, replete with Insular *prosodiae* and banderoles.[38] In the late eleventh century, a new Bible, Dijon BM 2, was prepared for Saint-Bénigne in *fere* canonically separated script.

The charters of Saint-Bénigne, written after the election of Abbot Halinard, were also separated. Robert, duke of Burgundy's charter of relief dating from 1031–46 was written in script separated by 2 times the unity of space, with terminal forms that included the capital *S*.[39] His charter of restitution dating from 1034–39 was also written in separated script, with proper names denoted by all capitals.[40] However, when in about 1066 Saint-Bénigne's monks produced copies of both a genuine and a fake papal bull from Benedict VIII (1012–24), they were subtle enough to employ aerated script, exhibiting a sensitivity to the historicity of that text format for an Italian charter.[41]

Elsewhere in France before 1050, the emergence of word separation had no apparent correlation with the date of a particular abbey's acceptance of Cluny's customs. At Fécamp, as we have already seen, word separation occurred with the election of the reform abbot, John. Fleury and Saint-Micy, which had accepted the customs of Cluny from Abbot Odon, did not adopt word separation until the time of Abbo. At Saint-Maur-des-Fossés, the Abbey of Saint-Pierre had accepted the customs of Cluny at the time of Maïeul, abbot from 954 to 994, but separated writing was not introduced until between 1029 and 1058.[42] At the Abbey of Saint-Denis, which had also accepted Cluny's customs from Maïeul, word separation emerged in the middle third of the eleventh century,[43] and at the Abbey of Saint-Pierre-le-Vif of Sens, unseparated writing prevailed until at least 1045.[44]

Saint-Martial of Limoges

In southern France, the acceptance of word separation came in the second half of the eleventh century. The fact that the evolution in text format transpired over three-quarters of a century later in the south than in the north of France was the consequence of several factors. First, because of the closeness of written Latin and the spoken vernacular of southern France, the graphic innovations of intense aeration and word separation were perceived to be less urgent for the reading and comprehension of intellectually difficult texts than in other regions of France.[45] Second, although the texts of Bede, Alcuin, and the Insular grammarians were long familiar in southern France, its geographic remoteness from England also made it less susceptible to Anglo-Saxon graphic practices.[46] Finally, the dissemination of the new protoscholastic learning associated with Gerbert, Abbo, and Heriger, although indebted to Mozarabic Catalonia, was centered in northern France, Lorraine, and Germany, from whence its influence was slow to permeate the schools of southern France.

The Cluniac Order, established as an administrative structure under Abbot Hugh, became the major avenue for the penetration of both the customs of Cluny and word separation south of the Loire. Two large abbeys, in particular, adopted word separation as a corollary to reform at the hands of Abbot Hugh, Saint-Martial of Limoges and Saint-Pierre of Moissac. At Saint-Martial, hierarchical word blocks were the customary medium for written composition throughout the ninth and tenth centuries. Paris, BN lat. 5, the two-volume ninth-century Bible of the abbey, was written in hierarchical word blocks still occasionally exceeding twenty characters in maximum length.[47] In the tenth century, Paris, BN lat. 5239, was written in hierarchical word blocks exceeding twenty characters in maximum length.[48] Paris, BN lat. 5301, a lectionary prepared for the use of Saint-Martial in about 1000 and containing Odon of Cluny's *Vita* of Gerard of Aurillac, was written in hierarchical word blocks occasionally exceeding twenty characters in length.[49]

Word separation came to Saint-Martial in the course of the eleventh century, and two dates establish the chronology. The first is 1031, the date of the Synod of Limoges, which recognized Martial as an apostle. By felicitous circumstance, the *fond* of Saint-Martial *codices* at the Biblio-thèque Nationale includes the richest collection of liturgical books from any eleventh-century abbey. Following Martial's elevation to apostolic status, Saint-Martial's scribes methodically went through their liturgi-cal books (trope books, that is, chant books; also hymnals and Psalters) and altered the designation of the patron saint of the abbey by erasing the word *confessor* and writing in *apostolus*. All books with these re-visions can be dated to before 1031. Conversely, all Saint-Martial books in which Martial was designated *apostolus* by the original hand were writ-ten after 1031.

No manuscript originally designating Martial as *confessor* was writ-ten in separated script, indicating that the change in Martial's status antedates the adoption of word separation by the abbey's scriptorium. Furthermore, Paris, BN lat. 1119 and lat. 887, two trope books written with Saint Martial as *apostolus* and therefore after 1031, were unsepa-rated.[50] Paris, BN NAL 1871, a third and closely related trope book listing Martial as *apostolus*, but prepared for use at the Abbey of Saint-Pierre of Moissac, was copied without separation, either at Saint-Martial or at Moissac by a scribe from Saint-Martial. A *Versus de sancto Martiale* describing his acts and qualifying him as an apostle was added to Saint-Martial's lectionary, Paris, BN lat. 5301, after 1031, in unseparated script.[51]

The second date for determining the adoption of word separation at Saint-Martial was the death in 1034 of Adémar of Chabannes, a monk of the Cluniac Abbey of Saint-Cybard of Angoulême, who worked at Saint-Martial as a chronicler, scribe, and illuminator. The nine surviving books that he copied, either in their entirety or in part, comprise the largest corpus of work by any single French scribe of the eleventh century. All were copied either at Angoulême or Limoges in hierarchical word blocks exceeding twenty characters in length.[52] Adémar's pattern of aeration was totally unaffected by the size and page format of his codices, disproving the oft-stated idea that scribes omitted space in order to write as much text as possible on a limited quantity of parchment. Adémar's books are also proof that in the eleventh century, the absence of regular word sepa-ration was not a sign of a low level of literacy or defective Latinity. Adé-mar was one of the more competent chroniclers of his age, and his grasp of Latin grammar was no less perfect than that of his contemporaries to the north and east, who wrote with word separation.

Adémar's writing in hierarchical word blocks was not merely an anti-quated habit maintained by a venerable scholar in old age. Born in about

988, he was less than fifty at his death in 1034, and manuscripts like Paris, BN lat. 3784, in hierarchical word blocks exceeding twenty characters in length, were written in part by other and probably younger men, under his supervision.[53] The use of unseparated script at Saint-Martial's was a matter of preference, not of ignorance, for separated books were known to the abbey well before 1034. In his *Sermo III*, Adémar related that in 1031, King Canute of England (1016–35) sent an illuminated liturgical book to the Synod of Limoges.[54] A codex copied in England at this time would certainly have been written in separated script, and the decoration of Saint-Martial's Terence, Paris, BN lat. 7903, copied in hierarchical word blocks ca. 1000, already shows the influence of the Anglo-Saxon art of illumination as it was perfected in word-separated codices copied at Ramsey in about the year 1000.[55] Indeed, Adémar himself supervised the copying of a codex containing a text by Abbo, Paris, BN lat. 2400, and given the word separation in Abbo's manuscript tradition, the exemplar was in all probability separated.[56]

By suppressing word distinctions in a separated text, Adémar and other Saint-Martial monks were only continuing a practice that was also part of the Continental textual tradition of Bede. Adémar also continued the earlier practice of providing marginal glosses with tironian notes. Glosses written in tironian *hybrida* served as entry points to Pseudo-Augustine's *De musica*, Paris, BN lat. 7231.[57] Adémar also used tironian notes in parts of Leiden, BR Voss. lat. O. 15,[58] and in his sermons, Adémar made regular use of the tironian note for *Amen*.[59]

In 1053, part of the abbey accepted the suzerainty of Hugh of Cluny, and in 1062, Hugh selected a second Adémar as abbot, marking the end of the strife between Cluniac and non-Cluniac elements. Codices likely to have been copied in the period of transition are particularly important for tracing the change from unseparated to separated writing. A group of Saint-Martial monks copied Adémar of Chabannes's *Chronicon* from an autograph codex then still at Saint-Martial. This manuscript, Paris, BN lat. 5927, was written partially in unsurely executed separated script and partially in word blocks.[60] Occasional split-line *traits d'union* confirm contact with the new practice of word separation. Paris, BN lat. 7562, containing Donatus's *De Grammatica*, was also written in this period, partly in word blocks and partly in separated script.[61] Because after ca. 1040 Cluny scribes usually observed word separation, its appearance in these books is probably related to the entry of Saint-Martial into the Order of Cluny. Paris, BN lat. 822, a sacramentarium for the use of

Saint-Martial, includes a feast for Odilon of Cluny that was not quali-fied as *sanctus*, and therefore that was copied after his death in 1049, but before his canonization in 1095.[62] Most likely written soon after 1053, the date of Saint-Martial's full affiliation with Cluny, the sacramentarium was copied in separated script with interword space equivalent to from 2 to 2.6 times the unity of space. Paris, BN lat. 5240, a seventeenth-century composite book formed from fragments of Saint-Martial manuscripts, contains as its first two quires an Easter table beginning in 1064 and a letter of Pope John XIX discussing the apostolic status of Saint Martial that is without doubt contemporary with the table.[63] The text was sepa-rated by interword space equivalent to 2 times the unity of space, and *prosodiae* included the acute accent on monosyllabic prepositions as a re-dundant sign of separation. The brief inscription on the tomb of Roger le Chantre (d. 1025) was written in the mid-eleventh century in script separated by space and interpuncts.[64]

Paris, BN lat. 2208, Gregory the Great's *Moralia in Job*, was, accord-ing to its colophon, copied by the scribes Arleius and Petrus for Abbot Adémar, and therefore must date from before his death in 1114.[65] The codex, today divided into two volumes, was transcribed in canonically separated script. *Prosodiae* consisted of hyphens to correct scribal errors and *traits d'union*. Monolexic abbreviations, including superscript forms and the Insular sign for *est*, were present in unprecedented numbers. The presence of protracted intraword letters and ligatures to fill out columns suggests that this manuscript was copied visually by a scribe trying to reproduce the page format of his exemplar. Abbot Adémar was also prob-ably responsible for the second two-volume Bible of Saint-Martial, Paris, BN lat. 8, copied from the unseparated text of lat. 5. Lat. 8 was written in canonically separated script.[66] This text format was totally appropriate to the new eleventh-century taste for books intended to facilitate reading. On folio 41 of the second volume, an illumination, replete with bande-role, depicted the prophet Eli and the messengers of the king.[67] The ban-derole thus followed the path of word separation, from north to south.

Word separation at Saint-Martial's can be identified with refinement in the use of *prosodiae*. Gregory the Great's *Liber regulae pastorolis*, Paris, BN lat. 2799, was transcribed under Abbot Adémar in canonically sepa-rated script.[68] Following the rules of Pseudo-Priscian's *Liber de accentibus*, acute accents were placed on the last syllable of adverbs that might other-wise have been misconstrued, such as *tanto* and *quanto*. They were also used for words divided at line endings in lieu of *traits d'union*. A varied pattern of green and red minor initials conferred a distinct mnemonic image to many leaves. In Paris, BN lat. 2056, Augustine's *De civitate Dei*, copied in about 1100, the vertical stroke of the *t* protruded above the horizontal, enhancing word shape.[69] South of Limoges, at the collegial church of Saint-Yrieix-la-Perche, a Bible now in the vault of the *mairie* of Saint-Yrieix was transcribed by monks from Saint-Martial in the second half of the eleventh century in separated script, with abundant use of the *trait d'union* and the acute accent.[70]

By the end of the eleventh century, the northern protoscholastic and devotional separated texts were increasingly present at Saint-Martial. In Paris, BN lat. 5239, a late-eleventh-century hand added Abbo's treatise on computation on folios 127v through 128 in *fere* canonically separated script.[71] John of Fécamp's prayer *Lassus penitentiae* was copied in separated script in a quire contained in Paris, BN lat. 544, ff. 141–42v, a composite book formed in the eighteenth century.[72] Also at the end of the eleventh century, a scribe at Saint-Martial, perhaps indirectly influenced by the example of Fleury, experimented with transcribing the Romance vernacular. In the poem *Sponsus*, transcribed in Paris, BN lat. 1139, the text was aerated, although the same scribe, when he wrote an adjacent text in Latin, separated words by from 1.3 to 4 times the unity of space and employed the *trait d'union*.[73] For an overview of word separation at Saint-Martial, see the Appendix, Table A7.

Saint-Pierre of Moissac

Saint-Pierre of Moissac, near Toulouse, follows the pattern of Saint-Martial. A tradition of writing there in hierarchical word blocks can be documented from the end of the ninth century. By the end of the eleventh century, as texts contained in BN lat. 7505 document, Insular writing and reading habits had penetrated into southern France. Priscian's *Institutiones grammaticae* in that collection was written at Moissac in the beginning of the eleventh century in hierarchical word blocks exceeding twenty characters in maximum length, accompanied by an added text and glosses written in tironian *hybrida*.[74] This codex, with those of Saint-Martial, was among the last to perpetuate the use of tironian notes, which word separation would soon render obsolete. By the second half of the eleventh century, a Moissac scribe added as a preface to the *De ordinatione constructionis* in BN lat. 7505 the same short explication of word order that was copied at Fleury at the time of Abbo.

The Moissac transcription, like the Fleury copy, was written in separated script, with interword space equivalent to 2 times the unity of space and with terminal forms such as the capital *M* and *S*.[75] *Prosodiae* included *traits d'union* and conspicuous intraword ligatures. To the unseparated text of Priscian's *Institutiones*, an emendator now added alphabetical construction notes consistent with the dictates of *De ordinatione* to help the reader recast Priscian's classical prose into a more logical, comprehensible, and by now more familiar word order.

Chicago, Newberry Library 1, a homilarium from Saint-Pierre of Moissac, documents the transition from hierarchical word blocks to separated script.[76] The homilarium was copied by several scribes, some of whom wrote in word blocks of over twenty characters in length, employing interword ligatures. However, the writing of one hand was canonically separated by interword space equivalent to 2 times the unity of space and denoted the double *ii* with acute accents.[77] Another transitional codex is a collection of patristic texts, including works of Augustine and Paschasius Radbertus, Paris, BN lat. 2077. It was copied mostly in hierarchical word blocks exceeding fifteen characters in maximum length,[78] but portions of it (for example, folios 122 through 173) were written in script separated by space varying from equivalence to 2 times the unity of space, with a small elevated *h* in lieu of the *dasia* at word beginnings. Some proper names were denoted by initial capitals. Acute accents, the *dasia*, and the small *h* were added to clarify the unseparated pages. Unlike their confreres in the north, the monks of Limoges and Moissac did not have to evolve ex nihilo their own conventions for separating Caroline script. They profited from Cluny's experience and rapidly emulated perfected models of northern separated script.

The earliest firmly datable manuscript written with word separation at Moissac is Oxford, BL d'Orville 45, a Psalter arranged for private devotion, which contains the feast of Odilon and is precisely datable from its Easter table to 1067.[79] Its script was separated, with interword space equivalent to 2.5 times the unity of space. *Prosodiae* consisted of the acute accent to denote the tonic syllable. The presence of Odilon in the calendar and the separation of the script indicate the Cluniac influence of Durand, abbot from 1048 to 1072, subsequently reinforced by that of Hunaud de Gavarret, abbot from 1072 to 1085. Both abbots, trained at Cluny, struggled to make Moissac conform to Cluny's standards of liturgical discipline and independence from secular authority.[80]

Valuable insight into the process of the introduction of word separa-

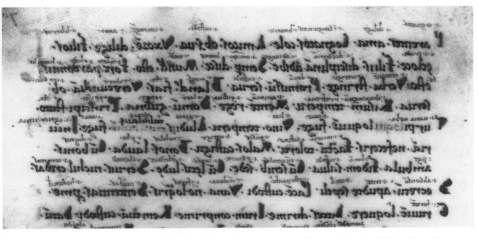

Figure 34. Pedagogical word separation by points and space in the *Dicta Leonis*.
Paris, Bibliothèque Nationale lat. 4886, f. 70 recto; reproduced by permission.

tion at Moissac and its dependencies may be gleaned from the text of the
Dicta Leonis in Paris, BN lat. 4886, ff. 69v–70.[81] The *Dicta Leonis* was a
ninth-century pedagogical text intended for teaching reading and augmenting vocabulary. The Moissac scribe who copied it, probably from
an unseparated exemplar, inserted both interpuncts and space between
words to emphasize the word as the basic graphic and pedagogic unit
(Figure 34). Acute accents were used to denote the tonic syllable and as a
sign of word continuation. Leiden, BR BPL 1822, containing Paschasius
Radbertus's *De corpore et sanguine Christi*, an important source for both
sides in the controversy between Berengar of Tours and Lanfranc over
the Sacrament, was copied at Saint-Pierre with interword space equivalent to 2.5 times the unity of space.[82] This highly legible book, small in
format and surely intended for personal study, contained over 250 abbreviations, among which monolexic ones, particularly superscript forms,
were numerous.

Two surviving eleventh-century volumes from Moissac containing
transcriptions of classical texts are particularly significant for their *prosodiae*. Josephus's *Antiquitatum iudaicarum libri* and Caesar's *De bello
Gallico*, in Paris, BN lat. 5056, were copied at the end of the century in
canonically separated script, with interword space equivalent to from 2
to 3 times the unity of space.[83] The scribe used the acute accent in combination with the hyphen to attach the enclitic conjunction -*que* that

he had originally separated by space. The scribe and an early emendator corrected other errors in word separation with the successor note to the *diastole*. On folios 89v through 139v, the scribe used the *dasia* as a redundant sign of separation. Paris, BN lat. 5058, containing Josephus's *De bello Iudaico*, copied at the end of the century, was written in script separated by 2.5 unities of space, with the *dasia* present as a redundant sign of separation.[84] Acute accents were used on second-conjugation infinitives and words ending with the enclitic particle *-ve*.

In a two-volume homilarium, Paris, BN lat. 3783, the acute accent was also employed to clarify compound words formed from proclitics and enclitics, and the elevated small *h* was used as a sign of word distinction.[85] In two late-eleventh-century manuscripts of Saint-Martial, Paris, BN lat. 17002, a collection of *Vitae sanctae*,[86] and lat. 4808, Aethicus's *Cosmographia*,[87] the vertical stroke of the letter *t* protruded above the horizontal stroke, a modification of form analogous to *prosodiae* in enhancing word shape, and as a consequence increased the reader's reliance on peripheral vision.[88] The final portion of Paris, BN lat. 5083, Cassiodorus's *Historia ecclesiastica tripartita*, was written in script separated by 3 times the unity of space, with protracted intraword ligatures indicating that the scribe, copying visually, had sought to replicate each leaf of his exemplar as a unity. For an overview of word separation at Moissac, see the Appendix, Table A8.

Other than the two short but highly important grammatical texts in lat. 7505, discussed in the next section below, and copies of classical authors, there is little evidence that Moissac was greatly influenced by the new learning of protoscholasticism. The oldest inventories of the library confirm the impression that texts on mathematics, astronomy, and logic were largely absent from the abbey.[89] Contact with Arabic culture was evident only in the abbey's lapidary inscriptions. However, an early modern catalogue of the library enumerated a "collection of the canons of Burchard in folio," now lost.[90] Since few copies of Burchard's work were produced after the twelfth century, this catalogue entry could refer to an eleventh-century codex of a text whose diffusion was closely linked to that of word separation.

An important codicological feature symptomatic of graphic change at Moissac was foliation. The use of foliation or the impulse to refer to folios in unfoliated codices was consistent with reading habits in which skimming and cross-reference occurred. In Paris, BN lat. 1961, Augustine's *Tractatus in Iohannis Evangelium*, a book begun in hierarchical word blocks and continued in separated script, the first 250 leaves were foliated in the upper center margin by an eleventh-century hand using Roman numerals and punctuated into decimal distinctions with interpuncts and the long *j* terminal form. Beginning on folio 251, the foliation was continued by the same twelfth-century hand that also foliated BN lat. 4212 and 17002, both from Moissac. The impulse toward foliation is also evident in a marginal note from the first half of the eleventh century in Paris, BN lat. 7505 on folio 46: "thus Priscian himself stated seven folios further on."[91] The examples of foliation noted in eleventh-century codices, rare as they were, mark some of the earliest attempts of scribes, emendators, and readers to define physical loci as places for cross-reference within the book. Although it would take another four centuries for foliation to become a more than rare phenomenon, it is not without significance that early experiments in foliation transpired at French monastic centers after the transition from aerated to separated script.[92]

The *Ars lectoria* in Aquitaine

The same Moissac scribe who copied the *De ordinatione constructionis* in the second half of the eleventh century added another prefatory text to lat. 7505, a fragment of an *Ars lectoria* textually related to the *Ars lectoria* of the Aquitanian monk Magister Siguinus, composed in ca. 1087–88.[93] The title, *Ars lectoria*, which first appears only in twelfth-century manuscripts, implied not only skills for correct pronunciation, but for correct comprehension as well. This treatise, like Pseudo-Priscian's *Liber de accentibus*, was addressed to both readers and scribes.[94] The fragment in lat. 7505 is one of the oldest extant manuscripts of any *Ars lectoria*. It was written in separated script exactly like that of the *De ordinatione constructionis*. Its anonymous author was concerned with reducing the ambiguity of the written page and proposed that scribes distinguish between nouns and verbs by the inclusion or suppression of the letter *u*.[95] Very similar notions were repeated by Siguinus.[96] The lat. 7505 *Ars lectoria* also distinguished between the pronunciation of the letter *x* of *ex* as a simple word and *ex-* as a syllable in a compound word, an oral distinction that may well be related to distinguishing the preposition *ex* from the syllable *ex-* by the insertion of interword space.[97] Similar ideas relating to clarity in written expression were developed by Siguinus, who explicitly referred to word separation, cautioning scribes to take care to write *dictiones compositas* as single units, a concern equally present in the copious use of *prosodiae* at Limoges and Moissac.[98] He insisted upon spellings that prevented misconstruction of word boundaries when nouns followed monosyllabic prepositions.[99] He also took cognizance of correct and incorrect punctuation.[100] Siguinus assumed word separation and word order when he recommended the postpositioning of *te* as a freestanding word as a convenient aid to distinguishing active and passive verbs.[101] He similarly emphasized the need to distinguish *c* and *t* in a manner that complemented the practice of the Saint-Martial and Moissac scribes, who made the vertical stroke of the *t* protrude above the transverse stroke.[102] Siguinus explained, too, how proper accenting corrected the ambiguity engendered by minim strokes,[103] and he specifically offered instructions for the emendators of codices who were so active in eleventh-century monastic libraries.[104]

Aimericus, another Aquitanian monk, composed in 1085–86 a third closely related *Ars lectoria*, dedicated to Adémar, bishop of Angoulême from 1076 to 1101.[105] It is quite possible that both Aimericus and Siguinus were monks at Saint-Martial of Limoges or at Saint-Cybard of Angoulême.[106] However this may be, it is certain that all three of these treatises reflect scribal habits current at Limoges, Angoulême, and Moissac and that the authors wished to reduce reader perplexity in a manner consistent with the efforts of Cluniac scribes south of the Loire in the second half of the eleventh century. Aimericus, in his *Ars lectoria*, went so far as to make explicit reference to the scribe's use of graphic signs of punctuation as adjuncts to syntax in order to clarify the meaning of biblical text. He followed ninth-century Insular grammarians in emphasizing the first syllable that was readily detectable in the extended parafoveal vision of separated script.[107] He carefully distinguished between monosyllables as freestanding words and unaccented monosyllables in composition, a distinction foreign to ancient grammatical tradition.[108] Like Pseudo-Priscian in the *Liber de accentibus*, Aimericus distinguished adverbs and prepositions from nouns and verbs by stating that they were accented on the last syllable,[109] a practice that, as we have seen, was followed by the Saint-Martial scribe of BN lat. 2799.

At the end of the eleventh century, a scribe in or near Arles, surely influenced by the text format that the Cluniac Order had propagated, wrote in Arles, BM 7, f. 249v, a few lines of instruction in verse on the art of writing in which he explicitly stated that space of equal quantity ought to be inserted between words (*partes*).[110] The verses evincing cognizance of word separation were written in separated script, with interword space equivalent to 2 times the unity of space. The terminal round *s*, the tironian symbol for the conjunction *et*, and the letter *t* with the vertical stroke protruding slightly above the cap were all present.[111]

Aurillac and Saint-Sever

At Saint-Géraud of Aurillac, a daughter abbey of Saint-Pierre of Moissac, Paris, BN lat. 1084, a trope book, was written in the mid-eleventh century in word blocks exceeding twenty-five characters in length.[112] In contrast, BN lat. 944, a pontifical written after 1070 but no later than 1135, was written in separated script.[113] The capital *S* was present as a terminal form, and *prosodiae* included *traits d'union*, as well as acute accents on the double *ii* and to denote the tonic syllable. At the Abbey of Saint-Sever in southwest Aquitaine, under the Cluniac reformer Grégoire of Montaner (d. 1072), Beato de Liébano's *Commentary on the Apocalypse and the Book of Daniel*, Paris, BN lat. 8878, was written in the second half of the eleventh century in separated script.[114] Terminal forms included the ampersand and the crossed capital *S* for -*orum*, and among its *prosodiae* were the *trait d'union* at line endings and beginnings and the acute accent as a sign of interline word continuation. Leaves, originally blank, were used to form a small cartulary of documents dating from the late eleventh century, the writing of which incorporated the accenting of the double *ii* and the Insular forms of emblematic punctuation.

The Reform of Saint-Victor of Marseille

The Abbey of Saint-Victor of Marseille became a center of Bene-dictine reform under the pontificate of Gregory VII (1073–85), whose circle employed word separation.[115] At the end of the century, Boethius's *In Categorias Aristotelis*, an element of the *Logica vetus*, was copied at Saint-Victor in separated and canonically separated hands, with inter-word space varying from 2 to 2.6 times the unity of space.[116] The clarity of the new writing was fully exploited. Terminal forms included the *et* ligature. *Prosodiae* included *traits d'union* at line endings and beginnings. The diples, which in books copied in word blocks were invariably placed in the margins, were here written within the text itself. Interlinear alpha-betical construction notes and schematic diagrams grammatically and pictorially clarified the sense of the text. Emblematic tie notes linked the gloss to the text. This separated copy of Boethius formed the con-cluding segment (folios 128 through 144) of BN lat. 1954. The first 127 leaves of the same codex, written not much earlier and containing Augustine's *De consensu evangelistarum*, was copied in hierarchical word blocks of greater than twenty-five characters in maximum length. On folio 2–2v, an interpage split-line *trait d'union* by the scribe is an unmistakable sign of contact with the new system of separated writing. Paris, BN lat. 14301, ff. 1–96, containing Isidore's commentary on Scripture, was also written partly in word blocks and partly in separated script.[117] Another early separated manuscript from Saint-Victor was Paris, BN lat. 2126.[118] The charters of Saint-Victor, bearing dates as early as 1005 and written in separated script, are clearly copies dating from the second half of the eleventh century.[119] The late-eleventh-century inscription of the tomb of Abbot Isarn in the crypt of Saint-Victor was written in separated script.[120]

La Grasse

The Abbey of La Grasse, near Carcassonne, was reformed in about 1070 by monks from Saint-Victor. A surviving original charter dated in 1038 was written in hierarchical word blocks exceeding twenty characters in length.[121] In contrast a *rituale*, Paris, BN lat. 933, datable to 1086–92, reveals the transition to separated and canonically separated script, with interword space consistently equivalent to 2 times the unity of space and with terminal forms such as the elevated *s*, the capital *S*, and the crossed capital *S* for *-orum*.[122] However, a hymn added on folios 109v through 110, which were originally blank, was written in hierarchical word blocks shorter than fifteen characters in length. Another aspect of this *rituale* suggesting transition to word separation is the original front flyleaf, formed from an eleventh-century leaf written in hierarchical word blocks exceeding fifteen characters in length. It is of particular interest that this fragment contains original acute accents on the double *ii*. In the northern centers, where word separation had supplanted word blocks well before the practice of using the acute accent for the double *ii*, the presence of this characteristic of canonical separation in the context of aerated script rarely occurred. Such hybridization at La Grasse was an important indication of the very rapid pace of transition from unseparated to canonically separated script south of the Loire.

Chapter 13

Italy

Word separation emerged in Italy, depending on the region and the center, from seventy-five to over one hundred years later than at Fleury and Reims.[1] The reasons for its tardiness were the same as for southern France. First, because of the great similarity between the Italian vernacular and Latin (Italian had evolved as a distinct language to an even lesser extent than Occitan), the innovations of word separation, word order, and a written vernacular were far less critical to reading. Second, the new disciplines of logic and mathematics took longer to penetrate Europe south of the Alps. The description of the general pattern of the adoption of word separation for Italy excludes the special case of the early medieval Irish monastic colonies in northern Italy such as Milan and Bobbio, where the earliest separated manuscripts were transcribed in the eighth century by Irish scribes. However, these codices left no permanent trace, and with the exception of a handful of manuscripts copied at Bobbio when Gerbert resided there as abbot, from 980 to 983, it was not until the final two-thirds of the eleventh century that word separation became prominent in Italian books and documents. Informal documents and draft notes were even later in employing separation, which did not become in any sense fully standard until the mid-thirteenth century.

The factors finally leading to the introduction of word separation in late-eleventh-century and twelfth-century Italy were diverse. They include the patronage of the Imperial court, particularly at Monte Cassino, the expanding influence of the orders of Cluny and Cîteaux (particularly in northwestern Italy, adjacent to France), the religious reform of Gregory VII at Rome, the Norman conquest of Sicily, and the renewed study of civil law at Bologna. All these forces, however, were not sufficient to establish separation definitively, and even in the late twelfth century, many formal Italian codices were still being written in aerated script.

The first major Italian monastery in the eleventh century to produce separated codices was the Abbey of Monte Cassino, located in southern Italy, where, as in Rome, the tradition of *scriptura continua* had been strong. Aerated writing at Monte Cassino continued uninterrupted throughout the ninth and tenth centuries and into the beginning of the eleventh. Under Theobaldus, abbot from 1022 to 1035, manuscripts were being copied in hierarchical word blocks half a century after word separation was regularly observed by the monks of Fleury, and over three centuries after its establishment in the British Isles.

Two Germans, Richerius, abbot from 1038 to 1055, and Frederick of Lorraine, abbot from 1056 to 1058, succeeded Theobaldus at Monte Cassino. These northerners brought separated Caroline codices to the abbey and thus began the process of introducing word separation to the indigenous Beneventan script. Nevertheless, in the first half of the eleventh century, the protoscholastic texts of Gerbert, Burchard of Worms, and the *Logica vetus* were copied as often in aerated as they were in separated script.

Even in the half century after Richerius and Frederick, because the Italian vernacular was closer to Latin, scribes at Monte Cassino often felt free to omit spaces between words, thus creating short word blocks without subdistinctions. A necrological calendar and *Ordo missae*, Vat Borg. lat. 211, attributed to the hand of Leo of Ostia, was written between January 30, 1094, and December 2, 1105, in solid word blocks (i.e., word blocks without significant subdistinction by minor spacing) shorter than fifteen characters in length, with the tripoint terminal punctuation carefully coordinated with initial capitals.[2] Three scribes copied Archivio Segreto Vaticano, Reg. Vat. 1, the register of Pope John VIII. The master scribe, "scribe A," wrote separated script; "scribe B" wrote in solid word blocks.[3] Manuscripts written at the time of Oderisius, abbot from 1087 to 1105, were still not consistently separated. In 1153, the Monte Cassino scribe Sigenulfus copied Malibu, California, J. Paul Getty Museum, Peter Ludwig Collection IX (olim Monte Cassino, 199), a Breviary in hierarchical word blocks exceeding twenty-five characters in maximum length.[4] Peter the Deacon's autograph script of ca. 1132–38, in Monte Cassino, Archivio della Badia 361, evinced hierarchical word blocks exceeding twenty characters in length.[5] His handwriting in Monte Cassino, Archivio della Badia 257, was also aerated.[6]

Prosodiae, monolexic abbreviations, and related modifications of script developed tardily in Beneventan codices. The association of the acute accent with the *i* (particularly in the tonic syllable and on the double *ii*) that had already evolved in Norman manuscripts in the last third of the eleventh century did not emerge in Beneventan writing until the thirteenth century.[7] The earliest examples of Beneventan *traits d'union* date from between 1099 and 1118,[8] and the use of terminal forms within the line was relatively sparse, even at line endings. The earliest successor notes to the *diastole* and interword vertical strokes in Monte Cassino manuscripts date from the early thirteenth century.[9] The signaling of proper names by the use of initial capitals was less frequent in comparison with eleventh-century French, German, Lotharingian, and English manuscripts. Colophons with personal messages from scribe to reader were late to develop in Monte Cassino, as were attempts to write in the vernacular.

In the north, the Abbey of Bobbio did not produce separated manuscripts with any regularity until the end of the eleventh century. In the early twelfth century, Cistercian abbeys like Santa Maria de Morimonde, near Milan, were producing word-separated codices that consistently emulated northern models.

In central Italy, particularly at Bologna, the emergence of word separation was closely tied to the renewal of juristic studies. Paris, BN lat. 4458A, ff. 1–306, containing the *Digestum vetus et novum*, written at the end of the eleventh century, was heavily glossed, and because of the content of these glosses, it is generally regarded as one of the earliest artifacts documenting legal study at Bologna.[10] The manuscript evinces incipient word separation. Produced by a number of scribes, the codex varies from hierarchical word blocks exceeding fifteen characters in length to canonical separation, with interword space equivalent to 3 times the unity of space. The scribes of the separated portions used *traits d'union*, and they appear to have gone back to correct the aerated writing of the codex with the successor note to the *diastole* in an attempt to make the manuscript equally legible throughout. The glosses, too, show signs of ongoing graphic evolution. Earlier ones were without tie marks; later ones were linked to the text by emblematic tie marks. Acute accenting was used occasionally to resolve ambiguities in the separation of compound words and to denote monosyllabic prepositions, space after monosyllabic prepositions often being omitted. In one instance, the letter *i* was accented.[11] Folios 169 through 239, perhaps written slightly later than folios 1 through 168, also show a variety of spacing patterns, ranging from hierarchical word blocks to separation, with space omitted after monosyllabic prepositions and with contemporary or nearly contemporary attempts by emendators to use the successor note to the *diastole*, the *J* form of *diastole*, and the *trait d'union* to resolve ambiguities due to the absence of regular separation.

The same transition can be seen in codices containing the *Leges Langobardorum*. Paris, BN lat. 4613, of central Italian origin, was written at the end of the tenth century or in the early eleventh in hierarchical word blocks exceeding fifteen characters in length.[12] London, BL Add. 5411, copied in northern Italy at the end of the eleventh century or early in the twelfth, was separated, with interword space equivalent to from 2 to 3.5 times the unity of space.[13] *Prosodiae* included split-line *traits d'union* and *traits d'union* at line endings only. Terminal forms included the crossed capital *S* for *-orum*, and in the final section and in certain revisions, the elevated round *s*. The contemporary gloss was separated and also contained *traits d'union*. Another hand, probably of the mid-twelfth century, added schematic diagrams similar to those that in the previous century were used in the manuscripts of Reims, Fleury, and Chartres. Paris, BN lat. 4617, copied at the end of the twelfth century, was canonically separated, with interword space regularly equivalent to 2 times the unity of space and with terminal forms that included the round *s*.[14] Monolexic abbreviations consisted of the tironian sign for *et* and, in the gloss, the Insular sign for *est*. *Prosodiae* included *traits d'union* and the acute accent on the double *ii*. Insular-type tie marks joined the gloss to the text.

At the Abbey of Saint Sylvester of Nonantola, just north of Bologna, a group of twenty manuscripts produced for Peter Damian, nephew of the famous saint and reformer of the same name and abbot of Nonantola between 1089 and 1110, are now in the Vatican Library's Fonte Avellana and in the Biblioteca Nazionale Centrale Vittorio Emanuele II in Rome. These Nonantola books exhibit word separation and many related northern graphic traits, including split-line *traits d'union*, suspended ligatures, and the acute accent as a sign of interline continuation.[15]

In Rome and its surroundings, from the eighth century to the tenth, both written Latin and Greek were less aerated than north of the Alps, and in some codices, word blocks exceeded twenty-five characters in length, approaching *scriptura continua*.[16] In the eleventh century, two religious reformers, Saint Peter Damian (d. 1072, the uncle of the abbot of Nonantola) and Pope Gregory VII, whose pontificate ran from 1073 to 1085, became closely associated with a reform of scribal practices patterned on northern models. Gregory had spent considerable time in Germany and France, and he was intimately involved in the controversy surrounding Berengar of Tours. The authorial manuscript of Gregory VII's *Dictatus Papae*, Archivio Segreto Vaticano, Reg. Vat., 2, was written in consistently separated script (Figure 35).[17] Terminal forms included the capital *S* and the crossed capital *S* for *-orum* and *-mus* and the long *j* in numbers. Numbers were punctuated by points and space into decimal distinctions. Proper names were designated by all capitals, capital initials, and suspension abbreviations. Anselm of Lucca and Cardinal Deusdedit compiled two principal canon law collections to buttress the arguments for papal authority, and these were diffused exclusively in separated script.[18] Deusdedit's collection contained a more sophisticated subject index than that of the *Libri viginti decretorum* of Burchard of Worms, a text that was a source for Anselm's work. Vat. lat. 1363 of the late eleventh century, containing recension "B" of the *Collectio* of Anselm of Lucca, was canonically separated by 3 times the unity of space. Terminal forms included the capitals *R* and *S*, the latter especially present at line endings and at the end of sentences, where it was coordinated with the tripoint note of termination.[19] The vertical stroke of the *t* frequently protruded above its cap (as in the writings of Gerard of Florennes and at Mont Saint-Michel, Limoges, and Moissac), thereby enhancing clarity of each word's global image.

Just north of Rome, at the Abbey of Farfa, word separation appears to have been observed only late in the eleventh century.[20] The abbey's lectionary, Rome, BN Vittorio Emanuele II, Farfa 32, was written perhaps as late as the third quarter of the eleventh century, in hierarchical word blocks shorter than twenty characters in length.[21] However, a *fere*-contemporary emendator annotated the manuscript with *prosodiae*, including the acute accent, the interpunct, and the vertical stroke to distinguish words. A group of manuscripts associated with Gregorio di Catino (d. 1132), a member of Gregory VII's circle of reformers, was written in a Farfa variety of Caroline minuscule. Badia, Codex 3, a Breviary judged by its decoration to have originated at Farfa, apparently written at this time, was inscribed in separated script incorporating the capital *S* as a terminal form.[22] Vat. lat. 8487, the *Regestum Farfense* of Gregorio di

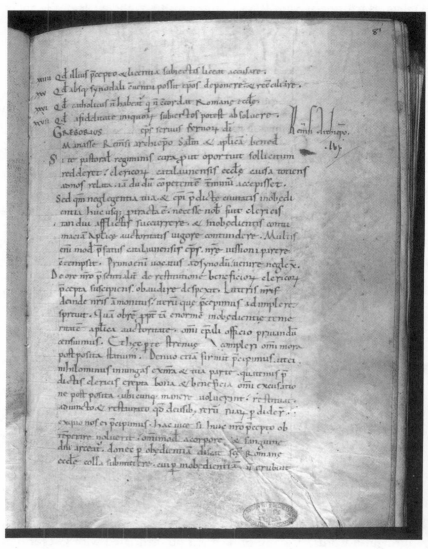

Figure 35. Word separation in Pope Gregory VII's *Dictatus Papae*. Archivio Segreto Vaticano, Reg. Vat., 2, f. 81 recto; reproduced by permission.

Catino (ca. 1060–1132), or as the author entitled it, *Liber gemniagraphus sive cleronomialis ecclesiae Farfensis*, compiled from 350 documents between 1092 and 1125, was written in script separated by 3 to 4 times the unity of space.[23] Terminal forms consisted of the capital *S*, the elevated *s*, and the long *j* in numbers.

Gregorio's second and more specialized cartulary, the *Liber largitorius*, which he called the *Liber notarius*, Rome, BN Vittorio Emanuele II, Farfa 2, in its sophistication surpassed any of the northern cartularies.[24] Written in 1103 in script separated by 2 times the unity of space, with initial capitals denoting proper names, it placed charters of endowment in chronological order, prefaced by an extensive, alphabetically arranged table of geographic locations. The worth of each endowment was evaluated. The codex was foliated, and the table provided reference to folios and to sequential letters of the alphabet placed at the apposite loci in the codex's margins. These letters were similar to those found in the margins in certain manuscripts from Saint-Amand, but Gregorio di Catino's system of explaining both foliation and alphabetical sequential notes went far beyond any surviving artifact of northern origin (see Figure 17).

South of Rome, excluding Monte Cassino, with its special connections to Germany and Lorraine, the ancient Roman tradition of *scriptura continua* was firmly entrenched and continued until the Norman conquests of the second half of the eleventh century brusquely brought about revolutionary changes in text format. Before the arrival of the Normans, the charters of Amalfi, Naples, and Sorrento resembled more closely than did any other western European documents of the central Middle Ages the ordinary cursive writing of ancient Rome.[25] Into this milieu dominated by ancient tradition, the Normans' conquest of Sicily in 1060 and subsequent domination of southern Italy simultaneously introduced Caroline script and separated writing, and a penumbra of Norman influence in the form of word separation spread in books and documents written in Beneventan script. For example, the apparently original charter of Giordano, Prince of Capua, dated May 31, 1000, from the archives of the monastery of San Lorenzo di Amersa, was transcribed in separated Beneventan script.[26] By the middle of the twelfth century, separation and canonical separation were increasingly practiced in southern Italian books and documents written in Caroline script. Paris, BN lat. 6637, a copy of Boethius's *Commentarii in Porphyrii Isagogen* and Aristotle's *Categoriae*, both texts of the *Logica vetus* fundamental to the protoscholastic curriculum of Gerbert, were written in the middle of the twelfth century in separated script, with interword space varying from 2 to 3 times the unity of space and with space omitted after monosyllabic prepositions.[27] Monolexic abbreviations included the tironian conventional sign for *et*, and the manuscript was replete with contemporary *traits d'union*.

Chapter 14

Reading and Writing in Northern Europe in the Twelfth and Thirteenth Centuries

The twelfth century has been widely recognized as an innovative period in law, theology, philosophy, and art in northern Europe. In reading and writing practices, it was primarily a time of continuity and consolidation, when canonical separation became the norm. The consolidation of reading and writing practices around canonical separation, however, both ratified and extended previous innovations and produced new innovations of its own. The former included the definitive shift of the responsibility to prepare a text for reading from the reader to the scribe, the regular use of schematic diagrams and other graphic aids to the display and retrieval of information, and the use of private reading for spiritual meditation. The latter, building on these, included the beginnings of individual authorship as we know it, the textual expression of intimate feelings, including erotica, as well as private writing for one's own purposes and the possibility of a new intimacy linking author, text, and reader. The consolidation of canonical word separation also produced innovations in book production, grammatical theory, and the language of mathematics: technological improvements in the furnishings of the scriptorium, the copying of texts without conceptually processing them, in the manner of the modern typist, grammatical refinements based on the new sense of the word as an integral unit, and the enrichment of mathematical notation.

The Spread of Canonical Separation

One of the most striking examples of the new medium of word-separated communication can be found in the works of Guibert of Nogent (d. ca. 1125). Guibert's own script and that of his secretaries, preserved in Paris, BN lat. 2500, 2502, and 2900 from the library of the Abbey of Nogent-sous-Coucy, near Soissons, was canonically separated, with terminal forms that included the capital *S* to accentuate the image of the word.[1] Guibert employed monolexic abbreviations for short function or linking words, for example, the ampersand for the conjunction *et* and the tironian sign for the verb *est*, and the *trait d'union*.

The manuscripts of Hugh of Saint-Victor (d. 1141), including the oldest ones from the Augustinian Abbey of Saint-Victor in Paris, were canonically separated, with the usual terminal signs for *-us*, *-tur*, *-m*, and *-orum* and the terminal round *s*, all enhancing Bouma shape. *Traits d'union* were provided by the scribe. Paris, BN lat. 15009, the earliest copy of Hugh's *De tribus maximis circumstantiis gestorum*, included as monolexic abbreviations the tironian sign for the conjunction *et*, and among terminal forms, the crossed capital *S* for *-orum*, the capital *NS* ligature, and the capital *R*. Bonn, Universitätsbibliothek, S 292/1, containing the *De sacramentis Christianae fidei*, was copied in 1155, fourteen years after Hugh's death, for the Cistercian Abbey of Altenburg, and like most Cistercian manuscripts, it was canonically separated, with interword space 2 times the unity of space.[2] Initial capitals to indicate proper nouns were common in these and other early codices of Hugh's works.

In Hugh's hands, the graphic display of information with the aid of colored initials and the architectural motifs perfected by eleventh-century scribes at abbeys like Fécamp and Saint-Germain-des-Prés became a conscious pedagogical tool. To aid memorization, he placed colored initials on each opening to give each one a quasi-distinct image.[3] In his grammatical and historical works, he used page format to simplify the presentation of information. In the *De tribus maximis circumstantiis gestorum*, he counseled schoolboys to fix their gaze on the book and to remember its color patterns and letter forms as cues to the page position of specific information within the text.[4] For Hugh, the visual interaction between reader and book was an integral part of study.

Hugh theorized about the new modes of reading canonically separated script. In the *Didascalicon*, he explicitly set forth three modes of reading: reading to another, listening to another read, and reading to oneself by gazing (*inspicere*), that is, silent, private reading.[5] Hugh's application of the verb *inspicere*, with its visual connotation, to the activity of reading harks back to Anselm's use of the term and to seventh-century Insular and eleventh-century Continental scholars' use of *videre*, "to see," as a synonym for reading. According to Hugh, the reader first masters the grammatical construction (facilitated by the grouping of related words upon the page), then the literal sense, and finally proceeds to the more profound meaning in a procedure free of the ancient emphasis on oral articulation with correct accentuation.[6] It was precisely these largely visual processes that the eleventh-century restructuring of written language had facilitated. Hugh described the signs, or *notae*, of the ancient grammarians, including punctuation as marks normally present in books. They were to be inserted by the scribe to aid the reader in comprehending the text. In ancient times, it had been the reader, rather than the scribe, who had added signs to aid parsing. Hugh's presumption that it was the scribe's responsibility to prepare the text for the reader exemplified the transformed mentality that the previous century had wrought. In his *De grammatica*, Hugh included an extensive vocabulary for critical notes, and he was the first medieval grammarian to enumerate tie notes among the signs that scribes were to provide to the reader.[7] These notes presupposed the ocular gestures of silent consultation.

Hugh's contemporary, Hugues of Fouilloy, wrote the *Liber de rota verae religionis*, the *Liber avium*, and the *De pastoribus et ovibus*, in which the roles of reader of images and reader of text fully merged. The first work contained schematic illustrations that are an advanced form of the fusion of art and script that had characterized so many of the word-separated eleventh-century codices from the British Isles and northern France.[8] The *Liber de rota verae religionis* referred explicitly to its miniatures. In Brussels, BR II, 1076, a codex of the late twelfth century, the legends incorporated into the miniatures were canonically separated and displayed numerous terminal forms, including the capital *S*, the sign that had been the hallmark of eleventh-century protoscholastic writing. In these drawings, the "good abbot" is shown motionless in study, staring at an open book. This iconography of silent reading had its antecedents in eleventh-century book illuminations copied at the abbeys of Fécamp and Luxeuil.

The school of Chartres, where writing had been separated since the time of Fulbert, was an important center for the transmission of the eleventh-century protoscholastic graphic innovations to the twelfth century. The *Decretum* and the *Panamia* of Ivo of Chartres (d. 1116) were diffused north of the Alps exclusively in separated script, as was the *Decretum* of Gratian, which supplanted them. Abelard and John of Salisbury, both of whom studied at Chartres, composed and disseminated their works only in word-separated codices. John of Salisbury (ca. 1115–1180), like Hugh of Saint-Victor, distinguished in his vocabulary between the reading aloud of a master to a student (*prelectio*) and private, silent, visual reading (*lectio*).[9] Like the late-eleventh-century masters of the *Ars lectoria*, John viewed grammar as including the art of correct writing, and he regarded punctuation as paratextual signs of communication between author and reader analogous to the neumes used for the notation of music.[10] Also, in keeping with the tradition of monastic emendation as it had evolved in the previous century, John showed a keen awareness of the importance of correct word separation for maintaining the acute parafoveal vision necessary for the private scrutiny of manuscript texts.[11] Elsewhere in France, the pattern was the same. Gilbert of Poitiers affixed his emblematic critical notes, inspired by eleventh-century models, to manuscripts such as Troyes, BM 988, which were written in canonically separated script.

As in Italy, the Cistercian Order in the north was an important conduit for spreading canonical separation. The manuscripts produced both at the Abbey of Clairvaux and at its daughter abbey, Notre-Dame de Signy, founded in 1135, are typical of the Cistercian page.[12] Charleville, BM 187, a collection of *Logica vetus* texts from Notre-Dame de Signy that includes Boethius's monographs, was written in canonically separated script, with interword space equivalent to 2 times the unity of space, on lines ruled in pencil, the better to guide the reader's eye. Terminal forms were the usual signs for *-us*, *-tur*, and *-bus*, the elevated round *s*, and the capital *S*. Monolexic abbreviations included the Insular sign for *est*, the tironian sign for the conjunction *et*, and numerous superscript forms. *Traits d'union* were present, and the scribe employed acute accents to denote monosyllables and the double *ii*. Another Notre-Dame de Signy codex, Charleville, BM 196c, Jerome's *Commentarii in Prophetas minores*, was written in canonically separated script, with interword space equivalent to 2 times the unity of space and with the terminal elevated *s* and suspended ligatures.[13] A contemporary emendator added alphabetical construction notes, *traits d'union*, and the successor note to the *diastole*. Red and green alternating initials generated a quasi-unique image for each leaf. The scribe of Augustine's minor works, Charleville,

BM 202, wrote in a similar canonically separated script. Notre-Dame de Signy scribes who worked for Guillaume of Saint-Thierry in Charleville, BM 49 and 114, used canonically separated script.[14] The abbey also provides examples of twelfth-century foliation.

The Cistercian Abbey of Beaupré, near Beauvais, also established in 1135, produced in the twelfth and early thirteenth centuries a large quantity of canonically separated manuscripts replete with a panoply of prosodiae enhancing the visual images of words. Many of these codices were contemporaneously foliated. Paris, BN lat. 1777, Johannes Chrysostom's *Homiliae in Matthaeum*, was written in the second half of the twelfth century with interword space varying from 1.67 to 2 times the unity of space. The manuscript was contemporaneously foliated. Paris, BN lat. 2243 (I–II), Gregory the Great's *Homiliae in Ezechielem*, was written in canonically separated script, with frequent accenting of the double *ii* and the tonic syllable. This foliated codex contained a table giving reference to its foliation. At least twenty-two other early Beaupré manuscripts bear contemporary foliation, making this scriptorium one of the first in the Latin West to add foliation systematically to its books.[15]

The earliest manuscripts of Cistercian authors, including those not copied at Cistercian abbeys, were always separated or canonically separated. While no autograph or authorial manuscripts by Bernard of Clairvaux (d. 1153) are known, the autograph corrections by Geoffroy of Auxerre (d. after 1188) to his *Vita prima sancti Bernardi*, Paris, BN lat. 7561, were written in script separated by 2 times the unity of space, with *traits d'union*.[16] The text that Geoffroy corrected had been written by a secretary who had denoted proper names with capitals and had employed the elevated round *s* as a terminal form and the tironian symbol for the conjunction *et*. The earliest twelfth-century manuscripts of Bernard of Clairvaux's *opera* were all separated. In Munich, Staatsbibliothek Clm. 7950, written in canonically separated script at the Cistercian Abbey of Kaisheim, Bernard was represented in a miniature that exemplifies the fusion of image with personal names, inscriptions, and banderoles.[17] Bernard's intimate associate, Guillaume of Saint-Thierry (d. 1148), retired to the Abbey of Notre-Dame de Signy, leaving there a copy of his *Epistola ad fratres de Monte Dei* with autograph revisions, Charleville, BM 114, ff. 1–45 and 102–213.[18] His writing was canonically separated and incorporated the standard eleventh-century terminal forms. Monolexic abbreviations included the tironian sign for *et* and superscript forms, and he made regular use of *traits d'union*. Like Geoffroy of Auxerre, Guillaume employed emblematic punctuation as an intrinsic part of his textual composition. Chicago, Newberry Library 21.1, a copy of the *Anticlaudianus* of Alain of Lisle (d. 1201), was written not long after his death in canonically separated script, with *prosodiae* that included the *trait d'union* and prominent *ct* intraword ligatures. Emblematic punctuation was placed at the end of each line, in columns reserved for this purpose, a format presupposing an extended field of vision that only separated writing afforded.

Canonical separation and the intermixture of text and image at Cistercian abbeys were complemented by innovative patterns of punctuation. Cistercian scribes employed marks to indicate a presumed negative or positive response to questions in order to complement graphically the interrogative particles of the ancients.[19] The intratextual diple, and eventually underlining, were used in Cistercian manuscripts as marks of quotation.

For the Cistercians, individual reading was inextricably linked to, and indeed was a prerequisite for, meditation. Richalm, the Cistercian prior of Schöntal from 1216 to 1219, in his *Liber revelationum de insidiis et versutiis daemonum adversus homines*, contrasted silent and oral reading much as we would today when he recounted how demons forced him to read aloud, thereby disrupting his silent *lectio* and depriving him of inward understanding and spirituality.[20] Richalm's preference for silent reading was in harmony with Cistercian spirituality as articulated by Bernard of Clairvaux, Isaac of Stella (d. 1178), Guillaume of Saint-Thierry, and Aelrède of Rievaulx (d. 1167).[21] These Cistercian monks, who regarded the heart to be the locus of the mind, considered reading to be a principal tool for influencing the *affectus cordis*, or state of mind. Aelrède maintained the presence of books to be essential to the pursuit of the *via meditativa*. This ideal, which had first been enunciated by John of Fécamp and Anselm of Canterbury, became a pervasive one among Cistercians in the twelfth century. Guillaume of Saint-Thierry, in his *Epistola ad fratres de monte Dei*, considered *lectio* to be closely bound to *meditatio*.[22] The anonymous and probably Cistercian author of the *De interiori domo* described meditation by the metaphor of internal reading.[23] An indication of the exceptionally advanced character of the visual reading habits of Cistercians was their introduction, in the first half of the thirteenth century, of books of *distinctiones*, supplemented by sophisticated indexes, with a system of foliation and alphabetically designated locations on the page.[24]

The new techniques of reference consultation and silent reading were also well developed by certain twelfth-century Benedictines. Bernard Itier, monk of Saint-Martial, who died in 1225, used foliation in Paris, BN lat. 1338, as a means of organizing the preliminary notes for his *Chronicon*, placing, for example, the notes for the year 1112 on folio 112.[25] Peter of Celles (d. 1182), author of the *De disciplina claustrali*, who considered reading in silence to be a prerequisite for meditation, used the term *videre*, like authors of earlier centuries, as a synonym for reading.[26] Peter referred to the private reading in the cloister that stimulated meditation as being chained to silence. The *Liber de disciplina claustrali* survives only in canonically separated script.[27] A copy of Peter's *Sermones*, transcribed at Clairvaux within a generation after his death, Troyes, BM 253, was canonically separated, with monolexic abbreviations that included the tironian sign for *et*, superscript forms, and emblematic punctuation.[28] Oderic Vital, the English-born monk of Saint-Evroul, whose *Historia ecclesiastica* ranks among the principal Norman historical compilations of the first half of the twelfth century, was a paradigm of the scribal productivity that he described in his chronicle.[29] His own writing was separated by more than 2 times the unity of space, and he used capital letters both to denote proper names and as terminal forms.

The Author and the Book

In late antiquity and in the early Middle Ages, as we have seen, authors had generally composed by dictation to a scribe, in large measure because of the difficulty of composing while writing in *scriptura continua*.[30] The adoption of separated writing sparked an interest in autograph composition, creating the possibility of more intimate expression on the part of the author. With the renewed desire of authors to write their own works, certain of them, such as Othlon of Saint Emmeram in the eleventh century and Guibert of Nogent in the twelfth century, expressed sentiments hitherto not set down on parchment because of the lack of privacy when composition depended upon dictation to a secretary. Eschewing secretaries, Guibert wrote in private, and his mastery of the medium of separated script penetrated into his own consciousness as an author. In his *De vita sua sive Monodiarum libri tres*, he described the sense of privacy that would become characteristic of late medieval literate culture. Guibert secretly wrote erotic poems modeled on those of antiquity, which he then hid from his confreres.[31] He also secretly composed a commentary on Genesis that he concealed from his master Anselm.

Like his eleventh-century predecessor, Othlon of Saint Emmeram, Guibert felt secure enough to set down in this medium intimate details of his dreams. He was particularly fascinated by the relationship between outer written expression and interior feeling, repenting for his erotic poetry by accepting it as a written record of feelings he no longer possessed.[32]

In his final years, blindness forced Guibert to cease writing his own compositions and to dictate to a secretary. In his *Tropologiae in Osee, Amos ac Lamentationes Jeremiae*, he complained bitterly that his loss of vision obliged him to compose "only by memory, only by voice, without the hand, without the eyes."[33] He resented the interfering presence of a secretary and regretted that he could no longer glance upon his own written text to revise its style and improve his choice of words. Before becoming blind, Guibert, like other twelfth-century authors, had emended his compositions with interlinear additions, a mode of textual amplification that flourished with word separation. The authorial manuscripts, identifiable by their erasures, corrections, and interlinear additions, form a new genre of literary evidence, documenting a dimension of intellectual life that had not existed before the late tenth century.[34] Odon of Orléans, who also wrote erotic verse, as abbot from 1105 to 1113 restored the Abbey of Saint-Martin of Tournay and established a new scriptorium that produced canonically separated books.[35] The Cistercian statutes of 1144 implicitly looked upon composition as a private, written act subject to juristic control.[36]

Indeed, the existence of twelfth-century erotica was possible because of the new intimacy between author, reader, and book. While a greater sense of intimacy had marked the devotional works of John of Fécamp and Anselm of Canterbury, it was in the twelfth century that the equation of author and writer became increasingly evident, both in practice and in the Latinity of lettered men. Even Bernard of Clairvaux, who is known to have dictated a large portion of his corpus, wrote first drafts in his own hand.[37]

Spurred on by the new aids to facilitate reading, authors who wished to write their own works, rather than to compose by dictation, were frustrated by the difficulty of writing in formal book scripts that necessitated a slow and measured pace. As a consequence, in most authorial manuscripts of the eleventh and twelfth centuries, like those of Berengar of Tours, Geoffroy of Auxerre, and Guillaume of Saint-Thierry, the author was but one of the scribes participating in the final copy. In many instances, the author's assistants worked from an authorial text written on wax tablets or scraps of parchment. Manuscripts written entirely or pre-dominantly by the author, like Cambridge, Corpus Christi College 371, containing Eadmer's autograph of the *Vita Anselmi* and other of his compositions, were typically set down over extended periods of time.[38] Guillaume of Saint-Thierry, who rapidly produced large quantities of prose, was obliged to use secretaries as adjuncts to the process of compo-sition. However, the writer's desire to have a personal and direct control over his work, explicit in the case of Guibert of Nogent, is also implicit in the erasures and marginal and interlinear additions of word-separated authorial manuscripts.

The first miniatures showing authors writing their own compositions, as opposed to dictating them to scribes, date from the eleventh cen-tury.[39] The poet Notker Balbulus was depicted in three eleventh-century codices as a solitary writer composing in the isolation of his cell.[40] The earliest images of Bernard of Clairvaux as author, dating from the thir-teenth century, show him as an author-scribe.[41] In the twelfth century, the verb *dictare* lost its obligatory oral connotation and was used for writ-ten composition and visual copying.[42] In the thirteenth century, Alexan-der of Buxtehude was depicted writing under the legend "hic scribat et dictat" (this one writes and composes) in the presence of the Agnus Dei, with a banderole stating "I let drop from Heaven what I reveal to you to be written."[43] In the late fourteenth century, even the infant Jesus was depicted as a writer of the Pater Noster.[44]

These changes did not mean that the iconographic conventions for depicting authors that had originated in late antiquity and the early Middle Ages disappeared entirely in the twelfth century. Authors were still frequently shown as dictators or as scribes writing from dictation, and the evangelists were normally depicted in this manner.[45] The apostle Paul was regularly shown as the dictator of his Epistles or as a scribe taking dic-tation.[46] In Paris, BN lat. 11624, f. 94v, an eleventh-century codex origi-nating from Saint-Bénigne of Dijon, Ambrose was shown dictating over the shoulder of a scribe. A similar scene appears in an eleventh-century manuscript from Tours, Tours BM 291, f. 132. In a twelfth-century codex, Admont, Stiftsbibliothek 34, written in about 1175 in separated script, Abbot Irimbert was depicted dictating his *Expositio in libros Josue, Judi-cum et Ruth* to a scribe writing on wax tablets, and Saint Jerome in a miniature in the same codex was also shown dictating to a scribe with stylus and tablets.[47]

Book Production

The silent reading of word-separated texts also encouraged the transition from oral to visual modes of book production.[48] Visual copying was a feature of the scriptorium of Guibert of Nogent, and the twelfth-century scribe who visually copied Jerome's *Commentarii in Habacuc* in Canterbury, Cath. X.l.lla, using a Canterbury copy dating from the time of Lanfranc (now Cambridge, Trinity College B.3.5 [84]), carefully reproduced the punctuation, *prosodiae*, and many terminal forms of his exemplar.[49] When Hermanus, in the early twelfth century, described in his *Liber de restauratione sancti Martini Tornacensis*, the copying of manuscripts in the scriptorium set up by Odon of Orléans, he specifically noted that the scribes worked *in silentio* on specially constructed tables.[50]

New furnishings for the scriptorium appeared. Eleventh-century and twelfth-century miniatures had depicted scribes copying a codex placed upon their knees from an exemplar positioned on a table. In 1173, Gregory of Narek and Gregory of Nazianzus were shown in this position.[51] Other miniatures show scribes using a book stand for the exemplar and a table for the book. Innovation in thirteenth-century scriptorium furnishings allowed the scribe to replicate a page as a set of visual images in a routine mechanical manner and to dispense with oralization as an essential aid to short-term memory.[52] Specialized furniture for copying designed to minimize the degree of ocular displacement between the exemplar and the copy was described by John of Garland, and such furniture was abundantly depicted in miniatures of the late Middle Ages, especially in vernacular texts intended for the laity. Other miniatures and woodcuts depicting late medieval scriptoria show scribes with sealed lips, seated at special tables equipped with book stands, employing a variety of new mechanically controlled line markers to guide their eyes in following the text of the exemplar.[53]

In the thirteenth century, the exemplars of university stationers, codices used exclusively for copying, provided a slightly larger ratio of interword space, no doubt as a special aid to scribes who were expected to copy mechanically from them.[54] At the end of the Middle Ages, both Petrarch and Jean Gerson used the term "painter" (*pictor*) for scribes who visually replicated texts without understanding them.[55] The iconography of fifteenth-century books of hours assimilated the iconography of scribes and painters, particularly in scenes depicting the apostle Luke, the patron saint of painters, writing his Gospel.[56] In place of dictation, many depictions of the four evangelists showed them copying from an exemplar held by angels. The cognitive skills of the late medieval copyist increasingly came to resemble those of a typist, whose mechanical reading process differs from that of the normal reader.[57] The painter-scribe, like a typist, read with an invariable eye-hand span while mindlessly replicating the black-on-white images of his exemplar. Imposition, the writing of text on large sheets prior to folding, as in printed books, a process that was perfected in the fifteenth century, was predicated on this kind of mechanical visual copying. The intricate manipulations of the sheet that this process required would have been incompatible with dictation.[58]

Changes in Scholastic Grammatical Theory

Languages that exist only in oral form do not have a word for "word" because they do not have a conception of the linguistic unit that constitutes a word.[59] Scholastic grammarians, for whom canonical separation in written language was normal, articulated the even finer distinctions implicit in the scribal practice of rigorously differentiating monosyllabic prepositions and bound syllables on the basis of function, regardless of pronunciation.[60] Conscious of words as graphic units, they also refined the definitions of different kinds of words. The Dominican Johannes de Balbis, in his *Catholicon*, completed in 1286, enumerated the adjective and the noun as virtually independent parts of speech.[61]

Some of the changes in medieval Latin, such as the distinguishing of prepositions and other short words by the insertion of interword space or the addition of signs of interrogation to complement interrogative particles, were purely graphic, and therefore imperceptible when a text was pronounced aloud. Other changes that transformed the appearance of the Continental book between the late twelfth and the early thirteenth century were apparent whether a text was viewed or recited. Medieval Latin of the twelfth and thirteenth centuries as a whole, quite apart from the way it was written, was less ambiguous. The scribal innovation of placing space after unaccented function words was made all the more prominent by the greatly augmented use of these words in medieval Latin at the expense of parataxis. Other thirteenth-century linguistic innovations, like the placing of the adjective before the noun and the adverb before the verb, as well as the use of subject-verb-object word order, had been anticipated by Insular sequential construction notes. Scholastic grammarians postulated the subject-verb-object order of the vernacular as the natural one for Latin.[62] Guido Favo, in his *Summa dictaminis*, regarded it as the natural arrangement, appropriate for the clear exposition of an idea expressed in the artificial word order of ancient authors.[63] In the context of a Latinity governed by conventions of word order, the symbols formerly used as construction notes became scribal notes of revision.[64]

The tendency of ancient authors to compose periodic sentences in which clauses were intertwined in each other and verbs and adjectives were placed far from the nouns they governed waned as Latin became an analytical language consciously molded to be an unambiguous vehicle for expressing logical distinctions. In the mid-thirteenth century, Roger Bacon (ca. 1212–92), who set down principles for syntactic punctuation, recognized word order and word proximity as important for signifying meaning.[65] In 1348, Jean Bolant used this simplified word order and word grouping to explicate the intricate constructions of Ovid's *Metamorphoses*.[66] The late Middle Ages began to produce an increasingly larger proportion of prose texts formed by the accretion of syntactic distinctions. Greater use of graphic punctuation signs naturally accompanied Latin prose that incorporated compact, discrete distinctions of words with close grammatical relations.

The combination of the new, analytic character of scholastic Latin and the new text format of separated script accompanied by emblematic punctuation facilitated the extraction of meaning from texts and reduced the reliance upon aural memory as a component of reading. In place of the oral reading of antiquity, readers in the late Middle Ages read visually from texts that in their syntax and graphic expression were simple and analytic. Word separation, word order, emblematic punctuation, discrete clauses, the ordering of both words and clauses within complex sentences, and the use of conjunctions and adverbial conjunctions for the construction of compound and complex sentences all facilitated sequential understanding of meaning within the boundaries of clause and sentence. Whereas the ancient reader had relied on aural memory to retain an ambiguous series of sounds as a preliminary stage to extracting meaning, the scholastic reader swiftly converted signs to words, and groups of words to meaning, after which both the specific words and their order might quickly be forgotten. Memory in reading was primarily employed to retain a general sense of the clause, the sentence, and the paragraph.[67] Albertus Magnus, Thomas Aquinas, Roger Bacon, Duns Scotus, and William of Ockham, despite their divergent national origins, all wrote a similar scholastic Latin remarkable for its clarity and precision of expression, which was achieved at the sacrifice of classical rhythm, meter, and mellifluous sonority.

Changes in the Language of Mathematics

As early as the thirteenth century, exponential forms were used to designate decimal unities, as in $v^m ii^c$ for 5,200.[68] The exponential xx to abbreviate long numbers, such as $iiii^{xx}v$ (four score and five) for lxxxv, found in documents from the thirteenth century, aided the comprehension of readers who counted mentally in the vernacular.[69] In the early thirteenth century, the abacus gave way to algorithms written on the page, and the earliest fully symbolic arithmetical statements evolved from a synthesis of Arabic numerals, decimal punctuation, monolexic abbreviations, and conventional signs borrowed from Latin prose to denote roots, multiplication, and division.[70] Medieval symbols for mathematical operations, unknown in antiquity, were modeled on Insular emblematic signs of punctuation, tie notes, and monolexic abbreviations.[71] The conventions of order for writing mathematical operations closely resembled those for Latin and vernacular prose written in separated script. The operation preceded the product, much as the verb preceded the object.[72] By the beginning of the thirteenth century, the emblematic representations of fractions were supplanted by the modern form of notation of Arabic origin, but incorporating right-to-left sequencing.[73] Arabic symbols thus ultimately superseded the Insular symbols for the transcription of fractions, as they did for the transcription of integers.

Chapter 15

Written Culture at the End of the Middle Ages

By the thirteenth century, all of western Europe, from Scotland and Denmark in the north to Spain and Italy in the south, had adopted a single and generally homogeneous form of written Latin that incorporated both the graphic conventions of canonical separation and the principles of word order and syntactic word grouping. This new Latin, which was so different from the Latin of antiquity, became the medium of intellectual discourse for scholars. It was a medium with minimal ambiguity, compared with the writing systems that had preceded it, and well suited to communicating the increasingly complex and subtle ideas of such authors as Albertus Magnus, Bonaventure, Duns Scotus, and William of Ockham.

Among scholars, the general adoption of canonically separated writing transformed authorship and writing practices, university pedagogy, and the nature and uses of libraries. The rapid silent reading that it made possible also had direct and unsettling effects on Christian doctrine. But the effect of separated writing on culture was not limited to the scholastic world at the end of the Middle Ages. The spread of separated writing to the vernacular and to texts destined for lay readers likewise affected writing and reading practices at royal courts and among the aristocracies and urban elites. In Italy, it was deeply connected with the rise of humanism. Throughout Europe, the reading that separated script made possible profoundly affected the nature of thought and culture across a range of phenomena, from political subversion and pornography to the intensification of personal piety. With the general acceptance of separated script and the practices it made possible, Europe entered the modern world as we know it.

Gothic Cursive Script and the Manuscript Book

In the thirteenth century, the silent reading of word-separated texts was a normal practice of literate society. The late Middle Ages (i.e., the era encompassed by the thirteenth, fourteenth, and fifteenth centuries) was the period in which the changes in the textual format of Latin and its linguistic alterations of the previous centuries bore fruit in an explosion in the quantity of logical writings.

The late medieval appetite for using writing as a means of refining the subtleties of intellectual discourse had profound consequences on the mode of composing texts. Scholastic authors could no longer articulate their ideas within the confines of cumbersome wax tablets and Gothic *textualis*. The task of composing lengthy works of synthesis ultimately led to the development of the author's autograph manuscript, written in fully separated Gothic cursive script. Composition on quires and sheets of parchment, rather than on wax tablets, meant that authors, without assistance, could rapidly revise and rearrange their texts while composing them. Thirteenth-century scholastic writers could prepare texts rich in cross-references, which presupposed that the reader, like the author, would flip from folio to folio in order to relate arguments to their logical antecedents and to compare comments on related but disparate passages of Scripture. The medium of the tablet had inhibited the development of a flowing and looped cursive script, much as it had in ancient Rome. Thirteenth-century authors, writing in the margins of parchment codices, could compose marginal notes and commentaries and modify the letter forms of glossular script to create a separated script that was fast and easy to write, first on parchment and later on paper. At first, Gothic cursive script was idiosyncratic and often difficult to read, even for contemporaries, but by 1400 it had become fluid, standardized, and often highly legible.[1]

Before the fourteenth century, writing in Gothic *textualis* on parchment had been a physically arduous task. The writing hand was poised so that only the point of the pen touched the support. In early illuminations, scribes were drawn writing with a pen in one hand and a knife in the other. In addition to aiding erasure and cutting the pen, the knife served to balance the raised hand holding the pen and anchored the parchment support used for formal books, for writing the bold strokes of Gothic *textualis* required pressure that changed direction with the frequent liftings of the pen.[2] The adoption of informal Gothic cursive on unbound quires and sheets in the fourteenth century made the physical act of writing less laborious and more compatible with intellectual activity. In fourteenth-century miniatures, authors composing in the new cursive script were depicted in more relaxed positions. The support, whether parchment or paper, which was easier to write on, was usually held in place by the hand, in the modern fashion.[3] As depicted in miniatures, the author alone in his study or on occasion in an idyllic pastoral setting, using Gothic cursive, was at once freed from both the labors of writing and the reliance on secretary-scribes.

The new ease in writing further enhanced the author's sense of intimacy and privacy in his work. In solitude, he was personally able to manipulate drafts on separate quires and sheets. He could see his manuscript as a whole and by means of cross-references develop internal relationships and eliminate the redundancies common to the dictated literature of the twelfth century. He could also at his leisure easily add supplements and revisions to his text at any point before forwarding it to a scriptorium for publication. Initially, composition in written form had been used only for Latin texts, but by the mid-fourteenth century, vernacular forms of cursive scripts provided the same advantages.

The Classroom

The new and more intimate way in which authors silently composed their texts, in turn, raised the expectation that they would be read silently. This expectation extended to the classroom. In antiquity and the early Middle Ages, as we've seen, when texts were composed orally, authors expected them to be read aloud. In the fourteenth century, when learned texts were composed in silent isolation in cursive script, authors expected them to be read silently. Nicolaus de Lyra, the great Franciscan biblical commentator of the fourteenth century, addressed himself to the reader, and not to the listener.[4] Jean Gerson advised the reader of Scripture to place himself in the affective state of the writer.[5] Fourteenth-century scholastic texts composed in cursive script were marked by a visual vocabulary, indicating that both the author and the reader were expected to have the codex before them.

While private, silent reading became increasingly pervasive in the thirteenth, fourteenth, and fifteenth centuries, public lectures continued to play an important role in medieval university life. However, because of the complexity of the subject matter, visual reading by the listener was essential for comprehension. While the professor read aloud from his autograph commentary, the students followed the text silently from their own books. This was a change from the reading aloud of holy texts in late antiquity and the early Middle Ages, when one monk had read aloud to others, who listened without the aid of a written text. In 1259, the Dominican house of the University of Paris required that students, if possible, bring to class a copy of the text expounded upon in public lectures. The new practices of the schoolroom, in turn, affected liturgical reading. Humbert of Romans (ca. 1194–1277) held that collective prayer could be enriched by individuals gazing on the text of a written prayer as it was collectively pronounced.[6] Regulations requiring students to bring books to class also existed in Paris at the College of Harcourt and at the universities of Vienna and Ingolstadt.[7] In 1309, Pierre Dubois, the most celebrated of the legists in the service of Philip the Fair, observed that students who did not have a copy of the text before them could profit little from university lectures.[8] Students too poor to purchase their own copies could borrow them from libraries like that of the Cathedral of Notre Dame of Paris, which received bequests especially for this purpose.[9] The statutes of the Sorbonne provided for lending books against security deposits.[10]

Additional changes in the text format of thirteenth-century and fourteenth-century manuscripts transpired simultaneously with the spread of silent reading in private and in the classroom. Oral reading had usually consisted of a continuous reading of a text, or of a substantial section of it, from beginning to end. Many Caroline codices, like ancient scrolls, had not been divided into sections shorter than the chapter. The *Regiensis Livy*, Vat. Reg. lat. 792, for example, had not been divided even into chapters. From the thirteenth century to the fifteenth, subdivisions were introduced into classical and early medieval texts.[11] In some cases, works that had already been subdivided into chapters in late antiquity were more rationally subdivided by university scholars.[12]

This new mode of presenting old texts was also an integral part of the structure of newly composed texts, which were arranged in terms of chapters and chapter subdivisions, termed *distinctiones*. Using the points of reference established by the new divisions, tables of chapter headings, alphabetical tables by subject, and running headings became standard features of the scholastic codex.[13] A new form of punctuation, the colored paragraph mark, from the early thirteenth century onward came into common use to isolate units of intellectual content.[14] Illuminated capitals were employed in the fourteenth century to help clarify the new sequential argumentation, in the fashion *ad primum, ad secundum*, and so on. The system of sequential marginal notes using letters of the alphabet to denote location on the page, a technique that had first appeared in the books of Benedictine abbeys of northern France in the late tenth century, was adapted for juristic texts.[15] At the end of the fourteenth century, sequential marginal notes were also employed to gloss literary texts. In the fifteenth century, we find alphabetical tie notes used for attaching the glosses of Nicolaus de Lyra in incunable editions.[16] The intricate schematic tree diagrams accompanying scholastic texts had direct antecedents in the diagrams accompanying protoscholastic works when they had first been diffused in separated script at Fleury. Like them, scholastic tree diagrams were understandable only to the reader who held the codex in his own hands.[17] These diagrams continued to be an important accoutrement of the page in the new humanist translations of Aristotle, and even after the invention of printing, scribes added them to incunables as part of the printed codex's final stage of confection.[18] The complex structure of the written page of a fourteenth-century scholastic text presupposed a reader who read only with his eyes, going swiftly from objection to response, from table of contents to the text, from diagram to the text, and from the text to the gloss and its corrections.[19]

Scribes of the late Middle Ages continued the practice of copying texts visually, and the oft-reported thesis that scholastic books were normally written by students transcribing professorial dictation during professional lectures is unsubstantiated by contemporary descriptions of the medieval classroom or by paleographical evidence.[20] Iconographic evidence supports the conclusion of visual copying. A fifteenth-century miniature suggests that the *Flores Augustini de civitate Dei* of François of Mayronnes was analogous to the notes made by a secretary during a lecture, and not a codex copied from dictation.[21] While some early modern engravings may show the classroom dictation of textbooks, there are no fourteenth-century or fifteenth-century miniatures depicting classroom scenes of students taking down verbatim transcriptions of professorial lectures. Indeed, late medieval writing did not possess a shorthand system that would have permitted precise copies to be made.[22] Instead, the illuminations typically show the professor lecturing from his text to students, who, with the occasional exception of the recording scribe, either had no pens or books or more usually were holding already written books.[23]

In medieval education, dictation was primarily a pedagogical device for instructing the young in writing and orthography, and it was in this form that it was represented in medieval miniatures. When dictation was used for university book production, the books were produced separately from and prior to the professorial lecture on the text. Thus, at the new University of Louvain (founded in 1425), when the stock of schoolbooks was still inadequate and libraries were wanting, professors arranged special dictation sessions so that students could come to class with the required books.[24] At Paris in 1355, the university recognized that a pace of lecturing slow enough to enable students to transcribe extensive class notes interfered with their need to focus their attention on the subtleties of the master's lecture.[25] Other and more efficient means for the dissemination of written texts existed outside the classroom. By the thirteenth and fourteenth centuries, the professional scribes of the *pecia* system at the University of Paris provided highly legible, standardized copies of the basic texts of the university curriculum.[26] In the fifteenth century, scribes at the University of Angers were capable of producing copies of professorial lectures in a month's time at relatively low cost. These manuscripts may even have been circulated before the lectures, so that the student could silently read along with the professor to grasp more easily the subtle arguments.[27] In the final years of the fifteenth century, the printing press provided the copies needed for classroom use.[28]

If access to books was important for comprehending the complexities of public lectures, it was even more necessary for private study, which was an increasingly acknowledged part of university life. Paintings and illuminations of the fourteenth and fifteenth centuries in vernacular books intended for the lay reader showed motionless scholars reading in libraries, both in groups and in isolation, with their lips sealed, an unmistakable iconographic statement of silence (Figure 36).[29] Inexpensive Latin and vernacular compendia of large treatises became popular to serve the growing student need for private study.[30] Pierre Dubois recommended their production as fundamental to his scheme of educational reform.[31] Nicolaus de Lyra, in the prologue to his *Tractatus de differentia*, declared that he had written this epitome of his lengthy *Postilla* so that poor students could afford to purchase copies for their own study.[32]

Libraries

Changes in reading also effected changes in libraries. The cloister libraries of the twelfth century had been suited to a culture where oral and silent reading had cohabitated.[33] The spacious cloister and carrels,

Figure 36. Silent reading in the mid-fifteenth century, an illumination from Jacque Le Grand's *Livre des bonnes moeurs*. Chantilly, Musée Condé 297, f. 23 recto; reproduced by permission. (Photo: Photographie Giraudon)

divided by stone walls, had allowed monks to read aloud or in a muffled voice to themselves, or to compose by quietly dictating to a secretary, without disturbing the contemplation or silent reading of their confreres. Because monastic authors had retained large amounts of sacred Scripture by rote oral memorization, formal collections of reference books were not always essential.

At the end of the thirteenth century, library architecture and furnishings began to change dramatically. At Oxford and Cambridge colleges and at the Sorbonne and other Paris colleges, libraries were installed in central halls and were furnished with desks, lecterns, and benches where readers sat next to one another.[34] Important reference books were chained to lecterns so that they could always be consulted in the library. The first such reference collection was established in Merton College, Oxford, in 1289.[35] A similar one was created in the Sorbonne in 1290.[36] In the mid-fifteenth century, the arts faculty of the University of Louvain created a wide-ranging scholastic reference library.[37] Chained reference books typically included alphabetical dictionaries and concordances, the Summas of Thomas Aquinas, the biblical commentaries of Hugh of Saint-Cher and Nicolaus de Lyra, and other lengthy works frequently cited by scholars. The statutes governing libraries emphasized that chained books were provided for the common good so that all could consult them.[38] The library was henceforth clearly regarded as a place where professors and students could go to read, write, and study.[39] Charles V installed just such a library in the Louvre and stocked it with specially commissioned French translations of classical and scholastic authors.

It was in the chained libraries of the late thirteenth century that the reader's need for silence was first professed. In the late antique library and early medieval monastery, where readers had read aloud, each reader's own voice had acted as a neurophysiological screen, blocking out the sounds of the adjacent readers.[40] When readers began to read visually, any oral reading became a source of potential distraction. Even quiet oral reading at the crowded desks of the chained reference collection in the medieval library would have made study difficult. Humbert of Romans, in the *De instructione officialium*, demanded that each Dominican house establish a common reading room in a silent location within the convent.[41] At Oxford, the regulations of 1412 recognized the library as a place of quiet.[42] The statutes of the library of the University of Angers of 1431 forbade conversation and even murmuring.[43] The statutes of the Sorbonne library, written down in the late fifteenth century, but reflecting practices established at an earlier date, proclaimed the chained library of the college to be an august and sacred place, where silence should prevail.[44] A similar rule existed in the library of the popes, reestablished in Rome after the Great Schism.[45]

Reference tools intended for rapid visual perusal within the library included aids for the use of the library itself, such as catalogues with alphabetical author indexes and special union catalogues representing the holdings of libraries in a city or region.[46] The supervised emendation of previously written manuscripts by the addition of *prosodiae*, punctuation, and textual variants had been, since the eleventh century, a regular practice of scribes and rubricators of monastic communities.[47] However, visual reading encouraged private readers to use books as instruments of study by noting passages in the margin with brief phrases, symbols, and doodles, enhancing subsequent visual recall. In the highly individualistic world of the late medieval university, rules were necessary to limit these activities in order to ensure that all annotations were suitable for common use.[48]

Private Study and Heresy

The transition to silent reading and composition, by providing a new dimension of privacy, had even more profound ramifications for both the lay and scholastic culture of the late Middle Ages. Psychologically, silent reading emboldened the reader because it placed the source of his curiosity completely under personal control. In the still largely oral world of the ninth century, if one's intellectual speculations were heretical, they were subject to peer correction and control at every moment, from their formulation and publication to their aural reception by the reader. Dictation and public *lectio*, in effect, buttressed theological and philosophical orthodoxy. Already in the eleventh century, heresy was linked to solitary intellectual curiosity and speculation. Berengar of Tours, who belonged to the second generation to write in separated script, lapsed into heterodoxy when he applied the logical techniques of Aristotle and Boethius to the Eucharist.[49] Reading with the eyes alone and silent, written composition removed the individual's thoughts from the sanctions of the group and fostered the milieu in which the new university and lay heresies of the thirteenth and fourteenth centuries flourished. These heresies were spread by the privately read *tractatus*.[50] Alone in his study, the author, whether a well-known professor or an obscure student, could compose or read heterodox ideas without being overheard. In the classroom, the student, reading silently to himself, could listen to the orthodox opinions of his professor and visually compare them with the views of those who rejected established ecclesiastical authority.[51] A forbidden text could be read even during the performance of public liturgy. Private, visual reading and private composition thus encouraged individual critical thinking and contributed ultimately to the development of skepticism and intellectual heresy. In England, the mere possession of Lollard writings was legal grounds for formal charges of heresy.[52]

University professors of the late Middle Ages were aware that they were addressing visual readers other than those who attended their lectures, and the anxiety created by the silent diffusion of ideas outside the lecture hall was reflected in contemporary university regulations. In the thirteenth century, university statutes forbade attendance at the public readings of forbidden books.[53] In the fourteenth century, the forbidden writings themselves were ferreted out and destroyed, as in 1323, when the general chapter of the Dominican Order decreed that all privately held writings on the prohibited art of alchemy be burned.[54] In 1346, the University of Paris declared that the writings of Nicolaus of Autrecourt were to be incinerated.[55] However, some copies of heretical works were necessary, if only for the theologians who wrote to refute them. The medieval rules of the library of the Sorbonne supposed that heretical writings in the library should be used only by professors of theology, for composing corrections of doctrinal errors. But how were individual scholars to be supervised when they read silently? In 1473, Louis XI offered a response when he ordered not only that nominalist doctrines not be taught, but that all nominalist books in the libraries of the University of Paris be chained.[56] The king realized that to forbid the teaching of nominalist doctrines was meaningless if nominalist writings could be easily read in numerous manuscripts in the libraries of the university.

Lay Society and Vernacular Texts

The transformation from an early medieval oral, monastic culture to a visual, scholastic one had at first only a limited effect on the reading habits of lay society, particularly in northern Europe, where oral reading and dictation of vernacular texts were commonly practiced until at least the thirteenth century. Until the mid-fourteenth century, French nobles and kings rarely read themselves, but were read to from manuscript books prepared especially for this purpose. When princes such as Saint Louis could read, they frequently read aloud, in small groups.[57] In addition to liturgical texts, the literature read to princes consisted of chronicles, *chansons de geste*, romances, and the poetry of troubadours and trouvères. Most of these works were in verse and were intended for oral performances. Thirteenth-century prose compilations, such as the *Roman du Lancelot* and the *Histoire ancienne jusqu'à César*, were also composed to be read aloud. The nobleman was expected to listen to the feats of his predecessors or of ancient worthies.[58] However, the illustrations, which from the twelfth century onward were more common in vernacular books prepared for the laity than in Latin ones meant for scholars, suggest that vernacular codices were also at times intended for private, visual reading.

Perhaps the fact that vernacular texts were meant for the listener, and not just for the reader, helps to explain why the practice of composing by dictation seems to have persisted longer for them than for Latin scholastic works.[59] Joinville dictated his *Histoire de saint Louis*, and the author of the *Roman du Lancelot* was depicted dictating.[60] The tardy development of vernacular protocursive and cursive scripts both reflected and encouraged the widespread practice of dictating vernacular texts. Much of medieval vernacular poetry and prose was composed, memorized, and performed orally and only later set down in writing.[61] In the thirteenth century, when Latin writers were beginning to write their own compositions in unbound sheets and quires and to develop cursive handwriting for this purpose, vernacular texts were still written down in *textualis* after having been composed orally. Word separation in vernacular books at the end of the Middle Ages continued to lag behind the norms of Latin codices. It was still often imperfect in early-thirteenth-century vernacular manuscripts, especially in Italy. In France, as late as 1300, scribes who knew that Latin texts had word separation were often unsure where to insert space between groups of syllables or morphemes in order to constitute correctly written vernacular words.[62] Separation of function words, normal for Latin, had still not been realized in 1500 for the Romance vernacular tongues. The article was one part of speech possessed by ancient Greek that had not been adopted into Boethius's translations of the *Logica vetus*.[63] The graphic definition of prepositions and articles remained more ambiguous in the vernacular than in Latin, where the article, which was adopted into scholastic Latin in the thirteenth century from French, was treated by university scribes as a separate graphic entity. In vernacular texts, the lack of orthographic uniformity between copies confirms that the letters within words were the principal signs of a decoding process that remained profoundly oral.[64]

Word-separated medieval Latin texts, nevertheless, had a profound effect on vernacular text format, grammar, and orthography. The various conventions of word order and the word separation that characterized the written vernacular after 1200 encouraged the dropping of inflection that had aided the ancient reader of *scriptura continua* to recognize properly and accent words and to identify their grammatical roles, a function that was no longer necessary in separated vernacular texts. Word separation, particularly in Middle French and English, allowed vernacular spelling to be less phonetic than that of Latin, for once vernacular words had a distinct image, the original spelling was retained, even when gradual changes in pronunciation rendered certain letters silent.[65] In the late Middle Ages, university-trained scribes, without intending to alter pronunciation, often inserted silent consonants into vernacular words in order to make them visually closer to the Latin from which they were derived, giving to words a purely visible etymology equivalent to that occurring with Chinese characters, but totally lacking in ancient Latin.[66] Mid-thirteenth-century scribes copying vernacular texts preferred to use well-separated exemplars, replete with terminal forms that included the terminal round *s*, punctuation, and *prosodiae*. These exemplars were analogous to those used by the professional scribes of the *pecia* system.[67] From the thirteenth century onward, certain vernacular texts were copied visually, with uniform page and text format similar to the editions of standard scholastic texts produced by university stationers. The copies of Guillaume Fillastre's *Thoison d'Or*, produced in the 1460's for the Burgundian Order of the Golden Fleece, were marked by the same striking similitudes in text and page format first evident in eleventh-century Latin books.[68] Vasque de Lucène's French translation of Quintus Curtius's *History of Alexander*[69] and Henri Romain's *Compendium historial* were other examples of texts reproduced in this manner for the Burgundian and French courts.[70]

In the early fourteenth century, when Gothic cursive was fully developed, authors began to employ it in conjunction with standardized word separation to compose vernacular documents and, at a slightly later date, literary texts. At the royal court of France, the task of administering the realm had become too complex to be mastered by illiterate princes who depended solely on the services of readers and scribes. Royal secretaries began to use cursive vernacular scripts to prepare drafts for the king's perusal; Charles V corrected drafts of his letters in his own hand and signed the originals.[71] A century later, certain royal letters were expected to be written in the king's hand, and many others were expected to bear his autograph signature.[72] Unlike the earlier Latin charters, which were composed by dictation and written in a rhythmical prose to be read aloud, the new royal documents were written in a prose as arrhythmical as scholastic Latin and were decorated with miniatures. They were clearly texts meant to be placed before the eyes of the sovereign.[73]

In the mid-fourteenth century, the French nobility began to accept the same practice of silent reading and composition for vernacular literary texts that had become established for the Latin literature of the universities during the previous century. The reign of John II marked the beginning of a major effort to translate Latin literature into French.[74] Because the syntax of scholastic texts closely resembled that of the vernacular in eliminating an excessive burdening of short-term memory, they tended to be far more successful in translating them than the ancient Latin authors, whose periodic sentences medieval readers found difficult to understand.[75] After John's death in exile, Charles V continued the royal patronage of translations, and he was the first king to assemble a true royal library, which was located in a tower of the Louvre. The king equipped the library with furnishings modeled on those used in contemporary university libraries.[76] In a miniature, he was painted seated in his library, motionless, not declaiming, reading with sealed lips in silent and tranquil isolation. Manuscripts also depicted the king attending lectures, visually following a copy of the text in the university fashion as he listened to the lecture.[77] New portable, private books of prayer intended to be brought to Mass contained vernacular texts to be read silently during the public recitation of the apposite Latin texts.[78] While theologians held that liturgical texts of the canonical hours had to be read aloud, even if they were not understood, devotional texts were to be read silently, with comprehension.

The monastic term *in silentio* had often referred to quiet, muffled oralization in *submissa* or *suppressa vox*. In the fifteenth century, vernacular authors employed a new, explicit vocabulary of silent reading, describing mental devotion from a written text as reading with the heart, as opposed to the mouth.[79] In the fifteenth century, the verb *veoir* and the vernacular phrase "to read with the heart" (*lire au coeur*) were used in French aristocratic texts to refer to private, silent reading, much as in earlier centuries *videre*, "to see," and *inspicere*, "to gaze," had been used as alternatives to *legere*, "to read."[80] At the same time, the word *écrire*, "to write," became, like *scribere*, its Latin equivalent, synonymous with composition.[81] In the illuminations decorating their manuscripts, authors close to the French royal house, including Jean Froissart and Christine de Pisan, were shown writing.[82] Even princes of the blood were depicted writing their own compositions. Charles V's grandnephew, René d'Anjou, a prolific author, was shown writing out his own texts in the manner of contemporary authors of Latin works.[83]

Silent, private reading by the king and great princes of the realm had a dramatic effect on the number and kinds of books prepared for royal and aristocratic courts. Just as fourteenth-century and fifteenth-century university libraries far surpassed the size of earlier monastic collections, royal and aristocratic libraries after 1350 grew to be far larger than their predecessors. Like the contemporary schoolmen, whose appetite for books increased when they adopted the habit of rapid, silent reading, laymen also acquired a taste for a greater quantity of reading material, particularly books of hours and vernacular works. The new vernacular texts composed for princes were almost exclusively in prose, in contrast to their earlier preference for literature in verse. The new aristocratic books were replete with the tables of contents, alphabetical glossaries, subject indexes, running heads, and intellectual complexities characteristic of thirteenth-century, fourteenth-century and fifteenth-century scholastic codices. Glosses with intricate cross-references accompanied the new French translations of the Bible, Saint Augustine, Aristotle, and Valerius Maximus, forming compound texts that would have been awkward to read aloud by a professional reader, but that were highly suited to visual perusal and study. These were the texts that Jean Gerson specifically recommended for the education of Charles VI.[84] In them, orthography became increasingly standardized, enabling the reader to recognize words by their global image, as in Latin, rather than to decode them phonetically by an ad hoc synthetic combination of phonemes. In the first half of the fifteenth century, French authors composed for the nobility new reference books, including alphabetical dictionaries of saints and gazetteers.[85] The number of illustrations increased in vernacular aristocratic books as miniatures evolved to play a more direct role in the comprehension of the text, serving a didactic function analogous to that of the diagrams accompanying scholastic literature.[86] In the form of banderoles, written text permeated the miniatures of vernacular texts, much as it had Latin works. As in Latin books, vernacular banderoles presupposed the reader's ability to decode simultaneously text and image.[87]

The growing practice of silent reading among the aristocracy stimulated important changes in the script of books copied for lay patrons. Before 1300, during the era when princes were read to, vernacular books could be written in the same *textualis* as Latin texts because those who read to princes normally had university training. The absence of most monolexic abbreviations other than the tironian sign for *et*, used as an ideograph to represent *et* in French and in English, and the inconsistent use of phonetic spelling were signs of the oral reading of these translations. When nobles began to read to themselves, in the fourteenth century, they found Gothic *textualis* difficult. A major source of difficulty was the confusion in recognizing the letters *m, n, i,* and *u,* composed of identical minim strokes, that had troubled earlier readers of Latin. To eliminate ambiguity in the representation of these letters more effectively than by the use of acute accent marks, scribes preparing books for the aristocratic market in the last two decades of the fourteenth century began to employ a form of *cursiva formata,* or formal cursive script, closely resembling that used by the royal chancellery for the preparation of vernacular documents.[88] A new vocabulary, *lettre de note, lettre de court,* and *lettre courante,* was created to denote this new cursive book script.[89]

In the first half of the fifteenth century, *cursiva formata* evolved into a new, unlooped form for which no equivalent documentary script existed. Contemporaries called this script *lettre bâtarde* to indicate that it was part cursive and part *textualis.*[90] Modern paleographers, who often refer to the Latin equivalent of this script as *hybrida,* have not been able to determine the exact date and place of its invention. One variety was used at an early date by the Brothers of the Common Life, who copied many books of devotion for sale to the Dutch laity. Another variety was used primarily for the French-speaking nobility.[91] Unlike Gothic cursive, *lettre bâtarde* or *hybrida* appeared almost simultaneously in vernacular and Latin texts.[92] This fact marks a singular change in the relationship between the written vernacular and Latin, for the former was no longer written in scripts that had evolved for the transcription of the latter, but rather, the vernacular played an active role in the evolution of new scripts. This is particularly true of the most legible form of *bâtarde,* the *lettre bourguignonne,* exemplified by the handwriting of David Aubert.[93] In France, *lettre bâtarde* became the standard script for both vernacular and Latin books copied for secular patrons in the latter portion of Charles VII's reign. At a slightly later date, it was frequently used in place of *textualis* for the vernacular pious treatises produced in large numbers for laymen and members of religious orders. In the mid-fifteenth century in aristocratic circles, the use of the less legible Gothic *textualis* was gradually restricted to Latin Bibles and liturgical books, which contained intensively read texts habitually read aloud.[94] Many laymen who could read Latin liturgical texts only by pronouncing them aloud, phonetically, without understanding, read vernacular texts silently, with full comprehension. In certain vernacular *lettre bâtarde* books, punctuation was borrowed from Latin university books and was calculated to guide the eye of the private reader, rather than to regulate the voice of a professional reader.[95] Aristocratic books of the fifteenth century regularly used paragraph signs, underlining, and capitalization to divide texts into intellectual, rather than rhetorical units.

Italy

Although the text format of Italian Latin manuscripts had been retrograde from the tenth century to the twelfth, lagging behind that of the north even in the fourteenth century, the habit of private, silent reading among laymen seems to have begun in Italy in the first half of the fourteenth century, that is, at least half a century earlier than in northern Europe. The earliest manuscripts of Dante's *Inferno* and *Paradiso* were intended to be held under the eyes of the reader.[96] The scribes who copied these texts for the libraries of aristocrats and great urban families used a new variety of highly legible Italian *cursiva formata* that seems to have been developed especially for the transcription of lay literature.[97] In the second half of the fourteenth century, the burgeoning lay readership stimulated experimentation with hybrid scripts to achieve greater legibility in vernacular codices transcribed for lay patrons.[98] Experimental Italian *hybrida* scripts traveling northward via the Rhine Valley may have inspired the northern *hybrida* and *lettre bâtarde*, but *hybrida* was not generally adopted in Italy for texts intended for lay readers in the early fifteenth century because, under the influence of humanism, scribes and authors turned to Caroline *textualis* as an alternative method of achieving superior legibility. A relatively larger number of fifteenth-century lay Italian readers were minimally literate in Latin, which even at the end of the Middle Ages was easier for Italians to understand.

Although Italian scribes deviated from canonical separation in Italian, and even in Latin, far more frequently than those of the north, Italian humanists never questioned the desirability of word separation, even though they knew quite well that their beloved ancients had written in *scriptura continua*.[99] To the scholars of the Renaissance, the advantages of word separation for maintaining textual integrity were indisputable.[100] The introduction of word separation into texts contained in ancient manuscripts was a normal part of editing, and the use of medieval signs of punctuation was an integral part of humanistic authorship.[101] Only on rare occasions did fifteenth-century scribes ever emulate ancient *scriptura continua*, and then only in display scripts.[102] Humanistic script was created by emulating the writing found in word-separated twelfth-century models, rather than in aerated ninth-century and tenth-century codices. Among the distinctive elements of eleventh-century and twelfth-century script that humanists imitated were the *ct* ligature and the protruding vertical stroke of the letter *t*, both of which served to enhance Bouma shape and thus augmented the rapidity of reading. Terminal capitals and capitals to denote proper names also were emulated.[103] So, too, was the use of *prosodiae*, especially the acute accent (frequently for mono-syllables), the *trait d'union*, and the suspended *ct* ligature, an alternative mode of signaling the continuation of a word divided at a line ending. Foliation, particularly with very un-Roman Arabic numerals, was com-mon in Italian humanist books.

Ancient scribes, at least after separation by interpuncts had been abandoned, had used no punctuation marks, and when they read Cicero, it had been the reader's responsibility to articulate the metrical *clausu-lae*, the Roman aural equivalent of punctuation.[104] The punctuation of humanist texts was more influenced by the visual achievements of the separated northern European Caroline texts of the eleventh and twelfth centuries than by Italian Gothic script. Humanist scribes invented mod-ern quotation marks by rediscovering the diple, which had been used in twelfth-century manuscripts to separate text from commentary, and they systematically employed it as a substitute for Gothic red underlining.[105]

Building on twelfth-century precedents, humanist scribes employed full syntactical sentence punctuation, with the characteristically modern usage of signs equivalent to the comma and period.[106] They integrated punctuation marks with the syntactical patterns of late Gothic capital-ization in order to achieve optimal conditions for silent reading. The humanist scribe's most original contribution was the parenthesis, a mark designed to give a graphic representation of the aside, a device of ancient oratorical eloquence.[107] The parenthesis in fifteenth-century humanist texts permitted the private, silent reader to recreate vicariously what in antiquity had been an oral experience.[108] Used in printed Latin far more than in manuscripts, the parenthesis served as a construction sign for parsing difficult syntax that had no direct equivalent in oral rhetoric. These volumes were printed in a rejuvenated *littera antiqua*, that is to say, humanistic textual script, highly suitable for private, silent reading.[109]

Private, Silent Reading and Personal Expression

The spread of *lettre de court, lettre bâtarde,* and the humanistic *tex-tualis* in the late fourteenth and fifteenth centuries throughout western Europe reflected and encouraged a dramatic change in the reading habits of the aristocracy and the urban elite of the cities of Italy and the lower Rhine Valley. Saint Louis had read aloud surrounded by an entourage. In the paintings of Memling and Van Eyck, Charles V, Louis XI, Lorenzo de Medici, and Flemish merchants read to themselves in inner solitude. Vernacular authors of the late fourteenth century increasingly assumed that their audience was composed of readers, rather than of listeners. Thus, Froissart expected that young noblemen would "look into" and read his *Chroniques.*[110] Between 1388 and 1392, Philippe de Mezières, anticipating that the young King Charles VI would personally read the *Songe du vieil pelerin,* included a special table designed to guide the secular reader through the complex, long histories told in parables and symbols.[111]

The visual mode of lay reading led authors to enrich vernacular texts with scholastic complexities that had hitherto been the restricted province of Latin literature. Just as separated written Latin had facilitated the birth of scholasticism, separated vernacular writing allowed for the transference of the subtleties of fully developed scholastic thought to a new lay audience. In northern Europe, the penetration of vernacular literature by Latin scholasticism became prevalent in the fourteenth and fifteenth centuries. Questions pertaining to the quarrel between nominalists and realists were discussed in the vernacular glosses accompanying Nicolas Oresme's translation of Aristotle and in the extensive corpus of treatises prepared for the Burgundian court.[112] The polemical tracts generated in the dispute between Philip the Fair and Boniface VIII were translated for the edification of Charles V and Charles VII.[113] Complex arguments, such as that over the nature of the Holy Blood of Christ, were presented in vernacular treatises composed by university masters for aristocratic patrons close to Louis XI.[114] Vernacular meditations, inspired by the Latin genre invented in the eleventh century by John of Fécamp and Anselm of Canterbury, were composed for lay aristocratic readers.[115] The new corpus of vernacular literature and the silent mode of reading imbued the aristocracy with a sense of private piety and made possible individual intellectual judgments on scholastic positions similar to those made by university scholars. In the numerous debates composed for great princes, it was the lay reader who was forced to decide between two or more subtly defined positions.[116]

The privacy afforded by silent reading and writing increased the display of irony and cynicism. The chronicles of France in the royal copy of the *Rozier de guerre*, which presented itself as the work of Louis XI, were marginally annotated with sarcasms, which kings, two centuries before, reading orally in a group, would never have permitted themselves to express.[117] Even more importantly, private reading provided a medium for expressing subversive political thoughts. Charles of France, the rebellious brother of Louis XI, left a copy of Cicero's *De officiis* with underlined passages justifying rebellion and the assassination of tyrants.[118] Guillaume Fillastre, in the epoch of the War of the Public Good, used arguments modeled on those of the conciliarists to justify the deposition of tyrannical kings. In the second half of the fifteenth century, the privately read aristocratic manuscript book became the principal medium for disseminating ideas justifying resistance to royal authority, much as the Latin *tractati* of the fourteenth century had provided a medium for those advocating resistance to papal authority.[119]

The new privacy afforded by silent reading also had dramatic and not entirely positive effects on lay spirituality. Private reading stimulated a revival of the antique genre of erotic art. In ancient Greece and Rome, material that today might be termed pornographic was read orally and was displayed openly in a tolerant, pagan society. Before the thirteenth century, erotic decorations in books were usually oblique, suggesting the repressed illicit desires of the chaste, rather than artfully crafted graphic fantasies intended to excite the reader.[120] In fifteenth-century France, where pornography was forbidden, private reading encouraged the production of illustrated salacious writings intended for the laity, writings that were tolerated precisely because they could be disseminated in secret. Miniatures of French and Flemish vernacular texts depicted bordello scenes of carnal lust with explicit and seductive realism.[121] Inspired by Boccaccio's *Decameron*, an anonymous Burgundian author prepared for Duke Philip the Good the *Cent nouvelles nouvelles*, an illustrated summa of sexual escapades that attributed licentious acts to the same reformed monks and friars who championed poverty and chastity. The author of the *Cent nouvelles nouvelles* anticipated that the prince would read it privately as an "exercise in reading and in study."[122] Like scholastic texts, the *Cent nouvelles nouvelles* was preceded by a table that gave in abbreviated form the high points of each adventure, so as to help the reader to browse and choose among the stories. This illustrated text was circulated in modest format so that it could be discreetly passed from reader to reader, much as the forbidden texts of William of Ockham and Marsilio of Padua had been surreptitiously disseminated among university scholars a hundred years earlier.[123]

By the end of the fifteenth century, the intimacy of silent reading permitted explicit graphic representations of human sexuality to permeate religious literature. In books of hours, enticing miniatures accompanying the penitential Psalms depicted David spying upon Bathsheba in her bath. Other miniatures illustrating the calendar showed embracing naked male and female figures representing the month of May and other suggestive scenes of fondling.[124] Illuminated borders displayed both heterosexual and homosexual encounters. In analogous fashion, the new habit of silent autograph composition allowed lay writers to breach matters of erotic intimacy in handwritten notes and letters. Philip the Good, writing in his own hand to his companion John of Cleves, discussed sexual escapades in frank and earthy language.[125]

The freedom of expression that private, silent reading gave to hitherto suppressed sexual fantasies also paradoxically intensified the depth of lay religious experience. Private, silent reading in the vernacular gave lay readers the means of pursuing the individual relationship to God that had been the aspiration of erudite Christians since Saint Augustine. The *De imitatione Christi*, written by Thomas à Kempis for his fellow monks, was soon after its composition translated into French and circulated at the Burgundian court.[126] Scores of other religious texts, including translations and original compositions, stressed the importance of reading, vision, and silence in achieving spiritual solace. In the prologue to his *Vie de Christ*, Jean Mansel declared that the spoken word is fleeting, while the written word endures, and he called upon knights and princes disposed to devotion for the profit of their souls "to see" (*voir*) the content of his book.[127] Proceeding from the reading of the life of Christ, Mansel urged each person to meditate using the "eyes of his contemplation."[128] The vernacular life of Peter of Luxembourg described a scion of an aristocratic family who spent his silent, nocturnal hours reading sermons, saints' lives, and patristic texts.[129] In the vernacular literature intended for lay readers, separation from the group for the purpose of private reading and silent prayer was emphasized repeatedly. Peter of Luxembourg stressed the need for private prayer and silent study.[130] Ludolf of Saxony's *Life of Christ*, translated for Louis of Bruges, advocated the solitary reading of Scripture as a principal element of the contemplative life.[131] Through the translation, the author now advised pious laymen to place before their eyes the deeds and words of Christ.[132] Books of hours, produced in increasing number for lay readers, were tailored to serve the need for individualized spiritual experience.[133] Both vernacular and Latin devotional books intended for the laity incorporated certain of the para-textual aids to reading that had been introduced into Continental Latin books in the eleventh century, including punctuation, capitalization, *traits d'union*, and the successor to the *diastole*, to aid in the distinction of words in Gothic *textualis*.[134]

Isolated, private reading and prayer as the pathway to salvation, in turn, may have fostered insecurities about the worthiness of each individual's faith and devotion and stimulated zeal for religious reform. The reformed mendicant orders of the fifteenth century found their strongest supporters among the urban merchants and the aristocratic families, who silently read vernacular religious manuscript books. Three generations later, many scions of these same families would become the supporters of John Calvin. On the eve of the Protestant Reformation, the mode of the dissemination of ideas had been so revolutionized that lay readers, like university scholastics, could formulate dissenting views in private and communicate them in secret. The iconography of motionless, silent reading in Gerard Dou's portrait of Rembrandt's mother had its antecedent in the iconography of the silent devotional reading practiced by the Virgin at the moment of the Annunciation. The printing press would play an important role in the ultimate triumph of Protestantism, but the formulation of reformist religious and political ideas and the receptivity of Europe's elite to making private judgments on matters of conscience owed much to a long evolution that began in the late seventh century and culminated in the fifteenth century in the manner in which men and women read and wrote. This enhanced privacy represented the consummation of the development of separated writing and constituted a crucial aspect of the modern world.

Appendix

Characteristics Relating to Word Separation in Manuscripts Surveyed

The following tables provide an overview of word separation and related characteristics in manuscripts pertaining to persons and monastic foundations surveyed in this book.

Each codex is identified by library and shelf-mark. Where these manuscripts are described in the text, the salient textual information may be obtained by consulting the Index of Manuscripts Cited. For the others, the reader should consult the library catalogues as well as the analytical descriptions provided in this book for specific bibliographical details. The textual complexity of many of these volumes makes it impractical to give a summary description of their contents in the context of the tables. Specific foliation references are given only for modern composite volumes.

Each codex is assigned a date as best as I have been able to establish it. Many dates are given in abbreviated forms: *s. X* means tenth century; *s. X*^{1} means the first half of the tenth century; *s. X*^{2} means the second half of the tenth century; *s. X in* means the first third of the tenth century; *s. X med* means the middle third of the tenth century; *s. X ex* means the final third of the tenth century; *a. 1011* means ante 1011; *p. 1011* means post 1011.

Fourteen types of word spacing characteristics are included. They are listed here with explanations of the kinds of information as presented in the tables.

Format. Abbreviations for formats are as follows. *Sep.* means words are separated; *sep. 2* means separation by 2 times the unity of space; *sep. 1–3.33* means separation varying from 1 to 3.33 unities of space, and so forth. *Can. sep.* means canonical word separation. *Aerated* means that the script is aerated and *not* separated. *HWB* means the manuscript is written in aerated script forming hierarchical word blocks. *HWB < 15* means that these blocks are less than the designated number of characters in length, measuring from one major space to another; *HWB > 15* means that they are greater than the designated number. A / between format types means that the script varies from one text format to another.

Syllabic Space. Conspicuous failure to suppress syllabic space in separated manuscripts is noted; this is an important vestigial attribute of aerated script.

Space after monosyllabic prepositions. The regular omission of such space is indicated, another vestigial attribute of aerated script.

Traits d'union. *Yes* indicates that original *traits d'union* are present; *split-line* indicates that they are sometimes present in the split-line form, that is, at line beginning as well as at line ending.

Suspended ligatures. The presence of this alternative to the *trait d'union* for scribal indication of words divided at line ending is indicated.

Terminal forms. Special abbreviations or letters used to designate word endings such as the abbreviation for *tur*, the capital *S*, or the *N* ligature.

Monolexic abbreviations. The use of these abbreviations for short words is noted. *Amp.* indicates that the ampersand set off by space represents *et*; 7 indicates that the tironian sign is used for *et*. Distinction is made between —· for *est*, the tironian sign common in manuscripts close to Fleury at the time of Abbo, and ÷, the usual sign for *est*, which is of Insular origin.

Successor note to the diastole. Its use as a contemporary sign indicating the omission of interword space is noted.

Acute accents on tonic syllable, on monosyllables, for word continuation, and on ii. These record various uses of the acute accent to remove ambiguity from word shape and to indicate interline word continuation.

Suspension abbreviations. Use of abbreviations such as *R.* for Robertus, a system by which one letter always represents one word, is noted.

Other characteristics. These include, for early word-separated manuscripts, signs for fractions, the capitalization of proper nouns, emblematic punctuation, and especially the presence of schematic or tree diagrams.

For ease of reading, only those characteristics that appear in a manuscript are listed.

TABLE AI
Early Manuscripts of Works by Gerbert

Library, shelf-mark, and date	Spacing characteristics
Milan, Biblioteca Ambrosiana C 128 inf 980–83	*Format*: sep. 3 *Other characteristics*: emblematic punctuation
Paris, Bibliothèque Nationale lat. 13955, ff 105v–106 s. X	*Format*: can. sep. 2–3
Paris, Bibliothèque Nationale lat. 7696 (Fleury) s. X²	*Format*: sep.
Paris, Bibliothèque Nationale lat. 16678, ff 1–8 (Fleury) s. X ex	*Format*: sep. by space (1–3), terminal, and conventional signs *Space after monosyllabic prepositions*: omitted *Trait d'union*: split-line *Terminal forms*: us, m, tur, NT, R *Monolexic abbreviations*: yes; –·, =, est
Leiden, Bibliotheek der Rijksuniversiteit Voss Q 17 (Micy) s. X ex	*Format*: sep. 4.67 *Terminal forms*: us, m *Monolexic abbreviations*: superscript forms *Other characteristics*: proper names capitalized
Paris, Bibliothèque Nationale lat. 8663 (Fleury) ca. 1000	*Format*: sep. 2–6 *Space after monosyllabic prepositions*: omitted *Terminal forms*: for syllables; long j in numbers *Monolexic abbreviations*: yes
Munich, Bayerische Staatsbibliothek CLM 14436 ff 24v–41v (St. Emmeram) s. XI in	*Format*: sep. 1.5–2.33 *Syllabic space*: not suppressed *Space after monosyllabic prepositions*: omitted *Monolexic abbreviations*: superscript forms, 7 *Suspension abbreviations*: for proper names *Other characteristics*: Insular fractions
Montpellier, Bibliothèque de l' Ecole de Médecine H 491 s. XI in	*Space after monosyllabic prepositions*: omitted *Terminal forms*: elevated o, N̄ for syllables *Successor note to diastole*: vertical strokes added
Leiden, Bibliotheek der Rijksuniversiteit Scaliger 38 s. XI in	*Format*: sep. 2 *Monolexic abbreviations*: vel., amp.
Leiden, Bibliotheek der Rijksuniversiteit Voss Q 54 (Micy) p. 1011	*Format*: sep. 1–3.33 *Syllabic space*: not suppressed *Space after monosyllabic prepositions*: omitted *Terminal forms*: us, m, orum, elevated o, long j in numbers *Monolexic abbreviations*: superscript forms, 7, ÷ *Suspension abbreviations*: for proper names *Other characteristics*: emblematic punctuation
Munich, Bayerische Staatsbibliothek CLM 14735 (St. Emmeram) s. XI¹	*Format*: sep. 2 *Terminal forms*: us, tur
Paris, Bibliothèque Nationale lat. 11127 (Echternach) s. XI¹	*Format*: sep.
Vatican Library Vat. Reg. lat. 733 s. XI med	*Format*: can. sep., Greek aerated *Trait d'union*: yes *Terminal forms*: elevated s *Monolexic abbreviations*: amp., ÷, =, est *Other characteristics*: emblematic punctuation

TABLE A1 *(continued)*

Library, shelf-mark, and date	Spacing characteristics
Monte Cassino, Archivio della Badia 189 s. XI	*Format*: aerated
Paris, Bibliothèque Nationale lat. 7377c s. XI ex	*Format*: can. sep. *Terminal forms*: us, tur *Monolexic abbreviations*: superscripts *Other characteristics*: schematic tree diagrams
Vatican Library Vat. Reg. lat. 1071 s. XI ex	*Format*: sep. 2 *Trait d'union*: split-line *Terminal forms*: tur, m, orum, elevated o, ę, long j in numbers *Monolexic abbreviations*: amp., 7
Paris, Bibliothèque Nationale NAL 886 s. XI ex	*Format*: can. sep. 2/2.33 *Trait d'union*: yes *Suspended ligatures*: yes *Terminal forms*: S at line ends, orum, tur, ę *Monolexic abbreviations*: amp. *Other characteristics*: schematic tree diagrams

TABLE A2

Early Manuscripts of Works by Adson

Library, shelf-mark, and date	Spacing characteristics
Paris, Bibliothèque Nationale lat. 13764 ff 1–48 c. 1000	*Format*: sep. 2–3 *Trait d'union*: yes *Successor note to diastole*: diastole only *Acute accent on tonic syllable*: in proximity to i *Acute accent on monosyllable*: yes *Acute accent for word continuation*: yes *Other characteristics*: proper names capitalized
The Hague, Koninklijke Bibliotheek 70.H.50 ff 1–12v s. X–XI	*Format*: sep. 3–4 *Terminal forms*: M, N̄, elevated s *Acute accent on tonic syllable*: yes *Acute accent on monosyllable*: yes *Other characteristics*: proper names capitalized
London, British Library Add 21917 s. X–XI	*Format*: sep. 4 *Trait d'union*: yes *Suspended ligatures*: yes *Terminal forms*: m, tur, orum, et, us, N̄, N̄ur *Monolexic abbreviations*: amp. *Other characteristics*: proper names capitalized
Orléans, Bibliothèque Municipale 17 p.6 (Fleury) s. XI	*Format*: sep.
Wolfenbüttel, Herzog August Bibliothek Aug. 76.14 ff 15–17 s. X.I	*Format*: sep. *Trait d'union*: yes *Acute accent on ii*: as terminal form
Vatican Library Vat. lat. 1783 s. XI med	*Format*: sep.
Paris, Bibliothèque Nationale 3454 (St. Martial) s. XI ex	*Format*: can. sep.

TABLE A3

Early Manuscripts of Works by Abbo of Fleury

Library, shelf-mark, and date	Spacing characteristics
London, British Library Add. 10972 (Fleury) p. 982	*Format*: sep. by space, terminal, and conventional signs; can. sep. *Trait d'union*: split-line *Suspended ligatures*: yes *Terminal forms*: us, m, NS, N̄ *Monolexic abbreviations*: yes *Acute accent on monosyllable*: yes *Other characteristics*: proper names in all caps
Vatican Library Vat. Reg. lat. 596 (Fleury) p. 982	*Format*: HWB < 15/ sep. *Space after monosyllabic prepositions*: regularly omitted *Monolexic abbreviations*: yes; —
Paris, Bibliothèque Nationale NAL 1611 and Orléans, Bibliothèque Municipale 267 (Fleury) s. X	*Terminal forms*: us, m, S, R *Monolexic abbreviations*: yes *Acute accent on monosyllable*: yes
Orléans, Bibliothèque Municipale 277 (Fleury) s. X ex	*Format*: sep. 2 *Terminal forms*: m, tur, N̄
Paris, Bibliothèque Nationale lat. 6638, ff 1–16 s. X ex	*Format*: sep. by space, terminal, and conventional signs *Terminal forms*: tur, bus, us, m, orum, S at line end
Leiden, Bibliotheek der Rijksuniversiteit BPL 139 B s. X ex	*Format*: sep. by space (z), terminal, and conventional signs *Space after monosyllabic prepositions*: regularly omitted *Monolexic abbreviations*: yes; amp., = *Other characteristics*: schematic tree diagrams
Paris, Bibliothèque Nationale lat. 7518, ff 36–37 (Fleury) s. X ex	*Format*: sep. 2
Paris, Bibliothèque Nationale lat. 17868, ff 15–16 s. X ex	*Format*: sep. by space, terminal, and conventional signs
London, British Library Harley 2506, ff 30–33v (Fleury) s. X ex	*Format*: sep. 1–2 *Trait d'union*: yes *Terminal forms*: long j in numbers, tur, bus, orum, elevated o, S, N̄ *Monolexic abbreviations*: ÷, l for vel
Paris, Bibliothèque Nationale lat. 7518, ff 25–36 s. X ex	*Format*: sep. 2 *Terminal forms*: tur, bus, us, m, orum, S at line end
Berlin, Staatsbibliothek 138 s. X ex	*Format*: sep. (1.5–2), terminal forms, and conventional signs *Trait d'union*: yes *Suspended ligatures*: ct *Terminal forms*: us, tur, orum, bus, amp., S, N, N̄, long j in numbers *Acute accent on monosyllable*: yes, ó *Other characteristics*: Insular fractions
Vatican Library Vat Reg. lat. 1573 (Ferrieres) s. XI in	*Format*: sep. *Trait d'union*: yes *Monolexic abbreviations*: yes

TABLE A3 (*continued*)

Library, shelf-mark, and date	Spacing characteristics
Bamberg, Staatsbibliothek Class. 53 c. 1000	*Format*: sep. 2 *Space after monosyllabic prepositions*: occasional *Suspended ligatures*: yes *Terminal forms*: m, tur, orum, bus, US, S at line end, N' at line end *Acute accent on monosyllable*: on prepositions *Other characteristics*: schematic tree diagrams
Leiden, Bibliotheek der Rijksuniversiteit Voss lat. F.96 (Fleury) p. 1039	*Format*: sep. 1.5 *Terminal forms*: N', long j in numbers *Monolexic abbreviations*: ÷, amp., 7
Vatican Library Vat. Reg. lat. 1864 f. 73 s. XI med	*Format*: sep. 2 *Terminal forms*: S, long j in numbers
Paris, Bibliothèque Nationale lat. 12117 1030–60	*Format*: sep. by space, terminal forms, and conventional signs
Paris, Bibliothèque Nationale lat. 2400 (St. Martial) a. 1034	*Format*: HWB
Vatican Library Vat. Reg. lat. 8591 s. XI[1]	*Format*: sep. can. sep. 2.5–4 *Terminal forms*: US, bus, long j in numbers *Monolexic abbreviations*: ÷, l. for est *Acute accent on monosyllable*: yes *Other characteristics*: schematic tree diagrams

TABLE A4

Early Manuscripts of Works by Fulbert

Library, shelf-mark, and date	Spacing characteristics
Paris, Bibliothèque Nationale lat. 14167 (St.-Père) p. 1028	*Format*: sep./can. sep. *Trait d'union*: split-line *Terminal forms*: m, us, orum, tur, bus, e cedilla *Monolexic abbreviations*: ÷, superscripts *Successor to diastole*: yes *Acute accent on tonic syllable*: in Arabic *Suspension abbreviations*: for proper names *Other characteristics*: proper names capitalized, Insular fractions
Paris, Bibliothèque Nationale lat. 2872 s. XI med	*Format*: sep./can. sep., 2 *Trait d'union*: yes *Suspended ligatures*: ct, e *Terminal forms*: m, us, orum, tur, bus, long j, N, S *Acute accent on monosyllable*: yes, 6 *Acute accent on ii*: yes
Leiden, Bibliotheek der Rijksuniversiteit Voss lat. Q.12 p. 1037	*Format*: sep. 2.5/3.5 *Syllabic space*: suppressed except at ligature *Space after monosyllabic prepositions*: sometimes *Trait d'union*: split-line *Suspended ligatures*: yes *Monolexic abbreviations*: superscript forms, l for vel., ÷, 7 *Successor to diastole*: yes *Acute accent on tonic syllable*: Hebrew names *Acute accent on monosyllable*: yes *Acute accent on ii*: yes *Suspension abbreviations*: for proper names *Other characteristics*: emblematic punctuation, proper names capitalized, fractions

TABLE A4 *(continued)*

Library, shelf-mark, and date	Spacing characteristics
Vatican Library Vat. Reg. lat. 1783 ff 97–128 s. XI med	*Format*: sep. 2/2.7 *Space after monosyllabic prepositions*: sometimes *Trait d'union*: yes, at feet *Terminal forms*: m, tur, us, orum, S, N̄ *Monolexic abbreviations*: superscript forms, Insular enim, 7, –· *Suspension abbreviations*: for proper names *Other characteristics*: Hyphen to correct interword space, tree diagrams
London, British Library Add 17808, f.73 c. 1040	*Format*: can. sep. *Trait d'union*: yes *Other characteristics*: symbols for fractions
Paris, Bibliothèque Nationale lat. 13955 s. XI²	*Format*: sep. 2–3
Montpellier, Bibliothèque de l'Ecole de Médecine H 137 (B) s. XI²	*Format*: sep./can. sep. *Space after monosyllabic prepositions*: split- line *Terminal forms*: long j in numbers *Acute accent on ii*: in numbers
Boulogne-sur-Mer, Bibliothèque Municipale 83 (St. Vaast) s. XI	*Format*: sep.
Dijon, Bibliothèque Municipale 30 (St. Vaast) s. XI	*Format*: sep.
Rouen, Bibliothèque Municipale 1378 (Jumièges) s. XI	*Format*: sep.
Oxford, Bodleian Library Bodley 852, ff 1–31 (Jumièges) 1049–72	*Format*: can. sep. *Trait d'union*: yes *Terminal forms*: R *Monolexic abbreviations*: amp. *Other characteristics*: architectural table, banderoles
Paris, Bibliothèque Nationale NAL 1455 (Cluny) p. 1049	*Format*: sep.

TABLE A5

Early Manuscripts Originating from the Abbey of Mont Saint-Michel

Library, shelf-mark, and date	Spacing characteristics
Avranches, Bibliothèque Municipale 50 p. 969	*Format*: HWB < 15
Avranches, Bibliothèque Municipale 78 s. X²	*Format*: HWB < 15
Avranches, Bibliothèque Municipale 109 s. X²	*Format*: HWB

TABLE A5 (*continued*)

Library, shelf-mark, and date	Spacing characteristics
Leiden, Bibliotheek der Rijksuniversiteit Voss lat. F39	*Format*: sep. 1–3 *Terminal forms*: N̄
991–1009 and Paris, Bibliothèque Nationale lat. 5920 991–1009	*Format*: sep. 1–3 *Terminal forms*: N̄
Avranches, Bibliothèque Municipale 97 991–1009	*Format*: sep. 1–3
Avranches, Bibliothèque Municipale 229 1009–27	*Format*: HWB > 20 and sep. *Successor to diastole*: added *Acute accent on monosyllable*: added *Acute accent on ii*: added *Other characteristics*: diple added
Paris, Bibliothèque Nationale lat. 8055, ff. 141–72 s. X[1]	*Format*: sep. *Acute accent on tonic syllable*: near minims
Paris, Bibliothèque Nationale lat. 8070, ff 1–129 s. X[1]	*Format*: sep. *Syllabic space*: suppressed
Avranches, Bibliothèque Municipale 91 1015–40	*Format*: sep. 1.3
Avranches, Bibliothèque Municipale 101 1030–45	*Format*: sep. 1.66–2 *Trait d'union*: split-line *Acute accent on tonic syllable*: near minims
Rouen, Bibliothèque Municipale 427 a. 1033	*Format*: sep. 2 *Syllabic space*: suppressed *Trait d'union*: yes *Acute accent on monosyllable*: yes
Avranches, Bibliothèque Municipale 59 1030–45	*Format*: sep. *Acute accent on monosyllable*: yes
Avranches, Bibliothèque Municipale 90 1050–65	*Format*: sep. 2 *Trait d'union*: split-line
Avranches, Bibliothèque Municipale 103 a. 1072	*Format*: fere can. *Other characteristics*: punctus elevatus
Avranches, Bibliothèque Municipale 58 s. XI[2]	*Format*: sep.
Avranches, Bibliothèque Municipale 107 s. XI[2]	*Format*: sep.
Avranches, Bibliothèque Municipale 163 1065–80	*Format*: sep. 1–2 *Terminal forms*: S *Other characteristics*: punctus elevatus

TABLE A6

Early Manuscripts Originating from Cluny

Library, shelf-mark, and date	Spacing characteristics
Paris, Bibliothèque Nationale NAL 1452 c. 946–54	*Format*: HWB > 15 and > 25 *Successor to diastole*: added *Acute accent on monosyllable*: added *Other characteristics*: hyphens added
Paris, Bibliothèque Nationale NAL 1460 950–91	*Format*: HWB > 25
Paris, Bibliothèque Nationale NAL 1461 s. X²	*Format*: HWB > 25
Paris, Bibliothèque Nationale NAL 1438 s. X	*Format*: HWB ≥ 15
London, British Library Add 22820 948–94	*Format*: HWB > 20
Paris, Bibliothèque Nationale NAL 2253 998–1008	*Format*: HWB > 30
Bamberg, Staatsbibliothek Bibl. 126 1002–24	*Format*: HWB
Paris, Bibliothèque Nationale NAL 1447 s. XI¹	*Format*: HWB > 25 *Trait d'union*: split-line *Successor to diastole*: yes
Paris, Bibliothèque Nationale 15176 s. XI¹	*Format*: sep. 2 *Trait d'union*: yes *Terminal forms*: m, us, tur, ꝫ, N, N̄, long j in numbers *Successor to diastole*: yes *Acute accent on tonic syllable*: near minims, Hebrew names *Acute accent on monosyllable*: yes *Acute accent for word continuation*: yes *Other characteristics*: punctus elevatus
London, British Library Add 11783 s. XI¹	*Format*: HWB, sep., can. sep.
Paris, Bibliothèque Nationale NAL 2248 s. X¹	*Format*: sep. 1
Paris, Bibliothèque Nationale NAL 1478 s. X–XI¹	*Format*: HWB and sep. *Terminal forms*: et ligature *Monolexic abbreviations*: superscripts *Other characteristics*: proper names capitalized
Paris, Bibliothèque Nationale NAL 1485 and 17275 c. 1049	*Format*: HWB/sep. 1.5–2 *Terminal forms*: et ligature, N̄, N, ꝫ, elevated s *Acute accent on tonic syllable*: near minims and on compounds, Hebrew names *Acute accent on monosyllable*: yes, ó
Paris, Bibliothèque Nationale NAL 1496 1049–61	*Format*: sep. 2 *Acute accent on monosyllable*: in lieu of space *Acute accent on ii*: yes

TABLE A6 *(continued)*

Library, shelf-mark, and date	Spacing characteristics
Paris, Bibliothèque Nationale NAL 2246 p. 1061	*Format*: sep. 1.5 *Trait d'union*: yes *Acute accent on tonic syllable*: yes
Paris, Bibliothèque Nationale NAL 638 p. 1083–86	*Format*: can. sep. *Terminal forms*: S, elevated s *Monolexic abbreviations*: 7, superscripts, monogram for *require* *Acute accent on ii*: yes *Other characteristics*: Roman numerals punctuated
Paris, Bibliothèque Nationale lat. 12601 p. 1061	*Format*: can. sep. *Trait d'union*: yes *Terminal forms*: round s
Paris, Bibliothèque Nationale lat. 17742 1085–97	*Trait d'union*: yes *Acute accent on tonic syllable*: yes

TABLE A7
Early Manuscripts Originating from Saint-Martial of Limoges

Library, shelf-mark, and date	Spacing characteristics
Paris, Bibliothèque Nationale lat. 5[1-2] s. IX	*Format*: HWB > 28
Paris, Bibliothèque Nationale lat. 1897 s. IX[2]	*Format*: HWB > 15 *Successor to diastole*: interpunct
Paris, Bibliothèque Nationale lat. 5239 c. 950	*Format*: HWB > 28
Paris, Bibliothèque Nationale lat. 5301 c. 1000	*Format*: HWB > 20
Paris, Bibliothèque Nationale lat. 7903 c. 1000	*Format*: HWB > 20
Paris, Bibliothèque Nationale lat. 1969 947–1007	*Format*: HWB
Paris, Bibliothèque Nationale lat. 1240 931–934	*Format*: HWB < 15 (chant)
Paris, Bibliothèque Nationale lat. 1121 a. 1054	*Format*: HWB < 15 (chant)
Paris, Bibliothèque Nationale lat. 1119 p. 1031	*Format*: HWB < 15 (chant)

TABLE A7 *(continued)*

Library, shelf-mark, and date	Spacing characteristics
Paris, Bibliothèque Nationale lat. 887 p. 1031	*Format*: HWB < 15 (chant)
Paris, Bibliothèque Nationale NAL 1871 p. 1031	*Format*: HWB < 15 (chant)
Paris, Bibliothèque Nationale lat. 3784 a. 1034	*Format*: HWB > 20
Paris, Bibliothèque Nationale lat. 2400 a. 1034	*Format*: HWB > 20
Paris, Bibliothèque Nationale lat. 7231 a. 1034	*Format*: HWB ≥ 20 *Other characteristics*: marginal tironian notes
Paris, Bibliothèque Nationale lat. 5927 1053–62	*Format*: HWB < 15/ < 20/sep. 1 *Trait d'union*: split-line
Paris, Bibliothèque Nationale lat. 7562 1053–62	*Format*: HWB/sep.
Paris, Bibliothèque Nationale lat. 822 1049–95	*Format*: sep. 2.6
Paris, Bibliothèque Nationale lat. 5240 (quire 1) c. 1064	*Format*: sep. 2 *Acute accent on monosyllable*: yes *Other characteristics*: proper names capitalized
Paris, Bibliothèque Nationale lat. 5240, ff 43–109 c. 1064	*Format*: sep. 1.5 *Space after monosyllabic prepositions*: yes *Trait d'union*: split-line *Terminal forms*: N̄, S, elevated s *Acute accent on tonic syllable*: compounds *Acute accent on monosyllable*: yes
Paris, Bibliothèque Nationale lat. 2208$^{1-2}$ a. 1114	*Format*: can. sep. 2.5 *Syllabic space*: suppressed, except ct and rt *Trait d'union*: yes *Monolexic abbreviations*: superscripts *Other characteristics*: hyphen
Paris, Bibliothèque Nationale lat. 8$^{1-2}$ a. 1114	*Format*: can. sep. 3 *Trait d'union*: yes *Terminal forms*: S, R, N̄ *Other characteristics*: banderole
Paris, Bibliothèque Nationale lat. 2799 a. 1114	*Format*: can. sep. 6 *Terminal forms*: N̄ *Acute accent on tonic syllable*: compounds *Acute accent on monosyllable*: yes *Acute accent for word continuation*: yes *Other characteristics*: accent on last syllable of adverbs, punctus versus and elevatus
Paris, Bibliothèque Nationale lat. 2056 c. 1100	*Format*: sep. *Terminal forms*: S, R *Acute accent on tonic syllable*: Hebrew names *Acute accent on ii*: yes *Other characteristics*: c/t distinction

Manuscripts Originating from Saint Pierre of Moissac

Library, shelf-mark, and date	Spacing characteristics
Paris, Bibliothèque Nationale lat. 2989 s. X ex	*Format*: HWB
Paris, Bibliothèque Nationale NAL 1871 p. 1031	*Format*: HWB < 15 (chant)
Paris, Bibliothèque Nationale 7505 s. XI in	*Format*: HWB > 20 *Acute accent on ii*: yes
Chicago, Newberry Library 1 s. XI med	*Format*: HWB > 20/can. sep. 2
Paris, Bibliothèque Nationale lat. 2077, ff 122–73 s. XI med	*Format*: HWB > 15/sep. 1–2 *Suspended ligatures*: yes *Successor to diastole*: dasia and elevated h *Acute accent on tonic syllable*: near minims, in compounds *Other characteristics*: proper names capitalized
Oxford, Bodleian Library Orville 45 c. 1067	*Format*: sep. 2.5 *Acute accent on tonic syllable*: yes
Paris, Bibliothèque Nationale lat. 4886 s. XI med	*Format*: sep. 2–3 *Space after monosyllabic prepositions*: yes *Terminal forms*: S, elevated s, long j in numbers
Leiden, Bibliotheek der Rijksuniversiteit BPL 1822 s. XI[2]	*Trait d'union*: yes and split-line *Suspended ligatures*: yes *Terminal forms*: Ń *Monolexic abbreviations*: copious *Successor to diastole*: after monosyllabic prepositions *Acute accent on monosyllables*: yes
Paris, Bibliothèque Nationale lat. 1961 s. XI[2]	*Format*: sep. 2 *Space after monosyllabic prepositions*: yes *Terminal forms*: S, Ń, long j in numbers *Acute accent on tonic syllable*: the i within tonic syllable
Paris, Bibliothèque Nationale lat. 5056 s. XI ex	*Format*: can. sep. 2–3 *Trait d'union*: yes and split-line *Suspended ligatures*: yes *Successor to diastole*: yes and dasia *Acute accent on tonic syllable*: compounds *Acute accent for word continuation*: yes *Acute accent on ii*: yes
Paris, Bibliothèque Nationale lat. 5058 s. XI ex	*Format*: sep. 2.5 *Trait d'union*: yes *Terminal forms*: crossed S for orum, R *Successor to diastole*: dasia *Acute accent on tonic syllable*: compounds and second conjugation verbs *Acute accent on ii*: yes
Paris, Bibliothèque Nationale lat. 1217 s. XI ex	*Format*: sep. 2–3 *Space after monosyllabic prepositions*: yes *Suspended ligatures*: yes *Acute accent on tonic syllable*: near minims in compounds *Acute accent on monosyllables*: yes *Acute accent on ii*: yes
Paris, Bibliothèque Nationale lat. 3783[1–2] s. XI ex	*Format*: sep. 1–2 *Successor to diastole*: elevated h *Acute accent on tonic syllable*: minims compounds *Acute accent on monosyllables*: yes
Paris, Bibliothèque Nationale lat. 17002 s. XI ex	*Other characteristics*: c/t distinction
Paris, Bibliothèque Nationale lat. 4808 s. XI ex	*Other characteristics*: c/t distinction

Reference Matter

Notes

The following abbreviations are used in the Notes.

ACA	Archivo de la Corona de Aragón, Barcelona
BEC	*Bibliothèque de l'École des Chartes*
BL (London)	British Library
BL (Oxford)	Bodleian Library
BM	Bibliothèque Municipale
BN	Bibliothèque Nationale
BR (Brussels)	Bibliothèque Royale
BR (Leiden)	Bibliotheek der Rijksuniversiteit
EETS	Early English Text Society
HBS	Henry Bradshaw Society
IMU	*Italia medioevale e umanistica*
JL	Janua Linguarum
IRHT	Institut de Recherche et d'Histoire des Textes, Paris
MA	*Le Moyen Age*
MBMRF	Münchener Beiträge zur Mediävistik und Renaissance Forschungen
MGH	*Monumenta Germaniae historica*
RB	*Revue bénédictine*
RHE	*Revue d'histoire ecclésiastique*
SHN	Société de l'Histoire de Normandie

Works cited by abbreviations not listed here will be found in the first section of the References, beginning on p. 437, as will works cited by shortened title only. Works cited by author's last name and a short title will be found in the second section of the References, beginning on p. 439.

Chapter 1

1. Saenger, "Silent Reading"; Roger Chartier, ed., *The Culture of Print* (Princeton, 1989), pp. 1–10, and Roger Chartier, "Les pratiques de l'écrit," in *Histoire de la vie privée,* vol. 3, *De la Renaissance aux Lumières* (Paris, 1986).

2. See Tzeng and Hung, "Linguistic Determinism"; Shen-Ping Fang, Ovid J. L. Tzeng, and Liz Alva, "Intralanguage versus Interlanguage Stroop Effects in Two Types of Writing Systems," *Memory and Cognition* 9 (1981): 609–17; Soja Park and Tannis Y. Arbuckle, "Ideograms Versus Alphabets: Effects of Script on Memory in *Biscriptural* Korean Subjects," *Journal of Experimental Psychology: Human Learning and Memory* 3 (1977): 631–42; de Kerckhove, "Logical Principles" and "Critical Brain Processes"; Alan Pavio and Ian Begg, *Psychology of Language* (Englewood Cliffs, N.J., 1981), pp. 321–23.

3. For a summary of the contrasting characteristics of ancient and modern European languages, see Antoine Meillet, *Esquisse d'une histoire de la langue latine*, 4th ed. (Paris, 1938), pp. 256–58, 271–73.

4. Antoine Meillet, "Le caractère concret du mot," *Journal de Psychologie* (1923): 246 ff., and "Remarques sur la théorie de la phrase," *Journal de Psychologie* (1921): 601 ff., both reprinted in his *Linguistique historique et linguistique générale*, 2 vols. (Paris, 1938), 2: 9–23 and 2: 1–8. See also Joseph Vendryes, *La Langue: Introduction linguistique à l'histoire* (Paris, 1921).

5. William S. Y. Wang, "Language Structure and Optimal Orthography," in Tzeng and Singer, *Perception of Print*, pp. 229–31; Viviane Alleton, *L'Ecriture chinoise*, 3d ed. (Paris, 1983); and Edwin O. Reischauer and John King Fairbank, *East Asia: The Great Tradition* (Boston, 1960), pp. 39–44. Hindu and Urdu are other examples of the same languages written with different script; see Jyotsha Vaid, "Effect of Reading and Writing Direction on Nonlinguistic Perception and Performance," in Insup Taylor and David R. Olson, eds., *Script and Literacy: Reading and Learning to Read Alphabets, Syllabaries, and Characters* (Dordrecht, 1995).

6. Marcel Cohen, in *L'Ecriture et la psychologie des peuples*, pp. 47, 319.

7. Tzeng and Hung, "Linguistic Determinism," p. 249; Taylor, "The Korean Writing System," pp. 67–82.

8. For differing skills inherent in reading Chinese and English, see Fang, Tzeng, and Alva, "Intralanguage versus Interlanguage Stroop Effects in Two Types of Writing Systems," pp. 609–17; Thomas W. Turnage and Elliott McGinnies, "A Cross-Cultural Comparison on the Effects of Presentation Mode and Meaningfulness of Short-Term Recall," *American Journal of Psychology* 86 (1973): 369–82.

9. Rebecca Treiman, Jonathan Baron, and Kenneth Luk, "Speech Reading in Silent Reading: A Comparison of Chinese and English," *Journal of Chinese Linguistics* 9 (1981): 116–25. Silent reading is not characteristic of Burmese, whose script is alphabetic; see the description of solitary oral reading among adult Burmese laborers in A. W. Smith, "Working Teak in the Burma Forests," *National Geographic Magazine* 50 (1930): 243, cited by Eugene S. McCartney, "Notes on Reading and Praying Audibly," *Classical Philology* 43 (1948): 185.

10. William S. Gray, *The Teaching of Reading and Writing: An International*

Survey (Paris, 1956); Insup Taylor, "Writing Systems and Reading," in *Reading Research: Advances in Theory and Practice* 2 (1981): 17–18. However, more recent research may suggest modifications to this conclusion because of the similarity of Chinese characters in peripheral vision; Taylor, "Writing Systems and Reading," p. 43; Taylor and Taylor, *The Psychology of Reading*, p. 38.

11. See Takahiko Sakamoto and Kiyoshi Makita, "Japan," in Downing, *Comparative Reading*, pp. 440–65; Tzeng and Hung, "Linguistic Determinism," p. 249; and Taylor and Taylor, *The Psychology of Reading*, pp. 77–91.

12. S. Sasanuma, "Impairment of Written Language in Japanese Aphasics: Kana versus Kanji Processing," *Journal of Chinese Linguistics* 2 (1974): 141–57; S. Sasanuma and K. Fujimura, "Selective Impairment of Phonetic and Non Phonetic Transcription of Words in Japanese Aphasic Patients: Kana vs. Kanji in Visual Recognition and Writing," *Cortex* 7 (1971): 1–18; S. Sasanuma, "Kana and Kanji Processing in Japanese Aphasics," *Brain and Language* 2 (1975): 369–83; Sakamoto and Makita, "Japan"; Pavio and Begg, *Psychology of Language*, p. 345; Taylor and Taylor, *The Psychology of Reading*, pp. 73–74; cf. Peter Meodell, "Dyslexia and Normal Reading," in *Dyslexia Research and Its Applications to Education*, ed. George T. Pavlidis and T. R. Miles (New York, 1981). The transcription of English into Braille also results in an apparent redistribution of cerebral functions; Ennio De Renzi, *Disorders of Space Exploration and Cognition* (New York, 1982), pp. 18–19. Recent research suggests that a simple model of right-hemisphere reading for logographic script and left-hemisphere reading for syllable and alphabetical scripts may be inadequate; see Reiko Hasuike, Ovid J. L. Tzeng, and Daisy L. Hung, "Script Effects and Cerebral Lateralization: The Case of Chinese Characters," in *Language Processing in Bilinguals: Psycholinguistic and Neuropsychological Perspectives*, ed. J. Vaid (Hillsdale, N.J., 1986), pp. 275–88; Ovid J. L. Tzeng, Daisy L. Hung, D. L. Chen, J. Wu, and M. S. Hsi, "Processing Chinese Logographs by Chinese Brain Damaged Patients," in *Graphonomics: Contemporary Research in Handwriting*, ed. Henry S. R. Kao, Gerard Van Galen, and Rumjahn Hoosain (Amsterdam, 1986), pp. 357–74.

13. Ho Sai Keung and Rumjahn Hoosain, "Right Hemisphere Advantage in Lexical Decision with Two-Character Chinese Words," *Brain and Language* 37 (1989): 606–15.

14. Alfonso Caramazza and Argye E. Hills, "Lexical Organization of Nouns and Verbs in the Brain," *Nature* 349 (1991): 788–90; *Johns Hopkins Magazine*, April/June 1991, p. 99.

15. See Michael E. Phelps, "Position Computed Tomography for Studies of Myocardial and Cerebral Function," *Annals of Internal Medicine* 98 (1983): 339–59; Michael E. Phelps and John C. Mazziota, "Proton Emission Tomography: Human Brain Function and Biochemistry," *Science* 228 (1985): 799–809; Ovid J. L. Tzeng and Fritz Tsao, review of *Left Side, Right Side: A Review of Laterality Research*, by Alan Beaton, *American Journal of Psychology* 102 (1989): 135–36.

John R. Skoyles suggests interesting avenues of inquiry in "Did Ancient People Read with their Right Hemispheres? A Study in Neuropalaeography," *New Ideas in Psychology* 3 (1958): 243–52.

16. Sakamoto and Makita, "Japan"; cf. Wang, "Language Structure and Optimal Orthography," in Tzeng and Singer, *Perception of Print.*

17. Sakamoto and Makita, "Japan."

18. Taylor, "The Korean Writing System," pp. 72–74; Park and Arbuckle, "Ideograms Versus Alphabets," p. 633.

19. See V. A. Mann, "The Relation Between Temporary Phonetic Memory and the Acquisition of Japanese Kana and Kanji," *Papers Presented at the Third International Symposium on Psychological Aspects of the Chinese Language,* Hong Kong, July 1984, summarized by Hasuike, Tzeng, and Hung, "Script Effects and Cerebral Lateralization," p. 276.

20. Sakamoto and Makita, "Japan"; see also, Taylor and Taylor, *The Psychology of Reading,* pp. 70, 114; Taylor, "The Korean Writing System," p. 71; Taylor, "Writing Systems and Reading," pp. 22, 25, 32.

21. Sakamoto and Makita, "Japan." Another graphic tradition in which oralization as a cognitive activity preliminary to word recognition is important to young readers is that of modern Hebrew. See Dina Feitelson, "Israel," in Downing, *Comparative Reading,* pp. 426–39. In Hebrew, the similarity in the form of many characters, even when both vowels and regular interword spacing are present, makes word recognition by word shape more difficult than in languages transcribed with Latin characters. As a result, Israeli educators in the 1960's rejected the emphasis of the previous decade on the global recognition of words as images. (This preference for phonetic reading seems to run counter to aspects of the thesis recently suggested by John R. Skoyles, "The Origin of Classical Greek Culture: The Transparent Chain Theory of Literacy/Society Interaction," *Journal of Social and Biological Structures* 13 [1990]: 321–53. Whole-word recognition is important to mature readers of Hebrew. See de Kerckhove, "Critical Brain Processes," p. 402.) This technique had been borrowed from the "whole-word method" of reading instruction used both in the English-speaking world and in Denmark, where it had been effective because English and Danish alike have large numbers of silent letters and letter combinations that help to distinguish visually the entire word but that hinder consistent decoding of a word through the synthesis of phonetic cues. See Feitelson, "Israel," p. 430. For the similarity of Danish and English pedagogy, see Mogens Jansen, "Denmark," in Downing, *Comparative Reading,* pp. 285–307.

The vernacular languages of India are an example of a modern graphic tradition in which oral processes are even more important for achieving lexical access than in the modern languages of western Europe. See Chinna Oommen, "India," in Downing, *Comparative Reading,* pp. 403–25. In Hindi, syllabic characters accompanied by vowels are admirably suited for accurate transcription of the component sounds of words, but because of the similarity of numerous signs, the Indian characters, like those of Hebrew, fail to bestow upon each word a unique and unequivocal global image, even when they are set off by interword spaces, as they are in twentieth-century script and printed books. This ambiguity in transcription has created a pedagogical tradition for young readers that stresses synthetic reading, oral recitation, and rote memorization of texts. In modern India, as in Greco-Roman antiquity, recitation from memory while following the text in an open book is an activity commonly regarded as a form of reading. See Marrou, *Histoire de l'éducation dans l'antiquité*, p. 234. See also Ugo Enrico Paoli, "Legere e recitare," *Atene e Roma* (1922): 205–7.

22. Sylvia Scribner and Michael Cole, *The Psychology of Literacy* (Cambridge, Mass., 1981); cf. Tzeng and Hung, "Linguistic Determinism," p. 249; Olson, *The World on Paper*, pp. 20–44.

23. Examples of ancient Greek and Roman *continua* are most easily consulted in B. L. Ullman, *Ancient Writing and Its Influence*, ed. Julian Brown (Cambridge, Mass., 1969). More satisfactory reproductions are to be found in Steffens, *Lateinische Paläographie*.

24. For a description of ancient oral reading habits, see Saenger, "Silent Reading."

25. See Sokolov, *Inner Speech and Thought*.

26. Harry Levin and Eleanor L. Kaplan, "Grammatical Structure and Reading," in Levin and Williams, *Basic Studies on Reading*, p. 119.

27. L. L. Lamme, *Growing Up Writing* (Washington, D.C., 1984), pp. 50–52, 79–80, 132–39; Scholes, "On the Orthographic Basis of Morphology."

28. On the residual aural tendencies of less skilled readers, see Scholes and Willis, "Prosodic and Syntactic Functions of Punctuations," pp. 13–20.

29. On the eye-voice span, see Levin and Addis, *The Eye-Voice Span*. The broad eye-voice span of modern separated script and Chinese logographs represents, in effect, incipient silent reading before the act of pronunciation.

30. Dennis F. Fisher, "Spatial Factors in Reading and Search: The Case for Space," in *Eye Movement and Psychological Processes*, ed. R. A. Monty and J. W. Senders (Hillsdale, N.J., 1976), pp. 417, 427, 453–55. Cf. Julian Hochberg, "Components of Literacy: Speculations and Exploratory Research," in Levin and Williams, *Basic Studies on Reading*.

31. An example in French would be *à/a* and *ou/où*. Here, distinctions or word meanings are conveyed by unpronounced grave accent marks. In English, certain variations in spelling and words spelled with silent letters denote ideas directly; see Josef Vachek, *Written Language: General Problems and Problems of English* (The Hague, 1973), pp. 12–13, 55. In English, the number of words more explicit in their graphic form than in their pronunciation is far fewer than in written Chinese; see Taylor and Taylor, *The Psychology of Reading*, p. 107. On the

phonemic process in *scriptura continua*, see de Kerckhove, "Logical Principles," p. 156; and "Critical Brain Processes," pp. 402–3.

32. Lucian, *Adversus indoctum*, 2; Quintilian, *Institutiones*, 1.1.32; Aullus Gellius, *Noctes Atticae*, 12.31.4–13. The commentary on Lucian by Bernard M. W. Knox, "Silent Reading in Antiquity," *Greek, Roman, and Byzantine Studies* 9 (1968): 424, unfairly represents the balanced analysis of G. L. Hendrickson, "Ancient Reading," *The Classical Journal* 25 (1929): 192–93. For additional examples of this phenomenon, see Parkes, *Pause and Effect*, p. 10.

33. Fisher, "Spatial Factors in Reading and Search," pp. 422–23, 426.

34. On the relationship of eye movement and brain processes, consult John Downing and Che Kan Leong, *Psychology of Reading* (New York, 1982), p. 33; and John W. Senders, Dennis F. Fisher, and Richard A. Monty, *Eye Movement and Higher Psychological Functions* (Hillsdale, N.J., 1978). The recent research by Joshua A. Solomon and Denis G. Pell, "The Visual Filter Mediating Letter Identification," *Nature* 369 (1994): 395–97, sheds important light on the direct link between interference in "low-level" physiological processes and reading. I am grateful to Brian Stock for this reference.

35. For an analysis of the complexities of syllable parsing, even with the artificial aid of interword space, see Adams, "What Good Is Orthographic Redundancy?," pp. 210–17. The diacritical marks enumerated in Pseudo-Priscian's *Liber de accentibus* represented in part the medieval scribes' attempt to alleviate syllabic ambiguity. See the text in Keil, *Grammatici latini*, 3: 519–28.

36. The oral nature of classroom reading has been well described by Michel Banniard, *Genèse culturelle de l'Europe: V⁻–VIII⁻ siècle* (Paris, 1989), pp. 35–36; cf. Taylor and Taylor, *The Psychology of Reading*, pp. 227–32. See also the remarks of Emile Faguet, *L'art de lire* (Paris, 1912), pp. 1–3.

37. The ancients complained about such unexpressive reading, in which the reader's voice betrayed a failure to grasp the meaning of words before pronouncing them. In early modern Europe, peasants and other members of the lower classes have frequently been described in literature and represented in paintings as reading aloud in order to understand. See the lines of Labiche's *La cagnotte*, cited by Chartier in "Les pratiques de l'écrit," p. 126.

38. The space contained within the letter *O* provides a useful unit of measurement for comparing interletter space in ancient and modern script. Medieval manuscripts and early printed books intended for beginning readers also followed the practice of inserting additional interletter space; see Paris, BN lat. 8093, ff. 84–86, the *Breves sententiae* of the *Disticha Catonis*, Giovanni Antonio Tagliente's *Libro maistrevole* (Venice, 1524), and Johannes Gropper's *Libellus piarum precum* (Cologne, 1546).

39. See, for example, Servius's *De finalibus* and Bede's *De arte metrica*. This tradition continued into the fifteenth and sixteenth centuries; see, for example, the *Babuino* (Perugia, 1531) described by Piero Lucchi, "La Santacroce, il Sal-

terio, e il Babuino: Libro per imparare a leggere nel primo secolo della stampa," *Quaderni storici*, no. 38 (1978): 608–9; and Tagliente, *Libro maistrevole*, described by Anne Schutte, "Teaching Adults to Read in Sixteenth-Century Venice," *Sixteenth Century Journal* 17 (1986): 1–16. For related works, see Giuseppe Manacorda, "Libri scolastici del Medio evo e del Rinascimento," *La Bibliofilia* 18 (1916–17): 244–45.

40. Henri-Irénée Marrou, *Saint Augustin et la fin de la culture antique*, Bibliothèque des écoles françaises d'Athènes et Rome, vol. 145 (Paris, 1938), pp. 24–26.

41. See Augustine, *Confessiones*, ed. Pierre de Labriolle (Paris, 1941), bk. 6, ch. 3, well explicated by Fabienne Gégou, "Son, parole et lecture au Moyen Age," in *Mélanges de langue et de littérature du moyen âge*, part 1, a special edition of *Cahiers d'études médiévales* (Nagoya, 1973). For remarks on the silent study practices of Ambrose, see his *Epistula XLVII* to Sabinus, in *PL* 16: 1150–51; and in English, trans. Mary Melchio Beyenka, Fathers of the Church, vol. 26 (New York, 1954), pp. 127–29. When Augustine refers to the heart, he means the mind; see Saenger, "Books of Hours," p. 146. When Carruthers translates comments on this passage in *The Book of Memory*, pp. 170–71, she projects on the text attitudes that are entirely postclassical. No ancient writer ever refers to reading as "scanning" or *meditatio*.

42. The distinction between "silent oral reading" and "true silent reading" is pertinent in this context; see Tony Pugh, "The Development of Silent Reading," in *The Road to Effective Reading: Proceedings of the Tenth Annual Study Conference of the United Kingdom Reading Association*, ed. William Latham (Totley, Thornbridge, 1973), p. 114. For children, imposed silence does not increase reading speed; see Levin and Addis, *The Eye-Voice Span*, p. 25. For examples of ancient private reading, see Josef Balogh, "Voces paginarum," *Philologus* 82 (1926–27): 92–93, 100–101.

43. Ovid appears to describe truly silent reading when Cydippe writes to Acontius "scriptumque tuum sine murmure legi." When Octavien de Saint-Gelais translated this line in the early sixteenth century, he used the term *en cuer*, meaning, clearly, "silent reading." Saenger, "Books of Hours," p. 146. Other references to reading referring to *tacitus* and *in silentio* are more ambiguous, since these terms in the Vulgate Bible, the Rule of Saint Benedict, and in medieval monastic customaries connoted vocal activities, including chanting, which although relatively quiet were not entirely mental; see Saenger, "Books of Hours," p. 145. Horace, *Saturae*, 2.5.68, describes the quiet reading of a will, and Plutarch, *Moralia*, 34a and *Brutus*, 5, describes the similar reading of letters, but in these instances it is uncertain whether inaudible mumbling or truly silent reading is implied. However, Isidore's preference for *lectio tacita*, *Sententiae*, 3.14.9, in *PL* 83: 689, clearly refers to the former, for he states, "vox legentis quiescat et sub silentio lingua movetur." In contrast, Augustine states

of Ambrose: "occuli ducebantur per paginas et cor intellectum rimabatur, vox autem et lingua quiescebant." Similarly ambiguous examples have been gleaned by Knox from fifth-century and fourth-century Greek literature; see "Silent Reading in Antiquity," pp. 432–34.

44. Maximus Victorinus, *Ars grammatica*, in Keil, *Grammatici latini*, 6: 188.

45. On vowels and syllable recognition, see Adams, "What Good Is Orthographic Redundancy?," pp. 197–221. Cf. her "Models of Word Recognition," *Cognitive Psychology* 11 (1979): 133–76.

46. Cohen, *La Grande invention*. On separation in Latin before the end of the second century A.D., see Wingo, *Latin Punctuation in the Classical Age*, pp. 4–17; Anderson, Parsons, and Nisbet, "Elegiacs by Gallus from Qasr Ibrim," p. 131.

47. De Kerckhove, "Logical Principles," p. 156. See also James Barr, "Reading a Script Without Vowels," in William Haas, ed., *Writing Without Letters* (Manchester, 1976), pp. 89–90; A. R. Millard, "*Scriptio Continua* in Early Hebrew: Ancient Practice or Modern Surmise?" *Journal of Semitic Studies* 15 (1970): 2–15; Moses Maimonides, *Mishneh Torah: The Book of Adoration*, ed. and trans. Moses Hyamson (Jerusalem, n.d.), p. 129b, gives traditional Hebrew criteria for adequate space for word separation. The medieval secret writing based on vowel deletion was also predicated on word separation.

48. Michel Lejeune, review of *L'écriture*, by Marcel Cohen, *Revue des études anciennes* 56 (1954): 429; Richard Harder, *Kleine Schriften* (Munich, 1960), p. 101; Eric G. Turner, *Greek Manuscripts of the Ancient World* (Princeton, 1971), p. 9.

49. Norman K. Gottwald, *A Light to the Nations: An Introduction to the Old Testament* (New York, 1959), pp. 40–48. In contrast to the ancient Hebrew of the Dead Sea Scrolls and like Carolingian writing, Masoretic script was written in word blocks.

50. A. L. Basham, *The Wonder That Was India* (New York, 1959), pp. 394–99; and Jean Filliozat, "Les écritures indiennes: Le monde indien et son système graphique," in *L'Ecriture et la psychologie des peuples*, pp. 147–66; W. Sidney Allen, *Sandhi: The Theoretical, Phonetic, and Historical Bases of Word-Juncture in Sanskrit*, JL, vol. 17 (The Hague, 1962), pp. 16–17; Florian Coulmas, *The Writing Systems of the World* (Oxford, 1989), p. 189.

51. Ernst Z. Rothkopf, "Incidental Memory for Location of Information in Text," *Journal of Verbal Learning and Verbal Behavior* 10 (1971): 608–13; cf. Turnage and McGinnies, "A Cross-Cultural Comparison," pp. 377–79.

52. Consult the observations of Edmond S. Meltzer, "Remarks on Ancient Egyptian Writing with Emphasis on Its Mnemonic Aspects," in *Processing of Visible Language* 2, pp. 43, 58–62, 63–64.

53. An example of a Greek text transliterated into Latin characters and separated by interpuncts is Revilo Oliver, "The First Medicean MS of Tacitus and the Titulature of Ancient Books," *Transactions and Proceedings of the American Philological Association* 82 (1951): 242 n. 19, referring to PSI 743 (end of the first

or early second century); Wingo, *Latin Punctuation in the Classical Age*, p. 15; cf. Turner, *Greek Manuscripts*, p. 9 n. 3.

54. See Roberts and Skeat, *The Birth of the Codex*, pp. 50–51, 73–74. W. Clark in his note, "Ancient Reading," *The Classical Journal* 26 (1931): 698–700, appears frustrated by his inability to find explicit evidence of modern "eye reading."

55. Balogh, "Voces paginarum," pp. 84–109, 202–40; Parkes, *Pause and Effect*, p. 9.

56. See the remarks of Colette Sirat, "The Material Conditions of the Lateralization of the Ductus," in de Kerckhove and Lumsden, *The Alphabet and the Brain*, pp. 197–98.

57. Seneca, *Epistula*, 40.11; *Sénèque: Lettres à Lucilius*, ed. François Préhac (Paris, 1969–79), 1: 165–67.

58. The *genuit* sequence from the Gospel of Matthew of Turin, Biblioteca Universitaria G.VII.15, is a virtually unique example; see Carlo Cipolla, *Codici Bobbiesi della Biblioteca Nazionale Universitaria di Torino* (Milan, 1907), pl. 15; cf. *CLA* 4 (1947): 465.

59. Jean Mallon, *La Paléographie romaine* (Madrid, 1952), pp. 95–97; Colette Sirat, *L'examen des écritures: L'oeil et la machine; essai de méthodologie* (Paris, 1981), p. 38.

60. Eric G. Turner, *The Typology of the Early Codex* (Philadelphia, 1977), p. 75; and Lehmann, "Blätter, Seiten, Spalten, Zeilen," pp. 1–59.

61. Müller, *Rhetorische und syntaktische Interpunktion*, pp. 16, 22, 35.

62. On the ancient mode of pronouncing monosyllables, see Harold Hagendahl, *La prose métrique d'Arnobe: Contributions à la connaissance de la prose littéraire de l'empire*, Göteborgs Högskolas Årsskrift, vol. 42 (Göteborg, Sweden, 1937), pp. 14–17; Carolus Zander, *Eurythmia vel compositio rythmica prosae antiquae*, 3 vols. (Leipzig, 1910–14), 2: 466–92.

63. This generalization is based on an examination of the photographs of the Greek manuscript collections that can be consulted in the Département des manuscrits in the Bibliothèque Nationale, Paris. Cf. *L'Ecriture et la psychologie des peuples*, pp. 180–81. In Italy, fifteenth-century printers of Greek did not regularly separate words by space, even though the same printers separated Latin words.

64. For some pertinent illustrations, see André Vallant, "L'écriture cyrillique et son extension," in *L'Ecriture et la psychologie des peuples*, pp. 301–12.

65. As late as 1724, documents in southern India were still being transcribed without interword space; Arthur Coke Burnell, *Elements of South-Indian Palaeography from the Fourth to the Seventeenth Century A.D.*, 2d ed. (London, 1878), pl. 32b.

66. The ancient Romans had no musical notation. As subsequent discussions will show, the birth and spread of medieval music notation are closely related to the introduction of word separation.

67. Meillet, "Le caractère concret du mot"; and "Remarques sur la théorie de la phrase"; see also Vendryes, *La Langue*, pp. 67–76.

68. The best modern synthesis is provided by Scaglione, *The Classical Theory of Composition*, pp. 105–22; and, more recently, by Anneli Luhtala, "Syntax and Dialectic in Carolingian Commentaries on Priscian's *Institutiones Grammaticae*," *Historia Linguistica* 20 (1993): 174–80. For Italian and Italian Renaissance Latin, see Raffaele Spongano, "Un capitolo di storia della nostra prosa di arte," in *Due saggi sull'Umanesimo* (Florence, 1964), pp. 39–78; and Ronald G. Witt, *The Earthly Republic: Italian Humanists on Government and Society* (Philadelphia, 1978), p. 14.

69. See Ulrich Ricken, "L'ordre naturel du français, naissance d'une théorie," in *La grammaire générale des modistes aux idéologues*, ed. André Joly and Jean Stéfanini, Publications de l'Université de Lille, vol. 3 (Villeneuve-d'Ascq, 1977), pp. 201–16; *Grammaire et philosophie au siècle des lumières: Controverses sur l'ordre naturel et la clarté du français*, Publications de l'Université de Lille, vol. 4 (Villeneuve-d'Ascq, 1978).

70. Havet, *Manuel de critique verbale*, p. 245 (1030); Christine Mohrmann, *Etudes sur le latin des Chrétiens*, 4 vols. (Rome, 1961–77), 2: 177–78; Monfrin, "Les traducteurs et leur public," p. 260.

71. John Percival Postgate, "Flaws in Classical Research," *Proceedings of the British Academy* 3 (1907–8): 166–67.

72. Antoine Meillet and Joseph Vendryes, *Traité de grammaire comparée des langues classiques* (Paris, 1968), p. 578. On the free word order of Greek, see Thomas Dwight Goodell, "The Order of Words in Greek," *Transactions of the American Philological Association* 21 (1890): 547; E. Kieckers, *Die Stellung des Verbs im griechischen und in den verwandtern Sprachen* (Strasbourg, 1911); H. Frisk, *Studien zur griechischen Wortstellung* (Göteborg, Sweden, 1932); and P. Chantraine, "Les Recherches sur l'ordre des mots en grec," *Annales de filogia clasica* (Buenos Aires) 5 (1952): 72–80; and, most recently, K. J. Dover, *Greek Word Order* (Cambridge, 1960). On the even less constrained word order in Latin, see J. Marouzeau, *Traité de stylistique latine*, 3d ed. (Paris, 1954), pp. 1–11, 228–45; and *L'Ordre des mots dans la phrase latine* (Paris, 1922–53). See also N. I. Herescu, *Entretiens avec J. Marouzeau* (Turin, 1962), pp. 21, 75–78; and H. Dubourdieu, "Etude sur l'ordre des mots en latin: Enclave et disjonction d'après César, *Guerre des Gaules*, V, VI, et VII," *L'information littéraire* (1957): 175–180. The question has most recently been reviewed by J. N. Adams, "A Typological Approach to Latin Word Order," *Indogermanische Forschungen* 81 (1976): 70–99. Attempts to detect the traces of an anterior word order in ancient Latin literature are purely speculative. On this, see also W. Lehmann, "Contemporary Linguistics and Indo-European Studies," *PMLA* 87 (1972): 976–93.

73. For an example, see Tore Janson, "Word, Syllable, and Letter in Latin," *Eranos* 65 (1967): 49–64.

74. See the complaints of medieval translators of classical texts enumerated by Monfrin, "Les traducteurs et leur public," p. 260. Bersuire found Livy's "constructions si suspensives, si trachées et si brièves," that they were difficult to understand. The role of short-term memory in ancient reading is to be contrasted to the role of short-term memory today, clearly elucidated by Eric Wanner, *On Remembering, Forgetting, and Understanding Sentences*, JL, series minor, vol. 170 (The Hague, 1974). See also N. Johnson-Laird and Rosemary Stevenson, "Memory for Syntax," *Nature* 227 (1970): 412.

75. Albert Dauzat, *Histoire de la langue française* (Paris, 1930), pp. 402–3, 425–27, 435–39); and *Les étapes de la langue française* (Paris, 1948), pp. 26, 46, 65–66. The study of medieval Latin syntax, and in particular the grouping of syntactically related words and conventions for word order and clause order within sentences, has been largely ignored by some of the standard works on medieval Latin, e.g., Karl Strecker, *Introduction to Medieval Latin*, English trans. and rev. Robert B. Palmer (Berlin, 1957), pp. 63–68. For useful statements on the subject, see M. Hubert, "Quelques aspects du latin philosophique aux XIIe et XIIIe siècles," *Revue des études latines* 27 (1949): 211–33; Joseph Herman, *Le Latin vulgaire*, 2d ed. (Paris, 1970), pp. 83–90; K. Harrington, *Mediaeval Latin* (1925; Chicago, 1972), pp. xxvi–xxviii; and Scaglione, *The Classical Theory of Composition*, pp. 105–22.

76. Guillaume de Conches uses the phrase "de continuatione vel expositione littere"; see Edouard Jeauneau, "Deux rédactions des gloses de Guillaume de Conches sur Priscien," *Recherches de théologie ancienne et médiévale* 27 (1960): 225; and *Guillaume de Conches: Glossae super Platonem*, Textes philosophiques du Moyen-Age, vol. 13 (Paris, 1965), 67.

77. Roger Bacon, *Sumulae dialectices*, ed. Robert Steele, in *Opera hactenus inedita Rogeri Baconi* (Oxford, 1948), 15: 340; Alain de Libera, "De la logique à la grammaire: Remarques sur la théorie de la *determinatio* chez Roger Bacon et Lambert d'Auxerre (Lambert de Lagny)," in *De Ortu Grammaticae: Studies in Medieval Grammar and Linguistic Theory in Memory of Jan Pinborg*, ed. G. L. Bursill-Hall, Sten Ebbesen, and Konrad Koerner (Amsterdam, 1988), p. 218. See the remarks of Johannes de Balbis on *adjectiva* in the preface to the *Catholicon* (Mainz, 1460).

78. J. Golling, "Einleitung in die Geschichte der lateinischen Syntax," in *Historische Grammatik der Lateinischen Sprache*, vol. 3, part 1, ed. Gustav Landgraf (Leipzig, 1903), pp. 28, 37.

79. Thurot, "Notices et extraits," pp. 341–50.

80. See the comments of the ninth-century Irish monk Murethach, *In Donati Artem maiorem*, ed. Louis Holtz, in *CCCM* 40 (1977): 244; *Ars Laureshamensis expositio in Donatum maiorem*, ed. Bengt Löfstedt, in *CCCM* 40A (1977): 231–35; Sedulius Scottus, *In Donati Artem maiorem*, ed. Bengt Löfstedt, in *CCCM* 40B (1977): 384–85; cf. Quintilian, *Institutiones oratoriae*, 7.3.62; 9.1.3;

9.1.6; 9.1.13; *Quintilian: Institution oratoire*, 7 vols., ed. Jean Cousin (Paris, 1975–79).

81. See the close relationship between contiguous order and syntax in Roger Bacon's exposition of the notes of punctuation in his *Opus tertium*, ed. J. S. Brewer, in *Fr. Rogeri Bacon opera quaedam hacternus inedita*, rolls series, vol. 1 (London, 1859), pp. 248–56.

82. "Un sens total . . . énoncé par plusieurs propositions qui se succèdent rapidement, et dont chacun a son fini qui semble complete." Nicolas Beauzée, *Grammaire générale ou exposition raisonnée des éléments nécessaires du langage pour servir de fondement a l'étude de toutes les langues* (Paris, 1762), p. 783, cited by Scaglione in *The Classical Theory of Composition*, p. 220; cf. Parkes, *Pause and Effect*, pp. 69–70.

83. See J. N. Adams, *The Vulgar Latin of the Letters of Claudius Terentianus (P. Mich. VIII, 1977)* (Manchester, n.d.), pp. 467–72; and *The Text and Language of a Vulgar Latin Chronicle (Anonymous Velesianus II)*, University of London Institute of Classical Studies Bulletin, supplement no. 36 (London, 1976), pp. 135–37.

84. Mohrmann, *Etudes sur le latin des Chrétiens*, 1: 48–49. For Hebrew word order, see M. O'Conner, *Hebrew Verse Structure* (Winona Lake, Ind., 1980), pp. 116–18. For word order in the Greek of the time of the apostles, see Paul Barth, "Zur Psychologie der gebundenen und der freien Wortstellung," *Philosophische Studien* 19 (1902): 46; W. Wundt, *Völkerpsychologie*, vol. 1, *Die Sprache* (Leipzig, 1900), p. 369.

85. Parkes, *Pause and Effect*, p. 15.

86. See Q. I. M. Mok, "Un traité médiéval de syntaxe latine en français," in *Mélanges de linguistique et de littérature offerts à Lein Geschiere, par ses amis, collèques et élèves* (Amsterdam, 1975), pp. 42, 45.

87. Hugh of Saint-Victor, in his chapter *De ordine legendi*, outlined the logical process in which first the syntax and then the sense was mastered; Charles Henry Buttimer, ed., *Hugonis de Saint Victor: Didascalicon de studio legendi*, Studies in Medieval and Renaissance Latin, vol. 10 (Washington, D.C., 1939), p. 58.

88. Levin and Addis, *The Eye-Voice Span*, pp. 109–47. The diagrams on p. 116 curiously resemble those of the modists. Cf. G. L. Bursill and Irène Rosier, "La grammaire speculative," *Collection THTL*, 2d ser., no. 1 (1982): 22.

89. See G. A. Klein and H. A. Klein, "Word Identification as a Function of Contextual Information," *American Journal of Psychology* 86 (1973): 399–406. See also Levin and Kaplan, "Grammatical Structure and Reading," in Levin and Williams, *Basic Studies on Reading*, p. 120; and Taylor and Taylor, *The Psychology of Reading*, pp. 124, 151. Although one might speculate that the constraints of word sequence of rhymed poetry might enhance the eye-voice span, this has not been investigated; see Levin and Addis, *The Eye-Voice Span*, p. 23.

90. Ian Begg, "Recognition Memory for Sentence Meaning and Wording," *Journal of Verbal Learning and Verbal Behavior* 10 (1971): 180; Jacqueline Strunk Sachs, "A Study of the Deep Structure Hypothesis: Memory in Reading and Listening in Discourse," *Memory and Cognition* 2 (1974): 99. See also Vendryes, *La Langue*, p. 390.

91. See Robert Blake, "Syntactic Aspects of Latinate Texts of the Early Middle Ages," in *Latin and Romance Languages in the Early Middle Ages*, ed. Roger Wright (London, 1991), pp. 219–32.

Chapter 2

1. On the importance of the word as a unit to the modern reader, see Jerome S. Brunner and Donald O'Dowd, "A Note on the Informativeness of Parts of Words," *Language and Speech* 1 (1958): 98–101; P. M. Merikle, M. Coltheart, and D. C. Lowe, "On the Selective Effects of a Patterned Masking Stimulus," *Canadian Journal of Psychology* 25 (1971): 264–79.

2. The name comes from the Dutch psychologist Herman Bouma; see Herman Bouma, "Visual Interference in the Parafoveal Recognition of Initial and Final Letters of Words," *Vision Research* 13 (1973): 762–82; Taylor and Taylor, *The Psychology of Reading*, pp. 186–94.

3. Hsuan-Chih Chen, "Reading Comprehension in Chinese: Implications from Character Reading Times," in Chen and Tzeng, *Language Processing in Chinese*, pp. 177–78.

4. On the relative importance of the absence of word separation and ambiguous letter forms as a source of textual corruption, see Wallace M. Lindsay, *An Introduction to Latin Textual Emendation Based on the Text of Plautus* (London, 1896), pp. 14–16, 40, 82–84.

5. See Colette Sirat, *L'examen des écritures: L'oeil et la machine; essai de méthodologie* (Paris, 1981), pp. 35–57.

6. Bradley, "On the Relation Between Spoken and Written Language," p. 214.

7. Alphonse Dain, *Les manuscrits*, 3d ed. (Paris, 1975), pp. 42, 149. The distinguished editor of Cassiodorus, James L. Halporn, has told me that he uses a tape recorder to collate codices written in *scriptura continua*. The 1741 Florence typographical facsimile of the *Codex Mediceus* inserted generous quantities of space between words.

8. See E. C. Poulton, "Peripheral Vision, Refractoriness, and Eye Movements in Fast Oral Reading," *British Journal of Psychology* 53 (1962): 409–19.

9. See L. Cohn and R. Rübenkamp, *Wie sollen Bücher und Zeitungen gedruckt werden?* (Braunschweig, 1903), p. 14; Oskar Messmer, "Zur Psychologie des Lesens bei Kindern und Erwachsenen," *Archiv für die gesammte Psychologie* 2 (1903): 273–74; W. Pickert, "Deutsche oder lateinische Buchstaben," *Allgemeine Deutsche Lehrerzeitung* 63 (1911): 133–40; Max Lobsien, *Über Lesbarkeit von Frak-*

tur und Antikva (Langensalza, 1918); R. Wolf, "Fraktur und Antikva," in *Deutsche Werbung* 1 (1934); Rudolf Schwegmann, *Experimentalle Untersuchung zur Lesbarkeit von Fraktur und Antiqua und von Gross- und Kleinschreibung* (Göttingen, 1935); A. Schachwitz, "Die experimentalle Lösung des Schriftstreits," *Flugblätter des Bundes für deutsche Schrift* 20 (1936); G. W. Ovink, *Legibility, Atmosphere Value, and Forms of Printing Types* (Leiden, 1938); Bror Zachrisson, *Studies in Legibility of Printed Text* (Stockholm, 1965), pp. 35–36. On Italic versus Roman type, see Miles A. Tinker and D. G. Patterson, "Influences of Type Form on Speed of Reading," *Journal of Applied Psychology* 12 (1928): 359–68. Miles A. Tinker, "The Influence of Form of Type on the Perception of Words," *Journal of Applied Psychology* 16 (1932): 167–74. See also Miles A. Tinker, "The Relative Legibility of Modern and Old Style Numerals," *Journal of Experimental Psychology* 13 (1930): 453–61.

10. See, for example, Stiennon, *Paléographie du Moyen Age*, pp. 94–103; and Bernhard Bischoff, *Paläographie des römischen Altertums und des abendländischen Mittelalters* (Berlin, 1979), pp. 218–19.

11. Olga Dobiache Rojdestvensky, "Quelques considerations sur les origines de l'écriture dite gothique," in *Mélanges d'histoire du Moyen Age offerts à M. Ferdinand Lot* (Paris, 1925), pp. 691–721; and Jacques Boussard, "Influences insulaires dans la formation de l'écriture gothique," *Scriptorium* 5 (1951): 238–64, have attributed this development to changes in the writing instrument.

12. A most dramatic instance of this concerns the manuscripts of Bobbio; see the comparative table of Paolo Collura, *Studi paleografici: La precarolina e la carolina a Bobbio* (1943; reprint, Florence, 1965), pp. 232–36. Northern manuscripts have also stimulated similar disagreements, for example, Paris, BN lat. 3182, containing Irish penitential texts; see McNeill and Gamer, *Medieval Handbooks of Penance*, p. 62.

13. Edward Maunde Thompson, *An Introduction to Greek and Latin Paleography* (Oxford, 1912), p. 57. Curiously, the primacy of Irish manuscripts with regard to separation is one aspect of Insular handwriting upon which the great Scottish paleographer Wallace M. Lindsay seems never to have remarked. E. A. Lowe also never discusses it specifically; see his *CLA* 4 (1947): viii. Müller, *Rhetorische und syntaktische Interpunktion*; James J. John, "Latin Paleography," in Powell, *Medieval Studies*, p. 46; and, most recently, Malcolm B. Parkes, *The Scriptorium of Wearmouth-Jarrow* (Jarrow, 1982), 17, have noted the precociousness of English and Irish scribes in respect to word separation.

14. *CLA* 4 (1947): viii.

15. E. A. Lowe, *Scriptura Beneventana*, 1: nos. 16, 17.

16. Claude W. Barlow, "Codex Vaticanus Latinus 4929," *Memoirs of the American Academy in Rome* 15 (1938): 91. See also Olga Dobiache Rojdestvensky, "Le Codex Q.v.I. 6–10 de la Bibliothèque de Léningrad," *Speculum* 5 (1930): 25.

17. Bischoff, *Paläographie des römischen Altertums*, pp. 218–19; cf. Riché, *Écoles et enseignement*, p. 112.

18. Jean Mabillon, *De re diplomatica* (Paris, 1681), p. 51. The extensive collection of charters of the Abbey of Cluny in the Bibliothèque Nationale offers a number of examples of this phenomenon. Following this criterion, I find the genuineness of Chilperic's diplomas of March 16, 716, in *ChLA* 14 (1992): no. 591, to be suspect. Patrick Périn and Laure-Charlotte Feffer, *La Neustrie: Les pays au nord de la Loire de Dagobert à Charles le Chauve (VIIe–IXe siècles)* (Paris, 1993), p. 106.

19. Charles François Toustain and René Prosper Tassin, *Nouveau traité de diplomatique*, 6 vols. (Paris, 1750–65), 3: 466, 489.

20. Ibid., 3: 491.

21. Natalis de Wailly, *Eléments de Paléographie*, 2 vols. (Paris, 1838), 1: 685–86, 690–92.

22. Jean Vezin, "Les manuscrits datés de l'ancien fonds latin de la Bibliothèque Nationale de Paris," *Scriptorium* 19 (1965): 86; and *Les scriptoria d'Angers*, p. 156.

23. Etienne Sabbe, "Étude critique sur le diplôme d'Arnoul Ier Comte de Flandre pour l'Abbaye de Saint-Pierre à Gand (941, juillet 8)," in *Etudes d'histoire dédiées à la mémoire de Henri Pirenne par ses anciens élèves* (Brussels, 1937), p. 306. Reusens does not broach the question; see *Eléments de paléographie*, pp. 9, 11, 145.

24. Petrucci, "Lire au Moyen Age," p. 606.

25. See Robert Marichal, "La critique des textes," in *L'histoire et ses méthodes*, ed. Charles Samaran (Paris, 1961), p. 1258; cf. Marichal, "L'écriture latine et la civilisation occidentale," p. 230 n. 1, where he places the beginning of separation in the twelfth century.

26. In this conclusion, I am in complete accord with Malcolm B. Parkes, personal communication, August 1992.

27. For example, Oxford, BL Laud misc. 141, the Lorsch copy of Augustine's *De genesi ad litteram*, copied ca. 800; Ganz, "The Preconditions of Caroline Minuscule," pp. 28–29.

28. Lupus also did not use the *trait d'union*. On his word division, see C. H. Beeson, *Lupus of Ferrières as Scribe and Text Critic: A Study of His Autograph Copy of Cicero's "De oratore"* (Cambridge, Mass., 1930). For a full list of Lupus's manuscripts, consult Robert J. Gariépy, "Lupus of Ferrières: Carolingian Scribe and Text Critic," *Medieval Studies* 30 (1968): 90–105; Bernhard Bischoff, "Paläographie und frühmittelalterliche Klassiküberlieferung," in *Mittelalterliche Studien*, 3: 66–67.

29. Most of these are conveniently listed in Julian Brown's edition of B. L. Ullman, *Ancient Writing and Its Influence* (Cambridge, Mass., 1969).

30. Ibid., pp. viii–ix.

31. For a list of these publications, see *Les manuscrits datés: Premier bilan et perspectives Neuchâtel, 1983*, Rubricae, vol. 2 (Paris, 1985).

32. Whenever practicable, the original codex has also been examined.

33. Delisle, *Cabinet des manuscrits* (Paris, 1868–81).

34. See especially Avril et al., *Manuscrits enluminés d'origine italienne*; Avril et al., *Manuscrits enluminés de la péninsule ibérique*.

35. This generalization is the result of an examination of reproductions of classical Latin papyri based on the lists provided by Wingo, *Latin Punctuation in the Classical Age*, pp. 134 ff. See, for example, P. Oxy. 1379; P. Oxy. 2086; and P. Berlin P. 8334, in Heinz Kortenbeutel, ed., *Ein Kodizill eines Römischen kaisers*, Abhandlungen der Preussischen Akademie der Wissenschaften, 1939, Philosophisch-historische klasse, no. 13 (Berlin, 1940). Even where interpuncts received space greater than normal interletter space, that quantity of space was usually only equal or inferior to the unity of space, i.e., the maximal intraletter space, here based on the letter *H*. In P. Mich, III, 159, interword space was one-half the unity of space; in P. Mich, VII, 456, interword space was equivalent to .66 the unity of space; and in P. Oxy I, 32, it was approximately .43 times the unity of space. A similar pattern exists in lapidary inscriptions: see Gordon and Gordon, *Palaeography of Latin Inscriptions*, p. 150; and Gordon, *Illustrated Introduction to Latin Epigraphy*, pp. 13–14. The summary statement on this question by René Cagnat, *Cours d'épigraphie latine*, p. 28, is misleading.

36. Sandys, *Latin Epigraphy*, p. 54. For an example, see Parkes, *Pause and Effect*, p. 304.

37. On the physiological consequences of the use of symbols rather than space to fill words, see Julian Hochberg, "Components of Literacy: Speculations and Exploratory Research," in Levin and Williams, *Basic Studies on Reading*, pp. 87–89; Dennis F. Fisher, "Spatial Factors in Reading and Search: The Case for Space," in *Eye Movement and Psychological Process*, ed. R. A. Monty and J. W. Senders (Hillsdale, N.J., 1976), pp. 417–27.

38. Fisher, "Spatial Factors in Reading and Search," p. 419, table 1, no. 5.

39. On measurement in print, see Robert Proctor and Miles A. Tinker, *Bases for Effective Reading* (Minneapolis, 1966), pp. 116–17. Some of the early modern modes of measuring interword space relative to letter height are potentially of far greater value; see Davis and Carter, *Moxon: Mechanical Exercises*, p. 297, cf. p. 103; *La science pratique d'imprimerie contenant des instructions très faciles pour se perfectionner dans cet art* (Saint-Omer, 1723), p. 16. It is interesting to note that young children prefer space to other graphic modes for framing only as their neurophysiological skills mature; L. L. Lamme, *Growing Up Writing* (Washington, D.C., 1984), pp. 50–52, 79–80.

40. A. K. Bowman and J. D. Thomas, *Vindolanda: The Latin Writing Tablets*, Britannia Monograph Series, no. 4 (London, 1983), p. 69.

41. Moses Maimonides, *Mishneh Torah: The Book of Adoration*, ed. and trans. Moses Hyamson (Jerusalem, n.d.), p. 129b.

42. Maimonides relates interword space to interletter space, the breadth of a strand of hair.

43. A historical precedent for this definition of the unit of space can be

found in the writings of the celebrated sixteenth-century calligrapher Ludovico degli Arrighi; see Paul Standard, *Arrighi's Running Hand: A Study of Chancery Cursive, Including a Facsimile of the 1522 "Operina," with Side by Side Translation* (New York, 1979), p. 19. Using a measure relative to the script is now also the practice of cognitive psychologists determining ocular saccade length; see Robert E. Morrison and Albrech Werner Inhoff, "Visual Factors and Eye Movements in Reading," *Visible Language* 15 (1981): 135.

44. Printed books since the introduction of movable type always provide a minimum of 1.5 unities of space and usually 2 unities of space. See, for example, Johann Gutenberg's *Catholicon* and Geoffroy Tory's *Le Champ fleury*, where interword space is equivalent to modern separation. For the concern of early printers with adequate space separation, see Davis and Carter, *Moxon: Mechanical Exercises*, p. 207 and passim; *La science pratique d'imprimerie*, pp. 17–18.

45. Ariane Levy-Schoen and Kevin O'Regan, "Control of Eye Movements," in *Processing of Visible Language 1*, p. 18; George W. McConkie and Keith Rayner, "The Span of an Effective Stimulus During a Fixation in Reading," *Perception and Psychophysics* 17 (1975): 578–86; Kevin O'Regan, "Structural and Contextual Constraints on Eye Movements in Reading" (Ph.D. diss., Cambridge University, 1975); Taylor and Taylor, *The Psychology of Reading*, pp. 126–28; Keith Rayner and Alexander Pollatsek, *The Psychology of Reading* (Englewood Cliffs, N.J., 1989), p. 130; Eleanor J. Gibson and Harry Levin, *The Psychology of Reading* (Cambridge, Mass., 1975), p. 357; Keith Rayner, "Eye Movements in Reading," in *Processing of Visible Language 1*, pp. 62, 72–73.

46. Rayner, "Eye Movements in Reading," and Kevin O'Regan, "Moment to Moment Control of Eye Saccades as a Function of Textual Parameters in Reading," in *Processing of Visible Language 1*, pp. 49–60; Morrison and Inhoff, "Visual Factors," pp. 139–40.

47. Morrison and Inhoff, "Visual Factors," p. 136.

48. The highest ratio found was .667 in P. Mich, 456, and in London, Papyrus 745 (in *CLA* 2 [1935]: 207), the famous Anonymous, *De bellis macedonicis* fragment from a Roman pocket-sized codex of the first century. See Charles Higounet, *L'Ecriture* (Paris, 1955), pp. 79–85. Proportional spacing would have had to have been twice as great to reach the "minimal legibility" of separated medieval handwriting.

49. See Joseph Shimron and David Navon, "The Distribution of Visual Information on the Vertical Dimension of Roman and Hebrew Letters," *Visible Language* 14 (1980): 5–12. Even in modern print, the use of all capitals increases the number of saccades and reduces the eye-voice span in oral reading, and it slows silent reading, attenuating significantly the usual advantages of word separation. Taylor and Taylor, *The Psychology of Reading*, p. 186; Levy-Schoen and O'Regan, "Control of Eye Movements," p. 17; Fisher, "Spatial Factors in Reading and Search"; Tinker and Paterson, "Influences of Type Form on Speed of

Reading," pp. 359–68; Tinker, "The Influence of Form of Type on the Perception of Words," pp. 167–74.

50. For a perceptive observation on the relation of ligatures and fusion in separated writing, see Marichal, "L'écriture latine et la civilisation occidentale," p. 230.

51. On the physiological implications of graphic concision for the reading of numbers, see Miles A. Tinker, "Numerals versus Words for Efficiency in Reading," *Journal of Applied Psychology* 12 (1928): 190–99.

52. Ovink, *Legibility, Atmosphere Value, and Forms of Printing Types*, pp. 115–17.

53. For example, see Reusens, *Eléments de paléographie*, pp. 16–27. Emmanuel Poule, "Une histoire de l'écriture," *BEC* 135 (1977): 137–44.

54. Alphonse Juilland and Alexandra Roceric, *The Decline of the Word* (Saratoga, Calif., 1975), p. 33; André Martinet, "Le mot," in *Collection Diogène*, p. 40; J. Fourquet, "Le mot en allemand," in *Linguistic Studies Presented to André Martinet on the Occasion of His Sixtieth Birthday*, ed. Alphonse Juilland and A. Beltrano (New York, 1967–69), also published as vols. 23–25 of *Word: Journal of the Linguistic Circle of New York*. The conception of interword space is fundamental in modern Western culture and is inculcated at an early age; see Linnea C. Ehri, "Effects of Printed Language Acquisition on Speech," in *Literacy, Language and Learning: The Nature and Consequences of Reading and Writing*, ed. David R. Olson, Nancy Torrance, and Angela Hildyard (Cambridge, 1985), p. 361. On the discontinuity between the continuum of speech and segmented writing, see Florian Coulmas, *The Writing Systems of the World* (Oxford, 1989), pp. 172, 230. Cf. Charles Read, Zhang Yun-Fei, Nie Hong-Yin, and Ding Bao-Qing, "The Ability to Manipulate Speech Sounds Depends on Knowing Alphabetic Writing," *Cognition* 24 (1986): 31–44.

55. Christian missionaries have repeatedly faced the thorny problem of establishing efficacious principles for the introduction of word separation into languages without a written tradition; see H. Beck, "Problems of Word Division and Capitalization in East African Bantu Languages," in *Orthography Studies*, ed. William A. Smalley (London, 1963), pp. 156–60. For the problem of defining a word using criteria other than intraword space, see Knud Tageby, "Qu'est-ce qu'un mot," *Travaux du cercle linguistique de Copenhague* 5 (1949): 97–111; Robert J. Scholes, "On the Morphological Consciousness of Pre-Literate Man," *Journal of Literary Semantics: An International Review* 21 (1992): 27–44; and "On the Orthographic Basis of Morphology." The significance of the word as the fundamental unit of linguistic study has been challenged by linguists studying the American Indian languages and the traditions for which written word separation was an alien concept; see Juilland and Roceric, *The Decline of the Word*. Specialists in American Indian languages label the morpheme as the fundamental unit of language.

56. Of these erroneous assertions, perhaps the most frequent is that Carolingian manuscripts were separated. In fact, they were not. See Marichal, "L'écriture latine et la civilisation occidentale," p. 230. The absence of word separation in the circle of Charlemagne is evident from an examination of the *Libri Carolini*, Vat. lat. 7207, and other books of Charlemagne's library; see Bernhard Bischoff, "Die Hofbibliothek Karls des Grossen," in *Karl der Grosse: Lebenwerk und Nachleben*, 2: 42–62 and pls. 1–6. Cf. Rosamund McKitterick, "Carolingian Book Production: Some Problems," *The Library*, ser. 6, 12 (1990): 1–5, 7–9. A few Carolingian manuscripts are so intensely aerated that they appear to be separated, but on close examination they are not, e.g., Paris, BN lat. 261 (Le Mans), lat. 2423.

57. It is important to remember that both in antiquity and the Middle Ages, "frequently omitted" does not mean "always omitted"; cf. Bowman and Thomas, *Vindolanda: The Latin Writing Tablets*, p. 69.

58. Harold Hagendahl, *La prose métrique d'Arnobe: Contributions à la connaissance de la prose littéraire de l'empire*, Göteborgs Högskolas Årskrift, vol. 42 (Göteborg, Sweden, 1937), pp. 14–17.

59. R. H. Robins, *Ancient and Mediaeval Grammatical Theory in Europe with Particular Reference to Modern Linguistic Doctrine* (London, 1951), pp. 20–21; R. H. Robins, *A Short History of Linguistics*, 2d ed. (London, 1967), pp. 56–57; Maurice Leroy, *Les Grands courants de la linguistique moderne*, 2d ed. (Brussels, 1971), p. 176; P. Swiggers, "Le Mot comme unité linguistique dans la théorie grammaticale au dix-huitième siècle," *Indogermanische Forschungen* 91 (1986): 1 nn. 1, 2.

60. Priscian, *Institutiones grammaticae*, in Keil, *Grammatici latini*, 3: 50–51.

61. See Malcolm B. Parkes, "The Contribution of Insular Scribes to the Grammar of Legibility," in his *Scribes, Scripts, and Readers* (London, 1991).

62. For the former, see Reusens, *Eléments de paléographie*, p. 145.

63. Hubert Vanderhoven and François Masai, *La Règle du maître: Édition diplomatique des manuscrits latins 12205 et 12634 de Paris*, Les publications de Scriptorium, vol. 3 (Brussels, 1953), pp. 107–8.

64. Shipley, *Certain Sources of Corruption in Latin Manuscripts*, pp. 7–8, 15–23.

65. For the *Regula magistri*, see Vanderhoven and Masai, *La Règle du maître*, pp. 103–13; for Hilary of Poitiers, see the extensive list of early manuscripts provided by P. Smoulders, "Remarks on the Manuscript Tradition," in *Studia Patristica*, ed. F. L. Cross (Berlin, 1961), 3: 129–30.

66. Rudolf Thurneysen, *A Grammar of Old Irish*, trans. D. A. Binchy and Osburn Bergin, rev. and enl. ed. with supplement (Dublin, 1946), pp. 24–25.

67. See Ruth Barbour, *Greek Literary Hands, A.D. 400–1600* (Oxford, 1981), p. xxvii; Parkes, *Pause and Effect*, pp. 23–24.

68. See the remarks by Petrucci, "Lire au Moyen Age," p. 606.

69. Examples include Saint Gall, Stiftsbibliothek, 1394, the Cathach Psalter,

the Springmount Bog Writing Tablets, and the fragment of Ruffinus's translation of Eusebius's *Historia ecclesiastica* recently discovered at the Folger Shake-
speare Library.

70. See Harry Levin and Eleanor L. Kaplan, "Grammatical Structure and
Reading," in Levin and Williams, *Basic Studies on Reading*.

71. Walter Dennison, "Syllabification in Latin Inscriptions," *Classical Philology* 1 (1906): 47–68; E. A. Lowe, *Beneventan Script*, pp. 281–82.

72. The *Antiphonary of Bangor* was written in this format.

73. Examples include the Book of Durrow, in *CLA* 2 (1935); A. A. Luce,
G. O. Simms, P. Meyer, and L. Bieler, eds., *Evangeliorum quattuor Codex Dur-
machensis*, facsimile ed. (Olten, Switz., 1960), and Milan, Biblioteca Ambrosiana
O. 212 sup., in *CLA* 3 (1938): 361; A. E. Burn, *Facsimiles of the Creeds from Early
Manuscripts*, HBS, vol. 36 (London, 1908), pls. 22–24; Kenney, *Sources for the
Early History of Ireland*, no. 520.

74. *MGH: Epistolae* 4 (1895): 285; cf. Ernst Dümmler, ed., *Alcuini carmina*,
in *MGH: Poetae latini aevi Carolini* 1 (1880): 320.

75. For example, Paris, BN lat. 2291, f. 1v; lat. 2832, ff. 123v–24.

76. Levin and Addis, *The Eye-Voice Span*, pp. 76–79; on the relationship of
musical notation to the syllable, see Leo Treitler, "The Early History of Music
Writing in the West," *Journal of the American Musicological Society* 35 (1982):
244–45; and "Reading and Singing: On the Genesis of Occidental Music Writing," *Early Music History* 4 (1984): 145–46. Certain early neumes, for example,
Oxford, BL Bodley 775, are scarcely more than syllable markers; see Treitler,
"The Early History," p. 273, pl. 1.

77. Denis Escudier, "Les Manuscrits musicaux," pp. 38–48.

78. P. Jaffé, ed., *Monachus Sangallenis: Gesta Caroli Magni*, in *MGH: Bibliotheca rerum Germanicarum* (Berlin, 1867), pp. 637–38; English trans., A. J.
Grant, *Early Lives of Charlemagne* (London, 1992), pp. 69–70; Hrabanus Maurus, *De clericorum institutione*, in *PL* 107: 303, 363–64.

79. Levin and Addis, *The Eye-Voice Span*, pp. 42, 93–94.

80. Modern cognitive studies using PET scanners indicate that the same
areas of a reader's brain are activated when viewing a phonetically plausible
pseudoword as when viewing a genuine word. In English, the view of a nonpro-
nounceable combination of letters does not elicit this reaction. The exposure to
long word blocks is likely to have resulted in a similar confusion.

81. For examples, see Bischoff, *Die südostdeuchen Schreibschulen*.

82. Roger Wright, *Late Latin and Early Romance in Spain and Carolingian
France* (Liverpool, 1982); Marc van Uytfanghe, "Histoire du latin, protohistoire
des langues romanes, et histoire de la communication," *Francia* 11 (1983): 601;
and "Le latin des hagiographes mérovingiens et la protohistoire du français . . .
à quelle epoque a-t-on cessé de parler latin?" *Romanica Gandensia* 16 (1976):
57, 75.

83. Thurneysen, *A Grammar of Old Irish*, pp. 24–25; A. Campbell, *Old English Grammar* (Oxford, 1959), p. 14; Virginia J. Cyrus, "Linguistic Features of Scribal Spacing," *Visible Language* 5 (1971): 101–10.

84. Gordon and Gordon, *Palaeography of Latin Inscriptions*, pp. 159–60.

85. Pellegrin, "Les Manuscrits de Loup de Ferrières," p. 20.

86. The space cloaked by the *ct* ligature indicated that the syllable boundary lay between the *c* and the *t*, and not after the *t*, as ancient grammarians had taught. Pedagogical manuscripts originating on the Continent confirm that the syllable, and not the graphic word, constituted the fundamental unit of reading aerated script of the Carolingian age. In order to aid the beginning reader, a ninth-century scribe placed interpuncts between all the syllables of the Psalms contained in Karlsruhe, Badische Landesbibliothek Aug. Fragment 8, a text written in hierarchical word blocks (see Figure 8). The Psalms regularly served as the first text for young readers. Similarly, a tenth-century scribe, possibly at Fleury, copied Pseudo-Cato's *Breves sententiae*, fifty-six very simplified sentences of two to four words used for the instruction of schoolboys, in Paris, BN lat. 8093, ff. 84–86, using a special exaggerated form of hierarchical word blocks, with syllables separated by points and space. See Munk-Olsen, *L'Étude des auteurs classiques latins*, 1: 74–75; Mostert, *The Library of Fleury*, p. 224. I am indebted to François Dolbeau for directing me to this source. Both manuscripts were likely meant as models that schoolboys could pronounce and copy onto wax tablets. The *Breves sententiae* forms part of Pseudo-Cato's *Disticha*; see Marcus Boas and Henricus Johannus Botschuyver, eds., *Disticha Catonis* (Amsterdam, 1952), pp. 11–30. On the *Disticha Catonis*, see Pierre Riché, "Apprendre à lire et à écrire dans le haut Moyen Age," *Bulletin de la Société Nationale des Antiquaires* (1978–79): 194.

87. Lupus of Ferrières systematically expunged the ampersand when it was written within words in certain manuscripts that he corrected; cf. Virgilius Maro Grammaticus, *Epistolae*, ed. G. Polara (Naples, 1979), pp. 310–13. For an example of the restricted use of the ampersand in the early twelfth century, see Monique-Cécile Garand, "Le scriptorium de Guibert de Nogent," *Scriptorium* 31 (1977): 15.

88. In certain manuscripts, however, the quantity of space after these short words, particuarly the monosyllabic prepositions *in* and *de*, was consistently less than the normal interword space.

89. Hagendahl, *La prose métrique d'Arnobe*, pp. 13–17; Dag Norberg, *Manuel pratique de latin médiéval* (Paris, 1968), p. 88.

90. A similar discordance between written and oral separation is that semi-literate peasants in the early years of this century had difficulty in correctly inserting interword space; see Marcel Jousse, *L'anthropologie du geste*, 2 vols. (Paris, 1974–78), 1: 340.

91. See G. L. Bursill-Hall, *Speculative Grammar of the Middle Ages: The Doc-*

trine of Partes Orationis of the Modistae (The Hague, 1971); G. L. Bursill-Hall, ed. and trans., *Thomas Erfurt, Grammatica Speculativa: An Edition with Translation and Commentary* (London, 1972).

92. Sten Ebbesen et al., eds., *Simon of Faversham: Quaestiones super libro eclenchorum*, Studies and Texts, vol. 60 (Toronto, 1984), pp. 91–93; Bacon, *Opus tertium*, ed. J. S. Brewer, in *Fr. Rogeri Bacon opera quaedam hactenus inedita*, 1: 238–43; cf. Dag Norberg, *Introduction à l'étude de la versification latine médiévale*, Studia latina Stockholmiensia, vol. 5 (Stockholm, 1958), pp. 7–28.

93. Rayner and Pollatsek, *The Psychology of Reading*, p. 133.

94. Rayner, "Eye Movements in Reading," p. 62; Keith Rayner and George W. McConkie, "What Guides a Reader's Eye Movements," *Vision Research* 16 (1976): 829–37; Kevin O'Regan, "Saccade Size Control in Reading: Evidence for the Linguistic Control Hypothesis," *Perception and Psychophysics* 25 (1979): 501–9; Taylor and Taylor, *The Psychology of Reading*, p. 132.

95. On the importance of short words in eye movement, see O'Regan, "Moment to Moment Control of Eye Saccades"; and Rayner, "Eye Movements in Reading," p. 62. The modern reader is particularly prone to recognize short function words by their Bouma shape; see Taylor and Taylor, *The Psychology of Reading*, p. 186. On the increased presence of function words as part of the simplification of medieval Latin, see Antoine Meillet, *Esquisse d'une histoire de la langue latine*, 4th ed. (Paris, 1938), pp. 256–58, 271–73; and "Le caractère concret du mot," in *Linguistique historique et linguistique générale*, 2 vols. (Paris, 1938), 2: 9–23; Albert Dauzat, *Les étapes de la langue française* (Paris, 1948), pp. 14, 24.

96. The scribes of Saint-Pierre of Moissac wrestled with this problem; see, for example, Paris, BN lat. 3783, a Breviary, f. 62, and especially Paris, BN lat. 5056, Caesar, *De bello gallico*, ff. 111, 116v, and 120; Paris, BN lat. 5058, Josephus, f. 7. Medieval practice here seems to argue against the thesis proposed by André Martinet that written language favors the delineation of word beginnings; Martinet, "Le mot," pp. 44–45.

97. André Martinet, *A Functional View of Language* (Oxford, 1962), p. 92.

98. For examples, see Albert Derolez, *The Library of Raphael de Mercatellis, Abbot of Saint Bavon's, Ghent, 1437–1508* (Ghent, 1979), pp. 60, 113; Jean Destrez, *La pecia dans les manuscrits universitaires du XIIIᵉ et du XIVᵉ siècles* (Paris, 1935), pl. 24; and Chicago, Newberry Library 101.

99. Saenger and Heinlen, "Incunable Description," p. 244.

100. See T. C. Skeat, "The Use of Dictation in Ancient Book Production," *Proceedings of the British Academy* 42 (1956): 179–208; and, for more recent work, Pierre Petitmengin and Bernard Flusin, "Le livre antique et la dictée: Nouvelles recherches," in *Mémorial André-Jean Festugière: Antiquité païenne et chrétienne*, ed. E. Lucchesi and H. D. Saffrey, published as vol. 10 of *Cahiers d'orientalisme*.

101. Cicero, *Epistula ad Atticum*, 13.25.

102. Dain, *Les manuscrits*, pp. 40–47; Klaus Junack, "Abschreibpraktiken

und Schreibergewohnheiten in ihrer Auswirkung auf die Textüberlieferung," in *New Testament Textual Criticism, Its Significance for Exegesis: Essays in Honor of B. Metzger*, ed. Eldon Jay Epp and Gordon D. Fee (Oxford, 1981), pp. 277–95. See also Havet, *Manuel de critique verbale*, pp. 245, xi–xiii, 155–57; Willis, *Latin Textual Criticism*, pp. 63–73, 87–91, 133–37.

103. On the lack of writing tables in antiquity, see Bruce M. Metzger, "When Did Scribes Begin to Use Writing Desks?" in *Akten des XI, internationalen Byzantinenkongress* (Munich, 1958), pp. 355–62, reprinted in his *Historical and Literary Studies: Pagan, Jewish, and Christian* (Grand Rapids, Mich., 1968), pp. 123–37 and pls. 3–19b; George M. Parássoglou, "Some Thoughts on the Posture of the Ancient Greeks and Romans When Writing on Papyrus Rolls," *Scrittura e Civiltà* 3 (1979): 5–21.

104. The earliest unambiguous illumination depicting a scribe writing a book on a writing table occurs in the *Lindisfarne Gospels*, copied in England in fully separated script; T. D. Kendrick, ed., *Evangeliorum quattuor Codex Lindisfarnensis . . . Cottonianus Nero D. V* (Olten, Switz., 1956–60), f. 93v.

105. Willis, *Latin Textual Criticism*, esp. pp. 57–62; Havet, *Manuel de critique verbale*, pp. 204–5, 209–10, 242–46.

106. Jacqueline Strunk Sachs, "A Study of the Deep Structure Hypothesis: Memory in Reading and Listening in Discourse," *Memory and Cognition* 2 (1974): 95–100; Ian Begg, "Recognition Memory for Sentence Meaning and Wording," *Journal of Verbal Learning and Verbal Behavior* 10 (1971): 176–81.

107. Jacqueline Strunk Sachs, "Recognition Memory for Syntactic and Semantic Aspects of Connected Discourse," *Perception and Psychophysics* 2 (1967): 437–42; John R. Anderson, "Verbatim and Propositional Representation of Sentences in Immediate and Long-Term Memory," *Journal of Verbal Learning and Verbal Behavior* 13 (1974): 149–62; Ian Begg and Wayne A. Wickelgren, "Retention Functions for Syntactic and Lexical vs. Semantic Information in Sentence Recognition Memory," *Memory and Cognition* 2 (1974): 353–59; Samuel Fillenbaum, "Memory for Gist: Some Relevant Variables," *Language and Speech* 9 (1966): 217–27; N. Johnson-Laird and Rosemary Stevenson, "Memory for Syntax," *Nature* 227 (1970): 412; Wanner, *On Remembering, Forgetting, and Understanding Sentences*, JL, series minor, vol. 170 (The Hague, 1974).

108. "Tres digiti scribunt, duo oculi vident, una lingua loquitur, totum corpus laborat." In Wallace M. Lindsay, "Dictation," *Palaeographia latina* 4 (1925): 85.

109. *Echardi IV casus Sancti Galli*, cap. 10, in *MGH: Scriptores* 2 (1829): 122, cited in T. Julian Brown, "Latin Palaeography since Traube," *Transactions of the Cambridge Bibliographical Society* 3 (1959–63): 361–81.

110. Charles Plummer, *Vitae sanctorum Hiberniae partim hactenus ineditae*, 2 vols. (Oxford, 1910), 2: 133, para. 11. For Mulling's boast, see Chapter 4, note 1.

111. Whitley Stokes, ed., *Book of Lismore* (Oxford, 1890), p. 226.

112. Plummer, *Vitae sanctorum Hiberniae*, 2: 24; R. I. Best, "On the Subscriptions of the *Book of Dimma*," *Hermathena* 43 (1922): 88.

113. Saenger, "Word Separation and Its Implications," pp. 41–50. The narrowly separated Wearmouth-Jarrow biblical codices do not evince this trait.

114. See Colgrave and Mynors, *Bede's Ecclesiastical History of the English People*, pp. xlvi–xlvii; J. Stevenson, ed., *Bede: History of England* (London, 1838), facsimile opposite 1; James J. John, "Latin Paleography," in Powell, *Medieval Studies*, p. 47.

115. This pattern is noticeable in the corpus of Burchard of Worms and Fulbert of Chartres, among others.

116. A total lack of visual similitude between copies of a text related by their *Überlieferungsgeschichte* (text transmission history) is characteristic of manuscripts before the acceptance of word separation; for examples, see Saenger, "Word Separation and Its Implications."

117. F. 169v, "Mac Regol depinexit hoc evangelium: quicumque legerit et intelligerit istam narrationem orat pro Macreguil scriptori." Louis Gougaud, "Les scribes monastiques d'Irlande au travail," *RHE* 27 (1931): 296. For later examples of painter-scribes, see Carruthers, *The Book of Memory*, p. 24.

118. John J. O'Meara, "Giraldus Cambrensis in Topographia Hiberniae," *Proceedings of the Royal Irish Academy* 52, Sec. C (1949): 151–52; Bieler, *Ireland Harbinger of the Middle Ages*, p. 114.

119. Levin and Addis, *The Eye-Voice Span*, pp. 71–76, 79. Confirmation of an enhanced visual dimension in copying is suggested by the curious entirely visual manner in which Irish scribes divided words at line endings without any regard to syllabic boundaries. They thus exhibited an insensitivity to the syllable as a unit in a manner similar to the profoundly deaf. See, for example, Milan, Ambrosiana C. 103 inf., described by R. I. Best, *The Commentary on the Psalms with Glosses in Old Irish* (Dublin, 1936), p. 20. On the problem posed by syllabic boundaries for the deaf, see Suzanne Abraham and Frederick Weiner, "Efficacy of Word Training vs Syllable Training on Articulatory Generalization by Severely Hearing-Impaired Children," *The Volta Review* 87 (1985): 96–105. In the early medieval Irish scriptorium, marginal conversational notes provide the first explicit evidence that scribal work had become a visual and silent task. In these written notes, the masters rebuked scribes silently, and the scribes silently lamented the conditions under which they worked. See Lindsay, *Early Irish Minuscule Script*, p. 42; and his "Conversational Jottings," *Palaeographia latina* 2 (1923): 24–25; Louis Gougaud, *Les chrétientés celtiques* (Paris, 1911), pp. 332–33; and "Les scribes monastiques," pp. 294–95; R. A. S. Macalister, *Muiredach Abbot of Monasterboice 890–923*, The Margaret Stokes Lectures, 1913 (Dublin, 1914), p. 65. Among codices so annotated is Laon BM 26, a ninth-century copy of Cassiodorus's *Commentum in Psalmos*. The Latin text of Cassiodorus was

separated by 2 to 3 times the unity of space, with space inserted after many monosyllabic prepositions. Monolexic abbreviations included the Insular signs for *est* and *enim* and the tironian note for the conjunction *et*. Microfilm at the IRHT; Kuno Meyer, "Neu aufgefundene altirische Glossen," *Zeitschrift für Celtische Philologie* 8 (1912): 175–76. However, the Old Irish text of the scribal conversations was written in morphemic hierarchical word blocks.

Chapter 3

1. J. Moreau-Maréchal, "Recherches sur la ponctuation," *Scriptorium* 22 (1968): 62. My translation. The original notes a development from "un système qui sépare les mots par des signes et les unités de sens par les blancs" to one "qui sépare les mots par des blancs et les unités par des signes."

2. Scholes and Willis, "Prosodic and Syntactic Functions of Punctuations."

3. This is the term used by Donatus in the *Ars maior*; it is also used by Isidore in *Libri etymologiarum*, ed. Wallace M. Lindsay (1911; reprint, Oxford, 1985), bk. 1, ch. 18. See Parkes, *Pause and Effect*, pp. 9–14. Like separation by space, the presence of *prosodiae* has rarely been noted in the description of medieval manuscripts. E. A. Lowe's description of the emergence of *prosodiae*, considered apart from word separation, is a starting point for documenting both phenomena in Southern Italian manuscripts; see E. A. Lowe, *Beneventan Script*, pp. 274–79.

4. Sandys, *Latin Epigraphy*, p. 54; Gordon and Gordon, *Palaeography of Latin Inscriptions*, pp. 150, 183–85; Gordon, *Illustrated Introduction to Latin Epigraphy*, p. 13; Anderson, Parsons, and Nisbet, "Elegiacs by Gallus," p. 131.

5. For an example in a particularly long word block, see John J. Contrini, *Codex Laudensis 468: A Ninth-Century Guide to Virgil, Sedulius, and the Liberal Arts*, Armarium codicum insignium, vol. 3 (Turnhout, 1984), f. 9. See also Wallace M. Lindsay, "Separation of Words by Dots," *Palaeographia latina* 2 (1923): 16–17.

6. See, for example, Karlsruhe, Badische Landesbibliothek Aug. Fragment 8; Alfred Holder, *Die Reichenauer Handschriften* 2 (1914): 368. I am indebted to J. P. Gumbert for this reference. Precedent for this practice existed in certain late antique inscriptions; see Walter Dennison, "Syllabification in Latin Inscriptions," *Classical Philology* 1 (1906): 49, re *CIL*, 6: 26353, 64-64 (106 examples); Cagnat, *Cours d'epigraphie latine*, p. 29, re *CIL*, 8: 4919; Gordon and Gordon, *Palaeography of Latin Inscriptions*, p. 184; Gordon, *Illustrated Introduction to Latin Epigraphy*, pp. 13–14, 37.

7. Marquise de Maillé, *Les Cryptes de Jouarre* (Paris, 1971), p. 228, fig. 102.

8. Paul Deschamps, *Etudes sur la paléographie des inscriptions lapidaires de la fin de l'époque mérovingienne aux dernières années du XII' siècle* (Paris, 1929), pp. 21–35. For examples at Moissac, see Dufour, *Scriptorium de Moissac*, pls. 77–78.

9. "Punctum est signum segregans intellectus et spiritum recreans prolateris,

vel punctum est signum scriptum quod convenit dictioni." Charles Fierville, *Une grammaire latine inédite du XIIIe siècle extrait des manuscrits no. 465 de Laon et no. 15462 (fonds latin) de la B.N.* (Paris, 1886), p. 119.

10. Bernard P. Grenfell and Arthur S. Hunt, *The Oxyrhynchus Papyri* (London, 1889–).

11. For example, Gaetano Panazza, *Lapidi e sculpture paleocristiane e preromaniche di Pavia* (Turin, 1950).

12. Lindsay, "Separation of Words by Dots," pp. 16–17.

13. See Eric G. Turner, *Greek Manuscripts of the Ancient World* (Princeton, 1971), p. 13.

14. Donatus attributes to it this function; see Holtz, *Donat et la tradition de l'enseignement*, p. 611; Michel Banniard, "Le lecteur en Espagne Wisigothique après Isidore de Séville: De ses fonctions à l'état de la langue," *Revue des études augustiniennes* 21 (1975): 119–20. Banniard accurately reproduces the shape of the *diastole*, but his examples are distorted by the anachronistic presence of interword space. In certain manuscripts of Donatus and Bede, the note for the *diastole* was that of the interpunct.

15. Jacob Christiansen, *De apicibus et I longis inscriptionum latinarum dissertatio* (Husum, 1889); on the use of the *apex*, see Quintilian, *Institutiones oratoriae*, 1.7.2–3; and Terentius Scaurus, *De orthographia*, in Keil, *Grammatici latini*, 7: 33; Gordon and Gordon, *Palaeography of Latin Inscriptions*, pp. 148–49.

16. Quintilian, *Institutiones oratoriae*, 1.4.10; 1.7.2.

17. Henri Weil and Louis Benloew, *Théorie générale de l'accentuation latine suivé de recherches sur les inscriptions accentuées* (Paris, 1855), pp. 293–94, 306–7. See also Beaulieux, *Histoire de l'orthographie française*, 2: 2–5. For an example of accents denoting long vowels, see C. H. Roberts and Eric G. Turner, *Catalogue of the Greek and Latin Papyri in the John Rylands Library, Manchester*, 4 vols. (Manchester, 1911–52), 4: 95–96.

18. For an interesting modern example of ambiguity reduced by the presence of accents, see Ernst Pulgram, *Syllable, Word, Nexus, Cursus*, JL, series minor, vol. 81 (The Hague, 1970), pp. 31–33 n. 13. Scholastic authors, among them William of Sherwood (d. 266–72) and Simon of Faversham, saw accentuation and rules of word order as playing analogous roles in reducing the ambiguity of logical texts; see Charles H. Lohr, "William of Sherwood, *Introductiones in logicam*: Critical Text," *Traditio* 39 (1983): 281, lines 200–201; Sten Ebbesen et al., eds., *Simon of Faversham: Quaestiones super libro eclenchorum*, Studies and Texts, vol. 60 (Toronto, 1984), pp. 91–93; cf. Alain de Libera, "De la logique à la grammaire: Remarques sur la théorie de la *determinatio* chez Roger Bacon et Lambert d'Auxerre (Lambert de Lagny)," in *De Ortu Grammaticae: Studies in Medieval Grammar and Linguistic Theory in Memory of Jan Pinborg*, ed. G. L. Bursill-Hall, Sten Ebbesen, and Konrad Koerner (Amsterdam, 1988), pp. 210–11.

19. C. H. Roberts, "The Antinoe Fragment of Juvenal," *Journal of Egyptian*

Archaeology 21 (1935): 202. This usage does not conform to the medieval rules set forth by Pseudo-Priscian's *Liber de accentibus*, in Keil, *Grammatici latini*, 3: 521.

20. Marrou, *Histoire de l'éducation dans l'antiquité*, p. 240.

21. F. G. Kenyon, "Two Greek School Tablets," *Journal of Hellenic Studies* 29 (1909): 39.

22. Isidore, *Libri etymologiarum*, ed. Lindsay, bk. 1, ch. 18.

23. In antiquity, accent signs were used by scribes when copying Homer and other texts for which the reader required special aids because of their unfamiliar dialect; see Turner, *Greek Manuscripts*, p. 13.

24. Françoise Henry, *The Book of Kells* (New York, 1974), p. 214, convincingly argues that the model for the symbols of the apostles on the first folio of the Book of Kells must have been in a book read from right to left, and this could only imply a Syriac codex, since Coptic is always read from left to right. For Syriac *prosodiae*, see J. B. Segal, *The Diacritical Point and the Accents in Syriac* (London, 1953); and J. P. P. Martin, *Traité sur l'accentuation chez les Syriens orientaux* (Paris, 1889). On Syriac and other Eastern influence on the decoration of Irish manuscripts and related decorative arts, see Walter Read Hovey, "Sources of Irish Illuminated Art," *Art Studies: Medieval Renaissance and Modern* 6 (1928): 110–12, 114, 118; Arthur Kingley Porter, *The Crosses and Culture of Ireland* (New Haven, 1928), pp. 18–19; Geneviève L. Micheli, "Recherches sur les manuscrits irlandais décorés de Saint-Gall et de Reichenau," *Revue archéologique*, ser. 6, 7 (1936): 199–200. Françoise Henry, *Art in the Early Christian Period* (London, 1940), pp. 45–46, 49, 51, 61, 65–66; (2d ed., London, 1965), p. 180; Carl Nordenfalk, "Eastern Style Elements in the Book of Lindisfarne," *Acta Archaeologica* 13 (1942): 166 n. 10; François Masai, *Essai sur les origines de la miniature dite irlandaise*, Les publications de Scriptorium, vol. 23 (Brussels, 1947), pp. 15–28; Ludwig Bieler, review of *Essai sur les origines*, by François Masai, *Speculum* 23 (1948): 496; E. Rosenthal, "Some Observations on Coptic Influences in Western Early Medieval Manuscripts," *Homage to a Bookman: Essays on Manuscripts, Books and Printing Written for Hans P. Kraus on His 60th Birthday, Oct. 12, 1967* (Berlin, 1956), pp. 57, 65; Martin Werner, "The Madonna and Child Miniature in the Book of Kells," *Art Bulletin* 54 (1972): 14, 129–30. Syriac may also have provided the model for the scribal colophons characteristic of Irish texts; see William Henry Paine Hatch, *An Album of Dated Syriac Manuscripts* (Boston, 1946), pp. 17–18. Certain variants found only in Irish Latin Bibles originate from the Syriac version of the New Testament; see Samuel Berger, *Histoire de la Vulgate pendant les premiers siècles du Moyen Age* (Paris, 1893), p. 34. On Syriac influence on Irish liturgy and private devotion, see Edmund Bishop, *Liturgica Historica: Papers on the Liturgy and Religious Life of the Western Church* (Oxford, 1918), pp. 161–63, 178 n. 3; and Carlo A. Lewis, *The Silent Recitation of the Canon of the Mass*, Excerpta ex dissertatione ad Lauream in Facultate Theologica Universitatis Gregorianae (Bay Saint Louis, Miss., 1962), pp. 42–45, 57, 72.

On the general question of the presence of Syrians in western Europe in the early Middle Ages, see Louis Bréhier, "Les colonies d'orientaux en Occident au commencement du Moyen Age," *Byzantinische Zeitschrift* 12 (1903): 1–39. On Asia as a source for the colorings used in Insular art, see Louis Gougaud, "Les scribes monastiques d'Irlande au travail," *RHE* 27 (1931): 306.

25. Leiden, Bibliotheek der Reijksuniversiteit Perizonus F. 55, ff. 46–48v. See Pseudo-Priscian, *Liber de accentibus*, in Keil, *Grammatici latini*, 3: 519–28.

26. For examples of interpunct-separated inscriptions as they would have been still visible in the early Middle Ages, see Brigitte Galsterer and Hartmut Galsterer, *Die römischen Steinschriften aus Köln* (Cologne, 1975).

27. Cologne presents one example of such influence; see Leslie Webber Jones, *The Script of Cologne from Hildebald to Hermann* (Cambridge, Mass., 1932), pls. 16, 30, 41, 65, 78.

28. See Lowe, *Beneventan Script*, pp. 276–77.

29. Pseudo-Priscian, *Liber de accentibus*, in Keil, *Grammatici latini*, 3: 520–21. For additional manuscripts of this text, see G. L. Bursill-Hall, *A Census of Medieval Grammatical Manuscripts* (Stuttgart, 1981), p. 325.

30. These marks have been briefly noted by Beaulieux, *Histoire de l'orthographie française*, 2: 6–7. For examples, see fig. 11, Cambrai, BM 470, *Philippus in Job*; *CLA* 6 (1953): 570, notes the marks and dates them to the twelfth century. In my judgment, the late eleventh century is more likely for most of these emendations.

31. See Poitiers, BM 95, f. 139v, a vernacular collection of pious texts written in an exceptionally dense Gothic *textualis* script; A. Lievre and A. Molinier, *Catalogue général des manuscrits des départements* 25 (1894): 33–34.

32. See Paris, BN lat. 7562, f. 8v, from Saint-Martial of Limoges, written in the first half of the eleventh century; for bibliographical references, see Holtz, *Donat et la tradition de l'enseignement*, p. 417. In Paris, BN lat. 7490, f. 45, the *diastole* is midway between the *J* form and an enlarged comma.

33. This note is present in the emendations of an unseparated Terence manuscript thought to have been copied at Reims, Paris, BN lat. 7899, f. 10; for bibliography, see Leslie W. Jones, *The Miniatures of the Manuscripts of Terence Prior to the Thirteenth Century* (Princeton, n.d.). It is used as an insertion sign in the so-called Ramsey Benedictional, BN lat. 987, f. 30 (s. 10); for bibliography, see Backhouse, *The Golden Age*, no. 39; E. Temple, *Anglo-Saxon Manuscripts, 900–1006*, no. 25. Another example is Paris, BN lat. 272, f. 119, plate facing p. 284, in Vezin, "Manuscrits des dixième et onzième siècles."

34. L. M. J. Delaissé, *Le Manuscrit autographe de Thomas à Kempis et l'Imitation de Jésus-Christ*, 2 vols. (Brussels, 1956), 1: 24; cf. Saenger and Heinlen, "Incunable Description," p. 244.

35. At the Abbey of Saint-Pierre of Moissac in the eleventh century, an interlinear *dasia* was frequently placed at the beginning of words; for represen-

tative manuscripts, see Dufour, *Scriptorium de Moissac*, pp. 64, 97–154 passim. For an example of construction notes placed so as to parse a word block, see Paris, BN lat. 2772, f. 92.

36. Cohen, *La Grande invention*, 2: 183, 235. Terminal forms were employed in the Dead Sea Scroll fragments, where words were also well separated by space. For Arabic, see also Agnes Smith Lewis and Margaret Dunlop Gibson, *Forty-one Facsimiles of Dated Christian Arabic Manuscripts*, Studia Sinaitica, no. 12 (Cambridge, 1907); and Johannes Pedersen, *The Arabic Book*, trans. G. French (Princeton, 1984), pp. 6, 76–77. For Syriac, see Hatch, *Album of Dated Syriac Manuscripts*, pp. 38–40. A system of diacritical dots equivalent to Latin *prosodiae* was introduced by Hajaj in the first Islamic century. For Syriac, similar signs were introduced far earlier; see Segal, *The Diacritical Point and the Accents in Syriac*; Shelomo Morag, *The Vocalization Systems of Arabic, Hebrew, and Aramaic: Their Phonetic and Phonemic Principles*, JL, series minor, vol. 13 (The Hague, 1962).

37. Léopold Delisle and Ludwig Traube, "De l'emploi du signe abréviatif, à la fin des mots," *BEC* 67 (1906): 591–93; Vezin, "Manuscrits des dixième et onzième siècles," pp. 292–93; Armando Petrucci, "Censimento dei codici dei secoli XI–XII: Instruzioni per la datazione," *Studi medievali*, ser. 3, 9 (1969): 1115–26. Robert Marichal notes the use of terminal capitals in the twelfth century in his "L'écriture latine et la civilisation occidentale," p. 230.

38. For ancient practices, see Gordon and Gordon, *Palaeography of Latin Inscriptions*, pp. 202–7, cf. pp. 185–201. For definitions of *parole* and *langue* in this context, see Jonathan Culler, *Ferdinand de Saussure*, rev. ed. (Ithaca, N.Y., 1986).

39. See especially Jerome S. Bruner and Donald O'Dowd, "A Note on the Informativeness of Parts of Words," *Language and Speech* 1 (1958): 98–101. Eleanor J. Gibson and Harry Levin, *The Psychology of Reading* (Cambridge, Mass., 1975), p. 358; Leonard M. Horowitz, Margaret A. White, and Douglas W. Atwood, "Word Fragments as Aids to Recall: The Organization of a Word," *Journal of Typographical Research* 2 (1968): 143–56.

40. This is particularly true in manuscripts of the *Logica vetus*; Saenger, "Separated Script at Reims and Fleury."

41. Shipley, *Certain Sources of Corruption in Latin Manuscripts*, pp. 20–21. In the seventeenth century, Joseph Moxon remarked on the relationship of capitalization to space in distinguishing words; Davis and Carter, *Moxon: Mechanical Exercises*, p. 207.

42. Taylor and Taylor, *The Psychology of Reading*, p. 116.

43. William Reeves, ed., *The Life of Saint Columba* (Dublin, 1857), p. xix. The relation of these accent marks to actual pronunciation is problematic; cf. Dag Norberg, *Manuel pratique de latin médiéval* (Paris, 1968), p. 163. For possible ancient precedents for this use of accenting, see Gordon and Gordon, *Palaeography of Latin Inscriptions*, p. 149.

44. Wallace M. Lindsay, "Collectanea varia," *Paleographia latina* 2 (1923): 18–19.

45. Wallace M. Lindsay, "The Letters in Early Latin Minuscule," *Palaeographia latina* 1 (1922): 27–28.

46. The scribes of the *Antiphonary of Bangor*, Milan, Ambrosiana, C. 5 inf., written ca. 680–91, so denoted the initial vowel of certain polysyllabic words, a use that can also be found in the eighth-century Anglo-Irish *Book of Kells*; *CLA* 2 (1935): 274.

47. Bern, Burgerbibliothek 363, is an early example, on which see Cesare Questa, "Il metro e il libro: Per una semiologia della pagina scritta di Plauo, Terenzio, Prudenzio, Oracio," in *Atti del convegno internazionale il libro e il testo Urbino, 20–23 settembre 1982*, ed. Cesare Questa and Renato Raffaelli (Urbino, 1984), pls. 30–40. The practice of reserving special letter forms to denote the limits of words has been discussed in paleographic literature chiefly as a clue to date and provenance. See, for example, Françoise Gasparri, "Textes autographes d'auteurs victorins du XIIe siècle," *Scriptorium* 35 (1981): 278. Paleographers have quite accurately linked the terminal capital *R* and *A* to the Insular scribal tradition, and their presence is useful for tracing the geographic origins of particular scribes. See Vezin, "Manuscrits des dixième et onzième siècles," p. 293. The terminal capital *A* occurs in Paris, BN lat. 7696.

48. The terminal capital *S* is present in Bern, Burgerbibliothek 363. See also Ker, *Catalogue of Manuscripts Containing Anglo-Saxon*, p. xxx. It is noteworthy that Poggio Bracciolini's early experimentation in reviving the terminal long *s* in humanistic *littera antiqua* was rejected by subsequent humanist scribes; see A. C. de la Mare, *The Handwriting of the Italian Humanists* (Oxford, 1973), 1: fasc. 1, pls. 15–16. Even Niccolò Niccoli often used the round *s* as a terminal form. Ibid., 54.

49. T. Julian Brown, "The Irish Elements in the Insular System of Scripts to circa A.D. 850," in *Die Iren und Europa im früheren Mittelalter*, ed. Heinrich Löwe (Stuttgart, 1982), p. 101.

50. The capital *T* and *M* were also used at word endings. For early examples of the terminal *R* in an Insular center on the Continent, see Jones, *The Script of Cologne*, pls. 61, 64.

51. Jean Destrez, *La pecia dans les manuscrits universitaires du XIIIe et du XIVe siècles* (Paris, 1935), pls. 23–24; in pl. 24, vertical strokes add to the distinction of words. Numerous excellent examples of juridical manuscripts without adequate space separation are to be found in Anthony Melnikas, *The Corpus of the Miniatures in the Manuscripts of Decretum Gratiani* (Rome, 1975).

52. Lindsay, *Notae Latinae*, pp. 376–79, 381–84. The apostrophe was of Continental origin, but in Insular manuscripts, it was for the first time restricted to the terminal *-us*. For the Continental origin of the apostrophe for the terminal *-s*, see Delisle and Traube, "De l'emploi du signe abréviatif," p. 592. Paris, BN

lat. 1092, listed by Traube and written in word blocks, is now identified in the catalogue as Italian, late tenth or early eleventh century. Paris, BN lat. 5748, also contains the terminal capital *S*. On the relation of the long *j* and Insular script, see Wallace M. Lindsay, "I Longa," *Palaeographia latina* 2 (1923): 30.

53. Pontano used the capital *T*, *S*, and *X* at line endings. B. L. Ullman, "Pontano's Handwriting and the Leiden Manuscript of Tacitus and Suetonius," *IMU* 2 (1959): 1–27. See also Chicago, Newberry Library 93.6, -94, 97.1, and 97.5, for examples of the crossed capital *R*, *R*, and *NT* ligatures at line endings.

54. In seventh-century England, the *e* cedilla acted as a primitive construction note when it aided a reader in linking a noun to the adjective modifying it.

55. On the physiological implications of graphic concision, see Miles A. Tinker, "Numerals versus Words for Efficiency in Reading," *Journal of Applied Psychology* 12 (1928): 190–99.

56. Ralph N. Haber and Robert M. Schindler, "Error in Proofreading: Evidence of Syntactic Control of Letter Processing?" *Journal of Experimental Psychology: Human Perception and Performance* 7 (1981): 573–79.

57. Turner, *Greek Manuscripts*, p. 14; Roberts, *Greek Literary Hands*, p. 1.

58. See Isidore, *Libri etymologiarum*, ed. Lindsay, bk. 1, ch. 21.

59. The *Book of Mulling*, written before 692, evinces a fully developed array of monolexical abbreviations. The same is true of Abbot Dorbéne's transcription of Adomnan of Iona's *Vita Columbae*, Schaffhausen, Stadtsbibliothek Generalis 1, copied before 713.

60. G. Polara, ed., *Virgilio Marone grammatico: Epitomi ed Epistole* (Naples, 1979), pp. 310–13; Law, *The Insular Latin Grammarians*, p. 47. On Virgilius Maro's probable Irish origin, see Michael Herren, "Some New Light on the Life of Virgilius Maro Grammaticus," *Proceedings of the Royal Irish Academy* 79, Sec. C (1979): 27–71; Louis Holtz, "Les grammariens hiberno-latins étaient-ils des anglo-saxons?" *Peritia* 2 (1983): 177.

61. The monolexic abbreviations current in Insular script can be found enumerated, although not designated as a separate class of abbreviation, in the publications of Wallace M. Lindsay. See also Parkes, *Pause and Effect*, p. 24.

62. Malcom B. Parkes, "Tachygraphy in the Middle Ages: Writing Techniques Employed for *Reportationes* of Lectures and Sermons," *Medioevo e Rinascimento* 3 (1989): 164.

63. Isidore, *Libri etymologiarum*, ed. Lindsay, bk. 1, ch. 18. For an example, see P. Mich, III, 159.

64. For an early example, see Zurich, Zentralbibliothek C 57 (271), f. 197, in Bruckner, *Scriptoria medii aevi Helvetica*, 3: pl. 16.

65. Adriana Mariotti, "Testo letterario latino non identificato," *Athenaeum* 25 (1947): 166–70.

66. In lapidary inscriptions, this practice was rare; see Gordon and Gordon, *Palaeography of Latin Inscriptions*, pp. 183–84; Gordon, *Illustrated Introduction to*

324 Notes to Pages 65–68

Latin Epigraphy, p. 13; Cagnat, *Cours d'épigraphie latine*, p. 29. In manuscript books, the few surviving examples indicate that points were frequently omitted even when lines ended with complete words; Wingo, *Latin Punctuation in the Classical Age*, pp. 50–67. In P. Mich, III, 159, the absence of an interpunct at the end of line 3 seems to indicate continuation; Henry A. Sanders, "A Latin Document from Egypt," *Transactions and Proceedings of the American Philological Association* 55 (1924): 21–34, pl. 4 following p. 248.

67. *CLA*, supplement (1971): 1679, 1703. This has been observed by James J. John, "Latin Paleography," in Powell, *Medieval Studies*, p. 47; Jean Vezin, "Les Manuscrits datés de l'ancien fonds latin de la Bibliothèque Nationale de Paris," *Scriptorium* 19 (1965): 86; Vezin, "Manuscrits des dixième et onzième siècles," p. 287.

68. This practice occurs in the *Book of Durrow*, the *Antiphonary of Bangor*, and the Leningrad Bede. The Irish had a special name for this scribal innovation, *ceann fa eite* (head under wing). John O'Donovan's *Grammar of the Irish Language* (Dublin, 1845), p. 434.

69. Bede, *De orthographia*, in Keil, *Grammatici latini*, 7: 273, 279.

70. Ker, *Catalogue of Manuscripts Containing Anglo-Saxon*, pp. xxxv–xxxvi.

71. Bernhard Bischoff, *Paläographie des römischen Altertums und des abendländischen Mittelalters* (Berlin, 1979), p. 217 n. 53, listing *CLA* 9 (1959): 1302; *CLA* 10 (1963): 1478; and Oxford, BL Marshall 19 (beginning of the ninth century).

72. The term *semipunctus* is used for the *trait d'union* in Paris, BN lat. 10922, f. 58v. Martin Hubert, "Corpus stigmatologicum minus," *Bulletin du Cange* 37 (1970): 168; and Thurot, "Notices et extraits," p. 416. Guillaume Tardif used the term *virgula* for the *trait d'union* in his *Grammatica* (N.p., n.d.); Paris, BN Rés. X 1570.

73. Paris, BN lat. 16258, the *Liber qui dicitur Oculus aureus*, a text drawn from the writings of Anselm of Laon, was copied in 1185 in aerated script, with interword space varying from 1.75 to 2.8 times the unity of space. *Traits d'union* were erroneously provided by the scribe in one instance after a monosyllabic preposition. At the beginning of the thirteenth century, the *Decretum* of Gratian was copied in central Italy in Paris, BN NAL 1576. Word separation was poorly produced and prone to degenerate into hierarchical word blocks of fewer than fifteen characters in length. *Traits d'union*, the tironian conventional symbol for *et*, and the terminal capital *S* were present.

74. Many of these forms have been added to Cambrai, BM 470.

75. For a clear statement of these rules, see Wallace M. Lindsay, *A Short Historical Latin Grammar*, 2d ed. (Oxford, 1915), pp. 25–28.

76. On this system, see E. A. Lowe, *Beneventan Script*, p. 276. The Beneventan examples discussed by Lowe are late and derived from Anglo-Saxon antecedents.

77. Venice, Marcianus Z. L. 497, ff. 15–19. See Francis L. Newton, "Tibullus

in Two Grammatical *Florilegia* of the Middle Ages," *Transactions of the American Philological Society* 93 (1962): 263, 275.

78. The form of the hyphen is reproduced by Banniard, "Le lecteur en Espagne Wisigothique," p. 119. The separation of words in the example is anachronistic.

79. Cf. Parkes, *Pause and Effect*, p. 12. On the use of wax tablets in ancient schools, see Marrou, *Histoire de l'éducation dans l'antiquité*, pp. 234–35, 259, 267, 406, 602, and passim.

80. Roberts, *Greek Literary Hands*, gives no examples of the hyphen in Greek papyri; Turner, *Greek Manuscripts*, nos. 13, 14, 27, 36, 50, gives examples of the hyphen, and in nos. 23 and 34 gives two examples of the *diastole*, all in Greek. Gordon and Gordon, *Palaeography of Latin Inscriptions*, record no instance of either in lapidary use; and Wingo, *Latin Punctuation in the Classical Age*, gives no examples from Latin papyri. I know of no example of either the hyphen or *diastole* in surviving Latin codices or documents from the patristic age.

81. See *CLA* 4 (1947): viii; Wingo, *Latin Punctuation in the Classical Age*, pp. 127–31. Lapidary examples of space as punctuation include Arthur Earnest Gordon and Joyce S. Gordon, *Album of Dated Latin Inscriptions*, 4 vols. (Berkeley, 1958–65), pls. 28a, 109; manuscript examples include *CLA* 8 (1959): 1031, *CLA* 3 (1938): 295, *CLA* 1 (1934): 1a, *CLA* 4 (1947): 445, 491; see Müller, *Rhetorische und syntaktische Interpunktion*, pp. 22–27; cf. Moreau-Maréchal, "Recherches sur la ponctuation," p. 59. The spaces present in the wooden tablets found at Vindolanda (England), dating from the end of the first century A.D., may be signs of rudimentary punctuation; cf. A. K. Bowman and J. D. Thomas, *Vindolanda: The Latin Writing Tablets*, Britannia Monograph Series, no. 4 (London, 1983).

82. See Michael Korhammer, "Mittelalterliche Konstruktionshilfen und Altenglische Wortstellung," *Scriptorium* 34 (1980): 18–58; and Fred C. Robinson, "Syntactical Glosses in Latin Manuscripts of Anglo-Saxon Provenance," *Speculum* 48 (1973): 443–75.

83. Gregory of Tours, prologue, *De gloria beatorum confessorum*, in *Les livres des miracles et autres opuscules*, 2 vols., ed. Henri Leonard Bordier (Paris, 1857–64), 2: 338–39.

84. The oldest codex with contemporary construction marks appears to be the Epistles of Paul, Würzburg, Universitätsbibl. M. P. TH. F. 12 (end of the eighth century); see the facsimile edition in Ludwig Christian Stern, *Epistolae beati Pauli glossatae glossa interlineali: Irisch-lateinischer Codex der Würzburger Universitätsbibliothek* (Halle, 1910), xiv; *CLA* 9 (1959): 47.

85. Research by Alfonso Caramazza conducted at the Johns Hopkins University, reported by the *Wall Street Journal*, October 12, 1993, A1–A8.

86. For the ninth-century Irish use of sequential construction signs, consult Martje Draak, "Construe Marks in Hiberno-Latin Manuscripts" in *Mededelingen der Kroninklijke Nederlandsche Akademie van Wetenschappen*, afd. Letter-

kunde, n.s., 20, no. 10 (1957): 261–82; and "The Higher Teaching of Latin Grammar in Ireland during the Ninth Century," in *Mededelingen der Kroninklijke Nederlandsche Akademie van Wetenschappen*, afd. Letterkunde, n.s., 30, no. 4 (1967): 109–44. For the impact of the written word and related graphic images as opposed to oralization on memory, see John T. E. Richardson, *Mental Imagery and Human Memory* (New York, 1980).

87. English scribes used letters in lieu of numbers in eighth-century calendars and as quire signatures. See H. A. Wilson, *The Calendar of Saint Willibrord from MS Paris Lat. 10883*7, HBS, vol. 55 (London, 1918), p. xii.

88. Parkes, *Pause and Effect*, p. 28.

89. V. L. Hanson and U. Bellugi, "On the Role of Sign Order and Morphological Structure in Memory for American Sign Language Sentences," *Journal of Verbal Learning and Verbal Behavior* 21 (1982): 621–33. On the brain's discrete and redundant aural and visual systems of short-term memory, see Alfonso Caramazza and Argye E. Hillis, "Lexical Organization of Nouns and Verbs in the Brain," *Nature* 349 (1991): 788.

90. Arthur T. Walker, "Some Facts of Latin Word Order," *The Classical Quarterly* 13 (1917–18): 652–57; cf. B. L. Ullman, "Latin Word Order," *The Classical Journal* 14 (1918–19): 405–6. On the diverging German and French approaches to punctuation of classical texts, see Henri Bornecque, *La prose métrique dans la correspondance de Ciceron* (Paris, 1898), pp. 205–9; Müller, *Rhetorische und syntaktische Interpunktion*.

91. Henri Bornecque, *Les clausules métriques latines* (Lille, 1907), p. xix; and *La prose métrique dans la correspondance de Ciceron*, pp. 206–9; Eugène Albertini, *La composition dans les ouvrages philosophiques de Sénèque* (Paris, 1923), p. 8.

92. See Arthur W. Hogman, "Latin Equivalents of Punctuation Marks," *The Classical Journal* 19 (1923–24): 408–9.

93. Malcolm B. Parkes, "Punctuation or Pause and Effect," in *Medieval Eloquence*, ed. J. J. Murphy (Berkeley, 1978), p. 127; Wingo, *Latin Punctuation in the Classical Age*.

94. Marrou, *Histoire de l'éducation dans l'antiquité*, 233, 406, 602–3; Parkes, *Pause and Effect*, pp. 10–19. For examples of a Greek text on a tablet, see Kenyon "Two Greek School Tablets," pp. 29–40; Wilhelm Schubart, *Einführung in die Papyruskunde* (Berlin, 1918), pl. 3, 3; Paul Beudel, *Qua ratione Graeci libros docuerint* (Münster, 1911), p. 41. For ancient descriptions of the method of instruction, see G. Goetz, ed., *Hermeneumata Pseudodositheana*, in *Corpus glossariorum latinorum* (Leipzig, 1883–1923), 3: 381; and Quintilian, *Institutiones oratoriae*, 2.54.

95. Augustine, *De doctrina christiana*, 3.2, in *PL* 34: 65–67; William M. Green, ed., *CSEL* 80 (1963): 79–80.

96. See Rufinus's preface to Origen's *Periarchon*, ed. H. Crouzel and M. Simonette, in *Origène, traité des principes* (Paris, 1978), 73–75; and Cassiodorus, *Institutiones*, in *PL* 70: 1109; and *Institutiones*, ed. R.A.B. Mynors (Oxford, 1937), 48–49. Rufinus probably meant textual corrections rather than

actual marks of punctuation; see Banniard, "Le lecteur en Espagne Wisigothique," p. 121 n. 49.

97. "Quasi quaedam viae sunt sensuum et lumina dictinum quae sic lectores dociles faciunt tamquam si clarissimis expositionibus inbuantur." Cassiodorus, *Institutiones,* 1.15.12.

98. On Insular characters of signs of punctuation, see Olga Dobiache Rojdestvensky, *Histoire de l'atelier graphique de Corbie 651 à 830, réflétée dans les manuscripts de Léningrad* (Leningrad, 1934), pp. 86–89; *CLA* 2 (1935): vii; and, for more recent work, Malcolm B. Parkes, "The Contribution of Insular Scribes to the Grammar of Legibility," in his *Scribes, Scripts, and Readers* (London, 1991).

99. C. R. Morey, Edward Kennard Rand, and Carl H. Kraeling, *The Gospel Book of Landevennec (The Harkness Gospels) in the New York Public Library* (Cambridge, Mass., 1931), p. 12; Parkes, *Pause and Effect,* pp. 30–34.

100. Hogman, "Latin Equivalents of Punctuation Marks," pp. 408–9.

101. Segal, *The Diacritical Point and the Accents in Syriac,* pp. 68–70.

102. Martin Harris, *The Evolution of French Syntax: A Comparative Approach* (New York, 1978), pp. 30–31.

103. See Patrick McGurk, "Citation Marks in Early Latin Manuscripts," *Scriptorium* 22 (1968): 3–13; cf. Turner, *Greek Manuscripts,* p. 17.

104. For a clear résumé on the origin of neumes, consult Solange Corbin in *Encyclopédie de la musique,* s.v. "Neume"; and for a more detailed treatment, see "Die Neumen," *Paläographie der Musik,* 1, 3 (Cologne, 1977). See, most recently, Kenneth Levy, "On the Origin of Neumes," *Early Music History* 7 (1987): 59–61.

105. Those manuscripts containing neumes attributed with certainty to the ninth century are: Sélestat, BM 1; Vat. Ottob. 313; Vat. Reg. lat. 215; Paris, BN lat. 2291, lat. 8093, and lat. 2832; and Munich, Clm. 9544. For the similarity between neumes and punctuation and *prosodiae,* see Leo Treitler, "Reading and Singing: On the Genesis of Occidental Music Writing," *Early Music History* 46 (1984): 186–203; Levy, "On the Origin of Neumes," pp. 62–63.

106. On the use of letters, see Alma Colk Santosuosso, *Letter Notations in the Middle Ages,* Musicological Studies, vol. 57 (Ottawa, 1989); J. Froger, "Epître de Notger sur les lettres sicnicatives," *Etudes grégoriennes* 5 (1962): 23–72; Joseph Smits van Waesberghe, "Les origines de la notation alphabétique au Moyen Age," *Annuario musical* 12 (1957): 3–16; Michel Huglo, "L'auteur du *Dialogue sur la musique* attribué à Odon," *Revue de musicologie* 69 (1955): 142–45; Escudier, "Les Manuscrits musicaux," pp. 40–42; Solange Corbin, "Valeur et sens de la notation alphabétique à Jumièges et en Normandie," in *Jumièges: Congrès scientifique du XIIIᵉ centenaire,* 2: 913–24; and the "Toner-Graduale of Saint Bénigne of Dijon," Montpellier bibliothèque de la faculté de médecine H. 159, printed in facsimile in *Paléographie musicale,* ser. 2, 8 (1901–5; reprint, Berne, 1972); Michel Huglo, "Le tonaire de Saint-Benigne de Dijon (Montpellier H. 159)," *Annales musicologiques: Moyen Age et Renaissance* 4 (1956): 7–18.

107. On the problem of textual clarity in manuscripts with musical nota-

tion, see Escudier, "Les Manuscrits musicaux," pp. 38–42; the Antiphonale of Saint Gregory, Laon, BM 239, *Paléographie musicale*, ser. 2, 10 (1909); Anne-Véronique Gilles, "La Ponctuation dans les manuscripts liturgiques au Moyen Age," in Maierù, *Grafia e interpunzione*, pp. 113–33.

108. Eligius Dekkers, "Les Autographes des pères latins," in *Colligere Fragmenta: Festschrift Alban Dold zum 70 Geburtztag am 7.7. 1952*, ed. Bonifatius Fischer and Virgil Fiala (Beuron in Hohenzollern, 1952), p. 138. See, for example, *CLA* 1 (1934): 12.

109. Ettore Cou, "Scrittura e cultura a Novara (secoli viii–x)," *Richerchi medievali* 6–9 (1971–74): 57–60.

110. On critical signs in ancient Greek, see Turner, *Greek Manuscripts*; E. A. Lowe, "The Oldest Omission Signs in Latin Manuscripts, Their Origin and Significance," in *Miscellanea Giovanni Mercati*, 6 vols. (Vatican City, 1946), 6: 76–78; reprinted in E. A. Lowe, *Palaeographical Papers*, 2 vols. (Oxford, 1972), 2: 378–80.

111. For published examples dating from the end of the eighth century, see Antonio Maria Ceriani, *Codex Syro-Hexaplaris Ambrosianus Photolithographicus Editus*, Monumenta sacra et profana ex codicibus praesertim Bibliotheca Ambrosianae, vol. 7 (Milan, 1874); the codex dates from the end of the eighth century and is rich in symbolic tie notes similar in form to subsequent Insular signs of punctuation.

112. These have been recently studied by Richard H. Rouse, "Statim invenire: Schools, Preachers, and New Attitudes to the Page," in *Renaissance and Renewal in the Twelfth Century*, ed. Robert L. Benson and Giles Constable (Oxford, 1982), pp. 201–25.

113. See Turner, *Greek Manuscripts*, p. 17, and Diogenes Laertius, III, 64–67 (life of Plato).

114. For examples, see Best, *The Commentary on the Psalms*; and Stern, *Epistolae beati Pauli glossatae*.

115. Devisse, *Hincmar, archevêque de Reims*, 2: 926; D. C. Lambot, "L'Homélie du Pseudo-Jérôme sur l'assumption et l'Evangile de la nativité de Marie d'après une lettre inédite d'Hincmar," *RB* 46 (1934): 269–70.

116. Roger Baron, ed., *Hugonis de sancto Victore opera propaedeutica* (Notre Dame, Ind., 1966), p. 127; Jean Leclerq, ed., "Le *De grammatica* de Hugues de Saint-Victor," *Archives d'histoire doctrinale et litteraire de Moyen Age* 14 (1943–45): 304.

117. E. A. Lowe, "The Oldest Omission Signs," pp. 76–78; reprint, Lowe, *Palaeographical Papers*, 2: 378–80.

118. Roberts and Skeat, *The Birth of the Codex*, pp. 24–29. See Saenger, "The Impact of the Early Printed Page."

119. Lehmann, "Blätter, Seiten, Spalten, Zeilen."

120. Turner, *Typology of the Early Codex*, pp. 74–76; Roberts and Skeat, *The*

Birth of the Codex, pp. 50–51. For an example, see Roberts, *Greek Literary Hands*, pl. 20c. On pagination of tablets, see Kenyon, "Two Greek School Tablets," p. 32.

121. See Lehmann, "Blätter, Seiten, Spalten, Zeilen," pp. 8–10; Bentley Layton, *Catalogue of Coptic Literary Manuscripts in the British Library Acquired Since the Year 1906* (London, 1987), includes numerous references to medieval Coptic pagination.

122. Vat. lat. 355 and 356, containing Jerome's *Opuscula* from the Abbey of Monte Cassino and dating from the tenth century, is said to be the oldest codex with contemporary foliation. The text is aerated, but not separated. The foliation is clearly Beneventan, but not, in my judgment, definitely contemporary with the codex. Among Latin manuscripts earlier than Vat. lat. 355 and 356, only an occasional instance of leaf signatures in Insular manuscripts has been detected.

123. Early examples come from Fleury, Saint-Pierre de Moissac, and in the twelfth century, the Cistercian Abbey of Beaupré. On the last, see Dolbeau, "Anciens possesseurs," pp. 183–238.

124. Gregorio di Catino, *Liber largitorius*, ed. Giuseppi Zucchetti, in *Liber largitorius vel notarius monasterii pharphensis* (Rome, 1913–32). No such tables citing foliation seem to have existed in Greek antiquity; cf. Turner, *Typology of the Early Codex*, p. 75.

125. Jean-François Vezin, Odile Berge, and Panicos Mavrellis, "Rôle du résumé de la répétition en fonction de leur place par rapport au texte," *Bulletin de Psychologie* 309 (1973): 163–67.

126. The manuscripts annotated at Fleury under Abbo are examples of such codices. Even earlier, the ninth-century author-scribe-emendator Lupus of Ferrières also combined both functions, although Lupus did not separate words in either his emendations or his script. See Pellegrin, "Les Manuscrits de Loup de Ferrières," p. 27.

127. See the remarks of D. F. McKenzie, "Speech-Manuscript-Print," in *New Directions in Textual Studies*, ed. David Oliphant and Robin Bradford (Austin, Tex., 1990), p. 104.

128. M. P. E. Littré, "Raimond Lulle," *Histoire littéraire de la France* 29 (1885): 75. For examples, see Charles Lohr, Theodor Pindl-Büchel, and Walburga Büchel, eds., *Raimundi Lulli Opera latinai, Supplementi Lulliani tomus, CCCM* 77 (1990).

129. Jean-François Vezin, "L'apprentissage des schémas: Leur rôle dans l'assimilation des connaissances," *L'année psychologique* (1972): 179–96. See also Oscar G. Darlington, "Gerbert, the Teacher," *American Historical Review* 52 (1946–47): 467, 472–73; and Saenger, "Separated Script at Reims and Fleury."

130. See, for example, Eleanore Stump, "Differentia and the Porphyrian Tree," in her *Boethius's "De topicis differentiis"* (Ithaca, N.Y., 1978), pp. 237–47.

131. Pseudo-Priscian, *Liber de accentibus*, in Keil, *Grammatici latini*, 3: 518–28; C. H. Kneepkens and H. F. Reijnders, *Magister Singuinus, Ars lectoria: Un*

art de lecture à haute voix du onzième siècle (Leiden, 1979), pp. 32–33, 78. The eleventh-century customary of Fleury and the twelfth-century *Liber ordinis* of the Austin canons of the Abbey of Saint-Victor in Paris testify to the importance of such emendations in medieval monasteries; see the *Consuetudines Floriacenses antiquiores*, in *Corpus consuetudinum monasticarum* 7, pt. 3 (1984); Marie-Thérèse d'Alverny, in her introduction to vol. 3 (1974) of *France: Manuscrits datés*, pp. xi–xii.

132. Paris, BN lat. 7585, a severely damaged late-ninth-century Continental copy of Isidore's *Libri etymologiarum* written in hierarchical word blocks, probably was brought to St. Augustine's, Canterbury, where it was restored and corrected in the second half of the tenth century. The English scribes who rewrote the missing portion of the text emended the late-ninth-century part using the *trait d'union*, acute accents, hyphens, and both the *J* form and the successor mark to the *diastole* to render the Continental Caroline script more legible. In some instances, the successor to the *diastole* closely resembled an acute accent (above) and a *diastole* (below). The successor mark to the *diastole* was used both where space was entirely omitted between words and where the scribe deemed interword space of fewer than 1.5 unities of space to be insufficient; T. A. M. Bishop, *English Caroline Minuscule* (Oxford, 1971), p. 4 and pl. 6; Ker, *Catalogue of Manuscripts Containing Anglo-Saxon*, no. 366; Gneuss, "A Preliminary List," no. 889. I am indebted to Jean Vezin for bringing Paris, BN lat. 7585, to my attention.

133. See the chapter *De officio armorii* of the *Liber ordinis* of the canons regular of the monastery of Saint-Victor, cited by d'Alverny in her introduction to vol. 3 of *France: Manuscrits datés*, p. xii; and the remark of Nicolaus de Lyra in his second prologue to the *Postilla super totam Bibliam*, 4 vols. (1492; reprint, Frankfurt am Main, 1971), 1: Aiiv.

134. Microfilm at the IRHT. Emile Chatelain, *Uncialis scriptora codicum latinorum novis exemplis illustratis* (Paris, 1901), pl. 92; *CLA* 6 (1953): 740.

135. Microfilm at the IRHT. *France: Manuscrits datés*, 5 (1965): 55 and pl. 242.

136. This codex is certainly from the region of Orléans. A microfilm is at the IRHT; for a list of the contents and general description, see Claude W. Barlow, "Codex Vaticanus Latinus 4929," *Memoirs of the American Academy in Rome* 15 (1938): 87–124 and pls. 11–18. The dating of many of the corrections pertaining to word separation to the ninth century by Barlow and subsequently accepted by Giovanni Billanovich, "Dall'antica Ravenna alle biblioteche umanistiche," *Aevum* 30 (1956): 329, 337 n. 1, is incorrect. For the provenance, see Richard H. Rouse and Mary A. Rouse, "The *Florilegium Angelicum*: Its Origin, Content, and Influence," in *Medieval Learning and Literature*, ed. Alexander and Gibson, pp. 77–78; Mostert, *The Library of Fleury*, BF 1317–20.

137. Added punctuation included the *punctus elevatus*.

138. It is interesting to note the emendation activity of scribes collaborating on a single codex or working in a single scriptorium during the period of transition to separated script on the Continent both north and south of the Alps. Characteristically, one scribe might write the text and some auxiliary signs, and another might clarify it by adding further auxiliary signs, including those of separation, such as the acute accent or the successor note to the *diastole*. Other emendations might include accenting of the double *ii*, *traits d'union*, and punctuation of sense. This division of labor is particularly in evidence in manuscripts written within a century of the introduction of separation by space. In the early juristic codices of Bologna, one scribe would incorporate certain auxiliary signs in the copying of his portion of a codex and then, acting as emendator, add the same signs into the text written by his collaborators. See Paris, BN lat. 4458A (eleventh century), described in Saenger, "Coupure et séparation des mots sur le Continent au Moyen Age." The collaboration between scribe and punctuator is less evident in the thirteenth century when the task of punctuation became increasingly a regular responsibility of the scribe as he wrote. See the remarks of Erasmus in *De recta latini graecique sermonis pronuntiatione*, ed. M. Cytowska, in *Opera omnia Desiderii Erasmi Roterdami*, ser. 1, 4 (1973): 38. However, it continued in modified form throughout the Middle Ages, and it was practiced extensively in the second half of the fifteenth century in incunables of monastic provenance. See Saenger and Heinlen, "Incunable Description," pp. 239–50.

139. The crucial factor for perception of punctuation is the breadth of parafoveal vision. On how this breadth is reduced by the absence of word separation by space, see George W. McConkie and Keith Rayner, "The Span of an Effective Stimulus During a Fixation in Reading," *Perception and Psychophysics* 17 (1975): 578–86; Ariane Levy-Schoen and Kevin O'Regan, "The Control of Eye Movements in Reading," and Keith Rayner, "Eye Movements in Reading," both in *Processing of Visible Language 1*, 17, 72.

Chapter 4

1. Alexander, *Insular Manuscripts, 6th to the 9th Century*, no. 45; *CLA* 2 (1935): 276–77; John Thomas Gilbert, *Facsimiles of National Manuscripts of Ireland* (Dublin, 1974–84), pl. 20; Lindsay, *Early Irish Minuscule Script*, pls. 7–8. I see no reason to deny the authenticity of the Mulling colophon for purely paleographical reasons, especially when paleographical chronology for this period is so uncertain for want of dated manuscripts. Comparison with Dorbéne's (before 713) copy of Adomnan's *Vita Columbae* (see below) makes the autograph character of the *Book of Mulling* entirely plausible. The mixed Vulgate text of Mulling is consistent with this date; see Peter Doyle, "The Text of Saint Luke's Gospel in the Book of Mulling," *Proceedings of the Royal Irish Academy* 73, Sect. C, no. 6 (1973): 199; H. J. Lawlor, *Chapters on the Book of Mulling* (Edinburgh, 1897); H. C. Hoskier, *Concerning the Genesis of the Versions of the New Testament*

Gospels, 2 vols. (London, 1910–11), 2: 278–378 (collation); Kenney, *Sources for the Early History of Ireland*, no. 456; Cordoliani, "Le texte de la Bible," pp. 9–10; cf. Brown, "The Irish Element," pp. 113–14; Peter Doyle, "The Latin Bible in Ireland: Its Origin and Growth," in *Biblical Stud.   e Medieval Contribution*, ed. Martin McNamara, Proceedings of the Irish Biblical Association, vol. 1 (Dublin, 1976), pp. 41, 45.

2. Anderson and Anderson, *Adomnan's Columba*, pp.   4, 101–5, and passim, four plates follow p. 176; *CLA* 7 (1956): 998; Lindsay, *Early Irish Minuscule Script*, p. 3 and pl. 2.

3. See Law, *The Insular Latin Grammarians*, pp. 46–47. Law, citing the edition by G. Polara and L. Caruso, *Virgilio Marone grammatico: Epitomi ed Epistole* (Naples, 1979), refers to the ampersand or *et* ligature. This sign appears in the surviving manuscripts. The *et* ligature was used in Irish manuscripts at an early date, even though Lindsay states that Insular script did not know the ampersand; see Lindsay, *Notae latinae*, p. 74.

4. "Et lector in aeclesia catholica ordinari non sinitur, nisi qui legere et scire potest syllabas et accentuum rationem et species et naturas dictionum et distinctiones sententiarum, ut Essidorus dicit in Libro de officialibus aeclessiae catholicae." Bernhard Bischoff and Bengt Löfstedt, eds., *Anonymus ad Cuimnanum expositio latinitatis*, in *CCSL* 133D (1992): 17; cf. Isidore, *De ecclesiaticis officiis*, ch. 12, in *PL* 83: 791.

5. "Intellegendum quoque generaliter praepositiones, nisi cassibus propriis iunguntur, transire in alterius partis significationem quod et Donatus ostendit; nam *invalidus prae me mecum profero, expresse praecedens absque circumcirca* in hac significatu in alias vel partes commotavit vel in earum quibus iecitur transit significationem. Quod sequitur *separari coniungi*, idest separantur in praepositiones cassui servientis aut in conpositionem figuras iunguntur." *Anonymous ad Cuimnanum*, p. 149.

6. "Figura quomodo definitur? Figura est forma rei vel nominis denuntiati." *Ars anonyma Bernensis*, in Keil, *Grammatici latini*, 8: 85. For the date, see Holtz, *Donat et la tradition de l'enseignement*, p. 434.

7. See *Aldhelm: The Prose Works*, ed. Michael Lapidge and Michael Herren (Totowa, N.J., 1979), pp. 1–3.

8. Miskolc (Hungary), Zrinyi Ilona Secondary School, fragment of the *Epistola ad Acircium*, in *CLA*, supplement (1972): 1792; Gneuss, "A Preliminary List," no. 850; see also Yale, Beinecke Library 401 and 401a (beginning of the ninth century), which was written by Continental scribes using Insular letter forms; cf. Barbara Shailor, *Catalogue of Mediaeval and Renaissance Manuscripts in the Beinecke Rare Book Library, Yale University*, 2 vols. (Binghamton, N.Y., 1984–), 2: 280–84; and *The Medieval Book* (Toronto, 1991), pp. 13–14 and pl. 11; Gneuss, "A Preliminary List," no. 853; M. Lapidge, "The Revival of Latin Learning in Late Anglo-Saxon England," in A. C. de la Mare and B. C. Barker-Benfield,

Manuscripts at Oxford: An Exhibition in Memory of Richard William Hunt (1908–1979) (Oxford, 1980), pp. 19–20. The early Continental manuscripts of Aldhelm are aerated and show numerous signs of Insular influence; see also Franz Unterkircher, *Sancti Bonifacii Epistolae: Codex Vindobonensis 751 der österreichischen Nationalbibliothek Faksimile-Ausgabe der Wiener Handschrift des Briefe des Heiligen Bonifatius* (Graz, 1971); Elias Avery Lowe, "An Eighth-Century List of Books in a Bodleian MS from Würzburg and Its Probable Relation to the Laudian Acts," *Speculum* 3 (1928): 8–9; *CLA* 7 (1956): 982.

9. "Prosodia est signum sermonis iter rectum faciens legenti." Aldhelm, *De metris et enigmatibus ac pedum regulis*, in *Aldhelmi opera*, ed. Rudolf Ehwald, *MGH: Auctores Antiquissimi* 15 (1919): 199; *PL* 89: 251B.

10. "Tonus autem aut petrahitur aut attrahitur, aut medietas syllabae bonam vocem habens . . . acutus tonus est nota per obliquum accendans in dexteram partem ut est *páx, píx, nóx*." *Aldhelmi opera*, ed. Ehwald, pp. 199–200; *PL* 89: 251C. The examples given appear to be of vowel length. The discussion of vowel length is obviously conflated with the definition of accent marks as defined by ancient grammarians of the second century.

11. "Dasia est qualitas syllabae juxta sonitum spirantis, ut est *homo, habitans, habens*." *Aldhelmi opera*, ed. Ehwald, pp. 199–200; *PL* 89: 251D. See the use of the letter *h* to denote word beginnings in Dorbéne's transcription of the *Vita Columbae* and in the *Book of Deer*, Cambridge University Library Li.6.32, written at the end of the ninth or early tenth century at Deer in northern Scotland; Alexander, *Insular Manuscripts 6th to the 9th Century*, no. 72; *PS*, 1: 210–11; Kenney, *Sources for the Early History of Ireland*, no. 502. See the diplomatic edition: John Stuart, ed., *The Book of Deer*, Spalding Club Publications, vol. 24 (Edinburgh, 1869).

12. J. Fourquet, "Le mot en allemand," in *Linguistic Studies Presented to André Martinet on the Occasion of His Sixtieth Birthday*, ed. Alphonse Juilland and A. Beltramo (New York, 1967–69), also published as vols. 23–25 (1967–69) of *Word: Journal of the Linguistic Circle of New York*.

13. "Passio est vox passibilis coniuncta et unita et divisibilia discernens." *Aldhelmi opera*, ed. Ehwald, p. 200; *PL* 89: 251D; cf. Aulus Gellius, *Noctes Atticae*, 13.31.10.

14. "Hyphen est coniunctio dictionis ex duabus perfectis imperfectis compositae, ut est luci̯fer, uni̯genitus, primo̯genitus. Hyperdiastoli est divisio compositarum litterarum propter ambiguitates, ut est: viridique in littore conspicituṛsus, ut non erret qui legat, ne pro *sus ursus* legat." *Aldhelmi opera*, ed. Ehwald, p. 200; *PL* 89: 234D–235A. I have amended the text by deleting an *r* from *prorsus* and adding spaces and *notae*. Cf. Donatus, *Ars maior*, in Holtz, *Donat et la tradition de l'enseignement*, p. 611; Parkes, *Pause and Effect*, p. 10.

15. For *figura* in Donatus, see Holtz, *Donat et la tradition de l'enseignement*, pp. 614, 624, 629, 630, 632, 637, 644, 646, 647, 651.

16. "*Figurae nominum quot sunt? Duae. Quae?* Simplex et conposita. *Sim-*

plex, ut decens, potens. 'Decens,' 'potens,' quomodo habet simplicem figuram? 'de' praepositio est, sed quia istud 'cens' nihil est, ideo Donatus simplici figura hoc posuit; 'po' nihil est, 'tens' similiter, et est simplex figura." Julian of Toledo, in *Ars Iuliani Toletani Episcopi,* ed. Maria A. H. Maestre Yenes, Vestigios del pasado, vol. 5 (Toledo, 1973), p. 22; cf. pp. 49, 99.

17. Maximus Victorinus, *Ars grammatica,* in Keil, *Grammatici latini,* 6: 8.

18. Bede, *Liber de orthographia,* in Keil, *Grammatici latini,* 7: 271; and ed. Charles W. Jones, in *Bedae opera pars I: Opera didascalica,* CCSL 123A (1975): 22. The modern editions based on late Insular and Continental codices do not attempt to reconstruct Bede's original placement of the *diastole* relative to spacing. Cf. *Ars Iuliani Toletani episcopi,* ed. Maestre Yenes, p. 175; Pompeius, *Commentum artis Donati,* pp. 132, 12, in Keil, *Grammatici latini,* 5: 132. Both Julian of Toledo and Pompeius clearly imply that the responsibility of separation lay with the reader pronouncing the text aloud, and not with the writer.

19. David Ganz, "An Anglo-Saxon Fragment of Alcuin's Letters in the Newberry Library, Chicago," *Anglo-Saxon England* 22 (1993): 175 n. 38; T. A. M. Bishop, "Notes on Cambridge Manuscripts," *Transactions of the Cambridge Bibliographical Society* 2 (1954–58): 187–89. Bishop, who does not note the well-developed word separation throughout, assumes that the book was brought to St. Augustine's, Canterbury, from the Continent. I think it more likely, given all the Insular qualities of this book, that it was the work of a Continental scribe or an English scribe of Continental training working at Canterbury. In London, BL Harley 3826, a tenth-century Continental copy written in hierarchical word blocks, the graphic representation of an oral error was achieved by the combined use of space and interpunct; see f. 38v, "Liberaperuit . reosmovit vestigacampos." On this codex, see Claudio Leonardi, "I codici di Marziano Capella," *Aevum* 34 (1960): 78–79.

20. *CSEL* 10 (1885): 81, line 235.

21. Early examples of separated Bede include Bückeburg Niedersächsisches Staatsarchiv/Münster, in Westfallen Staatsarchiv fragments of the *De temperorum ratione;* Darmstadt, Hessisches Landes- und Hochschulbibliothek 4264; the *Leningrad Bede,* Saint Petersburg, Public Library lat. Q. v. I. 18 (in part, possibly autograph); London, BL Cotton Tiberius A. xiv; London, BL Cotton Tiberius C. ii; Kassel, Landesbibliothek 4 Theol. 2; New York, Pierpont Morgan 826; and Oxford, BL Bodley 819. Of early Bede manuscripts, Cambridge, University Library Kk 5. 16, the *Moore Bede,* is the sole in English script that is not separated. I agree with Wallace M. Lindsay and Montague Rhodes James that this book, formerly in the cathedral of Le Mans and the Palace School of Aachen, was of Continental origin. Wallace M. Lindsay, "The Abbreviation Symbols of *ergo, igitur,*" *Zentralblatt für Bibliothekswesen* 2 (1912): 59; Montague Rhodes James, "The Manuscripts of Bede," in *Bede: His Life, Times, and Writings,* ed. A. H. Thompson (Oxford, 1935), p. 231. The "M" recension contained

in the Moore Bede is the oldest copy of the standard Continental version of the *Historia ecclesiastica*.

22. Isidore, *Etymologiae*, ed. Lindsay, bk. 1, ch. 19, 7. "Diastole, id est distinctio, quae e contratio separat, dextra pars circuli supposita versui, fit ita , .

23. Holtz, *Donat et la tradition de l'enseignement*, pp. 62, 64; Keil, *Grammatici latini*, 4: 32; 6: 194; 1: 435.

24. Bede, *De orthographia*, and *Bedae opera pars I*, ed. Jones, pp. 25, 35.

25. On separation in English books, see Parkes, *Pause and Effect*, p. 26; on separation in documents, see the charters of King Hlothere of Kent to Abbot Brihtwold, Oethelraed to Abbess Aethelbruh, and King Wihtred of Kent for the Abbey of Lyminge, all dating from before 700, in *ChLA* 3 (1963): nos. 182, 187, 220; see also the contributions by Pierre Chaplais to *Prisca Munimenta: Studies in Archival and Administrative History*, ed. Felicity Ranger (London, 1973).

26. *CLA*, 2 (1935): 273; A. A. Luce, G. O. Simms, P. Meyer, and L. Bieler, eds., *Evangeliorum quattuor Codex Durmachensis*, facsimile ed. (Olten, Switz., 1960). The suggestion of a Northumbrian origin for the Book of Durrow remains speculative; see Ludwig Bieler's review of François Masai, *Essai sur les origines de la miniature dite irlandaise*, *Speculum* 23 (1948): 495–502; T. Julian Brown, "Northumbria and the Book of Kells," *Anglo-Saxon England* 1 (1972): 219–46.

27. ".V. adiuncta .C. cum virga iacente superposita vir clarissimus, .V. geminata cum virga iacente superposita verbi gratia, .V. geminata cum .C. duplice viri clarissimi." Bede, *De orthographia*, in Keil, *Grammatici latini*, 7: 261; and *Bedae opera pars I*, ed. Jones, p. 7. The graphic forms of the abbreviations are reproduced here as the scribe entered them in the margin of Cambridge, Corpus Christi College 221.

28. For example, "L. sola Lucium significat, M. sola Marcum, N. sola Numerium, praeposita G. Gnaeum. sola Publium et cum R. populum Romanum, et subiecta R. rem publicam et praeposita C. litterae patres conscriptas sive post consulatum." Bede, *De orthographia*, in Keil, *Grammatici latini*, 7: 270; and *Bedae opera pars I*, ed. Jones, p. 7.

29. See examples of *notae iuris* in papyri reproduced by Steffens, *Lateinische Paläographie*, pl. 14. For example, in tenth-century Continental codices like Paris, BN lat. 4841 and 7530, the relationship between signs for words and syllables was totally ambiguous, just as it had been in the *notae iuris* of late antiquity.

30. This is apparent in his definition of *in*. "In praepositio significat modo id quod est valde et vim verbi cui praeponitur auget, ut increpuit insonuit in fregit; modo idem quod non, ut invalidus, infirmus; modo ponitur pro eo quod est inter ut benedicta tu in mulieribus; modo pro adversus, ut, 'duo in tres et in duos dividentur; modo pro spatio temporali, cum significat usque, ut dicimus, a mane in noctem, at volumus intelligi usque in noctem.'" Bede, *De orthographia*, in Keil, *Grammatici latini*, 7: 275; and *Bedae opera pars I*, ed. Jones, p. 29

and notes. The scribe of Cambridge, Corpus Christi College 221, inconsistently used the acute accent to distinguish the preposition *a*.

31. See Malcolm B. Parkes, *The Scriptorium of Wearmouth-Jarrow* (Jarrow, 1982), pls. 1, 3.

32. See Maria de Marco, ed., *Ars Tatvini*, in *Tatvini omnia*, CCSL 34 (1968): vi–x; and Law, *The Insular Latin Grammarians*, pp. 66–67, for the surviving codices of the eighth and ninth centuries: Vat. Palat. lat. 1746 (ninth century, in Caroline script), Paris, BN lat. 7560 (s. ix ex., in Caroline script); Paris, BN lat. 17959 (s. viii–ix, in Caroline script); Karlsruhe, Badische Landesbibliothek, Aug. Fragment 119; and Saint Paul in Carinthia, Stiftsbibliothek, a series of fragments (in separated Insular script, s. viii, ex., *CLA*, 8 [1959]: 1127). A manuscript of English provenance, Cambridge University Library Gg 5.35 (Gneuss, "A Preliminary List," no. 12), dates from the eleventh century.

33. Like Bede, Tatwine considered the suprascript line as an optional sign of abbreviation and therefore he implicitly accepted that space alone was sufficient for word demarcation. Tatwine, in *Ars Tatvini*, ed. de Marco, p. 6.

34. "Hae ergo a partibus orationis separare nequeunt, quia sollae positu intellectu carent et ob hoc cuicumque partium pareaeponitur eiudem partis sunt." *Ars Tatvini*, ed. de Marco, pp. 4, 87. Cf. Donatus, *Ars minor*, in Holtz, *Donat et la tradition de l'enseignement*, p. 648.

35. "Figura coniunctionum, ut in omnibus partibus orationis, duplex est aut enim simplex . . . aut composita." Tatwine, in *Ars Tatvini*, ed. de Marco, p. 85.

36. Tatwine, *Aenigma*, in Glorie, *Variae collectiones aenigmatum Merovingicae*, p. 171.

37. See Tatwine, in *Ars Tatvini*, ed. de Marco, e.g., p. 77; cf. Donatus, *Ars minor*, in Holtz, *Donat et la tradition de l'enseignement*, pp. 555–602.

38. Boniface, *Ars grammatica*, in *Bonifatii Ars grammatica*, ed. George John Gebauer and Bendt Löfstedt, CSEL 133B (1980): 20, 39, 76, 80, 98. See the observations by M. Roger, *L'enseignement des lettres classiques d'Ausune à Alcuin* (Paris, 1905), p. 335.

39. Wilhelm Alfred Eckhardt, "Das Kaufinger Fragment der Bonifatius-Grammatik," *Scriptorium* 23 (1969): 280–97 and pl. 99.

40. On Insular paradigms, see Law, *The Insular Latin Grammarians*, pp. 53–64.

41. Boniface, *Ars grammatica*, ed. Gebauer and Löfstedt, 71–73.

42. Bede, *De arte metrica*, ed. C. B. Kendall in *Bedae Opera pars I* (CSEL 123A [1975]), 94–104; Max Manitius, ed., "Micons von St. Riquier, *De primis syllabis*," *Münchener museum für Philologie des Mittelalters und der Renaissance* (1912): 154, lines 22–177. This portion of the text is the work of Dicuil; see A. Van de Vyver, "Dicuil et Micon de Saint-Riquier," *Revue belge de philologie et d'histoire* 14 (1935): 35.

43. See, with certain reservations, Martha Bayless, "*Beatus Quid Est* and the

Study of Grammar in Late Anglo-Saxon England," *Historiographia Linguistica* 20 (1993): 67–110, especially the plate of London, BL Harley 3271, f. 95. For possible origins of this scribal practice, see Erika Eisenlohr, "Alternate Letterforms in the *Book of Kells*," *Gazette du livre médiéval* 24 (1994): 13.

44. See the most recent edition, Bernhard Bischoff, Malcolm B. Parkes, et al., eds., *The Epinal, Erfurt, Werden, and Corpus Glossaries*, EEMF, vol. 22 (Copenhagen, 1988).

45. "Figura est sicut nomine ipso datur intelligi, quaedam conformatio dictionis a communione remota quam ostentationem et habitum possumus nuncupare." John Henry Hessels, ed., *An Eighth-Century Latin-Anglo-Saxon Glossary Preserved in the Library of Corpus Christi College Cambridge (MS no. 144)* (Cambridge, 1890), p. 77, line 182n; John Henry Hessels, ed., *A Late Eighth-Century Latin-Anglo-Saxon Glossary Preserved in the Library of the Leiden University (MS Voss. Qº. Lat. no. 69)* (Cambridge, 1906), p. 24, no. 57. The definition is remodeled from Cassiodorus; cf. Cassiodorus, *Expositio Psalmorum*, 2.2, CCSL 97 (1958): 41, 103.

46. In the circle of Charlemagne, Einhard and Lupus of Ferrières placed verbs in the final position more consistently than any classical author; see Arthur T. Walker, "Some Facts of Latin Word Order," *The Classical Journal* 13 (1918): 652–57. Other Carolingian writers like Hincmar observed a very free word order; see Devisse, *Hincmar, archevêque de Reims*, 2: 932.

47. Priscian, *Institutiones grammaticae*, xv, 39, in Keil, *Grammatici Latini*, 3: 89; Alain de Libera, "De la logique à la grammaire: Remarques sur la théorie de la *determinatio* chez Roger Bacon et Lambert d'Auxerre (Lambert de Lagny)," in *De Ortu Grammaticae: Studies in Medieval Grammar and Linguistic Theory in Memory of Jan Pinborg*, ed. G. L. Bursill-Hall, Sten Ebbesen, and Konrad Koerner (Amsterdam, 1988), pp. 211, 217.

48. Paul Grosjean, "Confusa caligo: Remarques sur les *Hisperica Famina*," *Celtica* 3 (1956): 79–83; Christine Mohrmann, "The Earliest Continental Irish Latin," *Vigiliae Christianae* 16 (1962): 216–33; François Kerlouégan, "Une mode stylistique dans la prose latine des pays celtiques," *Etudes celtiques* 13 (1972–73): 275–97; Michael Winterbottom, "Columbanus and Gildas," *Vigiliae Christianae* 30 (1976): 314–17; and "A Celtic Hyperbaton?" *Bulletin of the Board of Celtic Studies* 27 (1977): 207–12; Michael W. Herren, *Insular Latin Studies: Papers on Latin Texts and Manuscripts of the British Isles, 540–1066* (Toronto, 1981), pp. 7–8; Neil Wright, "Gildas's Prose Style and Its Origins," in *Gildas: New Approaches*, ed. Michael Lapidge and David Dumville (Woodbridge, Suffolk, 1984), pp. 107–28.

49. For Aldhelm's use of stylized noun and adjective combinations in verse, see his *Carmen de virginitate*, in *Aldhelmi opera*, ed. Ehwald, pp. 352–471; PL 89: 237–80. For his tendency in classroom books to use subject-verb-object order in his prose, see his *De metris et enigmatibus ac pedum regulis*, in *Aldhelmi opera*,

ed. Ehwald, pp. 59–204; *PL* 89: 161–238. In other prose, his syntax was exceedingly complex; see *Aldhelm: The Prose Works*, ed. Lapidge and Herren, pp. 3–4.

50. "Ordo ergo partium orationis non indecens ponitur, nam nomen ideo principatum et exordium obtenuit, quia unius cuiusque rei notitia nomine revelatur; nescis enim de qua re quis tecum loquutus sit, nisi nomine prius denudet, ut est: 'Dominus dixit ad me, filus meus es tu' et reliqua; tolle Domini nomen et incerta remanet sententia."

"Quod pronomen verbum praecedens, non principalitate sed ministrando nomini sequitur, cuius enim minister est et obsequio fungitur, eius vestigio adhere debet. Post hoc verbum merito principalite sua, quia secunda pars principalis est in ordinem procedit." Tatwine, in *Ars Tatvini*, ed. de Marco, p. 3.

51. On the variations of word order in Irish Bibles, see Kenney, *Sources for the Early History of Ireland*, p. 626; and Hoskier, *Concerning the Genesis*, 2: 230, 2: 356, and passim.

52. Bede, *De schematibus et tropis*, ed. Kendall, in *Bedae Opera pars I*, pp. 142–51. I am grateful to Malcolm Parkes for this reference.

53. Lloyd W. Daly, *Contributions to a History of Alphabetization in Antiquity and the Middle Ages*, Collection Latomus, vol. 90 (Brussels, 1967), pp. 27–44, 50–59. For an example, see Paul Collart, *Les papyrus Bouriant* (Paris, 1926), p. 19.

54. On the learning of Greek in ancient Rome, see Bernhard Bischoff, "The Study of Foreign Languages in the Middle Ages," rev. ed., in Bischoff, *Mittelalterliche Studien*, 2: 251–52.

55. See *CLA* 2 (1935): 251. See also Wolfenbüttel, Herzog August Bibl. Weissenb. 64, in *CLA* 9 (1959): 1388.

56. Facsimile edition, in Bischoff, Parkes, et al., eds., *The Epinal, Erfurt, Werden, and Corpus Glossaries*; Henry Sweet, *The Epinal Glossary* (London, 1893).

57. Bischoff, Parkes, et al., eds., *The Epinal, Erfurt, Werden, and Corpus Glossaries*; Hessels, *An Eighth-Century Latin-Anglo-Saxon Glossary*.

58. Peter Hunt Blair, *The World of Bede* (New York, 1970), p. 248.

59. See Wallace M. Lindsay, *The Corpus Glossary* (Cambridge, 1921), pp. iv–v.

60. See F. Unterkircher, *Notitiae regionum urbis Romae et urbis Constantinopolitane, Glossarium Latino-Theotiscum: Codex Vindobonensis 162*, Umbrae codicum occidentalium, vol. 2 (Amsterdam, 1960).

61. See, for example, the *Glossarium Ansileubi*, Paris, BN lat. 11529–11530; the *Reichenau Glossary*, Karlsruhe, Badische Landesbibliothek Augiens CCXLVIII; Hans Wilhelm Klein and André Labhardt, *Die Reichenauer Glossen*, 2 vols., Beiträge zur romanischen Philologie des Mittelalters (Munich, 1968–72), with two plates. The relation of word separation to alphabetical glossaries has been remarked on by Malcolm Parkes, in Bischoff, Parkes, et al., eds., *The Epinal, Erfurt, Werden, and Corpus Glossaries*, p. 15.

62. Alcuin, *Orthographia*, in *Alcuinus: De orthographia*, ed. Aldo Marsili (Pisa, 1952); *PL*, 101: 901–20.

63. See, for example, the Leiden Glossary, Leiden, BR Voss. Q. lat. 69, Hessels, *A Late Eighth-Century Latin-Anglo-Saxon Glossary*. Cf. Vat. lat. 3321, *Corpus IV*. Other glossaries, like the *Glossarium Ansileubi*, of which the earliest exemplar comes from Corbie, were compiled in alphabetical order; see Wallace M. Lindsay, J. F. Mountford, and J. Whatmough, *Glossaria latina* (Paris, 1926); cf. Wallace M. Lindsay, *The Corpus, Epinal, Erfurt and Leyden Glossaries* (Oxford, 1942), p. 1.

64. W. Schmitz, *Commentarii notaram tironianarum* (Leipzig, 1893); Paul Legendre, *Un manuel tironien du Xème siècle publié d'après le manuscrit 1597A de la Bibliothèque Nationale* (Paris, 1905); and *Études tironiennes* (Paris, 1907), pp. 51–53.

65. For examples of Byzantine Greek / Latin biblical texts, see Henri Omont, *Facsimilés des plus anciens manuscrits grecs en onciale et en minuscule de la Bibliothèque Nationale du IVe au XIIe Siècle* (Paris, 1892), pls. 5, 5 bis, 7. The bilingual conversations of the *Hermeneumata Pseudodostheana* were written in this format.

66. M. L. W. Laistner, *Bedae Venerabilis Expositio actuum apostolorum et Retractio* (Cambridge, Mass., 1939), p. xiii.

67. See, for example, the distance between reader and lectern in the illuminated miniatures of the sixth-century Vergilius Romanus, Vat. lat. 3867, facsimile edition, 1985. Ancient scribes also kept the support on which they wrote relatively distant; see Bruce M. Metzger, "When Did Scribes Begin to Use Writing Desks?" in *Akten des XI, internationalen Byzantinenkongress* (Munich, 1958), 355–62, reprinted in his *Historical and Literary Studies: Pagan, Jewish, and Christian* (Grand Rapids, Mich., 1968), pls. 3, 4B, 5, 6, 8 (a reader?), 10, 13, 17; George M. Parássoglou, "Some Thoughts on the Postures of the Ancient Greeks and Romans When Writing on Papyrus Rolls," *Scrittura e Civiltà* 3 (1979): pls. 2, 3, 5, 6.

68. See Martial's description of the exchange of gifts during a Saturnalia party, in Roberts and Skeat, *The Birth of the Codex*, pp. 24–29.

69. See Patrick McGurk, "The Irish Pocket Gospel Book," *Sacris Erudiri* 8 (1956): 249–70.

70. On this phenomenon, see Charles Plummer, "On the Colophons and Marginalia of Irish Scribes," *Proceedings of the British Academy* 12 (1926): 11–44. Louis Gougaud, "Les scribes monastiques d'Irlande au travail," *RHE* 27 (1931): 295–96. See also Drogin, *Medieval Scribes and the History of Book Curses*.

71. William Henry Paine Hatch, *An Album of Dated Syriac Manuscripts* (Boston, 1946), pp. 17–18.

72. "Finit. Amen. Finit. O tu quicumque scripseris vel scrutatus fueris vel etiam videris haec volumina, Deum ora . . . [m]issericorda sua . . . per clivosam

mundi viam . . . [a]dusque altissimum. Nomen scriptoris Mulling dicitur. Finiunt quatuor evangelia." Lindsay, *Early Irish Minuscule Script*, pp. 16–17. See above, note 1.

73. Whitley Stokes, *Lives of Saints from the Book of Lismore* (Oxford, 1892), p. 175.

74. C. R. Beazley, *The Dawn of Modern Geography*, 3 vols. (London, 1897–1906), 2: 608–12; facsimile in Kenneth Nebenzahl, *Maps of the Holy Land: Images of Terra Sancta through Two Millennia* (New York, 1986), pp. 30–31.

75. H. H. Glunz, *History of the Vulgate from Alcuin to Roger Bacon: Being an Inquiry into the Text of Some English Manuscripts of the Vulgate Bible* (Cambridge, 1933), pp. 15–22; Raphael Loewe, "The Medieval History of the Latin Vulgate," in *The Cambridge History of the Bible*, 3 vols., ed. G. W. H. Lampe (Cambridge, 1969), 2: 131; Doyle, "The Latin Bible in Ireland," pp. 34–37; Christopher Verey, "Notes on the Gospel Text," in *The Durham Gospels*, EEMF 20 (1980): 70–71; Bruce M. Metzger, *The Text of the New Testament*, 3d ed. (New York, 1992), p. 77.

76. On the textual analysis of Irish manuscripts, see Kenney, *Sources for the Early History of Ireland*, pp. 624–27; Hoskier, *Concerning the Genesis*, 1: 9–11; 2: 95–381; Samuel Berger, *Histoire de la Vulgate pendant les premiers siècles du Moyen Age* (Paris, 1893), pp. 29–45; Cordoliani, "Le texte de la Bible," 14; Hans Glunz, *Britannien und Bibeltext: Der Vulgatatext der Evangelien in seiner Verhältnis zur Irisch-Angelsächsischen Kultur der Frühmittelalters* (Leipzig, 1930), pp. 86–87; Loewe, "Medieval History of the Latin Vulgate," p. 131.

77. For an appreciation of the difficulty of manipulating text written in *scriptura continua*, see Célestin Charlier, "Les manuscrits personnels de Florus de Lyon et son activité littéraire," in *Mélanges E. Podechard* (Lyon, 1943), pp. 71–84, with two plates.

78. Lindsay, *Notae Latinae*, pp. 312–13; Bains, *A Supplement to Notae Latinae*, pp. 49–50.

79. William G. Rutherford, *A Chapter in the History of Annotation, Being Scholia Aristophonica*, vol. 3 of *Scholia Aristophonica* (London, 1905), pp. 47–60.

80. In so doing, they continued developments of ancient Vulgar Latin; see Mohrmann, "The Earliest Continental Irish Latin," pp. 216–33. For the best general overview of Vulgar Latin, see Joseph Herman, *Le Latin vulgaire*, 2d ed. (Paris, 1970).

81. On the assignment of these manuscripts to the ninth century and the presence of word separation, see Gonophore Morrish, "Dated and Datable Manuscripts Copied in England during the Ninth Century: A Preliminary List," *Mediaeval Studies* 50 (1988): 517–30; cf. Kenney, *Sources for the Early History of Ireland*, nos. 575–78; CLA 2 (1935): 204, 215, 199; PS, 1: 163; *Catalogue of Ancient Manuscripts in the British Museum*, 2 vols. (London: 1881–84), 2: 60–61 and pl. 21; 2: 61 and pl. 23; 2: 61–62 and pl. 22.

82. Another Irish reference tool associated with word separation is the peni-

tentiary. See Pierre Adnès, "Penitence," *Dictionnaire de Spiritualité*, 12, pt. 1 (1984), pp. 967–68; Gearóid MacNiocaill, "Fragments d'un coutoumier monastique irlandais du VIIIe–IXe siècle," *Scriptorium* 15 (1961): 228–33 and pl. 12.

83. Pierre Chaplais, "The Origin and Authenticity of the Royal Anglo-Saxon Diploma," in *Prisca Munimenta*, ed. Ranger, pp. 33–34.

84. Eduard Karl Heinrich Heydenreich, *Das älteste Fuldaer Cartular im Staatsarchiv zu Marburg: Das umfangreichste Denkmal in angelsächsischer Schrift auf deutschem Boden* (Leipzig, 1899), with two plates; Steffens, *Lateinische Paläographie*, pl. 54a; Edmund E. Stengel, *Urkundenbuch des Klosters Fulda* (Marburg, 1958), p. xx. The first true English cartularies, in London, BL Cotton Tib. A. xiii, come from the Benedictine priory of Worcester. They doubtless bear witness to the infusion of Continental influence after Abbo's death. See Neil R. Ker, "Hemmings Cartulary: A Description of Two Worcester Cartularies in Cotton Tiberius A. xiii," in *Studies in Medieval History Presented to F. M. Powicke*, pp. 49–75, pls. 1 and 2; Godfrey R. C. Davis, *Medieval Cartularies of Great Britain: A Short Catalogue* (London, 1958), p. 123, no. 1068. Cartularies were late to develop in Italy, and they appeared even later in Byzantium; see Franz Dölger and Johannes Karayannopulos, *Byzantinische Urkundenlehre* 1 (1968): 26.

85. *France: Manuscrits datés*, 3: 303 and pl. 5.

86. See A. Giry, *Manuel de diplomatique* (Paris, 1894), p. 28; H. Bresslau, *Handbuch der Urkundenlehre für Deutschland und Italien* 1 (1912): 94–101; Leiden, BR, Voss. lat. Q. 55; de Meyier, *Codices Vossiani latini*, 2 (1975): 138–39; Gysseling and Koch, *Diplomata Belgica*, pls. 5 and 6. For two eleventh-century German cartularies written at least in part in unseparated script, see *"Gerechtigkeit erhöht ein Volk": Recht und Rechtspflege in Bayern im Wandel der Geschichte*, exhibition catalogue (Munich, 1990), pp. 2–3 (with plates).

87. See the suggestive article by W. D. Elock, "La pénombre des langues romanes," *Revista Portuguesa de Filologia* 11 (1961): 1–19; and Marc van Uytfanghe, "Histoire du latin, protohistoire des langues romanes, et histoire de la communication," *Francia* 11 (1983): 601; and "Le latin des hagiographes mérovingiens et la protohistoire du français . . . à quelle epoque a-t-on cessé de parler latin?" *Romanica Gandensia* 16 (1976): 57, 75. The earliest surviving codices containing Old Irish, dating from the eighth and ninth centuries, are recorded by Martje Draak, "Construe Marks in Hiberno-Latin Manuscripts," in *Mededeelingen der Kroninklijke Nederlandsche Akademie van Wetenschappen*, afd. Letterkunde, n.s., 20, no. 10 (1957): 261–62. Written Irish existed from at least the eighth century; see R. I. Best, *MS 23 N 10 (formerly Betham 145 in the Royal Irish Academy)*, FCIM, vol. 6 (Dublin, 1954), p. v; Rudolf Thurneysen, *Zu irischen Handschriften und Litteraturdenkmälern*, Abhandlungen der königlichen Gesellschaft der Wissenschaften zu Göttingen, Philosophisch-Historische Klasse, n.s., vol. 14, pt. 2 (Berlin, 1912), pp. 22–30.

88. Ralph W. V. Elliott, *Runes: An Introduction* (Manchester, 1959), pp. 19–

20; R. A. S. Macalister, *Corpus inscriptionum insularum Celticarum*, 2 vols. (Dublin, 1945–59); Anthony Harvey, "Early Literacy in Ireland: The Evidence from Ogham," *Cambridge Medieval Celtic Studies* 14 (1987): 1–15. See also Seth Lerer, *Literacy and Power in Anglo-Saxon Literature* (Lincoln, Neb., 1991), p. 11; R. Derolez, *Runica Manuscripta: The English Tradition* (Bruges, 1934).

89. George Calder, *Auraicept na n-éces: The Scholar's Primer, Being the Texts of the Ogham Tract from the Book of Ballymote and the Yellow Book of Lecan and the Text of the Trefhocul from the Book of Leinster* (Edinburgh, 1917), pp. xlvii, 135; Rudolf Thurneysen, *A Grammar of Old Irish*, trans. D. A. Binchy and Osburn Bergin, rev. and enl. ed. with supplement (Dublin, 1946), pp. 24–25.

90. Virginia J. Cyrus, "Linguistic Features of Scribal Spacing," *Visible Language* 5 (1971): 101–10; A. Campbell, *Old English Grammar* (Oxford, 1959), p. 14.

91. C. E. Wright, *English Vernacular Hands from the Twelfth to the Fifteenth Centuries* (Oxford, 1960), pls. 1–2. For other examples of imperfect separation in eleventh-century Anglo-Saxon, see Marguerite-Marie Dubois, *Aelfric, sermonnaire, doctor, et grammarien: Contribution à l'étude de sa vie et l'action bénédictine en Angleterre au Xe siècle* (Paris, 1943), pl. 3 (depicting Paris, BN lat. 943); and the volumes of EEMF. For Irish manuscripts not fully separated, see J. H. Bernard and R. Atkinson, *The Irish "Liber Hymnorum"*, HBS, vols. 13–14 (London, 1898), 1: pl. 2; Françoise Henry and G. L. Marsh Micheli, "A Century of Irish Illumination," *Proceedings of the Royal Irish Academy*: Sec. C 62 (1961–62): 101–64, with 44 plates; R. I. Best and Eóin MacNéill, eds., *"Annals of Inisfallen," Reproduced in Facsimile from the Original Manuscript (Rawlinson B. 503) in the Bodleian Library with a Descriptive Introduction* [s. xi] (Dublin, 1933); James A. Geary, ed., *An Irish Version of Innocent III's "De contemptu mundi"* [s. xv] (Washington, D.C., 1931), pp. 8–12; Kathleen Mulchrone, ed., *The Book of Lecan* [s. xv ex.], FCIM, vol. 2 (Dublin, 1937); John Gwynn, ed., *"Liber Ardmachanus": The Book of Armagh* [s. ix] (Dublin, 1913); Edward Gwynn, ed., *Book of Armagh*, FCIM, vol. 3 (Dublin, 1937); R. A. S. Macalister, ed., *The Book of Mac Carthigh Riobhac, Otherwise, the Book of Lismore* [s. xv-xvi], FCIM, vol. 5 (Dublin, 1950); R. I. Best and Rudolf Thurneysen, eds., *"Senchas Mà": Facsimile of the Oldest Fragments from MS H. 2. 15 of the Library of Trinity College* [s. xiv], FCIM, vol. 1 (Dublin, 1931); cf. the edition by Rudolf Thurneysen, "Aus dem irischen Recht I," *Zeitschrift für celtische Philologie* 14 (1923): 338–92. A list of additional pertinent facsimiles is published by R. I. Best, *Bibliography of Irish Philology and Literature* (Dublin, 1942), pp. 61–64.

92. See Peter Rickard, "Système ou arbitraire? Quelques réflexions sur la soudure des mots dans le manuscrit français du Moyen Age," *Romania* 103 (1982): 470–505. The separation present in *Sermon sur Jonas* on the flyleaf of Valenciennes, BM 521 was exceptional. This text copied in the mid-tenth century was written in a unique form of tironian *hybrida* in which the tironian notes used for the Latin and Caroline letters were employed for the Old French

portion of the text that was generally separated; facsimile: Christine Ruby, "Les premiers témoins du français," in *Le livre au Moyen Age*, ed. Jean Glenisson (Paris, 1988), pp. 132–33 with plates; Guy de Poerck, "Le sermon bilingue sur Jonas du manuscrit Valenciennes 521 (475)," *Romanica Gandensia* 4 (1956): 31–66, and "Les plus anciens textes de la langue française comme témoins de l'époque," *Revue de linguistique romane* 27 (1963): 9–12; Edward Koschwitz, *Les plus anciens monuments de la langue française publiés pour les cours universitaires*, 6th ed. (Leipzig, 1902).

93. On the graphic word in French, see Jean-Claude Milner and François Regnault, *Dire le vers* (Paris, 1987), p. 21; Kendrick, *The Game of Love*, p. 35.

94. For an example of a variant form of the vertical stroke, see C. E. Wright, *English Vernacular Hands*, pl. 2; *PS*, ser. 2: pl. 133; Walter W. Skeat, *Twelve Facsimiles of Old English Manuscripts* (Oxford, 1892), pl. 4.

95. For examples of the *trait d'union*, see Ker, *Catalogue of Manuscripts Containing Anglo-Saxon*, pp. xxxv–xxxvi; C. E. Wright, *English Vernacular Hands*, pls. 1–2; EEMF, 13: 26, 16: 21. For its use in Irish, see *"Annals of Inisfallen,"* ed. Best and MacNéill.

96. Campbell, *Old English Grammar*, pp. 12–13; for examples in Anglo-Saxon, see Ker, *Catalogue of Manuscripts Containing Anglo-Saxon*, p. xxxv; for examples in French copied in England, see Beaulieux, *Histoire de l'orthographie française*, 2: 15.

97. One of the last to receive construction notes was Aldhelm's *De laudibus virginitate*; see Brussels, BR 1650 (s. x), facsimile ed. G. van Langenhove (Bruges, 1941); the manuscript's convoluted "Irish-Latin" artificial word order was no longer comprehensible two centuries later. In the twelfth century and later, the same signs were used to correct scribal error. Thus, the sequential notes added to Troyes, BM 496, one of the archetypes of Bernard of Clairvaux's *Sermones super cantica canticorum*, were added to emend the style, rather than to facilitate reading; see C. H. Talbot, "The Archetypes of Saint Bernard's *Sermones super Cantica*," *Scriptorium* 8 (1954): 231. These notes also disappeared from Latin texts composed after the eleventh century, when Latin word order began more regularly to approach that of the vernacular.

98. Robert Fawtier, *La vie de Saint Samson* (Paris, 1912), p. 108.

99. "Nos decem et septem genitae sine voce sorores . . . . / Tum cito prompta damus rogitanti verba silenter." Glorie, *Variae collectiones aenigmatum Merovingicae*, pp. 412–13.

100. Whitley Stokes and John Stiachan, *Thesaurus palaehibernicus: A Collection of Old Irish Glosses, Scholia, Prose, and Verse*, 2 vols. (Cambridge, 1901–3), 2: 293. The poem written in Old Irish is preserved only in Saint Paul in Carinthia, Stiftsbibliothek sec. xxv.d.86 (ninth century, from Reichenau). It has been retranslated by Kuno Meyer, *Selections from Ancient Irish Poetry* (London, 1928), pp. 83–84.

101. For a facsimile, see Bieler, *Ireland Harbinger of the Middle Ages*, p. 44.

102. William Levison, *England and the Continent in the Eighth Century* (Oxford, 1946), p. 293; Bernhard Bischoff, "Übersicht über die nichtdiplomatischen Geheimschriften des Mittelalters," *Mitteilungen des Instituts für österreichische Geschichtsforschung* 62 (1954): 16–17.

103. Saint Columba, the Irish missionary to Scotland and founder of Iona, was thus described in glosses to the Old Irish *Amra*: "He the tutor, used to sow the word of teaching. He was swift to interpret the glosses. He corrected the Psalms with obelus and asterisk," J. H. Bernard and R. Atkinson, *The Irish "Liber Hymnorum,"* 1: 173, 2: 67 (trans.), cited by Kathleen Hughes, "The Distribution of Irish Scriptoria and Centers of Learning from 730 to IIII," in *Studies in the Early British Church* (Cambridge, 1958), p. 243.

Chapter 5

1. In contrast, the history of manuscript illumination demonstrates that in Germany, the Low Countries, and northern France, Continental artists regularly emulated Irish and especially Anglo-Saxon models. Geneviève L. Micheli, *L'enluminure du haut Moyen Age et les influences irlandaises: Histoire d'une influence* (Brussels, 1939), pp. 63ff. and 131ff.

2. Acute accents were, however, employed at a few centers in Germany (e.g., Cologne and Freising in the ninth century) and in some abbeys near the English Channel (e.g., Arras in the tenth century).

3. Bernhard Bischoff, *Paläographie des römischen Altertums und des abendländischen Mittelalters* (Berlin, 1979), p. 217 n. 53.

4. For a rare example, see C. H. Beeson, *Lupus of Ferrières as Scribe and Text Critic: A Study of His Autograph Copy of Cicero's "De oratore"* (Cambridge, Mass., 1930).

5. See Wallace M. Lindsay, "Breton Scriptoria: Their Latin Abbreviation Symbols," *Zentralblatt für Bibliothekswesen* 29 (1912): 265. Microfilms at the IRHT. The manuscript, probably written at the Abbey of Saint-Pol-de-Léon, was later transferred to Fleury during the Norman invasions of the tenth century; see Mostert, *The Library of Fleury*, BF799; Bradshaw, *The Early Collection of Canons*, p. 33. *France: Manuscrits datés* 7 (1984): xxxviii, 491; Ludwig Bieler, *The Irish Penitentials*, Scriptores latini Hiberniae, vol. 5 (Dublin, 1963), pp. 12–13.

6. See Léon Fleuriot, *Dictionnaire des glosses en vieux breton* (Paris, 1904), pl. 1 (Cambridge, Univ. Libr. Ff. 4. 42), pl. 2 (Leiden, BR Voss lat. F. 96A), pl. 3 (Paris, BN lat. 10290), pl. 51 (Luxembourg, BN 89), pl. 71 (Angers, BM 477). On Voss. lat. F. 96A, see de Meyier, *Codices Vossiani latini* 1 (1973): 215 and 4 (1984): pl. 7e. See also J. Alexander, "A Note on the Breton Gospel Books," in Francis Wormald, *An Early Breton Gospel Book: A Ninth Century Manuscript from the Collection of H.L. Bradfer Lawrence 1887–1965* (Cambridge, for the Roxburghe Club, 1977), esp. pls. 15, 17–27; Lindsay, "Breton Scriptoria," p. 265, lists

Paris BN lat. 12021, *Cannones*; lat. 13029, cf. *France: Manuscrits datés* 3 (1974): 732, *Smaragadi Grammatica* (Corbie); Vat. Reg. lat. 296, Orosius; London, BL Cotton Otho E XIII, *Cannones*; Bern, Burgerbibliothek 167, Virgil.

7. Kenney, *Sources for the Early History of Ireland*, no. 496; Samuel Berger, *Histoire de la Vulgate, pendant les premiers siècles du Moyen Age* (Paris, 1893), pp. 47, 388; Rand, *A Survey of the Manuscripts of Tours*, no. 140 and pl. 151; Cordoliani, "Le texte de la Bible," pp. 15–16.

8. C. R. Morey, Edward Kennard Rand, and Carl H. Kraeling, *The Gospel Book of Landevennec (The Harkness Gospels) in the New York Public Library* (Cambridge, Mass., 1931).

9. Robinson, *Cambridge: Dated and Datable Manuscripts*, no. 140 and pl. 12; *NPS*, 1: pl. 109.

10. Henry R. Lyon, *A Wulfstan Manuscript Containing Institutes, Laws and Homilies: British Museum Cotton Nero A.I.*, EEMF, vol. 17 (1971), facsimile of ff. 47 and 194v in the appendix; Neil Ker, "The Handwriting of Archbishop Wulfstan," in *England Before the Conquest: Studies in Primary Sources Presented to Dorothy Whitelock*, ed. Peter Clemoes and Kathleen Hughes (Cambridge, 1971), pp. 328–30; Bradshaw, *The Early Collection of Canons*, p. 33. This codex also contains the *Capitulary* of Ansegisus.

11. McNeill and Gamer, *Medieval Handbooks of Penance*, pp. 56, 62 and pl. following p. 62; Bradshaw, *The Early Collection of Canons*, p. 33.

12. Kenney, *Sources for the Early History of Ireland*, no. 31; see François Kerlouégan, "Une mode stylistique dans la prose latine des pays celtiques," *Etudes celtiques* 13 (1972–73): 283–84; and Nora K. Chadwick, *The Age of the Saints in the Early Celtic Church* (London, 1963), pp. 155–56; Patrick Sims-Williams, "Thought, Word and Deed: An Irish Triad," *Eriu* 29 (1978): 85.

13. Marc van Uytfanghe, "Histoire du latin, protohistoire des langues romanes, et histoire de la communication," *Francia* 11 (1983): 579–613.

14. See Erich Petzet and Otto Glauning, *Deutsche Schrifttafeln des IX bis XVI Jahrhunderts aus Handschriften des K. Hof. und Staatsbibliothek in München*, 5 vols. (Munich, 1910–12), 1: pls. 3–14; Gerhard Eis, *Altdeutsche Handschriften* (Munich, 1949), pls. 20–45; Riché, *Écoles et enseignement*, pp. 235–36.

15. J. M. Clark, *The Abbey of Saint Gall as a Centre of Literature and Art* (Cambridge, 1926), pp. 55–57; Eis, *Altdeutsche Handschriften*, pl. 6.

16. Clark, *The Abbey of Saint Gall*, p. 57 and plate facing p. 68; *CLA* 7 (1956): 976; Drogin, *Medieval Scribes and the History of Book Curses*, p. 8; M. Drogin, *Medieval Calligraphy: Its History and Technique* (London, 1980), p. 13.

17. Lehmann, *Mittelalterliche Bibliothekskataloge Deutschlands und der Schweiz*, pp. 66–82.

18. Facsimile, *NCE*, 8: 721.

19. Riché, *Écoles et enseignement*, p. 91; Kenney, *Sources for the Early History of Ireland*, nos. 411–13. On the early unseparated charters, see Albert Bruckner,

"Paläographische Studien zu den älteren St. Gallen Urkunden," *Studi medievali,* n.s., 4 (1931): 119–30 with six plates dating from 744 to 817, all unseparated. See also *ChLA* 1 (1954): 40–108 and 2 (1956): 109–76, for unseparated charters of the eighth century. Moengal's separated writing is visible in two books: Basel, Universitätsbibliothek A. vii. 3, in Joseph Smits van Waesberghe, *Muzikgeschiedenis der Middeleeuwen* (Tilburg, 1939–42), pl. following p. 222; and Zurich, Zentralbibliothek C 57, in Bruckner, *Scriptoria medii aevi Helvetica,* 3: 124 and pl. 16; for charters written by him, see Hermann Wortmann, *Urkundenbuch der Abtei St. Gallen* (Zurich, 1863–82), 2: 44, 48, 60, 87.

20. For a list of the pertinent plates, see Albert Bruckner, "Paläographische Studien zu den älteren St. Gallen Urkunden (iii)," *Studi medievali,* n.s., 6 (1933): 291–93.

21. E. Dümmler, *MGH: Poetae Latini Aevi Carolini* 2 (1884): pl. 3. Under Abbot Salomo III (880–919), the scribe Sintram copied the *Evangelium longum,* Saint Gall, Stiftsbibliothek 53, with interword space varying between 1.5 and 2 times the unity of space. The *Saint Gall Psalter of Bamberg,* once in the library of Otto III, was also written in separated script. See Adolf Merton, *Die Buchmalerei in St. Gallen von neunten bis elften Jahrhundert,* 2d ed. (Leipzig, 1923), pls. 17 (St. Gall 77), 26 (St. Gall 23), 27 (Zurich, Zentralbibliothek C. 77), 34–36 (Einsiedeln 17, miniature with banderole).

22. The earliest example appears to be Munich, Bayerische Staatsbibliothek Clm. 954, f. 199v; Solange Corbin, in *Encyclopédie de la musique,* s.v. "Neume"; Bischoff, *Die südostdeutschen Schreibschulen,* 1: 203–4 and pl. 6d.

23. *Paléographie musicale,* ser. 1, 1 (1889).

24. *Paléographie musicale,* ser. 2, 1 (1900; new ed., 1970).

25. *Paléographie musicale,* ser. 2, 2 (1924; reprint, 1968).

26. Jammers, *Tafeln zur Neumenschrift,* pl. 8.

27. See Wolfram von den Steinen, *Notker der Dichter und seine geistige Welt,* 2 vols. (Bern, 1948), 2: pls. 3 and 4; J. Froger, "Epître de Notger sur les lettres signicatives," *Etudes grégoriennes* 5 (1962): 23–72; Smits van Waesberghe, *Muzickgeschiedinis der Middeleeuwen,* pp. 96, 165. See St. Gall 533 (end of the ninth or early tenth century); Merton, *Buchmalerei,* pl. 41; Pierre Riché, "Le rôle de la mémoire dans l'enseignement médiéval," in *Jeux de Mémoire: Aspects de la mnémotechnie médiévale,* ed. Bruno Roy and Paul Zumthor (Montreal, 1985), p. 40.

28. Scaglione, *The Classical Theory of Composition,* p. 109; Paul Piper, ed., *Die Schriften Notkers und seine Schule* (Freiburg in Breisgau, 1892–93), pp. xii ff.; Max Hermann Jellinek, *Geschichte der neuhochdeutschen Grammatik von den Anfängen bis auf adelung,* Germanische Bibliothek, vol. 7 (Heidelberg, 1914), pp. 426–32; L. M. de Rijk, "On the Curriculum on the Arts of the *Trivium* at St. Gall from c. 850–c. 1000," *Vivarium* 1 (1963): 53–54, 83–84; Anneli Luhtala, "Syntax and Dialectic in Carolingian Commentaries on Priscian's *Institutiones Grammaticae,*" *Historia Linguistica* 20 (1993): 174–77.

29. Zurich, Zentralbibliothek C 98, ff. 38v–66v. I am indebted to the Zentralbibliothek for providing me with a partial reproduction of these leaves.

30. See, for example, the Saint Gall copy of the *Benedictine Rule*, Saint Gall, Stiftsbibliothek 914; f. 103 reproduced in *NCE* 2: 284. Bruckner, *Scriptoria medii aevi Helvetica*, 3: 24, 26; 4: 39.

31. On Abbot Gregory, see M. B. Parkes, "A Note on MS Vatican, Bibl. Apost., lat. 3363," in *Boethius: His Life, Thought, and Influence*, ed. Margaret Gibson (Oxford, 1981), p. 426. For an Einsiedeln manuscript prepared under Gregory, see *Codex 121 of the Monastery Library Einsiedeln*, facsimile ed. (Weinheim, 1991).

32. Albert Bruckner, *Diplomata Karolinorum: Faksimile-Ausgabe der in der Schweiz liegenden originalen Karolinger und Rudolfinger Diplome* (Basle, 1969–74), esp. 2: nos. 46 ff.

33. See Bernhard Bischoff, *Lorsch im Spiegel seiner Handschriften* (Munich, 1974), pl. 9; Elmar Mittler, *Bibliotheca Palatina Ausstellung der Universität Heidelberg in Zusammenarbeit mit der Bibliotheca Apostolici Vaticana* (Heidelberg, 1986), 1: 126; 2: 82, 83, 90; Bernhard Bischoff, "Deutsche Karolingische Skriptorien in den Handschriften des Erzbischofs Laud," in A. C. de la Mare and B. C. Barker-Benfield, *Manuscripts at Oxford: An Exhibition in Memory of Richard William Hunt (1908–1979)* (Oxford, 1980), pl. 9.

34. See numerous plates in Daniel, *Handschriften des zehnten Jahrhunderts aus der Freisinger Dombibliothek*; Bischoff, *Die südostdeutschen Schreibschulen*, 1: pls. 2d–4d; Bischoff, *Kalligraphie in Bayern*, pls. 5–8.

35. Theodor Bitterauf, ed., *Die Traditionen des Hochstifts Freising*, Quellen und Erörterungen zur bayerischen und deutschen Geschichte, n.s., vol. 4 (Munich, 1905; reprint, Aalen, 1967), no. I, with plate.

36. Robert Amiet, *The Benedictionals of Freising*, HBS, vol. 88 (Maidstone, Kent, 1974). A partial microfilm is on deposit at the IRHT.

37. See, for example, Munich, Staatsbibliothek Clm. 6370, 6371, and 6372, written in separated script with minimal traces of Insular influence for the library of Bishop Abraham. Space was frequently inserted after monosyllabic prepositions; tree diagrams and iconic displays of syllogisms similar to those found at Reims and Fleury facilitated comprehension; see Daniel, *Handschriften des zehnten Jahrhunderts aus der Freisinger Dombibliothek*, pp. 143–44, 158–59, 175–76.

38. Chroust, *Monumenta Palaeographica*, ser. 1, 1: 3. Note the presence of the terminal capital *S*.

39. Chroust, *Monumenta Palaeographica*, ser. 1, 2: 1. However, a second cartulary was written between 891 and 894 in word blocks greater than fifteen characters in length. Chroust, *Monumenta Palaeographica*, ser. 1, 6. Bischoff, *Die südostdeutschen Schreibschulen*, 1: 223–24 and pl. 8c. Note use of the terminal capital *S*.

40. Bischoff, *Die südostdeutschen Schreibschulen*, 1: pls. 5d–8b; Bischoff, *Kalligraphie in Bayern*, pls. 1–4.

41. Georg Swarzenski, *Die Regensburger Buchmalerei des X. und XI. Jahrhunderts* (Leipzig, 1901), pl. 11; Bischoff, *Kalligraphie in Bayern*, pl. 22; Schramm and Mütherich, *Denkmale*, no. 111; Florentine Mütherich, "The Library of Otto III," in Ganz, *The Role of the Book*, 1: 20. See also the separated manuscripts written by the monk Hartwic, who studied at Reims and Chartres.

42. Chroust, *Monumenta Palaeographica*, ser. 2, 1; Bischoff, *Die südostdeutschen Schreibschulen*, 1: pls. 5a–5c; Bischoff, *Kalligraphie in Bayern*, pls. 10–14.

43. Chroust, *Monumenta Palaeographica*, ser. 2, 1: 6.

44. Klaus Gamber, "Das Salzburger Arno-Sakramentar," *Scriptorium* 14 (1960): 106–8 and pl. 13.

45. Bischoff, *Die südostdeutschen Schreibschulen*, 2: pls. 3a–8a.

46. Austria, *Katalog der datierten Handschriften* 1 (1969): no. 17 and pl. 17.

47. See Austria, *Katalog der datierten Handschriften* 5 (1981): nos. 146–47 and pls. 1–5; cf. 1 (1969): no. 83 (Cod. 12696) and pl. 18.

48. Paris, BN lat. 9389, a Gospel book written at Echternach or brought there from the Continent, was separated. On the Echternach Gospels, see Brown, "The Irish Element," pp. 109–12; Alexander, *Insular Manuscripts, 6th to the 9th Century*, no. 11; *CLA* 5 (1950): 578.

49. Ernst Dümmler, ed., *Alcuini carmina*, in *MGH: Poetae latini aevi Carolini* 1, pt. 1 (1880): 320; reprinted with English translation, Walter Horn and Ernest Born, *The Plan of Saint Gall*, 3 vols. (Berkeley, 1979), 1: 145.

50. See Edward Kennard Rand and George Howe, "The Vatican Livy and the Script of Tours," *Memoirs of the American Academy in Rome* 1 (1917): 19–56 and pls. 1–4, in conjunction with Bernhard Bischoff, "Die Hofbibliothek Karls des Grossen," in *Karl der Grosse: Lebenswerk und Nachleben*, 2: 42–62 and pls. 1–6; cf. D. Bullough, "Alcuino e la tradizione culturale insulare," *Settimane di studio del Centro Italiano di Studi sull'alto Medio-Evo* 20 (1973): 584–85. An English fragment of Alcuin, Chicago, Newberry Library frag. 15, is written in separated script. For other English copies of Alcuin, see Gneuss, "A Preliminary List," nos. 417, 418, 438, 511.

51. Bischoff, "Hofbibliothek Karls des Grossen," p. 55.

52. *CLA* 6 (1953): 707; L. W. Jones, "The Scriptorium at Corbie II: The Script and the Problems," *Speculum* 22 (1947): 385; Stiennon, *Paléographie du Moyen Age*, pp. 77–79, 96–97. For a facsimile opening, see Gérard Ooghe, "L'écriture de Corbie," in *Corbie abbaye royale* (Lille, 1963), pp. 277–78. On the relation of the script to Caroline minuscule, see Philippe Lauer, "La reforme carolingienne de l'écriture latine et l'école calligraphique de Corbie," *Mémoires présentés par divers savants à l'Academie des Inscriptions et Belles Lettres* 13 (1924): 417–40. The scribe of Amiens, BM 12, occasionally used a point to separate

short words; Wallace M. Lindsay, "Separation of Words by Dots," *Palaeographia latina* 2 (1923): 16.

53. See Stiennon, *Paléographie du Moyen Age*, p. 79. Ganz, "The Preconditions of Caroline Minuscule," pp. 26–27.

54. Mittler, *Bibliotheca Palatina*, 1: 120–21; 2: 76, 79; W. Braunfels, *Das Lorches Evangeliar: Faksimile Ausgabe* (Munich, 1967).

55. Bischoff, "Hofbibliothek Karls des Grossen," p. 62; Rand and Howe, "The Vatican Livy"; Parkes, *Pause and Effect*, p. 31.

56. *CLA* 5 (1950): 562. See L. D. Reynolds, *Texts and Transmissions: A Survey of the Latin Classics* (Oxford, 1983), p. 209.

57. For an interesting discussion of the relation between vowels and syllable divisions, see Adams, "What Good Is Orthographic Redundancy?," pp. 197–255.

58. Shipley, *Certain Sources of Corruption in Latin Manuscripts*, pp. 7–8. Understanding Livy's vocabulary and syntax remained problematic until the end of the Middle Ages; see Monfrin, "Les traducteurs et leur public," pp. 260–61.

59. Shipley, *Certain Sources of Corruption in Latin Manuscripts*, p. 17.

60. Ibid., pp. 18–21.

61. See the remarks of Abbo of Fleury, in Guerreau-Jalabert, *Abbon de Fleury: Quaestiones Grammaticales*, pp. 244–45 (28).

62. The same signs were present even more frequently in eleventh-century books written in separated script.

63. Willis, *Latin Textual Criticism*, p. 87; Havet, *Manuel de critique verbale*, p. 307 (sec. 1234).

64. Brussels, BR 10470-3, 10859, and Rouen, BM 1470, see A. Van de Vyver, "Dicuil et Micon de Saint-Riquier," *Revue belge de philologie et d'histoire* 14 (1935): 35.

65. Mario Esposito, "An Unpublished Astronomical Treatise by the Irish Monk Dicuil," *Proceedings of the Royal Irish Academy* 26, Sec. C (1906–7): 378–446 and pl. 22; cf. Tours, BM 803, in Rand, *A Survey of the Manuscripts of Tours*, no. 191, pl. 185.

66. Schramm and Mütherich, *Denkmale*, no. 95; Mütherich, "The Library of Otto III," p. 20; Bieler, *Ireland Harbinger of the Middle Ages*, p. 132 (facs.). See T. A. M. Bishop, "Autographa of John the Scot," in *Jean Scot Erigène et l'histoire de la philosophie: Laon 7–12 juillet 1975*, Colloques internationaux du CNRS, no. 561 (Paris, 1977), pp. 89–94, with plates of Reims, BM 875 and Laon, BM 81; Ludwig Traube and E. K. Rand, *Autographia des Iohannes Scottus*, in part 5 of Ludwig Traube, *Palaeographische Forschungen*, Abhandlungen der königlich-bayerischen Akademie der Wissenschaften, Philosophisch-philologische und historische Klasse, vol. 26, pt. 1 (Munich, 1912), esp. pls. 1–3, 6, 7; cf. Edward Kennard Rand, "The Supposed Autographa of John the Scot," *University of California Publications in Classical Philology* 5, no. 8 (1920): 131–41 and pls. 1–

11. The secretarial script in Laon, BM 81 also appears to be separated; Bishop, "Autographa of John the Scot," pl. 2. E. Jeauneau is currently preparing a monograph on Johannes Scottus's autograph writings.

67. John Contreni, *The Cathedral School of Laon from 850 to 930: Its Manuscripts and Masters*, MBMRF, vol. 29 (Munich, 1978), pls. 1–3; and "Le formulaire de Laon: Source pour l'histoire de l'école de Laon au début du Xe siècle," *Scriptorium* 27 (1973): 21–29; and "The Formation of Laon's Cathedral Library in the Ninth Century," *Studi Medievali*, ser. 3, 13 (1972): 919–35.

68. See, for example, Paris, Bibliothèque Mazarine, 561, Jean-Pierre Rothschild, "Traduire au Moyen Age," in *Le livre au Moyen Age*, ed. Jean Glenisson (Paris, 1988), p. 55 (pl. 39).

69. Ludwig Traube, *O Roma nobilis: Philologische Untersuchungen aus dem Mittelalter*, Abhandlungen der königlich-bayerischen Akademie der Wissenschaften, Philosophisch-philologische und historische Klasse, vol. 19, pt. 2 (Munich, 1891).

70. The manuscripts are listed by Kenney, *Sources for the Early History of Ireland*, no. 364.

71. See ibid., pp. 553–55.

72. Rudolf Thurneysen, *A Grammar of Old Irish*, trans. D. A. Binchy and Osburn Bergin, rev. and enl. ed., with supplement (Dublin, 1946; reprint, 1975), p. 6.

73. See Clark, *Abbey of Saint Gall*, pp. 55–57.

74. *NPS*, 1: pls. 32–33; Alexander, *Insular Manuscripts, 6th to the 9th Century*, no. 63; Kenney, *Sources for the Early History of Ireland*, no. 364, i; Lindsay, *Early Irish Minuscule Script*, pp. 36–40.

75. "Dubthach hos versus transcripsit tempore parvo Indulge, lector, quae mala [*sic*] scripta vides." Lindsay, *Early Irish Minuscule Script*, p. 36.

76. Cesare Questa, "Il metro e il libro: Per una semiologia della pagina scritta di Plauto, Terenzio, Prudenzio, Orazio," in *Atti del convegno internazionale il libro e il testo Urbino, 20–23 settembre 1982*, ed. Cesare Questa and Renato Raffaelli (Urbino, 1984), pls. 30–40; complete facsimile: H. Hagen, *Codex Bernensis 363*, Codices graeci et latini photographice depicti duce Scatone de Vries, vol. 2 (Leiden, 1897); Chatelain, *Paléographie des classiques latins*, 1: pls. 76–77; Kenney, *Sources for the Early History of Ireland*, no. 364, vii; Colgrave and Mynors, *Bede's Ecclesiastical History of the English People*, p. xlvi; Lindsay, *Early Irish Minuscule Script*, pp. 50–54. Mostert, *The Library of Fleury*, BF 174; Bieler, *Ireland Harbinger of the Middle Ages*, pp. 124–25 (facsimile of f. 167).

77. See, for example, with regard to Bern, Burgerbibliothek 363, Otto Keller and A. Holder, eds., *Quinti Horatii Flacci opera*, 2 vols. (Leipzig and Jena, 1899–1925), 1: xix–xxii; A. C. Clark, *The Descent of Manuscripts* (Oxford, 1918), pp. 27–31.

78. See William Reeves, ed., *The Life of Saint Columba* (Dublin, 1857), pl. 3.

For the attribution to the scribe of the text, see Anderson and Anderson, *Adomnan's Life of Columba*, p. 543 n. 12.

79. Kenney, *Sources for the Early History of Ireland*, no. 364, iii; Henri Omont, "Inventaire sommaire des manuscrits grecs," *Mélanges Charles Graulx* (Paris, 1884), pl. following p. 312. Samuel Berger, *Historie de la Vulgate pendant les premiers siècles du Moyen Age* (Paris, 1893), pp. 116, 411.

80. Kenney, *Sources for the Early History of Ireland*, no. 364, iv; Ludwig Bieler, *Psalterium Graeco-Latinum: Codex Basiliensis A. VII.3*, Umbrae codicum occidentalium, vol. 5 (Amsterdam, 1960); other facsimiles: August Baumeister, *Denkmäler des klassischen Altertums*, 3 vols. (Munich, 1885–88), 2: 1133; Smits van Waesberghe, *Muzikgeschiedenis der Middeleeuwen*, pl. following p. 223; Lindsay, *Early Irish Minuscule Script*, pp. 47–50.

81. Kenney, *Sources for the Early History of Ireland*, no. 364, v; complete facsimile: H. C. M. Rettig, *Antiquissimus quatuor evangeliorum canonicorum codex Sangellensis graeco-latinus* (Zurich, 1836); *PS*, 1: pl. 179; Steffens, *Lateinische Paläographie*, pl. 47; Bruckner, *Scriptoria medii aevi Helvetica*, 3: 28, 51, 60, 61 and pls. 13–14; Lindsay, *Early Irish Minuscule Script*, pp. 47–50.

82. Hermann Rönsch, "Zur biblischen Latinität aux dem cod. Sangallensis der Evangelien," *Romanische Forschungen* 1 (1883): 419–26; Berger, *Histoire de la Vulgate*, p. 114.

83. Kenney, *Sources for the Early History of Ireland*, no. 364, vi; complete facsimile: Alexander Reichardt, *Der Codex Boernerianus* (Leipzig, 1909); Lindsay, *Early Irish Minuscule Script*, pp. 47–50.

84. Tore Janson, *Prose Rhythm in Medieval Latin from the 9th to the 13th Century*, Studia latina Stockholmiensia, vol. 20 (Stockholm, 1975), p. 39.

85. Margaret Gibson, "The Continuity of Learning Circa 850–Circa 1050," *Viator* 6 (1975): 5.

86. "Figura a fingo verbo oritur. Ergo figura proprie dicitur limitatio quaedam membrorum seu formarum longitudine seu latitudine seu his omnibus consistens, dicta a fingendo, id est a componendo." Sedulius Scottus, *In Donati artem minorem*, ed. Bengt Löfstedt, in *CCCM* 40C (1977): 14.

87. Sedulius Scottus, *In Priscianum*, ed. Bengt Löfstedt, in *CCCM* 40C (1977): 73–75.

88. "*Figurae verborum quot sunt? Duae. Quae? Simplex, ut lego, conposita, ut neclego Quomodo?* . . . *Ex duobus integris, ut doleo: do uerbum est, leo nomen est.*" Julian of Toledo, in *Ars Iuliani Toletani episcopi*, ed. Maria A. H. Maestre Yenes, Vestigios del pasado, vol. 5 (Toledo, 1973), p. 75.

89. "Diastole secundum quosdam proprie est intercolomnium, id est spatium quod sit inter columnas; stola enim Grece, colomna dicitur Latine, inde separatio. Sed meilus 'interdictum' interpretatur, unde et Beda dicit: 'Diastole grece, Latine interdictum.'" Sedulius Scottus, *In Donati Artem maiorem*, ed. Bengt Löfstedt, in *CCCM* 40B (1977): 49.

90. Holtz, *Donat et la tradition de l'enseignement*, pp. 439–40.

91. *Ars Laureshamensis expositio in Donatum maiorem*, ed. Bengt Löfstedt, in *CCCM* 40A (1977): 45.

92. "... sunt quaedam praepositiones, quae separatae numquam ponuntur, sed semper coniuntae, ut di, dis, re, se, am, con. Et sunt quaedam, quae separate semper ponuntur et numquam coniunctae, *ut apud et penes* (Donatus 389, 28)." *Ars Laureshamensis*, ed. Löfstedt, p. 139.

93. "*Aut coniunguntur et separantur (Donatus, 389.26)*, Utrumque scilicet faciunt: et possunt separatae cum aliis iungi partibus, et coniunctae, prout voluntas loquentis exigit." *Ars Laureshamensis*, ed. Löfstedt, p. 139. Cf. André Martinet, *A Functional View of Language*, Waynflete Lectures, 1961 (Oxford, 1962), p. 92.

94. "Yfen Grece, Latine coniunctio dicitur, eo quod duas partes in unam pronuntiationem coniungat." *Ars Laureshamensis*, ed. Löfstedt, p. 183 (re Donatus, 372, 2).

95. "*Figura*. Figura dicitur a fingendo, id est, componendo, quia fingere dicere componere; unde, compositores luti figulos vocamus. Et est figura rerum forma, vel figura est res artificialis, quae aut ex una parte constat et simplex dicitur, aut ex pluribus et composita vocatur." W. Fox, ed., *Remigii Autissiodorensis in Artem Donati minorem commentum* (Leipzig, 1902), p. 13.

96. "*Antevolens (Donatus, 372, 2)*, id est praecurrens. In istis igitur verbis ne erret puer putando duas esse partes, subtus ponitur hyfen coniungens duo in unum. Est autem Graecum nomen, Latine sonat coniunctio. Coniungit enim male separata et interpretatur supposita coniunctio [In the manuscript containing this text, Einsiedeln, Stiftsbibliothek 172, p. 205, the scribe wrote the compound words *subterposita* and *antevolens* with minor spaces separating syllables]. Diastole, scilicet accentus dissimilis hyfen, quia, sicut ille coniungit, ita iste separat. Proprie autem diastole est intercolumnium, id est spatium, quod fit inter columnas. 'Stole' enim dicitur columna, inde diastole dicitur disiunctio, eo quod male coniuncta disiungat. *Ad imam*, id est ad finem. *Discernuntur*, id est separantur. *Cohaerentia*, id est, coniungentia ut 'virginis, ira' [In the manuscript *virginis, ira* is written *virgini s,sira*; Einsiedeln, 172, p. 207]." Keil, *Grammatici latini*, 8: 229. Microfilm at the IRHT.

97. David Ganz, *Corbie in the Carolingian Renaissance*, Beihefte der Francia, 20 (Sigmaringen, 1990), p. 42. In a conversation I had with Julian Brown in February 1985, he confirmed the absence of tironian notes in Insular manuscripts. To my knowledge, the earliest English examples of tironian notes date from the late eleventh century and are in Oxford, Saint John's College 17. The semi-syllabic, semi-ideographic conventions of Hangul, the Korean writing system, were invented in the fifteenth century; see Taylor, "The Korean Writing System."

98. Reusens, *Eléments de paléographie*, pp. 27–28; Chatelain, *Introduction à la lecture des notes tironiennes*, pp. 1–2.

99. Denis Muzerelle, "Analyse, transcription, et description des notes tironiennes (aperçu de quelques problèmes méthodologiques)," in Peter Ganz, ed., *Tironische Noten*, Wolfenbütteler Mittelalter Studien, vol. 1 (Wiesbaden, 1990), pp. 17, 27–29.

100. For examples, see the plates in Chatelain, *Introduction à la lecture des notes tironiennes*; and M. Prou and A. de Boüard, *Manuel de paléographie latine et française*, 4th ed. (Paris, 1924), pp. 117–18 and pl. 2.

101. For example, the signs for *et* and *est*.

102. In Bern, Burgerbibliothek 207, the Insular form of the *est* abbreviation was used instead of the usual tironian sign; Chatelain, *Introduction à la lecture des notes tironiennes*, p. 129.

103. The earliest tironian notes in an English manuscript date from the end of the eleventh century; Oxford, Saint John's College 17.

104. Paul Legendre, *Un manuel tironien du Xe siècle publié d'après le manuscrit 1597A de la Bibliothèque Nationale* (Paris, 1905).

105. See, for example, the following tironian Psalters: Paris, BN lat. 2178, 1327, 13160, and NAL 442. For an example of mixed notes and punctuation, see Bern, Burgerbibliothek 611, in Steffens, *Lateinische Paläographie*, pl. 56; Paris, BN lat. 2326; Arthur Mentz, "Die Tironischen Noten: Eine geschichte der Römischen Kurzschrift," *Archiv für Urkundenforschung* 17 (1942): pl. 5 and p. 261.

106. These columns are present in Paris, BN lat. 1327. In the Italian syllabic shorthand, such punctuation is not prominent; see the plates published by Luigi Schiaperelli, "Tachigrafia sillabica latina in Italia—Apponti," *Bolletino: Accademia italiana di Stenographia* 4 (1923); Carlo Cipolla, "Quattro documenti Astesi conservati nella biblioteca di sua maestà in Torino (955–1078)," *Miscellanea di storia italiana* 25 (1887): pl. 2; Julien Havet, "La tachygraphie italienne du Xe siècle," *Academie des inscriptions et belles lettres: Comptes rendus des séances*, ser. 4, 15 (1897): 351–75, reprinted in J. Havet, *Oeuvres* (Paris, 1896), 2: 483–503. The same absence of punctuation characterizes medieval Greek shorthand; see Michael Gitlbauer, *Die Ueberreste griechischer Tachygraphie im Codex Vaticanus Graecus 1809*, Denkschriften der Kaiserlichen Akademie der Wissenschaften; Philosophisch-Historische Classe, vol. 28, pt. 2 (Vienna, 1878), with 14 plates. For an eleventh-century manuscript with marginal musical notation that implied a similarly broad eye-voice span, see Robert G. Babcock, *Reconstructing a Medieval Library: Fragments from Lambach* (New Haven, 1993), fig. 21.

107. It is clear that the graphic concision that tironian notes offered for *scholia*, and not their supposed facility in oral transcription, was their principal appeal; see Legendre, *Etudes tironiennes*, p. 71; Paul Legendre, "Notes tironiennes du Vatic. lat. reg. 846," in *Mélanges Chatelain*, pp. 312–31 with one plate following p. 326.

108. Devisse, *Hincmar, archêveque de Reims*, 2: 952.

109. For an example of this type of script, see Bern, Burgerbibliothek 357;

Paris, BN lat. 7505, NAL 1595, lat. 9603; and Montpellier, Ecole de Médecine, 334, reproduced in Chatelain, *Introduction à la lecture des notes tironiennes*, pls. 1–6; Milan, Biblioteca Ambrosiana, M. 12. sup., reproduced in Steffens, *Lateinische Paläographie*, pl. 56c; see also Emile Chatelain and Paul Legendre, *Hygini astronomica: Texte du manuscrit tironien de Milan*, Bibliothèque de l'Ecole des Hautes Etudes, facs. 180 (Paris, 1909). Other excellent examples of *hybrida* are Paris, BN lat. 18554, e.g., ff. 85v and 87 (the gloss, from Notre Dame or Beauvais); and Leiden, BR Voss. lat. Q 98, Pliny the Younger, *Epistola* 1.1–2, reproduced in S. G. de Vries, *Exercitationes palaeographicas in bibliotheca universitatis Lugduno-Batavae* (Leiden, 1890). On the advantages of using tironian notes as a script for annotation, see Legendre, "Notes tironiennes du Vatic. lat. reg. 846," p. 313.

110. Legendre, *Etudes tironiennes*, does not record a single codex dated or datable by criteria rigorous enough to warrant inclusion in any of the catalogues of *manuscrits datés*.

111. Paris, BN lat. 1327 and 13160 are examples of tironian Psalters written with separated rubrics. In the glossaries contained in Paris, BN lat. 190, some of the definitions are written in separated script.

112. W. Schmitz, "Notenschriftliches aus der Berner Handschrift 611," in *Commentationes Wölfflinianae* (Leipzig, 1891), pp. 9–13; Legendre, *Etudes tironiennes*, p. 55; Mostert, *The Library of Fleury*, BF 222–23.

113. Chatelain, *Introduction à la lecture des notes tironiennes*, pp. 213–14 and pl. 3; Rand, *A Survey of the Manuscripts of Tours*, no. 58 and pls. 70–71, tironians not noted; Legendre, *Etudes tironiennes*, pp. 57–58.

114. Chatelain, *Introduction à la lecture des notes tironiennes*, pp. 214–21 and pls. 4–5; Rand, *A Survey of the Manuscripts of Tours*, no. 155 and pl. 163; Legendre, *Etudes tironiennes*, p. 57 (no. 50).

115. Chatelain, *Introduction à la lecture des notes tironiennes*, p. 120; Rand, *A Survey of the Manuscripts of Tours*, no. 172; Legendre, *Etudes tironiennes*, p. 64 (no. 107); Bede, *De natura rerum*, ed. Charles W. Jones, in *Bedae opera pars I*, CCSL 113A (1975): 180 (no. 88).

116. Chatelain, *Introduction à la lecture des notes tironiennes*, pp. 124–25; Rand, *A Survey of the Manuscripts of Tours*, no. 101 and pl. 117; Legendre, *Etudes tironiennes*, p. 64 (no. 108).

117. Paul Legendre, "Remarques sur les notes tironiennes du manuscrit 13 du Chartres (f. 4–7)" and "Commentaire sur la VIᵉ *Eclogue* de Virgile," in Legendre, *Etudes tironiennes*, pp. 1–41 and 71–88. This codex is no longer extant.

118. See, for example, the charter of an act of July 939 of Téotolon, archbishop of Tours, Archives Départementales d'Indre-et-Loire, reproduced in *Musée des archives départementales*, pp. 25–27 and pl. 10.

119. André Vernet, ed., *Histoire des bibliothèques françaises*, vol. 1 (Paris, 1988), p. 429 (pl. 7).

Chapter 6

1. See, for example, the early catalogues of the library of Saint Gall, in Lehmann, *Mittelalterliche Bibliothekskataloge Deutschlands und der Schweiz*, pp. 71–89.

2. On the effect of logic on the restructuring of medieval grammar, see especially de Rijk, *Logica modernorum*, pp. 97–125.

3. For an example of the new libraries characteristic of the eleventh century, see Jean Gessler, *Une bibliothèque scolaire du XIᵉ siècle*, rev. ed. (Brussels, 1935).

4. The ancient failure to define the word precisely may be contrasted to the modern linguistic assertion that graphic verbal boundaries in all languages are self-apparent; cf. Edward Sapir, *Language: An Introduction to the Study of Speech* (New York, 1921), pp. 34–35. Jack Goody and Robert Scholes have pointed out that in preliterate cultures, a word for "word" does not exist; see Jack Goody, *The Domestication of the Savage Mind* (Cambridge, 1971); and Scholes, "On the Orthographic Basis of Morphology." A corollary of this observation may be that in *scriptura continua* cultures, words for "word" remain ambiguous.

5. L. M. de Rijk, ed., *Garlandus Compotista: Dialectica, First Edition of the Manuscripts with an Introduction on the Life and Works of the Author and Contents of the Present Works*, Wijskerige Teksten en Studies, vol. 3 (Assen, 1959), pp. 64–65; cf. André Martinet, *A Functional View of Language*, Waynflete Lectures, 1961 (Oxford, 1962), p. 92.

6. R. H. Robins, *Ancient and Mediaeval Grammatical Theory in Europe, with Particular Reference to Modern Linguistic Doctrine* (London, 1951), pp. 20–22. Cf. Scaglione, *The Classical Theory of Composition*, p. 109.

7. Garland's dialectical *opera* as well as his computational tracts were copied exclusively in separated script.

8. On the general relation between syllogisms, writing, and graphic word separation, see Olson, *The World on Paper*, pp. 20–44.

9. L. M. de Rijk, *Petrus Abaelardus: Dialectica, First Complete Edition of the Parisian Manuscript*, Wijskerige Teksten en Studies, vol. 1, 2d rev. ed. (Assen, 1970), pp. 147–48.

10. De Rijk, *Petrus Abaelardus: Dialectica*, pp. 68–69; see Brian Stock, *Implications of Literacy: Written Language and Modes of Interpretation in the Eleventh and Twelfth Centuries* (Princeton, 1983), pp. 372–76; Jean Jolivet, *Arts du langage et théologie chez Abélard* (Paris, 1969), pp. 25–26.

11. Abelard, *Dialectica*, 176, 1–2; 194, 37–195, 1, cited by Jolivet, *Arts du langage*, p. 35.

12. Had the Romans of the second century not been intimidated by the superior level of Greek literature, grammar, and philosophy, it is doubtful that they would have discarded the separation of words by interpuncts.

13. Cohen, *La Grande invention*, 1: 235; A. R. Millard, "*Scriptio Continua* in

Early Hebrew: Ancient Practice or Modern Surmise?" *Journal of Semitic Studies* 15 (1970): 2–15.

14. Millard, "*Scriptio Continua* in Early Hebrew," pp. 2–15; Cohen, *La Grande invention*, 1: 231. See *Encyclopaedia Judaica*, 5: 1396–1407, for representative plates of the Dead Sea Scrolls.

15. Bradley, "On the Relation Between Spoken and Written Language," p. 214; James Barr, "Reading a Script Without Vowels," in William Haas, ed., *Writing Without Letters* (Manchester, 1976), pp. 92–93; de Kerckhove, "Logical Principles," p. 156.

16. Peter Brown, *The World of Late Antiquity A.D. 150–750* (London, 1971), p. 64.

17. In the *opuscula* of Fulbert of Chartres, for example; see Behrends, *The Letters and Poems of Fulbert of Chartres*, pp. 260–61.

18. See, for example, *Codices Graeci et Latini photographice depicti duce Scalone de Vries* 13 (1909).

19. Paul Ewald and Gustav Loewe, *Exempla scriptura Visigoticae* (Heidelberg, 1883), pl. 31. For an impression of Arabic-like demarcation of verbal boundaries in glosses, see Barcelona, ACA Ripoll 168 (s. xi), f. 5v, Boethius, *De arithmetica*; Beer, *Die Handschriften des Klosters Santa Maria de Ripoll*, 1: pl. 12.

20. For Barcelona, ACA Ripoll 106, see Millàs y Vallicrosa, *Assaig d'història*, pp. 214–19 and pl. 16.

21. Lindsay, *Notae Latinae*, p. 386; and "The Letters in Early Latin Minuscule," *Palaeographia latina* 1 (1922): 27; Léopold Delisle, "Manuscrits de l'abbaye de Silos acquis par la Bibliothèque Nationale," *Mélanges de paléographie et de bibliographie* (Paris, 1880), pp. 56–57.

22. C. Thulin, *Zur Überlieferungsgeschichte des Corpus Agrimensorum* (Göteborg, 1911), pp. 55–66, p. 65 (pl. of f. 82); Beer, *Die Handschriften des Klosters Santa Maria de Ripoll*, 1: 60–62, pls. 4–9; Millàs y Vallicrosa, *Assaig d'història*, pp. 214–19 and pl. 16; Riché, *Écoles et enseignement*, pp. 159–60.

23. The scribe used the Insular sign for *autem*. Terminal signs included an occasional long *j* in words and the consistent use of the long *j* in Roman numerals. The scribe also used a superscript vertical stroke for the terminal *m*.

24. Beer, *Die Handschriften des Klosters Santa Maria de Ripoll*, 1: 56, 94–95; Millàs y Vallicrosa, *Assaig d'història*, pp. 212–13; Riché, *Écoles et enseignement*, p. 159. The elevated round *s*, the capital *S*, the capital *NT* ligature were frequently used for word endings, and the capital *X* as a terminal form also appeared. The ampersand was restricted to the terminal position, and the usual symbols for terminal *-tur*, *-orum*, *-us*, and *m* were commonly employed.

25. Beer, *Die Handschriften des Klosters Santa Maria de Ripoll*, 1: 9, 98, 107 and pl. 12; Riché, *Écoles et enseignement*, p. 160. The capital *NT* ligature was used only at line endings, and the capital terminal *S* occurred only in headings written all in capitals where the penultimate letter was reduced in size. In

this codex, marginal glosses in Arabic are present, providing separated points of entry to the text.

26. See Riché, *Écoles et enseignement*, p. 159; and A. Mundó, "Moissac, Cluny et les mouvements monastiques de l'est des Pyrénées du Xe au XIe siècle," in *Pour un IXe Centenaire*, p. 213.

27. Delisle, *Cabinet des manuscrits*, 1: 512 (no. 40); *France: Manuscrits datés* 2 (1962): 133 and pl. 8; *Catalogue général des manuscrits latins* 3 (1952): 166–67; Avril et al., *Manuscrits enluminés de la péninsule ibérique*, no. 22; Jean Vezin, "Une importante contribution à l'étude du scriptorium de Cluny à la limite des XIe et XIIe siècles," *Scriptorium* 21 (1967): 318.

28. On the dates, see M. Alamo, *DHGE* 11 (1939): 330–32.

29. *France: Manuscrits datés* 4, i (1981): 351 and pl. 9.

30. See Archer M. Huntington, *Initials and Miniatures of the IXth, Xth, and XIth Centuries from the Mozarabic Manuscripts of Santo Domingo de Silos in the British Museum* (New York, 1904); A. Ruiz, *DHGE* 14 (1960): 623–27.

31. Paris, BN NAL 2171, f. 26; Marius Férotin, *Recueil des chartes de l'abbaye de Silos* (Paris, 1897), pp. 17–18. For another unseparated charter of 1020, see Paris, BN lat. 11832, no. 2.

32. Paris, BN lat. 11832, nos. 12 and 31.

33. In NAL 2170, ff. 1–233, Johannes Cassianus's *Collationes*, written in the tenth or early eleventh century in hierarchical word blocks exceeding twenty characters in maximum length, a late-twelfth-century emendator added separated marginal finding notes as well as the usual successor note to the *diastole*, and accents to distinguish words. On ff. 237–55 in the same codex, the *Vita Martialis*, copied in hierarchical word blocks of fewer than twenty characters in length, was emended by the accenting of monosyllables, the addition of hyphens, and the use of vertical strokes to clarify word boundaries. Avril et al., *Manuscrits enluminés de la péninsule ibérique*, nos. 17 and 27; Delisle, "Manuscrits de l'abbaye de Silos," pp. 78–79, no. x.

34. Cottineau, *Répertoire topo-bibliographique*, 1: 1435.

35. I am indebted to John Dagenais for indicating this manuscript to me and for providing me with a photograph of f. 176. On this codex, see T. Rojo, "La biblioteca del arzobispo don Rodrigo Jiménez de Rada y los manuscritos del monasterio de Santa Maria de Huerta," *Revista eclesiástica: Organo del clero español*, ser. 3, 1 (1929): 217–18.

36. F. 176v, "Pro misero peccatore qui hunc librum qualitercumque correxit et notulas accentum asicubi in pluribus dictionibus anotavit qui legerit aut viderit ex karitate suppliciter oret Dominum et dicat saltim, Domine missere super peccatore vel peccatoribus."

37. Emmanuel Poulle, "L'astrolabe médiéval d'après les manuscrits de la Bibliothèque Nationale," *BEC* 112 (1954): 84.

38. Millàs y Vallicrosa, *Assaig d'història*; Van de Vyver, "Les premières tra-

ductions," pp. 266–90. Gerbert wrote to Lobet of Barcelona for the translation of a treatise on the astrolabe which has been identified by modern scholars as the *De utilitatibus astrolopsus*; Bubnov, *Gerberti opera mathematica*, pp. 101–2; Lattin, *The Letters of Gerbert*, letter 32 (Havet 24), p. 69.

39. Beer, *Die Handschriften des Klosters Santa Maria de Ripoll*, 1: 57–59; Millàs y Vallicrosa, *Assaig d'història*, esp. pp. 150–51, 207–9, and pl. 7; cf. Van de Vyver, "Les premières traductions," p. 275 n. 38 [*sic*]; Werner Bergmann, "Der Traktat *De mensura astralabi* des Hermann von Reichenau," *Francia* 8 (1970): 89, 94; Federico Udina Martorell, "Gerberto y la cultura hispanica: Los manuscritos de Ripoll," in *Gerberto, scienza, storia e mito: Atti del Gerberti Symposium (Bobbio 25–27 Iuglio 1983)* (Bobbio, 1985), pp. 48–49; and in the same volume, Emmanuel Poulle, "L'astronomie de Gerbert" (pp. 611–12) and G. Beaujouan, "Les apocryphes mathématiques de Gerbert" (pp. 656–57), tend to support the Catalonian origin of Ripoll 225.

40. Microfilm at the IRHT; Mostert, *The Library of Fleury*, BF 1452; Pellegrin, *Les Manuscrits classiques latins* 2, pt. 1 (1982): 87–89; Millàs y Vallicrosa, *Assaig d'història*, p. 161 and pls. 10–11; Van de Vyver, "Les premières traductions," p. 276; Bergmann, "Der Traktat," pp. 89, 94; Karl Ferdinand Werner, "Zur Überlieferung der Briefe Gerberts von Aurillac," *Deutsches Archiv für Erforschung des Mittelalters* 17 (1961): 102–3; Bubnov, *Gerberti opera mathematica*, p. lxxxi; Guerreau-Jalabert, *Abbon de Fleury: Quaestiones Grammaticales*, p. 190.

41. There are numerous other examples, Paris, BN lat. 11248 (s. xi in.), contains the Latin astrolabe treatise on ff. 1–32. Poulle, "L'astrolabe médiéval," p. 101; Millàs y Vallicrosa, *Assaig d'història*, p. 177 and passim and pls. 9, 14–15; Van de Vyver, "Les premières traductions," p. 276; Delisle, *Inventaire des manuscrits latins*; Bergmann, "Der Traktat," pp. 93, 94. The text was canonically separated with interword space. A further indication of the scribe's consciousness of the word as a graphic unit was the presence, on f. 29v, of a suspended ligature. Diagrams were omitted in this transcription, but Arabic words in the text were set off by capitals and separated. On f. 5, an early emendator added a *trait d'union* in an Arabic name divided at the end of a line and accented the *i* in the Arabic name Algenubíe. In Bern Burgerbibliothek 196, ff. 1–8 (s. x ex. or xi in.), copied at Fleury, the treatise was also transcribed in separated script with interword space varying between 1.33 to 2 unities of space. I am grateful to Dr. C. V. Steiger, Librarian of the Bern, Burgerbibliothek, for providing me with a photocopy of this text. Mostert, *The Library of Fleury*, BF 105; Van de Vyver, "Les premières traductions," p. 276; Werner, "Zur Überlieferung," p. 103. In Vat. reg. lat. 1661 (s. xi ex.), formerly in the library of Pierre Petau, the astrolabe texts were copied on ff. 80–85v. A microfilm of this codex is at the IRHT; Pellegrin, *Les Manuscrits classiques latins* 2, pt. 1 (1982): 341–43; Millàs y Vallicrosa, *Assaig d'història*, p. 171 and pl. 8; Van de Vyver, "Les premières traductions," p. 282; Bergmann,

"Der Traktat," pp. 89, 94; Werner, "Zur Überlieferung," p. 103 n. 27. In Paris, BN lat. 14065 (s. xi ex.), the Lobet translations fell on ff. 47–52v of a composite manuscript. Poulle, "L'astrolabe médiéval," p. 101; Delisle, *Inventaire des manuscrits latins*, vol. 1. The scribe separated the text canonically, with interword space that was equivalent to 2.85 times the unity of space. He used suspended ligatures, and an apparently contemporary emendator added *traits d'union*. In Paris, BN lat. 7377C, ff. 32–33, the texts were also separated. In Paris, BN lat. 7412 (s. xi), a variant and perhaps earlier recension of the astrolabe translations that fell on ff. 1–19v, the scribe separated his words. On the recension, see Van de Vyver, "Les premières traductions," pp. 281–82; cf. Poulle, "L'astrolabe médiéval," p. 84. On Paris, BN lat. 7413, see also Poulle, "L'astrolabe médiéval," p. 102; Bergmann, "Der Traktat," pp. 92, 94. See also Marcel Detombes, "Un astrolabe carolingien et l'origine de nos chiffres arabes," *Archives internationales d'histoire des sciences* 58–59 (1962): 22–30, 43–45. The text was illustrated with schematic diagrams and charts with sequential alphabetical tie notes to link the Arabic names to the apposite stars. Van de Vyver, "Les premières traductions," pl. 3. In Munich, Staatsbibliothek Clm. 560, a manuscript written under French influence at a German center in the first half of the eleventh century, the same variant corpus falls on ff. 1–16. Millàs y Vallicrosa, *Assaig d'història*, p. 181 and passim; Van de Vyver, "Les premières traductions," p. 282; Bergmann, "Der Traktat," pp. 90, 94. Here, too, the scribe separated words by a combination of space, terminal forms, and monolexic abbreviations, with interword space varying from equivalence to 2 times the unity of space.

42. Van de Vyver, "Les plus anciennes traductions," pp. 666–84.

43. Ibid., pp. 666–67; Millàs y Vallicrosa, *Assaig d'història*, pp. 246–67 and pls. 18–19.

44. Van de Vyver, "Les plus anciennes traductions," pp. 666–68; Millàs y Vallicrosa, *Assaig d'història*, p. 248 n. 1. Folios 1–55v, written by another hand, contain the *Tractuli* of Guido of Arezzo; see Joseph Smits van Waesberghe, ed., *Tres tractuli Guidonis Aretini* (Buren, 1975), p. 36.

45. Van de Vyver, "Les plus anciennes traductions," pp. 666, 668.

46. John M. Burnham, *Palaeographia Iberica: Fac-similés de manuscrits espagnols et portugais (IXe–XVe siècles) avec notices et transcriptions*, fasc. 2 (Paris, 1920), no. 23. Burnham lists two additional plates. See also Van de Vyver, "Les premières traductions," p. 286; Guillermo Antolín, *Catalogo de los códices latinos de la Real Biblioteca del Escorial*, 5 vols. (Madrid, 1910–23), 1: 320–404; P. Ewald, "Reiserbericht," *Neues Archiv* 6 (1881): 236–41; 8 (1883): 357–59.

47. Intersyllabic space was largely suppressed, and interword space was 3.75 times the unity of space. The terminal forms of *m* and *-orum* were found in the usual form, as was the elevated terminal *s*.

48. Burnham, *Palaeographica Iberica*, no. 24. At San Millan of Cogolla,

the architecture was profoundly influenced by Arabic models; see Emile Mâle, *Art and Artists of the Middle Ages*, trans. Sylvia Stallings Lowe (Redding Ridge, Conn., 1986), p. 55. Terminal forms were identical to those in Escorial I. d. 2.

49. Folio 50v. On this manuscript, see *Archiv für altere deutsche Geschichtskunde* 8 (1839): 363–64; G. F. Hill, *The Development of Arabic Numerals in Europe* (Oxford, 1915). I am indebted to Dr. Martin Germann of the Manuscript Department of the Kantons-, Stadt-, und Universitätsbibliothek, Zurich, for generously providing me with a microfilm of this text.

50. Van de Vyver, "Les premières traductions," p. 286; Bubnov, *Gerberti opera mathematica*, pp. 101–2; Lattin, *The Letters of Gerbert*, letter 25 (Havet 17), pp. 64 n. 6, 68.

51. Hans Fischer, *Die lateinischen Pergamenthandschriften der Universitätsbibliothek Erlangen* (Erlangen, 1928), pp. 449–50; see also G. Friedlein, ed., *Boetii, De institutione arithmetica libri II; De Institutione musica libri V; Accedit geometria quae fertur Boetii* (Leipzig, 1867), collated as codex e, see pp. 395–401; G. Friedlein, *Gerbert, die Geometrie des Boethius und die Indischen Ziffern* (Erlangen, 1861), pl. 6; Hill, *The Development of Arabic Numerals in Europe*, pp. 28–29; Bubnov, *Gerberti opera mathematica*, p. xxxi. On the distinction between Pseudo-Boethius's *De geometria (in two books)* and *De geometria (in five books)*, see Lattin, "The Origin of Our Present System of Notation," pp. 189–90. Terminal forms included the conventional sign for *-bus* and *e* cedilla used at word beginnings. *Prosodiae* were the successor note to the *diastole* and suspended *ct* ligatures (added) and extended *ct* ligatures within words.

Prosodiae (which did not include the *trait d'union*) included the acute accent in Greek words and a rare instance of a hyphen used as a *trait d'union*, that is, as an interline sign of word continuation. In a later copy of Pseudo-Boethius's *De geometria (in two books)*, Paris, BN lat. 7377C, ff. 18v–34v, written in Lorraine in the middle or late eleventh century, Arabic numerals were present in canonically separated script with interword space 2 times the unity of space. The text was explicated on f. 18 by a schematic diagram. See Detombes, "Un astrolabe carolingien," pp. 38–39, no. 12; Bubnov, *Gerberti opera mathematica*, p. lvii. Gerbert included Arabic numbers in the table for the abacus attached to his *Regulae de numeroroum abaci rationibus*. In Paris, BN lat. 8663, f. 49, dating from ca. 1000 and probably copied at Fleury, this table was set in a text separated by space, terminal forms, and monolexic abbreviations indicating conventional signs. Detombes, "Un astrolabe carolingien," pp. 38–39, no. 9; Bubnov, *Gerberti opera mathematica*, p. lviii; Mostert, *The Library of Fleury*, BF 1157. In Montpellier, Bibliothèque de l'Ecole de Médecine H. 491, a book reported to originate from Chartres in the early eleventh century, Gerbert's table of Arabic numbers was set in separated script, with space often omitted after monosyllabic prepositions. Microfilm and *notice* are at the IRHT. Detombes, "Un astrolabe carolingien," pp. 38–39, nos. 10 and 11; Bubnov, *Gerberti opera mathematica*, pp. xxxix–xi. In another early eleventh-century copy of Gerbert's *Regulae de numerorum abaci rationibus*, Leiden, BR Scaliger 38, Gerbert's Arabic numerals were written in the context of separated script 2 times the unity of space.

Bernelinus, Gerbert's most distinguished mathematical student, composed a *Liber abaci* that also contained a table of Arabic numbers. In Vat. Reg. lat. 1661, dating from the end of the eleventh century, this table was set in separated script. Microfilm and *notice* are at the IRHT. This codex is described above among the manuscripts of the translations of Lobet of Barcelona. Bubnov, *Gerberti opera mathematica*, p. lxxxii. In Vat. Reg. lat. 1071, also of late eleventh-century French origin, the Arabic numerals in Bernelinus's *Liber abaci* were set in canonically separated script. In Rouen, BM 489, Gerbert's *Regulae de numerorum abaci rationibus* was transcribed at the reformed Abbey of Fécamp in Normandy at the end of the eleventh century in canonically separated script. Bubnov, *Gerberti opera mathematica*, p. lxxxv. For word separation in other copies of Gerbert's *Regulae*, see Appendix, Table A1. In Munich, Staatsbibliothek Clm. 14272, copied by Hartwic, a student of Fulbert's, at Saint Emmeram of Regensburg in the first quarter of the eleventh century, Arabic numerals were used as tie notes in a manuscript written in separated script, see f. 37v. On this codex, see Chapter 9, below. The last of the great treatises to explain the use of Arabic numbers and to present their *figurae*, Garland's *Regulae super abacum*, was composed in the second half of the eleventh century and survived only in separated and canonically separated manuscripts of the late eleventh century. For additional twelfth-century codices, see Detombes, "Un astrolabe carolingien," p. 39, nos. 20–22. Leiden, BR Voss. lat. O 95; Oxford, Saint John's College 17; London, BL Arundel 343.

52. "In geometria vero non minor in docendo labor expensus est; cuius introductioni abacum id est tabulam dimensionibus aptam, opere scutarii effecit. Cuius longitudini in XXVII diductae, novem numero notas omnem numerum significantes disposuit. Ad quarum etiam similitudinem mille corneos effecit caracteres, qui per XXVII abaci partes mutuati, cuiusque numeri multiplicionem sive divisionem designarent; tanto compendio numerorum multitudinem dividentes vel multiplicantes, ut prae nimia numerositate potius intelligi quam verbis valerent ostendi. Quorum scientiam qui ad plenum scire desiderat legat eius librum quem scribit ad C[onstantinum] grammaticum; ibi enim haec satis habundanterque tractata inveniet." Latouche, ed. and trans., *Richer: Histoire de France*, 2: 62–64.

53. While some of the manuscripts were written in Visigothic and others in Caroline letter forms, all were written either in separated or canonically separated script, and the transliterated Arabic terms, like the Greek citations embedded in Insular codices, were written all in capitals and always separated. Many of the manuscripts were accompanied by tables and schematic drawings to aid the reader in understanding the complicated astronomical and mathematical

relationships. In one of the tables, letters of the alphabet were used as tie notes for the explication of the diagram, in an adaption of Insular sequential signs, first used for syntax notes, to an analogous purpose predicating similar ocular gestures. The general appearance of the written page of the Arabic scientific translation was entirely brown or black with rubrics, and colored or illuminated initials were entirely lacking. Only two manuscripts possessed contemporary *traits d'union*, one sparsely and the other a single time. The acute accent and the successor note to *diastole* were not prominent in these books copied before 1050.

Chapter 7

1. See, for example, Cajori's magisterial *A History of Mathematical Notations*; Herbert Westren Turnbull, *The Great Mathematicians* (New York, 1961); Clarence Irving Lewis and Cooper Harold Langford, *Symbolic Logic*, 2d ed. (New York, 1959), pp. 3–26; and "History of Symbolic Logic," in James R. Newman, *The Word of Mathematics* (New York, 1956), pp. 1859–77; George A. Miller, "The Mathematicians Who Counted," a review of Newman, *The Word of Mathematics*, *Contemporary Psychology* 2 (1957): 38–39; Ernst Cassirer, "The Influence of Language upon the Development of Scientific Thought," *Journal of Philosophy* 39 (1942): 309–27. The parallel implications of changes in numerical and language notation have been described by Tzeng and Hung, "Linguistic Determinism," pp. 238–39. See also Bradley, "On the Relation Between Spoken and Written Language," p. 215.

2. Louis Couturat, *La Logique de Leibniz d'après des documents inédits* (Paris, 1901), pp. 85–87; cf. Miles A. Tinker, "Numerals versus Words for Efficiency in Reading," *Journal of Applied Psychology* 12 (1928): 190–99; and "How Formulae are Read," *American Journal of Psychology* 40 (1928): 476–83; and "The Relative Legibility of the Letters, the Digits, and of Certain Mathematical Signs," *Journal of General Psychology* 1 (1928): 472–95.

3. On the concept of iconic representation, see Charles S. Peirce, *Collected Papers* (Cambridge, Mass., 1931–58); Roman Jakobson, "Language in Relation to Other Communication Systems," *Selected Writings*, 8 vols. (The Hague, 1962–88), 2: 701; Terence Hawkes, *Structuralism and Semiotics* (Berkeley, 1977), pp. 128–29, 135; Leo Treitler, "The Early History of Music Writing in the West," *Journal of the American Musicological Society* 35 (1982): 239–41.

4. See the comments of Bradley, "On the Relation Between Spoken and Written Language," p. 212.

5. See Priscian, *De figuris numerorum quas antiquissimi habent codices*, in Keil, *Grammatici latini*, 3: 406–7.

6. Roy Harris, "How Does Writing Restructure Thought?" *Language and Communication* 9 (1989): 103.

7. David Eugene Smith, *History of Mathematics* (Boston, 1925); Georges

Ifrah, *From One to Zero: A Universal History of Numbers*, trans. Lowell Bair (New York, 1985), pp. 131–50, 313–20.

8. Ifrah, *From One to Zero*, pp. 203–7, 343–67, 387–96.

9. On the role of short-term memory in reading mathematical notation, see Couturat, *La Logique de Leibniz*, p. 95. On the parallels between oralization in verbal and numerical exercises, see Sokolov, *Inner Speech and Thought*, pp. 192–211.

10. The ancient Romans in daily life used other and less ambiguous number symbols equivalent to tironian notes; see Jean Mallon, *La Paléographie romaine* (Madrid, 1952), pp. 123–41.

11. G. Friedlein, *Die Zahlzeichen und das elementare Rechnen der Griechen und Römer und des christlichen Abendlandes vom 7. bis 13. Jahrhundert* (Erlangen, 1869), pp. 20–21; Cajori, *A History of Mathematical Notations*, 1: 37; Guy Beaujouan, "Le symbolisme des nombres à l'époque romane," *Cahiers de civilisation médiévale* 4 (1961): 163–64; P. Lejay, "Alphabets numériques latins," *Revue de Philologie, de littérature et d'histoire anciennes*, n.s., 22 (1890): 146–62.

12. Pseudo-Bede, *De loquela per gestum digitorum libellus*, in *PL* 90: 693. Cf. Cajori, *A History of Mathematical Notations*, 1: 37; Friedlein, *Die Zahlzeichen*, pp. 20–21.

13. Jean-Gabriel Lemoine, "Les anciens procédés de calcul sur les doigts en Orient et en Occident," *Revue des études islamiques* 6 (1932): 1–58; Florian Cajori, "Comparison of Methods of Determining Calendar Dates by Finger Reckoning," *Archeion* 9 (1928): 31–42; Florence A. Yeldham, "An Early Method of Determining Calendar Dates by Finger Reckoning," *Archeion* 9 (1928): 324–25; A. Cordoliani, "Un manuscrit de comput écclesiastique mal connu de la Bibliothèque Nationale de Madrid," *Revista de archivos, bibliotecas y museos* 57 (1951): 11–12 and plate following p. 16; Jean-Claude Schmitt, *La raison des gestes dans l'occident médiéval* (Paris, 1990), pp. 254–55.

14. For a list of the manuscripts of Bede's *De temporum ratione*, see *Bedae opera pars VI, 2*, ed. C. W. Jones, in *CCSL* 123B (1977). On the early manuscripts of Pseudo-Bede, see C. W. Jones, *Bedae Pseudepigrapha* (New York, 1939), pp. 53–54.

15. Bede, *De temporum ratione, Bedae opera pars VI, 2*, ed. Jones, pp. 272–73.

16. Dáibhí ó Crónin, "The Irish Provenance of Bede's *Computus*," *Peritia* 2 (1983): 229–47; C. W. Jones, *Bedae opera de temporibus*, Mediaeval Academy of America, 41 (Cambridge, Mass., 1943), pp. 105–10; Charles W. Jones, "The Lost Sirmond Manuscript of Bede's *Computus*," *English Historical Review* 52 (1937): 204–19.

17. For an example of a Roman/Greek concordance, see Vat. Reg. lat. 577, f. 58v, facsimile in R. H. Bautier and Monique Gilles, *Odorannus de Sens: Opera omnia* (Paris, 1972), pl. 2. For another example, see Leiden, BR Voss. lat. Q. 33

(s. x). See also Bernhard Bischoff, "The Study of Foreign Languages in the Middle Ages," rev. ed., in Bischoff, *Mittelalterliche Studien*, 2: 232.

18. On Ireland as the nexus between Eastern Mediterranean culture and Europe, see Hillgarth, "Visigothic Spain and Early Christian Ireland," pp. 177–78.

19. See, for example, a charter of Swaefred, King of Essex, in 704, *ChLA* 3 (1963): no. 188; a charter of Cenwulf, King of Mercia, in 799, *ChLA* 3 (1963): no. 223.

20. The Romans occasionally used the long *I* for the first in a series of *I* strokes at the beginning of or within a number; Mallon, *La Paléographie romaine*, p. 150. The use of the *I* longa in the terminal position in both words and numbers is not treated by W. M. Lindsay in his study "The Letters in Early Latin Minuscule," *Palaeographia latina* 1 (1922): 27–28.

21. On the *virga*, see Sandys, *Latin Epigraphy*, pp. 54–55; Gordon and Gordon, *Paleography of Latin Inscriptions*, pp. 166–82; Gordon, *Illustrated Introduction to Latin Epigraphy*, pp. 47–48; Ifrah, *From One to Zero*, p. 318.

22. Mallon, *La Paléographie romaine*, pp. 124–35.

23. For some examples, see Gillian R. Evans, "The Influence of Quadrivium Studies in the Eleventh- and Twelfth-Century Schools," *Journal of Medieval History* 1 (1975): p. 153, pl. 1.

24. *Prologus N. Ocreati in halceph ad Adelbordum Batensem magistrum suum*, ed. C. Henry, *Zeitschrift für Mathematik und Physik* 25 (1880): 129; David Eugene Smith and Louis Charles Karpinski, *The Hindu-Arabic Numerals* (Boston, 1911), pp. 119–20.

25. Cajori, *A History of Mathematical Notations*, 1: 58.

26. Cf. Lindsay, *Notae Latinae*, pp. 66–67, 129–30.

27. This form of abbreviation has been noted in passing by Richard Lemay, "The Hispanic Origin of Our Present Numeral Forms," *Viator* 8 (1977): 452–53.

28. Gordon and Gordon, *Paleography of Latin Inscriptions*, p. 171; Arthur Earnest Gordon and Joyce S. Gordon, *Album of Dated Latin Inscriptions*, 4 vols. (Berkeley, 1958–65), 1: 132 and pl. 60a; 4: 60; R. Schöne, "Zum Hildesheimer Fund," *Hermes* 3 (1869): 469–75; Theodor Mommsen, "Zahl- und Buchzeichen," *Hermes* 22 (1887): 605–11; Cagnat, *Cours d'épigraphie latine*, pp. 32–34; Fridericus Hultsch, *Metrologicorum scriptorum reliquiae*, 2 vols. (Leipzig, 1864), 2: xxv–xxviii; this table is based largely on Theodor Mommsen's edition of Volusius Maecianus, *De distributione*, in *Abhandlungen der Sachs. Gesellschaft der Wissenschaften* 3 (1853): 281; Friedlein, *Die Zahlzeichen*, pl. 2, no. 13, reproduced by Cajori, *A History of Mathematical Notations*, 1: 36.

29. Bede, *De temporum ratione, Bedae Opera pars VI*, 2, ed. Jones, pp. 278–83; the chapter *De ratione unicarum* was also diffused separately, *PL* 90: 699–702.

30. See Whitley Stokes and John Strachan, *Thesaurus Palaehibernicus: A Collection of Old-Irish Glosses, Scholia, Prose, and Verse* (Cambridge, 1901–3), 2:

xii. A. Van de Vyver, "Dicuil et Micon de Saint-Riquier," *Revue belge de philologie et d'histoire* 14 (1935): 34.

31. The oldest codex containing Vitruvius, *De architectura*, London, BL Harl. 2767, said to have been written in Northumbria, was transcribed in hierarchical word blocks in Caroline script, and therefore it was certainly not copied in England; microfilm at the IRHT. For the *notae* for fractions, see the edition by F. Granger (New York, 1931–34). See also Wilhelm Levison, *England and the Continent in the Eighth Century* (Oxford, 1946), p. 144.

32. Van de Vyver, "Dicuil et Micon de Saint-Riquier," pp. 33–34.

33. Calvin M. Bower, ed., *Boethius: Fundamentals of Music* (New Haven, 1989), pp. 93–94.

34. See W. van Christ, "Über das argumentum calculandi des Victorius und dessem Commentor," *Sitzungsberichte der königlichen bayerischen, Akademie der Wissenschaften zu München* 1 (1863): 100–152; Gottfried Friedlein, "Der Calculus des Victorius," *Bollettino di bibliografia e di storia delle scienze, matematiche e fisiche* 4 (1871): 42–79, and *Zeitschrift für Mathematik und Physik* 16 (1871): 443–63; Florence A. Yeldham, "Notation of Fractions in the Earlier Middle Ages," *Archeion* 8 (1927): 313–29, and "Fraction Tables of Hermannus Contractus," *Speculum* 3 (1928): 240–45; *Byrhtferth's Manual*, ed. S. J. Crawford (Oxford, 1929; reprint, 1966); Cyril Hart, "The Ramsey Computus," *English Historical Review* 85 (1970): 32–33.

35. In Garland's *Tractatus de abaco*, ed. B. Boncompagni, "Scritti inediti relativi al calcolo dell'abaco," *Bollettino di bibliografia e di storia delle scienze, matematiche e fisiche* 10 (1877): 595–647. For additional manuscripts, see B. de Vregille, "Gerland," *DHGE* 20 (1984): 883–85; and A. Cordoliani, "Notes sur un auteur peu connu: Gerland de Besançon (avant 1100–après 1148)," *Revue du Moyen-Age latin* 1 (1945): 419. To those listed, add Oxford, St. John's College 17. This passage from London, BL Arundel 343, destroyed by fire in 1865, has been reproduced in facsimile in James Orchard Halliwell, *Rara mathematica or a Collection of Treatises on the Mathematics and Subjects Connected with Them from Ancient Inedited Manuscripts* (London, 1839).

36. O. Guéraud and P. Jouquet, *Un livre d'écolier du IIIe siècle avant J. C.*, Publications de la Société Royale Egyptienne de Papyrologie, textes et documents (Cairo, 1938), pls. 1–3, 10; Roberts, *Greek Literary Hands*, pl. 5.

37. For early examples, see Carl Nordenfolk, *Die spätantiken Kanontafeln* (Göteborg, 1938).

38. Donatien de Bruyne, *Préfaces de la Bible latine* (Namur, 1920), pp. 153–55; *Dictionnaire d'archéologie chrétienne*, 2: pt. 2, 1900–1954. Cf. Jean Vezin, "Les divisions du texte dans les Evangiles jusqu'à l'apparition de l'imprimerie," in Maierù, *Grafia e interpunzione*, pp. 63–64.

39. That these tables were intrinsic to the text is not certain because no seventh-century Spanish copies of Isidore survive. The earliest existent Isidore

fragments are Insular. On the role of the British Isles in the dissemination of Isidore, see Hillgarth, "Visigothic Spain and Early Christian Ireland," pp. 180–85; *CLA* 3 (1938): 353; Franz Steffens, "Über die Abkürzungmethoden die Schreibschule von Bobbio," in *Mélanges Chatelain*, pl. after p. 352, of Milan, Biblioteca Ambrosiana L 99 sup.

40. See, for example, Garland's *Tractatus de abaco*, ed. Boncompagni, in "Scritti inediti," pp. 598, 599, etc.

41. H. P. Lattin, "The Eleventh-Century MS Munich 14436: Its Contribution to the History of Coordinates, of Logic, of German Studies in France," *Isis* 38 (1947–48): 205–25.

42. E. G. Turner, *Greek Manuscripts of the Ancient World* (Princeton, 1971), pls. 35 and 36.

43. "Sonus autem, quia sensibiles res est praeterfluit in pratereitum imprimiturque memoriae rationabili mendacio iam poetis favent ratione, Jovis et Memoriae filias Musas esse confictum est. Unde ista disciplina sensus intellectusque particeps 'musicae' nomen invenit." Augustine, *De ordine*, 16: 41, 434–35. "Et dicta musica per derivationem a Musis . . . sonus quia sensibilis res est et praeterfluit in praeteritum tempus imprimiturque memoriae. Inde a poetis Jovis et Memoriae filias Musas esse confectum est nisi enim ab homine memoria tenantur soni pereunt, quia scribi non possunt." Isidore, *Etymologiarum libri*, 3: 15, 1, cited by Marie-Elisabeth Duchez, "Des neumes à la portée: Elaboration et organisation de la discontinuité musicale et de sa representation graphique, de la formule à l'echelle monocordale," *Canadian University Music Review* 4 (1983): 22–25. See Leo Treitler, "Oral, Written and Literate Process in the Transmission of Medieval Music," *Speculum* 56 (1981): 471–91.

44. For an appraisal of the weight of Insular influence on the new notational system developed at Laon, see Joseph Smits van Waesberghe, "La place exceptionnelle de l'*ars musica* dans le développement des sciences au siècle des Carolingiens," *Revue grégorienne* 31 (1952): 82–83, 94–99; Paris, BN lat. 9488; *CLA* 5 (1950): 581, depicts very early neumes of the Saint Gall type added to a manuscript written in Anglo-Saxon majuscule separated by space.

45. For an interesting discussion of the effect of musical notation on page format, see Escudier, "Les Manuscrits musicaux," pp. 38–40. Escudier emphasizes the need for "lisibilité immédiate" in the text intended to receive musical notation.

46. Microfilm at the IRHT. See Leo Treitler, "Reading and Singing: On the Genesis of Occidental Music Writing," *Early Music History* 46 (1984): 145–46.

47. *Paléographie musicale*, ser. 1, 11 (1912); Jammers, *Tafeln zur Neumenschrift*, pl. 41. On the general question of the importance of the syllable in Western musical theory, see Treitler, "Reading and Singing," p. 179; and "The Early History," p. 244, where he cites Notker Balbulus (Jacques Froger, ed., "L'Epître de Notker sur les lettres significatives: Edition critique," *Etudes grégoriennes* 5

[1962]: 34–41) to the effect that "every movement of the melody should have a single syllable."

48. *Paléographie musicale*, ser. 1, 8 (1901–5); Michel Huglo, "Le tonaire de Saint-Bénigne de Dijon (Montpellier H. 159)," *Annales musicologiques* 4 (1956): 7–18.

49. Enrico Mariott Bannister, *Monumenti Vaticani de paleografia musicale latina* (Leipzig, 1913), pls. 18b and 27b.

50. Denis Escudier, "Des notations musicales dans les manuscrits non liturgiques antérieures au XII⁰ siècle," *BEC* 129 (1971): 37.

51. Kenneth Levy, "On the Origin of Neumes," *Early Music History* 7 (1987): 59–90.

52. See Gregorio Maria Suñol, *Introduction à la paléographie musicale grégorienne* (Paris, 1935), pp. 25–28, 39–42; Solange Corbin, in *Encyclopédie de la musique*, s.v. "Neume"; "Die Neumen," *Paläographie der Musik*, 1, 3 (Cologne, 1977). The relationship between neumes and ancient *prosodiae* is reflected in their nomenclature; see M. Huglo, "Les noms des neumes et leur origine," *Etudes grégoriennes* 1 (1954): 53–67.

53. Vat. Pal. lat. 235, f. 38v, cited by Peter Wagner, *Neumenkeunde: Paläographie des liturgischen Gesanges* (Leipzig, 1912), p. 355.

54. These included two manuscripts of the *Winchester Troper*, Cambridge, Corpus Christi College 473 (s. xi) and Oxford, BL Bodley 775 (s. x); Walter Howard Frere, *The Winchester Troper*, HBS, vol. 8 (London, 1894), with plate; and Montpellier, Bibliothèque de l'Ecole de Médecine H. 159; facsimile, *Paléographie musicale*, ser. 1, 7–8 (1901). See Huglo, "Le tonaire de Saint-Bénigne de Dijon," pp. 7–18; Solange Corbin, "Valeur et sens de la notation alphabétique à Jumièges et en Normandie," *Jumièges: Congrès scientifique du XIIIe centenaire*, 2: 912–24; see Jean René Hesbert, *Les manuscrits musicaux de Jumièges* (Macon, 1954), p. 87 and *passim*.

55. See Escudier, "Les Manuscrits musicaux," pp. 40, 41 (plate).

56. Treitler, "The Early History," pp. 254–62.

57. Ibid., p. 265.

58. Joseph Smits van Waesberghe, ed., *Guidonis Aretini Micrologus*, Corpus scriptorum de musica, vol. 4 (N.p., 1955), p. 36; Smits van Waesberghe, ed., *Tres tractatuli Guidonis Aretini: Guidonis Prologus in antiphonarium*, Divitiae Musicae Artis, A. III (Buren, 1975), p. 61; Duchez, "Des neumes à la portée," p. 24; cf. Odo of Saint-Maur (here, published under the name of Otto of Cluny) in Olivier Strunk, ed., *Source Readings in Music History* (New York, 1950), pp. 103–4.

59. "Item ut in unum terminentur partes et distinctiones neumarum atque verborum nec tenor longus in quibusdam brevibus syllabis aut brevis in longis obscoenitatem paret, quod tamen raro opus erit curare." Smits van Waesberghe, *Guidonis Aretini Micrologus*, pp. 173–74.

368 Notes to Pages 141–44

60. See the anonymous *Expositiones in Micrologum Guidonis Aretini*, ed. Joseph Smits van Waesberghe (Amsterdam, 1957), pp. 153–54; see also Calvin M. Bower, "The Grammatical Model of Musical Understanding in the Middle Ages," in Patrick J. Gallacher and Helen Damico, eds., *Hermeneutics and Medieval Culture* (Albany, N.Y., 1989), pp. 138–40.

61. For a list of the manuscripts, see the studies of Smits van Waesberghe, *Tres tractatuli Guidonis Aretini*, pp. 26–51. For plates, see ibid., pl. 2. See also Joseph Smits van Waesberghe, *De musico-paedagogico et theoretico: Guidone Aretino eiusque vita et moribus* (Florence, 1953), pls. 1, 2, 10, 11; *Muzikgeschiedinis*, 1: pls. of Munich Clm. 14663 and Darmstadt 1988; *Bernonis Augiensis abbatis de arte musica disputationes traditae, pars B; Quae ratio est inter tria opera de arte musica Bernonis Augiensis*, Divitiae Musicae Artis, A. VIb (Buren, 1979), pls. 2, 4; *Encyclopédie de la musique*, 2: 379; cf. Pietro Thomas in *Enciclopedia cattolica* 6 (1951): 1288. An ancient tradition links Guido to northern monastic centers in the Ile de France, Normandy, and England, where word separation had been definitively adopted either at the end of the tenth or in the first half of the eleventh century.

62. In referring to performers of musical instruments, psychologists refer to the eye-hand span; Levin and Addis, *The Eye-Voice Span*, pp. 71–76.

63. See James Grier, "The Stemma of the Aquitanian Versaria," *Journal of the American Musicological Society* 41 (1988): 249–88; and "Scribal Practices in the Aquitanian Versaria of the Twelfth Century: Towards a Typology of Error and Variant," *Journal of the American Musicological Society* 45 (1992): 373–427; Saenger, "Word Separation and Its Implications."

64. M. Huglo, *Les livres de chant liturgique*, Typologie des sources du Moyen Age occidental, vol. 52 (Turnholt, 1988), pp. 127–30.

Chapter 8

1. Latouche, ed. and trans., *Richer: Histoire de France*, 2: 64–65; Olleris, *Oeuvres de Gerbert*, p. 357; also in Bubnov, *Gerberti opera mathematica*, pp. 383–84; Lattin, "The Origin of Our Present System of Notation," p. 193.

2. Latouche, ed. and trans., *Richer: Histoire de France*, 2: 58–63; Oscar G. Darlington, "Gerbert, the Teacher," *American Historical Review* 52 (1946–47): 467–71.

3. Latouche, ed. and trans., *Richer: Histoire de France*, 2: 55–57.

4. For definitions of the *Logica vetus*, see de Rijk, *Logica modernorum*, 1: 14–15. De Rijk omits Cicero's *Topica*. See also Brian Stock, *Implications of Literacy* (Princeton, 1983), p. 365; and R. W. Southern, "Lanfranc of Bec and Berengar of Tours," in *Studies in Medieval History Presented to F. M. Powicke*, pp. 33, 41–42; André Van de Vyver, "L'Évolution scientifique du haut Moyen Age," *Archeion* 29 (1937): 12–20.

5. Darlington, "Gerbert, the Teacher," pp. 472–73.

6. On this kind of reading in a later context, see D. F. McKenzie, "Speech-Manuscript-Print," in David Oliphant and Robin Bradford, eds., *New Directions in Textual Studies* (Austin, Tex., 1990), p. 104.

7. See his Letter 15 (Havet 8), June 22, 983, in Lattin, The *Letters of Gerbert*, pp. 54–55.

8. Latouche, ed. and trans., *Richer: Histoire de France*, 2: 68–81; Gerbert, Letter 92 to Bernard of Aurillac, ed. F. Weigle, *Die Briefsammlung Gerberts von Reims, MGH: Die Briefe der Deutschen Kaiserzeit* 2 (Berlin, 1966): 121.

9. Paris, BN lat. 8663; Montpellier, Bibliothèque de L'Ecole de Médecine H. 491; Vat. Reg. lat. 1071, 1661.

10. M. Tosi, "Il governo abbaziale di Gerberto a Bobbio," in Tosi, ed., *Gerberto: Scienza, storia e mito: Atti del Gerberti Symposium, Bobbio, 25–27 Iuglio 1983* (Bobbio, 1985), pp. 125–30, 183–94, pls. following p. 192; cf. Bubnov, *Gerberti opera mathematica*, pp. 31–36.

11. A microfilm of this codex is at the IRHT. See de Meyier, *Codices Vossiani latini* 1 (1973): 131–35; Karl Ferdinand Werner, "Zur Überlieferung der Briefe Gerberts von Aurillac," *Deutsches Archiv* 17 (1961): 91–119.

12. Intersyllabic interference with word separation existed in some portions.

13. Mostert, *The Library of Fleury*, BF 1410; Bautier and Labory, *Helgaud de Fleury: Vie de Robert le Pieux*, pp. 21, 60–61.

14. Julien Havet, *Lettres de Gerbert (987–997)* (Paris, 1889), pp. 234–36; de Meyier, *Codices Vossiani latini* 2 (1975): 49; cf. ibid., 4 (1984): pl. 23e illustrating texts contained in the same fragment; Olleris, *Oeuvres de Gerbert*, pp. i, 3 and 483; "La bibliothèque de l'abbaye de Saint-Mesmin au IXe siècle," *Analecta Bollandiana* 23 (1904): 84.

15. Bubnov, *Gerberti opera mathematica*, pp. 46–97.

16. Bernhard Bischoff, "Literarisches und künstleris Leben in St. Emmeram (Regensburg) während des frühen und hohen Mittelalters," in Bischoff, *Mittelalterliche Studien*, 2: 81–82; Olleris, *Oeuvres de Gerbert*, pp. 572–73.

17. Olleris, *Oeuvres de Gerbert*, pp. 572–73; dated twelfth century, in Delisle, *Inventaire des manuscrits latins*.

18. Karl Strecker, ed., *Die lateinischen Dichter des deutschen Mittelalters, MGH: Poetae latinae medii aevi* 5, pt. 2 (1939): 474–75; Rudolf Peiper, ed., *De consolatione philosophiae* (Leipzig, 1871), pp. xl–xli. Bubnov, *Gerberti opera mathematica*, pp. 150–51.

19. Microfilm and *notice* are at the IRHT.

20. Bubnov, who did not know the Basel codex, found no basis for attributing this text to Gerbert. In the Basel codex, as in the other manuscripts, the text is anonymous.

21. *Catalogue général des manuscrits latins* 2 (1940): 444; *France: Manuscrits datés* 2 (1962): 115.

22. Olleris, *Oeuvres de Gerbert*, pp. 269–78, 565–67; *PL* 139: 170–78.

23. Chroust, *Monumenta Palaeographica*, ser. 1, 2: 23, 6.

24. Cf. Lattin, "The Origin of Our Present System of Notation," p. 193.

25. Florentine Mütherich, "The Library of Otto III," in Ganz, *The Role of the Book*, 1: 19. The manuscript was recorded in the twelfth-century catalogue of the cathedral of Saint Michael in Bamburg; *Archiv für deutsche Geschichtskunde* 21 (1895): 165–66; Latouche, ed. and trans., *Richer: Histoire de France*, 1: xii–xiii. G. H. Pertz discovered it and published it in *MGH: Scriptores* 3 (1839) with plate; cf. Latouche, ed. and trans., *Richer: Histoire de France*, 1: xii–xv; Schramm and Mütherich, *Denkmale*, no. 97 with plate. See also H. H. Kortum, *Richer von Saint Remi: Studien zu einem Geschichtschreiber des 10 Jhts.* (Stuttgart, 1985).

26. The instability of interword space may reflect the early date of this codex in the evolution of word separation on the Continent.

27. Latouche, ed. and trans., *Richer: Histoire de France*, 1: xiv, 104, 112, 118. This use of the suspension abbreviation for proper names was also evident in the manuscript tradition of the letters of Gerbert.

28. Eugène Martin, *DHGE* 1 (1912): 636; Eugène Martin, *Histoire des diocèses de Toul, de Nancy et de Saint-Dié*, 3 vols. (Nancy, 1900–1903), 1: 12 ff.; Riché, *Écoles et enseignement*, p. 168.

29. Lattin, *The Letters of Gerbert*, letter 15 (Havet 8), p. 54.

30. Lattin, *The Letters of Gerbert*, letter 88 (Havet 82), p. 125.

31. *Adso Dervensis: De ortu et tempore Antichristi*, ed. D. Verhelst, in *CCCM* 45 (1976): viii.

32. Riché, *Écoles et enseignement*, p. 129; Latouche, ed. and trans., *Richer: Histoire de France*, 2: 68–69.

33. *France: Manuscrits datés* 2 (1962): 275 and pl. 200.

34. H. Omont, "Catalogue de la bibliothèque de l'abbé Adson de Montier-en-Der," *BEC* 42 (1881): 157–60.

35. In the Montier-en-Der catalogue, interword space was 1.5 times the unity of space. Although brief, the catalogue contained the terminal signs for *-us*, and *m*, and reserved the *e* cedilla, the capital *S*, and the *NT* ligature for word endings in the manner characteristic of the enhancement of separation associated with Gerbert, Abbo, and Fulbert.

36. Robert Henri Bautier, *L'historiographie en France au Xe et XIe siècles* (Spoleto, 1979), pp. 842–43; *Adso: De Ortu*, ed. Verhelst, p. viii.

37. Leslie Webber Jones, "Dom Victor Perrin and Three Manuscripts of Luxeuil," *Bulletin of the John Rylands Library* 23 (1939): 174–78 and pl. 3.

38. Microfilm and *notice* are at the IRHT.

39. Lattin, *The Letters of Gerbert*, letter 14 (Havet 7), p. 53; cf. letter 42 (Havet 34), pp. 82–83; letter 66 (Havet 60), p. 107.

40. Chatelain, *Paléographie des classiques latins*, 1: pl. 19a; Hans Fischer, *Die Lateinischen Pergamenthandschriften der Universitätsbibliothek* (Erlangern, 1928), pp. 450–54; Emile Lesne, *Histoire de la propriété ecclésiastique en France*, 6 vols.

(Lille, 1938), 4: 103; L. D. Reynolds, *Texts and Transmissions: A Survey of the Latin Classics* (Oxford, 1983), pp. 105–6; Pierre Riché, "La bibliothèque de Gerbert d'Aurillac," *Mélanges de la Bibliothèque de la Sorbonne* 8 (1988): 96, 100.

41. Paris, BN Collection Porcher; *France: Manuscrits datés* 5 (1965): 241, and pl. 5; *Les plus beaux manuscrits de la Bibliothèque Municipale de Reims*, exhibition catalogue (Reims, 1967), p. 46, no. 68; Michel de Lemps and Roger Laslier, *Trésors de la Bibliothèque Municipale de Reims*, exhibition catalogue (Reims, 1978), no. 13 with a plate of the script; J. Deschusses, "Sur quelques anciens livres liturgiques de Saint-Thierry: Les étapes d'une transformation de la liturgie," in M. Bur, ed., *Saint-Thierry une abbaye du VIᵉ au XXᵉ siècle: Actes du colloque international d'histoire monastique Reims-Saint-Thierry* (1979): 141, 174–75. The colophon of this codex originally read "ex conditione Ayardi abbatis," but was emended to read "ex labore Ayardi abbatis." The scribe, however, does not appear to be the same hand as the writer of the Erlangen codex.

42. Tosi, "Il governo abbaziale di Gerberto a Bobbio," pp. 109–14, 173–83, pls. following p. 192; Lattin, *The Letters of Gerbert*, letter 16 (Havet 9), p. 55 n. 4; Franz Koehler, *Die Gudischen Handschriften*, in Otto von Heinemann, *Die Handschriften der Herzoglichen Bibliothek*, 4 (Wolfenbüttel, 1913), pp. 251–53. A microfilm of this codex is at the IRHT.

43. Scholars have identified two unseparated manuscripts predating Gerbert that are thought to have been used by him. The *Arcerianus* codex of the *Corpus agremensorum romanorum*, Wolfenbüttel, Herzog August Bibliothek, Aug. 36.32 2° (Teil A), written in *scriptura continua* in the sixth century and apparently used by Gerbert at Bobbio, was emended to separate words with acute accents on the *-is* termination and the successor note to the *diastole*. *Probationes pennae* and Latin verse were added in separated script. Bamberg, Staatsbibliothek Class. 42 (M.V.10), Pliny's *Historia naturalis*, also associated with Gerbert and written in hierarchical word blocks exceeding fifteen characters in length, was emended with the successor note to the *diastole*, the hyphen, and the acute accent used to denote the letter *i* in tonic syllables and the terminal position. While it is possible that some of the emendations in both codices were by Gerbert or his circle, no manuscript written close to the time of Gerbert, except those copied at Fleury, evince frequent use of the successor to the *diastole*.

44. Pierre Riché, "Nouvelles vies parallèles: Gerbert d'Aurillac et Abbon de Fleury," in *Media in Francia: Recueil de mélanges offerts à Karl Ferdinand Werner* (n.p., 1989), pp. 420–21; Cousin, *Abbon de Fleury-sur-Loire*, pp. 53–54, 213; Guerreau-Jalabert, *Abbon de Fleury: Quaestiones Grammaticales*, pp. 19–25.

45. See, most recently, Marco Mostert, *The Political Theology of Abbo of Fleury: A Study of the Ideas about Society and Law of the Tenth Century Monastic Reform Movement*, Middeleeuwse Studies en Bronnen, vol. 2 (Hilversum, 1987), pp. 17, 32, 48, 50 n. 35, 51; Lattin, *The Letters of Gerbert*, letter 204 (Havet 191), pp. 265–66 nn. 1–2.

46. Lattin, *The Letters of Gerbert*, letter 7, pp. 45–47 nn. 4–5.

47. Ibid., nn. 3, 4, 6, 7, p. 204.

48. For example, Paris, BN lat. 6620 and lat. 8663.

49. On Abbo's residence in England, see Marco Mostert, "Le séjour d'Abbon à Ramsey," *BEC* 144 (1986): 199–208; Cousin, *Abbon de Fleury-sur-Loire*, pp. 65–74, 213; Guerreau-Jalabert, *Abbon de Fleury: Quaestiones Grammaticales*, pp. 25–26; Dorothy Whitelock, "Fact and Fiction in the Legend of Saint Edmond," *Proceedings of the Suffolk Institute of Archaeology* 31, pt. 1 (1968 [for 1967]): 218–22; G. I. Needham, *Aelfric: Lives of Three English Saints* (Exeter, 1976), pp. 18–19; Winterbottom, *Three Lives of English Saints*, p. 8; Judith Grant, *La passion de Seint Edmund* (London, 1978), pp. 4–6; Walter W. Skeat, *Aelfric's Lives of Saints: Being a Set of Sermons on Saints' Days Formerly Observed by the English Church*, EETS, o.s., 76, 82, 94, 114 (1881–1900), 4: 315; Ursmere Bellière, "L'étude des réformes monastiques des Xe et XIe siècles," *Académie royale de Belgique de la classe des lettres et des sciences, morales et politiques* 18 (1932): 139–40. I have unfortunately not been able to consult M. Mostert's dissertation, "King Edmund of East Anglia (†869): Chapters in Historical Criticism" (University of Amsterdam, 1983).

50. "Tandem dicendum est quod vitando cavenda est collisio que solet inter duas partes fieri uel pronunciatione uel scripto, ut *ueni trex* pro eo quod est *uenit rex* et *par sest* pro *pars est* et *feli xes* pro *felix es*." Guerreau-Jalabert, *Abbon de Fleury: Quaestiones Grammaticales*, p. 245 (28), where it is accompanied by a clear French translation. This portion of the text, omitted in *PL* 139: 522–39 (=Angelo Mai, *Classici auctores* [Rome, 1828–38], 5: 329–49), was restored by Henry Bradley, "On the Text of Abbo of Fleury's *Quaestiones grammaticales*," *Proceedings of the British Academy* 10 (1921–23): 177–78.

51. Cf. *Excerpta Macrobii de differentiis et societatibus graeci latinique verbi*, in Keil, *Grammatici latini*, 5: 623, lines 18–20; printed from Paris, BN lat. 7186 (s. x–xi); written in hierarchical word blocks; from the library of Pierre Pithou.

52. *PL* 139: 419C–426A, e.g., *Epistola* 8, 14; cf. "Three Letters to St. Dunstan," in *Memorials of Saint Dunstan*, ed. W. Stubbs (London, 1874), no. 34, i–iii.

53. I have not been able to confirm the statement by Roger Wright, *Late Latin and Early Romance in Spain and Carolingian France* (Liverpool, 1982), p. 138, that a copy of the *Quaestiones grammaticales* exists in Vienna, Nationalbibliothek lat. 795, of which a microfilm copy exists at the IRHT. This codex is not recorded by Guerreau-Jalabert. Vienna, Nationalbibliothek lat. 795 is written in hierarchical word blocks.

54. Guerreau-Jalabert, *Abbon de Fleury: Quaestiones Grammaticales*, pp. 189, 200; Pellegrin, "Membra disiecta Floriacensia I," pp. 53–54; Van de Vyver, "Les oeuvres inédites," p. 125. Mostert, *The Library of Fleury*, BF 372–73. A microfilm and *notice* are at the IRHT.

55. A composite book of Pierre Daniel and Paul Petau: Guerreau-Jalabert,

Abbon de Fleury: Quaestiones Grammaticales, pp. 199–200; Pellegrin, "Membra disiecta Floriacensia II," p. 96. Abbo's *Quaestiones* formed one codex with Paris, BN lat. 6638, ff. 1–16; Van de Vyver, "Les oeuvres inédites," p. 126; Mostert, *The Library of Fleury*, BF 1438.

56. Van de Vyver, *Abbonis Floriacensis opera inedita*, pp. 23–24; Pellegrin, "Membra disiecta Floriacensia I," p. 14 n. 2; Mostert, *The Library of Fleury*, BF 1256, 725–27.

57. Virgilius Maro had called for avoiding the *et* ligature as a terminal form. In the ninth century, Lupus of Ferrières rejected the internal ampersand.

58. Although the mark of punctuation was not present in the three and one-half pages of Abbo's text, the scribe used the *trait d'union* in both Latin and Greek words in the preceding text, which was also separated by space.

59. Van de Vyver, *Abbonis Floriacensis opera inedita*, p. 25; Pellegrin, "Membra disiecta Floriacensia I," pp. 9–16; *France: Manuscrits datés* 7 (1984): 237 and pl. 7; Mostert, *The Library of Fleury*, BF 748.

60. Pellegrin, "Membra disiecta Floriacensia I," pl. following p. 14; Mostert, *The Political Theology of Abbo of Fleury*, p. 6 (pl.).

61. Van de Vyver, *Abbonis Floriacensis opera inedita*, pp. 24–25, and "Les oeuvres inédites," p. 133; Guerreau-Jalabert, *Abbon de Fleury: Quaestiones Grammaticales*, p. 193; Pellegrin, "Membra disiecta Floriacensia I," pp. 14–15; Mostert, *The Library of Fleury*, BF 275. This codex was in the library of Alexandre Petau.

62. Van de Vyver, *Abbonis Floriacensis opera inedita*, pp. 42–43. On the iconic aspect of the page, see Terence Hawkes, *Structuralism and Semiotics* (London, 1977), pp. 136–43; Umberto Eco, *Semiotics and the Philosophy of Language* (Bloomington, Ind., 1984), pp. 16–17.

63. Van de Vyver, *Abbonis Floriacensis opera inedita*, p. 25.

64. Leitschuh, *Katalog der Handschriften der Königlichen Bibliothek zu Bamberg* 1, 2, i (1966): 59–60; Van de Vyver, "Les oeuvres inédites," p. 139; Mostert, *The Library of Fleury*, BF 007.

65. Microfilm and *notice* at the IRHT; Mostert, *The Library of Fleury*, BF 134.

66. Van de Vyver, "Les oeuvres inédites," p. 152.

67. Ibid., pp. 150–52.

68. Ibid., p. 153; Mostert, *The Library of Fleury*, BF 1508.

69. Van de Vyver, "Les oeuvres inédites," p. 153. The acceptance of word separation probably reflected the influence of Fécamp and other reformed Norman abbeys.

70. Aimo in his early-eleventh-century *Vita Abbonis*, ch. 7, apparently refers to the *Collectio canonum* thusly: "assumptisque ex plurimorum patrum auctoritatibus sententiis, velut prudentissima apis variis favos composita [*sic*] floribus, mellitum defloravit opus. Quod licit ad presens non repperiatur, partim nostrorum negligentia, partim extraeorum subtractum cupiditate, certum tamen est

idcirco id eum excerpisse quo haberet munimen defensionis contra pontificem ęcclesię Aurelianensis non recta quędam ab eo exigentem." *PL* 139: 394A, as emended by Mostert, *The Political Theology of Abbo of Fleury*, p. 65; cf. pp. 52–53, 70–71.

71. Kasius Hallinger, ed., *Consuetudines floriacenses antiquiores*, in *Corpus consuetudinum monasticorum* 7: pt. 3 (Siegburg, 1984), p. 17. This text, dated to the tenth century, survives only in a fifteenth-century copy, Wolfenbüttel, Herzog August Bibliothek, Aug. 71.22. 2°, ff. 235v–52; Mostert, *The Library of Fleury*, BF 1557; cf. A. Davril, "Un coutumier de Fleury du début du XIe siècle," *RB* 76 (1966): 351–54.

72. Mostert, *The Political Theology of Abbo of Fleury*, pp. 71–75.

73. The principal text of lat. 11674 was written in hierarchical word blocks in a two-column format.

74. Mostert, *The Library of Fleury*, BF 1173; Delisle, *Inventaire des manuscrits latins*.

75. Mostert, *The Political Theology of Abbo of Fleury*, p. 64; Chatelain, *Paléographie des classiques latins*, 2: pl. 189; Legendre, *Études tironiennes*, p. 59; Ulrich Friedrich Kopp, *Paleographica critica*, 5 vols. (Mannheim, 1817–29), 1: 327–33; Mostert, *The Library of Fleury*, BF 194.

76. See ff. 55 and 71v–72.

77. See f. 81.

78. "Ego quidem corrigere per me, exemplar aliud non habens, si poteram, temptavi. Ergo, ubi minus potui R litteram apposui." E. Dümmler, "Ekkhart IV von St. Gallen," *Zeitschrift für deutsches Altertum*, n.s., 2 (1869): 21; see A. C. Clark, *The Descent of Manuscripts* (Oxford, 1918), p. 35.

79. On Paris, BN lat. 2278, see *Catalogue des manuscrits latins* 2 (1940): 382–83; and Cousin, *Abbon de Fleury-sur-Loire*, p. 8; Mostert, *The Library of Fleury*, BF 1028.

80. Other codices include Orléans, BM 267 (223), and Leiden, BR Voss lat. F.70; Saenger, "Separated Script at Reims and Fleury."

81. Guerreau-Jalabert, *Abbon de Fleury*, pp. 244–55 (28).

82. See Saenger, "Separated Script at Reims and Fleury."

83. For the geographical limits of Occitan, see Pierre Bec, *La langue occitane* (Paris, 1963), pp. 8–13.

84. Ernesto Monaci, *Facsimili di antichi manoscritti per uso della scuole di filologia* (Rome, 1881–92), p. vi and pl. 57. Bernhard Bischoff, "Panorama der Handschriftenüberlieferung aus der Zeit Karls des Grossen," in *Karl der Grosse: Lebenwerke und Nachleben*, 2: 250 n. 129; Bischoff, "Frühkarolingische Handschriften," p. 313; Ulrich Mölk, "A propos de la provenance du codex Vaticanus Regiensis latinus 1462 contenant l'aube bilingue du Xᵉ ou XIᵉ siècle," *Mélanges Rita Lajeune*, 2 vols. (Gembloux, 1969), 1: 37–43; for full bibliography, see Pellegrin, *Les manuscrits classiques latins*, 2, pt. 1 (1978): 222–24, and, most recently,

Paul Zumthor, "Un trompe-l'oeil linguistique: Le refrain de l'aube bilingue de Fleury," *Romania* 105 (1984): 171–92; Christine Ruby, "Les premiers témoins du français," in *Le livre au Moyen-Age*, ed. Jean Glenisson (Paris, 1988), pp. 124–25; Mostert, *The Library of Fleury*, BF 1503–4.

85. Monaci, *Facsimili di antichi manoscritti*, pls. 33–39; René Levaud and Georges Machicot, *Boecis: Poème sur Boèce (fragment); le plus ancien texte littéraire occitan réedité, traduit et commenté* (Toulouse, 1950); D'arco Silvio Avalle, *La letteratura medievale in lingua d'oc nella sua tradizione manoscritta* (Turin, 1961), pp. 28–31 and pl. following p. 32; P. Meyer, "Le poème de Boece revu sur le manuscrit," *Romania* 1 (1872): 227 n. 1; Alexander Vidier, *L'historiographie à Saint-Benôit-sur-Loire et les miracles de Saint-Benôit: Ouvrage posthume revu et annoté par les soins des moines de l'abbaye de Saint-Benôit-de-Fleury* (Paris, 1965), p. 240; Mostert, *The Library of Fleury*, BF 885–86.

86. Because the date of Zurich, Zentralbibliothek C 98, remains uncertain, the priority of the *Quomodo VII circumstantiae* has not yet been definitively established.

87. On this text, see Thurot, "Notices et extraits," pp. 87–89, analyzed by Scaglione, *The Classical Theory of Composition*, pp. 106–9. Printed from the Fleury codex, Orléans, BM 303, by Charles Cuissard, *Inventaire des manuscrits de la Bibliothèque d'Orléans, Fonds de Fleury* (Orléans, 1885), pp. 226–28. A seventeenth-century copy of the Fleury text exists in Paris, BN NAL 2056 (olim Arsenal 1008), ff. 1–3; Mostert, *The Library of Fleury*, BF 947. Very recently, another manuscript, said to date from the tenth century, has been brought to light; see Anneli Luhtala, "Syntax and Dialectic in Carolingian Commentaries on Priscian's *Institutiones Grammaticae*," *Historia Linguistica* 20 (1993): 177, 179. In fact, Florence, Biblioteca Medicea Laurenziana Plut 47,28, dates from the eleventh century and contains a Gerbert-related treatise on the abacus that includes the earliest Italian transcription of Arabic numbers. The text format is word-separated.

88. Roger Bacon predicated the same order; see chapter 14, note 65.

89. For a general consideration of the increasing intermixture of grammar and dialectic in the eleventh century, see de Rijk, *Logica modernorum*, 2: 95–127.

90. Mostert, *The Library of Fleury*, BF 804.

91. Guerreau-Jalabert, *Abbon de Fleury: Quaestiones Grammaticales*, p. 222 (14).

92. Ibid., pp. 77–80; Van de Vyver, *Abbonis Floriacensis opera inedita*, p. 27 n. 1.

93. See F. J. Worstbrock, "Heriger von Lobbes (Laubach)," in Wolfgang Stammler, ed., *Die deutsche Literatur des Mittelalters: Verfasserlexikon*, rev. ed. (1981), 3: 1044–48; C. R. Shrader, "A False Attribution to Gerbert of Aurillac," *Mediaeval Studies* 35 (1973): 189–91, 198–200; Lattin, *The Letters of Gerbert*, letter 233, pp. 299–302 (cf. *PL* 139: 1134A).

94. Robert Gary Babcock, "Heriger and the Study of Philosophy at Lobbes in the Tenth Century," *Traditio* 40 (1985): 317.

95. Bubnov, *Gerberti opera mathematica*, p. 205; text not recorded by the *Gesta abbatum Lobbiensium*, *PL* 139: 112–1154. The earliest surviving copies of this treatise dating from the eleventh century are anonymous, and it is attributed to Heriger in a manuscript for the first time only in the twelfth century.

96. Babcock, "Heriger and the Study of Philosophy," pp. 312–16.

97. Brussels, BR 5576–604. Other manuscripts are all of the twelfth century or later; see Shrader, "False Attribution," pp. 179–80; H. Silvestre, "Publications de sources et travaux," *RHE* 70 (1975): 877–79.

98. Verdun, BM 77. See K. Strecker, *MGH: Poetae latinae medii aevi* 5, pt. 1 (1937): 174–208; H. Silvestre, "Hériger de Lobbes (†1007) avait lu Dracontius," *MA* 69 (1963): 123. I am indebted to Denis Muzerelle for providing me with a photocopy.

99. Bamberg, Staatsbibliothek Hist. 161 (E.III.1); Leitschuh, *Katalog der Handschriften der Königlichen Bibliothek zu Bamberg* 1, 2, i (1966): 264–68. On this codex, see below, Chapter 13. The text of this *vita* is in *BHL* 2: no. 7113.

100. Babcock, "Heriger and the Study of Philosophy," pp. 307–11.

101. Ibid., p. 311. On this Lobbes codex, see below, Chapter 13; *BHL* 2: no. 7115; R. Köpke, *MGH: Scriptores* 7 (1846): 180–89; *PL* 139: 1149–68. See Robert Gary Babcock, *Heriger of Lobbes and the Freising Florilegium: A Study of the Influence of Classical Latin Poetry in the Middle Ages*, Lateinische Sprache und Literatur des Mittelalters, 1, 8 (Frankfurt-am-Main, 1984), pp. 180–85, 193–94.

102. Personal communication, November 1991.

103. Lapière, *Lettre ornée*, pp. 253, 256 (pl. 238), 413; Hoffmann, *Buchkunst und Königtum*, pp. 173–74 and pl. 49.

104. Brussels, BR II, 1180 (*olim* Phillipps 12459); Saint Gall, Stiftsbibliothek nos. 571 and 565; Trier, Cathedral no. 93; S. Balau, *Etude critique des sources de l'histoire du pays de Liège au Moyen Age* (Brussels, 1902–3), 1: 133–34; B. Krusch and W. Levison, eds., *Passiones vitaeque sanctorum aevi Merovingici*, *MGH: Scriptores rerum Merovingicarum* 5 (Hanover, 1903): 103.

105. Babcock, *Heriger of Lobbes*; Bischoff, *Kalligraphie in Bayern*, pp. 32–33 and pl. 24 (of f. 128); Hoffmann, *Buchkunst und Königtum*, pp. 210–11 and pl. 73.

106. E. Dümmler, "Zum Heriger von Lobbes," *Neues Archiv der Gesellschaft für ältere deutsche Geschichtskunde* 26 (1901): 755–59; R. Morin, "Les *Dicta* d'Heriger sur l'eucharistie," *RB* 25 (1908): 1–18; Shrader, "False Attribution," pp. 193–94 and passim; Jean-Paul Bouhot, *Ratramne de Corbie: Histoire littéraire et controverses doctrinales* (Paris, 1976), pp. 91ff., 139ff., 161–62; J. N. Bakhuizen van den Brink, *Ratraminus: De corpore et sanguine Domini, texte original et notice bibliograhique*, Verhandelingen der Kroninklijke Nederlandsche Akademie van Wetenschappen, afd. Letterkunde, n.s., 87, rev. ed. (Amsterdam, 1974), pp. 6–7, 29–32; cf. Babcock, *Heriger of Lobbes*, pp. 194–95; H. Silvestre's review of Bak-

huizen van den Brink, *Ratraminus*, in *Scriptorium* 30 (1976): 322–24; Silvestre, "Publications," p. 878. I have not been able to examine Liège, Séminaire 6. F. 30, which Morin judged to be of the eleventh century and older than Ghent, BR 909.

107. Bakhuizen van den Brink, *Ratraminus*, p. 13 and pls. 1, 5–7. The attribution is based on the Lobbes catalogue of 1094 (see below, Chapter 13), but the words of the entry "Herigeri abbatis exageratio plurimorum auctorum de corpore et sanguine domini" could equally well mean that this copy had belonged to Heriger; see Ernest Philip Goldschmidt, *Medieval Texts and Their First Appearance in Print*, Bibliographical Society Transactions, suppl. 16 (London, 1943), p. 98.

Chapter 9

1. Frederick Behrends, *DHGE* 19 (1981): 333–36; Behrends, *The Letters and Poems of Fulbert of Chartres*, p. xvii; Louis Halphen, "Note sur la Chronique de Saint-Maxent," *BEC* 69 (1908): 408n; P. Marchegay and E. Mabille, *Chronique des églises d'Anjou* (Paris, 1869), p. 385; *Chronicon Fontanallensis*, in M. Bouquet et al., eds., *Recueil des historiens des Gaules et de la France*, new ed., 24 vols. (Paris, 1869–1904), 10: 324; MacKinney, *Bishop Fulbert*, p. 6; Loren C. MacKinney, "Bishop Fulbert, Teacher, Administrator, Humanist," *Isis* 14 (1930): 286.

2. No photographs of this codex survive. On the destruction of the Chartres library, see Ernst Wichersheimer, "Textes mediévaux Chartrains de IXe siécle," in *Science, Medicine, and History: Essays Written in Honor of Charles Singer*, 2 vols., ed. E. Ashwood Underwood (London, 1953), 1: 164; and the report published in *Speculum* 29 (1954): 336–37.

3. Behrends, *The Letters and Poems of Fulbert of Chartres*, p. xvii.

4. Michael McVaugh and Frederick Behrends, "Fulbert of Chartres' Notes on Arabic Astronomy," *Manuscripta* 15 (1971): 172–77; Behrends, *The Letters and Poems of Fulbert of Chartres*, pp. x, xvii–xxviii and no. 148; Van de Vyver, "Les premières traductions," pp. 287–88 n. 84.

5. Behrends, *The Letters and Poems of Fulbert of Chartres*, pp. 256–61 (no. 147).

6. Bubnov, *Gerberti opera mathematica*, pp. lxi–lxii.

7. Cf. Barré, "Pro Fulberto," pp. 324–25.

8. Christian Phister, *De Fulberti Carnotensi episcopi vita et operibus* (Nancy, 1885), p. 24; Behrends, *The Letters and Poems of Fulbert of Chartres*, pp. xxxviii–xliv; Marie-Thèrese Vernet, "Notes de Dom André Wilmart (†) sur quelques manuscrits latins anciens de la Bibliothèque Nationale de Paris," *Bulletin d'information de l'Institut de Recherche et d'Histoire des Textes* 6 (1957): 22–25.

9. The scribes employed many of the standard terminal forms including *m*, *-us*, *-orum*, *-tur*, and *-bus*. Monolexic abbreviations included superscripts and the Insular sign for *est*, as well as the variant form *e* (beneath a *virga*). Initial

capitals, in addition to signaling the beginning of a sentence in conjunction with punctuation and increased space, denoted proper names. Numbers were written in Roman numerals set off by interpuncts in the presence of space.

10. This use of suspension abbreviations for proper names had Insular precedent in the abbreviations enumerated by Bede and Tatwine.

11. See f. 65.

12. Vernet, "Notes de Dom André Wilmart," pp. 20–23; Behrends, *The Letters and Poems of Fulbert of Chartres*, pp. xliv–xlv; *Catalogue général des manuscrits latins* 3 (1952): 179–83.

13. Monolexic abbreviations included superscript forms. In the presence of highly regular separation, *e* for *est* was written without interpuncts or *virga*, as were Roman numerals. Initial capital forms in the presence of augmented space and Insular-style emblematic punctuation were used to denote sentences. Emblematic forms of punctuation were reserved for text endings; the interrogation sign was used regularly.

14. Two Greek words in the text were also accented.

15. He used the *diastole* as an insertion mark only and left errors in word separation uncorrected.

16. Behrends, *The Letters and Poems of Fulbert of Chartres*, p. xliv; Bartoloméo Nogara, *Codices Vaticani latini* 3 (1912): 238–41. Microfilm and *notice* are at the IRHT.

17. Rouen, BM 471 (Fécamp), 1378 (Jumièges), 1388, 1390, 1418; Paris, Arsenal 372 (Fleury); Vat. Reg. lat. 490 (Reims); Dijon, BM 30 (Citeaux); Paris, BN lat. 3003, 3781, 14167, NAL 1436 (Cluny), NAL 1455 (Cluny); Châlons-sur-Marne, BM 217, 330; Reims, BM 295 (Cathedral of Reims); see the studies by J. M. Canal, "Los sermones marianos de San Fulberto de Chartres (†1028)," *Recherches de théologie ancienne et médiévale* 29 (1962): 33–51; "Texto crítico de algunos sermones marianos de San Fulberto de Chartres o a él atribuibles," ibid. 30 (1963): 55–87; and "Los sermones marianos de San Fulberto de Chartres: Adición," ibid. 30 (1963): 329–33. On the distinct textual tradition of the Sermones, see "Los sermones marianos de San Fulberto de Chartres: Conclusión," ibid. 33 (1966): 139–47; cf. Barré, "Pro Fulberto," pp. 324–30. Behrends, *DHGE* 19 (1981): 333–36.

18. René Merlet and l'Abbé Clerval, *Un manuscript chartrain du XIe siècle: Fulbert, évêque de Chartres* (Chartres, 1893); MacKinney, *Bishop Fulbert*, pl. 6. A microfilm is at the IRHT.

19. Interword space was 2.5 times the unity of space, with space present after monosyllabic prepositions. Syllabic space was present but hierarchically distinguished from interword space. Terminal forms included the usual signs for *m*, *-us*, *-tur*, and *-orum*. Monolexic abbreviations included the ampersand for *et*, which was not used within words.

20. This configuration is important for its implications on the use of peripheral vision.

21. See Bernhard Bischoff, "Literarisches und künstleriches Leben in St. Emmeram (Regensburg) während des frühen und hohen Mittelalters," *Studien und Mitteilungen zur Geschichte des Benedictiner-Ordens und seiner Zweige* 51 (1933): 101–42; reprinted in *Mittelalterliche Studien*, 2: 77–115; MacKinney, *Bishop Fulbert*, pl. 2. Hoffmann, *Buchkunst und Königtum*, pp. 524–25. A microfilm of Clm. 14272 is at the IRHT.

22. The text of the codex was written with separation by space complemented occasionally by separation by terminal forms and monolexic abbreviations. Interword space was 2 times the unity of space based on the letter *u*; syllabic space when present was hierarchically distinguished. Space after monosyllabic prepositions was occasionally inserted. Terminal forms included the usual signs for -*us*, *m*, -*tur*, and the capital *NT* ligature was reserved for section endings. Capitals seem to have been used only in conjunction with punctuation. The Greek citations contained in Boethius's *De musica* were separated, in the Insular mode, by both space and medial interpuncts. Numbers were punctuated by space into decimal distinctions, the *virga* being used as a sign for thousands, and on ff. 37–38v, Arabic numbers were used as emblematic tie notes. The marginal Insular critical sign *r* was present.

23. H. P. Lattin, "The Eleventh-Century MS Munich 14436: Its Contribution to the History of Coordinates, of Logic, of German Studies in France," *Isis* 38 (1947–48): 205–25; R. Derolez, *Runica Manuscripta: The English Tradition* (Bruges, 1954), pp. 251–53 and pl. 6.

24. Microfilm and *notice* at the IRHT. The codex has no shelf-mark.

25. Jean Vezin, *Les Scriptoria d'Angers*, p. 158.

26. In contrast, a scribe copied Bernard's text in ca. 1087 in Sélestat, BM 95, in canonically separated script that employed the *trait d'union* and used both the hyphen and the successor mark to the *diastole* to correct errors in canonical separation. The year 1087 is the foundation date of the Abbey of Sainte-Foy de Sélestat; cf. Cottineau, *Répertoire topo-bibliographique*, 2: 2980. For a list of the manuscripts of the *Vita*, see Auguste Bouillet, *Liber miraculorum sanctae Fidis* (Paris, 1897), pp. xv–xxv; Auguste Bouillet and L. Servières, *Sainte Foy, vièrge et martyre* (Rodez, 1910). Chartres, BM 1036 (1373) from the Abbey of Saint-Père was destroyed in 1944.

27. Wolfenbüttel, Herzog August Bibliothek Weissenburg 101; R. B. C. Huygens, "A propos de Bérenger et son traité de l'eucharistie," *RB* 76 (1966): 133–39, and *Beringerius Turoniensis, Rescriptum contra Lanfrancum*, in *CCCM* 84 (Turnhout, 1988), facsimile edition in preparation; Saenger, "Coupure et séparation des mots sur le Continent au Moyen Age"; R. W. Southern, "Lanfranc of Bec and Berengar of Tours," in *Studies in Medieval History Presented to F. M. Powicke*, p. 38n.

28. For examples of elongated descenders used as marks of insertion in Anglo-Saxon manuscripts, see Jean Vezin, "Manuscrits des dixième et onzième siècles," plate of Paris, BN lat. 272, following p. 284.

29. Brussels, BR 5576–604, ff. 157–63; van den Gheyn, *Catalogue* I (1901): 194–98; H. Silvestre, "Notice sur Adelman de Liège, évêque de Brescia (†1061)," *RHE* 56 (1961): 861; R. B. C. Huygens, "Textes latins du XIe au XIIIe siècle," *Studi medievali,* ser. 3, 8 (1967): 459. Other terminal forms in Weissenburg 101 were the elevated *s* and the crossed capital *S* for -*orum*. Berengar's monolexic abbreviations included the ampersand set off by space and the tironian sign for the conjunction *et* and the tironian sign for *est*, the same found in manuscripts close to Abbo.

30. Two early copies of his letter to Berengar of Tours survive, written in ca. 1049, disputing the latter's teachings on the Eucharist. In Admont, Stiftsbibliothek 769, the text was transcribed along with Adelman's letter to Herman II, archbishop of Cologne (1036–56). Word separation varied between 2 and 2.66 unities of space, with space after monosyllables often omitted. Terminal forms included the usual signs for -*us*, -*orum*, the capital *S*, and the *NT* ligature at line endings. Monolexic abbreviations consisted of superscript forms and the ampersand set off by space for the conjunction *et*. Proper names were denoted by capital letter suspension abbreviations; *prosodiae* included sparse *traits d'union*. Another early copy of Adelman's letter to Berengar was transcribed in Wolfenbüttel, Herzog August Bibliothek Aug. 18.4 2° ff. 116–24v, from the Abbey of Saint Erhard of Regensburg (Cottineau, *Répertoire topo-bibliographique*, 2: 2408–9), where the text was erroneously titled *Epistola Ieronimi*. This copy was also separated by space equivalent to from 2 to 3 times the unity of space, with terminal forms including the usual signs for -*tur*, -*us*, -*ra*, the round and elevated *s*, the *us* ligature and the capital *NT* ligature both reserved for line endings. Proper names were capitalized. On Adelman of Liège, see the important article (correcting numerous previous errors) by H. Silvestre, "Notice sur Adelman de Liège," pp. 855–71. Between 1028 and 1033, Adelman wrote an alphabetical poem *De viris illustribus sui temporis* (*PL* 143: 1295–98), listing the students of Fulbert's.

31. Backhouse, *The Golden Age*, no. 44; Temple, *Anglo-Saxon Manuscripts*, no. 32; and especially Paul Tannery and Jules-Alexandre Clerval, "Une correspondance d'écolâtres du XIe siècle," *Notices et extraits* 36, pt. 2 (1901): 491–93; Mostert, *The Library of Fleury*, BF 1083; Gneuss, "A Preliminary List," no. 886.

32. René-Jean Hesbert, *Manuscrits musicaux de Jumièges*, Monumenta musicae sacrae, vol. 2 (Macon, 1954), pp. 58–60 and pl. 63.

33. In Paris, BN lat. 7377C and Vat. lat. 3123. A fragment of the *De quadratura circuli*, copied on ff. 60v–61 of Paris, BN lat. 10444, written in separated script, contained the terminal elevated round *s*, the terminal capital *US* ligature, the terminal ampersand, and the capital *S* at the end of a paragraph. Geometric angles were represented by pictographs set off by interpuncts and unknown values variably by both capital and minuscule letters set off by space and interpuncts. *Prosodiae* were limited to the suspended *r* ligature as a sign of interline word continuation.

34. On Adalbero, see G. A. Hückel, "Les poèmes satiriques d'Adalbéron," *Bibliothèque de la faculté des lettres: Université de Paris* 13 (1901): 49–184; A. Regnier, *DHGE* 1 (1912): 437–38; Robert T. Coolidge, "Adalbéron, Bishop of Laon," *Studies in Medieval and Renaissance History* 2 (1965): 3–114, esp. pp. 106–11.

35. Microfilm and *notice* are at the IRHT; *Catalogue général des manuscrits des départements* 25 (1894): 322–23; J. Mangeart, *Manuscrits de Valenciennes* (Paris, 1860), pp. 300–304.

36. E. van Mingroot, *DHGE* 20 (1984): 742–51; L. Bethmann, ed., *Gesta episcoporum Cameracensium*, in *MGH: Scriptores* 7 (1846): 398–99 and pl. 3. I am grateful to Mr. W. J. van den Brink of the Department of Special Collections of the Koninklijke Bibliotheek for obtaining a microfilm of this codex.

37. See Bautier and Gilles, *Odorannus de Sens: Opera omnia*, p. 10; Bautier and Labory, *Helgaud de Fleury: Vie de Robert le Pieux*, p. 62. Ingon is not mentioned by Gerbert in his *Epistulae*.

38. U. Berlière, *DHGE* 1 (1912): 524–25; Lattin, *The Letters of Gerbert*, p. 301 n. 1.

39. Partial microfilm and *notice* at the IRHT; Bubnov, *Gerberti opera mathematica*, p. lxxi; P. Courcelle, "Etude critique sur les commentaires de la Consolatione de Boèce (IX–XVe siècle)," *Archives d'histoire doctrinale et littéraire* 12 (1939): 73–76, 126.

40. Bubnov, *Gerberti opera mathematica*, pp. 300–301.

41. *MGH: Scriptores* 4 (1841): 679–95. No medieval manuscripts of this text are recorded.

42. Paul Fournier, "Etudes critiques sur le Décret de Burchard de Worms," *Nouvelle revue historique de droit français et étranger* 34 (1910): 41–112, 289–331, 564; Fournier and Le Bras, *Histoire des collections canoniques*, 2: 384–419.

43. L. Weiland, *MGH: Legum sectio IV; Constitutiones et acta publica* 1 (1893): 639–44; Fournier, "Etudes critiques," pp. 43–44. No eleventh-century copies are recorded.

44. See the remarks of F. L. Ganshof, "Recherches sur les capitulaires," *Revue historique de droit français et étranger* 35 (1953): 209–12.

45. For the textual tradition, see Otto Meyer, "Überlieferung und Verbreitung des Dekrets des Bischof's Burchard von Worms," *Zeitschrift der Savigny-Stiftung für Rechtsgeschichte: Kanonistische Abteilung* 24 (1935): esp. 148–50; Gerard Fransen, "La tradition manuscrite du *Décret* de Burchard de Worms: Une première orientation," in Audomar Scheuermann and Georg May, eds., *Ius Sacrum: Klaus Mörsdorf zum 60. Geburtstag* (Munich, 1969), pp. 113–18.

46. A microfilm is at the IRHT. Winfried Hagenmaier, *Die lateinischen mittelalterlichen Handschriften der Universitätsbibliothek Freiburg im Breisgau* 1 (1974): 7–10; Hoffmann, *Buchkunst und Königtum*, pp. 208–9 and pl. 70.

47. *France: Manuscrits datés* 3 (1974): 99 and pl. 19. Part of the unseparated portion was written by scribe Wolkerius (f. 162, col. b).

48. Fransen, "La tradition manuscrite du *Décret*," p. 116.

49. See the early manuscripts of Hilary of Poitier's *De trinitate* enumerated and described by P. Smoulders in F. L. Cross, ed., *Studia Patristica* 3 (Berlin, 1961): 129–38.

50. Fournier, "Etudes critiques," pp. 43–44.

51. Lapière, *Lettre ornée*, pp. 9–42 (pls. 4–7, 12–13), 360; van den Gheyn, *Catalogue*, 2: 78; Bernard Lambert, *Bibliotheca Hieronymiana manuscripta*, 4 vols. (The Hague, 1959, 1972), 2: no. 207 for the text.

52. Space was occasionally inserted after monosyllabic prepositions and other monosyllables.

53. See the studies by André Boutemy; "Une page de notes de lectures de Sigebert de Gembloux," *Scriptorium* 3 (1949): 183–89; and "Fragments d'une oeuvre perdue de Sigebert de Gembloux: Le commentaire métrique de l'Ecclésiaste," *Latomus* 2 (1938): 196–209.

54. Other monolexic abbreviations included l for *vel*, superscript forms, and the Insular sign for *autem*.

55. M. B. Parkes, "The Influence of the Concepts of *Ordinatio* et *Compilatio* on the Development of the Book," in Alexander and Gibson, *Medieval Learning and Literature*, pp. 115–41.

56. He attributed this error to the corrupting influence of vulgar speech, which he did not clearly differentiate from Latin. Karl Manitius, *Gunzo Epistola ad Augienses*, in *MGH: Quellen zur Geistgeschichte des Mittelalters* 2 (Weimar, 1958): 27; Riché, *École et enseignement*, p. 153.

57. Manitius, *Gunzo Epistola*, pp. 14–15.

58. Microfilm at the IRHT; Pellegrin, *Manuscrits latins de la Bodmeriana*, pp. 147–48 and pl. 7.

59. Word separation was first in evidence in the eleventh-century copy of this text contained in Valenciennes, BM 298, ff. 89v–109v, originating from the monastery of Saint-Amand subsequent to the introduction of separation to this important scriptorium.

60. For Ratherius's autograph script and scripts closely related to his, see Bernhard Bischoff, *Anecdota novissima*, pp. 10–12; Claudio Leonardi, "Raterio e Marziano Capella," *IMU* 2 (1959): pls. 1–4; F. Weigle, "Die Briefe Rathers von Verona," *Deutsches Archiv für Geschichte des Mittelalters* 1 (1937): plate following p. 160; Giuseppe Billanovich, "Dal Livio di Raterio (Laur 63, 19) al Livio del Petrarca (BM Harley 2493)," *IMU* 2 (1959): pls. 5–10.

61. Valenciennes, BM 843, is an example. Microfilm and *notice* at the IRHT. See F. Weigle, "Zwei Fragmente von Rathers *Excerptum ex Dialogo Confessionali*," *Archiv für Urkundenforschung* 15 (1938): 136–44.

62. Odon's work were disseminated in the eleventh century in separated script; see Gabriella Braga, "Problemi di autenticità per Oddone di Cluny: L'epitome dei *Moralia* di Gregorio Magni," *Studi medievali* 18, pt. 2 (1977): 50–51 and pls. 2–4; André Wilmart, *Codices regienses latini* 2 (Vatican City, 1975):

154–55; Victor Saxer, "Un manuscrit démembré du sermon d'Eudes de Cluny sur Ste. Marie-Madeleine," *Scriptorium* 8 (1954): 119–23.

63. Chroust, *Monumenta Palaeographica*, ser. 1, 1: 18, 10; Jean Vezin, "Une importante contribution à l'étude du scriptorium de Cluny à la limite des XIᵉ et XIIᵉ siècles," *Scriptorium* 21 (1967): 317–18; Schramm and Mütherlich, *Denkmale*, p. 162, no. 126.

64. Léopold Delisle, "Notice sur les manuscrits originaux d'Adémar de Chabannes," *Notices et extraits* 35 (1896): 241–358 with 12 plates; notices for lat. 1121, 1978, 2355, 2400, 2469, 5288, 5296, 5943A, 6190, 7231, 13220, in *France: Manuscrits datés*, vols. 2 and 3; Jean Vezin, "Un nouveau manuscrit autographe d'Adémar de Chabannes (Paris, BN lat. 7321)," *Bulletin de la Société Nationale des Antiquaires de France* (February 24, 1965): 42–52; Bischoff, *Anecdota novissima*, pl. 2.

65. Paris, BN lat. 2400, ff. 154–62v, 183; *Catalogue général des manuscrits latins* 2 (1940): 444–45, 471–72.

66. Microfilm at the IRHT; Bautier and Gilles, *Odorannus de Sens: Opera omnia*, pls. 1–4.

67. Bautier and Labory, *Helgaud de Fleury: Vie de Robert le Pieux*, pp. 60–63.

68. Lattin, *The Letters of Gerbert*, letter 180 (Havet 171), pp. 208–9, 345, 386.

69. Mostert, *The Political Theology of Abbo of Fleury*, p. 19 and passim.

70. Behrends, *The Letters and Poems of Fulbert of Chartres*.

71. For the keen debate concerning who wrote English royal diplomas, see the contrasting views of Pierre Chaplais in Felicity Ranger, ed., *Prisca munimenta* (London, 1973); T. A. M. Bishop, *English Caroline Minuscule* (Oxford, 1971), pp. xix, 9; and Simon Keynes, *The Diplomas of King Aethelred, "The Unready," 978–1016: A Study of Their Use as Historical Evidence* (Cambridge, 1980), pp. 39–83. David Dumville, "English Libraries Before 1066: Use and Abuse of the Manuscript Evidence," in Michael W. Herren ed., *Insular Latin Studies: Papers on Latin Texts and Manuscripts of the British Isles 550–1066*, Papers on Latin Texts in Mediaeval Studies, vol. 1 (Toronto, 1981), pp. 163–64 and n. 41.

72. Françoise Gasparri, *L'écriture des actes de Louis VI, Louis VII et Philippe-Auguste*, Hautes études médiévales et modernes, vol. 20 (Geneva, 1973); "La chancellerie du roi Louis VII et ses rapports avec le scriptorium de l'abbaye de Saint-Victor de Paris," *Palaeographica, diplomatica et archivistica: Studi in onore di Giulio Battelli*, 2 vols. (Rome, 1979), 2: 151–58; and "Un copiste lettré de l'abbaye de Saint-Victor de Paris au XIIᵉ siècle," *Scriptorium* 30 (1976): 232–37.

73. Several canonically separated charters of Cluny have long been recognized as forgeries, e.g., Paris, BN Collection de Bourgogne, no. 76, pièce no. 1; see Delisle, *Fonds de Cluni*, p. 253.

74. See, for example, Georges Tessier, *Diplomatique royale française* (Paris, 1962), pl. 1, fig. 1 and pl. 2, fig. 2; *ChLA* 15 (1986): nos. 602, 605, 606; 19 (1987): nos. 673, 681.

75. J. J. Vernier, *Recueil de facsimilés de chartes normandes publiés à l'occasion*

du cinquantenaire de sa fondation (1869–1919) par la Société de l'Histoire de Normandie, SHN publication, 54 (Rouen, 1919), pl. 1.

76. Newman, *Catalogue des actes de Robert II,* no. 6; Jean Mabillon, *Acta sanctorum ordinis sancti Benedicti* (Paris, 1668–1701), Saecula VI, 1: 34; Joseph-Balthasar Silvestre, *Paléographie universelle* (Paris, 1839–41), pt. 3.

77. Archives Départementales de l'Yonne, reproduced in *Musée des archives départementales,* pp. 36–38 and pl. 13.

78. Paris, AN, K 18, no. 91; Newman, *Catalogue des actes de Robert II,* no. 3; *Recueil de fac-similes à l'usage de l'École des Chartes,* pls. 36 and 36 bis.

79. The subscription of *Giradus Hostiensis episcopus,* appended to this document in 1072–73, was written in clearly separated script with the capital terminal *S,* then firmly associated with the new mode of protoscholastic writing.

80. Archives de la Côte d'Or 2 H, liasse 2 (reg. 869), no. 14; Newman, *Catalogue des actes de Robert II,* no. 87; Chevrier and Chaume, *Chartes et documents de Saint-Bénigne,* 2: no. 260; Gautier, "Etude sur un diplôme," p. 276 and pl. 2; Clovis Brunel, *BEC* 71 (1910): 603–9; cf. Ernst Petit, *Histoire des ducs de Bourgogne,* 9 vols. (Dijon, 1885–1905), 2: x–xvi.

81. Archives de la Côte d'Or 9 H, liasse 2, 1ère layette, no. 2; Newman, *Catalogue des actes de Robert II,* no. 83; Chevrier and Chaume, *Chartes et documents de Saint-Bénigne,* 2: no. 233.

82. Archives de la Côte d'Or 2 H, liasse 2 (reg. 869), no. 15; Newman, *Catalogue des actes de Robert II,* no. 83; Chevrier and Chaume, *Chartes et documents de Saint-Bénigne,* 2: no. 296; reproduced in *Musée des archives départementales,* pl. 20.

83. Paris, AN, K 18, no. 8; Newman, *Catalogue des actes de Robert II,* no. 39.

84. Paris, AN, K 18, no. 7; Newman, *Catalogue des actes de Robert II,* no. 44.

85. Rouen, Archives de Seine Maritime, 9H 24; Newman, *Catalogue des actes de Robert II,* no. 74.

86. Monolexic abbreviations included the conventional tironian sign for *et* and superscript forms. Terminal forms included the usual symbols for *m, -us, -tur, -que,* and the round *s.*

87. Rouen, Archives de Seine-Maritime, 9H 1433; Newman, *Catalogue des actes de Robert II,* no. 75; Paris, AN, K 18, no. 6; Newman, *Catalogue des actes de Robert II,* no. 84.

88. Paris, AN, K 18, no. 85; Newman, *Catalogue des actes de Robert II,* no. 73 and Paris, AN, K 18, no. 5; Newman, *Catalogue des actes de Robert II,* no. 85.

89. *Recueil des fac-similes à l'usage de l'École des Chartes,* pl. 39; Frédéric Soehnée, *Catalogue des actes d'Henri Ier Roi de France* (Paris, 1907), no. 26.

90. Soehnée, *Catalogue des actes d'Henri Ier,* no. 80; Paris, BN Collection de Picardie, vol. 293, pièce no. 1.

91. Soehnée, *Catalogue des actes d'Henri Ier,* no. 102; Paris, AN, K 19, no. 52; *Recueil de fac-similes à l'usage de l'École des Chartes,* pl. 37; Tessier, *Diplomatique*

royale française, pl. 6; cf. Jean Mabillon, *De re diplomatica* (Paris, 1681), p. 392. Intersyllabic space varied between 1 to 2 times the unity of space. Terminal forms included the usual signs for *m, -us, -orum, -bus, -tur* (also used once within a word), the long *j*, and the capital *NT* at line endings. The long form for *j* was also used as a terminal form for numerals which were set off by space without interpuncts. In these diplomas, space was only occasionally inserted after monosyllabic prepositions.

92. Schramm and Mütherich, *Denkmale*, no. 65 and plate.

93. Wolfenbüttel, Niedersächsische Staatsarchiv G Urkunde 11; *Die Heiratsurkunde der kaiserin Theophanu 14 April 972: Faksimile Ausgabe* (Stuttgart, n.d.); Heinrich von Sybel and Theodor Sickel, *Kaiserurkunden in Abbildungen* (Berlin, 1881–89), 9: pl. 2; Schramm and Mütherich, *Denkmale*, no. 72; Louis Grodecki, Florentine Mütherich, Jean Taralon, and Francis Wormald, *Le siècle de l'an mil: 900–1050* (Paris, 1973); Hoffmann, *Buchkunst und Königtum*, pp. 176–77. On the handwriting, see Florentine Mütherich, "Ottonian Art: Changing Aspects," in *Studies in Western Art: Acts of the 20th International Congress of the History of Art* 1 (1963): 37–38 and pl. 10.

94. Stiennon, *L'écriture diplomatique dans le diocèse de Liège*, plates on pp. 58, 120–21; Sybel and Sickel, *Kaiserurkunden.*

95. Florentine Mütherich, "The Library of Otto III," in Ganz, *The Role of the Book*, 1: 15; Schramm and Mütherich, *Denkmale*, no. 94 with plate; Hoffmann, *Buchkunst und Königtum*, p. 368; Leitschuh, *Katalog der Handschriften der Königlichen Bibliothek zu Bamberg* 1, pt. 1 (1895): 36–39.

96. Hoffmann, *Buchkunst und Königtum*, pp. 303–53 and pls. 137–68.

97. Mütherich, "The Library of Otto III," p. 17; Schramm and Mütherich, *Denkmale*, no. 91 with plate; Leitschuh, *Katalog der Handschriften der Königlichen Bibliothek zu Bamberg* 1, pt. 1 (1906): 847–52.

98. Mütherich, "The Library of Otto III," pp. 19–20. Bamberg, Staatsbibliothek Patr. 46 (Q.VI.42), written in separated script, was another of Gerbert's gifts to his Imperial pupil. Mütherich, "The Library of Otto III," p. 20; Schramm and Mütherich, *Denkmale*, no. 96 with plate; Leitschuh, *Katalog der Handschrift der Königlichen Bibliothek zu Bamberg* 1, pt. 1, 3 (1903): 407–9.

99. Bamberg, Staatsbibliothek Lit. 140 and 143, Kassel Landesbibliothek, 4° Theol. 15; Schramm and Mütherich, *Denkmale*, nos. 116, 135, 136; Hoffmann, *Buchkunst und Königtum*, pp. 309, 407 and pls. 140, 219–20, 222.

Chapter 10

1. They include Dunstan's own schoolbook, Oxford, BL Auct. F. 4. 32; Augustine's *Expositio in Apocalypsim*, dating from 940–57, Oxford, BL Hatton 30 (SC 4076); the *Benedictional of Saint Aethelwold*, London, BL Add. 49598, written for Dunstan's intimate companion in ca. 971; the Missal of Robert of Jumièges, Rouen, BM 274 (Y.6), written after 1015; the *Ramsey Psalter*, London,

BL Harley 2904, written in the late tenth century; and the *Bosworth Psalter*, London, BL Add. 37517, which bears Dunstan's *ex libris*.

2. Lambeth Palace 362; Copenhagen, Kongelige Bibliotek GL. Kgl. S. 1588. See Winterbottom, *Three Lives of English Saints*, pp. 8–10; Cousin, *Abbon de Fleury-sur-Loire*, p. 9; M. R. James, "Bury St. Edmunds Manuscripts," *English Historical Review* 41 (1926): 258.

3. Oxford, Saint John's College 17; Cambridge, Trinity College, R. 15. 32 (945); London, BL Royal 13 A XI.

4. Backhouse, *The Golden Age*, no. 34; Temple, *Anglo-Saxon Manuscripts*, no. 35; Ker, *Catalogue of Manuscripts Containing Anglo-Saxon*, no. 363; Delisle, *Cabinet des manuscrits*, 3: 268; Leroquais, *Les pontificaux manuscrits*, 2: 6; *NPS* 1: pls. 111–12; Gneuss, "A Preliminary List," no. 879.

5. David Knowles, *The Monastic Order in England* (Cambridge, 1963), p. 50.

6. In an early Insular addition to the codex, a list of the bishops of Sherborne on f. iv, Aelthric (1002–ca. 1012) is the last bishop listed.

7. See T. A. M. Bishop, *English Caroline Minuscule* (Oxford, 1971), pp. xi n. 1, xxi–xxiv; Marguerite-Marie Dubois, *Aelfric docteur et grammarien: Contribution à l'étude de la vie et l'action bénédictine en Angleterre au Xe siècle* (Paris, 1943), pls. 1, 2, 4; Gneuss, "A Preliminary List," nos. 13, 115, 182, 331, 373, 403, 404, 435, 441, 442, 472 (end of the tenth century), 494, 670, 830, 918.

8. Delisle, *Cabinet des manuscrits*, 2: 446–47; D. de Bruyne, "Les manuscrits de Notre-Dame de Paris," *RB* 29 (1912): 483–85.

9. This Abbo might also be Abbo of Saint-Germain-des-Prés; U. Rouziès, *DHGE* 1 (1912): 51–52.

10. Microfilm and *notice* are at the IRHT; Verdun, BM 26, a collection of astronomical texts, and Verdun, BM 45, which included a *Life of Saint Ambrose* and Eusebius's *Ecclesiastical History*, were written in hierarchical word blocks with neither *prosodiae* nor capitalization prominent as aids to the discernment of words. Paris, BN Collection Porcher.

11. *Gesta episcoporum Virdunensium*, ed. G. Waitz, in *MGH: Scriptores* 4 (1841): 36–51; Kenney, *Sources for the Early History of Ireland*, no. 434; *Vita Richardi abbatis s. Vitoni Virdonensis*, ed. D. W. Wattenbach, in *MGH: Scriptores* 11 (1854): 280–90, chaps. 4–6; Kenney, *Sources for the Early History of Ireland*, no. 435.

12. *France: Manuscrits datés* 3 (1974): 423 and pl. 15; Riché, *Écoles et enseignement*, pp. 166–67.

13. G. T. Dennis, *NCE* 13 (1966): 218–19.

14. For editions and attribution of the authorship of the *Vita sancti Rodingi*, see Hubert Dauphin, *Le bienheureux Richard Abbé de Saint-Vannes de Verdun †1046*, Bibliothèque de la *RHE*, vol. 24 (Louvain, 1946), p. 232; Kenney, *Sources for the Early History of Ireland*, nos. 52, 435; *BHL* 2: no. 7281.

15. *BHL* 2: no. 8708.

16. Richard was elected October 28, 1004. Selected photographs on file in

the Section de paléographie, IRHT; *France: Manuscrits datés* 5 (1965): 531 and pl. 244; Dauphin, *Le bienheureux Richard Abbé de Saint-Vannes de Verdun*, plate of ff. 3v–4.

17. Riché, *Écoles et enseignement*, pp. 166–67.

18. Etienne Sabbe, "Notes sur la réforme de Richard de Saint-Vannes dans les Pays-Bas," *Revue belge de philologie et d'histoire* 7 (1928): 567.

19. *France: Manuscrits datés* 5 (1965): 533 and pl. 6; additional selected photographs on file in the Section de paléographie, IRHT.

20. Chicago, Newberry Library, 10, an eleventh-century copy of Boethius's *De consolatione philosophiae*, offers other examples of this phenomenon.

21. Richard simultaneously exercised both offices until 1033, when Bishop Reginard, Wolbodon's successor, dismissed Richard from Lobbes. All three codices copied by Rothardus were likely written during Richard's co-administration of the two abbeys.

22. *France: Manuscrits datés* 5 (1965): 633; selected photographs, Section de paléographie, IRHT; Paris, BN Collection Porcher.

23. *France: Manuscrits datés* 5 (1965): 634; photographs in the Section de paléographie, IRHT.

24. Verdun, BM 10, ff. 1–127, containing a calendar, a *martyrologium*, and the Regula sancti Benedicti, copied at approximately the same date at the Abbey of Saint-Airy of Verdun, confirms that canonical separation had become normal not only at Saint-Vannes but at adjacent Benedictine foundations by the end of the eleventh century.

25. See the discussion by Claude Gandelman, "By Way of Introduction: Inscription as Subversion," in *Inscriptions in Reading*, the special-issue title of *Visible Language* 23, nos. 2–3 (1989): 141–42. In contrasting Western and Oriental art, Gandelman does not consider the impact of the medieval changes in written format.

26. For some examples, see Mieczylaw Wallis, "Inscriptions in Paintings," *Semiotica* 9 (1973): 3–14.

27. *S. Gregorii Magni Registrum epistularum libri VIII–XIV*, ed. D. Norburg, in *CSEL* 140A (1982): bk. 9, 109; bk. 11, 10, 768, 873–76. See the remarks of Abbot Suger, in Erwin Panofsky, ed., *Abbot Suger on the Abbey Church of Saint-Denis*, 2d ed. (Princeton, 1979), pp. 62–63.

28. A recent study has begun to quarry one aspect of this material: D. Alexandre-Bidon, "Apprendre à lire l'enfant au Moyen Age," *Annales: Economies, sociétés, civilisations* 44 (1989): 953–92.

29. De Moreau, *Histoire de l'église de Belgique*, 2: 163–64; See A. Gauchie, *Biographie nationale*, 19: 256; Denis Escudier, "Le scriptorium de Saint-Vaast d'Arras des origines au XIIᵉ siècle: Contribution à l'étude des notations neumatiques du nord de la France," *Ecole Nationale des Chartes: Positions des thèses* (1970), p. 76.

30. *France: Manuscrits datés* 3 (1974): 645; Delisle, *Cabinet des manuscrits*,

3: 274 and pl. 31, no. 5; Léopold Delisle, "Mémoires sur d'anciens sacramen-taires," *Mémoires de l'Academie des Inscriptions et Belles-Lettres* 32 (1886): 188–90 (no. 56); Leroquais, *Sacramentaires et missels,* 1: 79–81.

31. Paris, BN Collection Porcher; Sigrid Schulten, "Die Buchmalerei des 11. Jahrhunderts im Kloster St. Vaast in Arras," *Münchner Jahrbuch der Bildenden Kunst,* ser. 3, 7 (1956): 79–81, no. 3, and pls. 6–7, 10, 14, 45–46; Escudier, "Le scriptorium de Saint-Vaast," p. 78.

32. Schulten, "Die Buchmalerei," p. 83, no. 10, and pl. 51.

33. Paris, BN Collection Porcher; Schulten, "Die Buchmalerei," p. 83, no. 9, and pls. 9, 23–24.

34. Schulten, "Die Buchmalerei," p. 86, no. 16, and pl. 27; "Bulletin codi-cologique," *Scriptorium* 24 (1970): p. 211, no. 428.

35. Schulten, "Die Buchmalerei," pp. 81–82, no. 6, and pls. 42–43; Escudier, "Le scriptorium de Saint-Vaast," p. 78.

36. Paris, BN Collection Porcher; Schulten, "Die Buchmalerei," p. 81, no. 5.

37. André Boutemy, "Notes de voyages sur quelques manuscrits de l'ancien archidiocèse de Reims," *Scriptorium* 2 (1948): 128 and pl. 18a.

38. The list of these books was added to Arras, BM 849 (294); Escudier, "Le scriptorium de Saint-Vaast," p. 76.

39. Word-separated codices with frequent terminal forms and *prosodiae* in-clude Brussels, BR 5478–83, 5571–72, and Paris, BN lat. 5795; Lapière, *Lettre orneé,* pp. 6–7 (pls. 1 and 2), 359; pp. 9, 12–41 (pls. 8–9, 22), 364; pp. 9, 366; André Boutemy, "Un manuscrit de Gembloux parmi les *codices Tornacenses* de la Bibliothèque Nationale de Paris (lat. 5795)," in *Mélanges Félix Rousseau: Etudes sur l'histoire du pays mosan au Moyen Age* (Brussels, 1958), pls. 1 and 2.

40. Anne-Catherine Fraeys de Veubeke, "Les *Annales Sancti Iacobi Leo-diensis minores,* seraient-elles originaires de Gembloux?" in *Hommages à André Boutemy,* pp. 117–28 and pl. 8.

41. Microfilm and *notice* at the IRHT; Lapière, *Lettre ornée,* pp. 41–43 (pl. 43), 346; van den Gheyn, *Catalogue* 1 (1901): 194–99.

42. De Moreau, *Histoire de l'église de Belgique,* 2: 165.

43. Microfilm and *notice* at the IRHT; *Catalogue général des manuscrits des départements* 25 (1894): 408–9.

44. Microfilm and *notice* at the IRHT; *Catalogue général des manuscrits des départements* 25 (1894): 359–60; Holtz, *Donat et la tradition de l'enseignement,* p. 401. For the various texts of Aristotle's *Categoriae,* see Lorenzo Minio-Palluelo, "The Text of the *Categoriae,*" *The Classical Quarterly* 39 (1945): 63–74.

45. See ff. 27–42v and 64v–65.

46. Léon Maitre, *Les écoles épiscopales et monastiques à l'occident depuis Charlemagne jusqu'à Philippe-Auguste* (Paris, 1886), pp. 283–85; Delisle, *Cabinet des manuscrits,* 2: 448–58.

47. Especially Orléans, BM 277 and Paris, BN NAL 1630.

48. For example, ff. 130–30v and 134.

49. Microfilm and *notice* at the IRHT; *Catalogue général des manuscrits des départements* 25 (1894): 384; Leslie Webber Jones and Christopher Morey, *The Miniatures of the Manuscripts of Terence Prior to the Nineteenth Century* (Princeton, 1930–31), p. 19.

50. Microfilm and *notice* at the IRHT; *Catalogue général des manuscrits des départements* 25 (1894): 370.

51. Microfilm and *notice* are at the IRHT; *Catalogue général des manuscrits des départements* 25 (1894): 370.

52. Similar alphabetical characters were present in the second cartulary of the Abbey of Farfa, the *Liber largitorius*, called by Gregory the *Liber notarius* (Rome, BN Vittorio Emanuele II, Farfa 2). In its sophistication, this volume surpassed any of the northern cartularies. The *Liber largitorius* was written in 1103 in script separated by 2 times the unity of space, with initial capitals denoting proper names. The codex was foliated, and the table provided reference to folio and to sequential letters of the alphabet placed at the apposite locus in the codex's margins.

53. Microfilm and *notice* at the IRHT; *Catalogue général des manuscrits des départements* 25 (1894): 260.

54. See A. C. Clark, *The Descent of Manuscripts* (Oxford, 1918), p. 35.

55. André Boutemy, *Manuscrits à miniatures (IXᵉ–XIIᵉ siècle) à l'exposition scaldis à Tournai* (n.p., 1956), p. 25, nos. 36–37; *Catalogue général des manuscrits des départements* 25 (1894): 208.

56. Microfilm and *notice* at the IRHT; *Catalogue général des manuscrits des départements* 25 (1894): 403–5; see, for plates, de Moreau, *Histoire de l'église de Belgique*, 1: pl. 4; *MGH: Poetae latinae aevi Carolini* 3 (1896): pl. 1.

57. Constantine the Abbot, *Vita Adelberonis II Mettensis episcopus*, in *MGH: Scriptores*, ed. G. H. Pertz, 4 (1841): 658–72; Kenney, *Sources for the Early History of Ireland*, nos. 432–33; Otto III charter of January 25, 992, to the monastery of Saint Symphoria of Metz, ed. T. Sickel, in *MGH: Diplomatum regum et imperatorum Germaniae* 2, pt. 2 (1888): 493; Kenney, *Sources for the Early History of Ireland*, no. 433; M. C. Chartier, "Les moines irlandais en Lotharingie aux Xᵉ et XIᵉ siècles," unpublished mémoire de maîtrise, Université de Paris X, 1975, cited by Riché, *Écoles et enseignement*, p. 125 n. 15.

58. Cf. de Moreau, *Histoire de l'église de Belgique*, 2: 172.

59. *France: Manuscrits datés* 2 (1962): 495; Jean Vezin, "Un manuscrit messin de la première moitié du XIᵉ siècle (Reims, BM 1429)," in *Miscellanea codicologica F. Masai dicata*, 1: 157.

60. Vezin, "Un manuscript messin," p. 164.

61. Colgrave and Mynors, *Bede's Ecclesiastical History of the English People*, p. lxiv; *Catalogue général des manuscrits des départements* 39, pt. 1 (1904): 666–67; Vezin, "Un manuscrit messin," pp. 157–60, pls. 19–20; *France: Manuscrits datés* 5 (1965): 601.

62. Watson, *Oxford: Dated and Datable Manuscripts*, no. 63 and pl. 22.

63. Archives de Meurthe et Moselle; *Musée des archives départementales*, pp. 30–32, no. 14, pl. 10.

64. *Ecriture et enluminure en Lorraine au Moyen Age*, exhibition catalogue, Musée Historique Lorraine (Nancy, 1984), no. 20, with plate.

65. A microfilm is at the IRHT. *France: Manuscrits datés* 7 (1984): pl. 7; *Catalogue général des manuscrits des départements*, ser. 4, 5 (1865): 107–9; see Wilmart, *Auteurs spirituels*, pp. 126–37.

66. *France: Manuscrits datés* 3 (1974): 107 and pl. 253; cf. Vezin, "Un manuscrit messin," p. 164. The script, marked by the presence of the Insular form of minuscule *r* descending below the line, included frequent intraword ligatures. Among the *prosodiae* were the hyphen and a form of the *trait d'union* attached to letter tops, strongly suggesting a suspended ligature. Terminal forms included the long *j*, the capital *R*, *S*, and *M* at the end of units of text and the long *j* at the end of Roman numerals.

67. On Poppon, see A. Cauchie, *Biographie nationale* 18 (1905): 43–53.

68. In the eleventh century, the decoration was rejuvenated, and the codex was emended with acute accents on monosyllables and the tonic syllable, the successor note to the *diastole*, and the *trait d'union* to clarify word boundaries. Punctuation was modified to elucidate larger divisions of text. Copies of charters addressed to Remaclus as abbot of Stavelot formed part of the original codex. To these, a scribe in about the year 1000 added in separated script on ff. 133v–40v transcriptions of three charters of Otto II dating from 953, 980, and 987. Also on ff. 5v–8v, a Bull of Gregory V, dated in 996 and sent via Notker of Liège to Abbot Ravengerus, was added in script separated by approximately 2 times the unity of space. In this section, proper names were distinguished by initial capitals. See Jos. Halkin and C.-G. Roland, *Recueil des chartes de l'abbaye Stavelot-Malmédy*, 2 vols. (Brussels, 1909–30), 1: xliv–xlv (under the number E.III); Lapière, *Lettre ornée*, pp. 250, 404.

69. Lapière, *Lettre ornée*, p. 253; Eric G. Millar, *The Library of Chester Beatty: A Descriptive Catalogue of the Western Manuscripts*, 2 vols. (Oxford, 1927), 1: no. 17, and pls. 43–45.

70. Lapière, *Lettre ornée*, pp. 258–60 (pl. 239), 407.

71. Jacques Stiennon, "Le scriptorium et la domaine de l'abbaye de Malmédy du Xe siècle au début du XIIIe siècle après les manuscrits de la Bibliothèque Vaticane," *Bulletin de l'Institut historique belge de Rome* 26 (1950–51): 5–41; *Libri manoscritti e stampati del Belgio nella Biblioteca Vaticana, secoli ix-xvii*, Vatican Library exhibition catalogue (Vatican City, 1979), p. 11.

72. Gilissen, *L'expertise des écritures*, pl. 7; Watson, *British Library: Dated and Datable Manuscripts*, pp. 70–71, no. 321 and pl. 52; Lapière, *Lettre ornée*, pp. 261–77 (pls. 245–49), 411.

73. Gilissen, *L'expertise des écritures*, pls. 4, 5; Lapière, *Lettre ornée*, pp. 266–69 (pl. 244), 407.

74. Georges Despy, "Le scriptorium de l'abbaye de Waulsort au XIe siècle:

Le provenance du psautier hymnaire Munich, Bayer. Staatsbibl. Clm. 13067," *MA* 59 (1953): 87–115; Lapière, *Lettre ornée*, pp. 312–17 (pls. 282–83), 417.

75. De Moreau, *Histoire de l'église de Belgique*, 2: 177.

76. Lapière, *Lettre ornée*, pp. 173–85 (pls. 172–75), 392.

77. P. Thomas, "Les imitations de Salluste dans la *Chronique de Saint-Hubert*," *Revue belge de philologie et d'histoire* 8 (1924): 589–92.

78. E. Brouette, *DHGE* 17 (1971): 579; E. van Mingroot, *DHGE* 20 (1984): 742–51.

79. Lapière, *Lettre ornée*, pp. 307–11 (pls. 275–77), 418.

80. See, for example, Brussels, BR 14650–59; François Masai and Léon Gilissen, *Lectionarium Sancti Lamberti Leodiensis tempore Stephani paratum 901–920*, Umbrae codicum occidentalium, vol. 8 (Amsterdam, 1963); Daniel Missione, "Etienne de Liège, le Psautier de Lothaire et le Legendier de Saint-Lambert," in *Miscellanea codicologica F. Masai dicata*, 1: 123–30 and pl. 18. Liège charters of the tenth century were aerated. See, for example, Stiennon, *L'écriture diplomatique dans le diocèse de Liège*, p. 112, figs. 91–92. Word-separated charters appear to have been written as early as 1050. Henri Pirenne, *Album belge de diplomatique: Recueil de fac-similes pour servir à l'étude de la diplomatique des provinces belges au Moyen Age* (Brussels, 1909), pls. 4–6; de Moreau, *Histoire de l'église de Belgique*, 2: 173. Jacques Stiennon, *Etude sur le chartrier et le domaine de l'abbaye de Saint-Jacques de Liège (1015–1209)*, Bibliothèque de la Faculté de Philosophie et Lettres de l'Université de Liège, vol. 124 (Paris, 1951), pp. 38–42 and pl. 1. Stiennon, *L'écriture diplomatique dans le diocèse de Liège*, pp. 132 (for 1050), 113 (for 1091), 85 (for 1092), 90 (for 1092), 114 (for 1097), etc. See also Jan Frederik Niermeyer Jr., *Onderzoekingen over Luikse en Maastrichtse Oorkonden en over de Vita Baldrici episcopi Leodiensis*, Bijdragen van het Instituut voor Middeleeuwsche Geschiedenis der Rijks-Universiteit te Utrecht, vol. 20 (Groningen, 1935), pls. 2–5.

81. De Moreau, *Histoire de l'église de Belgique*, 2: 167–68; Herman Vander Linden, *Biographie nationale* 27: 392–94.

82. Van den Gheyn, *Catalogue* 1 (1901): 372–74, no. 590; Maurice Coens, "Le Psautier de Saint Wolboden, écolatre d'Utrecht, évêque de Liège," *Analecta Bollandiana* 54 (1936): 137–42; François Masai, "Les manuscrits à peintures de Sambre et Meuse au XIᵉ et XIIᵉ siècles: Pour une critique d'origine plus methodique," *Cahiers de civilisation médiévale* 3 (1960): 174–76; *Treasures of Belgian Libraries*, Exhibition catalogue, National Library of Scotland (Edinburgh, 1963), p. 20 (no. 8). Lapière, *Lettre ornée*, pp. 6–9 (pl. 3). The attribution to Wolbodon is by Renier de Saint-Laurent (1120/30–1185/90), *Vita Wolbodonis episcopii Leodiensis*, ed. W. Arndt, in *MGH: Scriptores* 20 (1868): 569–70; cf. H. Silvestre, *Le Chronicon Sancti Laurentii Leodiensis dit de Rupert de Deutz: Etude critique*, Recueil de travaux, d'histoire, et de philologie de l'Université de Louvain, ser. 3, no. 43 (Louvain, 1952), pp. 252–61.

83. Max Schott, *Zwei Lüttischer Sakramentare im Bamberg und ihre Verwan-

denten (Strasbourg, 1931), pp. 183; Leroquais, *Sacramentaires et missels*, 1: 105–7; Delisle, "Mémoires sur d'anciens sacramentaires," pp. 244–45 (no. 95); Lapière, *Lettre ornée*, pp. 120–23 (pl. 117), 391. Other word-separated Saint-Laurent books are Munich, Staatsbibliothek, Clm. 23261, another sacramentarium copied before 1051, Brussels, BR 9349–54, 9534–36, 10260–63, 9381–82, 9742, and 9512–14. Karl Hermann Usener, "Das Breviar CLM. 23261 der Bayerischen Staatsbibliothek und die Anfänge der romanischen Buchmalerei in Lüttich," *Münchner Jahrbuch der bildenden kunst*, ser. 3, 1 (1950): 78–92; Lapière, *Lettre ornée*, pp. 128–40 (pls. 128, 130–34, 136, 138, 140), 391.

84. Lapière, *Lettre ornée*, pp. 57–60 (pls. 55, 57, 59), 370.

85. Niermeyer, *Onderzoekingen over Luikse en Maastrichtse Oorkonden*, p. 6 and pl. 1.

86. De Veubeke, "Les *Annales Sancti Iacobi Leodiensis minores*," pl. 8 following p. 120. For the contemporary prior portion of this codex, see Lapière, *Lettre ornée*, p. 369, etc.

87. Joseph Warichez and Désiré van Bleyenberghe, *L'abbaye de Lobbes depuis les origines jusqu'en 1200* (Louvain, 1900), pp. 71, 72, 154, 300.

88. Leitschuh, *Katalog der Handschriften der Königlichen Bibliothek zu Bamberg* 1, 1, i (1898): 139–41. Gift of Emperor Henry II (1002–1024) to the Cathedral of Bamberg; Schott, *Zwei Lüttischer Sakramentare*, pp. 181–82. I am indebted to the Bamberg Staatsbibliothek for providing me with photocopies of representative leaves.

89. *France: Manuscrits datés* 4, 1 (1981): 340; Hoffmann, *Buchkunst und Königtum*, p. 501, cf. pls. 272–302.

90. Carl Nordenfalk, "Der Meister des Registrum Gregorii," *Münchner Jahrbuch des bildenden Kunst*, ser. 3, 1 (1950): 61 (pl. 1); cf. Hoffmann, *Buchkunst und Königtum*, pp. 345, 489; Schramm and Mütherich, *Denkmale*, no. 82.

91. Wolfenbüttel, Herzog August Bibliothek Weissenburg 75; Hans Butzmann, *Die Weissenburger Handschriften* (Frankfurt-am-Main, 1964), p. 226; cf. Emile Lesne, *Les livres, scriptoria et bibliothèques du commencement du VIIIᵉ à la fin du XIᵉ siècle*, vol. 4 of *Histoire de la propriété ecclésiastique en France* (Lille, 1938), p. 707. Gerrichus III is paleographically a more plausible identification of the Gerrichus named in the colophon of the codex than Gerrichus II (†964).

92. On the reform of Lobbes, see Warichez and van Bleyenberghe, *L'abbaye de Lobbes*, pp. 69–71.

93. On Folcuin, see E. Brouette, *DHGE* 17 (1971): 744–48.

94. Daniel Haigneré, *Les chartes de Saint-Bertin d'après le grand cartulaire de Dom. Charles Joseph Dewitte*, 4 vols., Société des antiquaires de la Morinie (Saint-Omer, 1886–99), 1: xii–xiii. The authorial copies of Folcuin's major works, the *Gesta abbatum Sancti Bertini* and the *Gesta abbatum Lobbiensum*, were destroyed during the French Revolution, and these texts survive only in late medieval and early modern copies.

95. O. Holder Egger, *MGH: Scriptores* 15, pt. 1 (1887): 424–38; E. Brouette, *DHGE* 17 (1971): 750–51. Another copy, Boulogne-sur-Mer, BM 107, containing the complete text copied in the mid-eleventh century at the Abbey of Saint-Bertin, was written in separated script.

96. Microfilm and *notice* at the IRHT; *Catalogue général des manuscrits des départements* 25 (1894): 497; F. Weigle, "Zwei Fragmente von Rathers *Excerptum ex Dialogo Confessionali*," *Archiv für Urkundenforschung* 15 (1938): 136–44, "Ein Briefragment Rathers von Verona," *Deutsches Archiv für Erforschung des Mittelalters* 19 (1963): 489–93, and *Die Briefe des Bischoffs Rather von Verona*, in *MGH: Die Briefe der Deutschen Kaiserzeit* 1 (Weimar, 1949): 69–71.

97. François Dolbeau, "Un nouveau catalogue des manuscrits de Lobbes aux XIe et XIIe siècles," *Etudes augustiniennes* 14 (1979): 207–9; H. Omont, "Catalogue des manuscrits de l'abbaye de Lobbes (1049)," *Revue des bibliothèques* 1 (1891): 3–14.

98. A microfilm is at the IRHT; Ellen Jørgensen, *Catalogus codicum latinorum medii aevi bibliothecae Regniae Hafniensis* (Copenhagen, 1926), pp. 36–37.

99. A microfilm is at the IRHT; photograph of f. 24, Paris, BN Collection Porcher; *France: Manuscrits datés* 5 (1965): 632.

100. Watson, *British Library: Dated and Datable Manuscripts*, 1: 52, no. 873, 2: pl. 45; *PS* 1: pl. 61.

101. Dolbeau, "Un nouveau catalogue," p. 22, no. 107.

102. N. Huyghebaert, *DHGE* 21 (1986): 414–15; Brussels, BR 18018; Léon Gilissen, *L'éxpertise des écritures médiévales*; Emile Brouette, "Le plus ancien manuscrit de la *Vita Beggae*: Oeuvre inconnue de Goderan de Lobbes," *Scriptorium* 16 (1962): 81–84. The Bible of Lobbes is today preserved at the Grand Séminaire of Tournai, no shelfmark is recorded; Gilissen, *L'Éxpertise des écritures médiévales*, pl. 6; *Belgium: Manuscrits datés*, 1: pls. 3–7; J. van den Gheyn, *Album belge de paléographie* (Brussels, 1908), pl. 9.

103. De Moreau, *Histoire de l'église en Belgique* 1: 165–66.

104. André Wilmart, "Les livres de l'abbé Odbert," and "Note sur l'abbatiat d'Odbert," *Société des antiquaires de la Morinie: Bulletin historique trimestriel*, 14 (1924), 169–86, 187–88. See also William Hunt, *DNB* 6: 887.

105. William Hunt, *DNB* 18: 246.

106. Photographs of ff. 10v and 56 in Paris, BN Collection Porcher; Temple, *Anglo-Saxon Manuscripts*, no. 44; on Odbert's artistic oeuvre, see the works of A. Boutemy: "La miniature," in de Moreau, *Histoire de l'église de Belgique*, 2: 323–26; "Un grand enluminure du Xe siècle: L'abbé Odbert de Saint-Bertin," *Fédération archéologique et historique de Belgique: Annales XXXIIe session, Congrès d'Anvers 27–31 juillet 1947* (1950), pp. 247–54; "Odbert de Saint-Bertin et la seconde Bible de Charles le Chauve," *Scriptorium* 3 (1949): 101–2; "Encore un manuscrit décoré par Odbert de Saint-Bertin," *Scriptorium* 4 (1950): 245–46 and pl. 27b; "Influences carolingiennes dans l'oeuvre de l'abbé Odbert de Saint-Bertin (cir. ann. 1000)," in *Karolingische und Ottonische Kunst*, pp. 427–33.

107. Photographs of 148v and 149 in Paris, BN Collection Porcher; Wilmart, "Les livres de l'abbé Odbert," pp. 174–75.

108. Photographs of f. iv in Paris, BN Collection Porcher; Wilmart, "Les livres de l'abbé Odbert," pp. 172–73.

109. Wilmart, "Les livres de l'abbé Odbert," pp. 173–74; cf. Hagneré, *Chartes de Saint-Bertin* 1: 20–21. I am indebted to the librarians of the Bibliothèque Municipale for arranging for this codex to be microfilmed. See also *CLA* 6 (1953): no. 828.

110. Numerous photographs in Paris, BN Collection Porcher; Wilmart, "Les livres de l'abbé Odbert," p. 175; Temple, *Anglo-Saxon Manuscripts*, pp. 23, 67, 100, 116 and fig. 25; Boutemy, "Un grand enluminure," pl. 20; Victor Leroquais, *Les psautiers manuscrits latins des bibliothèques publiques de France*, 2 vols. (Macon, 1940–41), 1: 94–101 and pls. 15–21.

111. Paris, BN Collection Porcher; Wilmart, "Les livres de l'abbé Odbert," pp. 178–79.

112. E. Chatelain, *Codex Vossianus quadratus*, Codices Graeci et Latini photographice depicti duce Scatone de Vries, vol. 18 (Leiden, 1913); William E. Leonard and Stanley B. Smith, eds., *T. Lucreti Cari De rerum natura libri sex* (Madison, Wis., 1942), pl. 2; de Meyier, *Codices Vossiani latini* 2 (1975): 215–17 and 4 (1984): pl. 5c; Chatelain, *Paléographie des classiques latins*, 1: pl. 58. If the speculations of textual critics are correct, this process restored word separation to a textual tradition that had once been Insular; cf. Virginia Brown, "The Insular Intermediary in the Tradition of Lucretius," *Harvard Studies in Classical Philology* 72 (1967): 301–8.

113. Temple, *Anglo-Saxon Manuscripts*, no. 30 (xv); T. A. M. Bishop, "Notes on Cambridge Manuscripts, Part VII: Manuscripts Connected with Saint Augustine's Canterbury," *Transactions of the Cambridge Bibliographical Society* 3 (1959–63): 415, 420 n. 1, 421 (no. 21); Ker, *Catalogue of Manuscripts Containing Anglo-Saxon*, no. 7; Gneuss, "A Preliminary List," p. 50, no. 185; Fred C. Robertson, "Syntactical Glosses in Latin Manuscripts of Anglo-Saxon Provenance," *Speculum* 48 (1973): 443–44; Herbert Dean Meritt, *The Old English Prudentius Glosses at Boulogne-sur-Mer* (Stanford, Calif., 1959), pl. on p. 62.

114. Robertson, "Syntactical Glosses," p. 444 n. 2; Meritt, *Old English Prudentius Glosses*, p. 14.

115. Paris, BN Collection Porcher; Wilmart, "Les livres de l'abbé Odbert," p. 181; Boutemy, "Un grand enluminure," pl. 7.

116. The same text was copied at approximately the same date in separated script at Fleury under Abbo; London, BL Harley 2506.

117. De Moreau, *Histoire de l'église en Belgique*, 2: 164–65.

118. Thomas Symons, ed., *The Monastic Agreement of the Monks and Nuns of the English Nation* (New York, 1953). The two extant manuscripts of this text— Cambridge, Corpus Christi College 201, and London, BL Cotton Tiberius A.

III + Faustina B. III—were written in separated script; Gneuss, "A Preliminary List," nos. 65, 332, 363.

119. Gysseling and Koch, *Diplomata Belgica*; cf. Maurice Prou, "Examen d'un diplôme de Charles le Chauve pour Saint-Pierre de Gand," *Bulletin de la Commission Royale d'Histoire* 84 (1922): 41–63; Otto Oppermann, *Die älteren Ur-kunden des Kloster Blandinium und die Angänge der Stadt Gent*, Bijdragen van het Instituut voor Middeleeuwsche Geschiedenis der Rijks-Universeit te Utrecht, vol. I (Utrecht, 1928), pp. 29–41; Etienne Sabbe, "Etude critique sur le diplôme d'Arnoul Ier Comte de Flandre pour l'abbaye de Saint-Pierre à Gand (941, juillet 8)," in *Etudes d'histoire dédiées à la mémoire de Henri Pirenne par ses anciens élèves* (Brussels, 1937), pp. 299–330.

120. Apparently original charters of the mid-tenth century, including those of July 8, 941, and 950–53, were written in word and syllable blocks. The abbey's first cartulary dating from the tenth century (after 941), of which a fragment survives in Ghent, Archives, Suppl. no. 2 ter, was transcribed in hierarchical word blocks exceeding twenty characters in length. Arnold Fayen, *Liber traditionum Sancti Petri Blandinensis: Livre des donations faites à l'abbaye de Saint-Pierre de Gand depuis ses origines jusqu'au XIe siècle, avec des additions jusqu'au 1273* (Ghent, 1906), p. vii and pl. I (cf. p. 37); Gysseling and Koch, *Diplomata Belgica*, no. 49 and pls. 7–10. Even if this cartulary has been assigned too early a date and was actually copied in the late tenth or eleventh century, it is evidence that the monks believed that aerated script was appropriate for documents of the ninth century.

121. Gysseling and Koch, *Diplomata Belgica*, nos. 69, 70.

122. The scribes used initial capitals for proper names both in the subscription and the text. Numerals were set off by points and space and marked with superscript inflections. The Insular form of the minuscule *r*, frequently encountered in the books of Saint-Vaast and Saint-Bertin, was present.

123. Lattin, *The Letters of Gerbert*, letter 98 (Havet 96), pp. 133–34; cf. letter 44 of July 2, 984 (Havet 36), pp. 85–86. Lattin renders the abbot's name as Guy.

124. Lattin, *The Letters of Gerbert*, letter III (Havet 105), pp. 145–46.

125. Delisle, *Inventaire des manuscrits latins*; A. Verhulst, "L'activité et la calligraphie du scriptorium de l'abbaye Saint-Pierre-au-Mont-Blandin de Gand à l'epoque de l'abbé Wichard (†1058)," *Scriptorium* 11 (1957): 44.

126. See Verhulst, "L'activité et la calligraphie," pp. 37–49; Gysseling and Koch, *Diplomata Belgica*, pls. 41, 42, 44, 48, 49, 50–53.

127. Verhulst, "L'activité et la calligraphie," pl. 7b.

128. The acute accent was usual on the monosyllable *O*.

129. Gysseling and Koch, *Diplomata Belgica*, no. 61.

130. Fayen, *Liber traditionum*, pl. 2; Gysseling and Koch, *Diplomata Belgica*, pp. 87–121; Pirenne, *Album belge de diplomatique*, pl. 9.

131. Verhulst, "L'activité et la calligraphie," pl. 10a.

132. Jean Schroeder, *Bibliothek und Schule der Abtei Echternach um die Jahrt-*

ausendwende, Inaugural-Dissertation, Freiburg in Breisgau, pp. 67–81, offprint from *Publications de la Section Historique de l'Institut Grand-Ducal de Luxembourg* 91 (Luxembourg, 1967): 201–378.

133. Schroeder, *Bibliothek und Schule*, pp. 57–59; *Aristoteles latinus*, 1: 534; Delisle, *Inventaire des manuscrits latins*; Hermann Degering, "Handschriften aus Echternach und Orval in Paris," in *Aufsaetze Fritz Milkau gewidmet* (Leipzig, 1921), p. 80.

134. Schroeder, *Bibliothek und Schule*, pp. 59–60; *Aristoteles latinus*, 1: 534–35; Delisle, *Inventaire des manuscrits latins*; Degering, "Handschriften aus Echternach," p. 85.

135. Schroeder, *Bibliothek und Schule*, pp. 60–61; *Aristoteles latinus*, 1: 535; Delisle, *Inventaire des manuscrits latins*; Degering, "Handschriften aus Echternach," p. 85.

136. Schroeder, *Bibliothek und Schule*, pp. 55–57 and pls. 1, 7; Chatelain, *Manuscrits des classiques latins*, 1: pl. 53; Delisle, *Inventaire des manuscrits latins*; Degering, "Handschriften aus Echternach," pp. 80–81.

137. Paris, BN lat. 8912, 8922, 9528; *France: Manuscrits datés* 3 (1974): 97, 99, 125 and pls. 20, 19. Some of the aerated codices, for example, the *Golden Gospel Book* of the Germanisch National-Museum in Nürnberg, were prepared for the Imperial court. See Schramm and Mütherich, *Denkmale*, no. 85.

Chapter 11

1. Lilli Gjerløw, "The Good Friday Prayers of the *Regularis concordia*" (pp. 16–27) and "The Prayers of the Rouen Psalter," MS A. 44 [231] (pp. 132–47), in *Adoratio Crucis: The Regularis concordia and the Decreti Lanfranci* (Oslo, 1961). The *Adoro te* was particularly common in late medieval books of hours.

2. Thomas Symons, *Regularis concordia Anglicae nationis monachorum sanctimonialiumque* (London, 1953), pp. xxxiii, 15, 22, 26, 27, 53–55.

3. Jean Leclercq and Jean-Paul Bonnes, *Un maître de la vie spirituelle au XIe siècle: Jean de Fécamp* (Paris, 1946), pp. 98–100.

4. *PL* 147: 477–80; *PL* 184: 569; A. Wilmart, "Jean l'homme de Dieu auteur d'un traité attribué à Saint Bernard," *Revue Mabillon* 15 (1925): 5–29. Wilmart's arguments for denying authorship to John of Fécamp are plausible but, in the absence of early manuscripts, not convincing. For a translation of the relevant passage, see Ursmer Berlière, *L'ascèse bénédictine des origines à la fin du XIIe siècle* (Paris, 1927), pp. 190–91.

5. Berlière, *L'ascèse bénédictine*, pp. 75–76; Wilmart, *Auteurs spirituels*, pp. 127–28.

6. David Knowles, ed., *Decreta Lanfranci*, in *Corpus consuetudinum monasticarum* 3 (1967): xvii–xviii.

7. David Knowles, ed., *Decreta Lanfranci*, in *Corpus consuetudinum monas-*

ticarum 3 (1967): 27–28; cf. Knowles's edition of Lanfranc's *Monastic constitutiones* (London, 1951), p. 3.

8. When the ancients sought to denote what we would term silent reading, they explicitly described the lack of oral activity. Thus, Augustine described Ambrose as reading "vox autem et lingua quiescebant," and Ovid has Cydippe state "sine murmure legi." Augustine, *Confessions*, 6.3.21; Ovid, *Heroides*, 21.1. In contrast, in the sixth century, when Isidore refers in his *Sententiae* to "lectio tacita" and "sub silentio," he is explicitly referring to oral activity: "Amplius enim intellectus instruitur quando vox legentis quiescit et sub silentio lingua movetur." It is therefore clear that he meant quiet oral reading, that is, the murmuring that throughout the Middle Ages was compatible with the monastic *silentium* of the Rule of Saint Benedict, 3.14.9; *PL* 83: 689. My interpretation of this passage differs from that of Malcolm Parkes, *Pause and Effect*, p. 21, who fails to reproduce the final clause, which runs counter to his argument. In antiquity, the quiet oral reading of the *praelectio* stood in contrast to the formal declamation of a text before a master or other audience. In monastic and religious customaries, the terms *in silentio, sub silentio,* and *taciter* were regularly applied to reading, chanting, and prayer with suppressed voice. See Carlo A. Lewis, *The Silent Recitation of the Canon of the Mass*, Excerpta ex dissertatione ad Lauream in Facultate Theologica Universitatis Gregorianae (Bay Saint Louis, Miss., 1962), esp. pp. 5, 91; S. J. P. Van Dijk, "Medieval Terminology and Methods of Psalm Singing," *Musica Disciplina* 6 (1952): 9–10. In the cloister, even a bell could be rung *tacite*. Pseudo-Benedictus de Nursia, *Ordo monasticus*, in *PL* 66: 940. This text edited from an eleventh-century manuscript, Tours, BM 284. Neurophysiologically, barely audible quiet reading is still oral reading, and its recorded presence in the Middle Ages is not directly related to the transformation of the reading process that occurred with the introduction of word separation. After the introduction of word separation, the Latin verbs *videre* and *inspicere* came to be regarded as synonyms for reading. In this way, the transformation of medieval text format ultimately permitted the same vocabulary to be applied to the reading of a text as to the viewing of a painting.

9. *Decreta Lanfranci*, ed. Knowles, pp. 90–91.

10. Symons, *Regularis concordia*, p. lv; C. R. Dodwell, *The Canterbury School of Illumination 1066–1200* (Cambridge, 1966), p. 4 and pls. 2b and 3a; 2b shows microwriting in a book within the illumination; Temple, *Anglo-Saxon Manuscripts*, no. 100, ills. 313–14.

11. See, for example, the texts accompanying Rouen, BM 1408; René-Jean Hesbert, "Les manuscrits enluminés de l'ancien fonds de Jumiège," in *Jumiège: Congrès scientifique du XIIIᵉ centenaire*, 2: pls. following p. 728.

12. *S. Anselmi Cantuariensis archiepiscopi Opera omnia*, 6 vols., ed. F. S. Schmitt (Sekau, 1938–61; reprint, Stuttgart, 1981), 3: 2.

13. R. W. Southern, *Saint Anselm and His Biographer: A Study of Monastic Life and Thought 1059–c.1130* (Cambridge, 1963), pp. 52–53.

14. *S. Anselmi opera omnia*, ed. Schmitt, 1: 24–25.

15. Anselm, *Orationes et meditationes*, in *S. Anselmi opera omnia*, ed. Schmitt, 3: 3 and *Epistola ad Gondulfum monachum*, in ibid., 3: 136.

16. "Non sunt legendae in tumultu, sed in quiete, nec cursim et velociter, sed paulatim cum intenta et morosa meditationes." *S. Anselmi opera omnia*, ed. Schmitt, 3: 1. On the problem of rapid reading, see Emile Faguet, *L'art de lire* (Paris, 1912), pp. 1–2, cited by G. L. Hendrickson, "Ancient Reading," *The Classical Journal* 25 (1929): 195 n. 7.

17. R. Mittermüller, ed., *Expositio Regulae ab Hildemaro tradita*, vol. 3 of *Vita et Regula SS. P. Benedicti una cum expositione Regulae a Hildemaro tradita* (Regensburg, 1880), p. 430, cf. p. 481.

18. Yves Delaporte, "L'office fécampois de Saint Taurin," in *L'abbaye bénédictine de Fécamp: Ouvrage scientifique de XIIIe centenaire, 658–1958*, 3 vols. (Fécamp, 1959–63), 2: 175; *Catalogue général des manuscrits latins* 1 (1939): 352–53; Nortier, *Bibliothèques*, pp. 24, 26.

19. Solange Corbin, "Valeur et sens de la notation alphabétique à Jumièges et en Normandie," in *Jumièges: Congrès scientifique du XIIIe centenaire*, 2: 914.

20. On the autograph copies of John of Fécamp's compositions, see Jean Leclercq, "Prières attribuables à Guillaume et à Jean de Fruttuaria," in *Monasteri in alta Italia dopo le invasioni saracene e magiare (sec. X–XII): Relazioni e communicazioni presantate al XXXII Congresso Storico Subalpino, III convegno di storia della chiesa in Italia (Pinerolo 6–9 settembre 1964)* (Turin, 1966), pp. 162–63; Leclercq and Bonnes, *Un maître de la vie spirituelle*, p. 229. Cf. Jean Leclercq and J.-P. Bonnes, "Une *Lamentation* inédite de Jean de Fécamp," *RB* 5 (1942): 44–45.

21. See ff. 7–8, 103v, and 152. In copying a letter of the monks of Fécamp to William the Conqueror on f. 102v of the same codex, another and contemporary hand separated words by 3 times the unity of space and employed capital suspension abbreviations for proper names. The *Epistulae* of Jerome forming one of the principal texts of the codex was written in script separated by 2 times the unity of space, with terminal forms including the capital *R*, *S*, and *NT* ligature. *Traits d'union* and acute accents as alternative and redundant signs of word separation were present throughout. Punctuation included the tripoint terminal sign and other related emblematic marks of text termination. Catalogue of the eleventh century, no. 14, Betty Branch, "Inventories of the Library of Fécamp from the Eleventh and Twelfth Century," *Manuscripta* 23 (1979): 171; Nortier, *Bibliothèques*, p. 26; *Catalogue général des manuscrits latins* 2 (1940): 210.

22. Possibly the volume recorded in the catalogue of the twelfth century, no. 16, Branch, "Inventories," p. 171; Nortier, *Bibliothèques*, p. 26; *Catalogue général des manuscrits latins* 2 (1940): 244–45.

23. Corbin, "Valeur et sens de la notation alphabétique," p. 914.

24. The codex into which these two texts were added contained Augustine's *Epistulae* written in *fere* canonically separated script.

25. *Catalogue général des manuscrits latins* 4 (1958): 97; Leclercq and Bonnes, "Une *Lamentation*," pp. 44, 51–60. This fragment is not recorded by Nortier, *Bibliothèques*.

26. *Catalogue général des manuscrits latins* 2 (1940): 446; Nortier, *Bibliothèques*, p. 26.

27. Avranches, BM 58 (copied at Mont Saint-Michel), Paris, BN lat. 574 (copied at Saint-Martial of Limoges), Metz, BM 245 (from Saint-Arnoul of Metz), and Paris, BN lat. 1919 (of uncertain origin).

28. Catalogue of the twelfth century, no. 23, Branch, "Inventories," p. 169; *Catalogue général des manuscrits latins* 2 (1940): 252–53.

29. *Catalogue général des manuscrits latins* 3 (1952): 310; Nortier, *Bibliothèques*, p. 26; Avril, *Manuscrits normands*, p. 25, no. 11.

30. Nortier, *Bibliothèques*, p. 29; Avril, *Manuscrits normands*, p. 25, no. 10. The same painter decorated Rouen, BM 489, Paris, BN lat. 2101 and 2403, as well as Salisbury, Cathedral Library 89. Avril, *Manuscrits normands*, p. 24, no. 9; *Catalogue général des manuscrits latins* 2 (1940): 320; F. Wormald, "An Eleventh-Century Copy of the Norman *Laudes Regiae*," *Bulletin of the Institute of Historical Research* 37 (1964): 73–76.

31. Léopold Delisle, "Cérémonial d'une épreuve judiciare (commencement du douzième siècle)," *BEC* 18 (1857): 253; W. Foerster and E. Koschwitz, *Altfranzösisches Übungsbuch* (Heilbronn, 1884), cols. 161–62; *Catalogue général des manuscrits latins* 2 (1940): 446–47; Guy de Poerck, "Les plus anciens textes de la langue française comme témoins de l'époque," *Revue de linguistique Romane* 27 (1963): 12, 16.

32. Peter Rickard, "Système ou arbitraire? Quelques réflexions sur la soudure des mots dans les manuscrits français du Moyen Age," *Romania* 103 (1982): 470–505.

33. *France: Manuscrits datés* 7 (1984): 299 and pl. 13; Nortier, *Bibliothèques*, p. 29; Avril, *Manuscrits normands*, p. 24, no. 9 with plate; Bubnov, *Gerberti opera mathematica*, p. lxxxv, cf. pp. 1–3, 245 for related manuscripts.

34. In 1049–51, Paris, BN NAL 2196, an illuminated Gospel book begun at the Abbey of Saint Willibrord in Echternach in Lorraine, was completed at Luxeuil for presentation to Abbot Gérard. The portion written at Luxeuil was written in canonically separated script with interword space equivalent to 4 to 5 times the unity of space and with terminal forms including the ampersand. On f. 2, Abbot Gérard was depicted in the new posture of reading, motionless, staring at his open book, and on f. iv the miniature contained a banderole, the new form of decoration embodying the infusion of script into art; *France: Manuscrits datés* 4, pt. 1 (1981): 233. At Luxeuil, word separation had been established since the time of Adson.

35. The codex also contained prayers for William of Normandy accompanied by accentlike neumes. Wormald, "An Eleventh-Century Copy of the Norman *Laudes Regiae*," pp. 73–76; facsimile, Henri-Marie-Félis Loriquet, *Le graduel de l'église cathédrale de Rouen au XIIIᵉ siècle*, 2 vols. (Rouen, 1907), 1: pl. 1.

36. Nortier, *Bibliothèques*, p. 29; Barré, "Pro Fulberto," pp. 326–28.

37. Branch, "Inventories," pp. 168–72.

38. Alexander, *Norman Illuminations*, pp. 38–39; *France: Manuscrits datés* 7 (1984): 219 and pl. 9; D. Gremont and L. Donnat, "Fleury, Le Mont Saint-Michel et l'Angleterre à la fin du Xᵉ et au début du XIᵉ siècle à propos du manuscrit d'Orléans n. 127(105)," in *Millénaire monastique du Mont Saint-Michel*, 1: 751–93 and pl. 19; Temple, *Anglo-Saxon Manuscripts*, no. 3; Otto Homburger, "Eine Spätkarolingische Schule von Corbie," in *Karolingische und Ottonische Kunst*, p. 418 (pl. 184); Gneuss, "A Preliminary List," no. 867. An epitaph of Gauzelin occurs on p. 331; Mostert, *The Library of Fleury*, BF 538. A marginal dedicatory inscription on pp. 63–64 identifying the book as being commissioned for Fleury was written in unseparated script.

39. Alexander, *Norman Illuminations*, pp. 226, 229 and plate 1; de Meyier, *Codices Vossiani latini* 1 (1973): 85 and pl. 35f.

40. Microfilm is at the IRHT. Alexander, *Norman Illuminations*, p. 225; Van de Vyver, "Les étapes du développement philosophique," p. 449; *Aristoteles latinus*, 1: 433–38; *Supp.*, 82–83; Coloman Viola, "Aristote au Mont-Saint-Michel," in *Millénaire monastique du Mont Saint-Michel*, 1: 290; *France: Manuscrits datés* 7 (1984): 83 and pl. 11 (f. 1A).

41. Alexander, *Norman Illuminations*, p. 230; Chatelain, *Paléographie des classiques latins*, 2: pl. 131. Note the presence of the suspension abbreviation in the *lemmae* and the *punctus elevatus* in the gloss.

42. Paris, BN lat. 8055, ff. 141–72v, a copy of Persius's *Saturae*; Alexander, *Norman Illuminations*, p. 229; Chatelain, *Paléographie des classiques latins*, 2: 125; *Millénaire monastique du Mont Saint-Michel*, 2: pl. 55. Note the presence of emblematic tie notes and punctuation including *punctus versus*. And lat. 8070, ff. 1–129v, a copy of Juvenal's *Saturae*; Alexander, *Norman Illuminations*, p. 230; Chatelain, *Paléographie des classiques latins*, 2: pl. 131. Note the presence of the suspension abbreviation in the *lemmae* and the *punctus elevatus* in the gloss.

43. Bertrand de Broussillon, "Cartulaire de l'abbayette (997–1427)," *Bulletin de la Commission Historique et Archéologique de la Mayenne* 9 (1894): 9–12 and pl. 1.

44. Ibid., pp. 12–13 and pl. 2.

45. Paul de Farcy and Bertrand de Broussillon, *Cartulaire de Saint-Victor au Mans, prieuré de l'abbaye du Mont-Saint-Michel* (Paris, 1895), pls. 1–3.

46. Paris, BN NAL 1674, f. 4; a facsimile appears in the separately printed version of Léopold Delisle, "Charte normande de 1088," *Annuaire-Bulletin de la Société de l'Histoire de France* (1886): 177–84. I have not been able to examine

Saint-Lô, Archives de la Manche, H, fonds du Mont Saint-Michel, Faurraux, no. 133, a charter of 1054, cited by Alexander, *Norman Illuminations*, p. 42.

47. Thierry of Montgommeri, chosen in 1014 to be abbot by William of Volpiano, came directly from Fécamp; Julien Loth, ed., *Histoire de l'abbaye royal de Saint-Pierre de Jumièges par un religieux bénédictin de la Congregation de St. Maur*, 3 vols., SHN Publications, 16 (Paris, 1882–85), 1: 146.

48. *France: Manuscrits datés* 7 (1984): 261 and pl. 3; Alfred Cordoliani, "Le plus ancien manuscrit de comput écclesiastique du fonds de Jumièges," in *Jumièges: Congrès scientifique du XIIIe centenaire* 2: 691–702 and plate. However, an eleventh-century addition, the antiphon *Dum ortus fuerit*, was written on f. 62v in separated script accompanied by alphabetical pitch notation. The Caroline script of other additions was separated by 2 times the unity of space, and *prosodiae* included the acute accent on monosyllables. Terminal forms included the capital *S* and the capital *NT* ligature.

49. *France: Manuscrits datés* 7 (1984): 325 and pl. 7; Nortier, *Bibliothèques*, pp. 145, 171; Avril, *Manuscrits normands*, p. 8, no. 2; *Catalogue général des manuscrits des départements* 1 (1986): 344–45.

50. Alexander, *Norman Illuminations*, p. 10.

51. *France: Manuscrits datés* 7 (1984): 508; Nortier, *Bibliothèques*, pp. 146, 165; René-Jean Hesbert, *Les Manuscrits musicaux de Jumièges*, Monumenta musicae sacrae, vol. 2 (Macon, 1954), pp. 27–28 and pls. 43–50.

52. Loth, *Histoire de l'abbaye royal de Saint-Pierre de Jumièges*, 1: 147.

53. *France: Manuscrits datés* 7 (1984): 577; Backhouse, *The Golden Age*, no. 50 and color pl. 15; H. A. Wilson, *The Missal of Robert of Jumièges*, HBS, vol. 11 (London, 1896), pl. 15. On Robert of Jumièges's political role in England, see David Douglas, "Robert de Jumièges, archevêque de Canterbury, et la conquête de l'Angleterre par les normands," in *Jumièges: Congrès scientifique du XIIIe centenaire*, 1: 283–86; Marjorie Chibnall, "Les relations entre Jumièges et Angleterre du XIe au XIIe siècles," ibid., pp. 269–75; Gneuss, "A Preliminary List," no. 921.

54. The date has been established by John Basil Lowder Tolhurst, "Le missel de Robert de Jumièges, Sacramentaire d'Ely," in *Jumièges: Congrès scientifique du XIIIe centenaire*, 1: 287–92.

55. Marguerite-Marie Dubois, "Les rubriques en viel anglais du missel de Robert de Jumièges," in *Jumièges: Congrès scientifique du XIIIe centenaire*, 1: 305–8.

56. *France: Manuscrits datés* 7 (1984): 273 and pl. 186; Avril, *Manuscrits normands*, no. 85; Temple, *Anglo-Saxon Manuscripts*, no. 24; Backhouse, *The Golden Age*, no. 40; Nortier, *Bibliothèques*, pp. 146, 165; Gneuss, "A Preliminary List," no. 920.

57. Hesbert, *Les Manuscrits musicaux*, pp. 14–15 and pls. 2–3; Nortier, *Bibliothèques*, pp. 145, 165; G. H. Doble, ed., *Pontificale Lanaletense (Bibliothèque de la Ville de Rouen A. 27, Cat. 368): A Pontifical Formerly in Use at St. Germans,*

Cornwall, HBS, vol. 74 (London, 1937), esp. pp. xvi–xvii and pls. 2 and 4; Jean Stéphan, "Taristock et Jumièges: Nouvel Examen du Pontificale Lanalatense," in *Jumièges: Congrès scientifique du XIIIᵉ centenaire*, 1: 309–13; Leroquais, *Les pontificaux manuscrits*, 2: 287–300 and pls. 1–2; Gneuss, "A Preliminary List," no. 922.

58. Nortier, *Bibliothèques*, p. 167; Avril, *Manuscrits normands*, pp. 8–9, no. 3 with plate. The clarifications provided by the scribes were supplemented by the rubricator who on f. 4–4v acted as an emendator by adding *traits d'union*, acute accents, and *nota* marks.

59. M. Besson, "Achart," *DHGE* 1 (1912): 307; *BHL* 1: no. 182.

60. Watson, *Oxford: Dated and Datable Manuscripts*, no. 117 and pl. 23; Pächt and Alexander, *Illuminated Manuscripts in the Bodleian Library*, 1: no. 439 and pl. 36.

61. Charles Reginald Dodwell, "Un manuscrit enluminé de Jumièges au British Museum," in *Jumièges: Congrès scientifique du XIIIe centenaire*, 2: 737–41; not recorded by Nortier, *Bibliothèques*.

62. David Knowles, "Les relations monastiques entre la Normandie et Angleterre," in *Jumièges: Congrès scientifique du XIIIᵉ centenaire*, 1: 261–67.

63. J.-J. Vernier, *Recueil de fac-similés de chartes normandes publiés à l'occasion de l'histoire de Normandie* (Rouen, 1919), pl. 1; J.-J. Vernier, *Chartes de l'abbaye de Jumièges conservés aux archives de la Seine-Inférieure (v. 825 à 1204)* (Paris, 1916), pp. 14–15, no. v.

64. Vernier, *Chartes de l'abbaye*, pp. 16–19. I am indebted to M. François Burckard, Conservateur-en-Chef des Archives départementales de Seine-Maritime, for providing me with photographs of this and the following documents.

65. Vernier, *Chartes de l'abbaye*, pp. 20–23.

66. Ibid., pp. 23–25.

67. Ibid., pp. 43–46.

68. Ibid., pp. 53–56; Paul Chevreux and Jules Vernier, *Les Archives de Normandie et de la Seine-Inférieure: Recueil de fac-similés d'écritures du XIᵉ au XVIIIᵉ siècle accompagnées de transcriptions* (Rouen, 1911), pl. 3; Newman, *Catalogue des actes de Robert II*, no. 74; Frédéric Soehnée, *Catalogue des actes d'Henri Iᵉʳ Roi de France* (Paris, 1907), no. 8.

69. It is highly dubious that Lanfranc, who was trained as a jurist in Pavia, used separated writing in his youth, since no firmly datable manuscripts are known to have been written in northern Italy until the second half of the eleventh century. Anselm, born in Aosta in Piedmont, in all probability also learned word separation in the north.

70. For lists, see Dodwell, *The Canterbury School of Illumination*, p. 16 n. 1; and Nortier, *Bibliothèques*, p. 59.

71. Robinson, *Cambridge: Dated and Datable Manuscripts*, no. 342 and pl. 29; Z. N. Brooke, *English Church and the Papacy: From the Conquest to the Reign of John* (Cambridge, 1931), pp. 57–77; Dodwell, *The Canterbury School of*

Illumination, pp. 7, 16 and plates 4c–d; N. R. Ker, *English Manuscripts in the Century after the Norman Conquest* (Oxford, 1960), p. 25 and pls. 4–5; Montague Rhodes James, *The Ancient Libraries of Canterbury and Dover* (Cambridge, 1903), p. xxx; Gneuss, "A Preliminary List," no. 179 and pl. 22.

72. Dodwell, *The Canterbury School of Illumination*, pp. 7, 16, and pl. 4a; Ker, *English Manuscripts*, p. 25; Nortier, *Bibliothèques*, p. 59.

73. Reference from Paris, IRHT, Section de codicologie.

74. Henri Omont, in *Catalogue général des manuscrits des départements* 2 (1888): 385–94, nos. 81, 82, 128, 159, 160; cf. pp. 394–98, no. 49.

75. John Marenbon, *Early Medieval Philosophy* (London, 1983), pp. 90–110.

76. Helen Clover and Margaret Gibson, *The Letters of Lanfranc Archbishop of Canterbury* (Oxford, 1979), frontispiece.

77. See, for example, Oxford, BL Bodley 569, copied in Normandy. The first folio is reproduced by Margaret T. Gibson, *Lanfranc of Bec* (Oxford, 1978), frontispiece.

78. B. Smalley, "La *Glossa ordinaria*," *Recherches de théologie ancienne et médiévale* 9 (1937): 380–81.

79. B. Bischoff et al., *Nomenclature des écritures livresques* (Paris, 1954), pp. 10–11, pl. 3.

80. James, *The Ancient Libraries of Canterbury and Dover*, p. xxx; M. R. James, *The Western Manuscripts in the Library of Emmanuel College: A Descriptive Catalogue* (Cambridge, 1904), pp. 27–28.

81. Durham Cathedral Chapter B IV 24, ff. 47–73 (R. A. B. Mynors, *Durham Cathedral Manuscripts to the End of the Twelfth Century* [Oxford, 1939], no. 51; Gneuss, "A Preliminary List," no. 248); Cambridge, Corpus Christi College 130 (Gneuss, "A Preliminary List," no. 93); Cambridge, Peterhouse College 74, before 1096 (Mynors, *Durham Cathedral Manuscripts*, no. 50; Gneuss, "A Preliminary List," no. 149; Robinson, *Cambridge: Dated and Datable Manuscripts*, no. 280 and pl. 36); Hereford, Cathedral Library O. viii. 8 (Gneuss, "A Preliminary List," no. 265).

82. *Musée des archives départementales*, p. 51 and pl. 18.

83. See especially Anselm's *De grammatico*, in *S. Anselmi opera*, ed. Schmitt, 1: 145–68; on the prescholastic clarity of Anselm's prose, see Desmond Paul Henry, *The Logic of Saint Anselm* (Oxford, 1967), pp. 7–8, 12–30.

84. R. W. Southern, *The Life of Saint Anselm Archbishop of Canterbury by Eadmer* (London, 1962), pp. xxviii–xxx; George Gresley Perry, *DNB* 6: 309–10. Eadmer, Anselm's companion and biographer, wrote in canonically separated script and employed a sophisticated form of syntactical punctuation to signal the syntactical distinctions within his prose. Southern, *Saint Anselm and His Biographer*, frontispiece; Parkes, *Pause and Effect*, p. 153. The earliest collection of Anselm's letters, London, BL Cotton Nero A VII, ff. 41–112, probably originating from the Abbey of Bec, was written in *fere* canonically separated script

with the terminal capital *S* and original *traits d'union*. *S. Anselmi opera omnia*, ed. Schmitt, 3: 2 and frontispiece; Dodwell, *The Canterbury School of Illumination*, p. 16 n. 1; Clover and Gibson, *The Letters of Lanfranc*, p. 16.

85. Paul Grammont, "Jumièges et le Bec," in *Jumièges: Congrès scientifique du XIIIᵉ centenaire*, 1: 214; Hesbert, "Les manuscrits enluminés," pl. preceding p. 729.

86. *S. Anselmi opera omnia*, ed. Schmitt, 2: 222 and pl. following p. 230; Franciscus Salesius Schmitt, "Eine dreifache Gestalt der *Epistola de sacrificio azimi et fermentati des hl. Anselm von Canterbury*," *RB* 47 (1935): 217. Manuscripts of Anselm's works from Norman abbeys, Paris, BN lat. 13413 (written in 1077–82 at Saint-Martin of Séez), and Oxford, BL Rawlinson A 392 (written ca. 1085 at Saint-Martin of Troarn), were copied in separated script as were Arras, BM 455 (1021) from Saint-Vaast, and Metz, BM 248 from the Abbey of Saint-Arnoul. *S. Anselmi opera omnia*, ed. Schmitt, 1: 3 and pls. following pp. 14, 36. See also Vat. Reg. lat. 452 from ca. 1200, ibid., 2: 2 and pl. following p. 12, and Munich, Clm. 21248 from Ulm (first half of the twelfth century), ibid., 1: 176 with pl. following 176.

Chapter 12

1. Monique-Cécile Garand, "Copistes au temps de Cluny au temps de Saint Maieul (984–94)," *BEC* 136 (1978): 23–24, states incorrectly that the words "sont separés." Watson, *British Library: Dated and Datable Manuscripts*, 1: 64, no. 278 and 2: pl. 18; *PS* 2: pls. 109–10; H. Omont, "Manuscrit de Raban Maur offert par St. Maïeul à l'abbaye de Cluny," *Académie de Macon: Millénaire de Cluny: Congrès d'histoire et d'archéologie tenu à Cluny les 10, 11, 12 septembre 1910*, 2 vols. (Macon, 1910), 1: 127–29 and pl. 8.

2. *France: Manuscrits datés* 4, pt. 1 (1981): 337; Delisle, *Fonds de Cluni*, pp. 47–49 (no. 23).

3. Paris, BN NAL 1478 and NAL 340, containing elements of the *Logica vetus* dating from the eleventh century; see Delisle, *Fonds de Cluni*, pp. 160–65 (nos. 90–91).

4. *France: Manuscrits datés* 4, pt. 1 (1981): 239; Delisle, *Fonds de Cluni*, pp. 147–51 (no. 76).

5. Chroust, *Monumenta Palaeographica*, ser. 1, 1: 18, 10; Schramm and Mütherich, *Denkmale*, no. 126 and plate; Jean Vezin, "Une importante contribution à l'étude du scriptorium de Cluny à la limite des XIᵉ et XIIᵉ siècles," *Scriptorium* 21 (1967): 317–18.

6. *France: Manuscrits datés* 4, pt. 1 (1981): 167 and pl. 11; Monique-Cécile Garand, "Une collection personnelle de Saint Odilon de Cluny et ses compléments," *Scriptorium* 33 (1979): p. 163 n. 1; Delisle, *Fonds de Cluni*, p. 76 (no. 29).

7. Not recorded in Watson, *British Library: Dated and Datable Manuscripts*; Garand, "Copistes de Cluny," pp. 8, 17–18; Pierre Gasnault, "Dom Anselme le

Michel et les manuscrits de l'abbaye de Cluny," *BEC* 131 (1973): 218–19; *Catalogue of Additions to the Manuscripts of the British Museum in the Years 1841–1845* (London, 1850), p. 14. Paris, BN NAL 2248, was written by a similar and contemporary hand in separated script with interword space equivalent to or only slightly exceeding the unity of space. *France: Manuscrits datés* 4, pt. 1 (1981): 237 and pl. 118; Garand, "Copistes de Cluny," p. 32; Garand, "Une collection personelle," p. 163 n. 1; Delisle, *Fonds de Cluni*, pp. 103–4 (no. 43).

8. Delisle, *Fonds de Cluni*, pp. 160–62 (no. 90); Van de Vyver, "Les étapes du développement philosophique," p. 445; cf. *France: Manuscrits datés* 4, pt. 1 (1981): 338. In my judgment, Delisle's date is correct.

9. Vezin, "Une importante contribution," p. 316; *France: Manuscrits datés* 3 (1974): 409 and pl. 18; unrecorded in Delisle, *Fonds de Cluni*.

10. Delisle, *Fonds de Cluni*, pp. 337–38.

11. It was also used on monosyllables and on the tonic syllable, especially in proximity to the letter *i*. Terminal forms included *m*, *-us*, *-tur*, the *e* cedilla, the ampersand, the capital *N*, the *NT* ligature, and the long *j* in Roman numerals.

12. Garand, "Une collection personnelle," pp. 163–80 and pls. 17–19; *France: Manuscrits datés* 4, pt. 1 (1981): 43, 173–75 and pls. 1 and 13; Monique-Cécile Garand, "Giraldus Levita copiste de chartes et de livres à Cluny sous l'abbatiat de Saint Odilon (†1049)," in Jacques Lemaire and Emile van Balberghe, *Calames et cahiers: Mélanges de codicologie et de paléographie offerts à Léon Gilissen*, Les publications de Scriptorium, vol. 9 (Brussels, 1985), p. 41; Delisle, *Fonds de Cluni*, pp. 96–101 (no. 39).

13. *France: Manuscrits datés* 4, pt. 1 (1981): 43 and pl. 12; Garand, "Giraldus Levita," pp. 41–48 and pls. 3–4; Gasnault, "Dom Anselme le Michel," p. 214 n. 1; unrecorded in Delisle, *Fonds de Cluni*.

14. Paris, BN NAL 1455, ff. 25–31, 90–105. The only indication of graphic change in these leaves was the addition of the acute accent to denote the tonic syllable by an emendator who was quite possibly one of the scribes who subsequently expanded the volume.

15. See ff. 106v–33.

16. Paris, BN lat. 17275; cf. Garand, "Giraldus Levita," p. 46.

17. See *France: Manuscrits datés* 4, pt. 1 (1981): 175.

18. Interword space varied from 1.5 to 2 times the unity of space, and *prosodiae* included the acute accent used to designate Hebrew names, the tonic syllable in compound words, and as a redundant sign of separation for monosyllables such as the interjection *O* and the reflexive pronoun *se*. The medial interpunct was used to correct the omission of separation by space. Terminal forms included the elevated round *s*.

19. Paris, BN NAL 1496, ff. 27–58; NAL 2246, NAL 638, lat. 12601 and lat. 17742. Other separated codices of this period include Paris, BN lat. 13875 and NAL 1548.

20. Auguste Bernard and Alexandre Bruel, *Recueil des chartes de l'abbaye de Cluny*, 6 vols. (Paris, 1876), 1: xiv–xxviii; Delisle, *Fonds de Cluni*, pp. 229–32 (nos. 134–35).

21. Delisle, *Fonds de Cluni*, pp. 240–43 (no. 147), 253–54 (no. 155), 254–57 (no. 156), 237–39 (no. 145), 257–61 (no. 157).

22. Charter no. 87.

23. Charter no. 100.

24. See, for example, Schapiro, "A Relief in Rodez," p. 58 and pl. 17.21.

25. On this new genre, see Léopold Delisle, *Rouleaux des morts du IXe au XVe siècle* (Paris, 1866); A. Molinier, *Les obituaires français au Moyen Age* (Paris, 1880).

26. See Jacques Le Goff, *La naissance du purgatoire* (Paris, 1981), pp. 170–73.

27. *France: Manuscrits datés* 4, pt. 1 (1981): 73 and pl. 17; Joachim Wollasch, "Qu'a signifié Cluny pour l'abbaye de Moissac?" in *Pour un IXe centenaire*, pp. 13–24, and *Mönchtum des Mittelalters zwischen Kirche und Welt*, Münstersche Mittelalter Schriften, vol. 7 (1973), pp. 69, 71.

28. Veronika von Büren, "Le grand catalogue de la bibliothèque de Cluny," in *Le gouvernement d'Hugues de Semur à Cluny: Actes du colloque scientifique international, Cluny septembre 1988* (Cluny, 1990), pp. 247–48, 251. Exceptions include Paris, BN NAL 1478 and NAL 340; Delisle, *Fonds de Cluni*, pp. 160–63 (no. 91); *France: Manuscrits datés* 4 pt. 1 (1981): 71.

29. Christian Pfeister, *Etudes sur la règne de Robert le Pieux (996–1031)*, Bibliothèque de l'Ecole des Hautes Etudes, vol. 64 (Paris, 1885), pp. 3–4.

30. G. A. Hückel, *Les poèmes satiriques d'Adalbéron*, Bibliothèque de la faculté des lettres, vol. 13 (Paris, 1901); Robert T. Coolidge, "Adalbero, Bishop of Laon," *Studies in Medieval and Renaissance History* 2 (1965): 73–75.

31. André Wilmart, "Le couvent et la bibliothèque de Cluny vers le milieu du XIe siècle," *Revue Mabillon* 11 (1921): 89–124.

32. Cf. Monique-Cécile Garand, "Le scriptorium de Cluny, carrefour d'influences au XIe siècle: Le Manuscrit Paris, BN nouv. acq. lat. 1548," *Journal des savants* (1977): 257–83.

33. Dijon, BM 51; Paris, BN lat. 12637 and NAL 1618.

34. *Paléographie musicale* 7–8 (1901–5); Michel Huglo, "Le tonaire de Saint-Bénigne de Dijon (Montpellier H. 159)," *Annales musicologiques* 4 (1956): 7–18, and "L'auteur du *Dialogue sur la musique* attribué à Odon," *Revue de musicologie* 69 (1955): 144; Solange Corbin, "Valeur et sens de la notation alphabétique à Jumièges et en Normandie," in *Jumièges: Congrès scientifique du XIIIe centenaire*, 2: 915; Alma Colk Santosuosso, *Letter Notation in the Middle Ages* (Ottowa, 1989), pp. 67–80, 190–91, and pls. 28–35. It stands in contrast to other codices with alphabetic musical notation written at Fécamp and elsewhere in Normandy in separated script.

35. H. Bosse, *Die lateinische Handschriften der Sammlung Hamilton zu Ber-*

lin (Wiesbaden, 1966), pp. 40–42; Bernard de Vregille, "Le copiste Audebaud de Cluny et la Bible de l'abbé Guillaume de Dijon," in *L'homme devant Dieu: Mélanges offerts au Père Henri de Lubac*, Etudes publiées sous la direction de la Faculté de théologie S. J. de Lyon-Fourvière, vols. 56–58 (Paris, 1963–64), 2: 7–15.

36. *France: Manuscrits datés* 3 (1974): 125 and pl. 18; Alexander, *Norman Illuminations*, p. 233.

37. Paris, BN Collection Porcher, contains photographs of ff. 4v, 6, and 108v; Leroquais, *Les pontificaux manuscrits*, 1: 142, no. 48; Alexander, *Norman Illuminations*, p. 233; *Catalogue général des manuscrits des départements* 5 (1889): 32.

38. Paris, BN Collection Porcher; Charles Oursel, "La Bible de Saint-Bénigne de Dijon," in *Les trésors des bibliothèques de France* 1 (1926): 127–39 with 14 plates.

39. Dijon, Archives de la Côte d'Or 1 H, liasse 4; Chevrier and Chaume, *Chartes et documents de Saint-Bénigne*, 2: 87–89 (no. 310), 242 (pl.); Gautier, "Étude sur un diplôme," pl. 5.

40. Dijon, Archives de la Côte d'Or 1 H, liasse 208; Chevrier and Chaume, *Chartes et documents de Saint-Bénigne*, 2: 95–97 (no. 315), 242 (pl.).

41. Chevrier and Chaume, *Chartes et documents de Saint-Benigne*, 2: 37–39 (no. 245), 40–42 (no. 247), 240 (pls.); Gautier, "Étude sur un diplôme," pl. 4.

42. In 1029, during the brief abbacy of Eudes, Paris, BN lat. 12219, Augustine's *Adversus quinque haereses*, was written in hierarchical word blocks fewer than twenty characters in length, with the only sign of graphic change being the occasional presence of acute accents to denote tonic syllables. Terminal forms were few and limited to the usual signs for *-bus, -tur,* and *m*; *traits d'union* were absent. The year 1029 provides a date *post quem* for the normal use of word separation at Saint-Maur. Paris, BN lat. 3786, a homilarium was, according to its colophon, completed in 1058 after an interruption of many years. The original codex, dating from the beginning of the eleventh century, was copied in hierarchical word blocks fewer than fifteen characters in length. Two sections added in 1058 (ff. 240–43 and 252–59) were copied in part in separated script with interword space varying from equivalence to 2 times the unity of space and in part in canonically separated script with *prosodiae* including *traits d'union*, suspended ligatures, and acute accents to denote monosyllables. Terminal forms were the ampersand, the capital *S*, and the capital *NS* and *NT* ligatures; *France: Manuscrits datés* 3 (1974): 277 and pl. 249; *France: Manuscrits datés* 2 (1962): 195–97, pls. 10, 198; Maurice Prou, *Manuel de paléographie latine et française*, ed. Alain Boüard (Paris, 1924), p. 477 and pl. 9.

43. The abbey's eleventh-century sacramentorium, Paris, BN lat. 9436, and gradual, Bibliothèque Mazarine 384, were written in word blocks in the first half of the eleventh century.

44. Date of Odorannus's unseparated autograph codex.

45. In this light, it is not without significance that the earliest examples of written Occitan originated from Fleury, located in the zone of Langue d'oil, and not from Occitania.

46. For insight into the relations between England and Aquitaine, see George Beech, "The Participation of Aquitanians in the Conquest of England 1066–1100," in R. Allen Brown, ed., *Anglo-Norman Studies IX: Proceedings of the Battle Conference 1986* (Woodbridge, Suffolk, 1987), pp. 1–24.

47. Gaborit-Chopin, *Décoration à Saint-Martial*, pp. 176–77 and pls. 3, 5, 7–9, 11, 13–14, 16, 18, 21–22, 25, 27–29, 31–32, 35, 38–39, 44–45; Jean Porcher, *L'art Roman à Saint-Martial de Limoges*, exhibition catalogue (Limoges, 1950), pls. 8, 9; *Catalogue général des manuscrits latins* 1 (1939): 4–5.

48. Gaborit-Chopin, *Décoration à Saint-Martial*, p. 204.

49. Ibid., p. 206; Porcher, *L'art Roman à Saint-Martial*, pl. 10.

50. *France: Manuscrits datés* 2 (1962): 57 and pl. 9; Gaborit-Chopin, *Décoration à Saint-Martial*, pp. 182–83, 185–86 and pls. 78–79, 81; Jacques Chailley, *L'école musicale de Saint-Martial de Limoges jusqu'à la fin du XIᵉ siècle* (Paris, 1960), pp. 82–92, and "Les anciennes tropaires et sequentiares de l'école de Saint-Martial de Limoges (Xᵉ–XIᵉ)," *Etudes Grégoriennes* 2 (1957): 180; Chailley, *L'école musicale*, pp. 82–92, 101–2.

51. In contrast, the *vita* of Bernard of Angers, Fulbert's student, was added to the same volume in separated script with emblematic punctuation.

52. On the manuscripts of Adémar, see Léopold Delisle, "Notice sur les manuscrits originaux d'Adémar de Chabannes," *Notices et extraits* 35, pt. 1 (1896): 241–356; and the appropriate entries of *France: Manuscrits datés*.

53. *France: Manuscrits datés* 2 (1962): 193 and pl. 188.

54. Delisle, "Notice sur les manuscrits originaux," p. 289; *PL* 141: 122D.

55. Gaborit-Chopin, *Décoration à Saint-Martial*, p. 25.

56. Delisle, "Notice sur les manuscrits originaux," pp. 296–301; *Catalogue général des manuscrits latins* 2 (1948): 444–45; *France: Manuscrits datés* 2 (1962): 114 and pl. 188.

57. Jean Vezin, "Un nouveau manuscrit autographe d'Adémar de Chabannes (Paris, Bibl. nat. lat. 7231)," *Bulletin de la Société Nationale des Antiquaires de France*, 1965, 51; *France: Manuscrits datés* 4, pt. 1 (1981): 29 and pl. 12.

58. De Meyier, *Codices Vossiani latini* 2 (1975): 31–42, 4 (1984), pl. 24d; *Pays Bas: Manuscrits datés* 1 (1964): pls. 37–38; Bischoff, *Anecdota novissima*, pl. 2.

59. Delisle, "Notice sur les manuscrits originaux," p. 278.

60. Gaborit-Chopin, *Décoration à Saint-Martial*, pp. 104, 209; Jules Chavanon, ed., *Adémar de Chabannes: Chronique* (Paris, 1897), pp. xviii–xix.

61. Holtz, *Donat et la tradition de l'enseignement*, p. 417.

62. *France: Manuscrits datés* 2 (1962): 33; Gaborit-Chopin, *Décoration à Saint-Martial*, p. 182; cf. Leroquais, *Sacramentaires et missels*, 1: 203–4.

63. *France: Manuscrits datés* 2 (1962): 495; Gaborit-Chopin, *Décoration à Saint-Martial*, p. 204. In my judgment, the recently suggested attribution of this *libellus* to Adémar of Chabannes is erroneous; cf. Richard Landes, "A *Libellus* from St. Martial of Limoges Written in the Time of Adémar of Chabannes (989–1034): *Un faux à retardement*," *Scriptorium* 37 (1983): 178–204 and pls. 21–22. The same codex, on ff. 43–109, contains an evangelistary, apparently contemporary to the first quire, that qualifies Martial as an apostle (therefore, placing the book certainly after 1031). The text of the Gospels was written with words separated by 1.5 times the unity of space, with space often present after monosyllabic prepositions. To render words more recognizable, the scribe used acute accents to denote the tonic syllable in compound words and as redundant signs of separation for monosyllables. *Traits d'union* were present at line endings and beginnings. Terminal forms included the capital *NT* ligature, the capital *S*, and the elevated *s*.

64. The sarcophagus of Roger is today in the Musée Municipale, Limoges; see Maurice Ardant, "Rapport," *Revue des sociétés savantes des départements*, ser. 2, 2 (1859): 409.

65. *France: Manuscrits datés* 2 (1962): III; Gaborit-Chopin, *Décoration à Saint-Martial*, p. 195 and pls. 135–36.

66. Gaborit-Chopin, *Décoration à Saint-Martial*, pp. 177–78 and pls. 91, 93–98, 104–7, 110, 114–15; Porcher, *L'art Roman à Saint-Martial*, pls. 10–15; Philippe Lauer, *Les enluminures romanes des manuscrits de la Bibliothèque Nationale* (Paris, 1927), pls. 33, 37, 39, 43, 50; Samuel Berger, *Histoire de la Vulgate* (Paris, 1893), p. 83; *Catalogue général des manuscrits latins* 1 (1939): 7.

67. Gaborit-Chopin, *Décoration à Saint-Martial*, p. 200 and pl. 125.

68. Ibid.; *Catalogue général des manuscrits latins* 3 (1952): 95–96.

69. Gaborit-Chopin, *Décoration à Saint-Martial*, pp. 193–94 and pl. 137; *Catalogue général des manuscrits latins* 2 (1940).

70. Porcher, *L'art Roman à Saint-Martial*, pl. 18; Gaborit-Chopin, *Décoration à Saint-Martial*, p. 96 and passim, pls. 175, 181–83, 195, etc.

71. Gaborit-Chopin, *Décoration à Saint-Martial*, p. 204.

72. *Catalogue général des manuscrits latins* 1 (1939): 191–92.

73. Ibid., pp. 415–46; D'Arco Silvio Avalle, *La letteratura medievale in lingua d'oc nella sua tradizione manoscritta: Problemi di critica testuale* (Turin, 1961), pp. 27–28; D'Arco Silvio Avalle, ed., *Sponsus: Dramma delle vergine prudenti e delle vergine stolte* (Milan, 1965), includes a facsimile of the text; Robert A. Taylor, *La littérature occitane du Moyen Age: Bibliographie sélective et critique* (Toronto, 1977), nos. 688–89; Robert Bossuat, *Manuel bibliographique de la littérature française du Moyen Age* (Melun, 1951), nos. 3874–84; Guy de Poerck, "Les plus anciens textes de la langue française comme témoins de l'époque," *Revue de linguistique Romane* 27 (1963): 12, 16. For a similar example in a document of 1102, see Kendrick, *The Game of Love*, p. 35.

74. Delisle, *Cabinet des manuscrits*, 1: 519; Chatelain, *Introduction à la lecture des notes tironiennes*, pp. 211–12 and pl. 2; Legendre, *Études tironiennes*, p. 57, no. 49; Dufour, *Scriptorium de Moissac*, pp. 145–46, no. 97.

75. The capital *R* was present in the interior of the word, cf. ff. 6–10v; Dufour, *Scriptorium de Moissac*, p. 48.

76. For a full description, see Paul Saenger, *A Catalogue of the Pre-1500 Western Manuscript Books at the Newberry Library* (Chicago, 1989), pp. 3–9.

77. This separated portion manifests a consistent usage of the interior *ct* ligature that was only occasionally present in the unseparated text.

78. *Catalogue général des manuscrits latins* 2 (1940): 308–9; Dufour, *Scriptorium de Moissac*, pp. 120–21, no. 56, and pls. 15–16; Lilli Gjerløw, "MS Paris lat. 2077: A Note on the Hymn *Congregavit* and on the Bobbio Missal," in Gjerløw, *Adoratio Crucis: The Regularis concordia and the Decreti Lanfranci* (Oslo, 1961), pp. 148–49; Schapiro, "A Relief in Rodez," pp. 58–59, pls. 15.13 and 16.16.

79. Watson, *Oxford: Dated and Datable Manuscripts*, 1: 70, no. 436 and 2: pls. 28a–b; Dufour, *Scriptorium de Moissac*, pp. 108–9, no. 36; Pächt and Alexander, *Illuminated Manuscripts in the Bodleian Library*, 1: no. 432 and pl. 35; *Latin Liturgical Manuscripts and Printed Books*, exhibition catalogue (Oxford, 1952), no. 43 and pl. 6; A. C. de la Mare and B. C. Barker-Benfield, eds., *Manuscripts at Oxford: An Exhibition in Memory of Richard William Hunt* (Oxford, 1980), pp. 138–39, item xxx.3 and pl. 102; R. W. Southern, *Saint Anselm and His Biographer: A Study of Monastic Life and Thought* (Cambridge, 1963), p. 40 n. 1.

80. Jacques Hourlier, "L'entrée de Moissac dans l'Ordre de Cluny," in *Pour un IXe centenaire*, pp. 25–35; Dufour, *Scriptorium de Moissac*, pp. 3–4.

81. I am indebted to François Dolbeau for bringing this text to my attention. *PLS* 1: 194–96; J. B. Pitra, *Analecta sacra et classica* 5 (Paris, 1888): 117; *CPL* (under the name of Odus Cordubensis), no. 540; cf. *PL* 74: 815–48; the same text in Paris, BN lat. 1454 and 3842A; François Dolbeau, "Deux opuscules latins relatifs aux personnages de la Bible et antérieurs à Isidore de Séville," *Revue d'histoire des textes* 16 (1986): 89–90.

82. Dufour, *Scriptorium de Moissac*, pp. 106–7, no. 33, and pls. 29–30. *Prosodiae* included split-line *traits d'union* as well as *traits d'union* at line endings only. Suspended ligatures were used both in lieu of and in addition to *traits d'union*. Acute accents were used to denote monosyllabic prepositions in addition to and in lieu of space; they also denoted the tonic syllable. The scribe employed the successor note to the *diastole* to distinguish monosyllabic prepositions from their objects.

83. Delisle, *Cabinet des manuscrits*, 1: 519; Chatelain, *Paléographie des classiques latins*, 1: pl. 47; Charles Samaran, "Le *César* de Moissac," in *Pour un IXe centenaire*, pp. 117–20, esp. 119 n. 5; Jean Vezin, "Observations sur l'emploi des réclames dans les manuscrits latins," *BEC* 125 (1967): 31; Dufour, *Scriptorium de Moissac*, p. 140, no. 88, and pl. 44.

84. Delisle, *Cabinet des manuscrits*, 1: 519; Vezin, "Observations," p. 31; Dufour, *Scriptorium de Moissac*, pp. 48, 140–41, no. 89, and pl. 45.

85. Dufour, *Scriptorium de Moissac*, p. 153, no. 109.

86. Like many *Vitae sanctae*, this codex was augmented over an extended period of time; see Dufour, *Scriptorium de Moissac*, pp. 147–48 and pl. 22 (incorrectly titled; actually of f. 93v); cf. ibid., p. 50; Dolbeau, "Anciens possesseurs," p. 230.

87. Dufour, *Scriptorium de Moissac*, p. 138, no. 85, and pl. 43.

88. At Moissac, the evolution of this phenomenon may relate to a highly stylized form of the *ct* intraword ligature; e.g., Paris, BN lat. 2429, f. 17 (s. xii in.); Dufour, *Scriptorium de Moissac*, pl. 51.

89. Dufour, *Scriptorium de Moissac*, pp. 83–92.

90. Ibid., p. 86.

91. "Ita ipsa dixit Priscianus post vii folia." Cf. Lehmann, "Blätter, Seiten, Spalten, Zeilen," pp. 15–16.

92. A contemporary example of foliation occurred at Fleury. Many ancient classical authors, among them Virgil, Terence, Caesar, and Livy, seem only to have been consultable at Fleury in the eleventh century in older unseparated copies, and the Fleury codices of these works were often emendated so as to facilitate consultation. The reworking of Josephus's *De bello iudaico* in Paris, BN lat. 5763, ff. 113–80, was particularly interesting. On f. 156, an emendator left the following marginal note in separated script: "Quod est de de [*sic*] Archalao, require superius in xxx viij° folio sub hoc signo." The note does not refer to the current foliation of the book (which is modern), and the indicated critical mark cannot be found anywhere in the fragment of Josephus as it now stands. The note contains the split-line *trait d'union* at line ending and beginning, the terminal long form of the *i*, and a superscript inflected form of the number, all of which suggest a date in the eleventh century. The note suggests that foliation may once have been present in this book and then subsequently removed by trimming.

93. Thurot, "Notices et extraits," pp. 77–79; C. H. Kneepkens and H. F. Reijnders, *Magister Siguinus: Ars lectoria un art de lecture à haute voix du onzième siècle* (Leiden, 1979), pp. xxii–xxiv.

94. Keil, *Grammatici latini*, 3: 518–28.

95. Thurot, "Notices et extraits," p. 79.

96. Kneepkens and Reijnders, *Magister Siguinus*, p. 30; Roger Wright, *Late Latin and Early Romance in Spain and Carolingian France* (Liverpool, 1982), p. 225.

97. Thurot, "Notices et extraits," p. 79.

98. Caveat scriptor ne dictiones compositas disiungere uelit quandiu, quambonus, ubiubi, ámodo, usquémodo, usquequo . . . paulopost . . . unanimis. Firmissime tene quoniam due coniunctiones iuxta se posite in parte una et uno accentu reputantur: siquidem . . . veruntamen . . . itaque . . . etsi, acsi.

Kneepkens and Reijnders, *Magister Siguinus*, p. 32. The editors have followed manuscripts of the twelfth and thirteenth centuries in placing the acute accent on *ámodo* and *usquémodo*.

99. Kneepkens and Reijnders, *Magister Siguinus*, p. 45.

100. Ibid., p. 78; H. F. Reijnders, "Aimericus: *Ars lectoria*," *Vivarium* 10 (1972): 55.

101. Nota. Omne enim verbum cui accustativus pronominis monosillabus te supponitur absolute, aut desinens in -o activum est, ut "amo te" aut in -or commune est, ut precor te. Kneepkens and Reijners, *Magister Siguinus*, p. 76.

102. Ibid., p. 13.

103. Nomina vero Greca et Hebrea et notha et barbara si sint indeclinabilia in fine accentamus omnia, ut . . . Ruma, ut "sedet Abimelich in Ruma" Cubi quidam *m* in *i* et *n* per ignorantiam dividentes male "in ruina" dicunt. Ibid., p. 90.

104. Ibid., pp. xxxvi, 14, 21, 37, 49, 74.

105. Ibid., p. xxx; H. F. Reijnders, "Aimericus: *Ars lectoria*," *Vivarium* 9 (1971): 119–37, 10 (1972): 41–101, 124–76; Charles Thurot, "Documents relatifs à l'histoire de la grammaire au Moyen Age," *Académie des Inscriptions et Belles Lettres: Comptes rendus des séances de l'année 1870*, pp. 244–51.

106. Cf. Kneepkens and Reijnders, *Magister Siguinus*, pp. xxii–xxiv.

107. Ibid., pp. xxix–xxx.

108. Reijnders, "Aimericus: *Ars lectoria*," pp. 127–28.

109. Ibid., pp. 171–72.

110. "Partes discrete spaciis mediantibus eque." *A Fifteenth Century Modus Scribendi from the Abbey of Melk*, ed. Stanley Morison (Cambridge, 1948), p. xx.

111. A microfilm is at the IRHT, Paris. I am indebted to Mme. Anne-Véronique Raynal for providing me with a photocopy from it.

112. *Catalogue général des manuscrits latins* 1 (1939): 393.

113. Leroquais, *Les pontificaux manuscrits*, 2: 10–15; *France: Manuscrits datés* 2 (1962): 43 and pl. 191; Jean Vezin, "Les manuscrits datés de l'ancien fonds latin de la Bibliothèque Nationale," *Scriptorium* 19 (1965): 83–89; *Catalogue général des manuscrits latins* 1 (1939): 336.

114. *Commentaire sur l'Apocalypse et le Livre de Daniel: Edition en fac-similé du manuscrit de l'abbaye de Saint-Sever conservé à la Bibliothèque Nationale de Paris sous la cote MS lat. 8878* (Madrid, 1984).

115. See below, Chapter 13.

116. Paris, BN lat. 1954; *Catalogue général des manuscrits latins* 2 (1940): 258–59; *Aristoteles latinus*, 1: 497 (no. 357). On the medieval library of Saint-Victor of Marseille, see Jean Chelini, "La bibliothèque de Saint-Victor au Moyen Age," *Provence historique* 16 (1966): 520–27.

117. Delisle, *Cabinet des manuscrits*, 2: 413; Jean Anselme-Bernard Mortreuil, *L'ancienne bibliothèque de l'abbaye de Saint-Victor* (Marseille, 1854).

118. *Catalogue général des manuscrits latins* 2 (1940): 330; Delisle, *Cabinet des manuscrits*, 2: 413.

119. Paul Amargier, "Les *scriptores* du XIᵉ siècle à Saint-Victor de Marseille," *Scriptorium* 32 (1978): 213–20 and pls. 15–16.

120. Philippe Aries, *Images of Man and Death*, trans. Janet Lloyd (Cambridge, Mass., 1985), pl. 61; Schapiro, "A Relief in Rodez," pl. 17.20.

121. François Galabert and Clovis Lassalle, *Album de paléographie et diplomatique* (Toulouse, 1913), pl. 2.

122. *Catalogue général des manuscrits latins* 1 (1939): 330–31; Delisle, *Cabinet des manuscrits*, 1: 305.

Chapter 13

1. For a more detailed examination of this question, see Paul Saenger, "The Separation of Words in Italy," *Scrittura e civiltà* 17 (1993): 5–41.

2. Brown, *Handlist*, p. 163; Lowe, *Scriptura Beneventana*, 2: 77; P. Fadele, "Un codice autografo di Leone Ostense con due documenti veliterni del secolo XII," in *Bullettino dell'Istituto Storico Italiano* 31 (1910): 7–26 with two plates; Vincenzo Federici, *La scrittura delle cancellerie italiane dal secolo XII al XVII: Fac-simili per le scuole di paleografia degli archivi di stato* (Rome, 1934; reprint, Turin, 1964), no. 29 and pl. 29; Hartmut Hoffmann, "Der Kalender des Leo Marsicanus," *Deutsches Archiv für Erforschung des Mittelalters* 21 (1965): pls. 1–2; F. Newton, "Beneventan Scribes and Subscriptions with a List of Those Known at the Present Time," *Bookmark* 43 (1973): 26.

3. Brown, *Handlist*, p. 142; *Archivio Paleografico Italiano* 1 (1882): pl. 16; Dietrich Lohrmann, *Das Register Papst Johannes VIII (872–882)*, Bibliothek des Deutchen Historischen Instituts in Rom, vol. 30 (Tübingen, 1968), with 19 plates, esp. pls. 1, 4, 9; Lowe, *Scriptura Benevantana*, 2: pl. 69. On the register, see also Philipp Jaffé, *Regesta pontificum romanorum*, 2d ed., 2 vols. (Leipzig, 1885–88; reprint, Graz, 1956), 1: 376; and the edition of the *Register* in Antonio Carafa, *Epistolarum decretalium summorum pontificum*, 3 vols. (Rome, 1591), 3: 287–514.

4. Brown, *Handlist*, p. 11; Anton von Euw and Joachim M. Plotzek, *Die Handschriften der Sammlung Ludwig*, 4 vols. (Cologne, 1979–85), 2: 49–63; H. P. Kraus, *Monumenta codicum manu scriptorum* (New York, 1974), no. 12 and pls. on pp. 30, 120; Newton, "Beneventan Scribes and Subscriptions," pp. 13, 29.

5. Paul Meyvaert, "The Autographs of Peter the Deacon," *Bulletin of the John Rylands Library, Manchester* 38 (1955): 114–38, pls. 1, 2a; Mauro Inguanez, *Sexti Julii Frontini De aqueductu urbis Romae: Editio phototypica ex cod. Casin. 361, saec. XII* (Monte Cassino, 1930), ff. 22–33, 33–34, 34, 71; Clemens Herschel, *The Two Books on the Water Supply of the City of Rome of Sextus Julius Frontinus*, 2d ed. (New York, 1913), pl. of f. 71; Brown, *Handlist*, p. 84.

6. Meyvaert, "Autographs of Peter the Deacon," pl. 4a; Oderisio Piscicelli-

Taeggi, *Paleografia artistica di Montecasino* (Monte Cassino, 1876–84), *Latino*, pl. 62; Brown, *Handlist*, p. 78.

7. Lowe, *Beneventan Script*, p. 276.

8. Ibid., p. 278.

9. See Lowe, *Scriptura Beneventana*, 1: pl. 5 and 2: 70; Monte Cassino, Archivio della Badia 195; *Bibliotheca Casinensis*, vol. 4 (pl.).

10. Saenger, "Coupure et séparation des mots sur le Continent au Moyen Age," p. 454; Avril, *Manuscrits enluminés d'origine italienne*, 1: no. 143.

11. See f. 137.

12. Avril, *Manuscrits enluminés d'origine italienne*, 1: no. 22, pl. 5.

13. See Peritz, *Archiv der Gesellschaft für altere deutsche geschichtskunde* 8 (1839): 779–82; *MGH: Legum*, sect. 11, p. xvii; Charles M. Radding, *The Origins of Medieval Jurisprudence: Pavia and Bologna 850–1150* (New Haven, 1988), pp. 116–20. I am indebted to Professor Radding for permitting me to consult his microfilm of this codex.

14. Avril, *Manuscrits enluminés d'origine italienne*, 1: no. 156, pl. 55.

15. Mario Palma, "Da Nonantola a Fonte Avellana: A proposito di dodici manoscritti e di un *Domnus Damianus*," *Scrittura e civiltà* 2 (1978): 221–30 and pls. 1a–5b. Note esp. Vat. lat. 213, 455, Rome, BN Vittorio Emanuele II, Sessoriani 33, Vat. lat. 483, 4956, 285.

16. For example, see Armando Petrucci, "L'onciale romana: Origini, sviluppo e diffusione di una stilizzazione grafica altomedievale (sec. vi–ix)," *Studi medievali*, ser. 3, 12 (1971): 75–134 and 20 plates; Paola Supino Martini and Armando Petrucci, "Materiali ed ipotesi per una storia della cultura scritta nella Roma dela IX secolo," *Scrittura e civiltà* 2 (1978): 45–101 and 10 plates; Guglielmo Cavallo, "Interazione tra scrittura greca e scrittura latina a Roma tra VIII e IX secolo," in *Miscellanea codicologica F. Masai dicata*, 1: 23–29 and pls. 6–8.

17. *NCE*, 6: 763, pl. of ff. 80v–81; Wilhelm M. Peitz, "Das Original Register Gregors VII im vatikanischen Archiv (Reg. Vat. 2)," *Sitzungsberichte der Kaiserlichen Akademie der Wissenschaften: Philosophisch-Historische Klasse*, 165 (1911): 5 Abhandlung, pls. I–IV; Erich Casper, *Die Register Gregors VII*, in *MGH: Epistolae selectae* 2 (Berlin, 1920): vi.

18. Fournier and Le Bras, *Histoire des collections canoniques*, 2: 26–51. On Deusdedit, see also Rouse and Rouse, *Preachers, Florilegia and Sermons*, p. 5–6.

19. The manuscript must date from after 1081, date *post quem* of the text.

20. On the scriptorium of Farfa, see W. M. Lindsay, "The Farfa Type," *Palaeographia latina* 3 (1924): 49–51 and three plates; E. Carusi, "Cenni Storici sull'abbazia di Farfa," ibid., pp. 52–59; Giorgio Brugnoli, "Note sulla Minuscola Farfense," *Rivista di Cultura classica medioevale* 3 (1961): 332–41.

21. *Archivio paleografico italiano* 6 (1924; reprint, n.d.): pl. 98; *Italy: Catalogo dei manoscritti datati* 1 (1971): pls. 19–21; Brugnoli, "Note," p. 338.

22. Edward B. Garrison, "Random Notes on Early Italian Manuscripts," *La bibliofilia* 80 (1978): 197–201 with three plates.

23. I. Giorgi and Ugi Balzani, *Il registro di Farfa compilato di Gregorio di Catino,* 4 vols. (Rome, 1879–1914); *Archivio paleografico italiano* 6 (1924; reprint, n.d.), pl. 95; Hélène Tourbert, "Contribution à l'iconographie des psautiers: La commentaire des psaumes," *Mélanges de l'Ecole française de Rome* 88 (1976): 586 (pl. of f. 44v). For this and the other historical works by Gregorio, see Ugi Balzani, *Le cronache italiane nel medio evo,* rev. ed. (Milan, 1900), esp. p. 150; W. Kurze, "Zur Kopiertätigkeit Gregors von Catino," in *Quellen und Forschungen aus italienischen Archiven und Bibliotheken* 53 (1973): 407–56; Herbert Zielinski, "Gregor von Catino und das Regestum Farfense," *Quellen und Forschungen aus italienischen Archiven und Bibliotheken* 55–56 (1976): 361–404, pl. 2; G. Michiels, *DHGE* 21 (1986): 1489; Brugnoli, "Note," and pls. 1–4.

24. Giuseppi Zucchetti, *Libri largitorius vel notarius monasterii pharphenis,* 2 vols. (Rome, 1913–32); *Archivio paleografico italiano* 6 (1924; reprint, n.d.), pl. 100; *Italy: Catalogo dei manoscritti datati* 1 (1971): no. 2 and pls. 22–23.

25. *Archivio paleografico italiano* 7 (1906–29; reprint, 1974): pls. 52–58; cf. pls. 20 and 24 (Naples).

26. Ibid., pl. 59.

27. Avril, *Manuscrits enluminés d'origine italienne,* 1: no. 46 and pl. 14.

Chapter 14

1. See Monique-Cécile Garand, "La scriptorium de Guibert de Nogent," *Scriptorium* 31 (1977): 3–29, esp. p. 15 and pls. 1–3, and "Analyse d'écritures et macrophotographie: Les manuscrits originaux de Guibert de Nogent," *Codices manuscripti* 1 (1975): 112–23, esp. pls. 1–3.

2. Rudolf Goy, *Die Überlieferung der Werke Hugos von St. Viktor,* Monographien zur Geschichte des Mittelalters, vol. 14 (Stuttgart, 1976), p. 135, no. 8, and pl. 2.

3. See Ernst S. Rothkopf, "Incidental Memory for Information in Text," *Journal of Verbal Learning and Verbal Behavior* 10 (1971): 608–13.

4. Prologue to Hugh of Saint-Victor's *De tribus maximis circumstantiis gestorum,* ed. William M. Green, "Hugo of Saint-Victor: *De tribus maximis circumstantiis gestorum,*" *Speculum* 18 (1943): 490; English trans. in Carruthers, *The Book of Memory,* pp. 261–66.

5. Charles Henry Buttimer, ed., *Hugonis de Saint Victor: Didascalicon de studio legendi,* Studies in Medieval and Renaissance Latin, vol. 10 (Washington, D.C., 1939), pp. 57–58. See Ivan Illich, *In the Vinyard of the Text: A Commentary to Hugh's Didascalicon* (Chicago, 1993), pp. 86–87. Hugh reported the silent study habits of his *fere* contemporary Bernard of Chartres; Jerome Taylor, *The Didascalicon of Hugh of Saint Victor* (New York, 1961), p. 94 n. 61.

6. Buttimer, *Hugonis de Saint Victor: Didascalicon*, p. 58; cf. *Ars Victorini grammatici*, in Keil, *Grammatici latini*, 6: 188.

7. *Hugonis de Sancto Victore opera propraedeutica*, ed. Roger Baron (Notre Dame, Ind., 1966), p. 127.

8. Carlo de Clercq, "Le *Liber de rota verae religionis* d'Hugues de Fouilloy," *Bulletin du Cange* 29 (1959): 219–28 with two plates; and "Hugues de Fouilloy imagier de ses propres oeuvres?" *Revue du nord* 45 (1963): 31–42 with four plates.

9. John of Salisbury, *Metalogicon*, 1: 24, ed. Clement C. J. Webb (Oxford, 1929), pp. 53–54.

10. Ibid., 1: 20.

11. Ibid., 1: 21 (ed. Webb, pp. 50–51).

12. See André Vernet, *La Bibliothèque de l'abbaye de Clairvaux du XIIe au XVIIIe siècle* (Paris, 1979–), 1: pls. 1, 6; Monique-Cécile Garand, "Manuscrits monastiques et scriptoria aux XIe et XIIe siècles," in A. Gruys and J. P. Gumbert, eds., *Codicologica* 3 (1980): 16–18.

13. Microfilm at the IRHT; *France: Manuscrits datés* 5 (1965): 56 and pls. 236, 242. I am indebted to the staff of the IRHT for enabling me to consult the two volumes of this manuscript in Paris.

14. J.-M. Déchanet, "Un recueil singulier d'opuscules de Guillaume de Saint-Thierry: Charleville 114," *Scriptorium* 6 (1952): 196–212 and pls. 24–25; and "Les manuscrits de la *Lettre aux Frères du Mont-Dieu* et le problème de la préface dans Charleville 114," *Scriptorium* 11 (1957): 63–86 and pl. 12; *France: Manuscrits datés* (1965): 43, 51 and pls. 10–11.

15. See François Dolbeau, "Anciens possesseurs," pl. 3. The examples cited by Dolbeau have been supplemented by a list kindly provided to me by Patricia Stirnemann.

16. A. H. Bredero, "Un Brouillon du XIIe s.: L'autographe de Geoffroy d'Auxerre," *Scriptorium* 13 (1958): 27–60 and pls. 8–10.

17. Jean Leclercq, "Pour l'iconographie de saint Bernard," *Analecta Sacri Ordinis Cistercienis* 9 (1953): 43–44 and pl. 2; *Recueil des études sur Saint Bernard*, 2 vols. (Rome, 1962–66), 1: 9 n. 3, 77, 215, 247, 263.

18. For reference to the appropriate plates, see J.-M. Déchanet, "Les divers états du texte de la *Lettre aux Frères du Mont-Dieu* dans Charleville 114," *Scriptorium* 11 (1957): 85 n. 39.

19. These marks are present in Charleville, BM 196c. I am indebted to Mme. Anne-Véronique Raynal for indicating them to me.

20. Richalm, *Liber revelationum de insidiis et versutiis daemonum adversus homines*, in *Thesaurus anecdotorum novissimus seu Veterum monumentorum praecipue ecclesiasticorum ex Germanicis potissimum bibliothecis adornata collectio recentissima*, 4 vols., ed. Bernard Pez (Augsburg, 1721–29), 1: pt. 2, col. 390.

21. See Ursmer Berlière, *L'ascèse bénédictine des origines à la fin du XIIe siècle* (Paris, 1927).

22. Jean Mabillon, ed., *Sancti Bernardi abbatis primi clare-vallicensis Opera omnia*, 2 vols. (Paris, 1690), 2: 219–20.

23. *De interiori domo*, 24; *PL* 184: 520B–C, cited by Jean Leclercq, "Aspect spirituel de la symbolique du livre au XIIᵉ siècle," *L'homme devant Dieu: Mélanges offerts au Père Henri de Lubac*, Etudes publiées sous la direction de la Faculté de théologie S.J. de Lyon-Fourvière, vols. 56–58 (Paris, 1963–64), 2: 64. Absalon de Springkirsbach, *Sermo 25*, in *PL* 211: 1518-C, cited by Leclercq, "Aspect spirituel," p. 64.

24. Richard Rouse, "La diffusion en occident au XIIIᵉ siècle des outils de travail facilitant l'acces aux textes autoritatifs," *Revue des études islamiques* 44 (1976): 118, 120–23.

25. Monique-Cécile Garand, "Auteurs latins et autographes des XIᵉ et XIIᵉ siècles," *Scrittura e civiltà* 5 (1981): 98 and pl. 1.

26. Petrus Cellensis, *Tractatus de disciplina claustrali*, ch. 19 (de lectione); *PL* 202: 1125–26; Gérard de Martel, *Pierre de Celle: L'école de Cloître*, Sources chrétiennes, no. 240 (Paris, 1977), pp. 233–36.

27. De Martel, *Pierre de Celle*, pp. 74–78 with two plates.

28. Gérard de Martel, "Recherches sur les manuscrits des sermons de Pierre de Celle," *Scriptorium* 33 (1979): 3–17 and pl. 1.

29. Léopold Delisle, *Matériaux pour l'édition de Guillaume de Jumièges préparée par Jules Lair* (N.p., 1910), pp. 485–87.

30. Quintilian, who lived when script was separated by interpuncts, had recommended that authors write their own works; Quintilian, *Institutiones oratoriae*, 10.3.19–20.

31. Edmond René Labande, *Guibert de Nogent: Autobiographie* (Paris, 1981), pp. 136–39.

32. Ibid., pp. 136–37.

33. "Sola memoria, sola voce, sine manu, sine oculis." *PL* 156: 340.

34. See Monique-Cécile Garand, "Auteurs latins et autographes," pp. 88–97.

35. André Boutemy, "Odon d'Orléans et les origines de la bibliothèque de l'abbaye de Saint-Martin de Tournai," in *Mélanges Félix Grat*, 2: 179–222. For an example of the scriptorium of Saint-Martin, see Paris, BN NAL 2195; *France: Manuscrits datés* 4, pt. 1 (1981): 231 and pl. 17. *Prosodiae* include *traits d'union* and acute accents to denote the double *ii*. Paris, BN NAL 2195, a Psalter copied at Saint-Martin in 1107, was canonically separated with *prosodiae* including *traits d'union* and the acute accent on the double *ii*.

36. Josephus-Maria Canivez, ed., *Statuta capitulorum generalium ordinis cisterciensis*, 8 vols. (Louvain, 1933–41), 1: 26.

37. Jean Leclercq, "Saint Bernard et ses secrétaires," *RB* 61 (1951): 208–28; cf. Bernard, *Epistula 89*, in *PL* 182: 220–21.

38. R. W. Southern, ed., *The Life of Saint Anselm Archbishop of Canterbury by Eadmer* (London, 1962), pp. viii–xxiv; Southern, *Saint Anselm and His*

Biographer: A Study of Monastic Life and Thought 1059–1130 (Oxford, 1963), pp. 367–74. The frontispiece is a plate of the first leaf of the text.

39. For an overview, see P. Bloch, "Autorenbild," in Engelbert Kirschbaum, *Lexikon der christlichen Ikonographie*, 8 vols. (Rome, 1968–76), 1: 232–34.

40. Wolfram von den Steinen, *Notker Der Dichter und seine geistige Welt*, 2 vols. (Bern, 1948), 2: pls. 1–3.

41. Jean Leclercq, "Aspects littéraires de l'oeuvre de Saint Bernard," *Cahiers de civilisation médiévale* 1 (1958): 440 and pls. 3–4.

42. John J. O'Meara, "Giraldus Cambrensis: In topographia Hiberniae," *Proceedings of the Royal Irish Academy* 52C (1949): 151–52.

43. "Rorant e celo tibi que scribenda revelo." S. J. P. Van Dijk, *The Myth of the Aumbry: Notes on Medieval Reservation Practice and Eucharistic Devotion with Special Reference to the Findings of Dom Gregory Dix* (London, 1957), p. 80, pl. 10.

44. Lisbon, Gulbenkian Museum, lat. 148, f. 19v, and Paris, BN lat. 926, f. 2. The former is reproduced in James Marrow, *The Golden Age of Dutch Manuscript Painting*, exhibition catalogue (New York, 1989), pl. 1; the latter is in M. Meiss, *French Painting in the Time of Jean de Berry: The Late Fourteenth Century and the Patronage of the Duke* (New York, 1967), fig. 667. I am grateful to Professor Marrow for generously providing me with these references.

45. Examples include the evangelistary of Henry III, Bremen, Universitäts-bibliothek b.21, originating from Echternach; facsimile (Wiesbaden, ca. 1980); Paris, BN lat. 8551, f. 1, an evangelistary from Trier written in 1002–14; *France: Manuscrits datés* 3 (1974): 87, reproduction, Paris, BN Collection Porcher; Reims, BM 9, f. 23, reproduction, Paris, BN Collection Porcher.

46. Luba Eleen, *The Illustration of the Pauline Epistles in French and English Bibles of the Twelfth and Thirteenth Centuries* (Oxford, 1982), pls. 54, 55, 59, 61, 100.

47. *Beschreibendes Verzeichnis der Illuminierten Handschriften in Österreich* 4, 2 (1911): pls. 58 and 60.

48. Pierre Petitmengin and Bernard Flusin, "Le livre antique et la dictée: Nouvelles recherches," in Enzo Lucchesi and H. D. Saffrey, eds., *Mémorial André-Jean Festugière: Antiquité païenne et chrétienne*, Cahiers d'orientalisme, vol. 10 (Geneva, 1984), pp. 247–62, pls. 61, 71, 103; A. I. Doyle, "Further Observations on Durham Cathedral MS A.IV.34," in Gumbert and de Haan, *Litterae Textuales*, 1: 35–47.

49. Neil R. Ker, "Copying an Exemplar: Two Manuscripts of Jerome on Habakkuk," in *Miscellanea codicologica F. Masai dicata*, 1: 203–10 and pls. 30–33.

50. Georg Waitz, ed., *Hermani liber de restauratione s. Martini Tornacensis*, in *MGH: Scriptores* 14 (1983): 312–13.

51. Karl Kunstle, *Ikonographie der christlichen Kunst*, 2 vols. (Freiburg im Breisgau, 1926–28), 2: 442, 446.

52. See Saenger, "Word Separation and Its Implications."

53. See, for example, Dorothee Klein, "Autorenbild," *Reallexikon zur deutschen Kunstgeschichte* 1 (Stuttgart, 1937): 1312; Paris, BN lat. 415, f. 1.

54. For a plate of a well-spaced stationer's exemplar, see Bataillon, Guyot, and Rouse, *La production du livre universitaire au Moyen Age*. Vernacular exemplars were similarly well separated; see, for example, Paris, BN fr. 794 (s. xiii in.), described by Mario Roques, "Le manuscrit français 794 de la Bibliothèque Nationale et le scribe Guiot," *Romania* 73 (1952): 177–99.

55. Petrarch, *Epistolae familiares*, 23.19, in *Petrarca: Prose*, ed. G. Martrelotti (Milan, 1955), p. 1016; *Epistolae variae*, 15, in *Francisci Petrarcae: Epistolae de rebus familiaribus et variae*, 3 vols., ed. Joseph Fracassetti (Florence, 1859–63), 3: 332–33; Conrad H. Rawski, *Petrarch: Four Dialogues for Scholars* (Cleveland, Ohio, 1967), pp. 78, 138. Jean Gerson, *De laude scriptorum*, in Glorieux, *Oeuvres complètes*, 9: 424.

56. For examples, see Paris, BN lat. 1160, f. 3, and London, BL Add. 20694, f. 189 (St. Mark); Janet Backhouse, *Book of Hours* (London, 1986), p. 20, pl. 13.

57. Levin and Addis, *The Eye-Voice Span*, pp. 71–76, 79.

58. In the use of imposition, texts were copied in out-of-sense sequence; see G. I. Lieftinck, "Mediaeval Manuscripts with Imposed Sheets," *Het Boek*, ser. 3, 34 (1960–61): 210–20; Obbema, "Writing on Uncut Sheets." For related earlier examples of mechanical copying, see W. M. Lindsay, "Collectanea varia," *Palaeographia latina* 2 (1923): 26–28 and 4 (1925): 84–85; Doyle, "Further Observations on Durham Cathedral MS. A.IV. 34," pp. 35–47.

59. Scholes, "On the Orthographic Basis of Linguistic Constructs."

60. G. L. Bursill-Hall, *Speculative Grammars of the Middle Ages* (The Hague, 1971), pp. 258, 276; and *Thomas of Erfurt: Grammatica speculativa: An Edition with Translation and Commentary* (London, 1972), pp. 56, 57, 91–93.

61. *Catholicon* (Mainz, n.d.), ff. 12, 18, 24.

62. See Thurot, "Notices et extraits," pp. 341–50.

63. Remigio Sabbadini, "Sulla Constructio," *Revista di filogia e d'instruzione classica* 25 (1897): 102. See also Paris, BN lat. 11386, f. 30 (s. xiv); Thurot, "Notices et extraits," p. 344.

64. For an example, see C. H. Talbot, "The Archetypes of Saint Bernard's *Sermons super Cantica*," *Scriptorium* 8 (1954): 231.

65. In commentaries on Aristotle's discussion in the *De sophisticis elenchis* of the fallacies of composition and division, modist grammarians set forth the rule, lifted out of context from Priscian, that adjectives naturally preceded nouns and adverbs naturally preceded verbs, reducing the ambiguity of written prose much as *prosodiae* reduced the ambiguity of the individual word; Alain de Libera, "De la logique à la grammaire: Remarques sur la théorie de la *determinatio* chez Roger Bacon et Lambert d'Auxerre (Lambert de Lagny)," in *De Ortu*

Grammaticae: Studies in Medieval Grammar and Linguistic Theory in Memory of Jan Pinborg, ed. G. L. Bursill-Hall, Sten Ebbesen, and Konrad Koerner (Amsterdam, 1988), pp. 209–26.

66. Monfrin, "Les traducteurs et leur public," p. 261.

67. This process has been largely ignored by students of medieval and Renaissance mnemonics, e.g., Carruthers, *The Book of Memory*, p. 18. However, it has been studied by modern psychologists and psycholinguists; see Samuel Fillenbaum, "Memory for Gist: Some Relevant Variables," *Language and Speech* 9 (1966): 217–27; Jacqueline Strunk Sachs, "Recognition Memory for Syntactic and Semantic Aspects of Connected Discourse," *Perception and Psychophysics* 2 (1967): 437–42; John R. Anderson, "Verbatim and Prepositional Representation of Sentences in Immediate and Long-Term Memory," *Journal of Verbal Learning and Verbal Behavior* 13 (1974): 149–62; Eric Wanner, *On Remembering, Forgetting, and Understanding Sentences: A Study of the Deep Structure Hypothesis*, JL, series minor, vol. 170 (The Hague, 1974).

68. See Chicago, Newberry Library 24.1; Manuel Hoepli and Adriano Capelli, *Lexicon abbreviatorum: Dizionario di Abbreviature latine ed italiane* (Milan, 1973), pp. 413, 417, 418, 419, 420; Cajori, *A History of Mathematical Notations*, 1: 33.

69. Cajori, *A History of Mathematical Notations*, 1: 33; Hoepli and Capelli, *Lexicon abbreviatorum*, p. liv.

70. Cajori, *A History of Mathematical Notations*, 1: 90–91; Guy Beaujouan, "L'Enseignement de l'arithmétique élémentaire à l'université de Paris au XIIIe et XIVe siècles: De l'abaque à l'algorithme," *Homenaje a Millàs-Vallicrosa*, 2 vols. (Barcelona, 1954–56), 1: 95.

71. Cajori, *A History of Mathematical Notations*, 1: 90, 91, 252, 268, etc.

72. See the description of the operations of addition and subtraction by John of Sacrobosco in James Orchard Halliwell, *Rara mathematica or a Collection of Treatises on the Mathematics and Subjects Connected with Them from Ancient Inedited Manuscripts* (London, 1839), pp. 5ff.

73. Cajori, *A History of Mathematical Notations*, 1: 269.

Chapter 15

1. For examples of this proto-cursive writing, see the writing of Albertus Magnus, in S. Harrison Thomson, *Latin Bookhands of the Later Middle Ages* (Cambridge, 1969), no. 38; cf. that of Thomas Aquinas, in Antoine Dondaine, *Secrétaires de Saint Thomas* (Rome, 1956), pls. xxxvi–xxxviii.

2. Albert d'Haenens, "Ecrire en couteau dans la main gauche: Un aspect de la physiologie de l'écriture occidentale au XIe et XIIe siècles," in Rita Lejeune and Joseph Deckers, eds., *Clio et son regard: Mélanges d'histoire, d'histoire de l'art et d'archéologie offerts à Jacques Stiennon à l'occasion de ses vingt-cinq ans d'enseignement à l'université de Liège* (Liège, 1982), pp. 129–41; Obbema, "Writ-

ing on Uncut Sheets," p. 353. The frontispiece of the Morgan Library manuscripts of the *Bible moralisée* shows a scribe holding the page with his knife as he writes to dictation.

3. Jean Porcher, *Medieval French Miniatures*, trans. T. Julian Brown (New York, 1960), p. 93. For three different modes of authorship—dictation, writing *textualis* with the knife anchoring the page, and writing *cursiva* in the relaxed position—see Anne Tukey Harrison and Sandra Hindman, *The Dance Macabre of Women: MS fr. 995 of the Bibliothèque Nationale* (Kent, 1994), pp. 38, 51, 125.

4. Nicolaus de Lyra, prologue to his *Postilla* on the book of Genesis, *Postilla super totam Bibliam* (Strasbourg, 1492; reprint, Frankfurt, 1971), f. Ci verso.

5. "Nihilominus testimonium perhibeo vobis quale positum est in epistola mea Ad fratres de Monte Dei quod Scripturas Sacras nullus unquam plene intelliget qui non affectus scribentium induerit." Jean Gerson, *Sermo in festo S. Bernardi*, in Glorieux, *Oeuvres complètes*, 5: 334.

6. Humbert of Romans, *Expositio Regulae B. Augustini*, in *Humbertus de Romanis: Opera de vita regulari*, 2 vols., ed. Joachim Joseph Berthier (Rome, 1888–89), 1: 186.

7. H. Denifle and E. Chatelain, eds., *Chartularium Universitatis Parisiensis*, 4 vols. (Paris, 1889–97), 1: 386; du Boulay, *Historia Universitatis Parisiensis*, 4: 159; Hastings Rashdall, *The Universities of Europe in the Middle Ages*, ed. F. M. Powicke and A. B. Emden (Oxford, 1936), 423 nn. 1–2.

8. Pierre Dubois, *De recuperatione Terre Sancte*, ed. Angelo Diotti (Florence, 1977), p. 163.

9. In 1271, Jean d'Orléans, chancellor of Notre-Dame, mentions "libros tradendos et recuperandos pauperibus scolaribus in theologica studentibus"; Alfred Franklin, *Les anciennes bibliothèques de Paris*, 3 vols. (Paris, 1867–73), 1: 8 n. 5 (cf. 9 n. 1); Rashdall, *The Universities of Europe*, p. 423. At the Sorbonne in the fifteenth century, thirty manuscripts of the *Sentences* of Peter of Lombard were available for borrowing; see Jeanne Vielliard, "Le Registre de prêt de la bibliothèque du Collège de Sorbonne au XVᵉ siècle," *Mediaevalia Lovaniensia* 6 (1978): 291.

10. A. Tuilier, "La Bibliothèque de la Sorbonne et les livres enchaînés," *Mélanges de la Bibliothèque de la Sorbonne* 2 (1981): 22–23, 26.

11. L. D. Reynolds, *Texts and Transmissions: A Survey of the Latin Classics* (Oxford, 1983), p. 209.

12. Malcolm Parkes, "The Influence of the Concepts of *Ordinatio* and *Compilatio* on the Development of the Book," in Alexander and Gibson, *Medieval Learning and Literature*, pp. 124–25; Daniel A. Callus, "The 'Tabula super originalia patrum' of Robert Kilwardby O.P.," *Studia mediaevalia in honorem R. J. Martin* (Bruges, 1948), pp. 243–70; Richard W. Hunt, "Chapter Headings of Augustine's *De trinitate* Ascribed to Adam Marsh," *Bodleian Library Record* 5 (1954): 63.

13. Parkes, "The Concepts of *Ordinatio* and *Compilatio*," pp. 118–22; Rouse and Rouse, *Preachers, Florilegia and Sermons*, pp. 7–36.

14. Marichal, "L'écriture latine et la civilisation occidentale," pp. 237–40; Parkes, "The Concepts of *Ordinatio* and *Compilatio*," p. 121; Parkes, *Pause and Effect*, p. 44.

15. Paris, BN lat. 4436 and lat. 4523.

16. For example, the *Tragedies* of Seneca copied in 1397, Paris, BN lat. 8824. This system was used to attach Nicolaus de Lyra's *Postilla* to the text of the Bible in the Strasbourg edition of 1492 (see above, note 4).

17. D. F. McKenzie, "Speech-Manuscript-Print," in Dave Oliphant and Robin Bradford, eds., *New Directions in Textual Studies* (Austin, Tex., 1990), p. 104.

18. Saenger and Heinlen, "Incunable Description," p. 249.

19. Paul of Burgos's *Additiones* to the *Postilla* of Nicolaus de Lyra could be used only in this manner. For manuscripts of this text, see Friedrich Stegmüller, *Repertorium Biblicum medii aevi*, 8 vols. (Madrid, 1940–79), 4: 197.

20. The arguments presented by Philippe Delhaye for identifying Munich Staatsbibliothek Clm. 9559, ff. 18–22, as a quire copied in the classroom are scarcely convincing; *Siger de Brabant: Questions de la Phyique d'Aristote*, Les philosophes belges: Textes et études (Louvain, 1941), pp. 6–7; Jacqueline Hamesse, "Reportations, Graphies et Ponctuation," in Maierù, *Grafia e interpunzione*, p. 136 and pl. 2.

21. Dogaer and Debae, *La Librairie de Philippe le Bon*, pl. 33.

22. M. B. Parkes, "Tachygraphy in the Middle Ages: Writing Techniques Employed for *Reportationes* of Lectures and Sermons," *Medioevo e Rinascimento* 3 (1989): 159–69.

23. For an Italian example from the fourteenth century, see Astrik L. Gabriel, *Garlandia: Studies in the History of the Mediaeval University* (Frankfurt, 1969), pl. 25; for a French example from the thirteenth and fourteenth centuries, see Paris, Bibliothèque de la Sorbonne 31, f. 278, reproduced on the cover of the exhibition catalogue *La vie universitaire parisienne au XIIIe siècle* (Paris, 1974); Astrik L. Gabriel, *Student Life in Ave Maria College, Mediaeval Paris: History and Chartulary of the College*, Publications in Mediaeval Studies, vol. 14 (Notre Dame, Ind., 1955), pls. 25, 26. Duns Scotus was painted in the fourteenth century instructing students with books; Jacques Guy Bougerol, *Saint Bonaventure et la sagesse chrétienne* (Paris, 1963), p. 150. In the second half of the fifteenth century, the same iconography of the classroom is common in early printed books; see, for example, Guilhelmus of Gouda as a teacher, in Benjamin de Troeger and Leonide Mees, *Bio-bibliographia Franciscana neerlandica ante saeculum XVI*, 3 vols. (Nieuwkoop, 1974), 3: 77 (ill. 92).

24. A. Van Hove, "La bibliothèque de la faculté des arts de l'Université de Louvain," in *Mélanges d'histoire offerts à Charles Moeller à l'occasion de son jubilé*

de 50 années de professorat à l'Université de Louvain 1863–1913, 2 vols. (Louvain, 1914), 1: 616. See also Gerhardt Powitz, "Modus Scolipetarum et Reportistarum: Pronuntiatio and Fifteenth-Century University Hands," *Scrittura e civiltà* 12 (1988): 201–11.

25. The university wanted the professor to lecture in the manner of a preacher delivering a sermon; Denifle and Chatelain, *Chartularium Universitatis Parisiensis*, 3: 39, 642, 646. In the fourteenth and fifteenth centuries, the iconography of the preacher differed from that of the professor in that the preacher was usually shown speaking extemporaneously without a written text before him; see, for examples, Paris, BN lat. 646B, f. 1; lat. 17294, ff. 65v, 66v; lat. 17716, f. 43; fr. 147, f. 1; fr. 177, f. 315; fr. 244, f. 1; and fr. 824, f. 1. The effort to enliven the style of lecturing seems not to have taken hold, and in 1454, Cardinal Estouteville rescinded the prohibition of *legere ad pennam*, i.e., professors were permitted to read lectures so that a reporter could record them word for word; Denifle and Chatelain, *Chartularium Universitatis Parisiensis*, 4: 727; cf. Hamesse, "Reportations," p. 137 n. 11.

26. Jean Destrez, *La pecia dans les manuscrits universitaires du XIIIe et du XIVe siècle* (Paris, 1935); Bataillon, Guyot, and Rouse, *La production du livre universitaire au Moyen Age*.

27. At the University of Bologna in the fourteenth century, doctors disputing questions were obliged to deposit their manuscripts for inspection and transcription; H. Denifle, *Archiv für Literatur- und Kirchengeschichte des Mittelalter* (Berlin, 1885–1900), 4: 321–22. At Angers the lectures of the professor were made available for transcription by the library of the university; Celestin Port, "La bibliothèque de l'Université d'Angers," *Notes et notices angevines* (Angers, 1879), 34. The documents first published by Port have been reedited by Marcel Fournier, *Les statuts et privilèges des universités françaises*, 3 vols. (Paris, 1890–94), 1: 387–89. The hypothesis of transcriptions being made prior to oral presentation has been dismissed out of hand by H. Kantorowicz, "The *Quaestiones disputatae* of the Glossators," *Revue d'histoire de droit* 16 (1939): 41, but it would account for medieval miniatures which appear to show students silently reading from the very texts from which the professor is lecturing, e.g., Paris, BN lat. 14023, ff. 2, 123. In about 1300, an English theologian requested his pupils to submit their arguments in writing before redacting his lecture, an indication of the degree to which graphic communication may have paralleled and even anticipated oral presentation; P. Glorieux, *La littérature quodlibétique*, 2 vols. (Paris, 1925–35), 1: 52. On the relation between oral arguments and their published versions, see also Jean Acher, "Six disputations et un fragment d'une *repetitio* orléanaises," *Mélanges Fitting*, 2 vols. (Montpellier, 1907), 2: 300–301. In French law courts, written arguments also regularly amplified oral presentations. In the mid-fifteenth century, Thomas Basin suggested that oral arguments were therefore superfluous and could be discontinued; see P. Guilhiermoz, "De

la persistance du caractère oral dans la procédure civile française," *Nouvelle revue historique de droit français et étranger* 13 (1889): 21–65. The written pleas were especially needed in cases too complex to be understood orally. The court used the terms *dit de bouche* and *dit en escriptures* to distinguish between the two modes of presenting arguments, the logical structure of which closely paralleled the scholastic *quaestiones* of the law schools. The task of recording the oral pleas was assigned to a scribe and not to the reporter, who was one of the judges.

28. The colophon of Jacques Buyer's *Lectura decretalis*, apparently printed for use at the University of Valence, indicates that Buyer as printer and publisher was acting as a reporter for Laurentius Dozoli; Charles Perrat, "Barthélemy Buyer et les débuts de l'imprimerie à Lyon," *Humanisme et Renaissance* 2 (1935): 121; cf. James J. Murphy, "The Double Revolution of the First Rhetorical Textbook Published in England: The *Margarita eloquentiae* of Gulielmus Traversagnus (1479)," *Texte: Revue de critique et de théorie littéraire* (1989), pp. 367–76.

29. See, for example, Gozzoli's portrait of Saint Bonaventure (Bougerol, *Saint Bonaventure*, p. 163) and the representation of *scientia* (Paris, BN fr. 541, f. 108). In the sixteenth century, Geoffrey Whitney chose as an emblem of silence the scholar dressed in an academic gown poring over an open book; Raymond B. Waddington, "The Iconography of Silence and Chapman's *Hercules*," *Journal of the Warburg and Courtauld Institutes* 33 (1970): 29. See also the image accompanying the verse *In silentium* in Andrea Alciati's *Liber emblematum* (1st ed., 1531). I am indebted to François Dolbeau for indicating to me the illumination reproduced in Figure 36.

30. Martin Grabmann, "Abkürzende Bearbeitungen der Aristotilischen Schriften: *Abbreviationes, Summulae, Compendia, Epitomata*," *Sitzungsberichte der Bayerischen Akademie der Wissenschaften: Philosophisch-historische Abteilung*, pt. 5 (1939): 54–104. Nicolaus de Lyra stated specifically that the differences between the Hebrew Old Testament and the Vulgate, noted in the *Postilla*, could be more easily read (expeditius videri) in his *Tractatus de differentia*; Herman Hailperin, *Rashi and the Christian scholars* (Pittsburgh, 1963), p. 285 n. 22.

31. Dubois, *De recuperatione Terre Sancte*, p. 163.

32. Hailperin, *Rashi and the Christian Scholars*, p. 139.

33. The customary of the Augustinian convent of Springiersbach-Rolduc, written in ca. 1229, described as subaudible singing and reading what we would call mumbling or murmuring that did not violate the silence; Stephanus Weinfurter, *Consuetudines canonicorum regularium Springirsbacenses Rodenses*, in CCCM 48 (1978): 18, 67, 78, 82, 101. The *Liber Ordinis Sancti Victoris Parisiensis* set down rules for small groups of monks to practice liturgical recitation and the singing of psalms in a relatively quiet manner, which was held not to violate the general silence; Luc Jocqué and Ludo Milis, *Liber ordinis Victoris Parisiensis*, in CCCM 61 (1984): 145, 147, 149.

34. John Willis Clark, *The Care of Books* (Cambridge, 1909), pp. 145–64.

For a fifteenth-century miniature depicting such a library, see François Dolbeau, "Les usagers des bibliothèques," in André Vernet, ed., *Histoire des bibliothèques françaises*, vol. 1 (Paris, 1989), p. 394.

35. H. W. Garrod, "The Library Regulations of a Medieval College," *The Library*, ser. 4, 8 (1927): 315. For the growth of reference collections, see the bibliography provided by Richard H. Rouse, "The Early Library of the Sorbonne," *Scriptorium* 21 (1967): 60.

36. Rouse, "The Early Library of the Sorbonne," p. 59.

37. Van Hove, "La bibliothèque de l'Université de Louvain," pp. 602–25.

38. Delisle, *Cabinet des manuscrits*, 2: 181, no. 6.

39. See the statutes of the library of the University of Angers, in Port, "La bibliothèque de l'Université d'Angers," p. 28; for Oxford, see Henry Anstey, *Munimenta academica*, 2 vols., Rerum Britannicarum medii aevi scriptores, vol. 50 (London, 1868), 1: 263–66.

40. F. J. McGuigan and W. I. Rodier, "Effects of Auditory Stimulation on Covert Oral Behavior During Silent Reading," *Journal of Experimental Psychology* 76 (1965): 649–55; Robert M. Weisberg, *Memory, Thought, and Behavior* (New York, 1980), pp. 235–36, cf. pp. 159–60. In ancient libraries, oral reading was an accepted practice; see Optatus, Bishop of Mileve, *Contra Parmenianum Donatistam*, 7.1, ed. Karl Ziusa, in *CSEL* 26 (1893): 165.

41. *Humbertus de Romanis: Opera de vita regulari*, ed. Berthier, 1: 421; K. W. Humphreys, *The Book Provisions of the Medieval Friars* (Amsterdam, 1964), 136.

42. Anstey, *Munimenta academica*, 1: 263–64. ·

43. Port, "La bibliothèque de l'Université d'Angers, p. 31.

44. Delisle, *Cabinet des manuscrits*, 2: 201 correctly asserted that the text as given in Claude Héméré's manuscript *Sorbonae origines* dated from the establishment of a new building for the library ca. 1483. However, the inference drawn by Delisle that these rules were intended solely for printed books is not supported by fifteenth-century documentary evidence. Precedents for each of the Sorbonne regulations can be found in rules established for the fifteenth century. Moreover, in 1493, the Sorbonne library was still acquiring manuscript books; see Franklin, *Les anciennes bibliothèques de Paris*, 1: 256 n. 8. Manuscript and printed books were regularly intermixed in medieval libraries; see Dominique Coq, "L'incunable, un bâtard du manuscrit," *Gazette du livre médiéval* 1 (1981): 10–11.

45. Eugène Müntz, *La Bibliothèque du Vatican au XV* siècle d'après des documents inédits* (Paris, 1887), p. 140.

46. Rouse and Rouse, *Preachers, Florilegia and Sermons*; Pieter F. J. Obbema, "The Rooklooster Register Re-evaluated," *Quaerendo* 7 (1977): 326–53.

47. Saenger and Heinlen, "Incunable Description," pp. 239–50.

48. At Oxford, Angers, and Paris: Anstey, *Munimenta academica*, 1: 139–40; Port, "La bibliothèque de l'Université d'Angers," p. 32; Delisle, *Cabinet des manuscrits*, 2: 201.

49. Saenger, "Coupure et séparation des mots sur le Continent au Moyen Age," pp. 450–55.

50. After 1320, the *quodlibet* was no longer an important vehicle for discussing controversial issues. All of Ockham's writings were circulated as private tracts and were not intended for oral delivery to students in the classroom. On the demise of the *quodlibet*, see Gordon Leff, *Paris and Oxford Universities in the Thirteenth and Fourteenth Centuries: An Institutional and Intellectual History* (New York, 1968), p. 249.

51. It was perhaps for this reason that in 1259 the Dominicans forbade bringing to class any book other than the one read by the professor in his lecture; Denifle and Chatelain, *Chartularium Universitatis Parisiensis*, 1: 386.

52. Anne Hudson, "A Lollard Quaternion," *Review of English Studies*, n.s., 22 (1971): 442.

53. Denifle and Chatelain, *Chartularium Universitatis Parisiensis*, 1: 486, 543.

54. Ibid., 2: 271.

55. Ibid., p. 576.

56. Robert Gaguin reported the chaining of the books in a letter sent to Guillaume Fichet; Charles Samaran, *Auctarium chartularii Universitatis Parisiensis* 3 (1935): 259–60. Gaguin's report is confirmed by a letter of 1479 of Jean d'Estouteville to the rector of the University of Paris rescinding the order; du Boulay, *Historia Universitatis Parisiensis*, 5: 739.

57. Geoffroy of Beaulieu, *Sancti Ludovici vita*, in *Recueil des historiens des Gaules et de la France* 20 (Paris, 1840): 14–15; *Vie de Saint Louis par le confesseur de la reine Marguerite*, ibid., pp. 79–80.

58. Bernard Guenée, "La culture historique des nobles: Le succès des *Faits des Romains*, XIIIᵉ–XVᵉ siècles," in Philippe Contamine, ed., *La noblesse au Moyen Age XIᵉ–XVᵉ siècles: Essais à la mémoire de Robert Boutruche* (Paris, 1976), p. 268.

59. Gaston Paris and A. Jeanroy have written of the *Chronique* of Villehardouin that it has "l'air d'avoir été parlé, comme il était destiné à être écouté"; Paris and Jeanroy, *Extraits des chroniqueurs français* (Paris, 1912), p. 6.

60. Joinville speaks of having "fait escrire" his book, *Histoire de saint Louis*, chap. 1. He expected his book to be read aloud to listeners who would "orrez"; chap. 7 and passim. The author of the *Roman du Lancelot* is shown in a miniature dictating; Paris, BN fr. 342, f. 150, copied in 1274. In 1298, Marco Polo dictated *La description du monde*, ed. Louis Hambis (Paris, 1955), p. 2.

61. Only this process explains the textual variants, such as transposition of lines and stanzas, found in Provençal poetry. Guillaume Machaut described this process of oral composition and dictation when he declared in the *Livre du voir-dit*, "Quant j'eus fiat le dit et le chant, . . . Je le fis escrire et noter"; ed. Paulin Paris (Paris 1875), p. 180. A thirteenth-century Spanish miniature depicts the *Cantigas* in praise of Saint Mary being dictated to a scribe; Robert I. Burns, "Christian-Islamic Confrontation in the West: The Thirteenth-Century Dream

of Conversion," *American Historical Review* 76 (1971): 1416 (bottom left). Portraits also exist of scribes who appear to be taking down troubadour lyrics; Hendrik Van der Werf, *The Chansons of the Troubadours and Trouvères* (Utrecht, 1972), pls. 3–4.

62. See the recent discussion of twelfth-century Provençal texts by Kendrick, *The Game of Love*, p. 35. An analogous phenomenon is the difficulty in separating words when writing, which early-twentieth-century French peasants evinced; see Marcel Jousse, *L'anthropologie du geste*, 3 vols. (Paris, 1974–78), 1: 340.

63. Dag Norberg, *Manuel pratique de Latin médiéval* (Paris, 1968), p. 90.

64. See Kendrick, *The Game of Love*, pp. 31–32, 195–96.

65. *Fillastre* and *maistre* are good examples; by the end of the Middle Ages, the *s* was no longer pronounced.

66. In French, *devoir* became *debvoir*; *fevre* became *febvre*. In English, the *b* was introduced into debt. See Albert C. Baugh, *A History of the English Language* (New York, 1957), p. 250; and J. Vachek, "English Orthography: A Functionalist Approach," in W. Haas, *Standard Languages, Spoken and Written* (Manchester, 1982), pp. 37–56. Under the influence of humanism, departures from phonetic orthography in French reached their zenith in the first half of the sixteenth century but began to disappear after 1550, when Jacques Peletier, Louis Meigret, and Jean Antoine Baif led a campaign for the restoration of spelling that accurately expressed the sounds of words.

67. For an example, see Paris, BN fr. 794, described by Mario Roques, "Le manuscrit fr. 794 de la Bibliothèque Nationale et le scribe Guiot," *Romania* 73 (1952): 177–99. I am indebted to Geneviève Hassenohr for this reference.

68. Paul Saenger, "Colard Mansion and the Evolution of the Printed Book," *Library Quarterly* 45 (1975): 405–18.

69. D. J. A. Ross, *Alexander Historiatus: A Guide to Medieval Illustrated Alexander Literature* (London, 1963), pp. 69–71.

70. Monfrin, "Les traducteurs et leur public," p. 255.

71. Georges Tessier, *Diplomatique royale française* (Paris, 1962), p. 305.

72. Louis XI empowered his secretaries to imitate his hand in order to speed the flow of letters; Joseph Vaesen and Etienne Charavay, *Lettres de Louis XI roi de France*, 11 vols. (Paris, 1883–1909), 11: vi; Robert-Henri Bautier, "Les notaires et secrétaires du roi des origines au milieu du XVIᵉ siècle," in André Lapeyre and Rémy Scheurer, *Les notaires et secrétaires du roi sous les règnes de Louis XI, Charles VIII et Louis XII: Notices personnelles et généalogiques* (Paris, 1978), p. xxvii.

73. Tessier, *Diplomatique royale française*, frontispiece.

74. Pierre Bersuire's translation of Livy's *History of Rome* and Jean of Sy's translation of the Bible with Latin commentary are the principal literary monuments of King John's reign; see Delisle, *Cabinet des manuscrits*, 1: 16.

75. Monfrin, "Les traducteurs et leur public," pp. 260–62.

76. Delisle, *Cabinet des manuscrits*, 1: 201; Claire Richter Sherman, *The Portraits of Charles V of France (1338–80)* (New York, 1969), p. 13.

77. Sherman, *Portraits of Charles V of France*, fig. 11. Cf. a miniature depicting King Solomon as a teacher; Rosy Schilling, "The Master of Egerton 1070: Hours of René d'Anjou," *Scriptorium* 8 (1954): pl. 26.

78. Saenger, "Books of Hours," p. 153.

79. On the new vocabulary for reading, see Saenger, "Books of Hours," pp. 143–46. For an example of its use, see Pantin, note 129, below.

80. Saenger, "Books of Hours," p. 146; Jouvenal des Ursins stated that he had been instructed by Charles VII to go "en vos chambres des comptes, du Tresor de vos chartres et ailleurs pour veoir les lettres et chartres necessaires" for writing the *Traictie compendieux contre les Anglois*; cited by P. S. Lewis, "War Propaganda and Historiography in Fifteenth Century France and England," *Transactions of the Royal Historical Society* (1965): 16.

81. Jean Barthélemy used *écrire* in this sense; Paris, BN fr. 9611, f. 1. Jean du Chesne, in the prologue to his translation of the *Commentaries* of Julius Caesar, referred to the "Commentaires que Cesar mesmes escript de sa main" and qualified Caesar as an "escripvain"; BL Royal 16 G. VIII. Raoul Lefèvre, *L'histoire de Jason* (Frankfurt-am-Main, 1971), p. 125, referred to Philip the Good of Burgundy as the "pere des escripvains." In the mid-fourteenth century, however, Pierre Bersuire had found no ready French translation for the Latin *scriptor*, meaning author; see Jean Rychner, "La traduction de Tite-Live par Pierre Bersuire," in Fourrier, *L'humanisme médiéval*, pp. 170–71.

82. For Froissart, see BN fr. 86, f. 11; for Christine de Pisan, see Paris, BN fr. 603, f. 1; fr. 835, f. 1; and fr. 1176, f. 1.

83. Dogaer and Debae, *La Librairie de Philippe le Bon*, pl. 39.

84. Antoine Thomas, *Jean de Gerson et l'éducation des dauphins de France: Etude critique suivie du texte de deux de ses opuscules et de documents inédits sur Jean Majoris précepteur de Louis XI* (Paris, 1930), pp. 50–51.

85. See, for example, Jean Mansel's *Fleurs des histoires* in which the saints' lives were arranged "en ordre selon le A. B. C. pour plus legerement trouver ceulx donc len vouldra lire"; Paris, BN fr. 57, f. 9. On the early introduction of such tables to vernacular texts, see F. Avril, "Trois manuscrits des collections de Charles V et de Jean de Berry," *BEC* 127 (1969): 293.

86. Sherman, *Portraits of Charles V of France*, pp. 42ff.

87. For an example of vernacular banderoles, see Michel François, "Les rois de France et les traditions de l'abbaye de Saint-Denis à la fin du XVe siècle," in *Mélanges dédiés à la mémoire de Félix Grat*, pls. 7–8; Pierre Champion, *Louis XI*, 2 vols. (Paris, 1928), 2: pl. 20. In the sixteenth century, Martin Luther considered the banderole as part of the iconography of the Resurrection; see Catherine Delano Smith, "Maps as Art and Science: Maps in Sixteenth Century Bibles," *Imago Mundi* 42 (1990): 67.

88. An early example of *cursiva formata* used for an essentially literary text is Paris, Archives nationales, Registre JJ 28, dating from the reign of Philip the Fair. For literary texts, the script was first used regularly in the reign of Charles V; see, for example, Paris, BN fr. 16993. Cf. Léopold Delisle, *Recherches sur la librairie de Charles V* (Paris, 1905), p. 230.

89. Paul Saenger, "Geoffroy Tory et le nomenclature des écritures livresques françaises du XVe siècle," *MA*, ser. 4, 32 (1977): 493–520.

90. Geoffroy Tory, *Champ fleury*, ed. Gustave Cohen (Paris, 1913), f. 72.

91. Recently acquired Chicago, Newberry Library 116 contains Netherlandish texts written in the scripts usually reserved for French vernacular books.

92. G. I. Lieftinck, "Pour une nomenclature de l'écriture livresque de la periode dite gothique," *Nomenclature des écritures livresque du IXe au XVIe siècle* (Paris, 1954), pp. 23–24, suggests that *lettre bâtarde* was invented between 1420 and 1430, but his earliest dated example is 1436. Vernacular examples date from as early as 1441; Gerhard Eis, *Altdeutsche Handschriften* (Munich, 1949), pp. 82–83.

93. The term *lettre bourguignonne* has been suggested by G. I. Lieftinck, in *Pays Bas: Manuscrits datés* 1 (1964): xv. For examples of Aubert's script, see Dogaer and Debae, *La Librairie de Philippe le Bon*, nos. 64, 162, and passim.

94. For example, Gothic *textualis* was used in Louis XI's Latin Vulgate Bible, Paris, BN lat. 25. In an extensive survey of hundreds of fifteenth-century vernacular literary manuscripts from the circle of the royal court and the great nobility, I have found only a single example of a literary text written in *textualis*, Paris, BN fr. 19919.

95. See, for example, the use of capitalization and punctuation in Guillaume Fillastre's *Thoison d'Or*, Paris, BN fr. 139.

96. Erich Auerbach, *Literary Language and Its Public in Late Latin Antiquity and in the Middle Ages*, trans. R. Manheim (London, 1965), pp. 299–302.

97. Steffens, *Lateinische Paläographie*, no. 103.

98. See, for example, Lieftinck, "Pour une nomenclature," p. 33.

99. Silvia Rizzo, *Il lessico filologico degli umanisti* (Rome, 1973), pp. 104–5.

100. Erasmus, *De recta latini graecique sermonis pronuntiatione*, ed. M. Cytowska, *Opera omnia Desiderii Erasmi Roterodami*, ser. 1, 4 (1973): 38.

101. Terence O. Tunberg, "The Latinity of Lorenzo Valla's *Gesta Ferdinandi Regis Aragonum*," *Humanistica Lovaniensia* 37 (1988): 71–78.

102. For a French example written in Italian humanistic script, see Baltimore, Walters Art Gallery manuscript W. 452. I am indebted to Lilian Randall for this reference.

103. For particularly interesting examples, see James Wardrop, *The Script of Humanism* (Oxford, 1963).

104. Henri Bornecque, *La prose metrique dans la correspondance de Ciceron* (Paris, 1898), p. 205.

105. See, for example, Chicago, Newberry Library f. 101.1.

106. Geoffroy Tory, *Champ fleury*, ff. 65v–66, cited Byzantine grammarians for this use of punctuation. Cf. Aurelio Roncaglia, "Note sulla punteggiatura medievale e il segno di parentesi," *Lingua nostra* 3 (1941): 6–9.

107. The term and symbol of the parenthesis were known in the fourteenth century, but it was used with the sense of the classical rhetorical construction only in humanistic manuscripts and printed books in the fifteenth century.

108. Johann Fust in Mainz used parentheses in his 1464 edition of the *De officiis*. The parenthesis was used in manuscripts in semi-humanistic script in France in the reign of Louis XI. Tardif included it among the signs of punctuation in his treatise on grammar. In about 1500, the Parisian printer Jean Petit used the parenthesis in his editions of scholastic texts. At the end of the fifteenth century, the parenthesis was also used in vernacular texts, e.g., Paris, BN fr. 15456–57. The humanistic ideal of written eloquence is reflected by Guillaume Leseur, who wrote of royal historiographer Jean Chartier as a "très suffisant et elegant orateur" who "a bien sçeu escripte"; Guillaume Leseur, *Histoire de Gaston IV, comte de Foix*, ed. Henri Courteault (Paris, 1893–96), 1: xxiv.

109. Marichal, "L'écriture latine et la civilisation occidentale," p. 231.

110. Jean Froissart, *Chroniques*, 15 vols., ed. Simeon Luce (Paris, 1869–1975), prologue to book 1.

111. G. W. Coopland, ed., *Philippe de Mezières, Chancellor of Cyprus: Le songe du vieil pelerin*, 2 vols. (Cambridge, 1969), 1: 102.

112. Paul Saenger, "The Education of Burgundian Princes 1435–1490" (Ph.D. diss., University of Chicago, 1972), pp. 179–267.

113. Paul Saenger, "John of Paris: Principal Author of the *Quaestio de potestate papae*," *Speculum* 56 (1981): 41–55.

114. Pierre des Gros, *Jardin des nobles*, Paris, BN fr. 193.

115. See Saenger, "Books of Hours," pp. 148, 153–54.

116. For example, Guillaume Fillastre, *L'histoire de la Thoison d'Or*, Paris, BN fr. 140, f. 78, left it to his readers to judge whether an individual prince's highest loyalty should be to his family or to the *chose publique*.

117. Paulin Paris, *Les manuscrits françois de la Bibliothèque du roi*, 7 vols. (Paris, 1836–48), 4: 131–35.

118. Paris, BN lat. 6607.

119. Paul Saenger, "The Earliest French Resistance Theory: The Role of the Burgundian Court," *Journal of Modern History*, suppl. 51 (1979): 1225–49.

120. See, for example, a dog's tail suggesting anal penetration, Paris, BN lat. 12054 (s. xii), f. 330v.

121. A typical example illustrates a fifteenth-century copy of the French translation of Valerius Maximus, *Facta et dicta memorabilia*; Robert Melville, *Erotic Art of the West* (London, 1973), fig. 116. The miniature is misdated to the sixteenth century in the caption and the text. For other examples, see Edward Lucie Smith, *Eroticism in Western Art* (London, 1972). These manuscripts are

the direct antecedents of late-fifteenth-century and sixteenth-century erotic art, notably that of Hieronymus Bosch; see Anthony Bosman, *Jérôme Bosch* (Paris, 1962), p. 16; Otto Brusendorf and Paul Henningsen, *Love's Picture Book: The History of Pleasure and Moral Indignation from the Days of Classical Greece Until the French Revolution* (Copenhagen, 1960); Edward Fuchs, *Geschichte der Erotischen Kunst* (Munich, 1912), p. 175. The bordello was usually represented as a public bath.

122. An "exercise de lecture et d'estude." *Les cent nouvelles nouvelles*, ed. Franklin P. Sweetzer (Geneva, 1966), p. 22.

123. For a description of the surviving manuscripts, see Pierre Champion, *Les cent nouvelles nouvelles* (Paris, 1928), pp. xcvi–cxvii; and J. Gerber Young and P. Henderson Aitken, *A Catalogue of the Manuscripts in the Library of the Hunterian Museum in the University of Glasgow* (Glasgow, 1908), pp. 201–3.

124. Jean Harthan, *The Book of Hours* (New York, 1977), pp. 24, 26. Sotheby's November 1990 sale, lot no. 140, purchased by Pierre Berès. I am grateful to Christopher de Hamel for this reference.

125. A. Grunzweig, "Quatre lettres autographes de Philippe le Bon," *Revue belge de philologie et d'histoire* 4 (1925): 431–37.

126. *Thomas à Kempis et la dévotion moderne*, Bibliothèque Royale exhibition catalogue (Brussels, 1971), p. 34.

127. Paris, Arsenal 5205, f. "F." The image is drawn directly from the Latin of Ludolf of Saxony.

128. Paris, Arsenal 5206, f. 174.

129. Paris, BN fr. 982, f. 51v. A similar emphasis on private piety existed in England; W. A. Pantin, "Instructions for a Devout and Literate Layman," in Alexander and Gibson, *Medieval Learning and Literature*, pp. 406–7.

130. Paris, BN fr. 982, f. 56.

131. Paris, BN fr. 407, f. 5.

132. Paris, BN 407, f. 7.

133. Jacques Toussaert, *Le sentiment religieux en Flandre à la fin du Moyen Age* (Paris, 1963), pp. 351–52.

134. See, for example, Poitiers, BM 95, ff. 104, 139v.

Glossary

Terms in italics within a definition are themselves defined in this Glossary.

Aeration The practice of placing spaces between letters in a manner that does not regularly distinguish every word.

Alphabetical construction notes Interlinearly placed letters of the alphabet that sequentially link Latin words in periodic sentences so that the reader can mentally rearrange them into a particular order, e.g., subject, verb, object.

Ampersand A *monolexic abbreviation* for *et* in Latin formed when the *et* ligature is separated by space; its English name originates from the phrase "and *per se* and," a symbol which by itself means "and."

Banderole A ribbon bearing written text that assists in conveying the narrative of a medieval manuscript illumination or other work of art.

Bouma shape The shape of a word when written in upper- or lower-case letters and delimited by space, as defined by the Dutch psychologist Herman Bouma.

Canonical separation Word separation in which a minimum of unities of space are inserted between all words, including conjunctions and monosyllabic prepositions.

Cola et commata The Latin text format employed by Jerome in which each line represented either a phrase, a clause, or a sentence; some early medieval Bibles written in aerated script preserved this configuration (see Figure 2).

Dasia The Greek interlinear character for aspiration (ʽ), used by some medieval Latin scribes to denote word beginnings.

Diastole A large comma-shaped mark placed under the line to indicate word separation.

Diple Angular marks normally placed in the margin of an ancient or medieval text, such as the Bible, to set it off from the commentary.

Emblematic punctuation Encoded signs that delineate the grammatical structure of a text to aid comprehension; examples include the question mark and signs formed from fixed combinations of periods and commas that served as encoded notes to distinguish phrases, clauses, and sentences.

Fere canonical script Word separation that is *canonical* except that space is occasionally omitted after monosyllabic prepositions.

Fixation A principal point of focus as the eye moves in *saccades*, or jumps, across the page.

Foveal vision The portion of the eye's normal span of vision extending to a range of two to three characters to the right of the point of fixation; within this span, the reader can perceive individual letters in full detail.

Insular script Script using letter forms indigenous to Ireland, England, Wales, and Brittany.

Interpunct A point placed between words in ancient scripts; medieval scribes and emendators occasionally used interpuncts to facilitate word recognition.

J-shaped diastole A medieval J sign used to separate words.

Ligature A pen stroke that links two discrete letters within or between words.

Medial points *Interpuncts* or points used as signs of punctuation placed at mid-letter level.

Metron A point with a bow-shaped mark below it used to mark a major pause, usually at the end of a sentence, in Carolingian aerated scripts.

Minim strokes The short vertical strokes used to form the letters *m*, *n*, *u*, and *i*.

Monolexic abbreviations Clearly delimited signs that stand for words. Some, such as the ampersand, require surrounding space; others, like the signs in *tironian notes* for *et* and *est*, do not. Another example is ꝟ for *vero*.

Neume The earliest Latin form of musical notation, consisting of an accentlike mark denoting melodic movement (see Figure 29).

Nota sign A sign placed in the margin used to draw the reader's attention to a significant passage in the text.

Parafoveal vision The portion of the eye's normal span of vision beyond *foveal vision*, extending to a range of approximately fifteen characters to the right of the point of fixation. In it, the reader can perceive word shape, interword space, and *prosodiae*.

Peripheral vision The portion of the eye's normal span of vision beyond *parafoveal vision* in which the reader can perceive only gross characteristics of text, such as punctuation signs and major space delineating sentences and paragraphs.

Positurae The ancient Latin term for signs of punctuation.

Prosodiae The ancient Latin term for the signs complementing script that aided the reader in recognizing syllables and words and pronouncing them correctly.

Resumé note A brief summary, written in the margin, of the content of a portion of text.

Saccade The jumplike movement of the eye as it proceeds across the page.

Scriptura continua Script written in rows of letters uninterrupted by space.

Successor note to the diastole The most common eleventh-century sign used to separate words: ⫽ (see Figures 12 and 13).

Superscript forms The Insular variety of *monolexic abbreviations* in which one letter is superimposed over another to form a single graphic image of a commonly used word (see Figure 11).

Suspended ligature A purposefully placed incomplete ligature stroke at the end of the last letter on a line to indicate that it ought to be attached to the first letter of the next line because these form part of the same word.

Terminal forms Special letter forms (e.g., capital *S*), syllabic abbreviations (e.g., *-tur*), or accenting (e.g., *-is*) to denote the end of a word.

Textualis A formal script used primarily for the copying of manuscript books.

Tie-note A sign with variable forms linking a comment in the margin to the apposite point within the text.

Tironian hybrida A script written partly in *tironian notes* and partly in normal alphabetical characters.

Tironian notes A script derivative from ancient Roman shorthand in which discrete conventional signs represented words.

Tonic syllable The accented syllable in an ancient Latin word; the stressed syllable in a medieval Latin word.

Trait d'union The modern hyphen used at line ending as a sign of interline word continuation (see Figure 12).

Vertical strokes Strokes drawn between words to separate them; these strokes frequently slant slightly to the right.

Virga A line or bar drawn over an abbreviation or number in *scriptura continua* to denote letters that are not to be read as part of a word. In separated writing, its presence over a number was a sign of multiplication by 1,000, e.g., $\bar{X}$ = 10,000.

References

Sources Cited by Abbreviations and Shortened Titles

Aristoteles latinus
Lacombe, George. *Aristoteles latinus: Codices.* 3 vols. Rome, 1939–61.

BHL
Bibliotheca Hagiographica latina. 2 vols. Brussels, 1898–1901.

CCCM
Corpus Christianorum: Continuatio Medievalis. Turnhout, 1966–.

CCSL
Corpus Christianorum: Series latina. Turnhout, 1954–.

ChLA
Bruckner, Albert, and Robert Marichal, eds. *Chartae Latinae antiquiores: Facsimiles of the Latin Charters Prior to the Ninth Century.* Olten, Switz., 1954–.

CIL
Corpus inscriptionum latinarum. Berlin, 1862–.

CLA
Lowe, E. A. *Codices latini antiquiores: A Palaeographical Guide to Latin Manuscripts Prior to the Ninth Century.* 11 vols. Oxford, 1934–71.

CPL
Dekkers, Eligius. *Clavis patrum latinorum.* Sacris erudiri, vol. 3. Rev. ed. The Hague, 1961.

CSEL
Corpus scriptorum ecclesiasticorum latinorum. Vienna, 1866–.

Catalogue général des manuscrits des départements
Catalogue général des manuscrits des bibliothèques publiques de France: Départements. Paris, 1886–.

DHGE
Dictionnaire d'histoire et de géographie ecclésiastique. Paris, 1912–.

DNB
> *Dictionary of National Biography.* London, 1885–1900; rpr. 1963–65.

EEMF
> Early English Manuscripts in Facsimile. Copenhagen, 1951–.

FCIM
> Irish Manuscripts Commission: Facsimiles in Collotype of Irish Manuscripts. Dublin, 1931–54.

France: Manuscrits datés
> Samaran, Charles, and Robert Marichal. *Catalogue des manuscrits en éditions latines portant des indications de date, de lieu, ou de copiste.* Paris, 1959–.

Hommages à André Boutemy
> Combier, Guy, ed. *Hommages à André Boutemy.* Collection Latomus, vol. 145. Brussels, 1976.

Italy: Catalogo dei manoscritti datati
> *Catalogo dei manoscritti in scrittura latina datati o databili per indicazione di anno, di luogo o di copista.* Turin, 1971–.

Miscellanea codicologica F. Masai dicata
> Cockshaw, P., M.-C. Garand, and P. Jodogne, eds. *Miscellanea codicologica F. Masai dicata.* 4 vols. Les publications de Scriptorium, vol. 8. Ghent, 1979.

Musée des Archives départementales
> Ministère de l'Intérieur. *Musée des archives départementales: Recueil de facsimile héliographique de documents tirés des archives des préfectures, mairies et hospices.* Paris, 1878.

NCE
> *New Catholic Encyclopedia.* 15 vols. New York, 1966–79.

NPS
> *New Palaeographical Society.* 2 vols. London, 1903–30.

PL
> Migne, Jacques-Paul. *Patrologiae cursus completus . . . series latina.* 221 vols. Paris, 1844–64.

PLS
> Hamman, A. *Patrologiae latinae supplementum.* Paris, 1958–.

PS
> *Palaeographical Society.* 2 vols. London, 1873–94.

Pays Bas: Manuscrits datés
> Lieftinck, G. I. *Manuscrits datés conservés dans les pays bas.* Amsterdam, 1964–.

Processing of Visible Language 1
> Paul A. Kolers, Merald E. Wrolstad and Herman Bouma, eds. *Processing of Visible Language 1.* New York, 1979.

Processing of Visible Language 2
   Paul A. Kolers, Merald E. Wrolstad, Herman Bouma, eds. *Processing of Visible Language 2*. New York, 1980.

Recueil de fac-similes à l'usage de l'École des Chartes
   Album paléographique ou Recueil de documents importants relatifs à l'histoire et à la littérature nationales reproduits en héliogravure d'après les originaux des bibliothèques et des archives de France avec des notices explicatives par la Société de l'École des Chartes. Paris, 1887.

Studies in Medieval History Presented to F. M. Powicke
   Hunt, R. W., W. A. Pantin, and R. W. Southern, eds. *Studies in Medieval History Presented to F. M. Powicke.* Oxford, 1948.

Books and Articles

Adams, Marilyn Jager. "What Good Is Orthographic Redundancy?" In Tzeng and Singer, *Perception of Print*, pp. 197–221.

Alexander, J. J. G. *Insular Manuscripts, 6th to the 9th Century*. A Survey of Manuscripts in the British Isles, vol. 1. London, 1978.

———. *Norman Illuminations at Mont Saint-Michel 996–1100*. Oxford, 1970.

Alexander, J. J. G., and M. T. Gibson, eds. *Medieval Learning and Literature: Essays Presented to Richard William Hunt.* Oxford, 1976.

Anderson, Alan Orr, and Marjorie Ogilvie Anderson. *Adomnan's Life of Columba.* London, 1961.

Anderson, R. D., P. J. Parsons, and R. G. M. Nisbet. "Elegiacs by Gallus from Qasr Ibrïm." *Journal of Roman Studies* 69 (1979): 125–55.

Avril, François. *Manuscrits normands XIe–XIIe siècle.* Rouen, 1975.

Avril, François, Jean-Pierre Aniel, Mireille Mentré, Alix Saulnier, and Yolanta Zaluska. *Manuscrits enluminés de la péninsule ibérique.* Paris, 1992.

Avril, François, Marie-Thérèse Gousset, and Claudia Rabel. *Manuscrits enluminés d'origine italienne.* 2 vols. Paris, 1980–84.

Backhouse, Janet, D. H. Turner, and Leslie Webster. *The Golden Age of Anglo-Saxon Art, 966–1066.* Exhibition catalogue. London, 1985.

Bains, Doris. *A Supplement to Notae Latinae (abbreviations in Latin MSS of 850 to 1050 A.D.).* Cambridge, 1936.

Barré, Henri. "Pro Fulberto." *Récherches de théologie ancienne et médiévale* 31 (1964): 324–30.

Bataillon, Louis J., Bertrand G. Guyot, and Richard H. Rouse. *La production du livre universitaire au moyen âge: Exemplar et pecia; Actes du symposium tenu au Collegio San Bonaventura de Grattaferrata en mai 1983.* Paris, 1988.

Bautier, Robert-Henri, and Monique Gilles, eds. *Odorannus de Sens: Opera omnia.* Paris, 1972.

Bautier, Robert-Henri, and Gillette Labory, eds. *Helgaud de Fleury: Vie de Robert le Pieux (Epitoma Vitae regis Roberti Pii).* Paris, 1965.

Beaulieux, Charles. *Histoire de l'orthographie française.* 2 vols. Paris, 1927.

Beer, Rudolf. *Die Handschriften des Klosters Santa Maria de Ripoll*. Sitzungsberichte der Kaiserliche Akademie der Wissenschaften, Philosophisch-
historische Klasse, vol. 155, pt. 3 and vol. 158, pt. 2. Vienna, 1907–8.
Behrends, Frederick. *The Letters and Poems of Fulbert of Chartres*. Oxford, 1976.
Bieler, Ludwig. *Ireland Harbinger of the Middle Ages*. London, 1963.
Bischoff, Bernhard. *Anecdota novissima: Texten des vierten bis sechszehnten Jahr-
hunderts*. Stuttgart, 1984.
———. "Frühkarolingische Handschriften und ihre Heimat." *Scriptorium* 12
(1968): 306–14.
———. *Kalligraphie in Bayern achtes bis zwolftes Jahrhundert*. Exhibition cata-
logue. Wiesbaden, 1981.
———. *Mittelalterliche Studien: Ausgewählte Aufsätze zur Schriftkunde und li-
teraturgeschichte*. 3 vols. Stuttgart, 1966–81.
———. *Die südostdeutschen Schreibschulen und Bibliotheken in der Karolinger-
zeit*. 2 vols. 3d ed. Wiesbaden, 1974–80.
Bradley, Henry. "On the Relation Between Spoken and Written Language with
Special Reference to English." *Proceedings of the British Academy* (1913–14):
211–32.
Bradshaw, Henry. *The Early Collection of Canons Known as the Hibernensis: Two
Unfinished Papers*. Cambridge, 1893.
Brown, T. Julian. "The Irish Element in the Insular System of Scripts to circa
A.D. 850." In Heinz Löwe, ed., *Die Iren und Europa in früheren Mittelalter*.
1:101–19. Stuttgart, 1982.
Brown, Virginia. *Handlist of Beneventan Manuscripts*, published as vol. 2 of Elias
Avery Lowe, *The Beneventan Script: A History of the South Italian Minuscule*.
1914. 2d ed., prepared and enlarged by V. Brown. Rome, 1980.
Bruckner, Albert. *Scriptoria medii aevi Helvetica: Denkmäler schweizerischer
Schreibkunst des Mittelalters*. 13 vols. Genf, 1935–78.
Bubnov, Nicolaus. *Gerberti postea Silvestri II Papae opera mathematica (972–
1003)*. Berlin, 1899; repr. Hildesheim, 1963.
Cagnat, René. *Cours d'épigraphie latine*. 4th ed. Paris, 1914.
Cajori, Florian. *A History of Mathematical Notations*. 2 vols. Chicago, 1928–29;
repr. New York, 1993.
Carruthers, Mary J. *The Book of Memory: The Study of Memory in Medieval Cul-
ture*. Cambridge, 1990.
Chatelain, Émile. *Introduction à la lecture des notes tironiennes*. Paris, 1908; repr.,
New York, 1963.
———. *Paléographie des classiques latins*. Paris, 1884–1900.
Chen, Hsuan-Chih, and Ovid J. L. Tzeng, eds. *Language Processing in Chinese*.
Advances in Psychology, vol. 90. Amsterdam, 1992.
Chevrier, Georges, and Maurice Chaume. *Chartes et documents de Saint-Bénigne,
prieurés et dépendances des origines à 1300*. Dijon, 1943.

Chroust, Anton. *Monumenta Palaeographica: Denkmäler der Schreibkunst des Mittelalters.* Munich, 1902–17; Leipzig, 1927–.

Cohen, Marcel. *La Grande invention de l'écriture et son évolution.* 3 vols. Paris, 1958.

Colgrave, Bertram, and R. A. B. Mynors. *Bede's Ecclesiastical History of the English People.* Oxford, 1969.

Collection Diogène: Problèmes du langage. Paris, 1966.

Cordoliani, A. "La Texte de la Bible en Irlande du Ve au IXe siècle." *Revue Biblique* 57 (1950): 5–39.

Cottineau, L.-H. *Répertoire topo-bibliographique des abbayes et prieurés.* 2 vols. Macon, 1939.

Cousin, Patrice. *Abbon de Fleury-sur-Loire.* Paris, 1954.

Daniel, Natalia. *Handschriften des zehnten Jahrhunderts aus der Freisinger Dombibliothek: Studien über Schriftcharakter und Herkunft der nachkarolingischen und ottonischen Handschriften einer Bayerischen Bibliothek.* Münchener Beiträge zur Mediävistik und Renaissance Forschungen, vol. 11. Munich, 1973.

Davis, Herbert, and Harry Carter, eds. *Mechanical Exercises on the Whole Art of Printing (1683–84) by Joseph Moxon.* 2d ed. Leiden, 1962.

de Kerckhove, Derrick. "Critical Brain Processes in Deciphering the Greek Alphabet." In de Kerckhove and Lumsden, *The Alphabet and the Brain*, pp. 401–21.

———. "Logical Principles Underlying the Layout of Greek Orthography." In de Kerckhove and Lumsden, *The Alphabet and the Brain*, pp. 153–72.

de Kerckhove, Derrick, and Charles J. Lumsden, eds. *The Alphabet and the Brain: The Lateralization of Writing.* Berlin, 1988.

Delisle, Léopold. *Le Cabinet des manuscrits de la Bibliothèque Nationale.* 3 vols. Paris, 1868–81.

———. *Inventaire des manuscrits de la Bibliothèque Nationale: Fonds de Cluni.* Paris, 1884.

———. *Inventaire des manuscrits latins conservés sous les numéros 8823–18613.* 4 vols. Paris, 1863–71; repr. as 1 vol., Hildesheim, 1974.

de Meyier, K. A. *Codices Vossiani latini.* 4 vols. Leiden, 1973–84.

de Moreau, Edouard. *Histoire de l'église de Belgique.* 5 vols. Brussels, 1945–52.

de Rijk, L. M. *Logica modernorum: A Contribution to the History of Early Terministic Logic.* 2 vols. Wijskerige Teksten en Studies, vol. 16. Assen, 1962–67.

Devisse, Jean. *Hincmar, archevêque de Reims, 845–882.* 3 vols. Geneva, 1975–76.

Dogaer, Georges, and Marguerite Debae. *La Librairie de Philippe le Bon: Exposition organisée à l'occasion du 500e anniversaire de la mort du duc.* Brussels, 1967.

Dolbeau, François. "Anciens possesseurs des manuscrits hagéiographiques latines conservés à la Bibliothèque Nationale de Paris." *Revue d'histoire des textes* 9 (1979): 183–238.

Downing, John. *Comparative Reading: Cross-National Studies of Behavior in Reading and Writing*. New York, 1973.

Drogin, Marc. *Anathema: Medieval Scribes and the History of Book Curses*. Totowa, N.J., 1983.

du Boulay, César Égasse. *Historia Universitatis Parisiensis*. 6 vols. Paris, 1665–1773; repr. Frankfurt am Main, 1966.

Dufour, Jean. *La bibliothèque et scriptorium de Moissac*. Hautes études médiévales et modernes, vol. 5. Geneva, 1972.

L'Écriture et la psychologie des peuples. Ed. Marcel Cohen. Centre international de synthèse, XXIIe semaine de synthèse. Paris, 1963.

Escudier, Denis. "Les Manuscrits musicaux du moyen-âge (du IXe au XIIe siècle, Essai de typologie." In J. P. Gumbert, M. J. M. de Haan, and A. Gruys, eds., *Codicologica* 3 (1979).

Fournier, Paul, and Gabriel Le Bras. *Histoire des collections canoniques en occident depuis les fausses décrétales jusqu'au Decret de Gratien*. 2 vols. Paris, 1931–32.

Fourrier, Anthime, ed. *L'humanisme médiéval dans les littératures romanes du XIIe au XIVe siècle: Colloque organisé par le Centre de Philologie et de Littérature romanes de l'Université de Strasbourg du 29 janvier au 2 février 1962*. Actes et colloques, 3. Paris, 1964.

Franklin, Alfred. *Les anciennes bibliothèques de Paris*. 3 vols. Paris, 1867–73.

Gaborit-Chopin, Danielle. *La décoration des manuscrits à Saint Martial de Limoges et en Limousin*. Mémoires et documents publiés par la Société de l'École des Chartes, 17. Paris, 1969.

Ganz, David. "The Preconditions of Caroline Minuscule." *Viator* 18 (1987): 23–43.

Ganz, Peter, ed. *The Role of the Book in Medieval Culture: Proceedings of the Oxford International Symposium 26 September–1 October 1982*. 2 vols. Turnhout, 1986.

Gautier, P. "Etude sur un diplôme de Robert le Pieux pour l'abbaye de Saint-Bénigne de Dijon." *Le Moyen Age*, ser. 2, no. 22 (1909): 225–85.

Gilissen, Léon. *L'expertise des écritures médiévales: Récherche d'une méthode avec application à un manuscrit du XIe siècle: Le lectionnaire de Lobbes codex Bruxelliensis 18018*. Les publications de Scriptorium, 6. Ghent, 1973.

Glorie, François. *Variae collectiones aenigmatum Merovingicae aetatis*. Corpus Christianorum: Series latina, 133. Turnhout, 1968.

Glorieux, Palémon, ed. *Oeuvres complètes de Jean Gerson*. 10 vols. Paris, 1961–73.

Gneuss, Helmut. "A Preliminary List of Manuscripts Written or Owned in England Up to 1100." *Anglo-Saxon England* 9 (1981): 1–60.

Gordon, Arthur E. *Illustrated Introduction to Latin Epigraphy*. Berkeley, 1983.

Gordon, Arthur E., and Joyce S. Gordon. *Contributions to the Palaeography of Latin Inscriptions*. University of California Publications in Classical Archeology, vol. 3. Berkeley, 1957.

Guerreau-Jalabert, Anita. *Abbon de Fleury: Quaestiones Grammaticales.* Paris, 1982.

Gumbert, J. P., and M. J. M. de Haan, eds. *Litterae Textuales: Essays Presented to G. I. Lieftinck.* 4 vols. Amsterdam, 1972–76.

Gysseling, M., and A. C. F. Koch. *Diplomata Belgica ante annum milesimum centesimum scripta.* Bouwstoften en Studien voor de Geschiedenis en de Lexicografie van het Nederlands, 1. Brussels, 1950.

Havet, Louis. *Manuel de critique verbale appliquée aux textes latins.* Paris, 1911; repr. Rome, 1967.

Hillgarth, J. N. "Visigothic Spain and Early Christian Ireland." *Proceedings of the Royal Irish Academy* 62, Sec. C (1962): 167–94.

Hoffmann, Hartmut. *Buchkunst und Königtum im ottonischen und frühsalischen Reich.* Stuttgart, 1986.

Holtz, Louis. *Donat et la tradition de l'enseignement grammaticale: Étude sur l'Ars Donati et sa diffusion (IVe–IXe siècle) et édition critique.* Paris, 1981.

Jammers, Ewald. *Tafeln zur Neumenschrift.* Tutzing, 1965.

Jumièges: Congrès scientifique du XIIIe centenaire, Rouen 10–12 juin 1954. 2 vols. Rouen, 1955.

Karl der Grosse: Lebenwerk und Nachleben. 5 vols. Ed. Wolfgang Braunfels. Dusseldorf, 1965.

Karolingische und Ottonische Kunst: Werden, Wesen, Wirkung. Forschungen zur Kunstgeschichte und Christliche Archäologie, 3. Wiesbaden, 1957.

Keil, Heinrich. *Grammatici latini.* 7 vols. Leipzig, 1855–80; repr. Hildesheim, 1961.

Kendrick, Laura. *The Game of Love.* Berkeley, 1988.

Kenney, James F. *The Sources for the Early History of Ireland: An Introduction and Guide.* Columbia University Records of Civilization. New York, 1929.

Ker, Neil Ripley. *Catalogue of Manuscripts Containing Anglo-Saxon.* Oxford, 1957.

Lapière, Marie-Rose. *La lettre ornée dans les manuscrits monans d'origine bénédictine (XIe–XIIe siècles).* Bibliothèque de la Faculté de Philosophie et Lettres de l'Université de Liège, vol. 229. Paris, 1981.

Latouche, Robert, ed. and trans. *Richer: Histoire de France.* 2 vols. Paris, 1930–37.

Lattin, Harriet Pratt. *The Letters of Gerbert with his Papal Privileges as Sylvester II.* New York, 1961.

———. "The Origin of Our Present System of Notation According to the Theories of Nicholas Bubnov." *Isis* 19 (1933): 181–94.

Law, Vivien. *The Insular Latin Grammarians.* Studies in Celtic History, vol. 3. Woodbridge, Suffolk, 1982.

Legendre, Paul. *Études tironiennes: Commentaire sur le VIe Éclogue de Virgile, tiré d'un manuscrit de Chartres, avec divers appendices et un fac-similé.* Paris, 1907.

Lehmann, Paul. "Blätter, Seiten, Spalten, Zeilen." In his *Erforschung des Mittelalters* (Leipzig and Stuttgart, 1941–62), 3: 1–59.

————. *Mittelalterliche Bibliothekskataloge Deutschlands und der Schweiz*, vol. 1. Munich, 1918; repr. 1969.

Leitschuh, Friedrich. *Katalog der Handschriften der Königlichen Bibliothek zu Bamberg*. Bamberg, 1895–.

Leroquais, Victor. *Les pontificaux manuscrits des bibliothèques publiques de France*. 3 vols. Paris, 1937.

————. *Les Sacramentaires et les missels manuscrits des bibliothèques publiques de France*. 3 vols. Paris, 1924.

Levin, Harry, and Ann Buckles Addis. *The Eye-Voice Span*. Cambridge, Mass., 1979.

Levin, Harry, and Joanna Williams, eds. *Basic Studies on Reading*. New York, 1970.

Lindsay, Wallace M. *Early Irish Minuscule Script*. St. Andrews University Publications, 6. Oxford, 1910.

————. *Notae Latinae*. Cambridge, 1915.

Lowe, Elias Avery. *The Beneventan Script: A History of the South Italian Minuscule*. Oxford, 1914; repr. Rome, 1980.

————. *Scriptura Beneventana: Facsimiles of South Italian and Dalmatian Manuscripts from the Sixth to the Fourteenth Century*. 2 vols. Oxford, 1929.

MacKinney, Loren C. *Bishop Fulbert and Education at the School of Chartres*. Texts and Studies in the History of Medieval Education, 6. Notre Dame, Ind., 1957.

McNeill, John T., and Helena M. Gamer. *Medieval Handbooks of Penance: A Translation of the Principi Libri Poenitentiales and Selections from Related Documents*. Columbia University Records of Civilization, vol. 29. New York, 1938.

Maierù, Alfonso. *Grafia e interpunzione del latino nel medioevo: Seminario internazionale Roma, 27–29 settembre 1984*. Lessico intellettuale Europeo, 41. Rome, 1987.

Marichal, Robert. "L'Écriture latine et la civilisation occidentale du Ier au XVIe siècle." In *L'Écriture et la psychologie des peuples*, pp. 199–247.

Marrou, Henri-Irénée. *Histoire de l'éducation dans l'antiquité*. Paris, 1965.

Mélanges dédiés à la memoire de Félix Grat. 2 vols. Paris, 1946–49.

Mélanges offerts à M. Émile Chatelain par ses élèves et ses amis. Paris, 1910.

Millàs y Vallicrosa, José María. *Assaig d'història de les idees físiques: Matemàtiques a la Catalunya medieval*. Barcelona, 1931.

Millénaire monastique du Mont Saint-Michel. 4 vols. Paris, 1966–71.

Monfrin, Jacques. "Les traducteurs et leur public en France au Moyen Age." In Fourrier, *L'humanisme médiéval*, pp. 217–64.

Mostert, Marco. *The Library of Fleury: A Provisional List*. Hilversum, 1989.

Müller, Rudolf Wolfgang. *Rhetorische und syntaktische Interpunktion: Untersuchungen zur Pausenbezeichnung im antiken Latin.* Inaugural Dissertation. Tubingen, 1964.

Munk-Olsen, Birger. *L'Étude des auteurs classiques latins au XIᵉ et XIIᵉ siècles.* 3 vols. Paris, 1982–89.

Newman, William Mendel. *Catalogue des actes de Robert II Roi de France.* Paris, 1937.

Nortier, Geneviève. *Les bibliothèques médiévales des abbayes bénédictines de Normandie.* Paris, 1971.

Notices et extraits des manuscrits de la Bibliothèque Nationale et autres bibliothèques. Paris, 1787–.

Obbema, Pieter F. J. "Writing on Uncut Sheets." *Quaerendo* 7 (1978): 337–54.

Olleris, Alexandre. *Oeuvres de Gerbert.* Clermont-Ferrand, 1867.

Olson, David R. *The World on Paper: The Conceptual and Cognitive Implications of Writing and Reading.* Cambridge, 1994.

Pächt, Otto, and J. J. G. Alexander. *Illuminated Manuscripts in the Bodleian Library, Oxford.* 3 vols. Oxford, 1966–73.

Parkes, Malcolm B. *Pause and Effect: An Introduction to the History of Punctuations in the West.* Berkeley, 1993.

Pellegrin, Elisabeth. *Bibliothèques retrouvés: Manuscrits, bibliothèques et bibliophiles du Moyen Age et de la Renaissance, recueil d'études publiés de 1938 à 1985.* Paris, 1988.

———. *Les manuscrits classiques latins de la Bibliothèque Vaticane.* Paris, 1975–.

———. "Les Manuscrits de Loup de Ferrières à propos du MS. Orléans 162 (139) corrigé de sa main." *Bibliothèque de l'École des Chartes* 115 (1958): 5–31; repr. Pellegrin, *Bibliothèques retrouves,* pp. 131–57.

———. *Manuscrits latins de la Bodmeriana.* Cologny-Genève, 1982.

———. "Membra disiecta Floriacensia I." *Bibliothèque de l'École des Chartes* 117 (1959): 5–57; repr. Pellegrin, *Bibliothèques retrouvés,* pp. 129–210.

———. "Membra disiecta Floriacensia II." In *Miscellanea codicologica F. Masai dicata,* 1: 83–103. Ghent, 1979; rpr. Pellegrin, *Bibliothèques retrouvés,* pp. 257–77.

Petrucci, Armando. "Lire au Moyen Age." *Mélanges de l'École Française de Rome: Moyen Age, temps modernes* 96 (1984): 603–16.

Pour un IXᵉ Centenaire: Moissac et l'occident au XIᵉ siècle: Actes du colloque international de Moissac 3–5 mai 1963. Toulouse, 1964.

Powell, James M., ed. *Medieval Studies: An Introduction.* 2d ed. Syracuse, N.Y., 1992.

Rand, Edward Kennard. *A Survey of the Manuscript of Tours.* Studies in the Script of Tours, 1. Cambridge, 1929.

Reusens, Edmond-Henri-Joseph. *Éléments de paléographie.* Louvain, 1899.

Riché, Pierre. *Écoles et enseignement dans le Haut Moyen Age.* Paris, 1979.

Roberts, Colin Henderson. *Greek Literary Hands, 350 B.C.–400 A.D.* 2d ed. London, 1983.

Roberts, Colin Henderson, and T. C. Skeat. *The Birth of the Codex.* London, 1983.

Robinson, Pamela. *Catalogue of Dated and Datable Manuscripts c. 737–1600 in Cambridge Libraries.* 2 vols. Cambridge, 1988.

Rouse, Richard H., and Mary A. Rouse. *Preachers, Florilegia and Sermons: Studies on the Manipulus florum of Thomas of Ireland.* Toronto, 1979.

Saenger, Paul. "Books of Hours and the Reading Habits of the Later Middle Ages." In Roger Chartier, ed., *The Culture of Print: Power and Uses of Print in Early Modern Europe,* pp. 143–73. Princeton, N.J., 1989.

———. "Coupure et séparation des mots sur le Continent au Moyen Age." In Henri-Jean Martin and Jean Vezin, eds., *La Mise en page du manuscrit,* pp. 451–55. Paris, 1990.

———. "The Impact of the Early Printed Page on the History of Reading." *Bulletin de Bibliophile,* no. 2 (1996): 237–301.

———. "Separated Script at Reims and Fleury at the Time of Gerbert and Abbo." In F. Barbier and F. Duprigrenet-Desroussilles, eds., *Le livre et l'historien: Etudes offertes à Henri-Jean Martin.* Forthcoming.

———. "Silent Reading: Its Impact on Late Medieval Script and Society." *Viator* 13 (1982): 366–414.

———. "Word Separation and Its Implications for Manuscript Production." In Peter Rück, ed., *Die Rationalisierung der Buchherstellung in Mittelalter und in der frühen Neuzeit,* pp. 41–50. Institut für historische Hilfurssenschaten. Marburg, 1994.

Saenger, Paul, and Michael Heinlen. "Incunable Description and Its Implications for the Analysis of Fifteenth-Century Reading Habits." In Sandra Hindman, ed., *Printing the Written Word: The Social History of Books c. 1450–1570,* pp. 225–58. Ithaca, N.Y., 1992.

Sandys, John Edwin. *Latin Epigraphy: An Introduction to the Study of Latin Inscriptions.* Cambridge, 1919.

Scaglione, Aldo. *The Classical Theory of Composition from its Origins to the Present: An Historical Survey.* Chapel Hill, N.C., 1972.

Schapiro, Meyer. "A Relief in Rodez and the Beginnings of Romanesque Sculpture in Southern France." *Studies in Western Art: Acts of the 20th International Congress of the History of Art* 1: 40–66 (1963).

Scholes, Robert J. "On the Orthographic Basis of Morphology." In his *Literary and Language Analysis,* pp. 73–95. Hillsdale, N.J., 1993.

Scholes, Robert J., and Brenda J. Willis. "Prosodic and Syntactic Functions of Punctuations: A Contribution to the Study of Orality and Literacy." *Interchange* 21 (1990): 13–20.

Schramm, Percy Ernst, and Florentine Mütherich. *Denkmale der deutschen*

Könige und Kaiser: Ein Beitrag zur Herrschergeschichte von Karl dem Grossen bis Friedrich II 768–1250. Munich, 1962.

Shipley, Frederick William. *Certain Sources of Corruption in Latin Manuscripts: A Study Based on Two Manuscripts of Livy: Codex Puteanus (Fifth Century) and Its Copy Codex Regiensis 762 (Ninth Century).* New York, 1904.

Sokolov, Aleksandr. *Inner Speech and Thought.* Trans. G. T. Onischenko and D. B. Lindsley. New York, 1972.

Steffens, Franz. *Lateinische Palaeographie.* Trier, 1909.

Stiennon, Jacques. *L'Écriture diplomatique dans le diocèse de Liège du XIᵉ au milieu du XIIIᵉ siècle.* Bibliothèque de la Faculté de Philosophie et Lettres de l'Université de Liège, 5. Paris, 1968.

————. *Paléographie du Moyen Age.* Paris, 1973.

Taylor, Insup. "The Korean Writing System: An Alphabet? A Syllabary? A Logography?" In *Processing of Visible Language 2,* pp. 67–82.

Taylor, Insup, and Martin Taylor. *The Psychology of Reading.* New York, 1983.

Temple, E. *Anglo-Saxon Manuscripts 900–1006.* A Survey of Manuscripts Illuminated in the British Isles, vol. 2. London, 1976.

Thurot, Charles. "Notices et extraits des divers manuscrits latins pour servir à l'histoire des doctrines grammaticales au moyen âge." *Notices et extraits* 22, pt. 2 (1868).

Tzeng, Ovid J. L., and Daisy L. Hung. "Linguistic Determinism: A Written Perspective." In Tzeng and Singer, *Perception of Print,* pp. 237–55.

Tzeng, Ovid J. L., and Harry Singer, eds. *Perception of Print: Reading Research in Experimental Psychology.* Hillsdale, N.J., 1981.

Van de Vyver, André. *Abbonis Floriacensis opera inedita.* Bruges, 1966.

————. "Les étapes du développement philosophique du Haut Moyen Age." *Revue belge de philologie et d'histoire* 8 (1929): 425–52.

————. "Les oeuvres inédites d'Abbon de Fleury." *Revue bénédictine* 47 (1935): 125–69.

————. "Les plus anciennes traductions latines médiévales (Xᵉ–XIᵉ siècles) de traités d'astronomie et d'astrologie." *Osiris* 1 (1936): 666–84.

————. "Les premières traductions latines des traités arabes sur l'astrolabe." In *Premier Congrès International de Géographie Historique: II Mémoires,* pp. 266–90. Brussels, 1931.

van den Gheyn, J. *Catalogue de manuscrits de la Bibliothèque Royale de Belgique.* Brussels, 1901–48.

Vezin, Jean. *Les Scriptoria d'Angers au XIᵉ siècle.* Paris, 1974.

————. "Manuscrits des dixième et onzième siècles copiés en Angleterre en minuscule Caroline et conservés à la Bibliothèque Nationale de Paris." In *Humanisme actif: Mélanges d'art et de littérature offerts à Julien Cain,* pp. 283–96. Paris, 1968.

Watson, Andrew G. *Catalogue of Dated and Datable Manuscripts c. 700–1600 in the Department of Manuscripts, the British Library.* 2 vols. London, 1979.

————. *Catalogue of Dated and Datable Manuscripts ca. 1435–1600 in Oxford Libraries.* Oxford, 1984.

Willis, James Alfred. *Latin Textual Criticism.* Illinois Studies in Language and Literature, 16. Urbana, 1972.

Wilmart, André. *Auteurs spirituels et textes dévôts du Moyen Age latin.* Paris, 1932; repr. Paris, 1971.

Wingo, E. Orthu. *Latin Punctuation in the Classical Age.* Janua Linguarum: Series practica, vol. 133. The Hague, 1972.

Winterbottom, Michael. *Three Lives of English Saints.* Toronto, 1972.

Index of Manuscripts Cited

Austria
  Admont
    Stiftsbibliothek   34   251
                      769   380
  Saint Paul in Carinthia
    Stiftsbibliothek sec. xxv.d.86   98, 343
    Fragments   336
  Vienna
    Nationalbibliothek, lat. 751   333
                lat. 795   372
Belgium
  Brussels
    Bibliothèque Royale 1650   71, 343
                 5478–83   388
                 5500–03   176, 189
                 5571–72   388
                 5576–5604   189, 376, 380
                 9188–89   193
                 9349–54   392
                 9512–14   392
                 9534–36   392
                 9581–82   392
                 10470–3   349
                 10859   349
                 14650–59   391
                 II 1639   192
                 II 1076   245
                 II 1179   46, 192
                 II 1180   192, 376
                 II 1639   192

Ghent
   State Archives Suppl. 2 bis   200
                  Suppl. 2 ter   395
   Bibliotheek der Rijksuniversiteit 224   200
                      909   164, 377
Liège
   Universiteitsbibliotheek 162   193
Namur
   Grand Séminaire 37   192
Denmark
  Copenhagen
   Kongelige Bibliotek GI. Kgl. S. 20   195
           GL. Kgl. S. 1588   386
England
  Cambridge
   Corpus Christi College 130   403
            144   89, 91, 337
            192   102
            201   394
            221   86
            337   251
            473   367
   Emmanuel College I.1.8   214
   Peterhouse College 74   403
   Trinity College B.3.5 (84)   252
           B.16.44 (405)   212
           R.15.32 (945)   386
   University Library Ff4.42   344
           Gg5.35   336
           Kk 5.16   110, 334, 335
           Li 6.32   333
  Canterbury
   Cathedral Library X.I.IIa   252
  Durham
   Cathedral Library A.IV.34   418, 419
           B.IV.24   403
  Hereford
   Cathedral Library O.VIII.8   403
   Lambeth Palace Library 362   386
  London
   British Library Add 5411   238
           10972   154, 283
           11873   216, 287
           17789   211
           17808   129, 285
           20694   429

21917	150, 282
22820	215
28106	192
28107	192
33293	55
37517	386
47967	42
49598	385
Arundel 343	361, 365
Cotton Nero A I	345
Cotton Nero A VII	213–14, 403
Cotton Otho E XIII	345
Cotton Tiberius A III	203, 395–96
A XIII	341
A XIV	50, 334
B V	94
C II	334
Egerton 609	102
1070	428
Faustina B III	395–96
Harley 2506	283, 395
2767	365
2904	386
2965	96
3271	337
3826	334
7653	96
Royal 2.A XX.	96
6.A.V.	195
13.A.XI	386
16.G.VIII	428
Oxford	
Bodleian Library Auct. F.4.32	383
T.1.23	191
Bodley 309	134
Bodley 569	403
Bodley 775	312, 367
Bodley 852	211, 285
Hatton 30	385
42	102
Laud. Gr. 35	91, 93
Laud. Misc. 141	307
Marshall 19	324
d'Orville 45	228

Rawlinson A.392 — 404

B.503 — 342

G.44 — 198, 200

Saint John's College 17 — 353, 361, 386

Salisbury

Cathedral Library 89 — 399

France

Amiens

Bibliothèque Municipale 6 — 107

7 — 107

9 — 107

11 — 67, 107

12 — 107, 348–49

Angers

Bibliothèque Municipale 477 — 344

Arles

Bibliothèque Municipale 7 — 232

Arras

Bibliothèque Municipale 455 (1021) — 404

484 (805) — 213, 214

559 (435) — 188

732 (684) — 188

734 (686) — 188

849 (294) — 388

860 (530) — 188

903 (589) — 188

909 (589) — 188

Avranches

Bibliothèque Municipale 50 — 228, 285

58 — 286, 399

59 — 286

78 — 285

90 — 286

91 — 286

101 — 286

103 — 286

107 — 286

109 — 285

159 — 212

163 — 286

229 — 208, 286

Boulogne-sur-Mer

Bibliothèque Municipale 9 — 188

11 — 196

20 — 196–97

83 — 285

107	393
188	197
189	197

Cambrai
Bibliothèque Municipale 470 — 58, 60, 81, 82, 320, 324

Châlons-sur-Marne
Bibliothèque Municipale 217 — 378

Chantilly
Musée Condé 297 — 261

Charleville
Bibliothèque Municipale 49 — 247
114 — 247, 412, 416
187 — 247
196c — 81, 82, 246, 416
202 — 246–47

Chartres
Bibliothèque Municipale 13 — 119
47 — 140
49 — 247
100 — 165
114 — 247
1036 (1373) — 379
nouv. acq. 4 — 167

Conques
Abbey of Sainte-Foy, *Vita Sanctae Fidis* — 169

Dijon
Archives de la Côte d'Or 1H liasse 208 — 407
1H liasse 4 — 407
1H liasse 2 (reg. 869), no. 15 — 384
2H liasse 2 (reg. 869), no. 14 — 384
Bibliothèque Municipale 2 — 222
30 — 285, 378
51 — 221
107 — 222
122 — 222

Laon
Bibliothèque Municipale 26 — 316
81 — 349, 350
465 — 318

Metz
Bibliothèque Municipale 245 — 191, 399
248 — 404
384 — 407

Montpellier
Bibliothèque de la Faculté de Médecine H 137(B)   285
                                    H 159   140, 221,
                                             327, 367
                                    H 334   354
                                    H 491   281, 360
Orléans
Bibliothèque Municipale 17   282
                        127 (205)   208
                        221 (193)   101, 102
                        267 (223)   155, 160, 183
                        277 (233)   155, 156, 160,
                                     183, 388
                        302 (255)   101
                        303 (256)   161, 375
                        444 (649)   160–61
Paris
Archives Nationales JJ 28   429
                 K 18, no. 5   384
                 K 18, no. 6   384
                 K 18, no. 7   384
                 K 18, no. 8   384
                 K 18, no. 91   384
                 K 19, no. 52   394
Bibliothèque de l'Arsénal 372   378
                      1008   375
                      5205   431
                      5206   431
                      8407   110
Bibliothèque Mazarine 384   407
                  561   350
Bibliothèque Nationale
    Collection Bourgogne, Vols. 76, 77, 78   219, 383
    Collection Picardie 293   384
    Français 57   428
            86   428
            139   429
            140   430
            147   423
            177   423
            193   430
            244   423
            342   426
            407   431
            541   424
            603   428

794	419, 427
824	423
835	428
982	431
995	421
1176	428
9611	428
15456–57	430
16993	429
Latin 5	223, 226, 286
8	226, 281
25	429
190	354
261	311
272	320, 379
544	227
574	399
646B	423
819	193
822	225, 289
887	224, 289
926	418
933	234
943	184–85, 342
944	233
987	320
989	204–05
1084	233
1119	224, 288
1121	288, 383
1139	227
1160	419
1176	428
1240	288
1327	353, 354
1454	410
1541	194
1597A	339, 353
1632	207
1684	207
1777	247
1850	189
1871	289
1872	205
1897	288
1919	399

1928	205, 206
1939	206
1954	234, 412
1961	230
1969	288
1978	383
2056	227, 289
2076	169
2077	228, 410
2079	206
2101	399
2126	234
2178	353
2208	226, 289
2243 (I–II)	247
2278	158–59, 374
2291	140, 312, 327
2355	383
2400	147, 158, 159, 225
2401	205, 289
2403	206, 399
2423	311
2429	411
2500	244
2502	244
2772	321
2799	226, 232, 289
2832	312, 327
2855	126
2872	166–67, 284
2900	244
2999	290
3003	378
3088	205
3182	102
3454	150, 282
3783	314
3784	289
3786	407
3781	378
3783	230, 314
3784	225
3842	410
4212	231
4458A	237, 331
4613	238

4617	238
4808	230
4841	335
4886	229
5056	229, 314
5058	230, 314
5083	230
5239	223, 227, 288
5240	226, 289
5288	383
5294	191
5296	383
5301	223, 224, 288
5547	149
5730	5, 107
5763	411
5795	388
5920	208, 286
5927	225, 289
5943A	178, 383
6190	383
6401	170
6607	430
6620	372
6637	241
6638	283, 373
7202	168
7207	311
7231	225, 383, 408
7321	289, 383
7377C	282, 359, 360, 380
7413	359
7490	320
7505	161, 227–28, 230, 231, 290, 354
7518	283
7530	335
7561	247
7562	225, 320
7585	330
7696	281
7899	320
7903	225
8055	286, 400

8070	286, 400
8083	229
8093	313
8551	418
8663	281, 360, 372
8824	422
8878	233, 412
8912	396
8922	169, 175, 396
9389	348
9392	191
9394	191
9436	407
9488	366
9518	222
9528	396
9603	118, 354
9611	428
10290	344
10444	146, 380
11127	200–01, 281
11128	201
11129	201
11248	358
11386	419
11529	338
11530	338
11624	251
11674	158–59
12021	345
12052	188
12054	430
12061	288, 405
12117	157, 284
12201	345
12205	311
12211	212
12285	198
12601	405
12634	311
12832	96
13029	345
13160	353, 354
13220	383
13413	404
13764	150, 282

13875	405
13955	165, 281, 285
14023	423
14065	359
14167	166, 284, 378
14301	234
15009	244
15176	216, 287
15393	186
15462	318
16258	324
16678	281
17002	230, 231
17275	217, 405
17294	423
17715	219
17716	423
17742	288, 405
17868	159
17959	336
18195	201
18554	354
Nouvelles Acquisitions latines (NAL) 161	283
340	404, 406
348	220
442	353
638	288, 405
886	282
1436	378
1438	287
1442	215
1447	216
1452	287
1455	217, 285, 405
1460	287
1478	216, 287, 404, 406
1485	287
1496	405
1497	218–19
1498	218–19
1548	405, 406
1576	324
1595	118, 354
1611	155, 157, 160
1612	118

	1630	160, 170, 388
	1674	400
	1871	224, 290
	2056	375
	2154	219
	2170	357
	2171	357
	2180	127
	2195	417
	2196	207, 399
	2246	288, 405
	2248	287, 405
	2253	216, 287
	2320	198
	2322	119
Syriac 27		76
Poitiers		
Bibliothèque Municipale 95		320, 431
Reims		
Bibliothèque Municipale 9		418
	250	151
	295	378
	875	109, 349
	1429	191, 389
Rouen		
Archives Départementales de Seine Maritime 9H24		384
	9H27	211
	9H29	212
	9H30	212
	9H106	211
	9H1433	211, 384
Bibliothèque Municipale 26 (A.292)		210
	231 (A.44)	210, 396
	274 (Y.6)	210, 385
	310 (A.293)	210
	368 (A.27)	210, 401
	395 (Y.127)	210
	427 (A.143)	286
	471 (A.291)	207, 378
	478 (A.7)	206
	484 (805)	214
	489 (A.254)	207, 361, 399
	511 (A.361)	212
	536 (A.389)	211
	539 (A.366)	214
	1378 (V.40)	210, 285, 378

1386 (U.158)	170
1390 (U.36)	378
1418 (U.115)	378
1470 (O.32)	349

Saint-Etienne
| Bibliothèque Municipale 104 (olim) | 167 |

Saint-Omer
Bibliothèque Municipale 168	196
342 bis	194, 196
350	197
765	196

Sélestat
| Bibliothèque Municipale 1 | 327 |
| 95 | 379 |

Tours
Bibliothèque Municipale 284	397
291	251
803	349

Troyes
Bibliothèque Municipale 253	249
496	343
988	246

Valenciennes
Bibliothèque Municipale 41	190
169	190
298	170, 382
337	140
386	108
390	189
406	189
408	190
410	190
448	190
502	190
510	189
521	342–43
843	194–95, 382

Verdun
Bibliothèque Municipale 2	186
7	187
10	387
24	195
26	386
45	386
50	187
75	187

Germany
  Bamberg
    Staatsbibliothek Bibl. 44 (A.I.14)   182
                    Bibl. 126 (B.I.8)   178, 216, 287
                    Can. 1 (P.III.20)   182
                    Class. 42 (M.V.10)   371
                    Class. 53 (H.J.IV.24)   156, 284
                    Hist. 5 (E.III.3)   147, 148, 149, 152
                    Hist. 161 (E.III.1)   192, 376
                    Lit. 3 (Ed.V.4)   193
                    Lit. 140 (Ed.II.16)   385
                    Lit. 143 (B.VI.15)   385
                    Patr. 46 (Q.VI.42)   385
                    Philos. 2 (HJ.IV.5–6)   109
  Berlin
    Staatsbibliothek 138 (Phillipps 1833) Stiftung Preussicher   157, 158, 283
                    Kulturbesitz Hamilton 82   221
  Bonn
    Universitätsbibliothek S 292/1   244
  Brement
    Universitätsbibliothek b.21   418
  Bükeburg
    Niedersachisches Staatsarchiv, Bede fragments   334
  Cologne
    Dombibliothek 141   188
  Darmstadt
    Hessische Landes-und Hochschulbibliothek 314   193
                                          523   193
                                          1988   368
                                          4264   354
  Dresden
    Staatsbibliothek A.145.b   111
  Erlangen
    Universitätsbibliothek 288   130
                          380   151
  Freiburg im Breisgau
    Universitätsbibliothek 7   174
  Karlsruhe
    Badische Landesbibliothek CXLVIII   338
                        Aug. Frag. 8   39, 313, 317
                        Aug. Frag. 119   336
  Kassel
    Landesbibliothek 4 Theol. 2   334
                    15   385

Munich
Staatsbibliothek Clm 560 359
                      6292 164
                      6370 347
                      6371 347
                      6372 347
                      6430 .... 105, 139, 347
                      7950 247
                      9544 327
                      9559 422
                      13067 .... 192, 391
                      14272 .... 168, 173, 361
                      14436 .... 168, 281, 366, 379
                      14663 368
                      14735 .... 146, 168, 281
                      14836 .... 146, 173
                      21248 .... 404 or 405
                      23261 392
                      29164 106
Münster in Westfallen
Staatsarchiv, Bede fragments 334
Nuremberg
Germanisches National Museum, Golden Gospel Book 396
Trier
Dombibliothek 93 376
Stadtbibliotek 171/1621 194
Wolfenbüttel
Herzog August Bibliothek, Aug.18 40 380
                 Aug.36.32 20 (Teil A) 371
                 Aug. 71.22 2° 374
                 Aug. 76.14 2° 282
                 Gud. lat. 335 151
                 Weissenburg 75 392
                      101 .... 60, 160, 379
Würzberg
Univeritätsbibliothek M.P.TH. F.12 .... 325, 328
Hungary
Miskolc
Zrinyi Ilona Secondary School fragments 332
Ireland
Dublin
Chester Beatty Library 17 192
Royal Irish Academy, Cathach Psalter 34, 311
                      23. N. 10 341

Trinity College 57 (A.IV.5)   87, 312, 324, 335
              58 (A.I.6)   319, 322, 335, 337
              59 (A.IV.23)   49, 316
              60 (A.I.15)   83, 94, 331,
                                                                 357–58

              H.II.15   342
Italy
  Florence
    Biblioteca Laurenziana Plut. 47, 28   130, 375
  Milan
    Biblioteca Ambrosiana C.5 inf.   35, 312, 322, 324
                          C.103 inf.   316
                          C.128 inf.   144, 145, 181, 281
                          C.313 inf.   328
                          M.12 sup.   354
                          O.212 sup.   36, 313
  Monte Cassino
    Archivio della Badia 3   239
                        189   146, 282
                        195   414
                        199   236
                        257   236
                        361   236
  Naples
    Biblioteca Nazionale VII, C. 43   150
  Rome
    Biblioteca Nazionale Centrale Vitorio Emanuele II, Farfa 2   78, 241, 389
                                                   Farfa 32   239
  Soria
    Biblioteca publica 31-H   127
  Turin
    Biblioteca Universitaria G.VII.15   301
  Venice
    Biblioteca Marciana Z L 497   82, 324
Luxembourg
  The Hague
    Bibliothèque Nationale 89   344
Netherlands
  The Hague
    Koninklijke Bibliotheek 75.F.12   171, 172
                           70.H.50   150
  Leiden
    Bibliotheek der Reijksuniveriteit Voss. lat. O.15   225
                                          Q.17   281, 284
                                          Q.33   363–64
                                          Q.54   146

Q.55	341
Q.69	89, 337, 339
Q.94	197
O.95	361
Q.98	119, 354
F.39	208
F.67	109
F.70	374
F.79	197
F.96	284
F.96A	344
BPL 139B	155
1822	229
Lipsianus 26	198, 199
Perizonius F.55	320
Scaliger 38	281, 361

Portugal
  Lisbon
    Gulbenkian Museum, lat. 148 — 418

Russia
  Saint Petersburg
    Public Library Q.V.I.6–10 — 306
    Q.V.I.18 — 50, 324, 334

Spain
  Barcelona
    Archivo de la Corona de Aragón, Ripoll 40 — 126
    42 — 126
    59 — 126
    74 — 126
    106 — 125, 126, 356
    168 — 126, 356
    225 — 128

  Escorial
    Escorial d.I.1 — 130
    d.I.2 — 127, 129, 130

Switzerland
  Basel
    Universitätsbibliothek A.VII.3 — 111, 112, 351, 369
    An.IV.2 — 147

  Bern
    Burgerbibliothek 167 — 345
    196 — 358
    250 — 156
    357 — 353
    363 — 350
    451 — 158, 159

611 118, 353
668 116, 117
Cologny
  Bodmer 80 177
Einsiedeln
  Stiftsbibliothek 121 103, 347, 352
       172 352
Saint Gall
  Stiftsbibliothek 23 346
       48 111
       53 346
       77 346
       339 103
       359 103
       390–91 103
       533 346
       565 376
       571 376
       728 103
       913 103
       914 347
       1394 311
Schaffhausen
  Stadtbibliotek, Generalia I 83, 110
Zurich
  Zentralbibliothek C 57 323, 346
       C 77
       C 78 130
       C 98 104, 347, 375
United States
  Baltimore, Maryland
    Walters Art Gallery W.452 429
  Chicago, Illinois
    Newberry Library 1 228
       1.5, no. 9 31
       10 56, 387
       21.1 248
       24.1 420
       93.6 323
       94 323
       97.1 323
       97.5 323
       101 314
       116 429
       frag. 1 16
       frag. 15 348

Malibu, California
  Getty Museum, Ludwig Collection IX   236
New Haven, Connecticut
  Beinecke Library 401–401a   332
New York, New York
  New York Public Library 728   103
                        Harkness Gospels   102, 345
  Pierpont Morgan Library 826   334
Vatican City
  Archivio Segreto Vaticano, Reg. Vat. 1   236
                                       2   239, 240
  Vatican Library Vat. lat. 215   327
                           355   329
                           356   329
                        1783   167
                        3123   380
                        3321   339
                        3363   347
                        4929   82, 306, 330
                        5755   137, 138
                        7207   311
                        8487   239
                        8591   80, 284
                 Ottob. 313   327
                 Pal. lat. 46   49
                         50   107
                        235   367
                 Reg. lat. 296   345
                        452   404
                        490   378
                        577   140, 178
                        596   154, 283
                        615   163, 192
                        733   281
                        762   37, 107, 108, 113, 259
                        846   353, 354
                      1071   282, 361
                      1462   160, 374–75
                      1573   157, 283
                      1661   358, 361
                      1783   285
                      1864   284

General and Topical Index

In this index, "f" after a page number indicates a separate reference on the next page; "ff" indicates separate references on the next two pages. A continuous discussion over two or more pages is indicated by a span of page numbers (e.g., "57–59"); *passim* is used for a cluster of references in close but not consecutive sequence. For individual manuscripts not listed here, see the Index of Manuscripts Cited, p. .

Abbo of Fleury, 65, 100, 130, 137, 143f, 147, 152–66 *passim*, 170–73 *passim*, 178–85 *passim*, 190, 195, 209, 215f, 220–27 *passim*, 283f, 394n116, 329n126

Abbreviations, monolexic, 32, 39, 43, 45, 63–64; use of by Richer, 147; use of at Fleury, 160; use of in tenth-century England, 184

Abbreviations, suspension, 32, 64–65, 87, 146

Abbreviations, terminal, 39, 41, 43, 62–63

Acute accent, on double *ii*, 21, 57; on tonic syllables, 55; on minim strokes, 56; as signs of word continuation, 54–57, 68f; to identify adverbs, 57; on *-is* termination, 55, 69, 84, 101; on monosyllables, 55, 69, 84, 101; in French royal charters, 181; in tenth-century England,184; at La Grasse, 234; at Monte Cassino, 237; presence of in Greek names, 55; presence of in Hebrew names, 184, 206, 217; presence of in vernacular, 98, 161

Adalbero, Archbishop of Reims, 149, 198

Adalbero of Laon, 170, 172, 180, 221

Adalberon II, Bishop of Metz, 191

Adalbold of Utrecht, 172–73, 176

Adélard, abbot of Saint-Germain des Près and Saint-Bénigne,157, 222

Adelman of Liège, 170, 189

Adémar, abbot of Cluny, 225f

Adémar, Bishop of Angoulême, 232

Adémar de Chabannes, 147, 178, 224f

Adjectiva, 253

Adoro te, 202

Adson, 149–51

Aelfric, 184–85

Aelrède of Rievaulx, 248

Aemericus, 232

Aenigmata, 98

Aerated script, 32–44, 100, 433; use by students of Gerbert, 172

Aethelgar, Archbishop of Canterbury, 196

Aethicus, 238

Aimard, abbot of Cluny, 219

Alain of Lisle, 248

Albert, abbot of Saint-Mesmin, 211

Albertus, scribe at Saint-Vaast, 188

Albertus Magnus, 24, 254, 256

Alcuin, 36, 92, 100, 106, 109, 123

Aldebaldus, scribe at Saint-Bénigne, 221

Aldhelm, 71, 84, 88–90 *passim,* 98f

Alexander of Buxtehude, 251
Alphabetical glossaries and reference
    books, 90–93, 269
Alphabetical reference tools, 269
Alphabetical tie notes, 76
Altenburg, Cistercian abbey of, 244
Amalarius, 205
Ambrose (pseudonym), *Sermo de infor-
    matione episcoporum* of, 147, 158; silent
    reading of, 8, 397; iconography of, 251
American Sign Language for the deaf, 71
Ampersand, 29, 62, 83, 313n87, 322n3
Angers, University of, 263
Anglo-Saxon grammarians, 83–90
Angoulême, 224, 232
Anonymous ad Cuimnanum, 83
Anselm of Canterbury, 202, 203–04,
    212ff, 245, 248, 250, 273
Anselm of Laon, 324n73
Anselm of Lucca, 239
Apex, 54, 84. *See also* Acute accent
Apuleius (pseudonym), 144, 163, 189, 200
Aquitaine, 140, 142
Arabic language and script, 4, 10, 13,
    59, 123–30, 159–60,165f, 186, 230,
    255; terminal forms in, 321n36; Latin
    transliteration of, 61, 124, 166, 184
Arabic numbers, *see* Numerical notation
Aramaic, 10, 124
Arator, 189
Architectural motifs, use of in tables,
    138–39
Aristotle, 17, 79, 103, 111, 121, 131, 143f,
    149, 152–55 *passim,* 162ff, 170, 189, 200,
    208, 214, 233, 241, 260, 264, 419n65
Arno, Bishop of Salzburg, 107
Arnoul of Chartres, 170
Ars anonyma Bernensis, 83
Ars Laureshamensis, 114
Ars lectoria, 231–33
Art history, contribution of to the study
    of word separation, 25–26
Astrolobe, 127–30
Augustine (pseudonym), 8, 14, 16, 72, 110,
    198, 212, 227–34 *passim,* 246; *Categories*
    of, 149, 189; *De musica* of, 225; monas-

tic rule of, 202; on reading, 299n41. *See
    also* Ambrose
Authorship, 249–51, 257–58
Autograph script, 249–51
Ayrard, 151

Babcock, Robert, 163
Baif, Jean Antoine, 427n66
Banderoles, 187, 222, 226, 433
Barlow, C. W., 22
Baudouin IV, Count of Flanders, 188f,
    196
Beato de Liébano, 233
Beaupré, Cistercian abbey of, 247
Bec, abbey of, 212–14. *See also* Lanfranc of
    Bec
Bede (pseudonym), 85–92 *passim,* 106,
    110, 113, 123, 133f, 137, 189, 192, 198, 225;
    computational treatises of, 133f
Benedict VIII, Pope, 222
Benedict, rule of, 202
Beneventon script, and introduction of
    word separation, 236–37, 241
Berengar of Tours, 60, 169, 189, 214, 250,
    264, 380n30
Bernard Itier, 249
Bernard of Angers, 169
Bernard of Clairvaux, 247, 250
Bernelinus, 185, 361n51
Bersuire, Pierre, 427n74, 428n81
Bible, 16, 65, 138, 192, 216–17, 223, 227;
    Old Testament, 210; Psalter, 76, 116,
    210, 228; Gospels, 129, 138, 188, 191,
    196. *See also* Pocket Gospel Books
Bischoff, Bernhard, 22, 164
Bobbio, abbey of, 89, 144, 151, 235, 237
Boethius (pseudonym), 17, 126, 140–49
    passim, 160, 163, 168, 170, 185, 189–90,
    200, 208, 216, 220, 233, 241, 246, 266;
    De geometria of, 126, 130
Bologna, 62, 235, 237–38
Bonaventure, 24, 256
Boniface, 88, 98, 106
Bonifilius, Bishop of Girone, 130
Book production, *see* Copying of sepa-
    rated script; Dictation; Visual copying

Bouma shape, 19, 21, 27–29 *passim,* 39, 63, 126, 172, 217, 244, 272, 314n95, 433
Bourgueil, abbey of, 211
Brain, allocation of hemispheres, 3, 79
British Isles, graphic culture and influence of, 4, 13, 15, 21, 34–43 *passim,* 48, 52–56 *passim,* 61–65 *passim,* 71–75 *passim,* 83–90, 115, 121, 123, 134–40 *passim,* 162, 236
Brittany, 41, 73, 98, 101–02, 140
Brown, Julian, 61
Bruno, Bishop of Toul, *see* Leo XI
Burchard of Worms, 173–77 *passim,* 207–08, 212, 230, 236, 239
Byzantium, 77

Caen, 214
Caesar, Julius, 149, 229, 411n92
Calvlin, John, 276
Cambridge, University of, 262–63
Canon tables, 138
Canonical separation, 44–52, 433; in vernacular, 97
Canterbury, 196–97, 203, 214
Canute, King of England, 225
Capitalization, 73; at word beginnings, 59, 61; at word endings, 61, 63, 101, 108; at Fleury, 160, 228
Carcassonne, 234
Caroline and Carolingian script, 20–21, 36, 40, 43, 56, 61; and hybridization with tironian notes, 118; word separation in, 139; use at Monte Cassino, 236; and English use of Caroline separata, 183–85, 330n132
Carthusian order, 142
Cartularies, 96, 106, 200, 218–20, 233
Cassiodorus, 72, 188, 230
Catalonia, 140
Cato (pseudonym), 313n86
Chad, Gospel of, 94
Chapters, division into, 260
Charlemagne, 21, 106–08 *passim,* 118, 311n56
Charles the Bald, German emperor, 109
Charles V, King of France, 263, 267f, 273

Charles VI, King of France, 269, 273
Charles VII, King of France, 270, 273
Chartier, Roger, ix, x
Chartres, 79, 140, 168, 219, 231, 238, 245. *See also* Fulbert of Chartres
Chayter, H. J., ix
Chelles, abbey of, 181
Children, historical parallels to, 3–6. *See also* China, Denmark, India, Israel, Japan
China, 123, 133; language and writing in, 2–4, 19, 297n31
Christine de Pisan, 268
Cicero, 16, 48, 148, 151, 163, 189, 274
Cistercian Order, 81, 127, 142, 235, 237, 244, 246–49
Clairvaux, Cistercian abbey of, 246, 249
Cluny, abbey of, 168, 178, 198, 215–21, 285–88 *passim;* customs and influence of, 181, 203f, 209, 215, 220–24 *passim;* Order of, 223–28 *passim,* 235
Cola et commata, 16, 32, 91, 113, 124, 433
Colissio, 108
Collectio Anselma dedicata, 186
Cologne, 109, 115
Columbanus, 89
Conques, abbey of, 169
Constantine of Fleury, 152
Constantinus, abbot of Saint-Symphorien (Metz), 191
Construction notes, 70–71, 95, 433
Coptic, 77
Copying of separated script, 48–61
Corbie, 107
Coronis, 64
Corvey, 115
Ct ligature, 313n86
Cursiva formata, script, 270f
Customaries, and monastic rules, 158, 202, 397n8
Cyrillic script, 10, 13

Daniel, Pierre, 129
Dasia, 58, 84, 110, 228, 433; in tenth-century England, 184; at Saint-Pierre of Moissac, 230

David Aubert, 270

Deafness, effect on visible language, 71, 317n119

Delisle, Léopold, 25

Denis (pseudonym), *Periegesis* of, 94

Denmark, 256; pedagogy for beginning readers in, 296n21

De ordinatione constructionis, 161, 227

Diastole, 54, 57, 85ff, 101, 114, 433; use in vernacular, 97

Diastole, J-shaped form of, 57, 434; presence at Saint-Amand, 190

Diastole, successor note to, 57, 81, 433; use in Spain, 127; absence from works of Richer, 149; first Continental use of, 159; in works of Fulbert, 166; use at Monte Cassino, 237

Diastole, vertical-stroke form of, 47–48, 57–58, 435

Dicta Leonis, 229

Dictation, 48, 261, 266

Dictio, 89, 113, 121

Dicuil, 88, 108f, 137

Digest, 237

Diomedes, 86

Diple, 74, 233, 248, 433

Dodolin, scribe at Saint-Bertin, 196

Dolbeau, François, xi

Dominic, abbot of Silos, 127

Dominican Order, 142, 259, 263, 265

Donatus, 57, 85–90 *passim,* 114, 189, 225

Dou, Gerard, 276

Dubthach, scribe, 110

Duns Scotus, 254, 256

Dunston, 183–85, 196f, 202, 216

Durand, abbot of Saint-Pierre of Moissace, 228

E cedilla, explication of, 29, 62

Eadmer, 251

Eberhard, Bishop of Constance, 174

Echternach, abbey at,106, 174–75, 200–01, 281

Egbert, Bishop of Freising, 164

Egmont, abbey of, 109

Egypt, 64, 133

Einhard, 337n46

Einsiedeln, abbey of, 105

Elevated points, system of punctuation, 72–73

Elsendis, scribe and nun, 220

Emblematic punctuation, *see* Punctuation

Emendation, 79–82, 331n138

Enclictic elements, 31, 44, 47, 57, 72, 229–30

England, 41, 73, 83–90, 96ff, 106, 141; contacts with France, 152

English Benedictine Reform, influence of, 183–85, 194–98 *passim,* 204, 210–11

English school of illumination, 188, 197, 206, 211, 225

Epinal Glossary, 91

Erotica, 274–75

Eudes, Bishop of Chartres, 211

Eye-voice span, 6, 33, 39, 52

Farfa, abbey of, 239–40, 389n52

Fécamp, abbey of, 58, 168, 204–10 *passim,* 221, 244f. *See also* John of Fécamp

Fere canonical script, 44, 434

Ferrières, 284. *See also* Lupus of Ferrières

Figura, 83–92 *passim,* 113–14

Fingen, abbot of Saint-Symphorien, 191

Fixations, *see* Ocular fixations

Fleury, abbey of, 59, 79, 82, 118, 126, 129, 152–62, 168, 180, 190, 206–09 *passim,* 219, 222, 228, 235, 236, 281, 283–84, 329n126, 408n45, 411n92

Folcuin, abbot of Lobbes, 194, 196

Folcuin, abbot of Saint-Vincent (Metz), 191

Foliation, 12, 77, 230–31, 241, 271

Footnotes, antecedents of 76

Foveal vision, use of, 6, 27, 32

Fractions, transcription of, 137–38, 156, 166, 255

Fraktur (type font), 29

Franciscan Order, 142

Franco of Liège, 170

Franco, scribe at Cluny, 217

François of Mayrones, 260

Frederick of Lorraine, abbot of Monte Cassino, 236

Freising, 102, 105, 139, 164

Froissart, 268

Fulbert of Chartres, 65, 147, 165–68, 170, 176, 212, 245, 284–85; Sermons on the Virgin of, 167f, 207, 210, 217, 220; students of, 168–70

Fulda, abbey of, 96, 102

Garland, 121f, 137, 185, 189

Gasparri, Francoise, 179

Gauzelin, abbot of Fleury, 208

Gembloux, abbey of, 189. *See also* Olbert of Gembloux; Sigebert of Gembloux

Geoffroy of Auxerre, 247

Gerald, abbot of Aurillac, 130

Gérard, abbot of Saint-Evre of Toul, 149

Gérard I of Florennes, Bishop of Cambrai, 171f, 192, 194

Gerberge, 149

Gerbert of Aurillac, 65, 130, 143–49, 151–52, 159–78 *passim*, 192, 198, 201, 207, 235f; curriculum of, 185–90 *passim*, 207–09 *passim*, 215–23 *passim*, 236, 241–42; students of, 146–52 *passim*, 170–72, 186, 221

Germany, 40, 73, 97–106 *passim*, 115, 120, 125, 127

Gilbert of Poitiers, 246

Gilda, 89

Giordano, Prince of Capua, 241

Giraldus Cambrensis, 50

Glagolitic script, 10

Goderan, scribe at Lobbes and Stavelot, 192

Gomesanus, scribe at Albelda, 126

Gothic cursive script, 257–58, 270

Gothic language, 10

Gothic textualis script, 47, 269–70, 276, 306n11

Gottescalcus, Bishop of Puy, 126

Gratian, 62, 174, 324n73

Greek, 4–14 *passim*, 34, 55, 64–69 *passim*, 75; use of in circle of Sedulius, 99, 110–11; use of at Saint-Amand, 190; use of in early medieval Italy, 238; Latin transliteration of, 6; use of foliation and pagination, 12, 77; use of tie notes, 75–76

Grégoire of Montaner, 233

Gregorio di Catino, 78, 239–41

Gregory the Great, 149, 186f, 194, 196, 212, 226, 247

Gregory V, Pope, 390n68

Gregory VII, Pope, 233–39 *passim*

Gregory of Narek, 252

Gregory of Nazianzus, 252

Gregory of Tours, 70

Guibert of Nogent, 244–51 *passim*

Guido of Arezzo, 141

Guido Favo, 254

Guillaume Fillastre, 267

Guillaume of Saint-Thierry, 247–51 *passim*

Gunzo of Novare, 177

H used for aspiration and word separation, 58, 83f, 228

Halinard, abbot of Saint-Bénigne, 221–22

Hangul, 2, 352n97

Hartgar, Bishop of Liège, 109

Hartwic, 146, 164, 168

Haymon, Bishop of Verdun, 186

Hebrew, language and writing, 10, 16, 19, 43, 48, 59, 124, 126; Latin transliteration of, 206; terminal forms in, 321n36

Hedera, 26–28

Helgaud of Fleury, 146, 178

Helperic, 185, 208, 212

Henri Romain, 267

Henry I, King of France, 181

Henry II, German emperor, 106, 163, 173, 178, 182, 216

Henry III, German emperor, 193

Heriger of Lobbes, 130, 143, 162–64, 172–77, 185, 194; students of, 172–76

Hérivé, scribe at Saint-Bertin, 196

Hermanus, monk of Saint-Martin of Tournay, 252

Hervardus, scribe at Mont Saint-Michel, 208
Hierarchical word blocks, 36–43
Hilary of Poitiers, 33
Hildegar, 166
Hildemar, 204
Hincmar, Archbishop of Reims, 76, 118
Hisperica famina, 89
Hlothere, King of Kent, 335n25
Horace, 190, 221, 299n43
Hugh, abbot of Cluny, 217, 219, 223
Hugh, Bishop of Bayeux, 211
Hugh Capet, 22, 180, 211
Hugh I, Count of Maine, 209
Hugues of Fouilloy, 245
Hugh of Saint-Cher, 263
Hugh of Saint-Victor, 76, 244–45
Humbert of Romans, O.P., 259, 263
Hunaud de Gavarret, abbot of Saint-Pierre of Moissac, 228
Hybrida script, 270f
Hyperbaton, 15
Hyphen, 66–70 *passim,* 85, 101; in vernacular, 98

Iddephonsus of Toledo, 126
Iliad, transcriptions of, 55
Incunabula, 76
India, language and scripts of, 10, 19, 301n65; pedagogy for beginning readers in, 297n21
Ingelard, scribe, 157
Ingon, 172
Inspicere ("to read"), 203, 245, 268, 397n8. See also *Veoir; Videre*
Institut de Recherche et d'Histoire des Textes (Paris), ix, 25
Interletter space, 27
Interlinear translations, 93
Interpunct, 9–10, 26, 53, 64f, 434
Intersyllable space, at the court of Charlemagne, 107
Intertextual space, 27, 33
Interword space, definition of, 26–27
Ireland, 43, 49–53 *passim,* 61–66 *passim,* 83, 90–95 *passim,* 125

Irimbert, abbot of Admont, 251
Irish monks at Metz, 191
Isaac of Stella, 248
Isidore (pseudonym*),* *Decretals* of, 174
Isidore of Seville, 36, 55, 73–74, 86, 129, 140, 186, 234, 299n43, 397n8
Israel, pedagogy for beginning readers in, 296n21
Italy, 62, 77, 130, 141, 221, 235–42, 271–2
Ivo of Chartres, 246

J-shaped diastole, *see* Diastole, J-shaped form of
Jacques Boyer, 424n28
Jacques le Grand, 261
Japan, 123; language and writing in, 3–6 *passim,* 63
Jean Bolant, 254
Jean Gerson, 252
Jean Mansel, 275
Jerome, 16, 124, 138, 176, 188, 246, 252; iconography of, 251
Johannes Cassianus, 190
Johannes de Babis, 15, 122, 253
Johannes Scottus, 1908–09, 123
John VII, Pope, 236
John XIV, Pope, 184
John XIX, Pope, 226
John II, King of France, 268
John Chrysostom, 190, 217, 247
John of Fécamp, 58, 191, 202–07, 227, 248, 250, 273
John of Garland, 252
John of Sacrobosco, 136, 420n72
John of Salisbury, 246
Joinville, 266
Josephus, 192, 229f
Josephus Hispanus, 130
Jouarre, abbey of, 53
Jouvenal des Ursins, 428n80
Julian of Toledo, 85, 113
Jumièges, abbey of Saint-Pierre at, 168, 180f, 209–12, 285
Juvenal, 190, 221

Kaisheim, Cistercian abbey of, 247

Kana, 63
Kanji, 63
Knox, Bernard, 298n32, 300n43
Korean language and script, 2, 4

La Grasse, abbey of, 234
Lanfranc of Bec, 189, 202f, 213–14, 229,
    252, 402n69
Lapidary inscriptions, 53, 64, 137, 230,
    323n66
Laurentius Dozoli, 424n28
Lectio, 264; *lectio tacita*, 299n43, 397n8
Le Fèvre, Nicolas, 166
Legere, 200, 268, 299n43
Leges Langobardorum, 238
Leibniz, 132
Leo IX, Pope, 191
Leo of Ostia, scribe at Monte Cassino,
    236
Lessay, abbey, 214
Letter blocks, 34
Lettre bâtarde, 270
Lettre courante, 270
Liège, 193
Ligatures, 21, 29, 434. *See also* Ct ligature;
    NT ligature; Suspended ligature
Limoges, 232; synod of 1031, 223, 225. *See
    also* Saint-Martial of Limoges
Lindsay, Walace M., 18, 54
Lire au coeur, 268
Livy, 5, 107f, 113, 411n92
Lobet of Barcelona, 128
Logica vetus, 17, 143, 152, 160–70 *passim*,
    189f, 212, 233, 236, 241, 246, 266. *See
    also* Apuleius; Aristotle; Boethius
Lorenzo de Medici, 273
Lorraine, 73, 127
Lothaire, King of Lotharingia, 180
Louis VII, King of France, 179
Louis XI, King of France, 273f
Louis IX (Saint Louis), King of France,
    265f, 427n72, 429n94
Louis of Bruges, 275
Louis the Pious, German emperor, 108f
Louvain, University of, 261, 265
Lowe, Elias Avery, 18, 22, 81

Ludolf of Saxony, 275
Luke, iconography of, 252
Lupus of Ferrières, 25, 307n28, 313n87,
    329n126, 337n46
Luxeuil, abbey of, 150, 207, 245
Lyminge (abbey), 335n25

Mabillon, Jean, 22
Mac Regol, scribe and abbot of Bire, 50
Macrobius, 200
Maecianus Volusianus, 137f
Máel Sechlainn, Irish king, 109
Maïul, abbot of Cluny, 215, 219, 222
Maimonedes, 27
Mainhard II, abbot of Mont Saint-
    Michel, 208f
Manuscrits datés, collections of, 25
Marcigny-sur-Loire, priory of Cluny, 220
Marichal, Robert, 23
Marsilio of Padua, 275
Martin of Braga, 176
Martin of Tours, 94
Maternus, Firmicus, 162
Maudramnus, abbot of Corbie, 107
Meigret, Louis, 427n66
Memory, short-term in reading and
    copying, 7–8, 142, 252
Metron, 73, 434
Metz, 109, 191, 205
Milan, 109, 237
Minim strokes, 26, 40, 270, 434. *See also*
    Acute accent
Monosyllables, graphic treatment of, 45,
    54, 67, 87
Mont Saint-Michel, abbey of, 202, 208–12
    passim, 285–86
Montataire, 181
Monte Cassino, abbey of, 22, 146, 236,
    282
Montier-en-Der, abbey of, 149, 169
Musica Enchiriadis, 140
Morphemes, 7, 31, 41, 47
Morphemic hierarchical word blocks, 41,
    97f
Mozarabic culture, 125–130, 223, 230

Münster, 109
Music, notation of, 36, 73–75 *passim,* 139

Narratio, 9
Neumes, musical, 36, 73–75 *passim,* 126, 434
Newton, Isaac, 132
Nicolaus de Lyra, 95, 258–63 *passim,* 424n30
Nicolaus of Aurtrecourt, 265
Nonantola, *see* Saint Sylvester of Nonantola, abbey of
Normandy, 73, 140–41, 181, 202–14, 219
Nota signs, 53, 75, 434
Notae iuris, 65
Notker Balbulus, 103, 251
Notker, Bishop of Liège, 162, 186, 390n68
Notre-Dame de Signy, 81, 246f
Notre Dame of Paris, 259
Numbers, graphic forms of, 70, 127–38 *passim,* 144, 255, 326n87
Numerical notation, Arabic, 134–38 *passim,* 144, 163, 255; Roman, 132–37 *passim;* Greek, 70, 125, 131–34; Hebrew, 132–34 *passim*

O, letter, internal space of as unit of comparative measurement, 26, 298n38; comparative proportions of in separated and unseparated writing, 30
Occitan, 160, 235, 408n45
Ocreatus, 136
Octavien de Saint-Gelais, 299n43
Ocular fixations, 7, 8, 33, 434
Ocular regressions, 7, 33
Ocular saccades, 7, 8, 39, 434
Odbert, abbot of Saint-Bertin, 196–97
Oderic Vital, 249
Odilon, abbot of Cluny, 178, 216–17, 219, 226, 228
Odon, abbot of Cluny, 178, 223
Odon of Beauvais, 76
Odon of Orléans, 250
Odorannus of Sens, 178
Olbert of Gembloux, 170, 175–76, 193
Old English, transcription of, 160

Oliva, abbot of Ripoll, 126
Orléans, 181
Orosius, 42
Oswald, Archbishop of York, 183
Othlon of Saint Emmeram, 249–50
Otto I, German emperor, 149, 182
Otto II, German emperor, 163, 182, 390n68
Otto III, German emperor, 144, 149, 163, 173, 182, 194
Ovid, 254, 299n43, 397n8
Oxford, University of, 262–63

Pagination, 12, 77. *See also* Foliation
Paleography, and study of word separation, 18–25
Papias, 92
Papyri, 27–30 *passim,* 53–55 *passim,* 64, 69, 75, 77, 137, 335n29
Parafoveal vision, 6, 27, 39, 63, 125, 434
Parentheses, 272
Paris, University of, 259–63 *passim*
Pars, 113f, 121, 232
Paschasius Radbertus, 228f
Peletier, Jacques, 427n66
Peripheral vision, 6, 434
Persius, 209, 221
PET scanners, 312n80
Peter Abelard, 121f
Peter Damian, 239
Peter of Luxembourg, 275
Petrarch, 25, 252
Petrucci, Armando, xi, 23
Phebi Claro, 160
Philippe de Mezières, 273
Philippus, 58, 81
Philip the Fair, 259, 273
Philip the Good, Duke of Burgundy, 274–75
Phoenician, 9, 43
Photography, role of in study of word separation, 25
Pictor, 252
Pierre Dubois, 259
Pius VII, Pope, 192
Plato, 79

Pliny the Elder, 90
Pliny the Younger, 119
Plutarch, 299n43
Pocket Gospel Books, 93–95
Pomponius Festus, 90
Poppon, 191–94 *passim*
Porcher, Jean, collection of at the Biblio-
    thèque Nationale, 25
Porphyry, 143, 149, 155, 168, 200, 208, 241
Positurae, 36, 72f, 85, 140, 434
Post-factum emendation, 79–82
Praelectio, 8, 13, 69, 142
Prayer books, 268
Prepositions, bound and unbound,
    graphic treatment of, 31, 45–47, 67, 86,
    114, 231
Priscian (pseudonym), 87, 110, 137, 151,
    228, 230; *Liber de accentibus* of, 55, 57,
    68, 81, 226, 231f
Prosodiae, 28, 50–59 *passim*, 68, 74f, 84f,
    114, 140
Punctuation, 71–77; emblematic, 73, 140,
    434
Punctus elevatus, 73
Punctus flexus, 73
Punctus versus, 73

Question mark, 74, 248
Quintilian, 54, 89
*Quomodo septem circumstantie rerum in
    legendo ordinande sint*, 103f
Quotation marks, 74

Rabanus Maurus, 215
Ragimbold of Cologne, 165, 170
Rainier, scribe at Saint-Symphorien
    (Metz), 191
Ramsey, abbey of, 152, 183, 225
Raoul de Presles, 95
Ratherius, Bishop of Verona, 177–78,
    194–95
Raymond Lull, 79
Reference reading, 4
Regensburg, 105–06
Regimbert, abbot of Echternach, 175, 201
Regula magistri, 33

Regularis concordia, 197, 200–03 *passim*
Reichenau, abbey of, 98
Reims, 78, 81, 119, 144–50 *passim*, 165, 172,
    185, 192, 235
Remi of Auxerre, 114–15, 189, 217, 219
René of Anjou, 268
Résumé notes, 53, 79, 434
Richalm, Cistercian monk, 248
Richard I, Duke of Normandy, 208
Richard of Saint-Vannes, 172, 186–97
    passim, 215f, 221
Richer, 65, 130, 143–52 *passim*, 182
Richerius, abbot of Monte Cassino, 236
Robert, Duke of Burgundy, 222
Robert II, Duke of Normandy, 209
Robert II, the Pious, King of France, 146,
    179–81, 221
Robert Champort, abbot of Jumièges, 210
Roger Bacon, 15, 95, 122, 254, 304n81
Roger le Chantre, monk of Saint-Martial,
    226
Romance, 15, 74
Rothardus, scribe at Sainte-Vannes,
    186–87
Rotoldus, abbot of Corbie, 188
Ruadri, Welsh king, 109
Rudolf, scribe at Saint-Vannes, 186
Rufinus, 192
Runes, 97–98

Saccades, *see* Ocular saccades
Saint-Amand, abbey of, 108, 189–90, 196,
    382n59
Saint-Arnoul of Metz, 191
Saint-Bénigne, abbey of, 58, 180, 221–22,
    251
Saint-Bertin, 196–97, 221, 395n122
Saint-Cybard of Angoulême, 224, 232
Saint-Denis, abbey of, 222
Saint Emmeram of Regensburg, 105–06,
    146, 168, 249, 281
Saint Erhard of Regensburg, abbey of,
    380n30
Saint-Etienne, abbey of, 214
Saint-Evre of Toul, abbey of, 149

Saint Gall, abbey of, 102–09 *passim,* 140, 182
Sainte-Geneviève, canons of, 180f
Saint-Géraud of Aurillac, abbey of, 233
Saint-Germain-des-Fossés, abbey of, 181, 222
Saint-Germain-des-Près, abbey of, 96, 157, 172, 222, 244
Saint-Germain of Auxerre, abbey of, 114
Saint Germans in Cornwall, 210
Saint-Hippolyte of Combertault, abbey of, 180–81
Saint-Hupert, abbey of, 192
Saint-Jean at Florennes, 192
Saint-Martial of Limoges, abbey of, 147, 150, 158, 178, 205, 223–27, 232, 239, 249, 282–88 *passim*
Saint-Martin of Albelda, abbey of, 125–29 *passim*
Saint-Martin of Autun, abbey of, 222
Saint-Martin of Massay, abbey of, 172
Saint-Martin of Séez, 404n86
Saint-Martin of Tournay, abbey of, 250
Saint-Martin of Troarn, 404n86
Saint-Martin of Tours, abbey of, 118
Saint-Maur-des-Fossés, 222
Saint Maximin, 194
Saint-Mesmin of Micy, abbey of, 144, 146, 211, 222, 281. *See also* Albert, abbot of Saint-Mesmin
Saint-Pelayo of Cerrato, abbey of, 127
Saint-Père, abbey of, 119, 166, 288
Saint Peter's of Ghent, abbey of, 96, 197–200, 208, 218–21 *passim*
Saint Peter's of Lobbes, abbey of, 194–95
Saint-Pierre, abbey of at Jumièges, *see* Jumièges, abbey of Saint-Pierre at
Saint-Pierre-le-Vif, abbey of, 178, 223
Saint-Pierre of Moissac, abbey of, 227–31, 233, 239, 290, 314n96, 320–21
Saint-Pierre of Senones, abbey of, 191
Saint-Remi, abbey of, 150
Saint-Sever, abbey of, 233
Saint-Sylvester of Nonantola, abbey of, 238, 239

Saint-Symphorien of Metz, 191
Saint-Thierry, abbey of, 151, 189
Saint-Vaast, abbey of, 188, 191, 196, 395n122
Saint-Vannes of Verdun, abbey of, 163, 185–87
Saint-Victor of Marseille, abbey of, 233–34
Saint-Vincent of Metz, 191
Saint Willibrord, *see* Echternach, abbey at
Saint-Yrieix-le-Perche, collegial church of, 227
Sallust, 151, 200f
Salzburg, 106
Samson, 98
San Millan of Cogolla, abbey of, 130
San Sevrino, abbey of, 150
Sanskrit, 2, 14
Santa Maria de Morimonde, Cistercian abbey of, 237
Santa Maria of Huerta, abbey of, 127
Santa Maria of Ripoll, abbey of, 125
Schematic diagrams, 79, 132, 144; at Fleury, 160; at Chartres 168; at Saint-Armand, 190; in Italy, 238
Schöntal, Cistercian priory of, 248
Scotland, 256
Scribere, 268
Scriptura continua, 9–52 *passim,* 64–95 *passim,* 124, 434; in vernacular, 97, 266; reading of, 116; in Greek, 12, 124; and numbers, 136; and tables, 138; and musical notation, 139–40; mixture of script and image, 187; in southern Italy, 241; in the Renaissance, 271; near Rome, 238
Sedulius, 86
Sedulius Scottus, 109–15, 121, 123
Semipunctus, 66
Seneca, 12, 151
Senones, 191
Sens, 223
Sermon sur Jonas, 342n92
Servius, 89, 110
Sicily, 235, 241

Sigebert of Gembloux, 162, 176–77, 189, 200
Sigenulfus, scribe at Monte Cassino, 236
Siguinus, Magister, 231–32
Silentium, 203, 252, 268, 397n8
Silos, abbey of, 127
Simeon of Syracuse, 186
Sirat, Colette, 19
Smaragdus, 211
Soissons, 244
Spain, 123–27 *passim,* 221
Springiersbach-Rolduc, Augustinian abbey of, 424n33
Stabilis, monk of, 144, 146
Statius, 221
Stavelot Malmédy, twin abbeys of, 163, 191–92
Stirnemann, Patricia, xi
Submissa vox, 268
Sucherius, 216
Suppressa vox, 268
Suspended ligature, explanation of, 67–68; postfactum addition of, 82
Suthard, abbot of Saint-Pierre of Senones, 191
Syllable blocks, 35
Syllables, relation to reading and word recognition, 1, 6–9 *passim,* 34–40 *passim,* 54–58 *passim,* 74
Sylvester II, Pope, *see* Gerbert of Aurillac
Syriac, 10, 48, 55, 59, 70–75 *passim,* 94–99 *passim,* 124, 129, 134, 186, 319n24; astronomical corpus, 129, 159; diacritical dots, 321n36

T, protruding vertical stroke, 20f, 172, 209, 230, 232f
Tacitus, 14
Tarsus, Theodore of, Archbishop of Canterbury, 134
Tassin, René Prosper, 22
Tatwine, 88, 90, 98
Tech Mulling, scribe, 49, 94, 315n110
Terence, 190, 198f, 221, 225, 411n92
Tergensee, abbey of, 106

Terminal capitals *T* and *M,* 62
Terminal forms, 41, 61–62; postfactum addition of, 82. *See also* Capitalization
Theoboldus, abbot of Monte Cassino, 236
Thierry, Bishop of Metz, 191
Thierry of Montgommeri, abbot of Jumièges, 210
Thomas à Kempis, 275
Thomas Aquinas, 254, 263
Thorn, 160
Tie notes, 75–76, 434
Tironian hybrida, 118–19, 159, 225, 435
Tironian notes, 92, 101, 115–19, 225, 227, 435; glossaries of, 92, 116
Toul, 149, 191
Tours, 36, 73, 100, 108, 118, 251
Toustain, Charles François, 22f
Trait d'union, 23, 50, 52, 65–70 *passim,* 81, 435; relation to Irish scribal practice, 66; use in vernacular, 98; use in Spain, 127; use in musical texts, 142; absence from Richer's writing, 149; presence in works of Abbo, 154; split-line form, 166; at Saint Peter's of Ghent, 210; at Monte Cassino, 237; Irish equivalent, 66, 324n68
Traube, Ludwig, 18, 109
Tree diagrams, *see* Schematic diagrams
Trier, 194
Trigon, 73
Tye marks, 75–76
Typists, cognitive skills of, 51, 175, 253

Underlining, to mark citations, 248. *See also* Diple
Unity of space, definition of, 26–30; in vernacular, 97
Unseparated script, definition of, 6, 7

Vai language, 4
Vasque de Lucène, 267
Vendôme, 134
Veoir ("to read"), 268
Vernacular, 96–98, 123, 132; at Fleury, 160–61

Vertical strokes, *see* Diastole, vertical-stroke form of

Vezin, Jean, x, xi, 23

Videre ("to read"), 39, 94, 200, 203, 268, 397n8, 424n30. *See also Inspicere*

Victorinus, 86

Victorius, 137, 156, 195

Vietnamese, 2

Vigila, scribe, 127, 129

Virga, 43, 87, 136, 435

Virgil, 19, 113, 119, 200, 208, 221, 411n92

Virgilius Maro, 64, 84

Virgula, 66

Visigothic script, 125–27

Visual copying, 49–51, 175, 252–53. *See also* Memory, short-term in reading and copying

Vita of Finnan Clonard, 49

Vita of Saint Lasrianus, 49

Vita Remacli, 163, 192

Vivarium, 76

Vowels, implications for word separation, 10–11

Vox, 121

Vulgar Latin, 74

Wailly, Natalis de, 23

Wales, 41, 98, 109

Waulsort, abbey of, 192

Wax tablets, 55

Wazo of Liège, 170, 176

Wearmouth-Jarrow, twin abbeys of, 85, 87

Weisenburg, abbey of, 194

Werden, abbey of, 96

Wichard, scribe at Saint Peter's of Ghent, 198f

Wido, abbot of Saint Peter's of Ghent, 198–200

Wihtred, King of Kent, 335n25

William of Ockham, 254, 256, 275

William of Volpiano, 204, 221

William the Conqueror, 398n21

Winchester, artistic school of, *see* English school of illumination

Wolbodon, bishop of Liège, 186, 193, 194

Wolfsin, 184

Word, definition of, 31, 229, 252

Word blocks, solid, definition of, 41, 44, 236

Word division, definition of, 25, 50

Word images, 58. *See also* Bouma shape; *Figura*

Word order, in the vernacular, 14, 74, 132; implications of for reading, 1, 14–17, 161–62, 227; in the early Middle Ages, 15, 49, 89–90, 131; in the Vulgate, 16; in late medieval Latin, 253–55; in mathematical notation, 132, 255

Word separation, definitions of and implications of for reading, 13–17 *passim,* 26–32, 103–04, 161–62; in vernacular, 206–07, 266

Wulfsin, Bishop of Sherborne, 184

Library of Congress Cataloging-in-Publication Data
Saenger, Paul Henry
    Space between words : the origins of silent reading / Paul Saenger.
  p.   cm. — (Figurae)
Includes bibliographical references (p.) and index.
  ISBN 0-8047-2653-1 (cl.)   :   ISBN 0-8047-4016-x (pbk.)
  1. Books and reading—History. 2. Silent reading—History.
1. Title. 11. Series: Figurae (Stanford, Calif.)
Z1003.S13 1997
028—dc20   96-35088
                                                         CIP

⊗ This book is printed on acid-free, recycled paper.

Original printing 1997
Last figure below indicates year of this printing:
06   05   04   03   02   01